Two Social
Psychologies

■

SECOND EDITION

Two Social Psychologies

Cookie White Stephan

Department of Sociology and Anthropology
New Mexico State University

Walter G. Stephan

Department of Psychology
New Mexico State University

Wadsworth Publishing Company
Belmont, California
A Division of Wadsworth, Inc.

Sociology Editor: *Serina Beauparlant*
Editorial Assistant: *Marla Nowick*
Text Designer: *MaryEllen Podgorski*
Cover Designer: *Juan Vargas*
Production Editor: *Harold Humphrey*
Print Buyer: *Karen Hunt*
Copy Editor: *Lura S. Harrison*
Technical Illustrators: *Alan Noyes, Guy Magallanes, Jeanne Schreiber*
Compositor: *Monotype Composition Company*
Cover Painting: *Georgia O'Keefe,* Oriental Poppies, *1928. Oil on canvas.*
H. 30″ × W. 40-⅛″. University Art Museum, University of Minnesota,
Minneapolis/Purchase 37.1.

Printed in the United States of America   34

3 4 5 6 7 8 9 10   94 93 92

Library of Congress Cataloging in Publication Data
Stephan, Cookie White.
    Two social psychologies/Cookie White Stephan, Walter G. Stephan.
—2nd ed.
        p.   cm.
    Previous ed.: Homewood, Ill.: Dorsey Press, 1985.
    Includes bibliographical references.
    ISBN 0-534-11706-6
    1. Social psychology.   I. Stephan, Walter G.   II. Title.
HM251.S776   1990
302—dc20   89-16573
                                                CIP

■

To Janie and Neil White,
and to the memory of Peg and Jim Stephan.

CONTENTS IN BRIEF

CHAPTER 1: The Two Social Psychologies   1

CHAPTER 2: Social Psychological Theories   21

CHAPTER 3: Methods in Social Psychology   53

CHAPTER 4: Socialization   83

CHAPTER 5: The Self   110

CHAPTER 6: Sex and Gender   134

CHAPTER 7: Conformity and Society   166

CHAPTER 8: Deviance   195

CHAPTER 9: Person Perception   220

CHAPTER 10: Attitudes and Attitude Change   255

CHAPTER 11: Attraction   284

CHAPTER 12: Prosocial Behavior   315

CHAPTER 13: Aggression   347

CHAPTER 14: Groups   385

CHAPTER 15: Intergroup Relations   419

CHAPTER 16: Collective Behavior   453

CHAPTER 17: Applications of Social Psychology   478

            Name Index   513

            Subject Index   515

CONTENTS IN DETAIL

Instructor's Preface   xiii

Student's Preface   xv

CHAPTER 1
The Two Social Psychologies 1

What Is Social Psychology?   2

Sociological Social Psychology   3

   Sociological Heritage   3

   Sociological Social Psychology's Two
Perspectives   5

   Content   5

   Level of Analysis   5

   Methodology   7

   Theoretical Perspectives   7

Psychological Social Psychology   9

   Psychological Heritage   9

   Content   12

   Level of Analysis   12

   Methodology   12

   Theoretical Perspectives   13

Why a Synthesis of Social Psychologies?   15

   The Robbers Cave Study: An Integrated
Strategy   17

Summary   18

References   19

CHAPTER 2
Social Psychological Theories 21

Symbolic Interactionism   24

   Premises of Symbolic Interactionism   24

   Symbols   25

   Two Schools of Symbolic Interactionism   26

   Offshoots of Symbolic Interactionism   29

Role Theory   31

   Role Expectations   32

   Types of Roles   33

   Multiple Roles   33

Social Learning Theory   37

   Enactive Learning   37

   Observational Learning   38

   Acquisition and Performance   41

   The Regulation of Behavior   41

Exchange Theory   44

   The Propositions of Exchange Theory   45

   Power and Exchange   46

   The Norm of Reciprocity   46

   Distributive Justice   47

   Equity   47

Summary   50

References   51

CHAPTER 3
Methods in Social Psychology   53

Magic and Science: A Comparison 54
   Magic 54
   Science 55
Surveys and Observational Methods 57
   Questionnaires and Interviews 57
   Unstructured Interviews 62
   Observational Techniques 63
Experiments and Field Studies 69
   Laboratory Experiments 69
   Field Experiments 72
   Field Studies 74
Ethics in Social Psychology 77
   Confidentiality and Privacy 78
   Deception 78
   Psychological Harm 79
Summary 80
References 81

CHAPTER 4
Socialization   83

What Is Socialization? 84
   The Goals of Socialization 84
   Language and Socialization 85
   The Two Social Psychologies and Socialization 85
The Agents of Socialization 87
   The Family 87
   Schools 88
   Peer Groups 89
   Mass Media 89
   Other Influences 89
The Process of Socialization 91
   Psychoanalytic Theory 91
   Social Learning Theory 93
   Cognitive Developmental Theory 94

Characteristics of Socialization 97
   Continuity and Change 97
   Reciprocal Socialization 98
   Socialization Across Societies 100
Socialization through the Life Cycle 100
   Socialization in Childhood and Adulthood 100
   Adult Socialization 101
   Erikson's Psychosexual Stages 102
   Resocialization 104
   Old Age and Beyond 105
Summary 107
References 108

CHAPTER 5
The Self   110

The Development of the Self 111
   The Looking-Glass Self 111
   Mead's View of the Self 112
   Significant Others 113
The Self-Concept 114
   Measuring the Self-Concept 115
   Identities and the Self 115
   The Changing Self 115
   The Mutable Self 117
Self-Perception 117
   Self-Perception Theory 117
   Self-Schemata 119
Self-Presentation 120
   Strategies of Self-Presentation 120
   Individual Differences in Self-Presentation 125
Self-Esteem 127
   Self-Efficacy and Self-Esteem 128
Summary 130
References 131

CHAPTER 6
Sex and Gender   **134**

Sex, Sex Stereotypes, Gender Roles, and
Sexual Preference   135
Gender-Role Socialization   136
    The Family   136
    The Schools   137
    Peers   137
    The Media   137
Sex Differences and Similarities   139
    Intellectual Abilities   139
    Personality Traits   140
Explanations for Sex Differences   141
    Biological Explanations   141
    Environmental Explanations   143
Why Are Inaccurate Sex Stereotypes
Believed?   146
    Consistency with Gender-Role
    Socialization   146
    Sex and Power   147
Consequences of Restrictive Gender Roles   148
    Negative Consequences for Women   148
    The Male Gender Role and Its Negative
    Consequences   157
How Is Restrictive Gender-Role Socialization
Maintained?   158
    Motherhood   159
    Women's Two Jobs   160
In Search of Equality   161
Summary   161
References   162

CHAPTER 7
Conformity and Society   **166**

Conformity to the Norms of Society   168
    Consensus Is Never Total   170
    Consensus Is Negotiated   172

Conformity to Group or Individual Norms   172
    Reference Groups and Pressures
    to Conform   173
    Types of Social Influence Producing
    Conformity   176
    Pressures Toward Conformity   182
    Overobedience to Authority   186
    Deindividuation   189
Summary   191
References   192

CHAPTER 8
Deviance   **195**

Deviance as Problematic Behavior   197
    Strain Theories   197
    Differential Association Theory   200
    Control Theory   201
    A Self Theory of Deviance   204
    Assessing the Perspectives on Deviance as
    Objective   204
Labeling Theory   205
    Self-Fulfilling Prophecy   207
    Blaming the Victim   208
    The Labeling Theory Perspective on Mental
    Illness   210
    General Critique of Labeling Theory   216
    Is Deviance Objective or Subjective?   216
Summary   217
References   218

CHAPTER 9
Person Perception   **220**

Impression Formation   221
Establishing Identities   222
    Definitions of the Situation   224
    Situated Identities   224
    Negotiating Identities   225

Correspondent Inference Theory   226

   Trait Inferences   227

   Confirmation and Disconfirmation of
   Expectancies   228

Actor-Observer Differences in Attributions   230

Cognitive Information Processing and Person
Perception   231

Biases in Information Processing   234

   Attention   234

   Encoding   238

   Storage   242

   Retrieval   248

Summary   249

References   250

CHAPTER   10
Attitudes and Attitude Change   **255**

Defining Attitudes   256

The Functions of Attitudes   257

The Measurement of Attitudes   258

Attitude-Behavior Consistency   259

   Reasons for Inconsistencies   259

   LaPiere's Classic Study   263

Attitude Change Based on Cognitive Factors   264

   Cognitive Dissonance Theory   264

   Self-Perception Theory   267

Attitude Change Induced by Persuasive
Communications   270

   Type of Communicator   271

   Type of Communication   272

   Type of Audience   273

   Problems with the Communicator/Message/
   Audience Approach   275

   The Elaboration Likelihood Model   275

Summary   279

References   280

CHAPTER   11
Attraction   **284**

Predispositions to Attraction   285

   Attraction Is Functional   286

   Spatial Proximity   286

   Familiarity   287

Theories of Attraction   288

   Reinforcement Theories   288

   Balance Theory   299

   Misattribution of Arousal   300

Being in Love   302

   The Relationship of Liking and Romantic
   Loving   302

   How Do I Love Thee? Let Me Count the
   Stages   306

   A Multi-Stage Theory of Love   306

   Relationship's End: Is Breaking Up Really Hard
   to Do?   308

   Critique of Theories of Romantic
   Attraction   310

Summary   310

References   311

CHAPTER   12
Prosocial Behavior   **315**

Sociobiology   318

   Biological Evolution   318

   Social Evolution   320

Bystander Intervention   322

   Stage I   322

   Stage II   324

   Stage III   324

   Stage IV   325

Helper/Situation/Recipient Approach   327

   The Helper   328

   The Situation   332

   The Recipient   339

Summary   342

References   343

CHAPTER 13
Aggression   347

Family Violence and Rape   350
   Wife Battering   350
   Child Abuse   353
   Rape   355
Aggressor/Situation/Target Model   362
   The Aggressor   362
   The Situation   367
   The Target   376
Summary   377
References   379

CHAPTER 14
Groups   385

Types of Groups   387
   Primary Groups   387
   Formal Task Groups, Informal Groups, and Aggregates   389
Group Structure   390
   Power Structures   390
   Communication Structures   393
   Interpersonal Attraction Structures   394
Group Performance   397
   Additive Tasks   398
   Disjunctive Tasks   398
   Conjunctive Tasks   399
   Complementary Tasks   400
Social Facilitation   400
Group Dynamics   402
   Group Cohesion   402
   Group Polarization   404
   Minority Influence   406
Leadership   407
   Leadership Traits   409
   Behavioral Style   410
   Bureaucracies   411
   Transactional Theories of Leadership   413

Summary   414
References   415

CHAPTER 15
Intergroup Relations   419

The Historical Approach to
Intergroup Relations   421
   Internal Colonialism   422
   Assimilation and Acculturation   422
   Blau's Macrosocial Theory of Structural Assimilation   425
   Institutional Racism   426
   Reactions to Minority Status   429
Cognitive Processes That Contribute to Prejudice and Stereotyping   431
   Categorization   431
   Perceptual Assimilation and Contrast   432
   The Principle of Least Effort   434
   The Norm of Ingroup-Outgroup Bias   434
   The Ultimate Attribution Error   435
   Ethnocentrism   436
   Ambivalent Attitudes and Polarized Responses   437
Reducing Prejudice and Stereotyping   439
   The Contact Hypothesis   439
   The Effects of Desegregation   441
   The Jigsaw Classroom   444
   Reducing Intergroup Ignorance   446
   Other Techniques   447
Summary   448
References   450

CHAPTER 16
Collective Behavior   **453**

What Is Collective Behavior?   454
Types of Collective Behavior   455
    Mass Behavior   456
    Crowds   461
    Social Movements   470
Summary   474
References   476

CHAPTER 17
Applications of Social Psychology   **478**

Social Psychology and the Criminal
Justice System   479
    Pretrial Influences   482
    Jury Selection   482

Presentations of Evidence   483
Judicial Instructions   488
Jury Decision Making   488
Concluding Methodological Note   490
Social Psychology and Medicine   491
    From Health to Illness   492
    Stress   493
    Cancer   496
    Heart Disease   498
    Preventing and Treating Disease   499
Summary   505
References   506

Name Index   513
Subject Index   515

INSTRUCTOR'S PREFACE

In this text we attempt to integrate sociological and psychological social psychology. For each of the topics we discuss we have tried to bring together and synthesize the theories and research of both disciplines.

We begin the book with three introductory chapters, starting with a discussion of the differences between the two social psychologies in theory, level of analysis, and methods. We show students that combining the two approaches yields a richer and more complete understanding of social behavior than using only one approach. In the second chapter we first present two sociological social psychology theories: symbolic interactionism and role theory. Then we present two theories used by both social psychologies: exchange theory and social learning theory. We present these theories to illustrate the range of theories used in the two disciplines and to provide students with a background in some of the theories we will rely on in subsequent chapters. Chapter 3 covers a wide variety of techniques employed by the two social psychologies. It starts with techniques employed primarily by sociological social psychologists including questionnaires, interviews, and observational techniques. This chapter then covers techniques more commonly employed by psychological social psychology including experiments and field studies.

Having laid the groundwork for an understanding of how the two social psychologies approach social behavior, we proceed to a discussion of specific topic areas. These chapters are arranged in an order that we find logical, but since each is a separate unit they may be covered in any order the instructor wishes. We begin with a chapter on the self because self cognitions have such an important impact on behavior. The chapter on the self and the following ones on socialization and gender roles rely heavily on both sociological and psychological approaches. We have paired conformity and deviance, even though traditionally the first has primarily been the domain of psychology and the second of sociology. We think these chapters, along with the ones on socialization and gender roles, provide students with an essential background in understanding the important influence that social structure exerts on social interaction.

Next we explore a set of topics that derive primarily from psychological social psychology, including person perception, attitude change, attraction, prosocial behavior, and aggression. Our discussions of each of these topics include contributions of sociological social psychologists that are often ignored in psychological social psychology texts. For instance, discussions of establishing and negotiating identities, sociobiology, charitable contributions, rape, child abuse, and wife abuse are included. These chapters illustrate the role that factors associated with social situations, as well as individual factors, play in shaping social behavior.

The chapters on groups, intergroup relations, and collective behavior show how effectively the two social psychologies can be combined to yield a more comprehensive picture of a given topic than relying on only one approach. The study of groups and their interrelations provides a perfect opportunity to demonstrate that individual behavior is embedded in social contexts, of which a prominent feature is the groups to which individuals belong.

We end the book by applying the two social psychologies to the criminal justice system and to health and illness. We do this to show students that social psychology can make contributions to our understanding of important social institutions.

The essence of our approach is well summarized by Sheldon Stryker in a review of this text: "You cannot think reasonably about human behavior without considering the impact of cultural, social, and interactional processes on the human who behaves."

We would like to thank Sheldon Stryker, Indiana University; J. Michael Armer, Florida State University; Charles M. Bonjean, University of Texas, Austin; Nathan Church; Kathleen T. Crittenden, University of Illinois, Chicago; Harry Gyman, Bowling Green State University; Cary S. Hart, University of Toledo; Judith A. Howard, University of Washington; Jerri Husch, Tufts University; Karl Pillemer, University of

New Hampshire; Jerome Rabow, UCLA; Sandra Stanley, Towson State University; and Paul D. Starr, Auburn University for reviewing the manuscript for this edition and providing us with such useful feedback. We would also like to thank Paul O'Connell and Marlene Chamberlain, formerly of Dorsey Press, and Serina Beauparlant, Marla Nowick, Theresa Coyne, Hal Humphrey, MaryEllen Podgorski, and Karen Hunt of Wadsworth Publishing Company for all they have done to create this book.

STUDENT'S PREFACE

We are all social psychologists at heart because we all share a fascination with social behavior. In this book we will try to teach you a systematic approach to understanding social behavior. We have made this text as "user friendly" as we can. This preface outlines what we have done to make this book easy to use. We also offer suggestions concerning how to read this book to achieve maximal learning.

Organization within the Chapters

Every chapter begins with an outline and ends with a summary. At the beginning of each chapter we briefly discuss the main topics to be covered. The material in the chapters is divided through the use of three levels of subheads. These subheads form a hierarchy. The primary subhead indicates the main topics to be presented. The second level of subhead is used to divide these main topics into subcategories. The third level of subhead is used for more detailed information. Generally the first and last paragraphs under each subheading contain the most valuable information. New ideas are presented and material is summarized in these paragraphs. Similarly, the first and last sentences of each paragraph are usually the most important. The central concepts in each chapter are italicized. Usually the definition of the concept is presented the first time the concept appears.

Each chapter contains extra material to lighten your reading. Boxes are used to supplement the ideas presented in the text. Pictures, figures, tables, and cartoons are included to make the material easier to understand or more interesting. To help you focus on the ideas and information presented in the book we have tried to minimize the use of names and dates. You can find the references to the material we cite at the end of each chapter.

Study Tips

To learn the material in our book, or in any other book, you must comprehend and organize the information you read. You will remember more if you follow a few simple rules.

First, you should read in blocks of time. How long these blocks should be depends on your reading rate, ability to concentrate, and alertness. When you are tired or distracted a half hour may be too much, but when you are able to give yourself fully to the job of reading it may be possible to go for hours. To make it easier to concentrate, try to read in an environment that is free from distractions or disruptions.

Second, prepare to read the material you are going to cover before you start. If you are beginning a chapter, read the outline. Then read the summary at the end of the chapter. You may not fully understand all the concepts and findings that are summarized, but don't be discouraged. What you do not understand tells you what you need to pay the most attention to as you read. Next, decide how much material you are going to read at this sitting. Preview this material by skimming the subheadings so you get a general idea of the topics covered in this section.

Why all this preparation? Memory depends on understanding and structuring information. Knowing the structure of the material beforehand gives you a framework into which you can fit information as you read it. The material will be easier to recall later if it is well organized to begin with.

Third, read for comprehension. If you cannot comprehend the information, you will not remember it. We have tried to help you comprehend the material by presenting it in a logical fashion, but ultimately you must do the work of comprehending it. This is an active, not a passive process. If you want to remember information you cannot simply try to understand it, you must actively engage it and challenge your own understanding in the process. Before you read a paragraph ask yourself relevant questions, such as "What is cognitive dissonance?" or "Is self-monitoring useful or harmful?" Try to think of examples of concepts or apply them to your own life or the lives of friends of yours. Relate the concepts to one another as you read.

Fourth, match your reading style to the material. If the material is unfamiliar or difficult, read more slowly and go back over it if necessary. Read illustrations or examples more quickly. Varying your reading rate will maintain your interest. Sometimes reading a little faster than usual will force you to concentrate harder and this can have beneficial effects. To make it easier to review the material later, and to force you to note what is worth remembering, underline the central concepts of theories and important research findings for each topic.

Fifth, recall what you have read. Recalling information is one of the best ways of improving memory for it. After you have read a paragraph or a section, try to recall the main points. If you cannot remember them immediately after reading them, you almost certainly will not be able to recall them later. If you have difficulty remembering the material, read it again. You can't answer questions about material you do not understand or remember. When you have finished reading all the material for this sitting spend an extra minute or two to see if you can recall the main points in order. Ask yourself what questions your instructor is likely to ask about this material. Could you answer them now? If not, you may want to spend some extra time on this material later.

Actively extracting the desired information from the text, asking yourself questions, thinking of examples, and trying to recall the information you have read are all useful in aiding memory. The reason is that these techniques make you process the information more thoroughly and relate it more effectively to what you already know than simply reading to understand. It may take a little more work, but it is more interesting and has a higher payoff than reading the lazy way.

Now if you are following this strategy, you should try to remember the points we have just made. This will give you an opportunity to practice this technique right now and increase the chances you will use it when reading the book.

We hope you enjoy reading our book. We learned from the first edition that students are the first to spot our mistakes. If you find one we would really appreciate it if you would write us. Also, if there are things you particularly like, or dislike, about the book, let us know. You can write us at the Department of Sociology and Anthropology or the Department of Psychology, New Mexico State University, Las Cruces, NM 88003.

Cookie White Stephan
Walter G. Stephan

CHAPTER 1

The Two Social Psychologies

What Is Social Psychology?

Sociological Social Psychology

Sociological Heritage

Sociological Social Psychology's Two Perspectives

Content

Level of Analysis

Methodology

Theoretical Perspectives

Psychological Social Psychology

Psychological Heritage

Content

Level of Analysis

Methodology

Theoretical Perspectives

Why a Synthesis of Social Psychologies?

The Robbers Cave Study: An Integrated Strategy

WHAT IS SOCIAL PSYCHOLOGY?

■ Jason and Andy are both second graders. Jason's mother wants him to be high in self-esteem, ambitious, and independent. Andy's mother wants him to be cooperative, obedient, and neat in appearance. Why do the mothers want such different behaviors in their children?

■ Our country has a sad history of racial discrimination, with social, economic, and political costs borne by generation after generation of minorities. During the last 20 years, however, minorities have made many strides. Our ideal is a society of equal opportunities. How close are we to our ideal?

■ Jennifer says she believes that people should obey traffic laws. Yet she chronically speeds and sometimes drives a bit recklessly. Why are her attitudes and behaviors inconsistent?

■ Senator Padilla has just attended hearings on the issue of acid rain. Soon he must vote for or against monies to be appropriated to alleviate this perceived problem. These hearings have made him think about the formation of social problems. In this society a number of social problems exist, but how and why do certain conditions but not others come to be defined as problems? Does acid rain constitute a social problem? Is it important enough? How can one determine its importance? If acid rain is a social problem, when did it start to be one? When would it cease to be a social problem?

■ Companies that advertise products on television want glitzy, attention-getting commercials for their products, and advertising executives are only too willing to produce them. Do these ads really sell products? Is it possible that we remember the ads but don't buy the products? What is the most persuasive type of communication?

These topics—socialization, racial discrimination, attitude-behavior inconsistencies, the definition of situations, and persuasion—are examples of the subject matter of social psychology. The questions asked in these examples are the types of questions social psychologists attempt to answer.

What is social psychology? Social psychology seeks to understand and explain human behavior in its social context. Social psychology is concerned with how people, and the social forces that impinge on them, affect one another's thoughts, feelings, and behavior (1).

Social psychology is studied in two disciplines, sociology and psychology. In this book we will present the entire field of social psychology, both sociological and psychological. Sociology and psychology have overlapping but somewhat differing contents, levels of analysis, methodologies, and theoretical perspectives on social psychology. The social psychology of sociologists and the social psychology of psychologists also have much in common. Clearly, the field of social psychology profits from interchanges between the two viewpoints, and you too will benefit from an approach that combines both views.

In this chapter we will first introduce the two social psychologies, sociological social psychology and psychological social psychology. For each social psychology, we will in turn explore some of its intellectual roots, its content, its level of analysis, its methodology, and its theoretical perspectives. Then we will discuss the similarities between the two social psychologies and the need to integrate them. Finally, we will examine a successful research synthesis of sociological social psychology and psychological social psychology.

What do we mean by the content, level of analysis, methodology, and theoretical perspectives of the two social psychologies?

■ *Content* specifies the subject matter to which each branch of social psychology pertains.

■ *Level of analysis* concerns the types of phenomena on which social psychologists focus. Some social psychologists study individuals and their

■ *Secret delight: Social psychology is concerned with how people affect one another's thoughts, feelings, and behaviors. (© Richard S. Orton 1990)*

behaviors or small groups of individuals. Other social psychologists examine the relationship between individuals and the society. Take, for example, the topic of racial prejudice. One group of social psychologists might study individuals, asking why some people in a group are high in prejudice while others in that group are low in prejudice. Another group of social psychologists might study groups within societies, asking why in a given society some groups of people are high in prejudice, while others are low in prejudice.

■ *Methodology* consists of the procedures by which social psychological knowledge is acquired and the types of information sought by social psychologists.

■ *Theoretical perspective* concerns the general principles employed by social psychologists to explain their findings.

■

SOCIOLOGICAL SOCIAL PSYCHOLOGY

Sociological Heritage

Sociology is the study of social interaction and its consequences—the creation of human society and social behavior. The major premise of sociology is that human behavior is shaped by the groups to which people belong and by the social interaction that takes place in these groups.

Sociologists Emile Durkheim, Max Weber, Georg Simmel, and W. I. Thomas were among the many intellectual precursors of modern sociological social psychology (2). Durkheim (1855–1917) emphasized the necessity of understanding people's social realities to comprehend and predict their behavior (3).

For example, Durkheim demonstrated that social facts such as the differing suicide rates in different countries should be explained by social—not merely individual—forces (4). He argued that people who were not integrated into the religious, family, and political institutions of modern society were more at risk for suicide than people who were more integrated into the society. Durkheim found support for his theory in European countries around the turn of the century. Recent support has also been found in the United States (5).

One of Weber's (1864–1920) contributions to social psychological thought was his recognition that people's views of the world are subjective and their interpretations of reality are keys to their actions (6). Weber understood that this interpretative process can have critical effects on society itself. He studied the changes in Western European societies that resulted from the values and beliefs of Protestantism. This study provides a classic example of a situation in which people's interpretations of reality led to actions that changed society (7). Weber argued

that Protestant religious doctrine generates values such as individualism, hard work, and frugality. People with these religious values apply them in the economic realm, thus bringing about capitalistic economies.

Simmel (1856–1916) studied the forms and content of social interaction, asking such questions as: "How do group affiliations influence personality?" (8). Like Durkheim, Simmel was concerned with the relationship between the individual and society. He viewed society as more than the sum of its individual members. Simmel felt the interactions among the individual members produce a unique social reality. He focused on the involvement of individuals in groups, which he believed to be the necessary condition for the creation of societies. Simmel noted that people tend to associate with *ingroups,* or other people of their own kind. However, since one has many ingroups (social class, religious, recreational, racial, educational, sex), one's ingroups are crosscutting. For example, one's religious ingroup is likely to contain members of both sexes and other racial

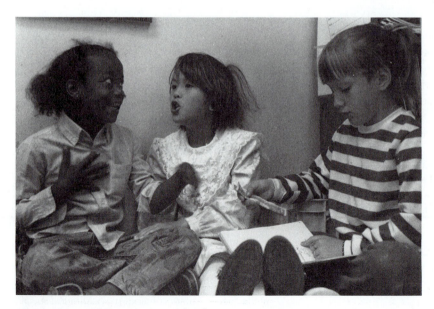

■ *Simmel noted that group memberships are crosscutting.*
(© Richard S. Orton 1990)

groups. Due to the cross-cutting nature of group memberships, it is often the case that the more contact we seek with ingroups, the more we are also brought into contact with outgroup members. Ironically, then, the greater our bias toward the ingroup, the more we must interact with outgroup members.

W. I. Thomas (1863–1947) emphasized human subjectivity. He defined a social situation as a combination of objective environmental conditions plus the subjective values, attitudes, and needs humans bring to a situation. His contributions to social psychological thought include his emphasis on the subjective over the objective aspects of social existence. This emphasis is exemplified in his concept of the *definition of the situation*. Individuals' definitions are meaningful because they have behavioral consequences. As Thomas wrote, "... if men define situations as real, they are real in their consequences" (9). Thus, people do not act solely on the basis of the objective reality, but are also influenced by their *perceptions* of reality.

Sociological Social Psychology's Two Perspectives

Two dominant perspectives within sociological social psychology are *symbolic interactionism* and the *personality and social structure perspective* (10). They are similar in many respects, because they both developed within the discipline of sociology, but they are different in others. In our discussion of sociological social psychology, we will present both perspectives and focus on some of the differences between them. As we explore the level of analysis, methodology, and theories of sociological social psychology, we will differentiate both the symbolic interactionist and personality and social structure perspectives.

Content

The two perspectives on sociological social psychology agree on its content. A sociological definition of social psychology is as follows:

Soc. S. P. def:

Social psychology ... is concerned with the behavior and psychological processes of individuals who occupy positions in social structures, organizations, and groups. On the one hand, social psychology is focused upon explaining the behavior of individuals as it is controlled, influenced, or limited by the social environment. On the other hand, it is concerned with the manner in which the behavior of individuals reacts upon, shapes and alters social structures and enters into the functioning of groups (11).

What is social structure? *Social structure* is the underlying framework of society, the regularity in patterns of relationships in a society. Social structures consist of such components as groups, *social statuses* (positions in society), *roles* (the expectations associated with a particular status), and *institutions* (patterns of behavior developed to fill a basic social need, such as education, the family, religion, politics, and the economy).

Sociologists thus emphasize the interdependence of individuals and the society. Like other sociologists, sociological social psychologists believe the individual and society are not distinct and separate units. Rather, they are determined by each other and neither can be understood without reference to the other. To understand individuals, one must examine the society which has shaped them and which is continually reshaping them. To understand a society, one must look to the individuals who constitute the society and who are constantly redefining it. For sociologists, the task of social psychology is to understand this reciprocal or two-way influence.

Level of Analysis

We can divide inquiry in social psychology into two types: *microsocial processes*, the events concerning individuals and small groups of individuals; and *macrosocial processes*, the events concerning larger groups, such as society's socioeconomic, ethnic, political, economic, and religious groups, or still larger groups, such as institutions or whole societies.

■ *Sociological social psychologists are interested in the ways positions in the social structure influence people's thoughts, feelings , and behaviors. (WGS)*

Most social psychology is microsocial, but some is macrosocial.

Sociologists who adopt the *symbolic interactionist perspective* are concerned primarily with micro-processes. They view the explanation of social interaction as a primary task of sociology. Topics of central interest to symbolic interactionists include the self, socialization, small groups, language, and roles.

Sociologists who take the *personality and social structure perspective* regard the link between micro-social individual characteristics and macrosocial characteristics of society as the primary topic of social psychology (12). Topics of interest from the personality and social structure viewpoint include the relationships between micro-level individual characteristics, such as personality traits, attitudes, values, or behavior and society's macro-level social institutions (occupational or religious organizations, social classes) or social processes (social mobility, urbanization) (13). Think back to Weber's study of the Protestant ethic, described above. This study provides one of the earliest examples of the link between micro-level events (individual values) with macro-level events (religious doctrine and economic structures).

If a symbolic interactionist were to study educational achievement, he or she might choose to study its particular meaning for individuals—for example, as a fulfillment of a desire to become a scholar or as a symbol of status unmatched by others in one's family. A sociologist from the personality and social structure perspective would be more likely to study the reasons for the different educational attainment (a micro-level variable) of members of various social classes (a macro-level variable). Do upper-class students receive more encouragement to continue in school than working-class students, or are financial resources the only important factor in their different levels of education?

Methodology

Some sociologists from the *symbolic interactionist perspective* feel human social behavior should not be studied out of context but in the natural "real life" setting. They insist that subjective methods *be* used that capture the world of the persons being studied (14). These symbolic interactionists feel such techniques as surveys and questionnaires should not be used because the objectivity of surveys means the perspective of the individual being studied is often ignored. They emphasize methods that incorporate the persons' views of themselves and of their worlds, such as the study of personal documents, rigorous observation (such as participating in the activities of the group under study), in-depth interviews, and discussions. Their methods are *qualitative;* they distinguish one object of study from another on the basis of type or kind (the preferences of men vs. women for political candidates, the differing views on marriage of lower-class vs. middle-class couples). These methods may be contrasted with *quantitative* methods, in which the magnitude of variables is measured (measuring agreement with the candidates' views on issues in a campaign as a predictor of voting patterns, measuring couples' levels of compatibility to predict marital success).

Other symbolic interactionists use a limited range of quantitative techniques (15). For example, these symbolic interactions use structured questionnaires designed to measure an individual's sense of self. Still other symbolic interactionists accept all quantitative measures as valid, and commonly use a variety of standardized objective measures, such as surveys and questionnaires (16).

Sociologists from the *personality and social structure perspective* believe social psychological concepts should be quantified and subjected to rigorous empirical tests. These sociologists are thoroughly quantitative in their approach, using the full range of quantitative measures employed by other social scientists.

Theoretical Perspectives

We will briefly introduce symbolic interactionism here, and discuss it in more detail in Chapter 2 (17). Symbolic interactionists focus primary attention on the *social construction of reality:* the way in which individuals define and continually redefine reality on the basis of social interaction. Symbolic interactionists believe meaning is determined through social interaction. For example, the way you view your home town is dependent upon your interactions with the people in it and with the physical surroundings. For this reason, your home town has a different meaning to you than to any other person.

In addition, behavior can only be understood in its social context. Behaviors exhibited in two different settings may have very different meanings. You may refuse a cup of coffee in the dorm cafeteria because you are not thirsty, but refuse a cup of coffee at a reception at the university president's house for fear of spilling it.

Howard Becker's research on becoming a marijuana user provides a classic example of research conducted from the perspective of the symbolic interactionist. More than 30 years ago, Becker studied the process by which people learn to use marijuana for pleasure by conducting in-depth interviews with marijuana users (18). Becker asked users to recount the history of their experiences with the drug. His method thus emphasized the subjective world of the informants, and the construction of meaning through social interaction.

Becker found that people use marijuana for pleasure only if they successfully pass through three stages. First, people must learn to smoke marijuana in such a way that its effects can be experienced. That is, individuals must learn how to smoke a "joint." Second, people must learn how to get "high"—they must learn the symptoms of being high

Symbolic Interactionism: A Research Example

As we have noted, symbolic interactionists focus on the social construction of reality, the ways in which meanings are derived from social interaction. One recent study of the "making" of meaning examines how missing children have come to be seen as a social problem (19).

Social problems are transitory, like all aspects of social reality. Some social problems (witchcraft) fade and others are created (AIDS). For a problem to be conceived as important, certain claims must be made and accepted. The phenomenon must be defined and estimates of the size of the problem must be sufficient to warrant attention. In addition, broad publicity given to "horror stories" associated with the problem tend to precede its recognition as a social problem.

In the case of missing children, United States Senate hearings were held in 1981. These hearings helped to establish the definition of missing children as a problem by drawing attention to the issue. The term "missing children" was officially defined to include runaways, children kidnapped by parents who do not have legal custody, and children abducted by strangers. In addition, the problem was further defined in terms of the types of danger to which such children were exposed (child molestation, prostitution, abuse) and the reasons for concern (children are blameless in their disappearance yet suffer tremendously as a consequence of it; they are priceless to society; they fall into the hands of criminals who use them to further criminal and immoral goals).

Organizations devoted to runaways were created. They distributed pamphlets claiming two million children were disappearing each year and focused attention on stranger abduction. A few cases of stranger abduction received national attention and companies began to run photographs of missing children on items such as milk cartons and in public service television announcements. Police departments cooperated through a program of fingerprinting children so they could be more readily identified if they disappeared.

This campaign was extremely successful in drawing attention to missing children. Ironically, the estimates of the magnitude of the problem were unbelievably overinflated. The actual number of children kidnapped by strangers is around 100–200 per year! The missing children "problem" is actually an extremely small one, but it *was* a large problem for several years during the 1980s because it was perceived as such. ■

and learn how to recognize these sensations in themselves. Typically, this learning takes place by observing the behavior of other users or through direct instruction by others. Third, people must learn to experience the sensation of being high as pleasurable. Becker found that naive users of marijuana often initially experienced these sensations as frightening, rather than as pleasant.

Only when people mastered all three steps did they use marijuana for pleasure. Thus, even what is usually considered to be a physiologically based sensation, getting high from smoking marijuana, is social in nature. It is largely a symbolically constructed activity that is shaped through interaction with other people.

For sociologists who work within the personality and social structure perspective, the major task of social psychology is to show how the individual (microsocial level of analysis) and society (macrosocial level of analysis) are linked. This perspective differs from symbolic interactionism because symbolic interactionists focus only on the microsocial level of analysis.

Sociologists working from the personality and social structure perspective employ a variety of social psychological theories in their research, such as role theory or exchange theory, both of which we will discuss in Chapter 2. They also use theories from other areas of sociology and mini-theories that apply to a given topic, such as occupational choice or intergroup relations. Since the uniqueness of this perspective lies in its attention to the link between microsocial and macrosocial events—and not in a single theoretical perspective—we will illustrate the personality and society perspective by describing a major research tradition from this school of thought. This work explores the association of social class and personality (20).

For many years, Melvin Kohn and his colleagues have studied the influence of social class on parental values and behavior regarding their children. It has been clear to sociologists for some time that social class is associated with many aspects of human life, but until recently it has not been equally clear why this is so. Kohn and his colleagues have found that upper-class people are more likely to value self-

direction and concern with internal psychological processes in their children, while lower-class people are more likely to value conformity and concern with appearance (21).

These values are associated with the parents' different work conditions (22). The work of upper-class parents is typically high in *occupational self-direction;* it is usually complex, unsupervised, and nonroutine. The work experiences of upper-class parents lead to world views that cause them to stress intellectual pursuits, self-motivation, and flexibility for their children. The work of lower-class parents typically is low in occupational self-direction; it is closely supervised, routine, and low in complexity. Their work experiences lead to world views that cause them to emphasize obedience to authority, conformity, and cleanliness in child-rearing.

Social class is not a personality or cultural variable; rather it is a structural variable because it is related to the underlying framework of the society. This research, conducted from the personality and society perspective, demonstrates how location in the structure of society influences beliefs and values. It is theoretically important because it provides an explanatory mechanism—work conditions—for the relationship of social class and child-rearing practices.

■

PSYCHOLOGICAL SOCIAL PSYCHOLOGY

Psychological Heritage

Like symbolic interactionism, psychology is the study of micro-level behavior. Unlike symbolic interactionists, however, psychologists attempt to understand the *cognitions* (thoughts), behavior, and *affect* (emotions) of humans, in order to understand how they would be likely to behave in a specified set of conditions.

Psychological social psychology counts psychoanalytic theory, learning theory, and field theory among its many intellectual roots (24). Psychoanalytic

■ *Holely preoccupied: The work of lower-class people typically is closely supervised, routine, and low in complexity. (WGS)*

theory, as exemplified in the pioneering work of Sigmund Freud (1856–1939), showed that thoughts not accessible to immediate awareness can have observable effects on human experience and behavior. In addition, Freud's work highlighted the conflict between an egotistical fulfillment of individual needs and a concern for the general welfare of all of society's needs (25). Motivation and equilibrium are key concepts in Freud's theory. Drives are created by physical or psychic frustrations; these drives must be met in order to return the human organism to a state of equilibrium. The psychoanalytic tradition has advanced social psychology through its recognition of the nonconscious and motivational nature of needs and the individual-society link.

One of learning theory's major contributions to

learning ⓣ

psychological social psychology derives from its discovery of the relationships between environmental stimuli and behavioral responses. According to the *law of effect,* a response closely followed by satisfaction will be more likely to reoccur, while a response closely followed by discomfort will be less likely to reoccur (26). For instance, let's say you study hard for a social psychology exam. If you are rewarded by receiving a high grade, you are more likely to study hard for your next social psychology exam than if you are punished by receiving a low grade. The knowledge that people's behavior is determined in part by the rewards and punishments they receive as a consequence of that behavior is useful in predicting behavior.

Learning theory directed the attention of social

BOX 1-2

Personality and Social Structure: A Research Example

The United States has a sad history of racial discrimination, and one of the many negative consequences of such discrimination is economic. One measure of economic disadvantage is underemployment, a combination of unemployment, employment at less than 35 hours per week, or employment in jobs with wages so low the workers cannot rise above the poverty level. A study of underemployment of urban black and white men from 1970 to 1982 was conducted to determine if this situation was changing, and if blacks were achieving greater economic gain than in the past (23).

This study thus seeks to link the macro-level or structural variable of ethnicity with the micro-level or individual-level variable of an individual's employment characteristics. In this instance, the macro-level variable is assumed to produce variations in the micro-level variable.

The data were not encouraging. Despite the fact that most people believe minorities have made great recent strides and more and more we are becoming a land of true equal opportunity, the underemployment data do not validate these beliefs. From 1970 to 1982 the underemployment gap between whites and blacks did not decrease. In fact, it increased substantially: The difference between black and white underemployment increased from 8 percent in 1970 to 18 percent in 1982. This underemployment gap occurred for all age groups, for all levels of education, and throughout the various shifts in the economy occurring during this time. ■

psychologists toward observable stimuli and responses, rather than toward unseen mental processes (27). Learning theory also focused attention on people's learned behavior, rather than on their biological characteristics. Social psychologists now understand that much human behavior is learned through positive and negative life experiences involving interaction with others and the environment.

Both social learning theory and exchange theory, to be discussed in Chapter 2, owe their existence to learning theory.

Kurt Lewin's (1890–1947) work on field theory directed attention toward the *Gestalt,* the total situation, in understanding behavior (28). For Lewin, behavior is a function of forces acting within the *life space,* which contains the *person* and his or her *psychological environment.* The physical world does not directly influence the individual. Instead, the person is influenced by events in the psychological environment, which is created through experiences with the physical world. The psychological environment includes the current situation and representations of the past and the future.

Lewin's interest in the influence of the psychological environment on the person led him to study the influence of groups on individual behavior. In one such study, he compared methods of persuasion, contrasting lectures with group discussions that ended with a public commitment to engage in behavior advocated by the persuasive communication. The combination of active group participation plus public commitment was much more effective in inducing behavioral change than the passive lecture method (29). Lewin's point is that much individual behavior cannot be understood apart from a group context.

Content

A psychological definition of social psychology is that social psychology is "an attempt to understand and explain how the thoughts, feelings, and behaviors of individuals are influenced by the actual, imagined, or implied presence of others" (30). Psychologists thus emphasize social cognition and social influence. For psychologists, the task of social psychology is to understand the behavior of individuals as a function of perceived social stimuli.

Level of Analysis

Psychological social psychology explores social cognition, affect, and behavior at the individual level. Social psychologists trained in psychology often study the influence of the current social situation on individuals' perceptions, feelings, and behaviors, as in the study of the influence of the number of bystanders on the likelihood that people will help in an emergency, or the influence of environmental cues that are associated with conformity (the pres-

ence of an authority figure) on the likelihood that people will conform. While sociological social psychology places greater emphasis on the structural forces that shape people's choices, the corresponding emphasis in psychological social psychology is on the immediate environment's influence on the person.

Typical topics of interest in psychological social psychology include attitude formation and change, racial prejudice, aggression, and conformity. These topics are also of interest to sociologists who employ the personality and social structure perspective of sociological social psychology. However, sociologists would be more likely to study these behaviors as a function of people's positions in society (the influence of social class of people's levels of aggressiveness), while psychologists would be more likely to study individuals' reactions to specific environmental events—for example, the influence of frustration on levels of aggression.

Methodology

Many of the social psychologists who work within psychological social psychology believe the complexity of social life must be reduced to facilitate the understanding of human behavior. These social psychologists frequently study behaviors in simplified or controlled social situations, such as laboratory settings (31). Social psychologists trained in psychology often control the situations they study, by allowing only one or a few dimensions of the setting to vary. They study the effects of these few variations on the behavior of people in that particular setting. For example, they might study how much prejudice people display in a particular situation by varying the race of another with whom the people are working. Thus, the methodology of psychological social psychology is largely experimental. While field experiments are sometimes conducted, most psychological social psychology research is conducted in laboratory settings. The research methodology of such social psychologists is almost exclusively quantitative (it measures the magnitude of variables).

BOX 1-3

Psychological Social Psychology: A Research Example

All of us use persuasion in an attempt to change others' attitudes and behaviors. As we know, some attempts are more successful than others. A cursory glance at typical television commercials shows advertising specialists clearly believe that vividness sells products. Commercials never calmly state the product's benefits. Instead, commercials grab our attention with some amusing or startling visual effect. The dialog is similarly vivid: the script may be provocative, outrageous, or humorous, but it is certainly ear-catching.

Does this strategy work? Recent studies of such vivid, colorful messages suggest it does not (2). In several studies, vividness was manifested in concrete and colorful language. In one, some people heard a vivid version of a news-story ("In one instance, a defenseless 70-year-old woman was jumped and brutally beaten in her garden"), while others heard a less vivid version ("Elderly people engaged in daily activities in and around their homes are often the victims of these juvenile crimes"). The results of these studies show that people are not more persuaded by vivid than by less vivid messages.

These studies also explain why advertising agencies continue to produce, and advertisers continue to buy, such ineffective messages. People recall vivid messages better than less vivid ones. In addition, people believe such messages are more persuasive, and further believe they and others are more persuaded by them. Both the audience and the advertisers are misled, by the greater recall of the messages, into believing these messages are also more persuasive. ■

persuasive vs recall

Theoretical Perspectives

Like the personality and social structure perspective within sociological social psychology, psychological social psychology does not have a single theoretical perspective. Some work in psychological social psychology is derived from social learning theory, exchange theory, and role theory, each of which we will discuss in Chapter 2. Beyond these general perspectives, psychological social psychology has developed mini-theories to explain certain categories of social behavior, such as helping and prejudice.

Figure 1.1 ■

The Theory of Reasoned Action

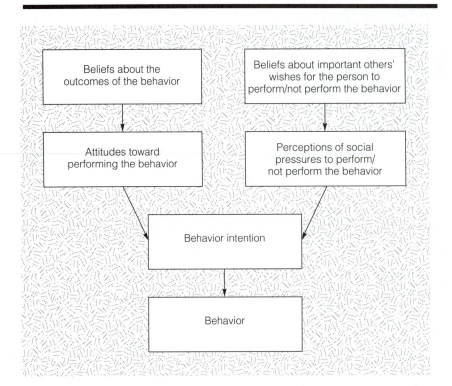

Because psychological social psychology has no single theoretical perspective, we will illustrate the use of theory in psychological social psychology by examining one psychological social psychology mini-theory linking attitudes and behaviors.

We all know that people do not always do what they say. Under what conditions are attitudes and behaviors linked? Martin Fishbein and Icek Ajzen have developed a *theory of reasoned action* linking behavior, behavioral intentions (intentions to engage in a certain behavior), attitudes (positive or negative evaluations toward a person or object), and beliefs (feelings of certainty about an issue or event) (32). According to this theory, people's behavioral intentions are the immediate determinants of their behaviors. Since intentions can change over time, the longer the interval between formation of the inten-

tion and the enactment of the behavior, the less likely the behavioral intentions will correspond to the behavior. Behavioral intentions are based on two factors: a personal factor, the person's attitudes toward the behavior in question, and a social factor, the person's perceptions of the social pressures to perform or not perform the behaviors. Both the person's attitudes and perceptions of social pressures are based on beliefs. Attitudes toward the behavior are based on beliefs about whether the behavior will lead to positive or negative outcomes. Perceptions of social pressures are based on beliefs that certain important individuals or groups want the person in question to perform or not perform the behavior. This theory is diagramed in Figure 1-1.

The theory of reasoned action has received considerable support. In one test of the theory,

Figure 1.2 ■

The Theory of Reasoned Action: An Example

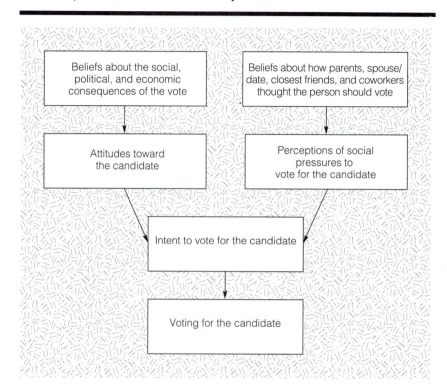

people's votes in a presidential election were predicted very accurately from their intentions to vote for a given candidate, which were measured a week before the election (34). These intentions were themselves accurately predicted from the individuals' attitudes toward the candidates and their perceptions regarding social pressures to vote for the candidates. In turn, the attitudes toward the candidates were predicted from the individuals' beliefs about the social, economic, and political consequences of their votes and their evaluations of these consequences. The perceptions of social pressures with respect to voting were predicted from their beliefs about how the voters' parents, spouses or dates, three closest friends, and coworkers thought they should vote (see Figure 1-2). This research is typical of psychological social psychology in that a mini-theory

was developed to understand and predict a specific behavior.

For a concise summary of all this discussion of the contents, levels of analyses, methodologies, and theoretical perspectives of the two social psychologies, see Tables 1-1 and 1-2.

■

WHY A SYNTHESIS OF SOCIAL PSYCHOLOGIES?

Now we ask a final question: Why study both sociological social psychology and psychological social psychology? There are three primary reasons.

First, the two approaches provide complemen-

Table 1.1 ■

The Two Social Psychologies: Heritage and Definition

	Heritage	Content
Sociological social psychology	Durkheim Weber Simmel Thomas	Study of the reciprocal influence of the individual and society
Psychological social psychology	Psychoanalytic theory Learning theory Field theory	Study of social influence

Table 1.2 ■

The Two Social Psychologies: Level of Analysis, Methodology, and Theoretical Perspective

	Level of analysis	Methodology	Theoretical perspective
Sociological social psychology Symbolic interactionism	Microsocial	Range within symbolic interactionism from only qualitative to a full range of methods	Symbolic interactionism
Social structure and personality	Link of microsocial and macrosocial	A full range of methods	Many theories (role, exchange) and mini-theories of a given topic (occupational choice, child-rearing)
Psychological social psychology	Microsocial	Quantitative	Many theories (social learning, exchange) and mini-theories of a given behavior (helping, aggression)

tary information about the same problems. The sociological social psychologists' focus on social interaction and the psychological social psychologists' emphasis on psychological processes within individuals can provide useful but distinct information on a single given issue. The psychologists' and symbolic interactionists' emphasis on individuals and interaction among individuals is complemented by the focus of the personality and society perspective within sociological social psychology on the influence of the social structure on individuals. Each of the views has weaknesses and strengths. Combining the approaches counterbalances some of the weaknesses of each school with the strengths of the other. For example, the limitation of the psychologists' methods of experimentation in controlled social situations is offset by the sociologists' focus on natural social environments. The combined approaches yield a richer and more complete understanding of a topic than any single approach can provide.

Second, the two views ultimately converge. All theories of social psychology attempt to understand individuals in their social context. All implicitly or explicitly recognize the reciprocal influence of the individual and society and the social construction of reality. Increasingly, the subject matter and the methods of the two social psychologies overlap.

Third, concern with the subjective world of the individual is a unique contribution of social psychology that is shared by sociological social psychology and psychological social psychology (36). Both perspectives emphasize the environment as perceived by the individual rather than the actual environment. Both social psychologies focus attention on cognitive interpretations of reality and on subsequent behaviors based on these interpretations.

The Robbers Cave Study: An Integrated Strategy

For many research problems the sociological social psychology and psychological social psychology approaches have been joined profitably. The following is one example of field research in which the

approaches of the two social psychologies were combined. Muzafer Sherif, a psychologist, Carolyn Sherif, a sociologist, and their colleagues conducted an elaborate field experiment to investigate intergroup relations (37). The Sherifs explored group formation, intergroup conflict, and techniques of reducing conflict. Their research subjects were 10- and 11-year-old boys attending Robbers Cave summer camp who were unaware they were participating in an experiment.

Group formation In phase one of the experiment the Sherifs examined the formation of groups, attraction to members of one's own group (the ingroup), and ingroup norms. Boys were assigned to one of two groups without knowledge of the existence of the other group. In each group the boys' activities demonstrated the formation of ingroup cohesion. Each group chose a name (the Rattlers, the Eagles) and developed a group hierarchy, special activities, favorite spots, and symbols of identification, such as a group flag. In addition, each group developed a set of norms for behavior: One group wished to be viewed as tough, while the other group wanted to be seen as well behaved. This ingroup formation appeared without encouragement or comment from the camp staff/experimenters.

Intergroup conflict When the Rattlers and the Eagles learned of each other's existence the members immediately felt intergroup competition. The groups turned spontaneous encounters with each other into competitive interactions. The results of this competition were strengthened ingroup ties and the development of feelings of hostility toward the other group (the outgroup). These feelings increased with each intergroup encounter. For example, after a game in which the Eagles were defeated, the Rattlers burned the Eagle flag. The Eagles then stole the Rattler flag. That act in turn provoked a raid on the Eagles' cabin, which led to an even more destructive raid on the Rattlers' cabin. Throughout the interactions, the outgroup was viewed in increasingly negative stereotyped terms, and the ingroup was seen in increasingly positive stereotyped terms. For example, in various competitions between the groups the boys overestimated the performance of their own group and underestimated the performance of the other group.

Intergroup cooperation In stage two of the experiment, the Sherifs tested several techniques to reduce the intergroup conflict that had developed. They first tried simple contact between the groups, but found that contact alone was not sufficient to reduce conflict. The groups merely used contact as an opportunity to escalate the level of hostility between them. A holiday picnic for the combined groups turned into a food fight!

The technique that was finally successful in reducing conflict was the introduction of *superordinate goals*—goals each group wished to achieve but which were impossible to achieve without the cooperation of the other group. One such goal was the restoration of water to the camp after a break in the water lines. The two groups worked jointly to find the break and to repair the line. A series of such encounters in which cooperation was required to reach common goals was successful in reducing hostility and in creating positive feelings across group lines. This was indicated by changes in ingroup and outgroup friendship choices.

This experiment combined techniques of both sociological social psychology and psychological social psychology. The Sherifs used the symbolic interactionists' techniques of observation by trained observers and in-depth interviews and combined them with the psychologists' technique of standardized questionnaires. The subjectivity inherent in observational processes was offset by the rigor of the standardized measurements. Problems resulting from the artificiality of these standardized measurements were lessened by the richness of the interview and observational data.

The Robbers Cave study exemplifies the common interest of all social psychologists in the subjective viewpoints of individuals. The study monitored changes over time in the group members' views of each other. The experimenters studied group formation from the perspectives of the boys themselves.

They were also able to observe the boys' changing attitudes and behaviors toward the ingroup and the outgroup members. Finally, this study combined both psychological and sociological levels of analysis. Feelings between the groups were measured by observations of individual attitudes and behaviors. At the same time, explanations for the behaviors of individuals were sought in the structured relations of the groups.

The Robbers Cave study demonstrates that sensitivity to the participants' viewpoint can be achieved within a structured setting. Qualitative and quantitative data can be used to complement each other. Analysis of individual-level and group-level factors can be merged effectively. Integrative studies of this nature combine the considerable strengths of the two social psychologies.

■

SUMMARY

Social psychology is the branch of the social sciences that examines how society influences individuals and, in turn, is influenced by them. Social psychology is studied in two disciplines, sociology and psychology. These two disciplines have overlapping but somewhat different contents, levels of analysis, methodologies, and theories of social psychology. The two social psychologies also have much in common and profit from an interchange of viewpoints.

Sociological social psychology has a rich sociological heritage. Its sociological precursors include Durkheim, Weber, Simmel, and Thomas.

There are two different perspectives within sociological social psychology: symbolic interactionism and the personality and social structure perspective. Both perspectives view the content of sociological social psychology as the interdependence of individuals and society.

Sociological social psychologists study both microprocesses (events concerning individuals and small groups of individuals) and macroprocesses (events concerning larger groups, institutions, or societies). Symbolic interactionists study micro-level social interaction. Sociologists, using the personality and social structure perspective, study the link between microsocial and macrosocial processes.

Some symbolic interactionists believe that the methods used in the study of interaction should be subjective. Thus, some symbolic interactionists use qualitative methods, some use a limited set of quantitative methods, and still others use the full range of quantitative methods. Sociologists from the personality and society perspective examine the relationships between individual characteristics (such as personality, attitudes, and values) and macrosocial events (such as society's institutions). They use the full range of quantitative methods in their investigations.

Symbolic interactionism is a major theoretical perspective in sociology. Symbolic interactionists are concerned with the ways in which reality is socially constructed on the basis of social interaction. Sociologists from the personality and society perspective do not have a unified theoretical perspective. They employ several of the major social psychological theories, mini-theories of specific topics, and other sociological theories. The use of mini-theories by sociologists from the personality and social structure perspective is exemplified by research investigating social class and child-rearing practices. Parental child-rearing practices are associated with the different work conditions of the social classes.

Psychological social psychologists attempt to understand the cognitions (thoughts), behavior, and affect (emotions) of humans, in order to understand how they would be likely to behave in a specified set of conditions.

Like sociologists from the personality and society perspective, psychological social psychologists do not have a unified theoretical perspective but use several major social psychological theories and mini-theories to explain specific behaviors. The theoretical perspective of psychological social psychology is illustrated by a theory relating beliefs, attitudes, behavior intentions, and behaviors. Each of these concepts imperfectly predicts the others.

Sociological social psychology and psychological social psychology should be studied together be- cause each view complements the other and each has weaknesses that the strengths of the other can partially offset; because the two views ultimately converge in their focus on individual human behavior, and because each is concerned with the subjective world of the individual.

■

REFERENCES

1. Rosenberg, M. and R. H. Turner, 1981, "Preface." In M. Rosenberg and R. H. Turner, *Social Psychology: Sociological Perspectives,* New York: Basic Books.

2. Turner, J. H., 1986, *The Structure of Sociological Theory,* 4th ed. Homewood, IL: Dorsey.

3. Durkheim, E., 1912, *The Elementary Forms of Religious Life,* New York: Free Press, 1954.

4. Durkheim, E., 1897, *Suicide,* New York: Free Press.

5. Breault, K. D., 1986, "Suicide in America: A Test of Durkheim's Theory of Religious and Family Integration, 1933–1980," *American Journal of Sociology,* 92:628–656.

6. Weber, M., 1947, *The Theory of Social and Economic Organization,* New York: Free Press.

7. Weber, M., 1904, *The Protestant Ethic and the Spirit of Capitalism,* New York: Scribners, 1958.

8. Wolff, K. H., 1950, *The Sociology of Georg Simmel,* New York: Free Press.

9. Thomas, W. I. and D. S. Thomas, 1928, *The Child in America,* New York: Alfred A. Knopf.

10. House, J. S., 1977, "The Three Faces of Social Psychology," *Sociometry* 40:161–177.

11. Lindesmith, A. R. and A. L. Strauss, 1968, *Social Psychology,* 3d ed., New York: Holt, Rinehart, & Winston.

12. Alexander, J., B. Giesen, R. Munch, and N. J. Smelser, 1987, *The Micro-Macro Link,* Berkeley: University of California Press; K. Knorr-Cetina and A. V. Cicourel (Eds.), 1981, *Advances in Social Theory and Methodology: Toward an Integration of Micro- and Macro-Sociologies,* Boston: Routledge & Kegan Paul.

13. House, J., 1981, "Social Structure and Personality," in M. Rosenberg and R. H. Turner, 1981, op. cit.; House, 1977, op. cit.

14. Blumer, H., 1969, *Symbolic Interactionism: Perspective and Method,* Englewood Cliffs, NJ: Prentice-Hall.

15. Kuhn, M. H. and T. S. McPartland, 1964, "An Empirical Investigation of Self-attitudes," *American Sociological Review* 19:68–76.

16. Stryker, S., 1980, *Symbolic Interactionism,* Menlo Park, CA: Benjamin/Cummings.

17. For an overview of this perspective see S. Stryker, 1981, "Symbolic Interactionism: Themes and Variations," in M. Rosenberg and R. H. Turner, 1981, op. cit.

18. Becker, H. S., 1953, "Becoming a Marijuana User," *American Journal of Sociology* 59:235–242.

19. Best, J., 1987, "Rhetoric in Claims-making: Constructing the Missing Children Problem," *Social Problems* 34:101–121.

20. The next section draws on material from J. House, 1981, op. cit.

21. Kohn, M. L., 1969, *Class and Conformity: A Study in Values,* Homewood, IL: Dorsey; M. L. Kohn and C. Schooler, 1969, "Class, Occupation, and Orientation," *American Sociological Review* 34:659–678.

22. Kohn, M. L. and C. Schooler, 1978, "The Reciprocal Effects of the Substantive Complexity of Work and Intellectual Flexibility: A Longitudinal Assessment," *American Journal of Sociology* 84:24–52; J. Miller, C. Schooler, M. L. Kohn, and K. A. Miller, 1979, "Women and Work: The Psychological Effects of Occupational Conditions," *American Journal of Sociology* 85:66–91.

23. Lichter, D. L., 1988, "Racial Differences in Underemployment in American Cities," *American Journal of Sociology* 93:771–792.

24. For a detailed discussion see G. W. Allport, 1985, "The Historical Background of Social Psychology," in G. Lindzey and E. Aronson (Eds.), *The Handbook of Social Psychology,* Vol. 1, New York: Random House.

25. For a compilation of Freud's work see J. Strachey (Ed. and Trans.), 1976, *The Standard Edition of the Complete Psychological Works of Sigmund Freud,* London: Hogarth Press.

26. Thorndike, E. L., 1911, *Animal Intelligence: Experimental Studies,* New York: Macmillan.

27. For a summary of this perspective see B. F. Skinner, 1974, *About Behaviorism,* New York: Vintage Books.

28. Lewin, K., 1951, *Field Theory in Social Science,* New York: Harper & Row.

29. Lewin, K., 1943, "Forces Behind Food Habits and Methods of Change," *Bulletin of the National Research Council* 108:35–65.

30. Allport, 1985, op. cit.

31. For a discussion of the experimentation in psychological social psychology see E. Aronson, M. Brewer, and S. M. Carlsmith, 1985, "Experimentation in Social Psychology," in G. Lindzey and E. Aronson (Eds.), op. cit.

32. Collins, R. L., S. E. Taylor, J. V. Wood, and S. C. Thompson, 1988, "The Vividness Effect: Elusive or Illusory?" *Journal of Experimental Social Psychology* 24:1–18.

33. Fishbein, M. and I. Ajzen, 1975, *Belief, Attitude, Intention, and Behavior: An Introduction to Theory and Research,* Reading, MA: Addison-Wesley.

34. Fishbein, M., 1981, "Acceptance, Yielding and Impact: Cognitive Processes in Persuasion," in R. E. Petty, T. M. Ostrom, and T. C. Brock (Eds.), *Cognitive Responses in Persuasion,* Hillsdale, NJ: Erlbaum.

35. McPhail, C., 1981, "The Problems and Prospects of Behavioral Perspectives," *American Sociologist* 16:172–175.

36. Cartwright, D., 1979, "Contemporary Social Psychology in Historical Perspective," *Social Psychology Quarterly* 42:82–93.

37. Sherif, M., O. J. Harvey, B. J. White, W. E. Hood, and C. W. Sherif, 1961, *Intergroup Conflict and Cooperation: The Robbers Cave Experiment,* Norman, OK: Institute of Group Relations.

CHAPTER 2

Social Psychological Theories

■

Symbolic Interactionism
Premises of Symbolic Interactionism
Symbols
Two Schools of Symbolic Interactionism
Offshoots of Symbolic Interactionism
Role Theory
Role Expectations
Types of Roles
Multiple Roles
Social Learning Theory
Enactive Learning
Observational Learning
Acquisition and Performance
The Regulation of Behavior
Exchange Theory
The Propositions of Exchange Theory
Power and Exchange
The Norm of Reciprocity
Distributive Justice
Equity

Before starting to read this chapter, look at the photographs on the facing page and identify the emotions these people are expressing.

We live in a complex and highly varied world. It is filled with people from diverse cultures who have different customs, values, norms, and attitudes. We do not speak the same languages nor do we dress in the same way. Yet, in spite of all these differences, we know we share a common humanity. But how do we know this? Yes, we are all confronted with the certainty of birth, death, and taxes, but isn't there a deeper kinship? Over a century ago, Charles Darwin theorized that humans the world over share the same emotional expressions. Other theorists disagreed, arguing that emotional expressions are learned and differ from culture to culture. If Darwin was right, then at a very fundamental level all people share the same human feelings. But if his opponents were right, we must look elsewhere for sources of our common humanity (1).

We will use this perplexing controversy to illustrate why theories are important in social psychology. *Theories* are sets of interrelated concepts that provide systematic explanations of behavior. Social psychological theories provide road maps that guide us over the sometimes difficult terrain of human behavior. We will examine the two theories of emotions presented above and then discuss studies testing the two theories. We will then use this example to discuss the value of theories and the qualities of good theories.

Darwin believed emotional expressions evolved over the course of human history and are inherited in much the same way as are the various senses (sight, hearing, taste, smell, touch). There are individual variations to be sure, but he thought the basic pattern for each emotion was biologically determined. Later in the century, the psychologist William James added to Darwin's theory the idea that people become consciously aware of the emotions they are experiencing on the basis of feedback from the muscles involved in emotional expressions. Emotional expressions are automatic responses to situations. Only following the emotional expression are we capable of being aware of what emotion we are

experiencing. Darwin's and James's theories do not deny that people can choose to display emotions (a forced smile), but rather argue that the most basic emotional expressions (fear, anger, sadness, happiness, disgust, surprise) are biologically preprogrammed, automatic responses to powerful stimuli.

The environmental theory suggests that emotional expressions are learned through socialization and vary from culture to culture. In essence, this theory implies that emotional expressions are like language. All people have a capacity to acquire a language; however, the language any given person speaks is determined by his or her culture. Just so with emotional expressions—they should differ as much from culture to culture as languages do. From this perspective, it is also argued that we are typically consciously aware of an emotion, say anger, before the emotional expression is displayed on our faces. Thus, emotional expressions are generally learned, voluntary products of conscious awareness.

It is often the case in social psychology that a given problem, in this case the cause of emotional expressions, can be explained by more than one theory. Research is then used in an effort to determine which theory provides the better explanation. The theories themselves frequently tell us what to look for to determine which explanation is better.

In the controversy over emotional expressions, it is necessary to determine if basic emotional expressions are universal or if they differ from culture to culture. Studies show that people in one culture can recognize the emotions people in a very different culture are feeling simply from looking at photographs (2). Thus, basic emotional expressions appear to be universal. Darwin's theory argues that emotional expressions are preprogrammed and inherited. Therefore, even small children and the blind should show the same basic emotional expressions. This too has been found to be the case (3). Darwin's theory also suggests we should find the same muscles involved in the expression of a given emotion in virtually all people. Research, using electrodes that measure minute muscle movements of the face, indicates that this too is the case (4). It would be consistent with James's theory if basic emotional

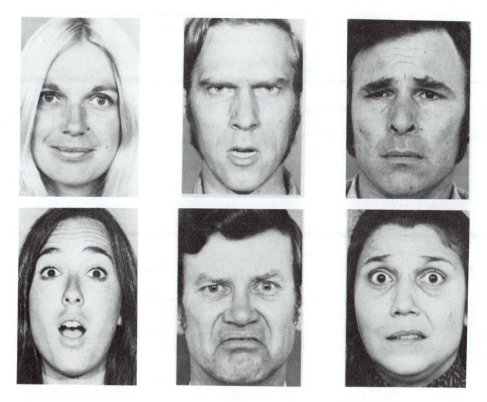

■ *What emotions are these people expressing? Compare your answers to those at the bottom of page 24. (Photos from* Unmasking the Face *(2nd ed.), by P. Ekman and W. Friesen, 1984. Used by permission of P. Ekman.)*

expressions occurred automatically, rather than being primarily the products of consciousness. The evidence supports this idea too, implying that spontaneous expressions of basic emotions are so automatic they are unlikely to be due to learning (5).

However, people are capable of learning to express emotions voluntarily, as fine actors constantly remind us. And when we deal with emotions other than the most basic ones or with complex emotions (grief, jealousy, love), it is clear that cultures differ in the circumstances under which these emotions can or should be displayed. Every culture has *display rules* that govern the expression of voluntarily controlled emotions. Thus, there are a number of basic emotions that do appear to be

unlearned and whose expression is automatic and universal, but these and other emotions can be voluntarily expressed and people learn the rules governing when they can be displayed.

The clash between these two theories illustrates the value of theories. Theories provide frameworks that can be used to understand the world around us. Good theories are simple and logical, yet wide in scope. Theories should be subject to test so they can be confirmed or disconfirmed. In the case of the two theories of emotions, Darwin's ideas concerning the universality of emotions were supported for basic emotions, while the environmentalists' ideas were supported for more complex emotions. Theories should be consistent with what is known,

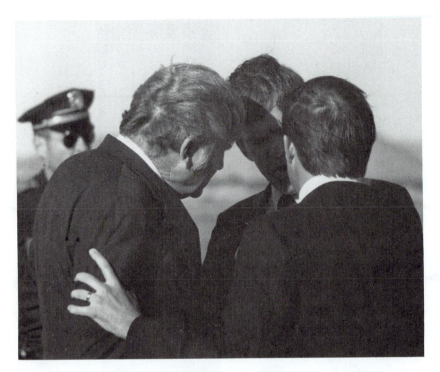

■ *Meaning is a product of social interaction. (WGS)*

but they should also point us in directions that will expand our knowledge. Ultimately, the best theories are effective in explaining, predicting, and changing behavior.

Social psychologists employ such an enormous range of theories in their work that we cannot attempt to cover them all in this chapter. Instead, we will present four theories that are widely used in social psychology. Two of these theories—symbolic interactionism and role theory—trace their roots primarily to sociological social psychology. The third theory—social exchange theory—traces its roots to both types of social psychology, while the fourth—social learning theory—traces its roots primarily to psychological social psychology. Our goal is to demonstrate how varied the theories in

Answer to the photo question on p. 23: From left to right, top to bottom, the faces express happiness, anger, sadness, surprise, disgust, and fear.

social psychology are as well as to provide you with a background in some of the theories we will employ in coming chapters.

■

SYMBOLIC INTERACTIONISM

Symbolic interactionism is certainly the most influential theoretical framework in sociological social psychology. We will examine symbolic interactionism itself and two additional theoretical traditions deriving from symbolic interactionism, the drama-turgical school and ethnomethodology.

As you remember from our discussion in Chapter 1, symbolic interactionism is concerned with the creation and modification of meaning through social interaction. Symbolic interactionists believe the individual and society are influenced by each other, and neither can be understood except in relationship to the other.

Premises of Symbolic Interactionism

Three major premises of symbolic interactionism are as follows (6). First, human beings act toward other people and objects on the basis of the *meanings* these people and objects have for them. In addition, the perspective of the actor, not merely the perspectives of outside observers, must be taken into consideration when attempting to understand human behavior (7). Symbolic interactionists feel the importance of meaning is often overlooked by other theorists, who search for causes of human behavior without exploring the meaning of the behaviors for the people engaging in them. Meanings are crucial because virtually no behavior is completely unambiguous to the observer. Even when we observe behavior in a situation where its meaning seems obvious, we may still misinterpret it. Suppose a student is accompanying her mother on a shopping trip. As they are entering the mall, the mother trips and takes a hard fall. A passerby quickly intercedes and helps the mother to her feet and picks up the scattered contents of her purse. Feeling relieved that her mother is unhurt, the student thanks the passerby for being so helpful. Later, when the mother tries to pay for a purchase she has made, she discovers the passerby has stolen her money. In this example, the obviously "helpful" behavior of the passerby was misinterpreted by the student.

Our *definition of the situation* allows us to assign meanings to the interaction. Even if our definition is inaccurate, as in the student's first definition of the above situation, we interpret situations in part on the basis of it. As W. I. Thomas wrote, "... if men define situations as real, they are real in their consequences" (8).

The second premise of symbolic interactionism is that meanings are the product of *social interaction*. Meanings do not reside within people or objects, nor are they developed by a single person. Instead, meanings are social products—the results of the ways people relate to each other and to objects. For example, what your school means to you is constantly

being modified through your experiences th[...]
through your [...]
initial percept[...]
that it was a lar[...]
know many p[...]
know everyone[...]
more students, [...]
been replaced [...]
a smaller and f[...]
ducted from the [...] perspective explores the ways in which individuals construct and modify the meanings of the situations they encounter.

The third premise of symbolic interactionism is that meanings are *modified* through *interpretations* people make in their dealings with other people and situations. Individuals construct meanings on the basis of the present situation and the people at hand. People are not simply passive recipients of meanings based on previous social interaction. Each person is an active creator of meanings. As the above example of the passerby demonstrates, our initial definition of the situation may change radically. On the basis of additional information we may come to see the original meaning we attributed to an interaction as being incomplete, simplistic, or in error.

As we continue to be exposed to a person or situation, our meanings are constantly being modified. For example, during your first semester in college you may have felt overburdened with course work since you were in a new environment that probably placed many more scholastic demands on you than your high school, and you hadn't yet adapted to the demands of college. Now that you have successfully made the transition to college and completed more demanding upper-division classes, you would probably view your first semester course load as light and those first few lower-division classes as relatively easy college credits.

Symbols

George Herbert Mead was symbolic interactionism's most influential theorist. According to Mead, a critical component of human communication is its use of *symbols*, abstractions that represent something else

(9). Our country's flag, a friend's wave of a hand, and a stop sign are all symbols. Symbols need not refer to something concrete to be understood. Many symbols, such as the concepts of "gravity" or "threat," have no physical representation, but are abstract concepts whose meanings we hold in common.

The ability to use symbols to communicate distinguishes us from other species. Animals can communicate, but only through the use of *gestures*— verbal or nonverbal behaviors that are predetermined by their physiology and have precisely fixed meanings. While learning is sometimes involved in the communication of higher animals, this communication does not involve shared meanings. When a chicken pecks another, it is a gesture enacted to gain the rewards of being high in the pecking order of the group. The gesture is elicited by specific environmental stimuli and its form is fixed. Although the peck is a communication, the chicken is not saying to itself, "I'll just go peck Tom to put him in his place." Nor can the chicken decide to substitute a push for a peck. Neither chicken knows the meaning of the peck for the other.

By contrast, humans communicate through the use of symbols, the most important of which are the words of our language. Humans think about their actions, *intend* to convey meanings to others, and are able to convey a single meaning in a variety of ways. Most important, human communication involves *significant symbols*, symbols that have shared meanings. In an argument, one person may shake his fist at another as a kind of threat. Both the person making the gesture and the recipient understand that this gesture conveys anger, and is a substitute for violent action. The term *symbolic interaction* is derived from the fact that social interaction depends on the shared meaning of symbols.

Since symbols can be stored in memory, they allow human beings to be consciously aware of the past and the future, as well as the present. The ability to retain the past allows us to pass culture and knowledge from generation to generation. It provides the basis for civilization, and makes the creation of societies possible. According to Mead, symbols also allow for the emergence of the self, a process we will discuss in Chapter 5. The idea that both the self and the society are derived from social interaction is a major tenet of symbolic interactionism (10).

Next we will examine a historical distinction between two schools of symbolic interactionism.

Two Schools of Symbolic Interactionism

The Chicago school Historically, two primary schools of symbolic interactionism developed—the Chicago school and the Iowa school. Each of these schools is named after the location of the university at which the early proponents of these schools of thought worked. The Chicago school is closely associated with Herbert Blumer. Of the two schools, its approach is more like Mead's version of symbolic interactionism. To the Chicago school, human behavior is a result of a continual interplay between the self and society. Human behavior thus arises through a dynamic and creative process. Like Mead, symbolic interactionists from the Chicago school stress the ongoing construction of behavior and the ability of humans to act, rather than merely to react (11).

Symbolic interactionists from the Chicago school feel it is inappropriate to study people's behavior as a function of their attitudes or roles because individuals are constantly constructing their own realities and not acting just on the basis of prior attitudes or social roles. They feel investigators should attempt to understand the subjective realities individuals construct for themselves in social situations. The emphasis is on individuals' active creation of meanings that emerge from an ongoing interaction.

Blumer felt symbolic interactionism needed its own research method because the study of human behavior is distinct from studies undertaken in other sciences (12). He thought attempts to understand people from an external or objective perspective would fail because this approach eliminated the information about people's subjective perspectives that uniquely determines their behavior. Blumer did not even believe that social psychologists should study specific variables (dimensions of interest to the researcher) or test hypotheses (causal statements about the effect of one variable on another) because this objective approach presupposes the existence of consistencies he thought were absent from human interaction. Instead, Blumer felt social psychologists should study human interaction with only *sensitizing concepts*, or ideas that suggest general directions in which to look to understand behavior. Think back to the examples of research conducted from the symbolic interactionist perspective cited in Chapter 1—learning to smoke marijuana and defining missing children as a problem. Both of these studies were conducted from the Chicago school perspective.

The Iowa school The Iowa school has followed Mead less closely than the Chicago school. Manford Kuhn, the symbolic interactionist most closely associated with the early Iowa school, believed symbolic interactionism should be investigated by using the same research methods used in the investigation of other theories in the natural and social sciences (13). He thus believed in imposing structures or controls on the assessment of behavior. Kuhn tested some of Mead's ideas and abandoned others he felt were inherently untestable. The technique Kuhn used most frequently in testing symbolic interactionist ideas was the Twenty Statements Test (TST) (14). In this test the respondent answers the question "Who am I?" by listing up to twenty open-ended responses. The results of the TST led Kuhn to emphasize the importance of a stable or "core" self in determining people's definitions of situations and subsequent actions. In Chapter 5 we will discuss other results obtained with this test.

The Iowa school's focus on the stable aspects of the self constitutes a second difference between the Iowa and Chicago school. While the Iowa school emphasizes the stability of personality and the predictability of the individual's behavior, the Chicago school's emphasis is on the creative and emergent aspects of the individual.

A third and related difference between the Iowa school and the Chicago school is the Iowa school's stress on the extent to which the self and society are dependent upon social structures (the division of society into social groups, statuses, roles, and institutions). All symbolic interactionists agree that social interaction is the means by which the concepts of the self and others are formed, situations are defined, and meanings are constructed. While the Chicago school emphasizes the creation of meaning, and ignores the influence of the social structure, a distinctive focus of the Iowa school is on the influence of the social structure on the person (15). Although it is recognized that the person's behavior is shaped by social interactions, the social structure puts limits on possible interactions. The social structure determines the differing types of social interaction people of different ages, sexes, social classes, and ethnic groups will have. For example, students attending a local community college will meet and interact with different people than will students attending an elite ivy league school. These limited interactions often influence the students' aspirations, expectations, viewpoints, and choice of friends.

At the same time, altering the possibilities for interaction can change the social structure (16). For example, as more minority students are able to attend elite schools, the races and ethnic backgrounds of people in powerful positions in this society may begin to change. With change in the types of people in power, changes in minority aspirations and expectations and changes in social policies are likely to occur.

Members of the Iowa school believe the social structure puts limitations on social interactions, but does not totally determine them. Symbolic interactionists from the Iowa school do not believe people are automatically and mechanically placed into predetermined social positions. To the contrary, people can often choose whether to perform the roles associated with such positions. The children of a company's founder may decide not to carry on the family business, but pursue careers more consistent with their own interests. They may even decide to cut family ties, and refuse to enact the roles of dutiful sons and daughters. In addition, people can modify their role performances to fit their own needs and interests. A child who does choose to carry on the family business may focus exclusively on the creative aspects of marketing and delegate other aspects of management, such as finances, to others.

BOX 2-1

Research Example from the Iowa School of Symbolic Interactionism: Identity Salience of Blood Donors

Some identities are alleged to be more a part of the self than others. Those that are most salient should have more influence on the self. These ideas were tested by examining the salience of the identity of blood donor among a group of people who had recently given blood (18). Those for whom the identity of blood donor was most salient should be more likely to define themselves as blood donors, evaluate others in terms of blood donation, and develop interpersonal relationships linked to blood donation.

Questionnaire responses were obtained from a number of individuals who had recently given blood at a Red Cross center. The salience of the identity of blood donor was measured by asking the donors if they agreed with such statements as "Blood donation is an important part of who I am."

All of the hypotheses were supported by the data. People for whom "blood donor" was a salient identity were more likely to evaluate others in terms of blood donation and to become friends with other blood donors than people for whom the identity of blood donor was less salient. In addition, the salience of the identity of blood donor was positively associated with the amount of blood given in a six-month time period: Those for whom the identity was more salient gave blood more times than those for whom the identity was less salient. ■

An example of work employing this perspective is provided by Sheldon Stryker's theory of *identity salience* (17). Stryker views the self as being comprised of a number of identities, each of which corresponds to a role played by the person. Stryker assumes identities differ in their salience or prom-inence. Both commitment to the identity and positive evaluation of it increase identity salience. The more salient the identity, the more likely a situation or event is to evoke that identity. For example, if Sharon's role as wife is extremely salient, because she is strongly committed to it and because she enjoys it a great deal, she may allow the role of wife to influence her choices outside it. She may choose not to pursue a career because she fears such outside work would interfere with her role as wife. But, if Janice's role as wife is less salient to her, she might not allow it to influence her career opportunities.

One can contrast the two schools of symbolic interactionism by comparing the way each school might conduct research on the same topic. If symbolic interactionists from the Chicago school were to study students' feelings about their universities, they might attempt to understand them by in-depth observations or unstructured interviews in which the students were asked to present their feelings and their reasons for these feelings. The researchers would try to avoid imposing their own ideas on the students in any way. If symbolic interactionists from the Iowa school were to study students' feelings about their universities, they would probably first formulate hypotheses about the factors that might influence students' feelings and would then attempt to test these hypotheses through a quantitative method such as survey research.

The historical distinction between the two schools of symbolic interactionism is not as important in symbolic interactionism today as it once was. This distinction is important, however, to understanding the considerable range in thought, theoretical issues, and methodologies among individuals who identify themselves as symbolic interactionists.

Offshoots of Symbolic Interactionism

As symbolic interactionism developed, various writers have borrowed and expanded ideas from symbolic interactionism and combined them with other theories to form new schools of thought. We will review two such offshoots of symbolic interactionism: the dramaturgical school and ethnomethodology.

The dramaturgical school Founded by Erving Goffman, the dramaturgical school differs from symbolic interactionism in being less concerned with individual-level analysis and more concerned with social interaction (mutual influences among individuals). Face-to-face interaction, the sole topic of the dra-

maturgical school, is only one of the many issues of concern to symbolic interactionists. The dramaturgical school's emphasis on face-to-face interaction recognizes its prime importance in forming our definitions of situations and our conceptions of the self.

Like the Chicago school of symbolic interactionism, the focus of the dramaturgical school is away from the social structure's influence on the individual and toward the creation of meaning in the course of interaction. Unlike the Chicago school, however, the primary topic of concern is the ways in which people work to create a particular impression of themselves in an ongoing interaction.

The dramaturgical school uses the metaphor of the theater to describe face-to-face interaction (19). For Goffman, there are similarities between the stage and real life. The ways people present themselves to others and attempt to control the impressions others form of them are similar to actors' performances of roles and their attempts to control the audiences' impressions of the characters they portray. In face-to-face interactions, each individual plays a role before an audience that consists of the others involved in the interaction. As a part of this performance the individual wears costumes, uses props, and "sets the stage" for the interaction. For instance, you probably take pains to present yourself as an interested student when interacting with your professors, or you may plan to present yourself as an appealing and fascinating person to a classmate to whom you are attracted. We will explore the issue of self-presentation in greater detail in Chapter 5.

One set of face-to-face interactions analyzed by Goffman is the interaction between stigmatized persons and "normals" (20). Goffman defines a *stigma* as a bodily sign people regard as evidence of something unusual and bad about the moral status of the person possessing it. There are three types of stigmata: physical deformities, blemishes of individual character such as alcoholism or mental illness, and tribal stigma (such as belonging to a minority race or religion). Goffman believes we treat stigmatized people as though they are not quite human.

The central issue in the life of a stigmatized

person is acceptance, for they are always uncertain of their reception by "normals." Goffman notes that normals often *pretend* to accept stigmatized people more than they actually do. As a consequence, stigmatized people often attempt social interaction with normals, only to find the latter may withdraw from full acceptance of them. For instance, a handicapped male may discover that his female acquaintances think he is a great "friend" but view him as a completely unacceptable date.

Goffman feels all of us know the perspective of the stigmatized as well as that of the normal. There is no person who meets all standards of perfection. We have all been judged lacking on some dimension, such as beauty, money, or talent, at some time in our lives. As Goffman put it, "In an important sense there is only one complete unblushing male in America: a young, married, white, urban, northern, heterosexual, male Protestant father, of college education, fully employed, of good complexion, weight, and height, with a recent record in sports" (21). Therefore, stigma management is not just a problem for a limited number of us. It is a general feature of society.

Goffman was also concerned with the ways in which we organize experience (22). He demonstrated that we use frameworks—mental structures that are used to interpret behavior—to respond to events. The types of frameworks used are culturally determined, and thus differ from group to group. Further, within a group, any event is ambiguous and thus is subject to more than one interpretation or *frame*. For example, are the two men who are pushing one another on the street corner fighting or kidding around? The two men may be using deception to influence the observers' choice of frames. Perhaps they wish to stage a fight to distract people from a robbery being conducted by an accomplice.

One's frame is an important component of one's definition of the situation. The interpretation of events is critical to our definition of a situation, yet people commonly disagree on interpretations, with resulting conflicting definitions. Most of us have had the experience of coming to a different understanding of an interaction with a friend, resulting in missed appointments, hurt feelings, or other negative consequences. The social costs of incorrectly framing events are obvious, and make clear our dependence on frames for the interpretation of reality. This type of analysis is close to that of *ethnomethodology*, another outgrowth of symbolic interactionism.

Ethnomethodology Like the dramaturgical school, ethnomethodologists are concerned with face-to-face interaction. Unlike the dramaturgical school, they ask the question, "How do techniques of interaction sustain a sense of social reality?" (23). That is, ethnomethodologists ask how a sense of reality is created and maintained through interaction.

While symbolic interactionists are concerned with the social construction of reality, ethnomethodologists address the *methods* by which reality is constructed. Ethnomethodologists view these methods as more interesting and important than the content of the reality that is created because they believe that these methods are the cement that holds society together. That is, it is not the nature of a society that is important, but the presumption by its inhabitants that the society *has* a specific nature. The important issue for investigation is how people construct a reality that is taken for granted and that allows for a sense of social order. The question, then, is not only "What are society's rules?" but "What methods do people use for seeing and describing these rules?" (24).

Since ethnomethodologists believe that people construct reality through social interaction, they feel we must discover the implicit rules regarding interaction in order to understand our methods of reality construction. For this reason, ethnomethodologists have attempted to discover implicit interaction rules (25). For instance, in interactions, actors must often wait for additional information to make sense of another's statement. When they wait for this information, rather than choosing not to understand or disrupting the interaction by asking for the information, they are exercising an important interaction rule—premature interruptions are dysfunctional.

We typically have no conscious awareness of these interaction rules. Our lack of awareness of these interaction rules is often so complete we only become conscious of them through their violation. For example, Harold Garfinkel exposed one of these unwritten rules by asking his students to question the ordinary comments that people made to them (26). To illustrate, in response to a friend's statement, "I had a flat tire," one of Garfinkel's students responded, "What do you mean, you had a flat tire?" The friend replied, "What do you mean, 'What do I mean?' A flat tire is a flat tire. That is what I meant. Nothing special. What a crazy question!" This response of surprise and hostility tells us an unwritten rule (commonly understood statements are not questioned) was violated. To expose society's unwritten rules is also to explore society's basic structure of reality.

You might also try violating an unwritten rule. Question the ordinary comments people make (be careful, they do get hostile), or break some trivial norm—perhaps standing in an elevator with your back to the door—and see for yourself the importance of rules of which we are not typically aware.

In summary, the dramaturgical school and ethnomethodology are offshoots of symbolic interactionism. Starting with the symbolic interactionists' focus on the individual and the creation of meaning, both offshoots focus more narrowly on face-to-face interaction. The dramaturgical school emphasizes impression management, while the ethnomethodologists emphasize methods of constructing reality and the implicit interaction rules used to do so.

Next we will consider role theory. Role theory and symbolic interactionism have many common points. Both theoretical perspectives are concerned with subjective experiences and performances, and both take the theater as a metaphor of social life. While the strength of symbolic interactionism lies in its ability to characterize the nature of social reality and social interaction, the strength of role theory lies in its ability to link the individual with the greater structure of the society (27).

■ ROLE THEORY

Role theory focuses on the networks of social statuses or positions found in all societies. *Roles* consist of the expectations for behavior characteristic of a recognized set of persons in a specific social position or *status*, such as father, teacher, delinquent, or friend (28).

The concept of role unites symbolic interactionisms and role theory. As we noted in Chapter 1, one can think of the self as being comprised of a number of identities, each of which corresponds to a role enacted by the person (29). For instance, identifying yourself as a student is associated with enacting the role of student, and identifying yourself as a son or daughter is associated with enacting these family roles.

Role theory bridges the gap between the microsocial level (individuals and small groups) and the macrosocial level of analysis (large groups, institutions, and societies) in two ways. First, roles are enacted by individuals, but the existing positions underlying them are determined by the society (30). In Chapter 5, we show how a child learns about his or her sense of self in part by playing at enacting the various roles available in the society. Second, roles transcend individuals. For instance, the position of elementary school teacher exists from generation to generation, even though varying people enact this role at different times. Social positions are a stable part of our society. Although the role enactment of teachers changes somewhat over time, as educational norms and values change, the position remains an important component of the structure of our society.

Mead and the Chicago school of symbolic interactionism emphasize the creative way in which individuals modify roles and make them their own. Roles are not merely enacted; roles are also made (31). Each individual determines his or her particular portrayal of the role. At any given time, a number of people occupy the position of student, but each student enacts the role differently from every other student. A student is *not* a student is *not* a student.

■ *These children's cooperative behavior conforms to role expectations. People are evaluated positively when their behavior conforms to role expectations.* (© Richard S. Orton 1990)

In contrast, role theorists and the Iowa school symbolic interactionists examine the manner in which statuses, as a part of the social structure, influence an individual's responses to situations. While individual behavior is constrained by the social structure, it is not wholly determined by the social structure. People modify role performances in accordance with the situation, the ongoing interaction, and their conceptions of themselves. To illustrate, not only does the role of daughter vary considerably across occupants of the role, but for any given occupant, the role of daughter demands different behaviors in different situations and changes substantially over time.

Role Expectations

Roles are comprised of expectations concerning appropriate conduct (32). These expectations derive from a number of sources, including societal norms,

other participants in a social interaction, and various audiences who may not even be present (such as one's deceased father, God, or future generations). Thus, when you are enacting the role of guest in someone's home, you may be helpful around the house, clean up after yourself, and leave after a short visit because these behaviors conform to our society's view of appropriate behavior for individuals occupying the role of guest. Your host expects these behaviors of you, and your mother probably taught you these rules and would expect you to obey them.

People tend to be evaluated positively to the extent that their behaviors conform to role expectations. Professors who miss classes without warning, come to class unprepared, and give unintelligible exams are evaluated more negatively by both students and university administrators than professors who conform to the expectations that they will be present, prepared, and intelligible. When people do not conform to role expectations, this may be due to individual interpretations of the role, poor skills at playing the role, low involvement with the role, or willful deviance from the role.

Role expectations vary on a number of dimensions (33). These dimensions determine the ease of portrayal of the role and its importance in our lives.

1. Role expectations vary in their *generality* or specificity. For some roles, such as that of father, the associated expectations are broad; individuals have considerable latitude in the ways they perform these role behaviors. For other roles, such as those performed in the military, specific expectations exist for the way role behaviors will be executed.

2. Role expectations vary in their *extensiveness*. Some roles, such as gender roles, affect many of our behaviors and, in part, determine which other roles we occupy. Other roles, such as the role of grocery shopper, are insignificant components of our lives.

3. Role expectations differ in their *clarity* or ambiguity. For some roles, such as student, the expectations are rather clear. Students should complete assignments, attend class, and pass course exams. For other roles, such as godmother, there may be considerable ambiguity about the expected behaviors.

4. Role expectations differ in degree of *consensus*. There is overall agreement that service station attendants at full service stations should put gas in cars, check oil and tire pressure, give directions, and make minor repairs. A good deal of disagreement currently exists, however, regarding the behaviors appropriate to the roles of male and female. Some people feel that these roles should be distinct, while others believe that they should be more similar.

Types of Roles

Two types of roles can be distinguished: ascribed and achieved (34). *Ascribed* roles are the expectations associated with statuses that people are born into or that are thrust on them without any effort or desire on their parts. For example, gender roles and most kinship roles (daughter, nephew) are ascribed roles. In contrast, *achieved* roles are the expectations that are associated with statuses the individual assumes after some effort or achievement. Such role performances usually require some skill or training. Occupational role behaviors such as butcher, baker, and candlestick-maker, as well as doctor and lawyer, provide examples of achieved roles. However, some roles are not readily classified as ascribed or achieved. The role of millionaire may be thrust on an individual at birth or may be the culmination of a lifetime of striving. The role of father may be sought after or accidentally filled. Our feelings regarding roles we have sought out, compared to roles thrust upon us, may of course be quite different. Ascribed roles are not chosen by us, and so achieved roles may seem to reflect more about our "true" selves. Yet many ascribed roles influence the ways our achieved roles are portrayed and the ways our role portrayals are viewed. One is not just a doctor, but may be a young, female, Hispanic doctor, and all those ascribed roles modify and influence the achieved role portrayal and its acceptance.

Multiple Roles

One occupies many roles in a lifetime and even during a single day. Some roles are enacted sequentially. For instance, you may move from the role of roommate to the role of student to the role of worker and then back to the role of roommate as you move through your day, enacting each of the roles in turn. We also exhibit multiple simultaneous roles. A person may be simultaneously middle-aged, black, male, and a lawyer.

The more roles in an individual's repertoire, the better the person will be able to function in society (see Box 2-2). Multiple roles facilitate adjustment to society because the ability to enact multiple roles equips people to deal with the wide range of situations in which the roles are enacted. Through taking the role of the other, they provide an understanding of the roles of other individuals. Other benefits of the accumulation of roles include the enjoyment of the benefits and privileges that accom-

■ *Can you identify both ascribed and achieved roles in this photo? (WGS)*

pany each role, being able to compensate for failure in a given role by succeeding in other roles, having multiple social relationships, and the achievement of accomplishments and perhaps prestige in the realms in which each role is enacted (36).

Role conflict   There are also costs to the enactment of multiple roles. Difficulty in meeting the obligations of multiple roles is labeled *role conflict*. One type of role conflict is *role overload*, which occurs when an individual's roles demand more time and effort than the individual has for them. To reduce role overload, individuals may drop some roles, perform some roles perfunctorily, or selectively fill only certain expectations of one or more roles. The importance of the role to the individual and the magnitude of the rewards and punishments associ-

ated with the role determine the individual's response to role conflict. Some women may find themselves pressed for time because they hold full-time jobs, want to spend time with their families, do all the housework, and have their own hobbies as well. When a woman confronts this role overload, it is much more likely that she will neglect her hobby, rather than her family or job, because these latter roles are more important—they bring her important rewards and she would incur costs by ignoring them.

Role conflict can also occur because separate roles are incompatible. For instance, a policeman whose nephew reveals a plan to start dealing street drugs will be torn between his professional role, which requires that he turn in his nephew, and his family role, which requires that he protect a member of his family.

BOX 2-2

Role Differentiation and Adjustment

A study your authors conducted in Chile illustrates the importance of knowing a variety of roles (35). The subjects were lower-class males who had either lived in Santiago, Chile all their lives or had moved to Santiago from rural areas during their adult lives. The subjects' average income was equivalent to $760 at the time, and their average education level was 4.7 years. We were interested in how effectively the migrants had made the transition from living in remote rural areas to living in a large metropolitan area with more than three million people. Our hypothesis, derived from role theory, was that the migrants who were most successful in understanding the different roles in their new environment would be better able to adjust and would be able to obtain and keep good jobs. We also believed that those migrants who were better at taking the roles of others would have an easier time adapting to the city.

To test for role differentiation and role-taking, we asked the migrants to tell us stories about drawings of typical urban social interactions. For some drawings, such as a scene of various people in a grocery store, the subjects were simply asked to describe the scene. For other drawings, such as one involving a person being interviewed for a job, the subjects were asked to take the role of one of the people in the picture. During the interview we also asked each person about his job history and his psychological well-being.

After tape-recording the interviews, we tabulated the number of different social roles the subjects had used to describe the people in the drawings, and we evaluated how effectively they had been able to take the roles we had asked them to take.

We found that (1) the migrants were not as good at differentiating roles as the life-long residents of Santiago, and (2) the migrants suffered from more psychosomatic symptoms than the life-long residents. We also found that the migrants who differentiated more roles tended to suffer fewer symptoms. The migrants who were better at role-taking also had fewer symptoms. In addition, we found that the migrants who were highest on role differentiation and role-taking abilities had obtained better jobs and kept them longer than the migrants who were low on these abilities. Clearly, the migrants who were best able to understand their social environments by placing others in roles and taking the roles of others were those who had adapted most successfully to their new lives. ■

Role strain Contradictory expectations can also be held about a single role. When one role contains incompatible expectations, *role strain* is said to occur. The manager of an office may find that she is expected to be a competent and firm supervisor as well as a warm and understanding friend to her employees. However, being a firm supervisor may preclude being an understanding friend. Thus, our roles are problematic as well as useful. They can create stress and conflict even as they tie us to the society and make life intelligible.

Roles and the self The roles that one is expected to enact may be more or less compatible with the self. We sometimes say a person is like a "square peg in a round hole," meaning the person's skills or personality traits do not suit her well for a role she is required to perform. Typically, the more congruent the role with the individual's characteristics, the better the role performance and the more involved the person is in the role. The various roles an individual enacts in large part determine the person's sense of self. Think how your sense of self changed as you left the role of high school student and took on the role of college student.

Other people often overidentify a person with the role he or she is currently enacting (37). This overidentification results in the perception of the person in terms of a single identity. For example, Lisa naively thinks of Dr. Garcia as merely a kindly old physician because that is the only role in which she sees him. Since she does not see him as husband, father, tennis player, gambler, and churchgoer, she does not recognize that all of these roles are also valid "selves" of Dr. Garcia.

Ralph Turner believes the identification of a person with a role can be justifiable in some instances (38). Turner points out that roles consistent with one's self-concept are played more frequently, more fully, and with more involvement than roles that are unimportant or inconsistent with the self-concept. Roles central to the person's self-concept have widespread influences on the person's personality. Thus, Dr. Garcia's role of physician may well exemplify his dominant "self," have shaped his personality and, in part, determine his portrayal of his other roles.

To the extent that role behavior carries over into a variety of situations, Turner speaks of a *role-person merger*.

A role-person merger has three characteristics. First, the person fails to compartmentalize roles. The role continues to be played, even in situations where it does not apply. The busy executive who carries his air of authority and competitiveness into relationships with his children provides an example of this characteristic. Second, the person resists giving up the role, even in situations where more advantageous or viable roles are present as alternatives. For example, a factory worker may reject a promotion to foreman because she is socially and emotionally involved in the role of worker. Thus, the role-person merger can entail costs for the individual. Third, this merger can be recognized by the existence of attitudes and beliefs appropriate to the role. The factory worker who resists promotion to foreman probably has a variety of pro-labor and anti-management attitudes that are important to her worldview.

When is a role-person merger likely to occur? The more comprehensive the role, the more likely it is that the person will be identified with it. A woman who does not work outside the home and whose duties and sphere of influence overlap little with those of her husband, may well come to be seen by others and by herself as a homemaker. It is unlikely, however, that she would be identified with the role of dental patient, even though she probably spends a small portion of her time in this role.

In addition, the better and more consistent the role portrayal, the more likely it is that the person will be identified with the role. A tennis player who plays extremely well clearly shows his or her own identification with the role. The player's skill will be seen by others as an unambiguous cue that the person values the role of tennis player. But, a tennis player who plays poorly may either be displaying noninvolvement with this role or lack of skill at a valued role. Information regarding poor performance is ambiguous and cannot be used by others in a definitive assessment of the person's role.

Finally, the more positive or negative the evaluation of a role, the more likely the person will be identified with it. A successful U.S. president or a notorious mass murderer is more likely to be identified with his or her role than a good grocery clerk.

Turner states that a person-role merger can have benefits for the person. By becoming associated with a major role, one becomes predictable and understandable. Moreover, an association with a single role allows people to use the roles they play well in a variety of situations, thus maximizing gratification in role-playing and minimizing the likelihood of having to play roles that they enact less well.

In summary, role theory provides a way of linking individual behavior with larger social groups through the concepts of status or position in society. An individual enacts the role, but the position underlying the role is determined by the society and exists apart from any individual enactment of it. We enact many roles, simultaneously and successively, with both costs and benefits to the person. We may be more or less suited to our roles, and we may even be overidentified with a single role.

We now turn to a theory that has its origins in psychological social psychology. As you read about it, think of the ways in which it differs from the two more sociological theories you have just read about in terms of their relative emphasis on the interdependence of individuals and society and the methods employed.

■
SOCIAL LEARNING
THEORY

The original basis for social learning theory was the learning theory developed by behavioral psychologists. However, social learning theory goes beyond behaviorism to emphasize the human capacity for cognition (thought). Social learning theory views human behavior as being determined by an interplay between the influence of the situation, the person's behavior, and the person's cognitions and emotions (39) (see Figure 2-1).

For instance, sometimes situations are so powerful they dominate our thoughts and behavior.

Figure 2.1 ■

The Reciprocal Influences of the Situation, Behavior, and Cognition

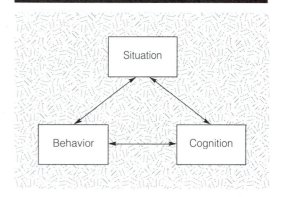

Adapted from Bandura, 1986.

Driving through a blizzard compels us to drive with care and not to let our thoughts wander. In other instances, our thoughts and behavior shape the situation as when a group of dorm residents decide to transform their dreary entrance hall for a Christmas party. There is also an interplay between cognitions and behavior. Sometimes our behavior is a product of our thoughts—for example, when you decide to quit studying and eat a snack. On other occasions, our thoughts result from our behavior, as would occur if you figured out that the snack you were eating was too salty and decided to stop eating it.

Social learning theorists suggest that behavior is learned through two processes, enactive learning and observational learning (40).

Enactive Learning

We learn many behaviors by *enacting* them and then directly experiencing the consequences of enaging in them. As children we learn which behaviors will be punished or cause us pain and which ones will be rewarded. We learn not to fight with children who are stronger than we are and that obeying adults usually brings rewards or at least helps us avoid punishments. This simple trial-and-error learning seems inefficient, but it works. Reinforcements and punishments can alter behavior, regardless of whether we are aware of the consequences of our behavior, but learning occurs faster when behavior is accompanied by conscious awareness of its consequences. If you are aware of what behavior is being rewarded in a given situation, you can modify your behavior accordingly. For instance, if you notice prospective employers seem interested in you when you discuss your computer skills, but seem bored when you discuss your work in drama, you can tailor your behavior to emphasize your computer background.

Observational Learning

If you had been obliged to learn everything you know through enactive learning, involving direct experiences with reinforcement and punishment, you probably would not have survived to read this book. Imagine learning to swim, drive, or cross Fifth Avenue in New York on the basis of the direct consequences of behavior. The first taxi barreling down Fifth Avenue would terminate the learning sequence, and you might not have lived long enough to figure out that you do not cross streets when the light is red (and on Fifth Avenue it helps to be careful even when it's green).

One of the most effective ways to learn is to *observe* the behavior of others. By observing others

we can learn about the consequences of behavior indirectly. People become aware of just how many behaviors are learned through observation when they enter an unfamiliar culture. The easiest way to learn what is appropriate in a foreign culture is to watch what other people are doing. What gestures do they use when greeting each other? What are the norms for eating? How do people excuse themselves (see Box 2-3)?

The distinction between enactive and observational learning can be seen in the behavior of different members of a mountain climbing team. As the leader of the team picks a path up the face of the mountain, he or she must make crucial decisions about handholds, footholds, where to insert chocks or picks, and which crevices to pursue. The punishment for mistakes can be long detours, injury, or even death. The rewards for making sound judgments are less energy expended, a greater margin of safety, and ultimately reaching the mountaintop. This is enactive learning. The other team members *watch* the leader and typically use the same handholds and footholds. They learn a safe path by observing the behavior of the person in front of them. In this instance, the rewards come from observational learning.

For behavior to be learned through observation, we must first direct our *attention* to a model who is engaging in the behavior (42) (see Figure 2-2). We are most likely to pay attention to models when we anticipate rewards for doing so. People who are

Figure 2.2 ■

The Modeling Sequence

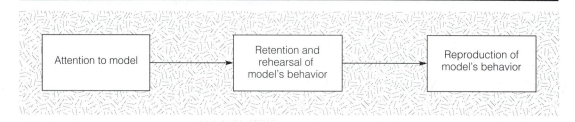

Adapted from Bandura, 1986.

BOX 2-3

The Diffusion of Behavior Change Through Modeling

Social learning theory has a number of practical applications. One application involves changing people's behavior through the use of modeling. When a society wishes to change the behavior of its members (for instance, by encouraging them to litter less, use solar water heaters, donate blood, or quit smoking), the leaders often try to encourage people to change. If the changes are immediately rewarding for the members of the society, as the adoption of a superior farming technique might be, then people may quickly change their behavior. Usually simply encouraging people to change is not very successful. Theories of modeling have been used to boost the adoption of desired behavior changes.

One such attempt occurred in Mexico where the government wished to reduce widespread illiteracy through the use of peer teaching programs (41). The idea was that people with reading skills could teach others to read using materials provided by the government. National advertisements for the program failed to ignite much enthusiasm. The government then turned to modeling to promote the peer teaching program. Soap operas are very popular in Mexico and thus could be used to reach a large audience. A set of soap opera programs was created in which peer teaching groups figured prominently. A popular soap opera performer played the role of group instructor. The story was made melodramatic to increase viewer attention. The benefits of literacy were graphically portrayed, and myths about the difficulty of learning to read were countered. Follow-up programs helped the viewers to retain the message of the program and to provide them with specific information on how they could start literacy training groups themselves. The actors in the program even demonstrated how to get the materials from the government centers. As a result of the television series, enrollment in the literacy programs jumped from 99,000 to 840,000 in one year.

A similar technique was used to encourage family planning. In a television series a small family was seen taking advantage of the family planning services and benefiting from them, while a large family was shown experiencing the distress of family discord and poverty. At the end of the programs, information on how to take advantage of the government's family planning agencies was provided. The year the program was aired, family planning centers reported a 32% increase in the number of new contraceptive users. Related programs have been used in this country to reduce the risk of heart disease (see Chapter 17). ■

learning to fly will closely observe the behavior of their instructors because they expect to learn something valuable by observing them. The reward, a safe flight, is a clear benefit of observing the model. Models who are expert, powerful, or to whom we are attracted are the most likely to command our attention.

Observing the behavior of others will not lead us to model their behavior unless we *retain* what we have observed. We often use language to condense a complex sequence of observed behaviors into an abbreviated form so we can retain it. For instance, in learning to ski, you can tell yourself to weight the downhill ski as you make a parallel turn. Symbolic encoding, involving the conversion of an observed sequence into language, is the most efficient way of retaining information, but we also retain information as visual images (43). Retention is further enhanced if we rehearse the behavior. This *rehearsal* can be either mental or behavioral. Immediate mental rehearsal is especially useful if a long delay occurs between the observation of the behavior and the attempt to imitate it.

For imitation to occur, the individual must have the physical and mental abilities to *reproduce* the behavior. Neither of your authors ever expects to perform like an Olympic gymnast—we could never imitate the behaviors, no matter how carefully we had attended to them, retained them or mentally rehearsed them. Even under the best of circumstances, it may take a number of practice trials before learners can adequately imitate a new or complex behavior they have observed.

When we observe the behavior of others, we note the *consequences* of their behaviors. The behavioral consequences provide us with information about the rewards and punishments we can anticipate if we imitate the behavior. If we see other people being rewarded for a given behavior, this information increases the chances we will imitate the behavior; if we see them being punished, this will decrease the chances of imitation. For instance, if you see

■ *Fishing for a solution to the generation gap: a child learning to fish by imitating his grandfather. (WGS)*

someone cheat on a test and get caught, you are less likely to cheat than if you see someone cheat and get away with it. In both cases, the behavior of the other person has been attended to and will probably be retained. However, only when the behavior is rewarded is it likely to be imitated.

One example of imitation based on behavioral consequences can be found in the incidence of airline hijackings (44). The most famous hijacking in the United States took place in November, 1974, when a man flying under the name D. B. Cooper hijacked a plane and demanded $200,000 plus two parachutes. When his demands were met, he parachuted from the plane carrying the money. The hijacking appeared to be successful, although it is not clear that he survived the jump. If imitation is the sincerest form of flattery, D. B. Cooper has been showered with flattery. A wave of similar hijacking attempts followed his hijacking. In the following month, there were two attempts, including one in which the hijacker demanded a parachute. In the following year, 19 attempts at hijacking for ransom occurred and in 15 the hijackers demanded parachutes. In contrast, unsuccessful hijacking attempts do not increase the rate of subsequent hijackings.

Acquisition and Performance

It is important to realize there is a distinction between the *acquisition* of behavior and its *performance*. In an experiment demonstrating this distinction, children were exposed to a model who behaved aggressively toward a Bobo doll (a plastic clown filled with air that pops upright after being hit) (45). The model's behaviors consisted of novel forms of aggression, such as hitting the Bobo doll with a mallet. After the model had beaten the Bobo doll, the experimenter entered the room and either complimented or criticized the model for hitting the Bobo doll.

Next, the children were given a chance to play with the Bobo doll. Children who had seen the model complimented imitated the model more than children who had seen the model criticized. The criticism of the model apparently inhibited the children from performing the aggressive behaviors. In this study, the consequences of the model's behavior clearly affected the children's willingness to *perform* it.

Following the opportunity to play with the Bobo doll, the children were offered rewards for showing the experimenter what the model had done to the Bobo doll. When the children who had seen the model criticized were offered these rewards, they were able to imitate as many of the model's behaviors as the children who had seen the model rewarded. This means that children who had seen the model criticized *acquired* the behavior, even though they did not perform it until they were asked to do so. It is often the case that people acquire new behaviors through observation, even though they do not immediately perform them.

The Regulation of Behavior

According to Bandura, behavior is regulated through three types of control processes: reinforcement control, stimulus control, and cognitive control. We will consider each control process in turn.

Reinforcement control Theories of learning are based on the idea that behavior is regulated by its consequences. Social learning theory expands on this idea by noting that the types of reinforcements and punishments regulating behavior include more than the direct experience of pleasure and pain. When we observe others, we observe the consequences of their behavior for them. The rewards and punishments others receive serve an informational function by indicating which of our behaviors are likely to be rewarded or punished.

The most important way in which reinforcement regulates behavior is through *self-reinforcement*. If our actions were controlled only by external reinforcements or punishments, our behavior would be situationally determined—responsive only to the reinforcements in a given situation. However, our behavior is often consistent across different situations because we have our own internal standards that we use to guide our behavior. For instance, your basic beliefs about right and wrong probably do not change to agree with those of the people you are currently with.

If we meet or exceed our standards we feel self-satisfied or proud of ourselves. This is *self-reinforcement*. If we fall below our standards we reproach ourselves, which is a form of *self-punishment*. Although our standards for social behavior, physical skills, and academic achievement are shaped by previous rewards and punishments, their continued use in adulthood is maintained through self-reinforcement and self-punishment. Thus, behavior can be regulated by internal rewards and punishments as well as by external ones.

Stimulus control The stimulus properties of situations also regulate some aspects of our behavior. We may develop phobias that lead us to respond with fear to such stimuli as spiders, rats, bats, snakes, and dentists. If we can, we avoid situations that cause us anxiety and seek those that elicit pleasure. The stimuli we either encounter or anticipate encountering in a situation regulate our behavior because of their association with events in our pasts.

Stimuli can also acquire significance through their association with reward and punishment. As children we learn that obeying our parents often results in their approval or at least allows us to avoid punishment from them. In this manner the dictates of authority come to be associated with rewards and punishments. Even when unfamiliar adult authority figures (firemen, teachers) tell us what to do, we are likely to obey them because of our past experiences with authority figures. This may be true even if we are not sure whether a particular authority figure has the power to reward or punish us. Thus, our prior learning often affects our responses to current stimuli to a greater extent than rewards or punishments that occur in the current situation.

Cognitive control Behavior is also controlled by internal thought processes. Cognitive control refers to our capacity to think, plan, and imagine our behavior and its consequences. *Anticipated* reinforcements or punishments are often more impor-

tant determinants of behavior than actual reinforcements or punishments. For example, we may plan to attend and then go to a concert because we expect it to be good. If the concert is not as good as we expected, we may lower our expectations about the quality of future concerts. These lowered expectations may then affect our decisions about whether to attend the next concert.

One particularly important type of expectancy concerns our beliefs about our ability to carry out a proposed activity. These judgments about *self-efficacy* often determine what actions we will undertake. People who feel they have the personal competence to act in an effective way are more likely to attempt a difficult task, like taking extra courses, than those whose judgments of self-efficacy are lower. We will have more to say about self-efficacy in Chapter 5.

Before acting, we often consider the alternative courses of action that are available to us. We weigh the anticipated rewards and punishments of each course of action and make the choice that will have the highest payoff. This type of foresight involves little or no stimulus or reinforcement control because we have not yet entered any of the situations we are contemplating. Instead, this type of control over behavior is entirely cognitive.

We are especially likely to use cognitive control when confronted with a new or complex situation. If you are thinking of taking one of several summer jobs, you will consider the pay and working conditions of each and then choose the one that has the most positive overall outcome for you. For well-learned routine behaviors like riding a bike or eating, we do not need to engage in such careful planning or consider different courses of action. Thus, well-learned behaviors are typically not under cognitive control.

All three types of control are often present in a single situation. However, the strength of the three types of control may vary in any given situation. In familiar situations, such as interacting with your family, stimulus control reigns. In unfamiliar situations, such as a job interview, we may employ cognitive control by using our past experiences to

"If reading is so much fun, how come she assigns three extra chapters for punishment!"

■ *These young social learning theorists understand that rewards and punishments are cognitively defined. (The Wall Street Journal.)*

decide upon the best plan of action. In unfamiliar situations, we would probably also use reinforcement control to modify our behavior in accordance with the rewards or punishments we receive in the situation. There is a constant interplay between the various types of control.

To illustrate, consider a group of loyal fans of your college football team. Thinking it would help the team to have some encouragement on the road and anticipating a good time, they plan to go to the next game played away from home (cognitive control). They attend the game and, just as they would do at home, they start cheering their team on and booing the referees when they make a call that goes against their team (stimulus control). However, when the fans of the home team start giving them a bad time, they tone down their enthusiasm and stop booing the referee (reinforcement control).

■ *Flying an airplane demands cognitive control of behavior. (WGS)*

Next we come to a theory that represents a synthesis of the two social psychologies—social exchange theory. The idea that social relations can be viewed as a type of exchange process has attracted theorists from both sociology and psychology. As you will see, this wide-ranging theory has been applied to relations between individuals, between individuals and groups, and between groups.

■

EXCHANGE THEORY

All men, or most men, wish what is noble but choose what is profitable; and while it is noble to render a service not with an eye to receiving one in turn, it is profitable to receive one. One

ought, therefore, if one can, to return the equivalent of services received, and to do so willingly.
Aristotle (46)

Rachel met Angie when Rachel was hired by the same company. Rachel immediately liked Angie and she asked Angie to help her learn her job. Soon they began going to lunch together and it wasn't long before they started spending some of their free time together. They both liked the same kind of movies and they shared an interest in horses. As they got to know one another better, they spent more time talking to each other about their pasts, exchanging views about their friends, and discussing their hopes for the future.

Gradually Rachel and Angie grew to trust and depend on one another. Each of them helped the other when help was needed. As the relationship

■ *Exchange theory suggests that interpersonal relationships are analogous to economic exchanges. (WGS)*

continued and deepened, there was an ongoing interchange. At times Rachel put more into the relationship—for instance, by caring for Angie when she was sick, but overall a sort of balance emerged. However, after they had known one another for some time Rachel started to feel the relationship was too one-sided. Rachel thought Angie was taking advantage of their friendship. The resentment this caused threatened to doom the relationship, although Rachel wanted very much to bring it back into their old balance.

Exchange theory provides a way of thinking about inputs and outcomes in relationships such as Rachel and Angie's. It focuses on what people put into relationships (such as time, effort, money, or emotional support), and what they get out of them (such as love, friendship, or prestige). The foundation of the theory is economic. The theory proposes that people will attempt to maximize the rewards they receive from relationships and minimize the costs they incur in them. Theories of learning have also contributed to exchange theory. Concepts from learning theories help us understand what relationships will be selected and maintained.

The Propositions of Exchange Theory

George Homans's version of exchange theory (47) centers on two-person relationships because he feels that all social interaction can be explained by the same rules that apply to them. His approach is based on a set of propositions derived from learning theory. The first proposition is that people will engage in actions that are rewarding. The frequency with which they will engage in rewarding actions depends on how soon the rewards occur after the action, the value of the rewards, and the pattern of the rewards. For instance, people can easily get caught up in playing slot machines because the rewards occur soon after pulling the lever, the rewards are valuable, and they are patterned randomly (a type of pattern that produces high rates of response).

The second proposition says the more similar the current situation is to one experienced in the past, the more likely it is that the actions that were rewarded then will be engaged in now. For example,

if in the past you received better grades when you underlined important points in the textbook (like the proposition you just read), then you will be more likely to underline as you are reading this book. (It isn't too late to start now.)

The third proposition suggests that rewards gain in value when we have been deprived of them and lose in value when we have received them very frequently. The first time your boyfriend or girlfriend says "I love you" it is music to your ears. However, by the 200th time you hear this (provided the relationship lasts this long), it may sound a bit flat.

In the next two propositions, Homans says that when we fail to obtain an expected reward we become angry, and when we obtain an unexpected reward we are pleased. Think of the grade point you expect to earn this semester or quarter. You will probably be angry (at the professors or yourself) if you get a much lower grade point, but you will be pleased if you get a higher grade point than you expected. Homans's final proposition is the most important. It says that the frequency with which a person engages in an action depends on the value of the outcome to him or her and the probability the action will lead to the outcome. This proposition is similar to the basic assumption of economics—people make rational choices among the alternatives available to them in an attempt to maximize their outcomes.

When the behavior of one person has an effect on another, the interaction can be viewed as an exchange between the two people. An exchange may consist of rewards, as would have occurred when Rachel helped Angie with her work and Angie thanked Rachel for her kindness. An exchange may also consist of punishments, as when Rachel confronted Angie about exploiting her and Angie got angry and said something that hurt Rachel's feelings. If a relationship is to be sustained, both participants must perceive that the rewards outweigh the punishments.

Mutually rewarding relationships lead to trust and liking, but this liking often declines if only the same rewards are always exchanged. Since rewards lose their power when given frequently, we sometimes get bored with the people we see very often.

Variety really is the spice of life, at least if you want enduring, mutually satisfying relationships.

A relationship is likely to be terminated if one of the members finds it burdensome, unless there are no better alternatives in sight. Rachel may keep Angie as a friend, even if she feels she is being exploited, as long as she believes she cannot find someone to replace Angie. In exchange theory, the consideration of alternatives to the present relationship is known as the *comparison level of alternatives*. Sometimes people remain in relationships where negative outcomes outweigh positive ones because the alternatives appear to be even worse. Women who are battered by their husbands do not leave them in some cases because they believe the alternatives would be even worse (trying to support themselves and care for their children by working at a minimum-wage job).

Power and Exchange

Rachel and Angie's relationship is one in which they are both equal. Mike is Angie's boss. When Angie disagrees with Mike, she often keeps her opinion to herself or changes it so she agrees with her boss. The reason is that in this relationship Mike has greater rewards and punishments to give Angie than Angie has to give Mike. This is the essence of *power* — the control of rewards and punishments (48).

In an exchange relationship, power exists when one member is dependent on the other for the receipt of rewards. Typically, this occurs when the dependent member has few or no other relationships in which he or she can receive these rewards. If Angie feels she cannot get as good a job as the one she has with Mike, then Mike has a lot more power over Angie than if Angie could easily find a comparable job. If the rewards are important to the dependent member, he or she is likely to do what the other person wants in order to obtain the reward. Thus, Angie may do all kinds of favors for Mike to ensure that her paycheck keeps coming in.

The power to punish is similar to the power to reward. Here, power derives from the fact that the punishment can be either given or withheld. When a punishment is withheld, this is a sort of reward—a reward that is given when the dependent member behaves as desired. Angie may find herself working overtime without pay to avoid being fired.

The person who has least to gain from an exchange has the greatest power in the relationship. If Mike doesn't really need Angie to do the job she is doing, but Angie desperately needs her job, then Mike has great power in the relationship. This type of relationship, where a male has extensive power over a female, is the seedbed for sexual harassment.

The Norm of Reciprocity

As Alvin Gouldner has noted, most exchanges are governed by the norm of reciprocity (49). This norm suggests that exchanges are rarely one-sided. When one person gives rewards to another, the other is expected to reciprocate. Usually, the rewards returned are not exactly the same as those received, but in some cases they may be. When Angie invites Rachel to dinner, then Rachel is likely to feel she should do something equally nice for Angie.

The norm of reciprocity says people should help those who have helped them. The repayment for a benefit received depends on the value of the benefit, which in turn, depends on the need of the recipient, the resources of the donor, and the constraints on the donor. Thus, Angie's debt to Rachel for caring for her would be greatest if Angie is really sick and if Rachel freely gives Angie something valuable (all her spare time) of which she has little.

The reciprocity norm helps to organize and stabilize social systems. It provides some of the "glue" that leads people to stick together. The norm of reciprocity makes people feel obligated to one another, and it discourages purely selfish exploitation of others. If you exploit others, they will feel little obligation to help you in your time of need. If Mike sexually exploited Angie, she might not come to his aid when he really needed her (she would now have the power because he would be dependent on her). We will have more to say about the norm of reciprocity in the chapter on prosocial behavior (Chapter 12).

Distributive Justice

On balance, people expect their relationships to be rewarding. Homans recognizes, however, that nearly all relationships involve costs as well as rewards. Whether individuals find the balance of rewards and costs satisfactory depends on two factors: (1) how much reward they expect compared with what they receive, and (2) the rewards and costs the other person experiences.

Homans's *law of distributive justice* states that each member expects the rewards of each person to be proportional to his or her costs. When the proportions of rewards and costs are not perceived to be equal, the disadvantaged party is likely to feel resentful and may try to terminate the relationship. The person who receives the unfair advantage may feel guilty. When Rachel felt she was putting a lot into the relationship, but getting little out of it, while Angie was putting little into it and getting a lot out of it, Rachel became dissatisfied. Then Rachel had to decide whether to try to make the relationship more equal or leave it. The law of distributive justice is not restricted to relations between individuals; it applies to relations between groups as well (see Box 2-4).

Equity

Homans's concept of distributive justice has been elaborated upon by several subsequent theorists (56). One of these elaborations revolves around the notion of equity. Each member of a relationship makes contributions to the relationship, called inputs (I), and receives things from the relationship, called outcomes (O). Inputs are usually negative, such as effort and time. Outcomes are usually positive, such as affection, money, knowledge, respect, and approval.

As was the case for distributive justice, *equity* exists when the ratio of one member's inputs and outcomes (person A) is equal to the other member's inputs and outcomes (person B). The formula for this relationship is:

$$\frac{I_a}{O_a} = \frac{I_b}{O_b}$$

It is the *perceived* value of the outcomes and inputs that are relevant, rather than their actual value. The perceptions of the values of the inputs and outcomes of the two members may differ. It is possible for one member in a relationship to consider it equitable, while the other member does not. Although Rachel clearly felt her relationship with Angie had become inequitable, Angie apparently did not share this view, and that is why she reacted so negatively when Rachel confronted her.

A fascinating example of the importance of perceptions for assessments of equity concerns the way husbands and wives feel about each other's earnings (57). Husbands feel *more* underpaid the more their wives earn, apparently because they feel they should earn more than their wives. In contrast, wives feel *less* underpaid the more their husbands earn, perhaps because they judge fairness in terms of the family's total income. In this situation, what is considered fair or equitable depends not on absolute earnings, but on how the relative earnings of husbands and wives are perceived.

Perceived inequity leads to attempts to restore equity. These attempts can take two forms, behavioral or psychological. There are five behavioral options open to disadvantaged parties.

- First, people can reduce their inputs. For example, an electronics factory worker who feels she is being underpaid can reduce her inputs by taking longer coffee breaks or working less intensely. $\downarrow I_p$

- Second, people can try to increase their outcomes. For example, the electronics employee could ask for a raise. $\uparrow O_p$

- Third, people can increase the other person's inputs. The electronics employee can attempt to increase the employer's costs of operation by joining other workers in demanding better working conditions and more fringe benefits. $\uparrow I_{\bar{p}}$

- Fourth, people can reduce the other person's outcomes. The electronics employee might do shoddy work so the products will be returned and the company will suffer. $\downarrow O_{\bar{p}}$

BOX 2-4

Social Class and Social Justice

The stratification of our society into social classes provides an interesting opportunity to apply theories of distributive justice. The key question is: Do the various social classes accept their positions as fair and just? Do people believe that the inputs of members of the upper classes to society are so much greater than those of members of the lower classes that they deserve more than those in the lower classes? If not, how do people account for the differential rewards received by members of the upper classes?

One theoretical position suggests people base their judgments of fairness on existing patterns of reward (50). They ask themselves if, in comparison to people like themselves, they are better or worse off. This theory predicts that people generally believe what "is" is what "ought" to be. Thus, the poor would be expected to compare themselves to others who are poor and to believe they are generally getting what they deserve.

In contrast, another version of distributive justice theory suggests that the relevant comparison in making judgments of fairness is some type of utopian standard that dictates that economic rewards should be distributed according to need (or that they should be distributed equally). Using such standards, the poor would be expected to feel like they are not being treated fairly by the social system.

Research findings indicate the upper classes adhere well to the first theory— the one that says that fairness is defined by what "is." Thus, it has been found that the more people earn, the more just they believe their incomes are (51). The lower classes adhere to the second theory—that fairness is defined by what one believes should be true.

The explanations of the rich and the poor for their economic positions vary correspondingly (52). Upper class people believe their wealth is due to personal drive, a willingness to take risks, initiative, and hard work. Lower class people see their poverty as due to a lack of jobs, low wages, poor schools, and discrimination (53). Thus, wealthy think they deserve their wealth because of their investments of ef____ while the lower classes tend to deny this. The poor tend to blame _____ ctural factors in society and thus do not feel they deserve to _____ disagree. They attribute poverty to lack of effort and ability _____ ment—an example of blaming victims for their misfortunes

_____ at people who feel they are underbenefitted are less _____ esteem than those who feel they are earning what they _____). These results illustrate a general principle in exchange _____ e more sensitive to being underbenefitted than they are to being _____ d. ■

■ Finally, if none of these avenues is deemed desirable, people can terminate the relationship.

Psychologically, the disadvantaged member of a relationship has four options. In this case it is not the actual inputs and outcomes that are altered, but the *perceptions* of the inputs and outcomes. Thus, (1) the electronics worker may decide that she really is not working all that hard (reducing her inputs psychologically), (2) or that she greatly enjoys working with her coworkers (increasing her outcomes psychologically). Alternatively, (3) she might decide that given the competitiveness in the electronics business, her employer is paying a very high wage (boosting her perception of her employer's inputs), (4) or that she is giving the employer a rather low rate of productivity (decreasing the employer's outcomes). Psychological means of restoring equity are often employed when behavioral remedies fail.

Restoring equity psychologically is preferred by people who receive a disproportionately favorable ratio of outcomes and inputs. People who experience inequitable advantages often do not wish to restore equity behaviorally by reducing their own positive outcomes or by increasing their inputs, nor do they wish to increase the burdens of the disadvantaged party. They would like to have their cake and eat it without discomfort—and without giving any of it away.

A psychological solution to this dilemma is to regard disadvantaged people as deserving the low ratio of outcomes to inputs they receive. This type of reasoning is consistent with the idea that people get what they deserve and deserve what they get— a phenomenon known as the *belief in a just world*. A belief that the world is just means that when we do not wish to change a disadvantaged person's situation or when we cannot change it, we often blame the person for causing his or her own problems. As indicated in Box 2-4, this tendency to blame the victim applies to the poor, but it also applies to people who have been victims of accidents or crime or who suffer from serious diseases (58).

In summary, each of the theories we have discussed describes one unique aspect of social psychological reality. Symbolic interactionism ex-

plores the social construction of reality, showing that meanings are created through the process of social interaction. Role theory describes one link between the individual and the society by demonstrating that roles transcend individuals and that roles are determined by society, even though they are enacted by individuals. Social learning theory views human behavior as an interplay between the influence of the situation, the person's behavior, and the person's cognitions and emotions. The focus of social learning theory is on the acquisition of behavior; it argues that substantial learning takes place indirectly, through observation. Exchange theory draws on learning theory and economics to focus on relationships, which it views as a balance between inputs and outcomes.

Each of these theories has its own strengths and weaknesses. In the past, symbolic interactionism's focus on meaning and social interaction tended to neglect the reciprocal influence of the individual and the society. Current formulations, however, place a greater emphasis on the influence of the social structure on the social construction of reality. Symbolic interactionism has also been criticized for imprecision in concepts, which has led to problems of testability. In contrast, role theory has focused on social expectations and the ways these social expectations structure human behavior. In the process, role theory has tended to neglect the role of the individual in determining his or her enactment of the roles. Symbolic interactionism and role theory are complementary in some ways. Symbolic interactionism starts with the person and his or her construction of reality and builds up to the society through the influence of the social structure on meanings. Role theory starts with the social structure by using the concept of role and builds down to the person through the individual role portrayed (59).

Social learning theory and exchange theory are also complementary in some respects. Each has psychological learning theory as an underlying premise, with its key concept that individuals seek rewards and avoid punishments. Social learning theory, however, has focused on micro-level factors such as cognitions and emotions in explaining the variety of ways that individuals learn. In general, the role of the society in determining what is rewarding and punishing to the individual has been neglected by social learning theory. By incorporating notions of power in relationships, exchange theory has begun to provide a link between individual interaction and the broader social structure. Yet exchange theory, with its focus on rewards and fairness, is limited in its ability to explain other facets of human relationships.

Each of these theories has been used to understand some social psychological topics but not others. Throughout the book we will apply these theories to the subject matter of social psychology when they are appropriate. Where more limited theories of human behavior have been suggested to explain a given subject, we will turn to these smaller mini-theories for explanations.

■

SUMMARY

Symbolic interactionists have a theoretical perspective that focuses on the social construction of reality; they believe that meanings are the product of social interaction. Symbolic interactionists believe that humans act toward people and objects on the basis of the meanings they have for them, that meanings are a product of social interaction, and that meanings are modified through interpretations people make in their dealings with other people and objects. Symbolic interaction is made possible through the use of symbols. There are two schools of symbolic interactionism. The Chicago school's methods are qualitative and oriented toward understanding the perspective of the person under study. The Iowa school differs from the Chicago school in its use of quantitative methods and in its stress on the dependency of the self and society upon social structures.

The dramaturgical school and ethnomethodology are outgrowths of symbolic interactionism. Both investigate face-to-face interaction. The dramaturgical school is concerned with impression management. Goffman has analyzed interactions between the stigmatized and "normals," noting that stigma-

tized people are treated as though their stigmata make them not quite human. Ethnomethodologists are more concerned with the ways in which a sense of reality is constructed. They have studied such topics as the unwritten rules of the society.

Role theory focuses on the existence of a variety of social positions with accompanying expectations regarding appropriate role behaviors. Roles are embedded in the social structure and they transcend individuals; they thus bridge the gap between the microsocial and macrosocial levels of analysis.

People tend to be evaluated positively to the extent that their role behaviors conform to role expectations. Role expectations vary on a number of dimensions—generality or specificity, extensiveness, clarity or ambiguity, and in degree of consensus. Roles can be ascribed or achieved. The more roles in an individual's repertoire, the better the person functions in society. However, multiple roles can lead to role strain or role conflict.

Social learning theory emphasizes the interplay between the situation, behavior, and cognition. It suggests that behavior is learned by enacting it and directly experiencing the consequences. Learning is enhanced if we are consciously aware of the consequences of behavior. We also learn through the observation of the behavior of others. Observational learning begins with attention to the model. The behavior must then be encoded, preferably symbolically. If the behavior is rehearsed it is more likely to be retained. The behavior will not be exhibited if the individual is incapable of reproducing it. Behaviors acquired through observational learning may not be subsequently exhibited, if the individual does not anticipate reinforcement for doing so.

One way behavior is regulated is by the meaning stimuli in the current situation, have due to their association with stimuli in the individual's past. A second way behavior is regulated is through the reinforcements and punishments that exist in the current situation. A third behavior regulation mechanism is through cognitively anticipating the consequences of behavior.

Exchange theory views relationships as exchanges of rewards and costs. Rewards lose their power when we receive them repeatedly, but gain in power when we have been deprived of them. Our attraction to a relationship depends on the types of rewards we can obtain from it and the probability of obtaining these rewards. Our satisfaction with a relationship depends on the degree to which we have received the rewards we expected and our perception of whether the proportion of rewards and costs each person is experiencing is equitable.

If the reward/cost ratio is perceived to be inequitable, attempts will be made, either behaviorally or psychologically, to restore equity. If these attempts fail, or if more rewarding relationships are available, the relationship is likely to be terminated.

■

REFERENCES

1. Buck, R., 1984, *The Communication of Emotion,* New York: Guilford Press; A. J. Fridlund and C. E. Izard, 1983, "Electromyographic Studies of Facial Expressions of Emotions and Patterns of Emotions," New York: Guilford Press; J. C. Hager and P. Ekman, 1983, "The Inner and Outer Meanings of Facial Expressions," in J. T. Cacioppo and R. Petty, *Social Psychophysiology,* New York: Guilford Press.

2. Ekman, P., 1973, "Cross-cultural Studies of Facial Emotions," in P. Ekman (Ed.), *Darwin and Facial Expression: A Century of Research,* New York: Academic Press.

3. Freedman, D. G., 1964, "Smiling in Blind Infants and the Issue of Innate vs. Acquired," *Journal of Child Psychology and Psychiatry* 5:171–184; C. E. Izard, R. R. Huebner, D. Rissner, G. C. McGinnes, and L. Dougherty, 1980, "The Young Infant's Ability to Produce Discrete Emotional Expressions," *Developmental Psychology* 16:132–140.

4. Fridlund, A. J. and C. E. Izard, 1983, op. cit.; W. E. Rinn, 1984, "The Neurophysiology of Facial Expression: A Review of the Neurological and Psychological Mechanisms for Producing Facial Expressions," *Psychological Bulletin* 95:52–77.

5. Ekman, P. "Expression and the Nature of Emotion," in K. R. Scherer and P. Ekman (Eds.), *Approaches to Emotion,* Hillsdale, NJ: Erlbaum.

6. Blumer, H., 1969, *Symbolic Interactionism: Perspective and Method,* Englewood Cliffs, NJ: Prentice-Hall.

7. Stryker, S., 1988, "Substance and Style: An Appraisal of the Sociological Legacy of Herbert Blumer," *Symbolic Interactionism* 11:33–42.

8. Thomas, W. I. and D. S. Thomas, 1928, *The Child in America.* New York: Alfred A. Knopf.

9. Mead, G. H., 1934, *Mind, Self, and Society,* Chicago: University of Chicago Press.

10. Stryker, 1988, ibid.

11. Cardwell, J. D., 1971, *Social Psychology: A Symbolic Interactionist Perspective,* Philadelphia: F. A. Davis; R. H. Lauer and W. H. Handel, 1977, *Social Psychology: The Theory and Application of Symbolic Interactionism,* Boston: Houghton Mifflin; B. N. Meltzer, J. W. Petras, and L. T. Reynolds, 1975, *Symbolic Interactionism: Genesis, Varieties, and Criticism,* London: Routledge & Kegan Paul.

12. Blumer, 1969, op. cit.

13. Lauer and Handel, 1977, op. cit.; Meltzer et al., 1975, op. cit.

14. Kuhn, M. H. and T. S. McPartland, 1954, "An Empirical Investigation of Self-Attitudes," *American Sociological Review* 19:68–76.

15. Stryker, S., 1984, "Symbolic Interactionism: Themes and Variations," in M. Rosenberg and R. H. Turner (Eds.), *Social Psychology: Sociological Perspectives,* New York: Basic Books.

16. Stryker, 1984, ibid.

17. Stryker, S., 1980, *Symbolic Interactionism,* Menlo Park, CA: Benjamin/Cummings.

18. Callero, P., 1985, "Role-identity Salience," *Social Psychology Quarterly* 48:203–214.

19. Goffman, E., 1959, *The Presentation of Self in Everyday Life,* Garden City, NY: Doubleday.

20. Goffman, E., 1963, *Stigma,* Englewood Cliffs, NJ: Prentice-Hall.

21. Goffman, E., 1952, "On Cooling the Mark Out: Some Aspects of Adaptation to Failure," *Psychiatry* 15:451–463.

22. Goffman, E., 1974, *Frame Analysis,* Cambridge: Harvard University Press.

23. Turner, J. H., 1986, *The Structure of Sociological Theory,* 4th ed. Homewood, IL: Dorsey.

24. Turner, 1986, ibid.

25. Garfinkel, H., 1967, *Studies in Ethnomethodology,* Englewood Cliffs, NJ: Prentice-Hall.

26. Garfinkel, 1967, ibid.

27. Heiss, J., 1981, "Social Roles," in M. Rosenberg and R. H. Turner (Eds.), *Social Psychology: Sociological Perspectives,* New York: Basic Books.

28. Biddle, B. J., 1979, *Role Theory: Expectations, Identities, and Behaviors.* New York: Academic Press.

29. Stryker, 1980, op. cit.

30. Turner, R. H., 1962, "Role-taking: Process vs. Conformity," in A. M. Rose (Ed.), *Human Behavior and Social Processes,* Boston: Houghton Mifflin.

31. Turner, 1962, ibid.

32. Heiss, 1981, op. cit.

33. Sarbin, T. R., 1968, "Role Theory," in G. Lindzey and E. Aronson (Eds.), *The Handbook of Social Psychology,* Vol. 1, 2d ed., Reading, MA: Addison-Wesley.

34. Linton, R., 1942, "Age and Sex Categories," *American Sociological Review* 7:589–603.

35. Stephan, W. G. and C. Stephan, 1971, "Role Differentiation, Empathy, and Neurosis in Urban Migrants and Lower-class Residents of Santiago, Chile," *Journal of Personality and Social Psychology* 19:1–6.

36. Seiber, S. D., 1974, "Toward a Theory of Role Accumulation," *American Sociological Review* 39:567–578.

37. E.g., Goffman, E., 1961, *Asylums,* Garden City, NY: Doubleday; Goffman, 1963, op. cit.

38. Turner, R. H., 1978, "The Role and the Person," *American Journal of Sociology* 84:1–23.

39. Bandura, A., 1986, *The Social Foundations of Thought and Action,* Englewood Cliffs, NJ: Prentice-Hall.

40. Bandura, A., 1986, ibid.; A. Bandura, 1971, *Social Learning Theory,* Morristown, NJ: General Learning Press.

41. Sabido, M., 1981, *Towards the Social Use of Soap Operas,* Mexico City: Institute for Communication Research, cited in A. Bandura, 1986, ibid.

42. Bandura, 1986, op. cit.

43. Bandura, A. and R. Jeffery, 1971, "Role of Symbolic Coding and Rehearsal Processes in Observational Learning," unpublished manuscript, Stanford University.

44. Holden, R. T., 1986, "The Contagiousness of Aircraft Hijacking," *American Journal of Sociology* 91:874–904.

45. Bandura, A., 1965, "Influence of Models' Reinforcement Contingencies on the Acquisition of Imitative Responses," *Journal of Personality and Social Psychology* 1:589–595.

46. Aristotle, 1968, *The Nichomean Ethics,* H. Rackham (Trans.), Cambridge, MA.: Harvard University Press.

47. Homans, G. C., 1961, *Social Behavior: Its Elementary Forms,* New York: Harcourt, Brace & World; Homans, G. C., 1974, *Social Behavior: Its Elementary Forms,* rev. ed., New York: Harcourt Brace Jovanovich.

48. Blau, P. M., 1964, *Exchange and Power in Social Life,* New York: Wiley.

49. Gouldner, A. W., 1960, "The Norm of Reciprocity: A Preliminary Statement," *American Sociological Review* 25:161–178.

50. Berger, J., M. Zeldich, B. Anderson, and B. Cohen, 1972, "Structural Aspects of Distributive Justice: A Status Value Formulation," in J. Berger, M. Zeldich, and B. Anderson (Eds.), *Sociological Theories in Progress,* Vol. 2, Boston: Houghton Mifflin.

51. Mirowsky, J., 1987, "The Psycho-economics of Feeling Underpaid: Distributive Justice and the Earnings of Husbands and Wives," *American Journal of Sociology* 92:1404–1434; N. J. Shepelak and D. F. Alwin, 1986, "Beliefs About Inequality and Perceptions of Distributive Justice," *American Sociological Review* 51:30–46.

52. Shepelak, 1986, op. cit.

53. Kluegel, J. R. and E. R. Smith, 1986, *Beliefs About Inequality,* New York: Aldine De Gruyter.

54. Robinson, R. and W. Bell, 1978, "Equality, Success, and Social Justice in England and the United States," *American Sociological Review* 34:125–143.

55. Alwin, D. F., 1987, "Distributive Justice and Satisfaction with Material Well-being," *American Sociological Review* 52:83–95; N. J. Shepelak, 1987, "The Role of Self-explanations and Self-evaluations in Legitimizing Inequality," *American Sociological Review* 52:495–503.

56. Adams, J. S., 1965, "Inequity in Social Exchange," in L. Berkowitz (Ed.), *Advances in Experimental Social Psychology,* Vol. 2, New York: Academic Press; E. Walster, G. W. Walster, and E. Berscheid, 1978, *Equity Theory and Research,* Boston: Allyn and Bacon.

57. Mirowsky, 1987, op. cit.

58. Lerner, M. J., 1965, "Evaluation of Performance as a Function of Performer's Reward and Attractiveness," *Journal of Personality and Social Psychology* 3:355–360; W. Ryan, 1971, *Blaming the Victim,* New York: Pantheon.

59. Stryker and Statham, 1985, op. cit.

CHAPTER 3

Methods in Social Psychology

Magic and Science: A Comparison

Magic

Science

Surveys and Observational Methods

Questionnaires and Interviews

Unstructured Interviews

Observational Techniques

Experiments and Field Studies

Laboratory Experiments

Field Experiments

Field Studies

Ethics in Social Psychology

Confidentiality and Privacy

Deception

Psychological Harm

MAGIC AND SCIENCE:
A COMPARISON

Magic

In the priests' retreats for rain they roll round stones across the floor to produce thunder, water is sprinkled to cause the rain, a bowl of water is placed upon the altar that the springs may be full, suds are beaten up from a native plant that clouds may pile up in the heavens, tobacco smoke is blown out that the gods may not withhold their misty breath (1).

This is a partial description of a religious ritual performed by the Zuni Indians. The Zuni have lived for centuries in pueblos in northern New Mexico. Agriculture has always provided an important source of food for the Zuni. The mountains and valleys of northern New Mexico are harsh and dry: nothing is more important to survival than rain. The rituals described by anthropologist Ruth Benedict are an attempt to control the rain. She labels these techniques "imitative magic" because they are designed to bring about the desired effect by imitating it.

Throughout history, imitative magic has been used in an attempt to control the occurrence of events in the natural world. In the next few paragraphs we will explore magic as a system of knowledge. Magic provides a historical and philosophical contrast to science as a system of knowledge. By contrasting magic and science, we hope to provide you with a better understanding of what science is and what it is not (2).

The greatest intellectual goal of humankind has always been to understand the world in which we live. There are many types of knowledge about the world. Imitative magic is one type of knowledge concerning the relationships of events in the world. Underlying the use of imitative magic is a set of assumptions. Practitioners of imitative magic believe the world operates according to principles that can be understood. They assume events in the world follow orderly sequences and that these events are determined. That is, they assume rules of cause and effect apply to events. Finally, people who practice imitative magic assume events can be controlled through the use of rituals—the performance of ceremonial acts.

These rituals tend to be rigid because they are based on the belief that performing the ritual correctly guarantees the desired results. Rituals employing imitative magic involve concrete assumptions about how to achieve desired results. Specifically, it is believed that imitation of the desired event will produce that event. Rituals employing imitative magic do not exist in isolation. Instead, they are woven into a complex tapestry of interrelated rituals. For example, many rituals are regularly scheduled among the Zuni, such as those concerning the growing and harvesting of crops and the summer and winter solstices. As noted by anthropologist Sir James Frazer, the most important quality of rituals is that so many of them work:

In many, perhaps in most cases, the desired event did actually follow, at a longer or shorter interval, the performance of the rite which was designed to bring it about; and a mind of more than common acuteness was needed to perceive that, even in these cases, the rite was not necessarily the cause of the event. A ceremony intended to make the wind blow or the rain fall, or to work the death of an enemy, will always be followed, sooner or later, by the occurrence it is meant to bring to pass (3).

The fact that rituals seem to be effective makes it exceedingly difficult to prove they are not the causes of the desired events. If the desired event does not occur, there is a ready explanation—the ritual was performed incorrectly. As Ruth Benedict observed of the Zuni:

If no rain comes during [a priest's] retreat, village gossip runs over and over his ceremonial missteps and the implications of his failure. Did the priest or the masked gods give offense to some supernatural being? Did he break his retreat by going home to his wife before the days were up? . . . At every step of the way, if the procedure is correct, the costume of the masked god traditional to the last detail, the offerings unimpeachable, the words of the hours-long prayer letter-perfect, the effect will follow according to man's desires . . . it is a matter of major importance if one of the eagle feathers of a mask has been taken from the shoulder of the bird instead of from the breast (4).

If the ritual is followed by the desired event, the ritual is perceived to have been the cause. Thus, despite the fact that imitative magic is unreliable and is based on an inaccurate understanding of causality, it is hard to replace (5). Magic provides the illusion of control. For this reason it has endured through the ages. As Frazer put it, magic is "an act of faith in a science yet to be born" (6).

You may think your own behavior is relatively free from magical beliefs. Perhaps, but how would you react to the following situation? Someone asks you to throw darts at a picture of someone you love. Could you do this as easily as throwing darts at a bullseye target? A recent study suggests not (7). Students were not nearly as accurate when throwing darts at the face of a liked person as they were at a neutral target. Throwing darts at the face of a liked person is apparently too similar to the voodoo imitative magic practice of sticking pins in dolls to cause harm to one's enemies.

Science

When science was born, how did it differ from magic? In some ways it did not differ at all. We will let Frazer count the ways:

The analogy between the magical and the scientific conceptions of the world is close. In both of them the succession of events is assumed to be perfectly regular and certain, being determined by immutable laws, the operation of which can be foreseen and calculated precisely; the elements of caprice, of chance, and of accident are banished from the course of nature (8).

In science, as in imitative magic, it is assumed that the events in the natural world obey the laws

of causality and, therefore, can be predicted and controlled. Both magic and science are based on observations of the natural world, and both constitute explanations of events in the natural world.

The scientific method Before you conclude that science is nothing more than magic, let us explore the differences between them. The principal difference between magic and science is the methods they employ to achieve the goal of understanding the world. The *scientific method* consists of techniques of systematically observing causal relationships between events. Science postulates a set of rules for testing causal relationships. The philosopher David Hume (1711–1776) wrote that to infer causality, we must observe a relationship between two events in which one (the effect) follows another (the cause) invariably, and neither occurs in isolation (9). For example, there is a well-known theory of aggression stating that frustration causes aggression. To determine the validity of this causal hypothesis, we need to determine if aggression is always preceded by frustration and if frustration is always followed by aggression.

Repeated observations must be made to establish a causal relationship. Since we can never observe every instance in which two events might occur together, we can never be absolutely certain about the causal inferences we draw from our observations. Thus, the scientist's idea of cause and effect is probabilistic, rather than absolute. Importantly, this concept of causality contains the possibility of disproof. If an event that is thought to be an effect is not preceded by its presumed cause, then the causal inference is wrong. For example, aggression occurring without prior frustration would provide evidence against the frustration-aggression hypothesis.

Hume's rigid definition of causality is no longer as accepted as it once was, for two primary reasons. First, it suggests each effect has a single cause. This definition of causality does not take into consideration the fact that effects often have multiple causes and causes often have multiple effects. To illustrate, frustration is only one of many causes of aggression, and aggression is only one of many different effects of frustration. Second, this definition considers only the presence or absence of a cause or effect. It fails to recognize that causes and effects vary in intensity, and that changes in intensity of a cause must coincide with changes in intensity of an effect. For example, as frustration increases, the amount of aggression should also increase.

A better definition of *causality* is that changes in the magnitude of the causal variable must be associated with corresponding changes in the variable that is regarded as the effect. Consider the saying, "birds of a feather flock together." This saying suggests that similar people will be attracted to one another. Using the revised definition of causality, we would expect that as similarity between people increases, so should their attraction to one another. This causal hypothesis does not deny that other factors may cause attraction, nor that increased similarity may have effects other than increased attraction (it may be that highly similar people work together better than dissimilar people).

The systematic application of the scientific method consists of observing situations in which the cause is present in order to determine whether the effect follows, and, if it does, the magnitude of the effect. Tests of a causal hypothesis are then repeated a sufficient number of times so it can be established, with a high level of confidence, whether the obtained results could or could not have been obtained by chance. The conditions of observation must be such that they can be repeated by other investigators.

Replicability, the independent verification of results, is an important component of the scientific method. Only when a given result has been obtained many times can we be confident that it represents a real cause-effect relationship. This is one reason why it is well to be cautious about acting on the latest medical findings concerning heart disease, cancer, or stress management if they are based on a single new study.

The particular cause-and-effect relationships scientists choose to test are typically derived from theory. As we have already noted, a *theory* is a set of interrelated propositions about relationships among classes of events. This means that scientific theories are abstract and thus may be contrasted with imitative magic, which tends to be more concrete. Science is abstract because it seeks the logic that lies behind whole classes of observable events.

For instance, cognitive dissonance theory suggests that when an individual who has a conflict between two cognitions (thoughts) or behaviors freely takes an action that has (or may have) negative effects, the individual will experience dissonance (10). An example of dissonance would be when a person who considers himself or herself to be honest (cognition 1) acknowledges the fact that he or she has just done something wrong, such as cheat on an exam (cognition 2). Here we have two dissonant cognitions and the clear possibility of negative consequences. Because dissonance is uncomfortable, the individual will attempt to reduce it. The need to reduce the conflict between dissonant cognitions depends upon the magnitude of the conflict, the importance of the cognitions, and the negative consequences. How the cognitions concerning honesty and cheating are reconciled in the example above will depend on such factors as how important honesty is to the person, how much he or she cheated, and what the penalties are for being caught. One avenue of dissonance reduction might be to justify the cheating by saying to oneself, "I had to cheat because everybody else did and I would have suffered if I hadn't."

Dissonance theory thus consists of a set of statements about relationships between cognitions, the importance of the cognitions, the negative outcomes, and the individual's subsequent behavior. In this theory, the cause (dissonance between cognitions) is specified, as is the effect (dissonance reduction). Both the cause and the effect are specified at an abstract level. The types of cognitions that can conflict are endless, and the ways in which dissonance can be reduced are likewise quite varied.

In sum, the scientific method differs from magic in four ways:

1. At the level of theory, science is abstract, involving tentative statements about relationships among classes of events.

2. Science is empirical. It is based on repeated, systematic observations of the relationship between events.

Table 3.1 ■

A Comparison of Science and Imitative Magic

| Shared Traits | Traits on Which They Differ | |
Magic/Science	Magic	Science
Founded on determinism	Emphasis is on concrete relationships	Emphasis is on abstract relationships
Goal is understanding events	Cannot be disproved	Open to test and disproof
Events can be predicted	Absolute knowledge of the world is possible	Only probabilistic knowledge is possible
Events can be controlled	Observational techniques are informal	Relies on systematic techniques of observation
	Rules for determining causality are unclear	Clear rules for determining causality are used
	Relatively rigid and unchanging	Constantly revised to account for new information

3. A concise conception of causality is employed.

4. It is possible to disconfirm causal hypotheses (see Table 3-1).

The scientific method is not the only valid technique of gathering information about human nature nor can it be applied to all questions. For instance, this method cannot be used to determine what system of moral values is best. However, the scientific method is a very effective technique for examining cause and effect questions when the causes and the effects are observable. As a technique, it demands keen observation, patience, careful analytical thought, skepticism, intuition, creativity, and sometimes a bit of luck or good timing.

We will now turn to an examination of the various empirical methods used by social psychologists. We will discuss the advantages and disadvantages of each method and present an example illustrating it. We will begin with methods that provide primarily descriptive information about people and social groups, such as questionnaires and interviews. These methods tend to be preferred by

sociological social psychologists to develop and test their theories. We then proceed to those methods that provide data that can be used to draw strong inferences about cause-and-effect relationships, such as laboratory and field experiments. These are the methods preferred by psychological social psychologists to develop and test their theories. In the final section of this chapter, we will discuss some of the ethical issues that social psychologists face when using these methods.

■

SURVEYS AND OBSERVATIONAL METHODS

Questionnaires and Interviews

There has been a revolution in race relations in the United States since World War II. Prior to the war, segregation permeated relations between the races.

It could be found in schools, hotels and restaurants, public transportation, hospitals, housing, and even in the gallery of the U.S. Senate. The laws that were used to maintain this social barricade were known as "Jim Crow" laws. The Jim Crow laws died a gradual death during and after the war. In 1941, President Franklin Roosevelt barred discrimination in war-related industries; in 1948, President Harry Truman integrated the armed forces; and in 1954, the Supreme Court unanimously mandated an end to segregation in the public schools.

In 1955, Rosa Parks, a black woman, decided to sit in the front of a Montgomery, Alabama bus, instead of sitting in the back—the only part of the bus where blacks were allowed. Her arrest led to the first civil rights march in the postwar period. The civil rights movement culminated, in 1964, in the passage of the first civil rights bill since the years after the Civil War. Racial discrimination was no longer legal. Gradually, the Justice Department began to enforce school desegregation. Whereas in 1964 only 1 percent of America's school children attended desegregated schools, by 1972, 38 percent of the black students in the South and 29 percent of the black students in the North attended desegregated schools (11). In a 1987 report, the U.S. Commission on Civil Rights found that 52 percent of the black students in the South, 31 percent of the black students in the North, and 44 percent of the black students in the West were attending racially balanced schools (12).

These facts are a matter of public record. But what about people's attitudes toward race relations? Did they change during this period? One way to answer this question is through the use of questionnaires. A *questionnaire* is a systematic procedure for asking the same questions of a number of people. A questionnaire may be presented during an interview or it may be completed privately by the respondent.

A questionnaire may be given to all the members of a *population,* which is the total group of interest to the investigator. Typically, however, the questionnaire is only given to a *sample* or subset of the population. To be able to generalize from the results of the sample to the population, one must use

random sampling. In *simple random sampling,* each member of the population has an equal chance of being selected for inclusion in the sample. In a refinement of random sampling, known as *stratified random sampling,* data are collected from a random sample of specified subgroups in a population. For instance, the country might be divided into the various religious groups and a random sample collected from each religious group. Random sampling ensures that the sample is representative of the population, with a known degree of error. Using this technique, a properly selected sample of 1500 people can be used to estimate the attitudes of the whole country to within a 2-3 percent margin of error (13). Questionnaires that do not employ random samples run the risk of arriving at false conclusions (see Box 3-1).

If we were interested in the changes in racial attitudes of all Americans, we could have a stratified random sample of Americans respond to the same set of questions. In addition, we would want to ask these questions every few years. Such a survey has been done periodically since World War II by the National Opinion Research Center (NORC) (16).

Interviews are conducted with a stratified random sample of between 1,000 and 1,500 Americans, rich and poor, old and young, men and women, North and South, Protestants, Catholics, and Jews, and so on. One question asked is whether the respondents endorse desegregated schools. In 1942, 32 percent of the white respondents accepted school desegregation. In 1956, the figure was 50 percent; in 1976, the figure was 84 percent; and in the 1980s the figures are consistently over 90 percent (see Figure 3-1) (17). A scale composed of five items concerning racial integration shows similar increases during this period (18). The increase occurred for all age groups, for all regions of the country, for people at all levels of educational achievement, and for people from every one of the religious backgrounds surveyed. The results of the NORC survey and those from other surveys indicate that private opinions kept pace with public policy. These surveys should not be taken to mean that America has solved its racial problems, but they do suggest that progress is being made (more on this topic in Chapter 15).

Figure 3.1 ■

Attitudes of Whites Toward School Desegregation

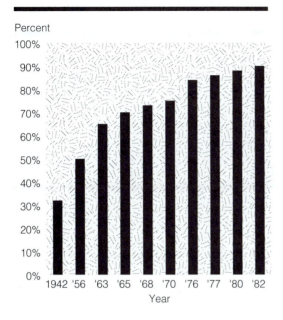

Percent

Note: The question was, "Do you think white students and black students should go to the same schools?" Adapted from Schuman, Steeh, and Bobo, 1985.

Many questionnaires are conducted for descriptive purposes and are not concerned with causal relations. Recently, however, new techniques have been developed that make it possible to use questionnaires to test causal hypotheses. For example, the NORC survey data could be examined to determine the origin of the above changes in attitudes. One could ask whether the changes in private opinions were brought about as a result of the changes in public policy, whether the changes in private opinion led to changes in public policy, or whether the two are unrelated. These analyses would make use of the causal logic of the scientific method. Policies and attitudes documented at an earlier time period can be used to infer causality about policies and attitudes documented at a later time period, but the reverse is not true. Later attitudes and policies cannot cause earlier attitudes and policies.

For instance, consider the effects of desegregation on the racial attitudes of students. To assess the effects of desegregation one should survey the students at least twice, once before desegregation and once afterwards. It would also be desirable to survey groups of students who continued to attend segregated schools during this same period as a natural control group. The attitudes of this control group would furnish information about changes over time in the racial attitudes of students who had not been exposed to desegregation. We could then compare the changes in this group to those in the desegregation group. Such studies have been done, although they did not always include all of the measurements or groups that would be desirable. The results of these surveys suggest that desegregation more often leads to positive than negative changes in the racial attitudes of blacks, but it more often leads to negative changes in whites—at least in the short-term (for more about this issue, see Chapter 15) (19).

Questionnaires are probably the most commonly used techniques of obtaining social information. All of us have completed countless questionnaires in our lives, including personality inventories, manufacturers' questionnaires, election polls, the U.S. Census, and course evaluations. The results of questionnaires are used by business executives to make market decisions, by political candidates to make campaign decisions, by television executives to make programming decisions, and by sociologists and psychologists to assess personality, opinions, and the effectiveness of social programs (to give but a few examples). Large amounts of information can be gathered quickly and efficiently using questionnaires. Questionnaires can be sent through the mail or interviews can be conducted over the telephone. In both cases, the respondents can often remain anonymous, which may allow them to be more candid than if their names were associated with their answers.

The use of questionnaires is widespread because the results of a sample of people can be generalized to the population of people from which the sample was drawn. This makes information about a target population available with a relatively small

BOX 3-1

Potential Pitfalls of Nonrandom Sampling

In 1987, Shere Hite published a report titled *Women and Love* in which she presented the results of a large-scale questionnaire. The results were very dramatic (14). Here is a sample of them:

84% of women are not satisfied emotionally with their relationships.

83% of women say they do not believe most men understand the basic issues involved in making an intimate relationship work.

84% of women say men frequently respond to things they say with an attitude of ridicule or condescension.

95% of women report forms of emotional and psychological harassment from the men with whom they are in love relationships.

64% of women say the love they receive is not satisfying to them.

87% of women say it is difficult to meet men they admire and respect.

70% of women married 5 years or more are having sex outside of their marriages.

76% of married women having affairs do not feel guilty.

87% of married women believe their husbands are faithful.

48% of single women are or have been having an affair with a married man.

87% of women married more than 2 years say they are not in love with their husbands.

Do these results sound right to you? They raised a firestorm of controversy when they were first published because they did not seem to fit with many people's

investment of time and energy. Another major advantage of questionnaires is they can provide us with information that is difficult to obtain in other ways. One of the best ways to determine what people think or feel is to ask them. This is almost the only way to gain access to such topics as people's future plans, past behavior, and internal experiences, like dreams.

Questionnaires are not without problems, however. These techniques rely on self-reports and it is

intuitive feelings nor did they accord well with earlier studies on related issues. Many questions were raised about Hite's methods, especially her sampling procedures.

Hite sent out 100,000 questionnaires to various women's organizations around the country including: walk-in centers for women and families in 43 states, women's rights organizations in 39 states, church groups in 34 states, professional women's groups in 22 states, and voting or political groups in 9 states. Of these questionnaires, 4,500 were returned partially or fully completed, a response rate of 4.5 percent. This response rate is quite low. In surveys that are mailed out, a response rate of 50 percent is only considered to be adequate (15).

Are these women typical of women in the United States? Hite reports that demographically her respondents mirrored quite closely the characteristics of women in the United States. Despite Hite's claims that the respondents were similar to women in general, her sample included a disproportionate number of women who had attended college and a substantial number who were lesbian or bisexual (18 percent). The women may not have been typical in other respects, as well. These women were willing to fill out a questionnaire concerning "women's points of view on . . . love, relationships, marriage, and monogamy" that contained 127 essay questions. It seems possible that it was primarily women who were intensely interested in these topics and who had a good deal of time to write about them who responded.

A second problem is that Hite built her statistics by looking at the written essays and "discovering patterns." Using "categories that more or less formed themselves," she then totaled the number of women in each category. This technique is highly subjective and may be even more difficult than it sounds. For instance, for the first statistic cited above, how dissatisfied must a respondent be with her current relationship to be counted? Must she be dissatisfied most of the time or with only one aspect of the relationship?

Hite defends her approach by arguing that she could only obtain meaningful responses with essay questions—that more "objective" questions would not have worked, and the questions could not be asked by an interviewer. Hite says, "The intention here was to permit women's own voices to emerge." She feels that, "If a study is large enough and the sample broad enough," one can generalize carefully. Her critics have questioned the representativeness, not the size, of her sample and the techniques she used to derive her generalizations. ■

assumed that people will respond honestly. The usefulness of questionnaires is restricted to topics where people are willing and able to report their feelings truthfully. Problems arise because people may wish to present themselves to others, and even to themselves, as possessing socially desirable traits and attitudes. When responding to sensitive topics, such as questions about racial attitudes or opinions on sexual practices, people may distort their true feelings.

Another problem is that people may respond to questions even when they have no clear opinions. Sometimes people fail to respond at all, particularly to questionnaires that are mailed. The consequence is that the sample of respondents may not be representative of the population. Interviewing can often overcome people's unwillingness to respond, and it may provide an opportunity to clarify ambiguous questions or to determine if people really have any opinion on a given issue. However, structured interviews, in which a fixed set of questions is asked, and standardized paper-and-pencil questionnaires are not well suited for assessing complex emotional issues, such as attitudes toward abortion or changing family patterns. The problem is that standardized questionnaires are rarely flexible enough to capture the subtleties of people's feelings concerning highly emotional issues. Each person's reasons for favoring or opposing abortion may be quite different, but standardized questions tend to overlook this information.

Unstructured Interviews

The unstructured interview is a technique that is effective for probing into complex and emotional issues (abortion, capital punishment, child abuse). In this technique, a small number of people are interviewed intensively about a specific issue or set of issues. The interviewers attempt to establish a close rapport with the respondent by being open and warm. This enables the interviewers to ensure that the questions are understood by the respondent and that they understand the respondent's answers. In her book *Worlds of Pain*, Lillian Rubin describes how she used this technique when interviewing working-class couples in their own homes:

the feel

> Talking for many hours with a single respondent made possible the kind of connection and rapport that allowed me to probe into places generally hidden from public view; to see and hear things I would ordinarily not have dared to ask about; or, if asked, people would be reluctant to answer. Perhaps more important, it taught

> me the things I ought to be asking, since in such situations people want to talk about their concerns as well as yours. Sometimes theirs were the same as mine; sometimes not—but always I tried to "hear" what was important to them (20).

Unstructured interviews are particularly useful in exploring new territory, where the issues are unclear and little previous theory or research can be used to generate hypotheses. Using this technique, a problem area can be defined and described and questions may be raised that will lend themselves to more systematic study in later investigations.

Earlier we reported there had been a revolution in race relations in this country, a revolution that is far from complete. It has also been claimed that we have experienced a revolution in the class structure of this country resulting in the disappearance of class differences. Rubin's book challenges this claim by examining working-class families and revealing class differences in family relationships. Her book is based on intensive interviews of 50 working-class families in the San Francisco area. The husbands all worked in traditional blue-collar jobs, the wives were all under 40, and all of the couples had at least one child. The interviews took up to 10 hours per person and they covered a wide range of topics: work, marriage, family, leisure, sexual relations, and hopes for the future. Rubin interviewed her own acquaintances and their friends to create a picture of working-class life. She also interviewed a comparison sample of 25 couples where the husbands were employed as professionals.

Here are some examples of the conclusions she has drawn. Notice in this first selection how she captures the ambivalence of working-class women's feelings about their husbands' authority:

> On the surface, working-class women generally seem to accept and grant legitimacy to their husbands' authority, largely because they understand his need for it. If not at home, where is a man who works on an assembly line, in a warehouse, or a refinery to experience himself as a person whose words have weight, who is "worth" listening to? But just below the surface,

there lies a well of ambivalence; for the cost of her compliance is high. In muting her own needs to be responsive to his, she is left dissatisfied—a dissatisfaction that makes her so uncomfortable she often has difficulty articulating it even to herself. "What right have I to complain?" she is likely to ask herself (21).

In another section she discusses the impact of having children soon after marriage, a common experience in her working-class sample:

Children born just months after the wedding added emotional as well as economic burdens to the adjustment process. Suddenly, two young people, barely more than children themselves, found their lives irrevocably altered. Within a few months—too few to permit the integration of the behaviors required by new roles in new life stages, too few to wear comfortably even one new identity—they moved through a series of roles: from girl and boy, to wife and husband, to mother and father. They often responded with bewilderment, filled with an uneasy and uncomprehending sense of loss for the past (22).

Finally, here is a summary of the quality of working-class marriage:

Yes, there is concern among these working-class women and men about the quality of life, about its meaning. Yes, there is a deep wish for life to be more than a constant struggle with necessity. The drinking, the violence, the withdrawn silences—these are responses of despair, giving evidence that hope is hard to hold on to. How can it be otherwise when so often life seems like such an ungiving, uncharitable affair—a struggle without end? In the early years, it's unemployment, poverty, crying babies, violent fights. That phase passes, but a whole new set of problems emerge—problems that often seem harder to handle because they have less shape, less definition; harder, too, because they are less understandable, farther outside the realm of anything before experienced. But if there is one remarkable characteristic about life among the working class, it is the ability to engage the struggle and to survive it—a quality highly valued in a world where life has been and often remains so difficult and problematic (23).

These few examples should give you a feeling for the strengths of unstructured interviews. They can provide a rich in-depth account of a given group. These strengths are offset by some major disadvantages. Unstructured interviews are time-consuming and the information is gathered in a form that is difficult to analyze. The samples of people who are interviewed are usually small and nonrandom, and it is unclear how representative of the total group they are. This means, for example, that it may not be reasonable for Rubin to talk about "working-class couples" because she has interviewed only a small sample of people from one region in the country. Precise comparisons between groups are often difficult to make with unstructured interviews. The questions are not standardized, and the response options are not fixed beforehand. Due to the lack of structure, it is difficult to make quantitative comparisons. For instance, Rubin is not specific about how much more violence and drinking working-class husbands engage in than husbands who work at professional jobs. Finally, the lack of structure in the interview situation means the interviewer's biases may be reflected in the questions that are asked and the answers that are received. Another example that illustrates the strengths and weaknesses of unstructured interviews appears in Box 3-2.

We turn next to a technique that goes a step beyond unstructured interviews in an attempt to view the world of the respondent from an insider's perspective, rather than from the outside.

Observational Techniques

Participant observation In participant observation the distinction between the investigator and the group being studied is eliminated. The investigator makes in-depth observations of the group, typically by becoming a member of it. This immersion in the group enables the investigator to view the situation

BOX 3-2

The Impact of Status in Forbidden Sexual Relationships

To examine the role of status differences in forbidden sexual relationships, Laurel Richardson conducted intensive interviews with 65 single women involved in sexual relationships with married men (24). In the relationships she studied, status differences in sex, age, socioeconomic rank, and marital situation typically coincided to give the men a distinct status advantage. She found that these status inequalities had effects on both of the stages through which such relationships progress: becoming confidantes and becoming a "we" or couple.

Because of the men's marital status, the relationships were private, there were time constraints, and they were thought of as being temporary (although some had gone on for as long as 25 years, and all of them had lasted for more than a year). These inherent aspects of forbidden relationships encourage intense intimacy and trust during the stage of becoming confidantes. Privacy increases intimacy because the couple tends to construct a world of their own, outside of the roles and norms of society. Time constraints promote intimacy because the couple spends only "quality" time together. As one woman commented, the relationship could not deteriorate into "a day-to-day domestic situation where demands are made that are unpleasant or mundane." Temporariness leads to intimacy because the women are relatively unconcerned about laying the groundwork for a future relationship. One interviewee said, "I don't have to keep myself under control because [the relationship] is not so dangerous because it can't go anywhere." The secret knowledge each person acquires about the other transforms two isolated individuals into intimates. This intimacy then generates a tendency among the women to idealize their partners—"Like no man ever known before" according to one woman.

from a perspective similar to that of other participants in the group. Contact with the group members is likely to be very high and involvement in the experience can become intense. Usually, the group members do not have the feeling they are being observed, and they behave as they normally would.

Reporters often do "inside" stories using this technique, and social psychologists use it as well.

A fascinating example of participant observation is a study conducted by David Rosenhan (25). The central question in his study was, "Does the environment of a psychiatric institution interfere with

The couple becomes a "we" through the creation of shared symbols that take on deep personal significance and through the sharing of private rituals. Secret languages or names for one another are developed, anniversaries are celebrated, and objects are collected that give the relationship meaning and provide it with a history. One interviewee showed Richardson "a bulletin board which held a dried bouquet, a Valentine's Day card, movie ticket stubs, and some postcards." It was positioned where she "can see it just before I turn the light off." Objects like these are used in place of the usual social confirmation that marks the existence of publicly acknowledged relationships, and thus the objects acquire great emotional meaning.

In addition to the objects that signify the existence of the relationships, private rituals are developed to further the impression of "we-ness." For example, a couple carrying on a long-range relationship wrote one another at the same time every day so they could feel like they were together.

In the process of becoming a couple, single women become more involved in the relationships than their married partners. The males are not dependent on the relationship for sex, they have an avenue of retreat to use if the relationship ends, and they have less reason to be concerned about being trapped. The secrecy protects the men more than it does the women and their higher status means the women are likely to be more damaged than the men if the relationship becomes public. The women sustain greater costs to maintain the relationship since they often become progressively more cut off from their normal social lives while the men do not. As the women's dependency increases, so does their commitment to continuing the relationship. Their dependency and commitment, combined with their low status, make it hard for the women to disengage from these relationships.

Richardson's study provides another example of the strengths of the unstructured interview approach. It yields a fascinating in-depth analysis of an issue that might be difficult to investigate otherwise. The limitations of this approach should also be apparent. We cannot be sure if her sample is representative, we have only one side of the story in one type of forbidden relationship, and the interviewer's interests and biases may have affected what she asked and what she was told. ■

the effective treatment of mental disorders?" To answer this question, Rosenhan and seven other people had themselves admitted to 12 different psychiatric institutions. These people (including a housewife, a painter, a pediatrician, and several psychologists) gained admission by reporting they heard voices saying things like "empty" and "hollow." Beyond these symptoms, each "pseudopatient" reported no other abnormal behavior and related his or her actual life history in response to questions.

After admission, the pseudopatients ceased reporting any symptoms and attempted to act com-

■ *A participant observer might join a cult to study its functioning. (WGS)*

pletely normally. Their task, in addition to observing the institution, was to gain their own release as soon as possible. Although none of the pseudopatients was detected as being sane by the staff, many of the real patients realized that the pseudopatients were sane. On the average, it took the pseudopatients 19 days to be released.

Why weren't these sane people detected? Rosenhan believes it is difficult to detect sane behavior in an institution for the insane. The problem is that once people have been labeled as insane (schizophrenic in this case), others' perceptions of their behaviors will be distorted so that they are consistent with the label. Another reason is that the staff spends too little time with the patients to chart their progress carefully. In the institutions studied, the professional staff (psychologists, psychiatrists, and caseworkers) spent an average of only seven minutes a day with these pseudopatients. In response to direct questions by pseudopatients, the most common reaction by

both the attendants (88 percent) and the psychiatrists (71 percent) was to ignore the question and to move on with their duties, eyes averted.

How did these experiences make the pseudopatients feel? First, they felt powerless. As Rosenhan put it, the patient "cannot initiate contact with the staff, but may only respond to such overtures as they make. Personal privacy is minimal. Patient quarters and possessions can be entered and examined by any staff member. . . . His personal hygiene and waste evacuation are often monitored" (26). Second, they felt less than human. "Depersonalization reached such proportions that pseudopatients had the sense that they were invisible, or at least unworthy of account. . . . Staff members went about their own business as if we were not there. . . . A nurse unbuttoned her uniform to adjust her brassiere in the presence of an entire ward of viewing men. One did not have the sense that she was being seductive. Rather, she didn't notice us" (27).

Nonparticipant observation This technique is similar to participant observation, except that the observer typically does not become a member of the group and may be recognized as a nongroup member by the people being observed. This may enable the observer to maintain a more objective viewpoint than participant observers, but it does so at the cost of making it clear to the group members that they are being observed.

David Snow and Leon Anderson employed this technique to study the homeless in Austin, Texas (28). Homelessness is an increasingly important problem in many U.S. cities. Estimates of the number of homeless people run as high as 4,000,000. In the little previous work that has been done on the homeless, the focus has been on their mental health, the threat they pose to the community (crime), or meeting their needs (food and shelter). Almost no research has been done on the inner lives of the homeless. How do these people maintain a sense of self-worth? This was the question Snow and Anderson sought to answer.

Using nonparticipant observation they attempted to understand the homeless by attaining an "intimate familiarity with the routines and situations that are part and parcel of [their] social worlds" (29). In 1984 the Salvation Army estimated that there were more than 11,000 homeless people in Austin. The authors spent time with 168 of them. Their approach was to "hang out with many of these individuals on a daily basis, spending time with them in varied settings (meal and shelter lines, under bridges, in parks, at day-labor pick-up sites)" (30). They engaged the homeless in conversation or eavesdropped on their conversations. While doing so, they recorded the statements the homeless made about identity and

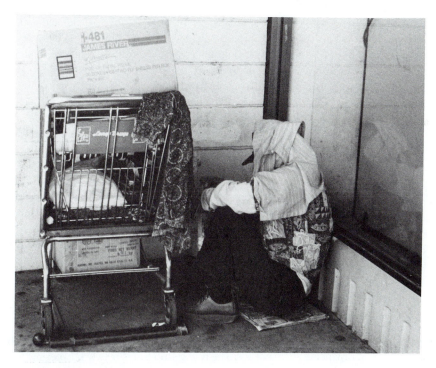

■ *The number of homeless people has increased dramatically during the last decade.* (WGS)

self-worth. Although the researchers wore old clothes, they made no attempt to conceal their identities and told many of the homeless what they were doing. During this time, they collected 202 statements concerning identity and self-worth.

Snow and Anderson found that the homeless acknowledge the difficulty of achieving a sense of self-worth in the face of overwhelming rejection by society. One person commented, "It's real hard to feel good about yourself when almost everyone around you is looking down on you" (31). To combat this rejection they use three strategies:

■ First, they attempt to *distance* themselves from the roles and institutions associated with the homeless. One person said, "I'm not like the other guys who hang out down at the Salvation Army. If you want to know about street people, I can tell you about them; but you can't really learn about street people from studying me, because I'm different" (32).

■ At the same time that they distanced themselves from the identity of being a homeless person, they claimed more favorable identities. They often did this by using the second strategy: *fictive storytelling*. In fictive storytelling the homeless embellish aspects of their pasts or fantasize futures that are more favorable than the present. The researchers described one "40-year-old homeless male who spent most of his time hanging around a transient bar boasting about having been offered a job as a Harley-Davidson mechanic at $18.50 per hour, while constantly begging for cigarettes and spare change for beer" (33). The fantasies for the future often involved respectable work, financial wealth, material possessions, or the opposite sex. For example, one homeless person said, "You might laugh and think I'm crazy, but I'm going to be rich. I know it. I just have this feeling. I can't explain it, but I am" (34).

■ In contrast to those people who used distancing and fictive storytelling to avoid negative self-evaluations, about a third of the homeless people said things that indicated they *embraced* their roles and did not evaluate these roles unfavorably. They rejected society's view of them and highlighted positive aspects of their situation or relationships, such as sticking up for one another. This group included people who had adopted nicknames such as Boxcar Billy and Gypsy Bill, which identified them as transients. One group thought of themselves as "hippies" and was proud of the fact that while others had changed their identities, they had stayed the same. The researchers suggest that, "For these streetpeople, there was little doubt who they were; they not only saw themselves as hippie-like tramps, but they embraced that identity both verbally and expressively" (35).

These findings indicate that even those at the bottom of the social hierarchy find ways of salvaging a sense of self-worth. For the homeless, as for all of us, identity emerges in part from our position in the social structure. Some of the homeless attempt to reject the definition implied by their position by distancing themselves, some try to fantasize better times to make the present more endurable, and others embrace the identity associated with their position, but reject society's rejection of them. To maintain this precarious sense of self-worth there is a norm among the homeless that prohibits probing too deeply into the identity claims others make for themselves. The researchers conclude that, "Whatever the limitations of this research tack, we think they are outweighed by the fact that it provides a relatively rare glimpse of the actual construction and use of personal identities in the course of everyday life among individuals at the bottom of society" (36).

Observational methods in general enable the observers to learn to see the world from the perspective of the participants in a way that is not possible with experiments or even with interviews. Observers may be told things or see things that experimenters and interviewers are not told or do not see. The role relationships between experimenters and subjects and between interviewers and interviewees are different than those between an observer and the person observed, particularly if the observed person is unaware of being observed. People who are aware of being observed may not behave in the same way as those who are unaware of being observed. Also, using observational techniques often enables observers to study events that take place over relatively long periods of time and to watch them unfold as they naturally would. Other approaches may be restricted to relatively brief time intervals (experiments) or may consist of people recounting their experiences with all the biases that may be introduced by faulty memory (interviews concerning past experiences).

However, observational techniques do suffer from some serious limitations. One drawback of participant observation is that the observers can become so emotionally involved in the situation they lose their objectivity. A participant observer in a center for victims of child abuse might become so outraged by the suffering of the victims that he or she can no longer view the problem dispassionately.

A second drawback is that the observers, like Rosenhan's pseudopatients, are not the same as real group members—and these differences may make it impossible for them to experience the situation in the same way as actual group members do. As Rosenhan writes, "I and the other pseudopatients in the psychiatric setting had distinctly negative reactions. We do not pretend to describe the subjective experiences of the patients. Theirs may be different from ours, particularly with the passage of time and the necessary process of adaptation to one's environment" (37).

A third drawback is that the observer may affect the behavior of the people being observed, just by his or her presence. Merely having a stranger around may affect their behavior or if the observer stays with the group for some time, his or her personality may affect the interpersonal chemistry in the group.

Finally, participant observation is usually limited to a single situation or group, and it may not be reasonable to generalize from such a small sample to other situations or groups. For instance, making generalizations regarding all homeless people from the small group studied in Austin may not be possible.

We now turn to a discussion of the empirical techniques preferred by psychological social psychologists.

EXPERIMENTS AND FIELD STUDIES

Laboratory Experiments

One of the primary functions of theories is to aid us in generating specific hypotheses about relationships between events. *Hypotheses* are statements about expected relationships between variables. To illustrate an experimental test of an hypothesis, we will consider a study of nonverbal behavior. Nonverbal behavior consists of gestures, facial expressions, body posture, eye gaze, voice intonation, and other facets of behavior that supplement and sometimes take the place of verbal behavior. They play a very important role in communicating dominance, liking, and approval, as well as many emotional states.

In the study we will discuss, Cecilia Ridgeway was interested in the effects of dominance on persuasion in small groups (38). You might ask yourself if, in your own experience, you find that people who behave in a dominant fashion when expressing themselves are more influential than people who tend strictly to business in expressing their opinions. Ridgeway hypothesized that nonverbal expressions of dominance are detrimental to task performance. She believes influence in small groups is based more on task performance than on expressions of dominance. In the absence of demonstrated task skills, a person who behaves in a dominant fashion may actually meet with resistance from the other members of the group.

To test her hypothesis, Ridgeway created a situation in which groups of three people were asked to consider a jury case and assign damages to the plaintiff. In the case a washing machine repairman was seeking $25,000 in damages due to an injury he had suffered on the job. Unbeknownst to the real subject, the other two people were working with the experimenter and their behavior was carefully scripted beforehand. During the discussion the actual subject witnessed an attempt by one confederate (A) to persuade the other (B) that a very low damage award was called for. This interaction was staged repeatedly using a different subject each time. For some of the subjects, confederate A behaved in a very dominant manner while discussing the case with confederate B. To convey dominance confederate A spoke in a loud voice with an angry, imperative tone, stared overtly at the other confederate with lowered eyebrows, used a straight, looming posture with high muscle tension, and pointed or used other intrusive gestures frequently.

For other subjects confederate A used a factual tone of voice, spoke fluidly and rapidly with few hesitations, maintained a steady direct gaze, and had a straight but relaxed posture. Although the nonverbal behavior of confederate A differed, there were no differences in verbal behavior. Confederate A always said exactly the same thing.

In all experimental studies, the experimenter attempts to set up conditions under which the hypothesized effect is expected to occur. The causal variable is called the *independent variable,* and it is this variable the experimenter controls. In the Ridgeway study, the dominant or task-oriented behavior of the confederate was the independent variable because the confederate's behavior was expected to have an impact on persuasion. The variable that is affected is called the *dependent variable* because it is hypothesized to depend upon the independent variable. In this study, the amount of persuasion was the dependent variable.

To determine if the independent variable has an effect on the dependent variable, at least two conditions must be included so a comparison can be made. In Ridgeway's study, the damages awarded to the plaintiff when confederate A behaved in a dominant manner were compared to the damages awarded when confederate A behaved in a task-oriented manner. The condition in which confederate A used

dominant nonverbal behaviors is the *experimental condition,* and the condition in which she used task-oriented behaviors is the *control condition*—the condition to which the experimental condition is compared.

In experiments, subjects are randomly assigned to conditions to ensure that all the groups are as equivalent as possible before the groups receive the experimental treatments. *Random assignment* consists of making certain each subject has an equal chance of being assigned to any given condition. In the Ridgeway experiment, this could have been accomplished by flipping a coin for each subject to determine whether she would be assigned to the dominant or task-oriented confederate. Random assignment is necessary to be able to draw the conclusion that any differences between the groups on the dependent measure are due to the experimental treatment, rather than to preexisting differences between the groups. Random assignment greatly reduces the chances that more people of a given type will wind up in one condition than another, and thereby bias the results. For instance, if a substantial number of people whose relatives had sustained on-the-job injuries listened to the task-oriented confederate, they might have recommended high awards, not because the confederate was persuasive, but because their personal experiences led them to believe high awards were needed. Random assignment solves this problem by ensuring that people of a given type will be assigned to each condition in approximately equal numbers.

In the Ridgeway study, the subjects were randomly assigned to one of the two conditions mentioned above. Then they read through the case and made their own initial judgment about the highest award to the plaintiff that would be acceptable to them. This initial award was made before the group discussion and provides a baseline against which the subjects' later awards can be compared. The initial judgments can also be used to examine the effectiveness of random assignment in this study. An indication that random assignment was successful may be seen in Table 3-2 which shows that the average initial judgments of the subjects in each condition were very similar. Thus, there were no

Table 3.2 ■

Highest Acceptable Award to the Plaintiff

	Type of Nonverbal Behavior Displayed by Confederate A	
	Dominant	Task Oriented
Initial judgments	$22,667	$22,780
Final judgments	$19,429	$15,350

Note: Low numbers for the final judgments indicate more persuasion.
Adapted from Ridgeway, 1988.

differences between the two conditions before the treatments were administered.

After the subjects made their initial judgements, they heard confederate A argue that the plaintiff should be awarded only $2,000 while using either dominant or task-oriented nonverbal behaviors. Following the discussion, the subjects again specified the highest award that would be acceptable to them. This second judgment was the dependent variable, and it was used to assess the amount of influence confederate A had on the subjects. To the extent that confederate A's arguments had an impact on the subjects' judgments, their second judgments should be lower than their first judgments. The hypothesis was that confederate A would be less persuasive when she used dominant than task-oriented nonverbal behaviors. An inspection of indicates that this prediction was supported. Lower awards were given to the plaintiff in the task-oriented than in the dominant condition.

This relatively simple study illustrates the basic elements of laboratory experimentation. In an experiment, the investigator manipulates the independent variable and assesses its effects on the dependent variable. Subjects are randomly assigned to conditions. The presence of the independent variable in one condition is compared with its absence in the control condition to determine if the experimental treatment had the hypothesized effect.

The sequence of steps in experimental studies is presented in Table 3-3.

Statistical tests are usually employed in assessing the effects of the independent variable. Such tests provide an estimate of the probability that a difference between the experimental and control conditions could have occurred by chance. In the Ridgeway study, a statistical test showed that the difference between the dominant and task-oriented conditions would have occurred by chance in fewer than 3 in 1,000 cases. The results of this study, therefore, support the hypothesis that dominant nonverbal behaviors have a negative impact on persuasiveness in small groups.

The great strength of experimentation is that it permits the investigator to draw strong conclusions about cause-and-effect relationships. The investigators carefully control the situation, so the only difference between the experimental and control groups is the one they intend to create (see Table 3-3). If there are differences between the groups on the dependent measure, the investigators can be fairly certain what caused the differences—their experimental treatments did. Because the situation is controlled in experiments, they tend to be *internally valid* which means that one can be confident the independent variable caused differences in the dependent variable. Thus, when the experiment is replicated the same results should be obtained.

Control in experiments is acquired at some cost. The situations created in the experimental laboratory are sometimes rather artificial. While it may be common enough to make decisions in small groups, it is unusual to do so in a setting where one's behavior is being observed. Because subjects may not behave naturally in the laboratory, experiments may not be *externally valid* which means that the results may not generalize from the laboratory to the real world.

In defense of experiments, the attempt is not necessarily to create *mundane realism,* the reality that corresponds to everyday life, for the subjects. Instead, the investigator attempts to create *experimental realism* by making the situation created in the laboratory a compelling and impactful one (39). If the subjects become involved in the experiment

Table 3.3 ■

The Sequence of Steps in Conducting an Experiment

1. A theory, developed by the investigator or someone else, forms the foundation of the study.
2. Hypotheses are derived from the theory.
3. The independent and dependent variables are translated into concrete operations.
4. Subjects are randomly assigned to the conditions in the study.
5. The treatment is administered.
6. The dependent measure is collected.
7. Statistical analyses are performed.
8. Conclusions are drawn about whether the data support the theory.

and take it seriously, then experimental realism has been created. Subjects who are involved in an experiment are likely to act normally, and this increases the chances that the results of the study can be generalized to the real world.

There are other potential problems with laboratory studies. It is difficult to study some groups of people in laboratory settings, such as working people and the elderly, because they are usually unavailable. Many laboratory studies have been conducted with college students and children, who may not be representative of the population in general. Thus, the generalizability of laboratory results may be limited because we can only be sure they apply to the types of people who have been studied. Another problem is that implicit pressures may be placed on the subjects to behave in ways that would support the experimenter's hypotheses. If the experimenters present a persuasive message, it may be obvious that they expect the subjects to be persuaded, and the subjects may behave accordingly because they think they are expected to do so. Obvious expectations in an experimental setting are referred to as *demand characteristics* (40).

Finally, in some laboratory experiments, subjects are deceived about the true purposes of the study. This deception raises an ethical issue regarding the conditions under which it is appropriate for exper-

imenters to be less than truthful about their studies. We will take up this and other ethical issues in the final section of the chapter.

Field Experiments

In field experiments, the experimental method is used in field settings. We can be fairly confident that the results we obtain in field experiments apply to the real world because they are conducted in natural settings where people typically do not know they are being observed. There are other advantages as well. In field experiments, the investigator randomly assigns subjects to the experimental and control conditions. As a consequence the investigator can be reasonably sure that any differences between groups on the dependent variable were caused by the independent variable. The Sherif study on intergroup conflict at a boys camp, which was discussed in Chapter 1, provides an example of a field experiment.

The value of field experiments can be illustrated by examining a study conducted by Jonathan Freedman and Scott Fraser (41). These researchers were interested in compliance—how people can be induced to do something they would rather not do. Short of putting pressure on people, how can you get them to do what you want? Freedman and Fraser

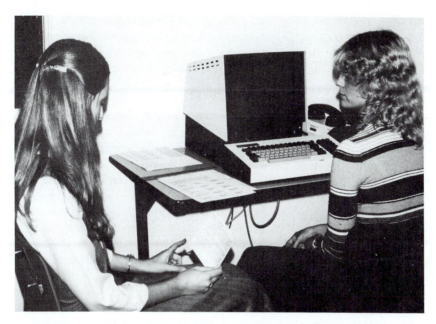

■ *A subject in a study is about to perform a computer trask under stress. Experimental realism is high, but mundane realism is low. (WGS)*

noted that people often respond to subtle differences in the ways requests are made of them. They reasoned that people might be more likely to comply with a request if it had been preceded by a smaller one first—a foot-in-the-door approach.

To test this idea, students who said they were representing the "Community Committee for Traffic Safety" interviewed housewives in Palo Alto. The students requested help in making citizens more aware of the need to drive carefully. Specifically, they asked if the housewives would be willing to put a small sticker in a window of their cars or homes that read "Be a Safe Driver." Almost all the housewives agreed to this small request. Two weeks later a different student, who said he or she represented "Citizens for Safe Driving," approached each housewife who had agreed to the first request and asked if she would be willing to put a large billboard concerning driving safety in her front yard. As these women could see, the billboard was not only large, it was also unattractive. What has just been described

was the manipulation for the experimental group; in the control group, only the second request was made. The foot-in-the-door technique was very successful. More than three fourths of the subjects in the experimental group agreed to put up the billboard; but without the small initial request compliance was quite low, only 17 percent.

Why does compliance with a small initial request lead to later compliance with a large request? It appears that people who comply with a small request convince themselves they are complying because they are the kind of people who agree to requests made for "good causes." This belief makes it likely they will comply with similar requests in the future, even if the requests are larger (42).

This study illustrates both the strengths and weaknesses of field experiments. Subjects were randomly assigned to conditions. The study incorporated a control condition, allowing the investigators to make strong statements about causal factors influencing compliance. It was conducted outside the laboratory in a situation where people almost certainly responded as they ordinarily would to requests that were made of them. Because field experiments are high on mundane realism their results are usually externally valid. The results are likely to generalize well to real world settings.

As with any technique, there are disadvantages associated with field experiments. The experimenter's control over the situation is far from optimal. For instance, compliance rates may have been influenced by a variety of factors other than those that were controlled. Time of day, the presence in the home of small children, or even the time of year (near Christmas) may have affected the housewives' willingness to help.

Field experiments are also limited to problems that can be studied in natural settings. Some types of behaviors occur too infrequently in natural settings to make field experiments feasible. Studies of intimate personal disclosures or of responses to emergencies are difficult to conduct in the field—emergencies because they occur infrequently, and personal disclosures because people avoid intimacy in publicly observable situations. Finally, ethical issues are raised by field experiments. The subjects typically do not know that their behavior is being studied, and sometimes they are not informed of the nature of the study even after it is completed. It is possible the subjects in these studies would not have consented to participate if given a choice. Some field experiments run the risk of invading people's privacy, while others may make people feel uncomfortable.

A field experiment designed to examine the stressful effects on an intrusion into personal space both invaded privacy and made people feel uncomfortable (43). In this study, men were surreptitiously observed when they entered a public lavatory to urinate. After the subject entered the lavatory, a confederate of the experimenter entered the lavatory and either stood at the adjacent urinal or stood one urinal away from the subject. Observing people in these circumstances would seem to be a clear invasion of privacy. The subjects in the study also experienced discomfort, as evidenced by the fact

that when the confederate stood next to them it took the subjects longer to begin urinating than when the confederate stood further away.

Field Studies

In field studies, investigators study the situation in which they are interested as it occurs in its natural setting. This technique can be used to study ongoing social processes, such as the decisions made by juries or interactions between doctors and their patients. Unlike field experiments, there is no manipulation of the independent variable. Thus, there generally is no control condition, with the result that strong causal statements cannot be made about the results of field studies. Typically, members of the group under observation know that they are being studied. The participants are likely to behave fairly naturally once they have adapted to being observed. The advantage of this technique is that it offers excellent opportunities to systematically collect data over an extended time period. Field studies represent a kind of compromise between the rigor of experiments and the insider's perspective afforded by participant or nonparticipant observation.

We can see the advantages of this technique in a study by Roger Bakeman and Robert Helmreich that was conducted with scientists working in an underwater diving station (44). Teams consisting of four scientists and one engineer lived and worked together for periods of two to three weeks. During these periods they were observed via television monitors by a team of psychologists located in a support ship. The behavior of each team member was recorded every six minutes, 24 hours a day. The question Bakeman and Helmreich examined was whether the most cohesive groups—those in which the members were most attracted to one another— were the most productive.

The investigators used time spent working as their index of productivity. They used the amount of leisure time the scientists spent conversing as a measure of cohesiveness. As predicted, at the end of their underwater stay, the most cohesive teams were more productive than the teams that were less cohesive. Bakeman and Helmreich measured this relationship with a correlation coefficient, which is symbolized by the letter *r*.

A correlation can vary between -1.00 and $+1.00$. It measures the type and degree of relationship between two variables. When the correlation is zero, there is no relationship between two variables (see Figure 3-2). A positive number indicates a positive correlation. A correlation is positive when high levels of one variable co-occur with high levels of the second variable. For instance, if highly cohesive teams tended to be highly productive, while low cohesive teams tended to be unproductive, the correlation coefficient would be positive. A negative number indicates a negative correlation. A correlation is negative when high levels of one variable co-occur with low levels of the second variable. For instance, if highly cohesive teams were low in productivity, whereas teams that were low in cohesiveness were highly productive, the correlation coefficient would be negative. The actual correlation coefficient between cohesiveness and productivity at the end of Bakeman and Helmreich's study was $+.73$, which indicates that cohesiveness and productivity are highly and positively correlated.

This study also illustrates some of the disadvantages of field studies. Although the investigators were able to systematically observe the scientists for an extended time, they observed only one situation. They could not contrast this situation with a more usual one, such as scientists working in typical work environments, so we do not know if these results generalize to more usual situations. Also, the scientists who participated in this study were not chosen at random. They may not be representative of people in general or even of scientists. Thus, although we know cohesiveness and productivity are related in this situation and for this group of people, we don't know whether this relationship would hold for other situations or groups of people. Field studies cannot help us to answer such questions because we cannot systematically compare different situations to which people have been randomly assigned.

When relationships emerge in field studies, it is not always clear what caused them. Often this is because only correlational relationships can be studied in field studies. You may have read that correlation does not imply causation. Even when we find a strong correlation, it is usually not possible to determine which variable caused the relationship.

In the Bakeman and Helmreich study, cohesiveness and productivity were strongly and positively correlated at the end of the study. Can we infer that high cohesiveness causes high productivity? No, because there are two other logical possibilities. First, it is possible that high productivity leads to high cohesiveness. This causal relationship could occur because people who are pleased with their accomplishments are likely to get along better with their coworkers than people who are less pleased with their accomplishments. Second, some third variable, such as length of acquaintance, could be the cause of both high cohesiveness and high productivity (see Table 3-4).

However, Bakeman and Helmreich did their study in a way that made it possible to make inferences regarding causality from the data. Their correlational evidence provides information on causality because data on cohesiveness and productivity were collected throughout the time the scientists were underwater. Using these data, one can look at cohesiveness at the beginning of the scientists' stay (Time 1) to see if it is correlated with productivity at the end of the stay (Time 2) (see Table 3-5). The groups that were initially highly cohesive were not much more likely to be productive at the end of their stay underwater than teams that were initially low in cohesiveness ($r = .13$). It appears that early cohesivenss did not cause later productivity.

But when Bakeman and Helmreich looked at productivity at the beginning of the scientists' stay (Time 1) and related it to later cohesiveness (Time 2), they found a strong positive correlation ($r = .72$). The teams that initially worked harder came to like each other more by the end of their stays. Since we know that productivity at Time 1 preceded cohesiveness at Time 2, we can infer that productivity caused cohesiveness. (Remember that to infer causality, one variable must precede the other in time, and the magnitude of the first variable must be

Positive Correlation

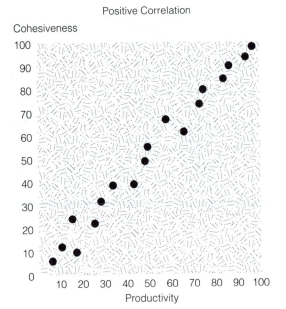

Negative Correlation

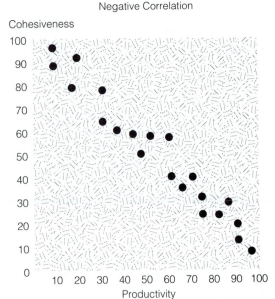

Zero Correlation

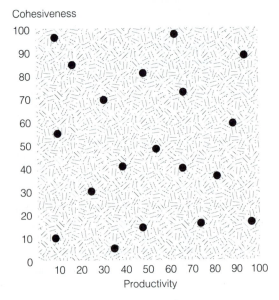

Figure 3.2 ■

Correlation Coefficients

Each dot represents the scores of one group on productivity and cohesiveness.

—In the positive correlation, high scores on productivity tend to co-occur with high scores on cohesiveness, while low scores on productivity co-occur with low scores on cohesiveness.

—In the negative correlation, high scores on productivity tend to co-occur with low scores on cohesiveness, while low scores on productivity co-occur with high scores on cohesiveness.

—In the zero correlation, there is no pattern in the relationship between scores on productivity and cohesiveness.

Table 3.4 ■

Causal Possibilities in Correlational Studies

  I. Variable A is unrelated to Variable B
     Example: Cohesiveness and productivity are unrelated

 II. Variable A causes Variable B
     Example: Cohesiveness causes productivity

III. Variable B causes Variable A
     Example: Productivity causes cohesiveness

IV. Variable C causes both Variable A and Variable B
     Example: Prior acquaintance causes productivity and cohesiveness

---

associated with corresponding changes in the second variable.) Thus, in this study, correlational data were used to make causal inferences. Although it is possible in some cases to draw causal inferences in field studies, this is usually possible only when data have been gathered over an extended period of time. Such studies are known as longitudinal studies. An example of a longitudinal study would be an examination of the relationship between self-esteem and academic achievement during all the secondary school years. Such a study would allow us to examine the correlations between self-esteem and achievement for each year separately, as well as allowing us to examine these correlations across several different years.

Table 3.5 ■

Correlations Between Cohesiveness and Productivity Among Scientists Working Underwater

	Cohesiveness	
	Time 1	Time 2
Productivity, Time 1	+.18	+.72
Productivity, Time 2	+.13	+.73

Adapted from Bakeman and Helmreich, 1975.

■

ETHICS IN SOCIAL PSYCHOLOGY

Each of the research techniques we have discussed raises ethical issues that involve the rights of subjects who participate in social research. Unlike medical researchers, social scientists are rarely concerned with causing or alleviating actual physical harm. The ethical issues of concern to social scientists are of a subtler nature, involving psychological rather than physical harm. Studies that lower subjects' self-esteem, cause them to behave in aggressive or other undesirable ways, or invade their privacy run the risk of causing psychological harm. Subjects have a right to confidentiality, privacy, self-determination, and to maintain their dignity when they participate in social research. Unfortunately, these rights are not always easy to maintain in the course of conducting research.

The degree to which these rights are violated should be weighed against the benefits of the research to the individual and to society. The purpose of social research is to advance our understanding of human behavior. The knowledge acquired through research often has valuable practical implications for public policy, the effectiveness of therapies and social programs, and the conduct of our everyday lives. Many social scientists feel an obligation to add to the existing body of knowledge on human behavior. Ethical problems arise when the pursuit of this obligation conflicts with the rights of the people who are being studied. We will consider three types of conflicts.

Confidentiality and Privacy

In most of the techniques we have reviewed, it is possible to identify the individuals who have provided answers to questions or who have behaved in particular ways. The people who provide this information have a right to expect that this material will be *confidential*. This right is rarely violated. Most researchers do not retain people's names in their data files, but keep only their responses. When the names are retained—for instance, when an investigator wishes to contact people at a later date—the names are separated from the data.

The data from most studies are analyzed in group form, which further ensures that specific people cannot be identified. For example, the responses of males may be compared with those of females, or subjects in the experimental condition may be compared with subjects in the control condition. In either case, it would be impossible for anyone other than the researcher to identify the responses of a specific subject.

Invasions of *privacy* are a greater problem than violations of confidentiality. The privacy of research subjects can be violated in situations where the subjects are unaware they are being observed. One-way mirrors, audio and visual recording, participant observation, and all other types of covert observation may violate people's privacy. People have a right to determine who will know about their behaviors, their past history, their beliefs, and their relationships. When they are being observed without their knowledge, their right to privacy may be violated. The preferred solution to this potential problem is to obtain informed consent before observing the behavior. To obtain *informed consent*, the investigator tells the subjects everything about the study that might influence their willingness to participate.

As a general guideline, informed consent is a valuable procedure. Unfortunately, for some prob-

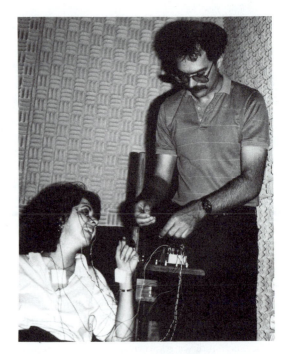

■ *Informed consent should be obtained in all studies, particularly those involving psycho-physiological measures. (WGS)*

lems that social psychologists study, informing the subjects beforehand of what is being investigated may alter their behavior. This is likely to be true for socially desirable or undesirable behaviors, such as helping, aggression, and prejudice. Here, the solution typically employed is to tell the subjects after the study what was being investigated. This is also the solution most commonly adopted in studies involving deception.

Deception

The majority of studies in psychological social psychology employ some deception while only a minority of studies in sociological social psychology employ deception (45). The Ridgeway study discussed earlier provides an example of deception in research. In this study, the subjects were not informed beforehand of the true goal of the research, which was to determine if nonverbal displays of dominance would diminish social influence. If the subjects had been told that nonverbal behavior was a focus of the investigation, it is likely that few subjects would have allowed the confederate's behavior to influence them, and the results would have presented a distorted picture of the impact of nonverbal behavior on persuasion. Most instances of deception are relatively harmless, involving mislabeling questionnaires or providing only incomplete information about the purpose of a study, but some types of deception such as those involving telling subjects they have failed on a task or inducing people to behave in socially undesirable ways (aggressively) are more problematical. Social psychologists generally agree that deception should not be used unless it is necessary, and then only a minimal amount of deception should be used.

Debriefing, a careful and thorough discussion of the study with each participant after the experimental session, is usually an effective means of dealing with deception. During debriefing the experimenter discusses the true purpose of the study, explains why deception was used, and attempts to alleviate any discomfort the subject may have experienced due to the deception. Interviews with subjects reveal that few of them have negative reactions after being debriefed, and most subjects report finding the experiments useful (46). There are situations, however, where debriefing is not entirely successful. In a study designed to explore potential problems in debriefing, the investigators gave their subjects false feedback on their performances on a task measuring social sensitivity (47). Half the subjects were told they were socially sensitive, and half of them were told they were socially insensitive. At the end of the study, both groups were debriefed, and they were told that the feedback they received did not reflect their actual performances.

Despite the debriefing, when these subjects were later asked to rate their social sensitivity, the subjects who had been falsely told that they had done well regarded themselves as being more socially sensitive than subjects who had been falsely told that they had done poorly. Fortunately, an even more thorough debriefing, which included an explanation of the perseverance of the effects of false feedback, eliminated this carryover effect. What this study shows is that debriefing must be done with extreme care—or it may not achieve its goal of returning the subjects to their preexperimental state.

Psychological Harm

Investigators have an obligation to prevent or minimize the possibility that any psychological harm may befall their subjects. The types of harm most likely to occur include shame, regret, loss of feelings of self-esteem, and discomfort over acquiring unwanted self-knowledge. Perhaps an example or two will clarify this issue. Studies of attraction have on occasion involved deceiving subjects into believing that others do not like them in order to investigate their reactions, studies of moral reasoning have sometimes placed people in situations where there is a high payoff for lying or cheating, and in studies of the effects of pornography on aggression subjects who have read pornographic materials are given an opportunity to harm another person. Informed consent is obtained when possible; but, when it is not possible, subjects are informed that they can cease to participate at any point in the research. Debriefing is used to process any negative reactions the subjects may have experienced as a result of the research. As an additional safeguard, nearly all institutions in which research on human subjects is conducted have review panels to guard against any psychological harm to subjects. Further, the American Sociological Association and the American Psychological Association have ethical guidelines that their members must obey to maintain membership in these organizations.

After all precautions have been taken to protect confidentiality and privacy and to minimize deception and harm, we must still ask: Is the topic of sufficient importance to justify the techniques that will be used? If the threat of harm or invasion of privacy is great, and if the knowledge to be gained is not deemed to be important, then the research should not be conducted. An example might be the restroom study in which the invasion of privacy was clear and the knowledge to be acquired about reactions to violations of personal space was not great. While the violation of privacy was not damaging to the individual, the knowledge to be gained was not sufficient to warrant conducting the research (48).

■ SUMMARY

We began this chapter with a comparison between magic and science. We found they were similar in a number of ways. For example, the goal of both magic and science is to be able to understand, predict, and control the events that occur in the world. Magic and science differ in how they achieve these goals. In magic, rituals are used to bring about desired events, and the rules of causality that are employed are unclear.

In contrast, the rule of causality used by scientists is clearly specified. The cause must precede the effect, and changes in the magnitude of the cause must be associated with changes in the magnitude of the effect. In testing causal relationships, scientists use systematic observational techniques. The use of systematic empirical techniques makes it possible to disprove scientific hypotheses. Scientific knowledge tends to be abstract, and it is always subject to revision and change.

Questionnaires are used to collect information systematically on people's attitudes, beliefs, feelings, and behavior. They can be used to describe a given population or to test causal hypotheses. Questionnaires are widely used because random sampling allows one to generalize from a sample to a population of respondents. Unfortunately, when responding to questionnaires, people sometimes give answers that present them in a favorable manner. In addition, some surveys suffer from low response rates.

Unstructured interviews allow the interviewers to probe more deeply into people's thoughts and feelings than is possible in questionnaires. Some of the problems with unstructured interviews are that they are time-consuming, only small numbers of subjects can be studied, and these samples usually are not randomly selected. Unstructured interviews are useful for presenting in-depth descriptions of specific groups and for generating hypotheses, but they are not as useful for testing hypotheses.

In participant observation, the investigator makes in-depth observations, often joining the group that he or she is studying. The investigator attempts to view the group from the inside, rather than as an outsider. In nonparticipant observation the observer does not join the group, and the group members may be aware they are being observed. One problem with these techniques is that the investigator may lose his or her objectivity. Another problem is that these techniques are usually used with only one or a small number of groups, so it is hard to know whether the knowledge acquired about them can be generalized to other groups.

Laboratory studies employ the experimental method. In this technique, theories concerning the relationships between classes of events are used to formulate hypotheses. Based on an hypothesis, experiments are designed in which the experimenter varies the independent variable (the cause) and examines its effects on the dependent variable (the effect). In conducting an experiment, the independent and dependent variables must be translated into concrete operations. Subjects are randomly assigned to the experimental or control group, and the effects of the experimental treatment are examined. Statistical tests are then used to determine if the results of the experiment support the theory.

Laboratory experiments make it possible to study events that do not occur naturally. In laboratory experiments, the investigator has more control over the situation than in any of the other techniques. The cost of obtaining this control is that laboratory experiments often take place in artificial settings. The investigator tries to create a realistic situation, even if it is not the same as a natural situation. Other drawbacks of laboratory experiments are that they often involve deception, and that they are typically performed on only certain social groups.

In field experiments, causal hypotheses can also be tested because, in this technique, the investigator systematically alters the situation to determine the effects of these alterations. An advantage of field experiments is that they occur in natural settings, and people usually do not know they are being studied.

Field studies take place in naturally occurring settings, where people typically behave normally. These settings make it possible to collect information systematically over extended time periods. Generally, field studies cannot be used to test causal hypotheses because the investigator has relatively little control over the situation.

Deception is one of the ethical issues confronted by social psychologists in conducting studies. Subjects in social research have a right to self-determination, privacy, and dignity and to be free from harm. Investigators have an obligation to ensure that the information they receive is maintained in confidence. If possible, informed consent should be obtained from research participants prior to their participation. Invasions of privacy should be minimized. If invasions of privacy or deception do occur in the course of conducting a study, the participants should be debriefed afterwards. Above all, investigators have an obligation to see that no harm befalls participants in research.

■

REFERENCES

1. Benedict, R., 1934, *Patterns of Culture,* Boston: Houghton Mifflin.
2. Monte, C., 1975, *Psychology's Scientific Endeavor,* New York: Praeger.
3. Frazer, J., 1922, *The Golden Bough: A Study in Magic and Religion,* New York: Macmillan, p. 68.
4. Benedict, 1934, op. cit.
5. Frazer, 1922, op. cit., p. 57.
6. Frazer, 1922, ibid., pp. 11, 19.
7. Rozin, P., L. Millman, and C. Nemeroff, 1986, "Operation of the Laws of Sympathetic Magic in Disgust and Other Domains," *Journal of Personality and Social Psychology* 50:703–712.
8. Frazer, 1922, op. cit., p. 56.
9. Hume, D., 1911 (originally published 1739–1740), *A Treatise of Human Nature,* ed. A. D. Lindsay, 2 vols., London: Dent.
10. Festinger, L., 1957, *A Theory of Cognitive Dissonance,* New York: Harper & Row.
11. Pettigrew, T. F., 1975, *Racial Discrimination in the United States,* New York: Harper & Row.

12. U.S. Commission on Civil Rights, 1987, *New Evidence on School Desegregation,* U.S. Government Printing Office: Washington D.C.
13. Oskamp, S., 1977, *Attitudes and Opinions,* Englewood Cliffs, NJ: Prentice-Hall.
14. Hite, S., 1987, *Women and Love,* New York: Knopf.
15. Babbie, E., 1983, *The Practice of Social Research,* 3d ed., Belmont: Wadsworth.
16. Greeley, A. M. and P. B. Sheatsley, 1971, "Attitudes Toward Racial Integration: The South Catches Up," in L. Rainwater (Ed.), *Social Problems and Public Policy I: Inequality and Justice,* Chicago: Aldine.
17. Schuman, H., C. Steeh, and L. Bobo, 1985, *Racial Attitudes in America,* Cambridge: Harvard University Press.
18. Taylor, D. G., P. B. Sheatsley, and A. M. Greeley, 1978, "Attitudes Toward Racial Integration," *Scientific American* 238: 42–49.
19. Stephan, W. G., 1986, "Effects of School Desegregation: An Evaluation 30 Years After Brown," in L. Saxe and M. Saks (Eds.), *Advances in Applied Social Psychology,* New York: Academic Press.
20. Rubin, L., 1976, *Worlds of Pain,* New York: Basic Books, p. 14.
21. Rubin, 1976, ibid., p. 113.
22. Rubin, 1976, ibid., p. 79.
23. Rubin, 1976, ibid., p. 113.
24. Richardson, L., 1988, "Secrecy and Status: The Social Construction of Forbidden Relationships," *American Sociological Review* 53:209–219.
25. Rosenhan, D. L., 1973, "On Being Sane in Insane Places," *Science* 173:250–258.
26. Rosenhan, 1973, ibid., p. 256.
27. Rosenhan, 1973, ibid., p. 256.
28. Snow, D. A. and L. Anderson, 1987, "Identity Work Among the Homeless: The Verbal Construction and Avowal of Personal Identities," *American Journal of Sociology* 92:1336–1371.
29. Snow and Anderson, 1987, ibid., p. 1338.
30. Snow and Anderson, 1987, ibid., p. 1342.
31. Snow and Anderson, 1987, ibid., p. 1340.
32. Snow and Anderson, 1987, ibid., p. 1349.
33. Snow and Anderson, 1987, ibid., p. 1359.
34. Snow and Anderson, 1987, ibid., p. 1361.
35. Snow and Anderson, 1987, ibid., p. 1355.
36. Snow and Anderson, 1987, ibid., p. 1365.
37. Rosenhan, 1973, op. cit., p. 257.
38. Ridgeway, C. L., 1987, "Nonverbal Behavior, Dominance, and the Basis of Status in Task Groups," *American Sociological Review* 52:683–694.
39. Aronson, E. and J. M. Carlsmith, 1968, "Experimentation in Social Psychology," in G. Lindzey and E. Aronson (Eds.), *The Handbook of Social Psychology,* Vol. 2, 2d ed., Reading, MA: Addison-Wesley.
40. Orne, M., 1962, "On the Social Psychology of the Psychological Experiment," *American Psychologist* 17:776–783.
41. Freedman, J. and S. Fraser, 1966, "Compliance Without

Pressure: The Foot-in-the-Door Technique," *Journal of Personality and Social Psychology* 4:195–202.

42. Freedman and Fraser, 1966, ibid.

43. Middlemist, R., E. Knowles, and C. Matter, 1976, "Personal Space Invasions in the Lavoratory: Suggestive Evidence for Arousal," *Journal of Personality and Social Psychology* 33:541–546.

44. Bakeman, R. and R. Helmreich, 1975, "Cohesiveness and Performance: Covariation and Causality in an Undersea Environment," *Journal of Experimental Social Psychology* 11:478–489.

45. Adair, G., T. W. Dushenko, and R. C. L. Lindsay, 1985, "Ethical Regulations and Their Impact on Research Practice," *American Psychologist* 40:59–73; A. Gross and I. Fleming, 1982, "Twenty Years of Deception in Social Psychology," *Personality and Social Psychology Bulletin* 8:402–408.

46. Smith, S. S. and D. Richardson, 1983, "Amelioration of Deception and Harm in Psychological Research: The Important Role of Debriefing," *Journal of Personality and Social Psychology* 44:1075–1082; K. Ring, K. Wallston, and M. Corey, 1970, "Mode of Debriefing as a Factor Affecting Subjective Reactions to a Milgram-type Obedience Situation," *Representative Research in Social Psychology* 1:67–85.

47. Ross, L., M. Lepper, and M. Hubbard, 1975, "Perseverance in Self-perception and Social Perception: Biased Attributional Processes in the Debriefing Paradigm," *Journal of Personality and Social Psychology* 32:880–892.

48. For a more detailed discussion of these issues see S. Cook, 1976, "Ethical Issues in the Conduct of Research in Social Relations," in C. Selltiz, L. Wrightsman, and S. Cook (Eds.), *Research Methods in Social Relations,* New York: Holt, Rinehart & Winston.

CHAPTER 4

Socialization

■

What Is Socialization?
The Goals of Socialization
Language and Socialization
The Two Social Psychologies and Socialization
The Agents of Socialization
The Family
Schools
Peer Groups
Mass Media
Other Influences
The Process of Socialization
Psychoanalytic Theory
Social Learning Theory
Cognitive Developmental Theory
Characteristics of Socialization
Continuity and Change
Reciprocal Socialization
Socialization Across Societies
Socialization Through the Life Cycle
Socialization in Childhood and Adulthood
Adult Socialization
Erikson's Psychosexual Stages
Resocialization
Old Age and Beyond

Kolya started to pull at the ball Mitya was holding. The action was spotted by a junior staff member who quickly scanned the room and then called out gaily: "Children, come look! See how Vasya and Marusya are swinging their teddy bears together. They are good comrades." The two offenders quickly dropped the ball to join others in observing the praised couple, who now swung harder than ever. (1)

This incident in a Soviet preschool illustrates the emphasis on cooperation in the socialization of Russian children. A researcher who has studied socialization practices in the United States and the Soviet Union describes the dominant methods of socialization by parents in one of these countries as follows:

> *They reason with the youngster, isolate him, appeal to guilt, show disappointment—in short, convey in a variety of ways, on the one hand the kind of behavior that is expected of the child; on the other, the realization that transgression means the interruption of a mutually valued relationship.*
>
> *The successful use of withdrawal of love as a disciplinary technique implies the prior existence of a gratifying relationship; the more love present in the first instance, the greater the threat implied in its withdrawal. . . . Our data indicate that it is primarily mothers who tend to employ "love oriented" techniques of discipline.* (2)

Can you guess which country's socialization practices were described here? While the description was written about American parents, it applies equally well to Soviet parents. Thus, while the content of socialization differs in these two countries, the methods of socialization appear similar. In this chapter we will explore aspects of socialization that transcend cultural boundaries.

■

WHAT IS SOCIALIZATION?

Socialization involves the process of teaching members of the society what they need to know to maintain social life. When infants are born, they do not exhibit any of the learned behaviors that characterize human beings and differentiate them from lower animals. They only have the capacity to learn these behaviors. Each society must face the question: "How are the human critters of this society to be transformed into socialized human beings?" (3).

Is socialization really important to human behavior? It certainly is! Its importance is dramatically illustrated by the behavior of human children who go unsocialized. Feral children, children who grow up in the wild, have occasionally been found. For example, two feral children were found living with wolves in India in 1920 (4). These children were wolfish in appearance, with hard calluses on their knees and palms from walking on them, and sharp-edged teeth. Their behavior was also wolflike: they sniffed and ate food like wolves, and they prowled and howled at night.

Another child, Isabelle, was discovered living in an attic in the United States in the 1930s (5). Her case demonstrates the effects of near-isolation from human society. Isabelle was an illegitimate child whose mother was a deaf mute. She lived with her mother in a darkened room without exposure to other humans. Isabelle and her mother communicated with gestures; the only sounds Isabelle made were low, croaking noises. After being discovered, Isabelle received intensive language training. Within about two months she was speaking in sentences. After two years, she had overcome the effects of her years of linguistic and social isolation. Isabelle's case not only illustrates the effects of isolation, it also shows the remarkable learning capacity of human children. In only a short time, she was able to become a socialized member of society. However, late socialization has limitations. After a certain age, lack of socialization creates permanent deficits.

The Goals of Socialization

The socialization practices of any society must accomplish at least two tasks (6). First, they must ensure *physical survival* so a new generation can be born. This requires the transmission of skills for satisfying our basic biological needs and for defense against danger. Second, socialization practices must ensure that people *understand* the system of norms and roles developed by society and *conform* to it. This involves teaching shared goals and means to achieve them and establishing a system of control over individuals. It is to accomplish these tasks that individuals are socialized into the culture of their society.

Socialization into the culture of the society is the occupation of childhood. Culture consists of all aspects of symbolic meaning in a society, including beliefs, values, rituals, art forms, ceremonies, language, stories, and habits of everyday life. Yet, every culture contains conflicting symbols—rituals, stories, and guides that suggest opposing behaviors. For example, we need only to think of some of our folk idioms ("Birds of a feather flock together," "Look before you leap," and "It's better to be safe than sorry") and compare them with others ("Opposites attract," "He who hesitates is lost," and "Nothing ventured, nothing gained") to discover guides that justify contradictory actions. Culture is not always internally consistent because different situations may call for dissimilar behaviors. We can think of culture as an information base from which we can select various data for different circumstances (7).

Language and Socialization

Language is an important prerequisite for socialization. Socialization cannot proceed without social interaction, and social interaction requires language. Without language, it would be impossible to communicate the rules and values of the society. Socialization typically begins in earnest only after the child has acquired language.

This important landmark of socialization, language, begins with the baby making random noises. When the baby makes sounds similar to those of the language of the parents, the parents give the baby attention and praise. The parents also modify and repeat the baby's language sounds in an effort to get the baby to imitate them. The closer the baby's sounds are to the desired language sounds, the more

the parents reward the baby. Because of these rewards, the baby is increasingly motivated to make these desired sounds.

Most researchers believe only human beings have the ability to acquire language. They feel this ability sets humans apart from other animals. This view of language as an exclusive characteristic of humans has been challenged by some researchers who believe a small number of nonhuman animals (chimps, gorillas, and dolphins) also have the capacity to acquire language. These researchers believe language capacity in nonhuman animals has been demonstrated because the animals have been taught to use sign language or other nonverbal communication systems (8).

However, most experts in the area argue that these animals have not demonstrated "true" language learning. Those arguing for this viewpoint feel the animals have demonstrated only limited abilities to use the nonverbal communication systems they have been taught. For instance, animals cannot teach the language they use to other animals, nor communicate about their ability to communicate. They have no sense of consciousness nor aesthetics, and they are unable to attribute intentions and beliefs that they do not themselves hold to others. The emphasis on whether animals possess language has perhaps been misplaced. Their relatively meager level of communication is only one measure of the cognitive gap between animals and humans (9). Only humans develop cultures, and require socialization practices to ensure the continuation of those cultures.

The Two Social Psychologies and Socialization

Although both sociologists and psychologists believe the study of socialization is critical to social psychology, these disciplines differ in their approaches to socialization. Sociologists tend to focus on the *characteristics* of socialization, such as continuity and change over time, the reciprocal nature of socialization, and socialization as a life-long process, including adult resocialization. Psychologists are more likely to study the *processes* involved in

■ *Fathers are an overlooked but important agent of socialization.* (WGS)

socialization—the ways in which socialization is accomplished. Unlike sociologists, many psychologists view socialization as developing through a series of life stages.

In this chapter we will first detail the primary agents of socialization and then explore the processes by which socialization is accomplished. Next, we will consider several characteristics of socialization. Finally, we will examine socialization through the life cycle. The development of a sense of self also occurs in the process of childhood socialization. The self is such an important topic that we devote all of Chapter 5 to it.

THE AGENTS OF SOCIALIZATION

Both sociologists and psychologists study the agents of socialization. Sociologists focus on the influence of social institutions on individuals, whereas psychologists stress the result of specific socialization practices of individuals (10).

The Family

Parents as well as other members of the immediate family are the primary socializers of children in their first few years. Many studies have explored the association between the mother's child-rearing practices and the behaviors of her children. Until recently, however, the father's role in socializing children was neglected. It is now recognized that fathers play a major role in socializing their children (11). In fact, in most societies fathers have more ultimate control over their children than mothers because fathers have more power in the marriages. Further, fathers frequently exercise this control and are often stricter with their children than mothers. Consistent with this status and behavior, children typically view fathers as more powerful and punitive than mothers. Fathers also play a more active role in some aspects of children's language development than mothers. For instance, fathers are more insistent that their

children give names of things and explanations of the functions of things than are mothers (12). In addition, siblings—especially older ones—help socialize their brothers and sisters.

Socialization differs from family to family because each family has different values and beliefs. Different families also provide varying opportunities for achieving success in the society. These opportunities influence socialization practices, as we saw in Chapter 1 when examining the influence of social class on childhood socialization. In addition, differences in values and norms among racial and ethnic groups are reflected in the socialization practices of these groups. For example, in Hispanic culture a greater emphasis is placed on cooperation, obedience to authority, and traditional gender-role relationships, relative to some other American ethnic groups (13). Such differences in values sometimes contribute to intergroup misunderstandings because each group judges members of the other group (the outgroup) by using its own values as standards. For example, Caucasian teachers of Native American Indians sometimes complain that their students are disrespectful because the students will not look their teachers in the eye when they are being addressed. What these teachers do not understand is that in Native American Indian culture, averting one's eyes is a sign of respect.

Also, families change over time with the result that children from the same family are not raised in an identical manner (14). Young parents interact differently with their first-born children than older, more experienced parents interact with later-borns. To illustrate, relative to treatment of their later-born children, mothers of first-borns interfere more with the child's attempts at problem solving and apply more pressure on the child to achieve. This differential treatment results both in more conflicts with first-born than with later-born children and in relatively greater achievement among first-born children (15). For instance, first-born children have higher Stanford Achievement Test (SAT) scores than later-born children.

Families also experience changes in occupation, geographic residence, and other facets of their lives that may cause their socialization practices to change over time. A couple who socialized their older children to be obedient and conforming may, after a change in occupations, socialize their younger children to be independent and achievement oriented. Parents who move from one community to another may change their child-rearing practices to conform to the standards of the new community in an attempt to ensure their children's acceptance by others outside the family.

Schools

By age three, many children in this society attend nursery school. Once children begin school, teachers become important socializers. The role of parents and teachers as socializing agents often overlaps in the years through elementary school (16). The schools provide an important socialization bridge between the family and the ultimate occupational setting. More than the family, the schools stress values that are important for success in the work place.

In school, children learn they will be judged on intellectual achievement, and their levels of self-esteem are greatly influenced by these judgments. Children are also judged on their ability and willingness to conform to other school demands, such as punctuality, neatness, and obedience. In addition, they may be judged on largely irrelevant criteria, such as social class and race. Many educational critics argue that education is a middle-class system run by middle-class adults for middle-class children, with the result that lower-class children have a greater chance of failure in the system. In Chapter 8 we will explore the influence of teacher expectations on pupil performance.

■ *Peers are important agents in the socialization of school-age children.*
(© Richard S. Orton 1990)

Peer Groups

Peer groups differ from the family and the schools in that the latter two institutions have socialization of children as an explicit goal. The child's peer group is his or her first voluntary group (17). Membership in a peer group provides the child with a way of exercising independence from and reacting against adult control. Children's peers—siblings, friends, and classmates—also socialize each other. In the later school years peers often become more important than parents as agents of socialization. Also, the later school years include a widening circle of different peer groups. Peers help to teach each other ways of presenting themselves in public, distinguishing appropriate from inappropriate behaviors, negotiating problems, and developing relationships with others (18). For example, peer friendships provide settings where children can explore their attitudes toward parents, school, sex, and the obligations of adult life.

Mass Media

The mass media, particularly television, also play an important role in the socialization of children (20). The average American child spends more hours per week watching television than attending school (21). The media teach children (and adults) about current trends, ranging from political thought to clothing styles. In addition, they represent a primary force in cultural diffusion; the media teach us about the variety of ways people live in this and in other countries. For instance, a small child in a southern rural setting is now integrated via the media into the larger, urban society and its values at an early age. Thus, differences among the segments of our society are being narrowed. At the same time, all segments of our society are able to see the material possessions of others and compare those possessions with their own.

The media have taken over many functions of the family, such as teaching values and giving advice on common problems. Of course, the values taught by the media may not be those to which a given family would subscribe. In addition, the media

provide information on standards for ideal families to which individual families may or may not conform or wish to conform. The media also provide the dominant form of recreation for many children and adults, one which has dramatically reduced time spent reading and in family interaction. Last, people's knowledge has been greatly expanded through the large informational output of the media.

Marshall McLuhan was one of the first social thinkers to express concern regarding the influence of mass media on people in technologically advanced societies. In his book, *The Medium is the Massage* (not Message), he argued that the mass media foster passivity and submission in their consumers (22). In addition, the manner in which the media present information shapes the attitudes of viewers.

Other critics have charged the media with producing an ideology of consumption through advertising and marketing, in which life is reduced to one's ability to purchase (23). In particular, concern has arisen over the influence of advertising on children who are too young to evaluate persuasion attempts that concern dangerous or expensive toys, food products low in nutritional benefit and high in sugar or cholesterol, or products associated with alcohol abuse in young people. Young children also cannot protect themselves from deception and misrepresentation in advertising, nor do they understand advertising as a calculated attempt to induce behavior financially beneficial to the advertiser.

As we move from a technological to an information society, individuals' future statuses are associated more and more with their degree of access to information. The nature of the labor market is already undergoing rapid change as more and more jobs become "high tech." As our dependency on information increases, the purveyors of information—the mass media—become ever more important in socialization.

Other Influences

In addition, many other persons (neighbors, other relatives) and institutions (the church) assist in the socialization of individuals. Religion provides both an important social setting and a moral training

BOX 4-1

Friendship and Delinquency

Because peers are important agents of socialization, researchers have been interested in the relationships between delinquents, who seem to represent some failure of socialization, and their peers. We seem to hold conflicting stereotypes of the friendships formed by delinquents. We hold one stereotype of the gang member, whose behavior is completely controlled by the gang, and another stereotype of the alienated, antisocial loner who has no friends at all. In a recent study of the friendships of delinquent and nondelinquent adolescents, neither stereotype was supported. The investigators found few differences between the friendships of delinquent and nondelinquent adolescents (19).

The researchers measured the perceived rewards of friendship, the frequency of interactions with friends, and the extent of conflict in friendships in delinquents and nondelinquents aged 12 to 19. Delinquents reported levels of caring and trust in their friendships equal to those reported by nondelinquents. Delinquent and nondelinquents also reported similar feelings of being able to be themselves in their friendships. In addition, delinquents and nondelinquents did not differ in the reported frequency of interaction with their friends. Interestingly, a significant difference in self-disclosure was found, with a lower rate of self disclosure among the most law-abiding adolescents. Delinquents did report higher levels of conflict with their friends than did nondelinquents.

On the basis of these data, we must conclude that delinquents are neither loners nor mindless gang clones. Whatever the factors that distinguish delinquents from nondelinquents, quality of friendships is not among them. Peers appear to play the same role in the socialization of delinquents as in the socialization of nondelinquents. ■

ground for a substantial proportion of children. Children's physical environments also provide lessons about the culture. While urban children are exposed to a greater variety of social roles than children from small towns, children from small towns are included in more aspects of social life than children in urban areas, who are more likely to be excluded from adult work roles and social events (24).

At any given time, then, multiple agents of socialization are acting on the child, and the values and behaviors these agents encourage may be inconsistent with one another. Furthermore, espoused values and behaviors vary with the child's social class, age, and ethnicity. While we sometimes think of socialization as being consistent within and across individuals in a society, it clearly is not. Socialization is dependent upon the social context.

■ *In an information society, status will be associated with access to information.*
(© Richard S. Orton 1990)

THE PROCESS OF SOCIALIZATION

How do we become socialized? We will present three theories suggesting differing mechanisms: psychoanalytic theory, social learning theory, and cognitive developmental theory. We will discuss each of these theories, paying special attention to their conceptions of the development of morality.

Psychoanalytic Theory

Sigmund Freud's conception of socialization has greatly influenced sociological and psychological views of personality and behavior. The cornerstone of his psychoanalytic theory is the concept of the unconscious. This concept lies at the heart of his theories of psychosexual stages and the dynamics of personality. We will explore each of these concepts in turn.

The unconscious As we mentioned in Chapter 1, one of Freud's most important contributions was his concept of the unconscious. Freud compared the mind to an iceberg: the top that shows is the region of consciousness, while the much larger portion below the water is the region of unconsciousness. The unconscious contains the ideas and urges that are consciously repressed because they are unacceptable to the conscious mind.

Freud believed all actions were attributable to *psychic energy,* the motivational states found within the person. The major motivating force is the *libido,* the source of energy for the life instincts, including survival and reproduction. Freud turned most of his attention to the part of the libido that encompasses the sexual drive. Since the sexual urges of the libido are often unacceptable to the conscious mind, they reside in the unconscious mind.

Unconscious ideas and urges influence the conscious thoughts and behaviors of the person. They may be displaced onto another object or the energy associated with them may be directed toward another activity. For example, a person with strong sexual urges that are unacceptable to her might develop a literary interest in expressions of intimacy and become a professor of literature. A person with strong feelings of hostility and resentment toward his father might express these feelings in an altered form by expressing hostility and resentment toward other authority figures.

Psychosexual stages One of Freud's most revolutionary ideas was that the sexual drive is active from birth onward (25). In Freud's conception, sexuality is not solely associated with the genital zone; many types of sexual pleasure exist, each associated with a different erogenous zone. He believed that socialization is accomplished by the individual's passage through four psychosexual stages between infancy and adulthood. These stages specify the major focus of the individual's sexual energy at a given time. Freud consistently emphasized the importance of early experience in the development of the individual. He believed early experiences during these stages had profound implications for adult development.

The child passes through three of the stages in the first five years of life. These first few years are the most critical ones for the formation of the personality. At each stage, satisfaction is achieved through a specific mode. If the appropriate satisfactions are not achieved at each stage, some of the child's psychic energy may become *fixated,* or arrested, at that stage. This fixation may interfere with later development and be manifested in personality traits exhibited in adulthood. In the course of normal development the child moves from stage to stage, with each stage contributing to the development of the individual.

The first stage, which occurs in the first year of life, is called the *oral stage.* During this stage the principal sources of pleasure are oral. Eating, sucking, and biting are important sources of satisfaction during this stage. According to Freud, a child who becomes fixated in the oral stage might become verbally aggressive and sarcastic or might become gullible. Feelings of dependency are prominent during this stage.

The second stage, which occurs from 1 to 3 years of age, is the *anal stage.* During it, the principal sources of pleasure derive from elimination. The interactions with the parents in the course of toilet training produce differing personality types. Freud believed that a child who experiences difficulties with her parents during toilet training could become an "anal retentive" adult—orderly, stingy, and acquisitive—or might become cruel or messy and disorderly. Issues of responsibility, creativity, and productivity arise during this phase.

Third, the *phallic stage* occurs during the years 3 to 5. In this stage, the child's own sex organs become the principle source of pleasure. The child discovers that the genitals can provide pleasure, and he or she begins to have sexual fantasies. According to Freud, a child who does not successfully pass through the phallic stage could suffer problems of gender identity. The child deals with issues of independence during this phase.

These three stages are followed by a prolonged *latency period* during which the child's impulses for pleasure are repressed—forced out of conscious awareness. The superego develops during this period, and the child moves from dependency on the parents to dependency on the peer group.

The final stage is the *genital stage,* in which one of the individual's principal sources of pleasure is derived from sexual contact with others. This stage begins at about 12 when adolescence reactivates the individual's impulses for pleasure and brings them into consciousness. Freud believed the individual enters adulthood during this stage. In the genital stage, the individual becomes a socialized adult, having moved by small increments away from the selfishness of infancy. In this stage, the child should become dependable, responsible, and competent. Concern for others has come to rule over individual pleasure seeking. While the final stage is the genital stage, the oral, anal, and phallic stages all contribute to the formation of the individual.

Personality and morality According to Freud, the personality is composed of three systems: the id, ego, and superego. The three systems work together. The *id,* which comprises biological drives, is the source of the psychic energy discussed above. The id has a twofold goal: to avoid pain and obtain pleasure. The id achieves this goal through wish-fulfillment—by fantasizing the satisfaction of its needs. It is thus both selfish and unrealistic.

In contrast, the *ego* deals with the objective world of reality. The ego's goal is to find a realistic way of satisfying the wishes of the id. It operates on the basis of reason, rather than fantasy. It decides what actions will be taken to satisfy the biological drives. It is the executive of the self, responding to the external world by integrating the demands of the other two systems.

The *superego* contains two components. The first, the conscience, consists of prohibitions against socially undesirable behaviors. The second is the ego-ideal, the individual's view of the person he or she ideally should be. The superego develops in response to the rewards and punishments children receive from their parents. On the basis of these rewards and punishments, a moral code is instilled in the child that results in self-control. The superego both inhibits the unacceptable impulses of the id and attempts to persuade the ego to substitute moralistic for practical solutions in a given situation. The child develops a sense of morality through the operation of the superego.

The individual's personality is influenced by the relationships among the id, ego, and superego. Freud believed people differ in the ways they deal with the struggle between the id and the superego, and its moderation by the ego. For example, one person's id may win more battles, while another's superego may win more often. The personality of the former person should be more impulsive, with this individual more prone to gratify physical and emotional pleasures. The latter person, by comparison, should be more moralistic and perfectionistic.

Social Learning Theory

Social learning theory was discussed in detail in Chapter 2. Here we will apply it to socialization. According to social learning theory, socialization is accomplished through two processes, direct learning and observational learning. Direct learning is a product of rewards and punishments. While reward increases the likelihood behaviors will be repeated, punishment decreases the likelihood behaviors will be repeated. For example, as a young child, you may have learned not to cross a busy street by being punished for crossing one.

Through the second process, observational learning, we learn by observing the behavior of others. From observing others in the society, we can determine the likely consequences of our own behaviors. As a young child you may also have learned not to cross a busy street by observing another child being punished for crossing such a street. Most of the socialization that occurs in our lives occurs through this second method.

Internalization and morality Over time, a child's behaviors become less dependent on the parents' rewards and punishments. Social learning theorists believe self-reinforcement is the most important form of behavioral regulation for older children and adults (26). When a child progresses from external reinforcement to self-reinforcement as a means of behavior control, *internalization* has occurred (27). Internalization exists when individuals conform because they believe in their actions and not for external rewards or punishments. The conformity is consistent with their values, and so conformity is self-rewarding. It is the means by which children truly acquire the values, attitudes, and beliefs of their parents and other socialization agents.

Social learning theorists believe the same two mechanisms that guide socialization in general—rewards and punishments and observational learning—also provide the sources of internalization. Internalization that derives from previous rewards or punishments was demonstrated in a study of 8–10-year-old children, who were placed in a room with an adult and two toys (28). One of the toys was much more attractive to the children than the other. The children were asked repeatedly to choose between the two toys. The adult rewarded the children with praise and candy when they selected the less attractive toy and said nothing when they picked the more attractive toy. After only two or three trials, the children consistently selected the less attractive toy. How did the researchers know this behavior had been internalized? After the adult had left the room most of the children reached for the less attractive toy first, even though the adult could not reward them for or even know of their choices.

Internalization also derives from observational learning. In Chapter 2 we described a study in which children saw an adult either rewarded or punished for playing aggressively with a Bobo doll (29). Later, when given an opportunity to play with this doll, children who had seen the adult punished for aggressive play imitated the adult less than children who had seen the adult rewarded for the play. This study demonstrates that the children had learned to control their behaviors by internal means through observation of another's outcomes.

Cognitive Developmental Theory

The emphasis of cognitive developmental theory is on cognitive maturation. Cognitive developmental theory was first proposed by the Swiss psychologist, Jean Piaget (30). According to Piaget, children pass through four stages in the course of their cognitive development. The first, the *sensorimotor stage,* lasts from birth to about 1½ years. During this stage, the child reacts to objects in terms of their physical characteristics. Thus, at this stage, children respond to their stuffed animals as soft, cuddly objects, rather than as toys or symbols of real animals.

The second stage, the *preoperational stage,* lasts from about 1½ to 7 years of age. During it, children become markedly more proficient in the use of symbols. To illustrate, children recognize the stuffed animal as a play animal, a toy, and the object that goes to bed with them at naptime. In this stage, children's thinking about an object centers on the most salient perceptual feature of that object. For example, children believe a cup of water poured into a tall, narrow glass contains a greater amount of water than the same cup of water poured into a short, wide glass.

The third stage is the *concrete-operational stage,* which occurs from ages 7 to 11. Here, children learn the principle of conservation of matter. Thus, chil-

dren now recognize a cup of water contains the same amount of water, regardless of the shape of the container that it is in. They also begin to think in relational terms at this stage. For example, children at this stage can correctly answer the question, "If Mark is older than Jason, and Jason is older than Kent, who is older, Mark or Kent?"

The fourth stage is *formal operations,* which starts at about age 11. This stage is marked by mature, conceptual thought characteristic of adult mental activity. The child is now capable of abstract and systematic reasoning.

Researchers today now think the stages are not as rigid as Piaget believed them to be (31). Cognitive skills develop gradually, rather than in sudden leaps. They further believe Piaget underestimated infants' and young children's cognitive skills. For example, first graders show evidence of concrete reasoning and sometimes even formal operations.

The cognitive stages are not simply a result of maturation; they also involve socialization. Experience and social interaction are critical to the child's movement from stage to stage. In fact, Piaget stressed the extent to which children are actively involved in their own learning and, thus, in their passages from one stage to the next. Children seek information and experiences that help them understand their worlds. Individual differences in socialization, such as children's experiences with family, peers, and school, facilitate or hinder passage through these stages. Some families expose their children to more abstract thinking than others, and this exposure facilitates the children's acquisition of formal-operational thinking.

The child's rate of passage through these stages is also influenced by cultural factors. Generally, children who live in urban centers and have attended school show greater cognitive skills than children who live in rural areas and have not attended school (32). However, such differences may be due only to the lack of familiarity with the stimuli being used to elicit cognitive skills, rather than to differences in cognitive abilities.

Moral development Piaget's early theory of moral development has been extended by Lawrence Kohlberg (33). According to Piaget, stages of moral development are parallel and dependent upon the four stages of cognitive development. Kohlberg believes three levels of morality exist. At each level there are two stages of moral development. According to Kohlberg, the stages form an invariant sequence. The stages are reached in a specific order, although an individual may stop developing at any stage. Each stage represents a different mode of moral thought, involving different ideas about what is right and different justifications for doing what is right.

At level one, *preconventional morality,* moral behavior is defined in terms of good and bad events, rather than by standards of behavior. Preconventional morality contains stages one and two. Individuals at the stage one level of development believe it is right to be obedient for the sake of obedience, and that one should not break rules that will result in punishment. They do what is right for two reasons: to avoid punishment and because authorities have superior power. People at stage two believe it is right to follow rules, but only when the rules are in their own best interests. Stage two individuals do what is right in order to be fair, but only as long as their own needs are also served. Their view of fairness is to trade favor for favor with others.

At level two, *conventional morality,* moral behavior is thought to consist of maintaining the conventional social order and meeting people's expectations. Conventional morality contains stages three and four. Individuals at stage three believe it is right to live up to the expectations of family and friends. Stage three individuals do what is right in order to be good people in their own eyes and in the eyes of others. Persons at stage four believe it is right to fulfill duties they have agreed to fulfill. They do what is right in order to avoid the breakdown of the social system.

At level three, *postconventional morality,* morality consists of conformity to individual as well as universal ethical principles. Postconventional morality contains stages five and six. People at stage five believe most rules are relative to the situation. For them, what is right depends upon the situation, although a few nonrelative or overriding rules (the support of liberty, the protection of life) exist. They do what is right out of a sense of obligation to the law and to culturally agreed upon moral principles. In stage six, individuals follow self-chosen ethical principles. People at stage six do what is right because of their belief in universal moral principles, such as justice.

A number of studies have shown that stage of moral development can be used to predict the incidence of prosocial and antisocial behavior in children and adults (36). In one study, 7-year-olds at higher levels of moral development were more likely to donate candy to poor children and to help a younger child complete a task than 7-year-olds at lower levels of moral development (37). However, other studies find inconsistencies in people's moral behaviors (38). An individual who would not cheat in one situation may lie in another. These findings are not consistent with Kohlberg's idea of a single stage of moral development that guides all behaviors.

Kohlberg believes these stages develop in a universal sequence, and most of the cross-cultural data support his view. These stages have been shown to develop in the same order in over 40 societies (39). For example, people in India (40), the United States, and Papua New Guinea (41) progress through the stages in the same way. However, progression to the final stages of moral development—postconventional reasoning—is only characteristic of people in complex urbanized societies (42). Some people in the United States and India, but none in Papua New Guinea, reach stages five and six. It is possible that people in folk societies do reach these stages, but the cultural biases of researchers have prevented them from detecting evidence of the higher stages in these societies (43).

Other evidence suggests men and women approach moral dilemmas in different ways (44). When using real life dilemmas, such as whether or not to have an abortion, men are oriented toward questions of justice (Is it right to have an abortion? Whose decision should this be?), while women are oriented toward caring and the relationships of those involved (Could I have a good relationship with this child? What responsibilities do I have toward my boyfriend?). One limitation of Kohlberg's system is

BOX 4-2

Measurement of Moral Development

How can an individual's level of moral development be determined? It can be measured by the person's responses to hypothetical moral dilemmas. Here is one moral dilemma used by Kohlberg:

In Europe, a woman was near death from a special kind of cancer. There was one drug that the doctors thought might save her. It was a special form of radium that a druggist in the same town had recently discovered. The drug was expensive to make, but the druggist was charging five times what it cost him to make it. He paid $400 for the radium, and charged $2,000 for a small dose of the drug. The sick woman's husband, Heinz, went to everyone he knew to borrow the money, but he could only get together about $1,000, half of what it cost. He told the druggist that his wife was dying, and asked him to sell it cheaper or let him pay later. But the druggist said, "No. I discovered the drug and I'm going to make money from it, so I won't let you have it unless you give me $2,000 now." So Heinz got desperate and broke into the man's store to steal the drug for his wife (34).

The individuals are then asked to answer a series of questions such as, "Should Heinz have done that?" "Was it actually right or wrong?" "Why?" The individuals' levels of moral development are assessed from their answers. The following responses to the Heinz dilemma provide examples of various stages of moral development (35).

that it focuses on justice orientations, but ignores relationship orientations.

In summary, three competing theories of socialization were presented. From the psychoanalytic viewpoint, socialization takes place through unconscious processes, as does the development of morality. Social learning theorists view observation as the primary learning mechanism and behavioral consequences as the determinant of imitation. In this view, morality is developed through internalization of society's values. According to cognitive developmental theorists, socialization as well as moral development occur as a result of cognitive maturation and cultural exposure.

Both psychoanalytic theory and cognitive developmental theory are stage theories, the former governed by unconscious processes and the latter by age-linked cognitive processes. In contrast, the social learning theorists view socialization as a continuous process, and focus upon learning rather than internal maturational processes. Of the three theories, social learning theory and cognitive developmental theory are more testable and are accepted by more social psychologists.

Stage One: Orientation toward Punishment and Obedience

Pro: "He should steal the drug. It isn't really bad to take it. It isn't like he didn't ask to pay for it first. The drug he'd take is only worth $200; he's not really taking a $2,000 drug."

Con: "He shouldn't steal the drug: it's a big crime. He didn't get permission, he used force, and broke and entered. He did a lot of damage, stealing a very expensive drug and breaking up the store, too."

Stage Three: Morality of Conventional Role-Conformity

Pro: "He should steal the drug. He was only doing something that was natural for a husband to do. You can't blame him for doing something out of love for his wife. You'd blame him if he didn't love his wife enough to save her."

Con: "He shouldn't steal. If his wife dies, he can't be blamed. It isn't because he's heartless or that he doesn't love her enough to do everything that he legally can. The druggist is the selfish and heartless one."

Stage Six: Morality of Individual Principles and Conscience

Pro: "This is a situation which forces him to choose between stealing and letting his wife die. In a situation where the choice must be made, it is morally right to steal. He has to act in terms of the principle of preserving and respecting life."

Con: "Heinz is faced with the decision of whether to consider the other people who need the drug just as badly as his wife. Heinz ought to act, not according to his particular feelings toward his wife, but considering the value of all the lives involved." ■

■ CHARACTERISTICS OF SOCIALIZATION

Continuity and Change

Sociologists emphasize continuity as well as change in both people and societies (45). Age norms produce a certain amount of continuity across generations. We divide human life into stages—infancy, childhood, adolescence, maturity, and old age. In each of these stages, norms and expectations exist regarding what individuals should be doing. Such events as education, entry into the labor market, marriage, birth of one's first child, and becoming a grandparent are a function of social as well as biological timing. The culture regulates the occurrence of these events, and the timing is rather precise. For instance, virtually all adults know whether they married "on time," or married early or late with respect to our society's norms about age of marriage. These age norms are a part of social time or of society's *age grading*.

Another dimension of time, the historical, ensures that socialization never results in a duplication of the last generation. Historical time interacts with social time, producing a unique social system in each generation. Because society changes, people age, or progress through social time, in different ways. People differ in the historical and cultural experiences to which their age group is exposed. During any historical period, we are influenced by the economic, political, and social events that occur during our lifetimes. For example, the Vietnam War radically influenced the lives of young people during the author's youth. The education, careers, and family lives of many young men were irrevocably changed by the onset of this war. Currently, student choices of college majors seem to be influenced by the relatively volatile state of the economy. Students now are more likely to ask whether they can get jobs when they graduate with a given major than they were in the past.

While cultural continuity thus is ensured through the socialization process, cultural change is also an inevitable result. The "generation gap" is one consequence of this change. Each generation of parents attempts to socialize its children as it was socialized. Parents view the current social climate as too permissive and believe that their children lack sufficient respect for the traditions they attempt to pass on. In turn, each generation of children reacts against the parents' rules, which it perceives as old-fashioned and repressive. Ironically, the hippies and flower children of the late 1960s and early 1970s are now the parents that today's relatively conservative college students are rebelling against.

Because each age group passes through social and historical time in its own unique way, it contributes to changes in the social structure. For example, childhood itself is a relatively late conception in Western European culture. Before the 17th century, childhood was not recognized as a distinct age phase. Children were treated as small adults, and their special needs were not recognized (46). The timing of family life events in the last ten years provides another example of this type of change. Because women are now having fewer children, they bear their last child at a relatively young age, compared with past generations of women. This is one of several changes that has led to a view of motherhood as a temporary stage, rather than a life-long occupation, for women.

Reciprocal Socialization

Both sociologists and psychologists recognize the reciprocal or bidirectional nature of socialization. Children are not passive agents in socialization, to be acted upon and changed by adults. Instead, children play an active and important role in their own socialization (47). Attention was first drawn to children's role in their own socialization by research findings difficult to interpret within the traditional framework of adults influencing passive children. To illustrate, siblings are often quite different in personality, even though they may be reared in apparently similar ways. Because of these personality differences, children sometimes react in dissimilar ways to the same child rearing practices, even to the same incident. One child, scolded for some misbehavior, may become repentant. Another may become even more persistent in performing the behavior. These personality differences between

"You're lucky—When I was your age, I had to walk to school on all fours."
(The Wall Street Journal.)

siblings are often apparent in the first few days of an infant's life. To be successful, socialization practices must be adapted to the individual's personality.

Many studies of parent-child socialization show a relationship between parental behaviors and characteristics of their children. In the past, these relationships were interpreted as showing the parents' influence on the children. Now, however, researchers realize the relationship also reflects the children's influence on the parents. In a study of reciprocal socialization, investigators examined the political, religious, and gender attitudes of a set of adults, their parents, and their grandparents (48). As expected, parental attitudes influenced their children's attitudes even after the children became adults. This was true both of the attitudes of the adults and their parents and of the parents and the grandparents. While parents' influence on their children decreased with age, the children's influences on parental attitudes remained relatively strong for both adult-parent and parent-grandparent dyads. As can be seen in Figure 4-1, the differences in attitudes are quite small, less than a single scale point for each dyad where the possible differences were over 15 points. The attitude consistency was a little stronger for the political and religious topics than for gender, probably because of the rapid changes in gender norms in the last few decades.

This reciprocal process of socialization is due in part to *role negotiation,* or attempts to define one's role and that of relevant others to one's own satisfaction (49). A preschool boy not only responds to his parents' expectations but also expects—and attempts to elicit—certain behaviors from them as well. Further, many roles are not highly regimented, so the person has considerable power in determining how the role expectations will be filled. A 5-year-old son may have to fulfill his parents' expectations of that role, but 5-year-old boys can exercise these obligations in different ways. Some boys are more independent than others at that age, and some families accept independence more easily. Each boy and his parents must together negotiate an acceptable level of independence for the boy, given the inclinations of each party.

Figure 4.1 ■

Mean Absolute Differences between Generations in Three-Generation Families

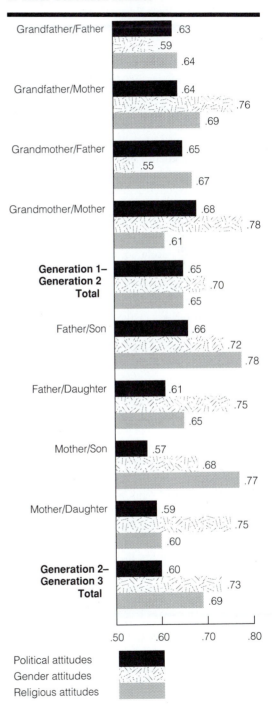

Socialization Across Societies

If one knows the society in which an infant will be socialized, one knows much about the ultimate social being the child will become (50). Societies with different cultural traditions instill different behaviors and attitudes in their members. Socialization practices are generally successful in producing the expected type of persons. We do not mean to suggest that different cultures require specific personality traits in their members. For example, not all U.S. citizens are socialized to be achievement oriented or competitive, even though those behaviors generally are rewarded. In a society as complex as ours, such specific socialization would be impossible. However, all societies define certain behaviors as unacceptable and attempt to control them and define others as desirable and attempt to promote them. The particular behaviors defined as acceptable and unacceptable vary from society to society. In the United States, for example, physical aggression is defined as unacceptable, and is punished, while competitive behavior is defined as desirable, and is rewarded. In other societies, where such a great distinction between acts of physical aggression and competition does not exist, both types of behaviors might be controlled or both promoted.

Socialization practices are also adapted to economic and political structures. All cultures utilize the technological and natural resources available to them, and socialization practices reflect these realities. In addition, gender-role socialization prepares individuals to function under exactly the type of economy that sustains the society (51). In hunting-and-gathering societies, where males hunt large game and women gather wild foods, gender-role differences are typically rather large. The males are socialized to be much more independent and self-reliant than are females. In societies such as ours, where the work of men and women is more similar, these differences are smaller.

Children are also trained to conform to the existing political system. As we mentioned earlier, children in the Soviet Union are socialized to be cooperative, since they are expected to comply with the rules of their socialistic government. Children in the United States do not receive such extensive training in cooperation. Rather, they are socialized early to be independent—a type of training compatible with our democratic political philosophy.

■

SOCIALIZATION THROUGH THE LIFE CYCLE

We typically associate socialization with childhood. However, socialization actually extends throughout the life cycle (52). Fortunately, we never stop learning and adapting to change! In this section we will discuss differences between childhood and adult socialization, and examine socialization in later life. We will then explore a theory of psychosocial stages, the life conflicts with which people must cope in their journey from infancy through old age. We will end this chapter with an examination of resocialization and of the last stage of socialization, into old age and dying.

Socialization in Childhood and Adulthood

Childhood and adult socialization differ on at least two dimensions. First, they differ in content (53). In childhood, much of the learning that takes place involves introduction to the society's system of values and norms. This type of learning applies to a variety of situations. For example, children learn the Golden Rule—that they should treat others as they wish to be treated. While some material learned in adult socialization is new, much adult socialization involves synthesizing what has been learned in other contexts. For instance, in scuba diving one learns to combine swimming, snorkling, and water safety skills. Further, in adulthood much of the learning involves specific behaviors appropriate for a given role, such as training for one's chosen profession.

Second, differences exist in adults' and children's motivations to learn. Much adult socialization is voluntary, such as acquiring the education needed to obtain a new position or the skills necessary to engage in a new activity. Adults thus do not need much external motivation to begin the learning process. Despite children's interest in learning new activities, a considerable amount of childhood socialization is not intrinsically rewarding. Children do not want to learn to be toilet-trained, eat with a fork, nor clean their rooms. As discussed earlier, much childhood socialization necessitates motivating the child to begin to learn—typically through the use of rewards and punishments.

Adult Socialization

We are not always aware of the extent to which we undergo socialization in adulthood. Important areas where adult socialization occurs include the work place, the family, and the community. One way in which adult socialization has been studied is by exploring the common changes adults experience in these domains (54).

The work place A person must choose an occupation and learn to perform it. During the course of our working lives, we are likely to be promoted, demoted, or change jobs. These changes will be accompanied by changes in interpersonal relationships at work and in levels of aspiration. These occupational changes require socialization, a task in which coworkers will play an active role. For example, when you take a new job, your co-workers will not only give you tips about performing it, but they will also share information with you on the informal norms of the organization and the characteristics of other employees. They may tell you, for example, that your boss hates tardiness and that the person at the next desk asks for help with his work, but never returns the favor. This information can be useful as you adjust to a new working environment.

Socialization among a group of Los Angeles prostitutes provides an example of occupational socialization (55). Socialization into this occupation is surprisingly similar to socialization into more accepted occupations. As in many occupations, pros-

titutes first consider entering prostitution after having contact with another person in that occupation. Like most individuals entering an occupation, prostitutes go through a formal training period. Prostitutes typically become apprenticed to another prostitute for a period of two or three months. The apprentice works out of an apartment, learning by supervised on-the-job training. She is also tutored by her teacher in such skills as telephone solicitation, physical hygiene, and dealing with problem situations. The apprentice is taught various norms of the profession, such as working quickly and limiting unnecessary interaction with customers. She is also exposed to values of the occupation that both promote identification with prostitution and help the apprentice reject the negative appraisals of the larger society regarding her occupation.

The family Changes also occur in the course of family life. Individuals who marry and have children must adapt to these roles, both of which constitute life crises that require major adjustments by individuals, even though they also provide major sources of personal satisfaction. Through the years, the relationships between the husband and wife and between the parents and children undergo many changes. During these changes, the family members attempt to socialize each other to their changing views of family life. For example, teenagers start demanding more freedom at the same time parents require greater responsibility from them.

Retirement is another major life adjustment that involves socialization. Men, in particular, have difficulty leaving the work place—the major source of their identity and esteem. In a recent cross-cultural study, women choose to retire from the labor force in old age more frequently than men, even in societies with low public pensions and no norm of retirement (57).

The community Within the community, people are likely to assume new roles and drop others. Most individuals will move from one community to another at least once during the course of their lives. Such changes require accommodation to new lifestyles and local norms. Here, too, role occupants

BOX 4-3

Socialization into New Occupations

Being socialized into a new job can be difficult enough, but what if the job is a newly created one? Is being socialized into a new job even more difficult than being socialized into an already existing one?

To answer this latter question, researchers explored the learning and adjustment of over 2,400 British managers taking new jobs in their companies, some of whom moved to jobs without previous occupants and some of whom moved to jobs with previous occupants (56). They found that socialization into a brand new job is indeed more difficult than socialization into an established one. Managers moving to newly created jobs found fewer sources of help in work adjustment than managers moving to established jobs. In addition, managers moving to newly created jobs found job training received from bosses, subordinates, colleagues, company literature, job specifications, and in-company training programs less useful than managers moving to established jobs. This more informal and ineffective job socialization had negative personal consequences. Managers moving to newly created jobs also felt they had to cope with more change on the job, felt work was less predictable, and believed their chances of career success were more the result of external forces, such as luck and office politics, than managers moving to established jobs. ∎

will assist newcomers in learning new roles. If, for example, your behavior conflicts with the norms of your new community because you drink and do not attend church, your neighbors are likely to let you know you are not meeting the standards of behavior of more established members of the community.

Like childhood socialization, adult socialization is undertaken by many agents who may attempt to impress conflicting values and goals on the individual. In adulthood, too, the particular forces that act on the individual vary by his or her social class, ethnicity, and sex. Just as childhood socialization is inconsistent within and across individuals in a given society, so too is adult socialization. Socialization cannot be separated from its social context.

Erikson's Psychosocial Stages

Emotional growth is another component of the life-long process of socialization. Throughout the course of life we learn to understand ourselves better and to resolve our problems more effectively. Certain conflicts and problems of identity seem to be an inevitable part of life, and learning to resolve them provides one mechanism of emotional growth.

Erik Erikson has developed a theory of psycho-social stages to describe eight types of life conflict which are experienced from birth through old age (58). Erikson believes every individual passes through these stages, each of which revolves around one primary conflict or identity problem. The individual may or may not resolve the conflict in question successfully. A successful resolution adds a healthy dimension to the individual's personality. Failure means an unhealthy dimension is added, and the issue involved may color the individual's attitudes and expectations throughout the remainder of life.

Stages one through five involve ego development from infancy through adolescence. These psychosocial stages parallel Freud's psychosexual stages (see Table 4.1 for a comparison of Freud's psychosexual and Erikson's psychosocial stages). According to Erikson:

■ Stage one involves *trust vs. mistrust*. Stage one occurs during the first year of life. The primary issue at this stage is whether the infant's needs are met in a reliable way. At the end of the first year, infants are left with a basic feeling of trust or of mistrust in people.

■ Stage two, during year two, involves feelings of *autonomy vs. doubt*. The principle issue at this stage is the young child's feelings of self-control. Children leave this stage with a sense of independence or with a sense of doubt and shame.

■ Stage three, during years 3 to 5, involves *initiative vs. guilt*. At this stage, the child attempts self-initiated activities. The child leaves this stage either with a sense of achievement or with a sense of guilt over committing unacceptable acts.

■ Stage four, during years 6 to 10, involves feelings of *industry vs. inferiority*. At this stage, the child is concerned with the issues of reasoning and obedience. The child leaves this stage feeling either productive or inadequate.

■ Stage five, during years 11 to 21, involves *identity vs. identity confusion*. Here, the primary issue is identity development. At this stage, the individual either comes to have a sense of self and a clear identity or fails to attain a strong sense of self.

Stages six through eight involve ego development in the adult years.

■ In stage six, during the years 22 to 35, the individual is concerned with *intimacy vs. isolation*. The primary task is to achieve intimacy with another person. This, of course, is the age at which most individuals marry and raise a family.

■ In stage seven, during the years 36 to 65, the person is concerned with *generativity vs. stag-*

Table 4.1 ■

Freud's Psychosexual Stages and Erickson's Psychosocial Stages

Year	Freud's Psychosexual Stages	Erickson's Psychosocial Stages
1	Oral	Trust vs. Mistrust
2	Anal	Autonomy vs. Doubt
3–5	Phallic	Initiative vs. Guilt
6–10	Latency Period	Industry vs. Inferiority
11–21	Genital	Identity vs. Confusion
22–35		Intimacy vs. Isolation
36–65		Generativity vs. Stagnation
65 and over		Integrity vs. Disgust and Despair

nation. The issue here is growth or lack of growth. The individual will either be productive and outer-directed or become self-absorbed.

■ The final stage, during the years 65 and over, concerns *integrity vs. disgust and despair*. The person either feels a sense of pride over life accomplishments or feels he or she has failed in life.

While we have argued that adults are more willingly socialized than children, this statement is not equally true of all adult socialization. In this final section we will explore adult socialization that is typically undertaken reluctantly by adults—resocialization and socialization into old age and beyond.

Resocialization

Resocialization refers to a process in which individuals are subjected to desocialization, or unlearning of a set of behaviors, norms, and values and then relearning of new behaviors, norms, and values. Typically, the resocialization process is forcible, and the behaviors, norms, and values to be unlearned have been deemed socially unacceptable and those to be relearned are more socially acceptable ones. Resocialization is commonly attempted by total institutions—institutions that bar individuals of a particular type from life in the outside world and attempt to completely control their behavior (59). Examples of total institutions include prisons, mental hospitals, nursing homes, and, to an extent, the military. Total institutions have a number of extreme socialization practices. For example, all aspects of life (work, play, living arrangements) are conducted in the same place and are governed by the same authority. Daily activities are strictly scheduled in accordance with the goals of the institution. These conditions have a single goal: the surrender of the inhabitant's autonomy.

■ *Life aboard a ship is an example of a total institution. (WGS)*

Total institutions deprive people of their individuality through a number of mechanisms. The inhabitants' appearances are typically made more similar through standard institutional clothing. Their individual possessions are severely limited. The inhabitants may even lose the use of their names. For example, prisoners may be called by number, and mental patients are typically called by their first names. Further, inhabitants are strictly required to obey the rules, which are backed by a system of rewards and punishments. At the same time, the inhabitants also lose their identification with life outside the institution: they no longer fulfill the occupational, familial, and recreational roles that formerly gave them a sense of identity.

The complete control desired by the total institution is never quite achieved, despite the intentions and practices of the authorities. Even in total institutions, there are methods by which the inhabitants can subvert the institution's complete control over them. These arrangements are called *secondary adjustments*. Inhabitants can make arrangements with employees of the institution for goods and services outlawed by the institution. They can use their jobs in the institutions to procure illicit goods and services or merely to avoid surveillance by the institutional staff. Inhabitants can create problems for the staff—either by uncooperative behavior, complaining, or by acts that subvert the staff members' duties. For example, mental patients can refuse their medicines, complain about the nurses, or bump into an orderly and cause him or her to drop a tray of medicine.

Total institutions exist in degree, not in kind. That is, even the most coercive institution involves some freedoms, and our society's institutions (the educational system, the family) involve some inflexibility and coercion. One can take any social institution and examine it for elements of total institutions and study the effects of these elements on those who are influenced by them.

Old Age and Beyond

Old age and death are the final life stages. Each of them requires socialization into its characteristics and components. Unfortunately, in our society much of the socialization into old age involves learning negative stereotypes, and socialization into death requires the giving up of life. The negative qualities of these types of socialization bear some resemblance to the process of resocialization.

The stigma of old age Old age is a stage of life that has only recently been given serious attention by researchers. However, increased longevity means the elderly now form a significant proportion of our population. As the numbers of elderly have increased, greater attention has been drawn to them.

"Old age" as a stage of life is an invention of the 20th century, largely attributable to increased lifespans and fixed retirement ages (60). When lifespans were shorter and retirement less common, few persons lived long after their working lives were over. Therefore, working adulthood was the final stage of life for most persons. Now there are many retired people who live longer, healthier lives.

Our concept of aging has also changed in this century. In the 19th century, aging was viewed as a natural process, associated with wisdom and survival of the fittest. Old age is still associated with status and wisdom in many societies, and among some minority groups in this society. In the 20th century, however, many of us have come to associate aging with deterioration, dependence, and physical unattractiveness. Forgetfulness is thought to be an almost inevitable consequence of aging. The combination of this negative view of aging and the loss of income associated with retirement has created a climate in which the aged often experience hardship and discrimination.

Researchers question the validity of the association of these negative characteristics with aging, asking if these states are really correlated with old age or if we have wrongly been socialized to perceive a nonexistent correlation of old age with them. It appears the latter may be the case. For example, only 14 percent of persons over 65 suffer from forgetfulness and less than one third of this 14 percent experience a severe form of this problem (61). As for physical attractiveness, it clearly exists

■ *Not just shuffling along. Contrary to stereotype, many elderly people are healthy and active. (WGS)*

in the eye of the beholder. Photographers and artists have long been fascinated by the beauty of old age.

Despite these and other data, evidence is growing that we have convinced our elderly they are infirm and incompetent when most of them are not. There have been recent demonstrations that, with encouragement, elderly persons considered to be incompetent can show increased competent behavior. In one study, when the environment in a nursing home was restructured so residents were given tangible rewards for remembering information, increased memory resulted. Further, these increases generalized to other behaviors. The residents also increased in alertness, mental activity, and social adjustment (62).

Because we have convinced the elderly in this society they are declining, physically and mentally, many older persons overestimate the decrements in their physical and mental capabilities attributable to old age (63). For example, the elderly tend to attribute their forgetfulness to aging. They do not notice that younger persons are forgetful also, nor do they recall their own forgetfulness when they were younger. Younger people not only overestimate the declines the elderly experience, they also add to the problems of the elderly by treating them as though they are incompetent. This acceptance of the negative characteristics of aging by most segments of the society leads to lowered motivation and self-esteem on the part of the elderly. These, in turn, result in an increase in their symptoms. Recently, the elderly have begun to organize and use their political power to protest the negative images of aging in this society and the resulting discrimination.

Death and dying   In the drama of life, the last act is death. Just as we pass through stages in the course of our lives, so also do we pass through stages in the course of dying. Elizabeth Kubler-Ross has proposed that people in modern western societies go through five stages in the course of dying (64). The first stage is *denial.* In this stage, dying individuals refuse to acknowledge the fact they will soon die. The second stage is *anger.* In it, the dying feel frustrated and angry they must die. In the third stage, *bargaining* takes place. People attempt to bargain for life, typically with God, but in some cases with medical personnel. They try to make deals in which they will do good deeds for humankind if only they will be allowed to live. The fourth stage is *depression.* As their diseases progress, people can no longer deny the fact that they are dying. Their anger turns to depression. This stage is accompanied by fear of death and withdrawal. The final stage is *acceptance.* Here, the individuals cease to struggle against death.

More recent research suggests that these stages may be typical only of middle-class majority group members (65). They might best be thought of as feelings the dying may experience. Some individuals experience other emotions while dying. Others may become fixated at one of the stages, may experience two stages at the same time, or may go back and forth between stages. Clearly, however, socialization into our culture, social class, and family influences how we leave life. We learn how to die, just as we learn how to live.

■ SUMMARY

Socialization involves the process of teaching members of the society what they need to learn to maintain social life. All societies are faced with this task. They must ensure physical survival for their members so new generations can be born, and they must make certain that individuals understand the system of roles the society has developed and conform to the system. Language is an important prerequisite for socialization, and many researchers believe only humans have language abilities.

The agents of socialization include the family, the school, the peer group, and the media. The family is the most important socialization agent in the early years. The mother, as well as the father, plays an important role in the socialization process. The school and the church also become important agents after the school years begin. Peers and the media further contribute to childhood socialization.

Three theories of the processes of socialization were presented: psychoanalytic theory, social learning theory, and cognitive developmental theory. Freud understood that the conscious mind is influenced by unconscious urges and ideas that are unacceptable to it. He believed that socialization is accomplished by the individual's passage through four psychosexual stages (oral stage, anal stage, phallic stage, latency period, and genital stage) between infancy and adulthood. These stages specify the source of the individual's sexual energy at a given time. The personality is composed of the id, ego, and superego. The child develops a sense of morality through the operation of the superego.

Social learning theory suggests we are socialized through two processes—direct reward and punishment and observational learning. However, self-reinforcement is the most important form of behavioral regulation for older children and adults.

Cognitive developmental theory suggests children pass through stages of cognitive development in which their reasoning becomes increasingly abstract and systematic. According to the cognitive developmental theory of moral development, individuals go through an invariant sequence of six stages of moral development, from an emphasis on obedience and punishment to an emphasis on universal moral principles.

Socialization has a number of characteristics. First, socialization is reciprocal: The child plays an active, rather than a passive, role in socialization. Second, socialization involves both continuity and change. Continuity in socialization is promoted through age grading. Socialization also promotes change because each generation lives in a different historical time. This means each generation is different from every other, and each generation promotes societal change. Third, socialization varies from family to family and society to society.

Socialization is a life-long process. Childhood and adult socialization differ in content (society's norms and values vs. synthesis of previous learnings) and in motivations to learn (reluctance vs. eagerness). Considerable adult socialization occurs in the work place, the family, and the community. Erickson's psychosocial theory suggests individuals pass through eight stages from birth to old age. Each of these stages deals with an identity conflict which must be resolved.

Resocialization is the unlearning of unacceptable behaviors, norms, and values and the relearning of more socially acceptable ones. Resocialization is commonly attempted in total institutions—institutions that attempt to bar individuals from the outside world and completely control their behaviors. Interestingly, total institutions fail to achieve the total social control they seek.

Socialization into old age and death bear some resemblance to resocialization. In our society the negative attitudes many people hold regarding aging result in the elderly being stigmatized. Kubler-Ross's theory of death and dying suggests there is a process through which people go in accepting their own deaths. She believes that the typical progression goes from denial to acceptance. However, there may be no typical way to die.

■

REFERENCES

1. Bronfenbrenner, U., 1970, *Two Worlds of Childhood,* New York: Russell Sage.

2. Bronfenbrenner, U., 1958, "Socialization and Social Class Through Time and Space," in E. E. Maccoby, T. M. Newcomb, and E. L. Hartley (Eds.), *Readings in Social Psychology,* New York: Holt, Rinehart & Winston.

3. Denzin, N. K., 1977, *Childhood Socialization,* San Francisco: Jossey-Bass.

4. Brown, R. W., 1972, "Feral and Isolated Man," in *Language,* V. P. Clarke et al. (Eds.), New York: St. Martin's.

5. Davis, K., 1940, "Extreme Social Isolation of a Child," *American Journal of Sociology* 45:554–565; K. Davis, 1947, "A Final Note on a Case of Extreme Isolation," *American Journal of Sociology* 52:432–437.

6. Inkeles, A., 1968. "Society, Social Structure, and Child Socialization," in J. A. Clausen (Ed.), *Socialization and Society,* Boston: Little, Brown.

7. Swidler, A., 1986, "Culture in Action: Symbols and Strategies," *American Sociological Review* 51:273–286.

8. Herman, L. M., D. G. Richards, and J. P. Wolz, 1984, "Comprehension of Sentences by Bottlenosed Dolphins," *Cognition* 16:129–219; F. Patterson, 1978, "Conversations with a Gorilla," *National Geographic* 154:438–465.

9. Premack, D., 1985, " 'Gavagai!' or the Future History of the Animal Language Controversy," *Cognition* 19:207–296; H. Terrace, 1979, *Nim: A Chimpanzee Who Learned Sign Language,* New York: Knopf.

10. The next three sections draw from V. Gecas, 1981, "Contexts of Socialization," in M. Rosenberg and R. H. Turner (Eds.), *Social Psychology: Sociological Perspectives,* New York: Basic Books.

11. This discussion draws from D. B. Lynn, 1974, *The Father: His Role in Child Development,* Belmont, CA: Wadsworth.

12. Masur, E. F. and J. B. Gleason, 1980, "Parent-Child Interaction and the Acquisition of Lexical Information During Play," *Developmental Psychology* 16:404–409.

13. Grebler, L., J. W. Moore, and R. C. Guzman, 1970, *The Mexican-American People,* New York: The Free Press.

14. Inkeles, 1968, op. cit.

15. Maccoby, E. E., 1980, *Social Development,* New York: Harcourt Brace Jovanovich.

16. Brim, O. G., Jr., 1968, "Adult Socialization," in J. A. Clausen, op. cit.

17. McCandless, B. R., 1969, "Childhood Socialization," in D. A. Goslin (Ed.), *Handbook of Socialization Theory and Research,* Chicago: Rand McNally.

18. Fine, G. A., 1981, "Friends, Impression Management, and Preadolescent Behavior," in J. Gottman and S. Asher (Eds.), *The Development of Children's Friendship,* New York: Cambridge University Press.

19. Giordano, P. C., S. A. Cernkovich, and M. D. Pugh, 1986, "Friendships and Delinquency," *American Journal of Sociology* 91:1170–1202.

20. This section draws from O. N. Larsen, 1964, "Social Effects of Mass Communication," in R. E. L. Faris (Ed.), *Handbook of Modern Sociology,* Chicago: Rand McNally.

21. National Institute of Mental Health, 1982, *Television and Behavior: 10 Years of Scientific Progress and Implications for the Eighties,* Vols. 1 and 2, Washington, DC: U.S. Government Printing Office.

22. McLuhan, M. and Q. Fiore, 1967, *The Medium is the Massage,* New York: Bantam.

23. Czitrom, D. J., 1982, *Media and the American Mind,* Chapel Hill: University of North Carolina Press.

24. McCandless, 1969, op. cit.

25. Freud, S., 1905, *Three Essays on the Theory of Sexuality,* New York: Avon Books, 1965; S. Freud, 1925, *Collected Papers,* Vol. 5, London: Hogarth, 1950. This section draws on G. E. Swanson, "Mead and Freud: Their Relevance for Social Psychology," in J. G. Manis and B. N. Melzer (Eds.), *Symbolic Interaction* (2nd ed.). Boston: Allyn & Bacon; and C. S. Hall and G. Lindzey, 1957, *Theories of Personality,* New York: Wiley.

26. Bandura, A., 1977, *Social Learning Theory,* Englewood Cliffs, NJ: Prentice-Hall; J. Aronfreed, 1968, *Conduct and Conscience: The Socialization of Internalized Control over Behavior,* New York: Academic Press.

27. Aronfreed, 1968, ibid.

28. Aronfreed, 1968, ibid.

29. Bandura, A., D. Ross, and S. Ross, 1963, "Imitation of Film-mediated Aggressive Models," *Journal of Abnormal and Social Psychology* 66:3–11.

30. Piaget, J., 1970, "Piaget's Theory," in P. H. Mussen (Ed.), *Carmichael's Manual of Child Psychology,* Vol. 1, 3d ed., New York: Wiley.

31. Flavel, J. H., 1985, *Cognitive Development,* 2nd ed., Englewood Cliffs, NJ: Prentice-Hall; R. Selman, 1980, *The Growth of Interpersonal Understanding,* New York: Academic Press.

32. Chi, M. T. H. and S. J. Ceci, 1987, "Content Knowledge: It's Role, Representation, and Restructuring in Memory Development," in H. W. Reese (Ed.), *Advances in Child Development and Behavior,* Vol. 20, New York: Academic Press; B. Rogoff, M. Gauvain, and S. Ellis, 1984, "Development Viewed in Its Cultural Context," in M. H. Bornstein and M. E. Lamb (Eds.), *Developmental Psychology: An Advanced Textbook,* Hillsdale, NJ: Erlbaum.

33. Kohlberg, L., 1969, "Stage and Sequence: The Cognitive-Developmental Approach to Socialization," in D. A. Goslin (Ed.), *Handbook of Socialization Theory and Research,* Chicago: Rand-McNally.

34. Kohlberg, 1969, ibid.

35. Kohlberg, 1969, ibid.

36. e.g., Brown, M. E., S. H. Schwartz, K. A. Feldman, and A. Heingarter, 1969, "Some Personality Correlates of Conduct in Two Situations of Moral Conflict," *Journal of Personality* 37:41–57; D. Krebs and A. Rosenwald, 1977, "Moral Reasoning and Moral Behavior in Conventional Adults," *Merrill Palmer Quarterly* 23:77–87.

37. Rubin, K. H. and F. W. Schneider, 1973, "The Relationship Between Moral Judgment, Egocentrism, and Altruistic Behavior," *Child Development* 44:661–665.

38. Hartshorne, H. and M. A. May, 1928, *Studies in the Nature of Character: Studies in Deceit,* Vol. 1, New York: McMillan.

39. Snarey, J. R., 1985, "Cross-cultural Universality of Social–Moral Development: A Critical Review of Kohlberg's Research," *Psychological Bulletin* 97:202–232.

40. Vasudev, J. and R. C. Hummel, 1987, "Moral Stage Sequence and Principled Reasoning in an Indian Sample," *Human Development* 30:105–118.

41. Tietjen, A. M. and L. J. Walker, 1985, "Moral Reasoning and Leadership Amnong Men in a Papua New Guinea Society," *Developmental Psychology* 21:982–992.

42. Snarey, 1985, op. cit.

43. Snarey, 1985, ibid.

44. Gilligan, C., 1982, *In Another Voice,* Cambridge: Harvard University Press.

45. This section draws from Bengtson, V. L. and Black, K. D., 1973 "Intergenerational Relations and Continuities in Socialization," in P. B. Baltes and K. W. Schaie (Eds.), *Life-Span Developmental Psychology: Personality and Socialization.* New York: Academic Press; B. L. Neugarten and N. Datan, 1973, "Sociological Perspectives on the Life Cycle," in P. B. Baltes and K. W. Schaie, op. cit.; and M. W. Riley, 1987, "On the Significance of Age in Sociology," *American Sociological Review* 52:1–14.

46. Wrong, D. H., 1961, "The Oversocialized Conception of Man in Modern Sociology," *American Sociological Review* 26:183–193.

47. e.g., R. Q. Bell and L. V. Harper, 1977, *Child Effects on Adults,* Hillsdale, NJ: Lawrence Erlbaum.

48. Glass, J., V. L. Bengtson, and C. C. Dunham, 1986, "Attitude Similarity in Three-generation Families: Socialization, Status Inheritance, or Reciprocal Influence?" *American Sociological Review* 51:685–698.

49. Goslin, D. A., 1969, "Introduction," in Goslin, op. cit.

50. This section draws from Inkeles, 1968, op. cit.

51. Barry, H., III, M. K. Bacon, and I. L. Child, 1957, "A Cross-cultural Survey of Some Sex Differences in Socialization," *Journal of Abnormal and Social Psychology* 55:327–332.

52. Bush, D. M. and R. G. Simmons, 1983, "Socialization Processes over the Life Cycle," in M. Rosenberg and R. H. Turner, op. cit.

53. Brim, 1968, ibid.

54. Brim, O. G., Jr., 1966, "Socialization Through the Life Cycle," in O. G. Brim, Jr., and S. Wheeler, *Socialization After Childhood: Two Essays,* New York: Wiley.

55. Bryan, J. H., 1965, "Apprenticeships in Prostitution," *Social Problems* 12:287–297.

56. West, M. A., N. Nicholson, and C. Rees, 1987, "Transitions to Newly Created Jobs," *Journal of Occupational Psychology* 60:97–113.

57. Pampel, F. C. and S. Park, 1986, "Cross-national Patterns and Determinants of Female Retirement," *American Journal of Sociology* 91:932–955.

58. Erikson, E. H., 1963, *Childhood and Society,* 2d ed., New York: W. W. Norton.

59. Goffman, E., 1961, Asylums. Garden City, NY: Anchor.

60. Hareven, T. K., 1978, "The Last Stage: Historical Adulthood and Old Age," in E. H. Erikson (Ed.), Adulthood, 2d ed., New York: W. W. Norton.

61. Rodin, J. and E. Langer, 1980, "Aging Labels: The Decline of Control and the Fall of Self-esteem," *Journal of Social Issues* 36:12–29.

62. Langer, E., J. Rodin, P. Beck, C. Weinman, and L. Spitzer, 1979, "Environmental Determinants of Memory Improvement in Late Adulthood," *Journal of Personality and Social Psychology* 37:2003–2013.

63. Rodin and Langer, 1980, op. cit.

64. Kubler-Ross, E., 1969, *On Death and Dying,* Toronto; Macmillan.

65. Fox, R., 1981, "The Sting of Death in American Society," *Social Service Review* 81:42–59; E. Schneidman, 1980, "Death Work and Stages of Dying," in E. Schneidman (Ed.), *Death: Current Perspectives,* Palo Alto: Mayfield.

CHAPTER 5

The Self

The Development of the Self

The Looking-Glass Self

Mead's View of the Self

Significant Others

The Self-Concept

Measuring the Self-Concept

Identities and the Self

The Changing Self

The Mutable Self

Self-Perception

Self-Perception Theory

Self-Schemata

Self-Presentation

Strategies of Self-Presentation

Individual Differences in Self-Presentation

Self-Esteem

Self-Efficacy and Self-Esteem

To thine own self be true, And it must follow, as the night the day, Thou canst not then be false to any man. Hamlet, Act 1, scene 3

We all know the meaning of the term, the self. In the words of the symbolic interactionist Charles Horton Cooley, the self is "simply that which is designated in common speech by the pronouns of the first person singular, 'I,' 'me,' 'my,' 'mine,' and 'myself'" (1). The self consists of the variety of persisting attitudes of the person toward himself or herself (2). Other issues with respect to the self are not so easily answered. How does our sense of self develop? Of what are our self-concepts composed? How do we decide what traits and characteristics we have? How do we attempt to control the impressions we make on others? How are our levels of self-esteem established? These are the questions sociological social psychologists and psychological social psychologists attempt to answer in their study of the self. We will explore each of these questions in turn.

■

THE DEVELOPMENT OF THE SELF

The development of the self is one focus of study of the symbolic interactionists. A primary tenet of symbolic interactionism is that the self is linked to the society through the interactions of individuals (3). We will trace the development of this idea from early psychology to present day symbolic interactionism.

George Herbert Mead's views of the development of the self have most profoundly influenced social psychology. Mead's view of the self was itself influenced by three contemporary social scientists, James, Dewey, and Cooley.

The psychologist William James (1842–1910) was the first American to study the concept of the self (4). James recognized that two aspects of the self exist: the capacities to develop self-attitudes and self-feelings (the self as *subject*), and the ability to respond to oneself (the self as *object*). He believed that we possess a social self composed of feelings about oneself derived from the reactions of others. Mead was strongly influenced by the concept of the dual nature of the self and the idea that others are important in the development of the self.

John Dewey (1859–1952) was a psychologist and educator. He believed the human capacity to think was the ability that set them apart from other animals. He studied consciousness in an effort to explore the workings of the mind. For Dewey, the mind was not an entity. Rather, it was the process of adjusting, and thinking and deliberating about various forms of action (5). From Dewey, Mead adopted the idea that the mind emerges through social interactions.

The Looking-Glass Self

The sociologist Charles Horton Cooley refined James's ideas regarding the development of the self. His concept of the looking-glass self is summarized in his couplet:

Each to each a looking-glass;
Reflects the other that doth pass. (6)

A looking glass is, of course, a mirror.

For Cooley, the sense of self always involves other people. According to Cooley, we (1) imagine how we appear to another person, (2) imagine that person's judgment of our behavior, and (3) experience some feeling with respect to the self (pride, embarrassment) based on the other's perceived judgment. Cooley felt that people respond to the attitude they *believe* the other has, not the actual attitude. Cooley stressed the fact that one's perception of the other's attitude is not necessarily accurate. But accurate or not, it is the *perception* of the other's attitude that determines the self-feeling, not the attitude itself. For example, Jared may think he is socially skilled because he believes others admire his social abilities. In reality, others may think he is a nerd. But Jared's perception of their opinion, not their actual opinion, is what influences his sense of self. As long as his perception of others' opinions of his social skills is positive, his own judgment of his social skills will be positive.

Mead's View of the Self

In Chapter 2 we discussed Mead's emphasis on the human ability to manipulate symbols. The conception of self is dependent upon the manipulation of symbols in the form of language. For this reason Mead believed the self begins to develop once the child's language skills are in place.

The "I" and the "me" Mead adopted James's view of the self as both subject and object. In Mead's terms, the self consists of two components: the "I" and the "me" (7). The "I" is the subject. It is spontaneous, energizing, and creative. The "I" is the active component of the self that commits the individual to action (8). In contrast, the "me" is the object. It is an organized set of attitudes and expectations common to the social group. The "me" gives direction, allowing the chosen actions to be carried out. It is goal-directed and conforming. The "I" and the "me" are united into a single self; neither could exist without the other.

Role-taking Like Cooley, Mead believed that people view themselves indirectly, by taking the point of view of others in the society (9). In *role-taking* the child assumes the perspective of others to see how reality is viewed from those perspectives. To illustrate, a child who is being scolded by her mother attempts to understand her mother's anger. Mead believed that role-taking is essential to human interaction and to the development of the self and society. Without role-taking skills, we could not understand one another, nor could we predict each other's behaviors. Cooperation, which is essential to the development of society, would be impossible without role-taking.

According to Mead, we develop selves by becoming objects to ourselves. This can happen only by taking the perspectives of others toward ourselves. A sense of self is developed through social interaction, where people learn to view themselves through the eyes of others. Mead believed that people first develop an awareness of others and only later develop an awareness of themselves. Mead discusses the development of this self-awareness using the metaphors of play and games.

Play, games, and the generalized other In the first stage of self-development, the child learns to take the role of particular others. During childhood play, a child tries out different roles and "plays like" a mother, a firefighter, or a teacher. He or she changes roles from moment to moment and learns the behaviors associated with each. During this play stage, the child may refer to herself as "Sandy" (third person), rather than as "I" (first person), for she does not yet have a unified self-conception. In addition to discovering that a number of different possible roles exist, the child also learns that some roles are related to or complement others. For example, to play hospital, patients, doctors, and nurses are required, so the child learns to assume the perspective of one or two others in addition to the self.

In the last stage of the development of the self, individuals learn to see themselves not just from the perspective of a particular other, but from the unified perspective of others. This process is analogous to playing games, in which children must learn to view their roles from the points of view of all the other children in related game roles. Games have rules governing the relationships among the players, and each player must follow them. To learn the rules, a child must learn the behaviors required of each player, not just those required for his or her own role. A child playing a game of baseball must be able to understand and anticipate the behavior of all the children on both his or her own and the other team. Mead called such an external unified perspective the *generalized other*, which he defined as the set of standards common to a social group.

The generalized other comprises different groups in differing situations. The generalized other for the child playing a game comprises the perspectives of all the other players in the game. However, the generalized other may comprise a broader and more abstract group. When children think of themselves as students, the generalized other includes all others whose attitudes are relevant to their statuses as

■ *Building sandcastles is serious business. A sense of self is developed in a process analogous to play and games. (WGS)*

students, such as teachers, principals, classmates, and parents. When children think of themselves as U. S. citizens, the generalized other consists of the even broader and more abstract group of all other citizens of the United States.

By taking the perspective of the generalized other, we are able to view ourselves as objects and to evaluate our own behaviors. Viewing oneself from the perspective of the generalized other, as well as the perspectives of particular others, enables one to develop a sense of self. A sense of self, as well as a sense of others, is essential for sustained symbolic interaction. The capacity to view oneself from the perspective of the generalized other marks the final stage in the development of the self.

Significant Others

Modern theorists believe the self is based primarily on the appraisals of *significant others*—those who are most important to the individual. Thus, if a person you know only slightly, perhaps another student in one of your classes, thinks you talk too much, this perception is unlikely to change your view of yourself. But, if your closest friends think you talk too much, this view is likely to influence your self-concept.

Parents are typically the most significant others to their children. In a recent look at their influence on children's appraisals of themselves, the self-appraisals of children from the 4th through 7th grades and the parents' appraisals of their children were measured (10). Each child and parent was asked to evaluate the child's academic and athletic abilities and the child's level of physical attractiveness. Both sets of parents' appraisals influenced their children's academic and athletic self-appraisals. As you can see in Table 5-1, the mothers' and fathers' scores are significantly correlated with their sons' and daughters' self-scores. Although a correlation does not demonstrate causality, additional statistical analyses showed a clear influence of the parents' appraisals on their children's self-appraisals. As you can also see in Table 5-1, the parents' assessments

■ *Family members are often significant others.*
(WGS)

of their children's physical attractiveness are not significantly correlated with their children's appraisals of their own physical attractiveness. The lack of influence on the children's self-appraisals of physical attractiveness may be due to the fact that the standards for judging attractiveness are ambiguous. Surprisingly, both parents had a stronger influence on children of the opposite than of the same sex.

Next we will examine the self-concept. The self-concept is studied by both sociological and psychological social psychologists. Sociologists focus on the influence of the society on the individual's self concept, while psychologists explore the role of social comparison in the formation of the self-concept.

■

THE SELF-CONCEPT

The *self-concept* comprises all of an individual's thoughts and feelings about himself or herself as an object (11). The self-concept is influenced by the person's social context—for instance, the similarity or dissimilarity of the individual to others in the surroundings in terms of race, religion, and social class. If people are dissimilar to others, they may

Table 5.1 ■

Correlations Between Control Variables and Ratings of Self and Parents

	Boys			Girls		
	Self	Mother	Father	Self	Mother	Father
Peer rating of physical attractiveness	.08*	− .02*	.07*	.09*	.11*	.17
Academic grades	.46	.45	.35	.49	.47	.32
Academic test scores	.36	.46	.49	.47	.50	.48
Athletic test scores	.41	.43	.41	.39	.44	.33

*Not significant at .05 level.

experience prejudice and discrimination, or they may be forced to conform to norms that are foreign to them. At the very least, they will lack relevant others with whom to compare themselves. This is not to say that racial or religious minority group members or members of lower social classes necessarily have low self-esteem. In fact, members of minority groups do not typically show lowered levels of self-esteem, apparently because they compare themselves primarily to others from their own group (12).

The process of *social comparison* plays a central role in the development of the self-concept (13). We all use others to evaluate ourselves, even though the other people may not be aware of their part in our evaluation. The more similar the other person is to us, the more likely the comparison will be useful. You can judge your social abilities by asking your friends about them or by inferring their judgments from their responses to you. You can also simply observe your friends' social abilities and judge yourself using their abilities as comparison. Whether we are shy or smart is a relative judgment that can only be made in comparison with others.

Measuring the Self-Concept

Who are you? Before you read further, please answer the question posed in Box 5-1. The answers that people give to this question contain some interesting similarities. These similarities give social psychologists clues to people's conceptions of the self.

The self-concept largely comprises dispositions, such as attitudes, traits, abilities, and values; social identities, such as one's age, sex, and race; and physical characteristics (15). What types of categories did you use in Box 5-1 to describe yourself?

Identities and the Self

The fact that people answer the question, "Who am I?" with a variety of identities is consistent with the symbolic interactionists' idea that the self is composed of identities, each of which is associated with a social role. Social roles link the individual to the society; roles exist prior to the person, and the society determines the roles and their interpretations. At the same time, each of us "makes" rather than "takes" our roles; our role portrayal is uniquely our own.

Roles and identities link us to the society in another way: As we mentioned in Chapter 2, the more committed the individual is to the identity, the more the individual will seek opportunities to perform in terms of the identity. Commitment to identities is determined in large part by the structure of society; the organization of the society greatly influences the individual's social relationships and their importance, and thus influences the identities the individual will enact (16). For instance, your identity at this time in your life as a student is not only a result of your individual desires, but also a result of the extent to which people of your age, sex, ethnic group, and social class find social barriers to or prescriptions for education.

Identities provide considerable continuity in the self across the lifetime (17). The roles one enacts provide stable identities that can endure throughout the life span. One's family and occupational roles, for example, are constant and important aspects of our "self." At the same time, identities and thus the self also change, as the individual moves through age-linked social roles. We are not expected to be the same person late in life as we were as a teenager, and the roles we enact and thus our identities change as we pass through age categories. For example, a teenager is probably still a student, while an elderly person typically is not. Even though a person may be a parent both as a teenager and an elderly person, being the parent of a pre-school child and an adult child are associated with rather different expectations.

The Changing Self

The sociologist Ralph Turner has suggested that individuals regard some of their attributes and roles as stemming from their real selves and others as not being part of their real selves (18). For example, we feel that some of our behaviors are prompted by

BOX 5·1

Who Are You?

In the 20 numbered blanks write 20 different answers to the simple question, "Who am I?" Answer as if you were giving the answers to yourself, not to somebody else. (14) Write the answers in the order they occur to you. Don't worry about logic or importance.

1. _____   6. _____   11. _____   16. _____
2. _____   7. _____   12. _____   17. _____
3. _____   8. _____   13. _____   18. _____
4. _____   9. _____   14. _____   19. _____
5. _____   10. _____   15. _____   20. _____

our honest feelings on an issue, while others result largely from the situation we are in and what is socially appropriate in that situation. According to Turner, individuals tend to locate their real selves in one of two domains—institution or impulse.

People who believe their real selves are institutional selves tend to believe their selves are revealed when they adhere to high standards and when they are in full control of their behaviors. The *institutional self* is based on the pursuit of society's goals and in the acceptance of group obligations. People whose real selves are institutional are concerned with achievement, and they are oriented towards the future.

People who believe their real selves are impulsive tend to feel their real selves are revealed in spontaneous behavior that occurs when one's inhibitions are lowered. The *impulsive self* is based on the pursuit of satisfaction of impulses that are not a part of society's goals. People whose real selves are

impulsive fear blindly following arbitrary rules, and they are oriented towards the present.

Turner believes that in recent decades most people have moved away from identification with the institutional self to identification with the impulsive self. He feels that people increasingly view institutions in terms of rules that limit expression of the true self. They prefer to emphasize self-fulfillment through the expression of their own values.

Data taken from diaries written in three time periods—1818–1860, 1911–1939, and 1949–1972—have been used to argue that the transformation from an industrial to a postindustrial society has created a change from the self as institution and product to a self as impulse and process (19). That is, the structure of the society has important effects on the selves of its members. The primary characteristics of the postmodern self are irrationality, mysticism, and self-concern. The conditions of a postindustrial society that are thought to have caused this self are changing social values and the contradictions of modern society.

The Mutable Self

Turner's analysis is consistent with that of Louis Zurcher (20). Zurcher used the Twenty Statements Test (TST) to study the self-definitions of college students. In this test, respondents provide 20 responses to the question, "Who am I?" just as you did in Box 5-1. Then these responses are divided into four categories. A-mode responses are those that identify the individual in terms of physical attributes or other information typically found on drivers' licenses (I am blond; I live in New York). B-mode responses describe socially defined statuses (I am a college student; I am Catholic). C-mode responses describe styles of behavior that are more independent of the social structure (I am a happy person; I like rock music). D-mode responses are so general that they give no reliable information about the individual (I am a living being; I am part of the universe).

Zurcher found that in the 1970s individuals were less likely to identify themselves with institutional roles (B-mode responses) and more likely to identify themselves as actors apart from the social structure (C-mode responses) than in the 1960s. He believed that C-mode responses are more adaptive during periods of social change than B-mode responses. Zurcher further suggested that the move from the social B-mode responses to the reflective C-mode responses culminates in a move to a "mutable self," in which all four modes of responding are integrated. The person with a mutable self is able to select among all four modes as the situation requires.

More recent investigations of the responses of college students of the late 1970s and early 1980s suggest they are more like the students of the early 1970s than the students of the 1960s (21). Like students of the early 1970s, students of the early 1980s characterize themselves by using reflective (C-mode), rather than institutional (B-mode) responses.

What do you think the students of the early 1990s are like? Look again at the answers that you gave to the question, "Who am I?" in Box 5-1. Can you classify yourself on the basis of your responses as identifying predominantly with the institutional or impulsive self? Can you classify your responses according to mode? If so, are your responses more like students of the 1960s or students of the 1970s and early 1980s?

The concepts of the impulsive self, the postmodern self, and the self characterized by C-mode responses draw upon Mead's ideas regarding the "I." Similarly, the institutional self and the self characterized by B-mode responses are based on Mead's conception of the "me." Much current work in social psychology has origins in classical theory.

■

SELF-PERCEPTION

While the self-concept consists of the individual's thoughts and feelings about the self, *self perception* involves the process of attributing characteristics to ourselves. Psychological social psychologists have been predominantly concerned with self-perception, an interest which stems from their cognitive approach and their resulting concern with the attributions or explanations that people give for their own and others' behaviors. We will describe two answers to the question of how attributions are made about the self—self-perception theory and self-schemata.

Self-Perception Theory

Self-perception theorists ask how people make attributions about themselves. According to Daryl Bem, people make attributions about themselves in the same way they make attributions about others—by observing their behaviors (22). On the basis of others' behaviors, we decide they are shy, honest, or kind. Similarly, we make attributions about ourselves by observing our own behaviors. We infer our likes and dislikes, our strengths and weaknesses, and our feelings in this manner.

However, not all of our behaviors can be used to infer what we are like. Behaviors performed solely to obtain a reward or to avoid a punishment cannot be used to infer our attitudes. Just because you study for your final exams does not mean you will conclude that you like studying. Rather, you will probably make the inference that you study because you do not wish to receive poor grades, a punishment. Similarly, working 20 hours a week at a job does not necessarily lead you to believe you enjoy working while going to school. You are more likely to assume you work for the rewards that working brings, such as money to pay for food, shelter, and tuition. But behaviors performed freely, because we want to perform them, are useful in inferring our attitudes. If you often swim at lunchtime when you have other options, such as eating with friends, studying, or going for a walk, you should make the inference that you like to swim or, perhaps, that you believe exercise is important.

Intrinsic motivation One implication of the reward–inference relationship is if you are rewarded for performing an act you enjoy for its intrinsic or inherent merits, you may believe you performed it only for the reward (23). Thus, ironically, rewards can decrease, rather than increase, your enjoyment of an activity. For example, as a child you may have loved to go to school and worked hard at learning for the sheer enjoyment of it. But, if your parents began to reward you by giving you money or special privileges for doing your homework, you may have redefined your behavior and come to believe you studied only for the money or special privileges. This effect has been termed *overjustification* since it involves unnecessary rewards. Thus, rewards can have the unintended effect of undercutting the intrinsic motivation to engage in an activity.

However, in many instances intrinsic interest in an activity is related to one's competence at the activity. If you perform an activity well, such as playing tennis, you are more likely to be interested in it than if you play it poorly. In addition, recognition of one's competence through rewards increases one's interest in the activity. In such instances, reward

■ *Fishing for self-esteem: Intrinsic interest is related to one's competence at the activity. (WGS)*

for good performance may well lead to increased enjoyment of it.

Thus, a reward may convey two different messages. The reward may convey the message that your behavior is being "bought" or controlled by the reward. On the other hand, rewards may also confirm your competence at certain activities. You have doubtless been given money, praise, or attention for highly competent behaviors. If the reward were given in a situation in which you felt honored for competent behavior (receiving a citizenship award in high school), then the reward should have had the opposite effect than if it were given to control your behavior (being loaned your roommate's car for having entertained her relatives).

In one study demonstrating this difference, young adults were asked to solve puzzles (24). In one situation, subjects were given a reward to control their behavior: They were offered a large amount of money for merely trying to solve the puzzles. In a second situation, subjects were given a reward to confirm their competence: They were told they would receive the money only if their performances were of high quality. All subjects were given the money. In the third situation, subjects were told nothing about the payment, but were unexpectedly given the money after completing the puzzles. The results show that subjects who were told they would be given money for attempting to solve the puzzles liked the puzzles less than subjects who did not expect money for solving them. But subjects who were told they were given money for high-quality performance liked the puzzles more than subjects who did not expect the money.

Self-Schemata

Schemata theorists explore a somewhat different aspect of the problem of self-perception: They ask how we organize information. Because there is so much information available in our worlds, we must be selective in the information that we take in. To help us in this selection process, we organize information into knowledge structures, or *schemata* (25). (See Chapter 9 for a more detailed discussion of cognitive information processing.) These schemata, which contain related bits of information, are used to organize and interpret new information. Without such organizational structures, it would be impossible to interpret incoming information.

One way in which individuals differ from each other is in the organization of their self-schemata. Due to their differing schemata, individuals perceive the world in different ways. For example, some people perceive themselves to be at the extremes on the continuum of optimism–pessimism. Of these people, those who perceive themselves to be extremely optimistic (positive in world view, always seeing the good aspects of life) have an optimism self-schemata, while those who perceive themselves as extremely pessimistic (negative in world view, always seeing the worst in a situation) have a pessimism self-schemata. Others, less extreme in their optimism or pessimism, are aschematic on this dimension; they have neither optimism nor pessimism self-schemata.

Self-schemata arise from repeated categorizations of our behavior on some dimension by both ourselves and others. If you and others often characterize your behavior as shy, you may develop a shyness self-schema. Typically, our self-schemata are organized around aspects of ourselves that either distinguish us from others or about which we have some comparative information. If you are of normal height and weight, you are less likely to have height and weight self-schemata than if you are unusually high or low on those dimensions. If you have played racquetball avidly for years, you are more likely to have a racquetball self-schema than if you have played little. In one study, grade school children were more likely to think about and describe themselves in dimensions on which they were distinctive, relative to dimensions on which they were not distinctive (26). For example, redheaded children were more likely to mention their hair color when describing themselves than were children with more common hair colors. Similarly, minority children in schools with predominantly majority group children were more likely to mention their racial or ethnic groups when describing themselves than were the majority children.

There are several consequences of being self-schematic in a particular area. First, individuals process information about themselves in that domain comparatively quickly and certainly. If you have an intelligence self-schema, you should easily and firmly categorize yourself as intelligent, in comparison to others who do not have an intelligence self-schema.

A second consequence of self-schemata is that people have a good memory for behavior in that domain. If you are schematic for intelligence, you are likely to attend to and remember your intelligent behavior. A third consequence is that individuals are successful at predicting their behavior on that dimension. An intelligence self-schema should mean you are good at predicting the behavioral consequences of your intelligence. Fourth, people are relatively resistant to information that runs counter to their self-schemata. When schematic for intelligence, you are likely to reject information that suggests you are not intelligent. Finally, individuals evaluate information with respect to their self-schemata. If you have an intelligence self-schema you are likely to examine new information about yourself for its relevance to intelligence.

Individuals also think about their potential and their future and derive scenarios called *possible selves.* (27) These possible selves represent our goals, motives, and fears. We think about all the selves we could become, that we would like to become, and that we fear becoming. Possible selves shape the individual's expectations and behaviors and provide a way of interpreting our behavior.

■

SELF-PRESENTATION

Self-presentation concerns the ways in which we manage (control, hide, enhance) information about ourselves. Sociologists and psychologists study slightly different aspects of this issue. In keeping with their emphasis on interaction, most sociologists are concerned with strategies of self-presentation; consistent with their focus on individuals, most psychologists study differences in people's self-presentation.

Strategies of Self-Presentation

The dramaturgical school According to Erving Goffman, all face-to-face interaction involves *impression management* (28). Each person tries to influence or manage the impression that others have of him or her. One of the strategies of impression management is to influence the definition of the situation that other people have. Each of the participants in the interaction tries to get the other people to accept his or her perceptions of the situation. To illustrate, if you are trying to sell your stereo to another student, you will present yourself as trying to help the student by selling an excellent piece of auditory engineering for a low price. The other student,

however, may well attempt to present himself as assisting you by taking an obsolete piece of junk off your hands for a considerable sum of money.

To say that we use impression management is not to imply that we always engage in deception when interacting with others. While it is true that individuals sometimes knowingly contradict reality in the impressions they present of themselves, there are many other patterns of "managed" self-impression. For example, sometimes people dress in certain ways to gain the approval of groups to which they belong. In general, we do not readily expose aspects of ourselves of which we are ashamed or which would lead others to have a negative impression of us.

Impressions are managed in part by the use of *settings,* or physical surroundings. The impression of expertise and power that doctors wish to convey to their patients is created through the display of diplomas and bookcases full of medical texts in the doctors' private offices, and by sophisticated-looking medical paraphernalia in the examination rooms, elegant furnishings, and expensive office space. Impressions are also managed by the performer's *personal front*—consisting of such things as sex, age, speech, hair style, and clothing—that are identified with the performer. For example, a young doctor, who learns that her patients are surprised and somewhat disappointed to find she is not a middle-aged man, may dress and speak in a way that makes her appear both older and more a part of the traditional medical establishment.

In almost every interaction something is concealed. Errors and mistakes are corrected before the performance takes place. For example, the smudge is removed from one's dress before the party, and misspelled words are corrected before handing in one's term paper. This necessity for concealment requires distinct regions where preparations and performances take place.

The place where the performance is given is the *front region.* Here standards consistent with the impression being fostered are carefully maintained. In contrast, the *back region* is the place where performances are practiced, the real work is conducted, and the actors "let down their hair." In the

■ *Uniforms are a component of the personal front. (WGS)*

back region the performances of the front region are routinely contradicted. For example, the front region in a gambling casino is the place where patrons gamble. In this region, the employees are cordial and polite to the patrons and to each other. In the back region, where patrons are not permitted to go, the employees ridicule the gambling habits of the patrons, complain about their jobs and each other, and relax from the demands of being courteous to patrons.

Why do we use self-presentational strategies? Three primary motives exist (29). First, impression management can help us fulfill personal goals: We may put our best foot forward to get a job, a girlfriend or boyfriend, or act in a way that makes us fit in with a social group. Second, impression management allows us to present a consistent and positive view of ourselves to the world. To be thought of as witty, we must be funny even if we are feeling grumpy or sad. Third, impression management is sometimes needed if we are to conform to social norms. If we are to show proper deference to our older, but not

always dearly loved, relatives or to show tact with our coworkers, we must sometimes hide our innermost feelings.

Situated identities and the self As we learned in Chapter 2, the roles that an individual plays are associated with self-identities. One has as many identities as roles that one portrays. A *situated identity* can be defined as the self that is identified with the person's current role (30). Situated identities define the relationship between an individual and the environment—including other individuals—as a given point in time. Stable characteristics of the actor and the perceiver in large part determine the identities that are defined.

People must establish identities before they can proceed with an interaction (31). This process is necessary because identities determine what people should do and what they feel others in the interaction should do. For instance, unless you and an older female establish that she is the physician and you are the patient, the appropriate interaction cannot take place. If you mistakenly identify her as a nurse, or she identifies you as a delivery person, the interaction will soon be disrupted by confusion.

People's actions provide information about their personal characteristics, even if they perform exactly and only the behaviors expected of them. Is she a kindly or an irritable doctor? Does she view herself as a modern technician or an old-fashioned healer of the sick? Even in the first few moments of this interaction, you will learn much about her. Similarly, while all patients describe their symptoms, allow themselves to be examined, and listen to the physician's diagnosis, the manner in which you enact these behaviors provides the doctor with a rich tapestry of information. The interaction of your doctor's and your definitions of the situation define your shared reality for the moment. This doctor, with another patient, and you with another doctor, may share a very different social reality.

People wish to create socially desirable identities. The process of establishing a positive identity is facilitated by *altercasting* (32). In altercasting, one projects an identity to be assumed by the other person in the interaction that is consistent with one's own goals. Thus, people project their own identities and define situations in such a way that others respond in the desired manner. A lawyer who wishes to undercut a client's fear regarding a legal problem may present his legal analysis in a positive way and respond to negative statements by the client by pointing out positive aspects of the case.

Accounts An analysis of *accounts* provides an example of establishing a positive identity through language (33). An account is a statement made by someone to explain a behavior of theirs that was unanticipated or in some way improper. Excuses and justifications constitute the two types of accounts.

Excuses are statements that lessen responsibility when conduct is questioned. Let us assume you arrive an hour late to meet a friend, and this friend is angry with you because of your lateness. You might blame the heavy rainstorm for your delay or you might blame your tardiness on your landlord's request to help him fix something in your apartment.

Justifications are arguments that the behavior in question actually had some positive value or was appropriate. Let's assume that Tim refused to help Helaine when she had car trouble, and she is irritated at Tim for his refusal. Tim might argue that Helaine did not really need him since she could call a garage for help or that Helaine did not deserve his help because she caused the trouble by not taking proper care of her car.

The use of accounts is relatively common. Sometimes they are accepted and sometimes not. Most of us have a wide repertoire of accounts that we use selectively, depending upon the situation and the others involved. The account, "I just couldn't get it together," might be acceptable in explaining why you were late in meeting a friend, but you are not likely to try it as an explanation to a professor for a late paper. "I've been depressed lately" will satisfactorily explain a variety of behaviors, but will not explain others, such as cheating on your spouse or your income tax. A single type of account used repeatedly by a person (I need to copy your homework because I didn't have time to do mine) is unlikely to be accepted indefinitely.

Altercasting is a prerequisite to accounts. The identities of the self and others provide the background against which accounts are offered and accepted or rejected. The offering of accounts is one aspect of negotiation over the current identity being claimed.

Self-enhancement People make claims to the most positive images they feel they can establish, taking into consideration both the probability of making a successful claim and the negative sanctions attached to making an unsuccessful claim. (35) Thus, a failing student is unlikely to claim to be an honor student, but a "C" student may claim to be a "B" student.

Not only do people claim positive images that are related to the roles they occupy, such as the student's claim to scholarship or the politician's claim to power and "inside information," but people also claim positive images that have little or no relationship to their roles. One example of this phenomenon is that of *BIRGing: basking in reflected glory* (36). Some people brag about their chance contacts with famous persons; others identify with

Talk About Excuses!

The following statements are actual explanations for accidents written on insurance claim forms. (34) Can you categorize any of these excuses using the classification system given for accounts?

I had been driving my car for forty years when I fell asleep at the wheel and had an accident.

An invisible car came out of nowhere, struck my vehicle, and vanished.

I had been shopping for plants all day, and was on my way home. As I reached an intersection, a hedge sprang up obscuring my vision. I did not see the other car.

A pedestrian hit me and went under my car.

The telephone pole was approaching fast. I was attempting to swerve out of its path when it struck my front end. ■

---

their professional baseball team, at least in a winning season; still others feel proud when a person from their community whom they do not know wins a national award. In a study of birging, college students who had attended a basketball game in which their team had either won or lost were asked to explain the outcome of the game (37). Many more students used the term "we" (we played well) when describing a victory than a defeat (they played sloppy ball). The students also tended to describe a victory in personal terms (our offense is great) and a defeat in situational terms (the referees were lousy).

Ingratiation   While most self-presentation is practiced, but not highly deceptive, some self-presentation is clearly aimed at deception. *Ingratiation* is the term that describes deceptive behaviors used illicitly by people to cause others to like them (39). There are four basic ingratiation tactics (40).

1. An individual can flatter the other person.

2. An individual can pretend to be more similar to the other person in attitudes and beliefs than he or she actually is. This tactic rests on the assumption that people like others who agree with them. As we will see in Chapter 10, this is a reasonable assumption.

3. An individual can do favors for the other person.

4. An individual can present himself or herself in a falsely favorable light—for example, by falsely claiming characteristics that are generally valued in the culture (intelligence, honesty, kindness).

Three primary factors determine the use of ingratiation tactics: (1) the value of a goal that can be achieved through ingratiation, and the availability of a target who can secure that goal for the ingratiator; (2) the subjective probability of success of the

BOX 5-3

Immortalizing the Self through Sport

The creation of an immortal self through sports provides one avenue of self-enhancement. (38) Sports participation allows for the creation of an immortal self because sports figures are cultural heroes, constant self-evaluation and record-keeping is a mandatory part of the participation, and winners are recognized through awards and other means. Through sports, one can both magnify the self and assure it a degree of permanence.

Interviews with sports figures confirm that they seek a place in sports history. As the baseball player Brooks Robinson said, "Being inducted into the Hall of Fame ... means immortality." They also think about their progress, and feel concern about failure to achieve desired progress. As Beth Daniel, a professional golfer once remarked, "If I were to quit golf today, I would go down in history as nothing."

While the ability to immortalize oneself through sports may be rare, the desire to do so is quite common. To illustrate, high school students in the 1950s and 1970s frequently wished to be remembered as athletic stars. ■

ingratiation technique; and (3) the perceived legitimacy of the use of such tactics. Perceived legitimacy refers to techniques through which individuals convince themselves that their use of illicit tactics is justified, and to personal traits that allow individuals to view ingratiation tactics as legitimate. For example, ingratiation is often used by people who are low in power because they feel they have no other way to influence more powerful individuals (41).

The effect of ingratiation depends both on how obvious the ingratiation attempts are and on the extent to which the ingratiator is dependent upon the other person. Frequent or flagrant ingratiation is likely to be unsuccessful if the ingratiator is highly dependent on the other person. Thus, since your boss knows how much you have to gain from a favorable impression, ingratiation tactics directed toward your boss should be muted if they are to be effective.

Self-presentation and social behavior Self-presentation may account for some of our behavior in the areas of helping others, comforming, making attitude changes and self-attributions, responding to evaluations, being aggressive, and in performing tasks (42). These behaviors may actually fulfill one of the two major self-presentational motives: pleasing the immediate audience or constructing a public self that is consistent with one's ideal self.

The goals underlying these two self-presentational motives differ. The purpose of pleasing the immediate audience is to obtain rewards, while the purpose of constructing an ideal public self is for personal self-fulfillment. Sometimes both motives are realized through the same behaviors. For instance, the motives of pleasing an immediate audience and constructing an ideal public self would both be realized if you helped someone in need. However, in some situations there is a conflict between the realization of the two motives. The motive of pleasing an immediate audience can entail behaviors that conflict with the overall public image the person wishes to present. Let's say you have a sister who wants your opinion of her new and obnoxious boyfriend. If you tell her the truth you may offend her or make her defensive and angry. To please the immediate audience consisting of your sister, you may have to violate an important component of your ideal public image: honesty.

Individual Differences in Self-Presentation

People differ in the degree to which they are aware of or focus on themselves in public and private, monitor the impressions they make on others, change their behaviors to fit the situation, and are willing to disclose information about themselves to others.

Self-awareness At times our attention is focused on the self; at other times attention is focused away from the self. When our attention is focused on the self we speak of self-awareness. We can be self-aware in two ways: aware of the private self and aware of the public self (43). The *private self* consists of the person's attitudes and feelings that cannot be seen by others. On the other hand, the *public self* consists of overt behavior and mannerisms that are portrayed to the public.

These types of self-awareness can be situationally induced. For example, in an experimental demonstration of self-awareness, one group of college students was asked to take a timed test alone (44). It was possible to increase one's score on the test by working beyond the time allotted—that is, by cheating. The experimenters found that 71 percent of the students cheated in this situation. A second group of students was given the same task and the same instructions, but worked in front of a large mirror. In this condition, cheating was reduced to only 7 percent. Why did cheating drop in this condition? The experimenters feel that the mirror increased subjects' levels of private self-awareness because seeing their images reminded the subjects of their personal standards and values. This increased private self-awareness made the self implications of any thoughts of dishonesty salient to them. Since the students' thoughts of cheating were at variance with their beliefs that they were honest, they could avoid negative feelings about themselves only by not cheating. In contrast, the subjects who were not working before a mirror were able to cheat because they were less aware of the implications of this action for their self-definitions.

People also differ in the degree to which they habitually attend to themselves. Thus, one can be chronically high or low in public and private self-awareness. Public and private self-awareness are separate dimensions, with the relationship between them being positive, but only moderate in strength.

In many situations, chronic levels of self-awareness have behavioral consequences. For example, one consequence of private self-awareness is increased accuracy of self-descriptions. In one study, people high in private self-awareness took less time to decide if a negative trait was characteristic of them than people low in private self-awareness. (45) One consequence of public self-awareness is increased accuracy in judging others' reactions to the self. In one experiment, people high in public self-awareness were better able to predict the effect on an audience of a videotape about themselves than people low in public self-awareness. (46)

Public and private self-awareness have been associated with a variety of other social behaviors, including conformity, reactions to coercive persuasion attempts, attitude change, judgments regarding justice, and the salience of norms. (47)

Self-monitoring People high in public self-awareness understand how their self-presentation affects others, but they are not necessarily willing to alter the impression they are making, and they do not necessarily have a high need for others' approval. However, some people are willing to alter their impressions in order to receive approval.

Self-monitoring is a personality dimension measuring the ability to modify one's self-presentation, and the extent to which this ability is used to fit the self to the situation. (48) One's abilities on this trait are measured by means of a 25-item true–false scale. The scale measures concern with the social appropriateness of people's self-presentation, attention to social comparison cues, ability to control and modify self-presentations, willingness to use this ability, and the extent to which people tailor their self-presentations to suit the situation. The items include the following: "When I am uncertain how to act in social situations, I look to the behavior of others for clues," and "In different situations, and with different people, I often act like very different persons."

High self-monitors are very sensitive to the verbal and nonverbal expressions and self-presentations of others in social situations. They use others' presentations as cues to guide their own verbal and nonverbal self-presentations. In contrast, low self-monitors do not attend much to others' presentations, nor do they have a well-developed range of self-presentations. In comparison to high self-monitors, low self-monitors appear to be controlled from within—by their own emotions and attitudes.

People who differ in levels of self-monitoring have different self-conceptions. High self-monitors regard themselves as flexible and adaptable. They see themselves as shrewdly fitting their social behavior to the situation. High self-monitors try to be the right people in the right places at the right times. Low self-monitors view themselves as principled individuals who do what they believe. They attempt to accurately communicate their feelings and attitudes to others. High self-monitors exhibit less consistency in behavior and attitudes than low self-monitors. Further, high self-monitors are better able to express and communicate various emotions than low self-monitors (49). As one would expect, professional actors have higher scores on the self-monitoring scale than university undergraduates.

The importance of self-monitoring lies not only in the fact that people high and low in self-monitoring engage in different behaviors. Since people also choose to enter situations that facilitate the enactment of their goals, characteristics such as self-monitoring can determine the situations people enter, the relationships they develop with others, and the types of relationships that develop. For example, high self-monitors are more concerned with the potential partner's physical attractiveness in the initiation of a romantic relationship, while low self-monitors are more concerned with the personality of the potential partner (50). In addition, low self-monitors prefer to be with the person they are dating in a variety of social situations, but high self-monitors prefer to be with more than one friend of the opposite sex (51). In general, low self-monitors seem more committed to their dating partners than high self-monitors.

Self-disclosure *Self-disclosure,* the act of revealing personal information to others, is a major avenue through which we regulate others' knowledge about ourselves (52). Self-disclosure can be viewed as having two dimensions, breadth and depth. *Breadth* of self-disclosure refers to the scope of the disclosure. *Depth* of self-disclosure refers to its level of intimacy. *Intimacy* of self-disclosure has several properties: uniqueness (I am a psychic), perceived vulnerability (I am seeing a psychiatrist), social undesirability (I love to gossip), and strong affect (I hate my sister).

Individuals take into consideration the time, place, and length of their relationship with another when they consider how much to self-disclose. Self-disclosure is viewed as more appropriate with a friend than with a stranger and with people of more similar than dissimilar ages (53).

Reciprocity of self-disclosure is usually desired. Both underintimacy and overintimacy are less satisfying than equal intimacy. Reciprocity can be viewed as a form of equal exchange, with an equal input–outcome ratio for partners in an interaction. A partner's lack of reciprocally intimate disclosure can make the other individual feel rejected. A partner's overintimate disclosure can make the individual feel uncomfortable and embarrassed. For example, highly intimate self-disclosures from strangers may provoke a need to protect one's privacy. Thus, if a disclosure

■ *Self-disclosure is viewed as most appropriate to friends and people of similar age. (WGS)*

from a stranger is viewed as too intimate, we may violate the norm of reciprocity and become less intimate rather than more intimate, in our subsequent self-disclosures (54).

However, the more intimate the relationship, the more readily the reciprocity rule can be broken. While a friendship would never flourish if lack of reciprocity was the rule, in long-standing friendships an intimate self-disclosure does not require a parallel self-disclosure. If your best friend tells you about breaking up with his girlfriend, you are likely to comfort him rather than respond with horror stories about your past breakups with girlfriends.

Level of self-disclosure is related to marital satisfaction. Happily married people are higher in overall levels of self-disclosure (Let me tell you about my day; I was proud of you last night) than unhappily married people, but unhappily married people are higher in negative self-disclosure (I've always hated the way you kiss) than happily married people. Sadly, levels of self-disclosure appear to decline with years of marriage (55).

Last, we turn to the topic of self-esteem. Self-esteem is studied by sociologists and psychologists alike.

■

SELF-ESTEEM

Self-esteem refers to one component of the self-concept: the level of positive or negative feelings about the self. Self-esteem is derived from some of the same sources as the self. Significant others provide one component of self-esteem, with the most significant others providing the most important inputs into self-esteem. In addition, social comparison and self-attributions contribute to self-esteem (56).

Many theorists stress one's own role in the development of self-esteem. Most people have high self-esteem. This is made possible through selective evaluation of one's characteristics. Our level of self-esteem is not based on our assessments of all of our qualities. Rather, it is based on our assessments of only those qualities that count (57). We tend to value those qualities at which we excel and devalue those qualities at which we consider ourselves poor. Virtually all people can feel good about themselves if they are able to choose the bases for their self-judgments.

There are four types of selectivity that allow us to choose the judgments we make about ourselves. First, behaviors can be *interpreted selectively*. Most behaviors can be viewed in a positive light. For example, you may think someone you do not like is calculating, but you will see the same behavior in yourself as clever or perceptive. Given the same evidence, you may view another person as insincere and gushy, but you will see yourself as warm and caring.

Second, standards can be *selectively set*. Absolute performance is less important than relative performance. Most people choose standards of performance that are well within their limitations. The authors of this book, for example, do not compare their skills in sports with their students' skills. Instead, they compare their athletic abilities with their friends who are professors, like themselves.

Third, people use *interpersonal selectivity*. We tend to expose ourselves to information consistent with our beliefs and to associate with people who like us. Friendship provides a good example of this type of selectivity. It is a clear instance of picking one's propaganda! One of the great rewards of friendship is the joy of mutual admiration. The even greater rewards of lovers are based in part on the even greater joy of mutual love and devotion.

Fourth, we *select our environments*. We seek environments in which we will be accepted and situations in which we feel we will excel. Do we select occupations in which we think we will fail? Hardly. We select occupations in which we have demonstrated some talent.

We are sometimes limited in the extent to which we can select our environments and the people in them. Parents provide the most important limit on selectivity. In childhood, one's main source of information about the self comes from one's parents. The child is just beginning to form a sense of self

and has little else on which to base self-evaluations. If the parents reject the child, it is difficult for him or her to have a positive sense of self. A self-fulfilling prophecy may well occur: A child labeled as bad (or dumb or even clumsy) may well become just that because he or she takes the perspective of the parents in judging himself or herself.

Self-esteem has important implications for behavior. Children who are high in self-esteem, relative to children who are low in self-esteem, tend to set higher standards for themselves and perform better scholastically (59). Both adults and children who are high in self-esteem have more confidence in their own opinions, and thus are more likely to influence others and are less likely to be influenced by others, than people low in self-esteem (60). Self-esteem is also associated with a number of indices of mental health. It is negatively associated with depression, anxiety, feelings of vulnerability, and submissiveness, and positively associated with satisfaction with life, self-acceptance, and self-respect (61).

Self-efficacy and Self-esteem

Self-efficacy is the sense of oneself as a free agent who acts and causes effects. People experience self-efficacy as a positive emotion, and seek instances in which to display self-efficacious behavior. One's self-esteem is derived in part from the experience of oneself as self-efficacious.

Researchers have studied the influence of success and failure on self-esteem and self-efficacy. Because almost any consequence of behavior can be attributed to personal or environmental factors, success does not necessarily lead to feelings of high self-esteem based on high self-efficacy nor does failure necessarily lead to feelings of low self-esteem based on low self-efficacy. People do not experience low efficacy-based self-esteem if their failures are attributable to external factors, but they do if their failures are attributable to internal factors (62).

One's feelings of self-efficacy also affect one's behaviors (63). People are influenced more by their feelings of efficacy than by their expectations about the outcome of events (64). In a study of women in labor, the roles of self-efficacy (the strength of the

BOX 5-4

Measuring Self-Esteem: An Example

Rosenberg's Self-Esteem Scale is one of the more reliable and better validated measures of self-esteem. (58) Respondents are asked to select the answer that best describes how they feel about themselves from among the following responses: strongly agree, agree, disagree, strongly disagree. The following are items taken from this scale:

1. I feel that I am a person of worth, at least on an equal basis with others.
2. I feel I have a number of good qualities.
3. All in all, I am inclined to feel that I am a failure.
4. I am able to do things as well as most other people.
5. I feel I do not have much to be proud of.
6. I take a positive attitude toward myself.
7. I wish I could have more respect for myself.
8. At times I think I am no good at all.
9. On the whole, I am satisfied with myself.
10. I certainly feel useless at times.

The self-esteem score is a sum of the items. Items 1, 2, 4, 6, and 9 are scored with: strongly agree = 4, agree = 3, disagree = 2, and strongly disagree = 1. Items 3, 5, 7, 8, and 10 are scored with: strongly agree = 1, to strongly disagree = 4. The higher the score, the higher the self-esteem or sense of self-worth. ■

woman's belief in her own ability to control pain during childbirth and delivery) and expected outcomes (the woman's belief in the effectiveness of pain-control techniques taught in her childbirth class) were compared (65). The woman's self-efficacy was a better predictor of the length of time in labor without pain medication than her expected outcomes.

Unfortunately, the extent to which a person can experience efficacy-based self-esteem may be de-

pendent upon his or her status in society (66). People must have an opportunity to engage in effective action to experience high efficacy-based self-esteem. Opportunities to engage in these actions are dependent upon the constraints on the individual's autonomy, the degree of control the individual experiences, and the resources available to the person to produce intended outcomes. Each of these factors is dependent upon the person's position in the society's power structure. Individuals with more

■ *Surf efficacy: The experience of self-efficacy is that of oneself as a free agent whose actions cause effects. (WGS)*

power will have more opportunities to engage in effective action than those with less power. In addition, the outcomes of powerful people (the settlement of an international monetary crisis by a negotiator) are valued more highly than the outcomes of less powerful people (the increase in monthly snow cone sales by a vendor). For this reason, the self-esteem of individuals in powerful positions may be based more on efficacy, while the self-esteem of less powerful individuals may be based more on reflected appraisals.

■
SUMMARY

The self consists of the variety of persisting attitudes of the person toward himself or herself. Cooley's concept of the looking-glass self suggests the self is based on the judgments that we believe others have of us. According to Mead, the self is composed of the "I" (the subject) and the "me" (the object). Mead believed people view themselves by assuming the perspective of others. A sense of self is developed through social interaction, where people learn to view themselves through the eyes of others. This self-awareness is developed in a process analogous to play and games. Once the child can see himself or herself from the unified perspective of others, the generalized other, the sense of self is fully developed. The self is based primarily on reflected appraisals of significant others, those who are most important to the individual.

The self-concept is composed of all our thoughts and feelings about ourselves as subjects. One's similarity or dissimilarity to others in the surroundings influences our self-concept. The self-concept largely comprises dispositions, social identities, and physical characteristics. Identities link us to the society through the roles we portray. Our commitment to our identities is also largely determined by the structure of the society and the opportunities it provides or denies to individuals. Identities provide continuity in the self throughout the life cycle. It seems likely that recently young people have begun to identify themselves less in terms of society's goals (the institutional self) and more in terms of self-fulfillment (the impulsive self) than they did in the past. People may be moving toward a mutable self that changes as the situation requires. From industrial to postindustrial times, the self has become more irrational, mystical, and self-concerned.

Self-perception involves the process of attributing characteristics to ourselves. Bem believes we make inferences about ourselves just as we make inferences about others: by observing our behaviors. Receiving rewards for behaviors complicates this inference process. If people are rewarded for intrinsically interesting activities, they will infer that they are disinterested in the activities, unless the reward is perceived as a confirmation of competence at the activity. We organize information about ourselves in self-schemata—cognitive structures that contain related pieces of information about the self. Self-schemata are organized around concepts that distinguish us from others.

Self-presentation consists of the ways we influence others' evaluations of ourselves. Many strategies of self-presentation exist. According to Goffman, all face-to-face interaction involves impression management. One of the strategies of impression management is to influence the definition of the situation that other people have. Impressions are also managed through the use of settings and by the performer's physical front. Something is concealed in every interaction.

People's identities change with the roles they portray. The situated identity is the self that is identified with the person's current role. Stable characteristics of individuals in large part determine the identities that are defined. People must establish identities before they can proceed with an interaction. This process is facilitated by altercasting—projecting an identity to be assumed by the other person that is consistent with one's own goals. Positive identities can also be established through the use of accounts, statements made to explain improper or unanticipated behavior.

People make claims to the most positive images they feel they can establish. People claim positive images to which they are entitled. They also claim positive images to which they have little or no relationship, as when they bask in reflected glory. While most self-presentation is practiced, but not highly deceptive, some self-presentation is clearly aimed at deceit. This type of self-presentation is called ingratiation. People have two motives in self-presentation: pleasing the immediate audience and constructing a positive public self. These motives may be fulfilled through such social behavior as helping, conforming, and changing one's attitudes.

Individual differences exist in self-presentation. People differ in self-awareness, self-monitoring, and self-disclosure. We can be more or less aware of ourselves. When attention is focused on the self, we are self-aware. One can be privately or publicly self-aware. The private self consists of the person's attitudes and feelings, while the public self consists of behaviors and mannerisms.

Individuals vary in the extent to which they are willing to control their self-presentations. High self-monitors are more concerned with self-presentation and are more sensitive to others' self-presentations than low self-monitors.

Self-disclosure is the act of revealing personal information to others. Typically, reciprocity guides disclosures: We self-disclose at about the same level of intimacy that our partner in the interaction has self-disclosed.

Self-esteem is the level of positive or negative feelings about the self. It is influenced by significant others, social comparison, and self-attributions. We maintain high self-esteem by basing our self-judgments on qualities at which we consider ourselves to be good. Self-efficacy, the feeling that the self is a free agent who acts and causes effects to be produced and changed, is an important component of self-esteem for higher status individuals.

■

REFERENCES

1. Cooley, C. H., 1902, *Human Nature and the Social Order*, New York: Charles Scribner's Sons.
2. House, J. S., 1981, "Social Structure and Personality," in M. Rosenberg and R. H. Turner (Eds.), *Social Psychology: Sociological Perspectives*. New York: Basic Books.
3. Stryker, S., 1988, "Substance and Style: An Appraisal of the Sociological Legacy of Herbert Blumer," *Symbolic Interactionism* 11:33–42.
4. James, W., 1890, *The Principles of Psychology*, Dover Publications.

5. Dewey, J., 1922, *Human Nature and Human Conduct,* New York: Henry Holt.

6. Cooley, 1902, op. cit.

7. Mead, G. H., 1934, *On Social Psychology,* Chicago: University of Chicago Press.

8. Miller, D. L., 1973, *George Herbert Mead,* Austin: University of Texas Press.

9. Mead, 1934, op. cit.

10. Felson, R. B. and M. Reed, 1986, "The Effect of Parents on the Self-appraisals of Children," *Social Psychology Quarterly* 49:302–308.

11. Rosenberg, M., 1981, "The Self-concept: Social Product and Social Force," in M. Rosenberg and R. H. Turner (Eds.), *Social Psychology: Sociological Perspectives,* New York: Basic Books.

12. Rosenberg, M., 1979, *Conceiving the Self,* New York: Basic Books.

13. Festinger, L., 1954, "A Theory of Social Comparison Processes," *Human Relations* 7:117–140; Rosenberg, 1979, op. cit.

14. Kuhn, M. H. and T. S. McPartland, 1954, "An Empirical Investigation of Self-attitudes," *American Sociological Review* 19:68–76.

15. Rosenberg, 1979, op. cit.

16. Stryker, S., 1987, "Identity Theory: Developments and Extensions," in K. Yardley and T. Honess (Eds.), *Self and Identity: Psychosocial Perspectives,* New York: John Wiley & Sons.

17. Wells, L. E. and S. Stryker, 1988, "Stability and Change in Self over the Life Course," in D. L. Featherman and R. M. Lerner (Eds.), *Life Span Development and Behavior,* New York: Academic Press.

18. Turner, R. H., 1976, "The Real Self: From Institution to Impulse," *American Journal of Sociology, 81:*989–1016.

19. Wood, M. R. and L. A. Zurcher, Jr., 1988, *The Development of a Postmodern Self: A Computer-Assisted Comparative Analysis of Personal Documents,* Westport, CT: Greenwood Press.

20. Zurcher, L. A., 1977, *The Mutable Self,* Beverly Hills: Sage.

21. Snow, D. A. and C. L. Phillips, 1982, "The Changing Self-orientations of College Students: From Institution to Impulse," *Social Science Quarterly* 63:462–476.

22. Bem, D., 1972, "Self-perception Theory," in L. Berkowitz (Ed.), *Advances in Experimental Social Psychology,* Vol. 6, New York: Academic Press; M. E. Enzle, 1980, "Self-perception of Motivation," in D. M. Wegner and R. R. Vallacher (Eds.), *The Self in Social Psychology,* New York: Oxford University Press.

23. Deci, E. L., 1975, *Intrinsic Motivation,* New York: Plenum.

24. Enzle, M. E. and J. M. Ross, 1978, "Increasing and Decreasing Intrinsic Interest with Contingency Rewards: A Test of Cognitive Evaluation Theory," *Journal of Experimental Social Psychology* 14:588–597.

25. This section draws from H. Markus, 1980, "The Self in Thought and Memory," in D. M. Wegner and R. R. Vallacher (Eds.), *The Self in Social Psychology,* New York: Oxford University Press; and H. Markus and J. Smith, 1980, "The Influence of Self-schemas on the Perception of Others," in N. Cantor and J. Kihlstrom (Eds.), *Personality, Cognition, and Social Interaction,* New York: Lawrence Erlbaum.

26. McGuire, W. J., C. V. McGuire, P. Child, and T. Fujioka, 1978, "Salience of Ethnicity in the Spontaneous Self-concept as a Function of One's Ethnic Distinctiveness in the Social Environment," *Journal of Personality and Social Psychology* 33:743–754.

27. Markus, H. and P. Nurius, "Possible Selves," *American Psychologist* 41:954–969.

28. Goffman, E., 1959, *The Presentation of Self in Everyday Life,* Garden City, NY: Doubleday.

29. Rosenberg, 1979, op. cit.

30. Alexander, C. N., Jr. and P. Lauderdale, 1977, "Situated Identities and Social Influence," *Sociometry* 40:225–233.

31. Goffman, E., 1961, *Encounters,* Indianapolis: Bobbs-Merrill; C. N. Alexander, Jr. and M. G. Wiley, 1981, "Situated Identities and Social Influence," in M. Rosenberg and R. H. Turner, op. cit.

32. Weinstein, E. A. and P. Deutschberger, 1963, "Some Dimensions of Altercasting," *Sociometry* 26:454–466.

33. Scott, S. and M. B. Lyman, 1968, "Accounts," *American Sociological Review* 33:46–62.

34. *The Toronto Sun,* July 27, 1977.

35. Schlenker, B. R., 1980, *Impression Management,* Monterey, CA: Brooks/Cole; Goffman, 1959, op. cit.

36. Cialdini, R. B., R. J. Borden, A. Thorne, M. R. Walker, S. Freeman, and L. R. Sloan, 1976, "Basking in Reflected Glory: Three (Football) Field Studies," *Journal of Personality and Social Psychology* 34:366–375.

37. Burger, J. M., 1985, "Temporal Effects on Attributions for Academic Performances and Reflected-glory Basking," *Social Psychology Quarterly* 48:330–336.

38. Schmitt, R. L. and W. M. Leonard II, 1986, "Immortalizing the Self Through Sport," *American Journal of Sociology* 91:1088–1111.

39. Jones, E. E., 1964, *Ingratiation,* New York: Appleton-Century-Crofts.

40. Jones, E. E. and C. B. Wortman, 1973, *Ingratiation: An Attributional Approach,* Morristown, NJ: General Learning Press.

41. Tedeschi, J. T., B. R. Schlenker, and T. V. Bonoma, 1973, *Conflict, Power and Games: The Experimental Study of Interpersonal Relations,* Chicago: Aldine.

42. Baumeister, R. F., 1982, "A Self-presentational View of Social Phenomena," *Psychological Bulletin* 91:3–26.

43. Scheier, M. F. and C. S. Carver, 1981, "Two Sides of the Self: One for You and One for Me," in J. Suls (Ed.), *Psychological Perspectives on the Self,* Vol. 1, Hillsdale, NJ: Lawrence Erlbaum; M. F. Scheier and C. S. Carver, 1980, "Individual Differences in Self-concept and Self-process," in D. M. Wegner and R. R. Vallancher, op. cit.

44. Froming, W. J., G. R. Walker, and K. J. Lopyan, 1982, "Public and Private Self-awareness: When Personal Attitudes Conflict with Societal Expectations," *Journal of Experimental Social Psychology* 18:476–487.

45. Turner, R. G., 1978, "Self-consciousness and Speed of Processing Self-relevant Information," *Personality and Social Psychology Bulletin* 4:456–460.

46. Tobey, E. L. and G. Tunnell, 1981, "Effects of Public Self-awareness and Acting, A Self-monitoring Subscale," *Personality and Social Psychology Bulletin* 7:661–669.

47. For a discussion of this literature see Scheier and Carver, 1981, op. cit.

48. Snyder, M., 1980, "Self-monitoring Processes," in L. Berkowitz (Ed.), *Advances in Experimental Social Psychology,* Vol. 1, New York: Academic Press; M. Snyder and B. H. Campbell, 1981, "Self-monitoring: The Self in Action," in J. Suls, op. cit.

49. Snyder, M., 1974, "The Self-monitoring of Expressive Behavior," *Journal of Personality and Social Psychology* 30:526–537.

50. Glick, P., 1985, "Orientations Toward Relationships: Choosing a Situation in Which to Begin a Relationship," *Journal of Experimental Social Psychology* 21:544–562.

51. Snyder, M. and J. A. Simpson, 1984, "Self-monitoring and Dating Relationships," *Journal of Personality and Social Psychology* 47:1281–1291.

52. This section draws from R. L. Archer, 1980, "Self-disclosure," in D. M. Wegner and R. R. Vallacher, op. cit.

53. Chaikin, A. L. and V. J. Derlega, 1974, "Variables Affecting the Appropriateness of Self-disclosure," *Journal of Consulting and Clinical Psychology* 42:588–593.

54. Archer, R. L. and J. H. Berg, 1978, "Disclosure Reciprocity and Its Limits: A Reactance Analysis," *Journal of Experimental Social Psychology* 14:527–540.

55. Hendrick, S. S., 1981, "Self-disclosure and Marital Satisfaction," *Journal of Personality and Social Psychology* 40:1150–1159.

56. Rosenberg, 1979, op. cit.

57. This section draws on M. Rosenberg, 1967, "Psychological Selectivity in Self-esteem Formation," in C. W. Sherif and M. Sherif (Eds.), *Attitude, Ego-involvement, and Change,* New York: Wiley.

58. Rosenberg, M., 1965, *Society and the Adolescent Self-image,* Princeton, NJ: Princeton University Press.

59. Coopersmith, S., 1967, *The Antecedents of Self-esteem,* San Francisco: Freeman.

60. Gergen, K. J., 1971, *The Concept of Self,* New York: Holt, Rinehart & Winston.

61. For a discussion of this literature see Rosenberg, 1979, op. cit.

62. E.g., A. Bandura and N. E. Adams, 1977, "Analysis of Self-efficacy of Behavioral Change," *Cognitive Therapy and Research* 1:287–308; A. Bandura, 1982, "Self-efficacy Mechanism in Human Agency," *American Psychologist* 37:122–147.

63. Bandura, A., 1982, ibid.; A. Bandura, 1981, "The Self and Mechanisms of Agency," in J. Suls op. cit.

64. Abramson, L. Y., M. E. P. Seligman, and J. D. Teasdale, 1978, "Learned Helplessness in Humans: Critique and Reformulation," *Journal of Abnormal Psychology* 87:49–74.

65. Manning, M. M. and T. L. Wright, "Self-efficacy Expectancies, Outcome Expectancies, and the Persistence of Pain in Childbirth," *Journal of Personality and Social Psychology* 45:421–431.

66. Gecas, V. and M. Schwalbe, 1983, "Beyond the Looking-glass Self: Social Structure and Efficacy-based Self-esteem," *Social Psychology Quarterly* 46:77–88.

CHAPTER 6

Sex and Gender

■

Sex, Sex Stereotypes, Gender Roles, and Sexual Preference

Gender-Role Socialization

The Family

The Schools

Peers

The Media

Sex Differences and Similarities

Intellectual Abilities

Personality Traits

Explanations for Sex Differences

Biological Explanations

Environmental Explanations

Why Are Inaccurate Sex Stereotypes Believed?

Consistency with Gender-Role Socialization

Sex and Power

Consequences of Restrictive Gender Roles

Negative Consequences for Women

The Male Gender Role and Its Negative Consequences

How Is Restrictive Gender-Role Socialization Maintained?

Motherhood

Women's Two Jobs

In Search of Equality

Is it a boy or a girl? This is probably the first question your mother, father, relatives, and parents' friends asked about you. The answer to this question has almost certainly affected much of your life—the manner in which you were raised, the ways you feel and behave in social situations, your hopes and dreams for the future, your occupational plans, and the primary activities to which you will commit your life. Certainly, men and women have very different life experiences in this and other societies. The differences are seen as natural and inevitable by many people. They are supported by gender-role socialization and by society's views that men and women have different abilities and personality traits.

In this chapter, we will answer six questions. First, how are gender roles learned? Second, what differences in intellectual abilities and personality traits exist between the sexes and what causes these differences? Third, why are inaccurate stereotypes regarding men and women believed? Fourth, what are the consequences of restrictive gender roles? Fifth, how are restrictive gender roles maintained? Last, what can be done to achieve equality between the sexes?

Both sociologists and psychologists study sex and gender. While sociologists tend to focus on the relative position of men and women in society and the influence society has on male and female behavior, psychologists search for sex differences and similarities, and attempt to understand the reasons for any differences found.

■
SEX, SEX STEREOTYPES, GENDER ROLES, AND SEXUAL PREFERENCE

Before we explore these questions further, we must make distinctions among the terms sex, sex stereotypes, gender roles, and sexual preference. *Sex* is a biological phenomenon, the division of people into genetic males and females. This division is based in part on chromosomal differences. All human beings have 46 chromosomes. For males, the sex chromo-

somes are composed of an X chromosome from the mother and a Y chromosome from the father. For females, the sex chromosomes are composed of two Xs, one from the father and one from the mother. Five other indicators of biological sex exist: gonadal sex, with the male having testes and the female having ovaries; hormonal sex, with the male having mostly androgens and the female having mostly estrogens and progestins; sex of the internal reproductive organs, with the male having a prostate gland, ejaculatory ducts, vas deferens, and seminal vesicles, and the female having a uterus and fallopian tubes; and the sex of the external reproductive organs, with the male having a penis and scrotum, and the female having the clitoris, labia, and vagina.

Sex stereotypes consist of overgeneralizations about the similarities within each sex and the differences between the sexes. Although they may be partially true, often they are completely inaccurate. Sex stereotypes provide a foundation and a rationalization for the society's gender roles.

Most cultures hold beliefs that males and females have different personalities and talents, although the beliefs of some cultures do not parallel those of ours. For example, Margaret Mead (1) found that the New Guinea tribe, the Tchambuli, expected males to be artistic, jealous, and emotionally dependent, while females were expected to be dominant, impersonal, and responsible. In the Western world, sex stereotypes have much in common with these stereotypes, but they are the reverse of those of the Tchambuli. In most Western cultures females are viewed as passive, dependent, emotional, submissive, interested in and aware of the feelings of others, and focused primarily on home and family. Males are viewed as aggressive, independent, unemotional, controlling, rational, and as having little concern with the feelings of others.

Gender roles consist of the behavioral expectations associated with the roles of male and female. These expectations are defined by the culture and are manifested in cultural definitions of masculinity and femininity. All societies have definitions of appropriate behaviors for men and women, and boys and girls. Socialization into gender roles is an important aspect of cultural training, and in all societies men and women are taught that conformity to society's gender roles is right and proper. Gender roles always support the society's current social organization—its family, economic, political, and legal arrangements.

The traditional view of gender roles in our society holds that men and women should have different roles in the society. This *dual sphere concept* relegates men, who are supposedly competitive, aggressive, and independent, to the economic market place and women, who are allegedly nurturant, timid, and dependent, to the home and family. Many people in our society were raised to believe that such differences exist. They hold such beliefs as "a woman's place is in the home," men should be the "head of the family," and "wives should leave decision making to their husbands."

However, society is never static, and views regarding gender roles have changed rapidly in the last twenty years, particularly among women (2). Many young people now reject the traditional view of gender that divides men's and women's worlds. They believe the "women's place is in the house—and in the Senate," and men are viewed as fathers and husbands, rather than only as providers of the family paycheck.

These ideological changes have been precipitated by important changes in the lifestyle of people in our society. Despite the ideal of the "traditional" family, few families in the United States consist of the traditional nuclear family, with a husband in the labor force, a wife who does not work outside the home, and their children. While in 1960, 70 percent of United States families were of this traditional type, in 1987 only 9 percent of United States families fit this pattern (3). Economic need has been the most important force in women's increased participation in the labor market.

Sexual preference designates whether an individual is *heterosexual,* sexually attracted to members of the opposite sex, or *homosexual*, sexually attracted to members of the same sex. Just as homosexuals and heterosexuals are of both sexes, so do homosexuals and heterosexuals exhibit a wide range of gender-role behaviors, personality characteristics, and abilities. For example, many aggressive, strong,

independent male homosexuals exist, just as there are many passive, artistic, gentle, male heterosexuals.

Having distinguished sex, sex stereotypes, gender roles, and sexual preference, we now turn to our first question: How are gender roles learned?

Gender-Role Socialization

The gender-role socialization of children is based on a society's views of the "natural" differences believed to exist between the sexes. Despite the fact that considerable change has occurred in the last twenty years in our society, these traditional views about differences between the sexes still prevail. They underlie gender role socialization in this country, which is largely successful in teaching traditional stereotypes of males and females. As we have seen, men's and women's gender roles are undergoing change as a result of lifestyle changes in the society. However, some cultural changes lag behind others. Gender-role socialization and the sex stereotypes that underlie it have not kept pace with the changing gender roles themselves.

Next we explore some of the institutions through which traditional gender-role expectations continue to be conveyed to males and females. Consistent with their emphasis on the reciprocal influence of the individual and the society, sociologists in particular are interested in the role society's institutions play in gender-role socialization.

The Family

The earliest and most powerful source of gender-role socialization is the family. Considerable data suggest that in most families boys and girls are treated quite differently. In fact, you are very likely to have grown up in a family in which this different treatment was the rule, starting at birth. In many families, small girls are dressed in pink, play with dolls, and sometimes wear frilly dresses. When older, they are assigned the chore of doing dishes, and recreation may include more feminine activities such as attending dance classes on Saturdays. In contrast, small boys are often dressed in blue (but never in pink!), play with footballs, sometimes wear miniature suits like daddy's, are assigned the chore of taking out the trash, and attend baseball practice on Saturdays.

Parents have gender stereotyped perceptions, expectations, and values for their children (4). Differing treatment based on these stereotypes begins quite early. For example, parents play more actively with male than female infants (5) and they interact more with same-sex children (6). By age 6, boys are allowed to be farther away from home, and with less supervision, than girls (7). Parents have higher educational and achievement expectations for boys than girls and respond more positively to physical activity in boys than girls. Girls are required to do more housework, and the housework assigned to children of both sexes is gender stereotyped (8).

In addition, siblings contribute to gender-role socialization. Siblings, particularly older ones, reinforce and model sex stereotyped interests and behaviors (9).

The Schools

While the schools are changing, and open schools in particular try to provide nonsexist education, schools still play an important role in traditional gender-role socialization. One researcher even calls the teaching of traditional gender roles the "second curriculum" in the schools (10).

Like parents, teachers often treat boys and girls differently. As in the home, boys receive more praise, punishment, and attention from their teachers than girls (11). In school, boys are rewarded almost exclusively for their academic behavior, while girls are rewarded predominantly for nonacademic behavior, such as obedience (12). Overall, the message girls receive from teachers is "be dependent and conforming." The message for boys is "be high-achievers."

Students also learn about the *sex-typing* of occupations—the fact that many occupations are held predominantly by one sex or the other—in the schools. Most elementary teachers are women, while men in elementary schools are often administrators. In high school there are more male teachers, and they usually teach math and the sciences. Language teachers tend to be women. Still, at the high school level, administrators tend to be men.

Students are still encouraged to take sex-typed courses, such as shop for boys and home economics for girls (13). (When your authors were in school these courses were required, and students were not allowed to enroll in classes designed for the opposite sex. In some schools, interest in cross-sex-typed course was thought to be a sign of emotional disturbance!)

Finally, male and female high school students with the same talents are given different vocational counseling. Males with high math abilities may be encouraged to pursue a career involving mathematics, while girls with these abilities are more likely to be encouraged to teach math. Nontraditional career counseling is still almost nonexistent (14). Girls with interests in science are steered into medical technician jobs and nursing, while boys with such interests are encouraged to prepare for medical school.

Peers

Children of all ages spend more time with same-sex than opposite-sex peers and peers typically model behavior consistent with traditional gender roles (15). In one recent study, girls were found to engage in play involving the same amount of motor activity as boys when alone, but not when with other children (16). It appears that boys' greater activity during play is a socially created difference. Children who play at cross-sex-type activities are often rejected by their same-sex peers, resulting in their eventual conformity to the expected gender-role behavior (17).

The Media

The public media still present a stereotyped view of males and females. Although the last decade has brought real improvement, the media presentation of men and women is far from balanced. For example, television news stories are seldom about women and, when they are, typically show the wives

■ *Teachers encourage high academic achievement more in boys than in girls.*
(© Richard S. Orton 1989)

of public officials. Women's accomplishments are rarely reported (18).

In television drama, more male than female characters are portrayed, and the starring roles are written predominantly for males. Males tend to be shown as autonomous and powerful, and females as powerless and dependent. Women typically are young and hold domestic roles; the professional women portrayed often have difficulties in their personal lives (19). In television commercials, women are shown mostly as housewives whose sole interest appears to be (having some man show them) how to clean a floor better, what detergent is more effective, or which soap and perfume will make them most attractive to men. The messages not-so-subtly conveyed are that women are not worth including on television, and that women do not have a place in the world of work.

Rock videos are dominated by white males, who are shown in more active and dominant roles than the relatively few women who appear (20). An analysis of popular music over three decades found

a tendency to characterize women as evil or as the possessions of men, to describe them in terms of physical characteristics, and to stress their need for men (21).

Children's books, both textbooks and other books, also underrepresent females and present stereotyped views of both sexes. The characters of most children's books are male. Although these books do a much better job than in the past of portraying male and female characters in similar activities, even picture books designed to be non-sexist show female characters who are less active, more nurturant, and more emotional than boys, thus inadvertently reinforcing some stereotypes (22).

The adult print media are similar in this respect to the children's print media. Most women's magazines still focus on the lives of housewives rather than working women (23). Even magazines designed to attract young single women often are filled with features about finding single men and getting them to propose marriage. An analysis of photographs in magazines for computer users showed this new type of magazine to portray decidedly traditional gender roles (24). Men were pictured twice as often as women, and shown as expert users of computers, computer store managers, and computer repairpersons. Women were shown as sex objects, and were depicted as rejecting computers.

Comic strips also portray traditional gender roles (25). Comic-strip males engage in a much more diverse set of activities, both professionally and recreationally, than do comic-strip females. Comic-strip males often read, while comic-strip females seldom do so. Many comic-strip females routinely wear aprons (typical apparel for women in the 1990s?)!

In summary, the family, the schools, peers, and the media all convey traditional gender-role information to children. In addition, boys and girls are treated in different ways in the family and in school. While in all institutions the stereotyping is less strong than a decade ago, traditional presentations of gender roles are still strongly entrenched. Taken together, these data present a powerful argument that males and females are socialized to have different personalities and behaviors. With such a consistent message portrayed on so many different fronts, we would expect strong sex differences to result.

Next we address this issue and ask: What are the actual differences between men and women and what are the causes of these differences? We first review the social science data on the differences between the sexes, and then examine biological and environmental causes for the sex differences that were found. A major contribution of psychological social psychology to the study of sex and gender has been through empirical studies designed to determine the actual differences between the abilities and personality traits of men and women.

■ SEX DIFFERENCES AND SIMILARITIES

What do we mean by a sex difference? A *sex difference* is an average difference between men and women on some physical or social dimension. Let's use as an example two differences we know exist between males and females—size and strength. Males are generally larger and physically stronger than females. Does this mean all males are larger and stronger than all females? Of course not. All of us know some men are smaller and less strong than some women. The statement that males are larger and stronger than females is a statement about *averages*. Thus, when we ask, "Are males more aggressive than females?" we do not ask if all males are more aggressive than all females, but if, on the average, males are more aggressive than females.

Differences between men and women are not necessarily large, even if they are statistically significant. These differences may be relatively small, but consistent. Many sex differences are so small that the overlap between males and females is almost complete. In such cases the difference is not a reliable predictor of male and female behavior or characteristics. In order to assess the importance of a sex difference, we need information regarding its size as well as its existence.

First, we review the literature on intellectual abilities and then turn to the literature regarding personality traits.

Intellectual Abilities

The sexes' intellectual abilities are actually most notable for their similarities. No overall sex differences in IQ or creativity exist (26). With the exception of those associated with size and strength, sex differences in motor abilities also are not found (27). However, in the realm of specific intellectual abilities, two small sex differences do exist.

Males often have higher quantitative (mathematical) abilities than females, with the difference beginning at about age 11 and continuing through adulthood (28). This difference is very small, accounting for about 1 percent of the variation in individual scores (29). In addition, the findings are inconsistent; they vary by age of subjects, type of test used, and the heterogeneity of the sample.

Females often have greater verbal ability than

males, again beginning at about age 11 and continuing through adulthood (30). Females are superior to males in vocabulary, grammar, spelling, comprehension, and writing. These differences are also quite small.

It is often stated that, beginning in adolescence, males have greater spatial abilities than females (31). *Spatial ability* is the capacity to visualize objects in three-dimensional space. Recently, however, inconsistencies in research findings and the small size of the differences between the sexes call into question the alleged sex difference in spatial abilities (32). Inconsistencies in measurement have led some researchers to doubt even the existence of a clearly definable concept of spatial abilities.

In summary, sex differences exist in mathematical and verbal abilities. However, these differences are so small in magnitude, and are affected by so many other factors, that the sex similarity in these abilities is the more noteworthy finding.

Personality Traits

A number of stereotypes of personality differences between males and females exist; interestingly most are not supported by data. Females are stereotyped as being more nurturant, dependent, and conforming than males. However, studies of these behaviors have *not* shown consistent sex differences for any of these characteristics (33). Males are thought to be more competitive than females, but neither is this assumption supported by the data (34). Whether the tests have been laboratory tests of the behavior or field studies of more naturally occurring behavior, males and females do not differ significantly on these traits.

Other sex differences that may provide a basis for sex stereotypes have been found. Data on aggression, social influence, locus of control, and helping isolate some differences.

Males are more aggressive than females, a difference apparent from the age of two (35). But, the size of the difference is moderate and decreases with age (36). It is also inconsistent, influenced by the kind of aggression measured (verbal vs. physical);

the method of measurement (observation vs. subjects' reports of their behaviors); and the design of the study (natural vs. experimental setting).

Some differences have been found in the effects of social influence on the sexes. Sex differences in this area differ by type of subject, study, and social influence measure (37). For both studies of *persuasion*—in which attitude change in response to a persuasive communication is measured—and studies of *group pressure*—conformity to an incorrect response to a task—sex differences are found using some statistical measures, but not others. Where differences are shown, females are more easily influenced than males, with the size of the difference being small to moderate (38). Thus, even though females are sometimes more subject to influence than males, it is an overgeneralization to say that an overall sex difference exists in social influence.

In addition, some researchers argue that sex differences exist in the trait of locus of control, the extent to which people believe their lives are controlled by external factors beyond their control or by internal factors that allow them control over their lives. It is said that females feel external factors control their lives more and internal factors control their lives less, compared to males (39). However, the most sophisticated and recent analyses suggest the findings are more complex. Males are more likely to attribute their outcomes, both positive and negative, to ability than females, and females are more likely to attribute their outcomes to luck (40). Thus, it appears to be an overstatement to argue that overall gender differences exist in locus of control.

Finally, males have been shown to be more helpful than females (41). This difference in helpfulness has been demonstrated in a variety of settings.

In summary, few clear sex differences in personality exist. Those that exist are small to moderate, and typically vary by age of subject, type of measure used, and methods of study (42).

Next we assess the explanations for the few sex differences that have been found.

EXPLANATIONS FOR SEX DIFFERENCES

The discovery of a sex difference does *not* tell us anything about its causes. While a difference could be due to biological factors, it could also be caused by environmental factors—different treatment of males and females.

The *age* at which a sex difference first appears is not an indicator of its cause. Differences appearing early in life, such as differences in aggression at age 2, are not necessarily due to biological factors. As we have seen, males and females are treated differently from early infancy. Thus, differential socialization could account even for sex differences manifested early in life. Correspondingly, differences appearing later on, such as differences in math ability at age 11, are not necessarily the result of socialization. Biological factors need not be evident at birth. For example, a sex difference caused by hormones might not be manifested until puberty, when large changes in hormonal levels occur.

Biological Explanations

The fact that sex differences are not uniform throughout humankind, but vary rather dramatically across cultures, suggests that biological factors are not the sole causes of sex differences. If sex differences were solely biological, men from all cultures should manifest the same behaviors and abilities, and correspondingly, women from all cultures should share the same characteristics. Further, biological and environmental factors are not mutually exclusive. To the extent that biological factors are influential in causing sex differences, they are surely modified by environmental factors. The more complex and interesting question is not which set of factors is the cause of sex differences, but which set is most influential.

Intellectual abilities The most common biological explanations for sex differences in intellectual abil-

ities involve chromosomes, hormones, differential hemispheric processing in the brain, and maturation, or some combination of these factors (43). However, the evidence for these explanations tends to be rather weak.

The *chromosomal explanation* stems from the fact that males and females have different sex chromosomes; males have one X and one Y and females have two Xs. Only one relatively clear effect of chromosomes on sex differences in IQ is known: An extra X or Y chromosome tends to lower IQ (44). For persons with normal chromosomal structures, no effect of chromosomes on sex differences in intellectual abilities is known to exist.

The *hormonal explanation* stems from the fact that females have predominantly estrogens and progestins, and males, mostly androgens. While some data suggest chromosomal or hormonal factors may influence spatial ability, the results of these studies are mixed (45).

The hypothesis regarding *differential hemispheric processing* in the brain stems from the finding that language ability is largely a function of the left cerebral hemisphere, and quantitative abilities of the right cerebral hemisphere. Since women's greater verbal abilities stem from the left hemisphere, and males' greater math abilities from the right, the question arises as to whether males' right hemispheres and females' left hemispheres are more dominant or active in intellectual functioning. Currently, no conclusive studies show that functional differences in the hemispheres contribute to sex differences in intellectual abilities (46).

However, it does appear that *lateralization*, the localization of function on a specific side of the brain, is more pronounced in males than in females (47). It is possible that this difference in lateralization could contribute to sex differences in verbal and quantitative abilities in a way not yet understood.

The hypothesis regarding *maturation rates* stems from the different rates of maturation of males and females. While females mature more rapidly than males (walk earlier, talk earlier), research exploring different rates of maturation as an explanation of

BOX 6-1

Sex Differences and Studies of Hermaphrodites

John Money's (50) research with *hermaphrodites*, persons of ambiguous gender, is consistent with the conclusion that sex differences are likely to have predominately environmental explanations. For hermaphrodites, the five indicators of biological gender are inconsistent or inconclusive (for example, the external genitals may not be clearly either male or female). This extremely rare condition is created prenatally. It can be caused by a number of factors, including an extra chromosome and errors, excesses, and insufficiencies of the hormone system. For example, for a variety of reasons (a male-hormone producing tumor), testosterone can be added to the bloodstream of a genetic-female fetus, causing the child to be born with an extremely enlarged clitoris or a penis and scrotum.

A decision must be made in infancy as to whether the hermaphrodite will be reared as a male or a female. Money's research has shown that, as long as the child is assigned a sex before the age of 18 months and is reared consistently as a member of that sex, most sexually ambiguous children successfully adapt to whatever sex is assigned. For instance, a hermaphrodite with male hormones or chromosomes would probably still have a strong and consistent identification as a female if that person were reared as a female from an early age. Even a completely normal male child was successfully reared as female after his penis was accidentally burned during circumcision.

For the assigned sex to be successfully adopted, the assignment must be made early, ideally before 18 months of age. In addition, corrective surgery must be done to make the external genitals consistent with the sex of assignment, and hormone treatments must begin in adolescence so the appropriate secondary sexual characteristics will develop. And, of course, the parents and all other persons in close contact with the child must be consistent in treating the child as a member of the assigned sex.

Thus, sex of assignment is the most important factor in gender identity, more important than chromosomes, hormones, or physical appearance. If environmental conditions determine our basic sense of identity as male and female, it is certainly likely that they contribute importantly in determining our intellectual abilities and personality traits. ■

sex differences in intellectual abilities has been inconclusive (48).

In summary, biological explanations for sex differences in mathematical and verbal ability have not been supported by experimental evidence.

Personality traits The biological explanations most commonly offered are chromosomal and hormonal (49). With the exception of aggression, little support exists for the idea that either chromosomes or hormones explain sex differences in personality traits. However, the male's Y chromosome may be associated with aggression. In addition, male hormones, androgens, seem to be associated with aggression. Although the data are not completely clear nor totally consistent, at present these biological factors appear to be associated with the greater aggressiveness of males. With few exceptions, the data do not strongly support biological explanations as the primary source of sex differences in personality traits.

Environmental Explanations

Since biological explanations do not appear to provide an adequate explanation of sex differences, we now examine environmental explanations for these differences. As is the case with theories of socialization in general, psychologists have contributed the primary theories regarding the learning of gender roles. This interest stems from the psychological focus on learning in general. First, we explore three theories of gender-role socialization—social learning theory, cognitive developmental theory, and psychoanalytic theory (51). After presenting these theories, we discuss the role of our society's institutions in gender-role socialization.

Social learning theory According to social learning theory, gender-role socialization occurs in the same manner as all other learning—primarily through observation (52). Children watch same-sex models to determine how members of their own sex behave. If the behaviors they observe cause others of the same sex to receive rewards or avoid punishments,

the models are likely to be imitated. Children also watch opposite-sex models to determine how *not* to behave. Like other types of learning, gender-role learning is facilitated when there is a nurturant relationship between the observer and the model, when the model is powerful, and when the model rewards appropriate behavior.

As we pointed out in Chapter 2, immediate rewards are not necessary for learning to take place. To illustrate, daughters follow their mothers around the house and watch their activities. Daughters often play "house" and play with dolls, imitating their mothers' child-care, housekeeping, and cooking activities. This imitation can happen whether or not the mothers reward the daughters' imitation.

However, rewards and punishments often accompany gender-role socialization. In many families little girls are likely to be rewarded for feminine behaviors and punished for masculine behaviors, while little boys are rewarded for masculine behaviors and punished for feminine behaviors. For instance, boys may be scolded for crying, but girls may be comforted for the same behavior.

Further, in many families the child's environment is sex-typed or differentiated on the basis of sex. For example, boys may be given "masculine" toys, such as cars, and girls may be given "feminine" toys, such as dolls. (If you think this practice is a thing of the past, thumb through the toy section of any Christmas catalog (53)!) In these families, children will likely believe certain toys are for boys, while others are for girls.

Of course, families differ in the extent to which they believe behaviors consistent with the traditional gender roles are important. While some families punish a male who plays with dolls, others simply ignore him but then give him attention when he plays with stereotypically masculine toys. In families in which the parents actively discourage sex-typing in their children, playing with cross-sex-typed toys may elicit rewards from the parents.

Social learning theory suggests children are responsive to whatever pattern of rewards and punishments exists. Since families differ in the behaviors they model and those they reward and punish in

■ *Not all families encourage traditional gender-role socialization. (WGS)*

middle-class families. The sex difference, with boys adopting sex-typed behaviors earlier than girls in either class, is probably attributable to the higher status of the male than the female role in this society.

The data on and the earlier pressure on boys to learn their gender role showing decreases in sex differences that coincide with exposure to cross-sex-typed experiences is consistent with social learning theory. For example, sex differences in mathematical ability have declined as females have begun to take more math courses (55).

Cognitive developmental theory Cognitive developmental theorists stress the active participation of children in their gender-role socialization (56). This theory assumes gender-role attitudes are developed largely as a result of the children's cognitive organization of their social worlds. They think all children progress through similar stages of gender-role development because all children go through a similar cognitive maturation process.

According to cognitive developmental theorists, gender-role socialization begins with children's *gender identity*, or categorization of themselves as boys or girls. This process of identification is learned early from their parents and others. Once adopted, gender identity is thought to be irreversible, and becomes an important determinant of the children's values. Once children learn their sex, they positively value objects and behaviors consistent with their sex identities. They attempt to be boy-like or girl-like, and they find successful attempts at being boy-like or girl-like reinforcing. This type of reinforcement is not just externally imposed, but provides an example of internal *self-reinforcement*. Thus, young children are very interested in observing older children and adults for cues as to what makes boy-ness and girl-ness. They note sex differences in clothing, hairstyles, toys, games, and personality traits and try to copy those of their sex.

Several mechanisms support the development of interests, behaviors, and values consistent with the gender role. These include the *egocentrism* or self-focus of childhood, in which children value anything like themselves; the belief found in younger children that conformity to one's own gender role

their children, social learning theory predicts children from different families will exhibit different gender-role behaviors and will differ in beliefs about the proper behavior of males and females. Children rewarded for traditional gender-role behavior will be traditional in values and behaviors, and those rewarded for nontraditional gender-role behavior will be nontraditional in values and behaviors.

Researchers often find social class differences in sex-typed behaviors. For example, lower-class boys have a preference for sex-typed toys by the ages of 4 to 5. This preference is not found for lower-class girls and middle-class boys until age 7 and for middle-class girls until age 9 (54). The social class difference is probably due to a more rigid gender-role differentiation in lower-class compared with

is moral and proper; and the tendency for positive values to be associated with each gender (femininity's association with nurturance and caring; masculinity's association with strength and power).

According to this theory, children's gender-role development does not vary much in response to differing family values, since gender-role development is primarily a result of the children's own cognitive organization and maturation. Regardless of the pattern of gender-role behavior in the family, children will seek out information on sex-typed behavior in the society—from peers, at school, on television, and so on.

Cognitive developmental theory and social learning theory thus make different predictions regarding gender-role variations as a function of the family's beliefs about these roles. Can we determine which of these theories is more valid by examining the behaviors of children in families with different beliefs about desirable gender roles? Unfortunately, we cannot. Children from different families ultimately exhibit different gender-role behaviors, as social learning theory predicts. However, early in life all children of a given sex exhibit very similar gender-role behaviors, as cognitive developmental theory predicts. Neither theory is consistent with all the data on children's gender-role behaviors.

Psychoanalytic theory We will present two psychoanalytic theories on sex differences, one about identification and gender-role learning and one about attachment and mothering.

Identification theory. David Lynn's psychoanalytic theory relates identification with the same-sex parent to gender-role learning (57). The initial identification for both male and female infants is with the mother. This identification with the mother occurs because the mother typically is the primary caretaker when the infant is small. For girls, gender-role socialization is a relatively simple process. Girls merely strengthen this initial identification with the mother. Further, many girls have their mothers or another adult female with them during most of their waking hours. This means girls can learn the female gender role through intense and intimate contact with females.

For males, however, gender-role socialization is a relatively more difficult process. First, boys must switch from their initial identification with the mother to an identification with the father. Second, boys typically do not have their fathers or another adult male with them during many of their waking hours. This means boys must learn the male gender role primarily from females. Since females do not enact the male role, they can only teach it secondhand. Females typically teach the masculine role by negative example, for example, by telling male children not to act like females. Boys also learn the male role from their peers, who are likely to have only a stereotyped and conventional view of masculinity.

Lynn believes gender-role socialization and sexual preference are also related. More females than males are heterosexual in sexual preference. While around 10 percent of males are exclusively homosexual throughout life, the figure for females is around 1–2 percent. Lynn thinks this numerical difference is due to the more difficult process of gender-role identification for males.

Males also undergo more pressure to achieve early gender-role identification. Girls are allowed to be "tomboys," but boys are not allowed to be "sissies," a role that has only negative connotations. Lynn believes the pressure for males to achieve early gender-role identification and the difficulty of doing so cause males to be anxious about gender-role identification. He also believes these pressures lead to a second result, hostility toward women, because women play a central role in this difficult process of gender-role learning.

Theory of mothering. Nancy Chodorow has offered a psychoanalytic view of why women, rather than men, engage in mothering (58). Although we tend to think of mothering as "natural" for women, since they bear and nurse children, the bearer of the child does not have to be the motherer. Since the advent of the baby bottle, neither has nursing been a biologically imposed role. Mothering could be done by men as well as women.

Chodorow argues that adolescent girls in our society remain attached to their mothers, and correspondingly, mothers continue to feel their daughters are like themselves. Girls emerge from adolescence feeling connected with others and with a strong basis for experiencing another's needs as their own. Their needs for relationships and psychological definitions of themselves as being in relationships commits them to mothering.

In contrast, adolescent boys break their attachment to the mother to identify with the father. Similarly, mothers view their sons as male opposites. Chodorow believes boys' gender-role identifications are not derived through attachment to the father, but through their *rejection* of their attachment to the mother. They leave adolescence without the same attachment and empathy of female adolescents. Males' gender-role socialization includes the message that they should not be emotionally available. This lack of emotional availability adds to males' lack of attachment and empathy to help ensure that women will be left to do the mothering. Clearly Chodorow's theory is inconsistent with the findings of few differences between the sexes in characteristics such as empathy and nurturance.

■

WHY ARE INACCURATE SEX STEREOTYPES BELIEVED?

We have seen that few sex differences in abilities and traits actually exist, and that the small number of differences that have been found are mostly due to the different gender-role socialization of males and females. In fact, the lack of sex differences is particularly striking, in light of the rather restrictive gender-role socialization we have described. We have also noted that conceptions regarding the gender roles of men and women are clearly changing in response to the changing economic and family roles held by men and women.

Given these changes in gender roles, it seems odd that restrictive gender-role socialization and traditional sex stereotypes are so persistent. Even as more and more women join the labor force and more men spend significant amounts of time with their families, people continue to believe the old

traditional sex stereotypes. Since the gender-role socialization of children is based on a society's sex stereotypes, it is important to ask how outmoded stereotypes can continue to exist. Two answers to this question are presented, one involving behavioral consistency with gender-role socialization and another involving sex differences in power.

Consistency with Gender-Role Socialization

Societies not only teach gender roles to men and women, they teach them to believe these roles are proper and correct. Even though the *roles* are changing, most adults were *socialized* into relatively traditional gender roles and our *sex stereotypes* reinforce these traditional views. For this reason, many men and women are unlikely to engage in or admit engaging in behaviors or feeling emotions inconsistent with their traditional gender-role socialization, particularly around members of the opposite sex. This hesitancy in behaving in a way inconsistent with the traditional gender role produces behavior consistent with the sex stereotype, due not to "natural" differences between the sexes but the social pressures to conform to one's gender role.

To illustrate, it is believed women are more empathic than men, but data typically show no sex differences in empathic skills. However, women *report* feeling more empathy than men (59). Since empathy is consistent with the female but not the male gender role, and thus seems more legitimate for women to express than for men, women are more likely than men to admit feeling empathy. In addition, women may feel it is more acceptable to show empathy in public.

Both men and women inhibit behaviors and interests they believe typical of the opposite sex in situations thought to be unsympathetic to their display. In high school, men may not pursue natural abilities in art or music for fear of being labeled a sissy or a wimp. In the same setting, women may hide their talent in science for fear of losing male companionship or being thought unfeminine.

■ *Many stereotypes about the sexes are inaccurate, as the close physical relationship between this father and son illustrates. (WGS)*

Sex and Power

A second explanation centers on sex and power. In the everyday world, differences between the behaviors of men and women do exist. However, these differences often stem largely from their unequal statuses, rather than from differing personality traits (60). Because women typically have less power and status than men, women engage in more nurturant, dependent, or conforming behavior. These behaviors are attributable to low status, not sex. While these differential behaviors are performed by men and women in natural settings, they are not found in the laboratory, where the confounding effect of unequal status has been removed. This explanation is consistent with the personality and social structure perspective of sociological social psychology, in which aspects of the social structure are thought to influence individual behaviors.

Stereotypes in which men are considered to be competitive, independent, and high in self esteem while women are thought to be timid, dependent, and low in self esteem may persist in this society because the allegedly male traits are exhibited by people high in power, while the allegedly feminine traits are those of people low in power. Let's explore one such characteristic in more detail.

It is commonly observed that men and women speak differently (61). Women's speech is said to be more tentative than men's speech and to contain more questions (Don't you think it's pretty?) and more qualifiers (I sort of think it's pretty), compared to men's more decisive speech (It's pretty). Women also speak less in conversations with men, and when they do speak they often ask questions about the man's opinions or accomplishments. In addition, women are interrupted more by men than vice versa. Many researchers believe these differences in interaction style exist, but are a function of status rather than sex. Women are often in lower power positions, relative to the men with whom they are speaking.

When the interactions of men and women who do not differ in power are examined, the "sex difference" in language disappears. The interactions of higher status women and lower status men show a reverse "sex difference" in language: Men become the hesitant, tentative, less talkative ones (62).

■
CONSEQUENCES OF RESTRICTIVE GENDER ROLES

We now turn to a consideration of our fourth question: What are the consequences of gender-role stereotypes? A large number of these consequences are negative for both men and women.

Negative Consequences for Women

We will focus on three consequences: negative attitudes toward women, women's lower wages relative to men's wages, and problems of mental and physical health experienced disproportionately by women in traditional marriages.

Negative attitudes toward women   One consequence of the false gender-role stereotypes labeling women with many negative qualities is that both men and women hold women in lower esteem than they hold men. Edwin Schur argues that women are stigmatized in our society (63). In short, femaleness is a devalued status. Females are considered to be deviant, and they:

with great regularity have been labeled—and they still are being labeled—"aggressive," "bitchy," "hysterical," "fat," "homely," "masculine," and "promiscuous." Judgments such as these . . . may not put the presumed "offender" in jail, but they do typically damage her reputation, induce shame, and lower her "life chances."

Schur argues that labeling women as deviant reinforces disparities in social and economic power between men and women. Because of this stigmatization, the society's reaction to offenses against women, such as rape, abuse, and sexual harassment, is ambivalence. The result is that the victims of such offenses are treated as deviants.

Other analysts argue that physical and emotional abuse of women is a terrorist tactic used by men to control women so they will be compliant in the face of a system of oppression (64). They argue that violence directed against women has been directly or indirectly approved in every society. The direction of blame to the *victims* rather than the perpetrators of rape, wife assault, and sexual harassment provides a current example of this process. Even victims of child sexual abuse are sometimes blamed for being "provocative."

Women and wages   Women earn considerably less money than men in this and many other societies. In a recent study of male and female workers in Austria, Denmark, Finland, Germany, Israel, the Netherlands, Norway, Sweden, and the United States, women earned substantially less than men in every country (65). The gender gap was *greatest* in the United States.

Other analyses are consistent with these findings. As can be seen in Table 6-1, in 1987 women in the United States earned a weekly median salary of $383, as compared to $433. As a further inspection of this table shows, men earn substantially more money than women in every occupational category. Why does this sex difference in wages exist?

Unequal pay for equal work. One answer to this question is that women are still not paid as highly as men for equal work. Despite the existence of a number of laws to ensure equal pay for equal work, such as the Equal Pay Act of 1963 and Title VII of the Civil Rights Act of 1964, inequities exist. One reason for this continued inequity has been the exclusion of many positions from these laws. Another problem has been lax enforcement by and understaffing in the federal agencies responsible for enforcing the laws.

A number of negative and unsupported myths regarding women workers exist which are based on false sex stereotypes and traditional gender-role socialization. They doubtless contribute to the tendency of employers to undervalue women and to believe it is "fair" to pay them less than men. This inequity in payment, of course, harms men as well as women, since it lowers total family earnings.

Stereotypes of females as submissive, dependent, nonobjective, and excessively emotional, and stereotypes of men as aggressive, independent, objective, and rational contribute to the tendency of employers to perceive men as more qualified for high-status, high-income jobs, and women as qualified only for low-status, low-income jobs. Yet dozens of studies of male and female managers fail to find differences in personality characteristics and work behaviors. In a recent review of the literature on sex and managerial style, the authors asked researchers to stop rediscovering the same lack of sex differences and turn to a more promising question: Why are nonexistent sex differences perceived to exist (66)?

Traditional gender-role socialization suggesting women have no need to work since they will be cared for by a man and that women are more concerned with family than a career also contribute to the devaluation of women's labor. Quite to the contrary, however, women do need to work. Over 90 percent of women will enter the labor force for some period in their lives. In 1985, 54.5 percent of all women aged sixteen and over were in the civilian

■ *The number of men and women holding nontraditional jobs is growing.* *(WGS)*

Table 6.1 ■

Full-Time Wage and Salary Workers—Number and Median Weekly Earnings, by Selected Characteristics: 1983 to 1987

Characteristic	Number of Workers (1,000)				Median Weekly Earnings			
	1983	1985	1986	1987	1983	1985	1986	1987
All workers[1]	70,976	77,002	78,727	80,836	$313	$343	$358	$373
Male	42,309	45,589	46,233	47,162	378	406	419	433
16 to 24 years	6,702	6,956	6,822	6,726	223	240	245	257
25 years old and over	35,607	38,632	39,410	40,436	406	442	462	477
Female	28,667	31,414	32,494	33,674	252	277	290	303
16 to 24 years old	5,345	5,621	5,513	5,526	197	210	218	226
25 years old and over	23,322	25,793	26,981	28,148	267	296	308	321
White	61,739	66,481	67,779	69,358	319	355	370	383
Male	37,378	40,030	40,471	41,150	387	417	433	450
Female	24,361	26,452	27,308	28,208	254	281	294	307
Black	7,373	8,393	8,654	9,050	261	277	291	301
Male	3,883	4,367	4,464	4,679	293	304	318	326
Female	3,490	4,026	4,190	4,371	231	252	263	275
Hispanic origin[2]	(NA)	(NA)	5,630	6,093	(NA)	(NA)	277	284
Male	(NA)	(NA)	3,622	3,874	(NA)	(NA)	299	306
Female	(NA)	(NA)	2,008	2,219	(NA)	(NA)	241	251
Family relationship:								
Husbands	28,720	30,260	30,491	30,932	410	455	475	487
Wives	14,884	16,270	16,820	17,496	257	285	299	313
Women who maintain families	3,948	4,333	4,512	4,709	256	278	290	300
Men who maintain families	1,331	1,313	1,411	1,508	377	396	397	399
Other persons in families:								
Men	5,518	6,173	6,239	6,385	219	238	247	263
Women	4,032	4,309	4,328	4,469	201	213	222	235
All other men[3]	6,740	7,841	8,085	8,333	350	380	395	405
All other women[3]	5,803	6,503	6,841	7,004	274	305	316	326
Occupation, male:								
Managerial and professional	10,312	11,078	11,333	11,555	516	583	608	636
Exec., admin., managerial	5,344	5,835	5,980	6,117	530	593	620	647
Professional specialty	4,967	5,243	5,353	5,438	506	571	599	625
Tech., sales, and admin., support	8,125	8,803	8,977	9,241	385	420	437	453
Tech. and related support	1,428	1,563	1,597	1,533	424	472	490	500
Sales	3,853	4,227	4,373	4,580	389	431	447	479
Admin. support, incl. clerical	2,844	3,013	3,006	3,128	362	391	403	402

Service	3,723	3,947	3,987	4,143	255	272	284	296
Private household	11	13	14	16	(B)	(B)	(B)	(B)
Protective	1,314	1,327	1,433	1,481	355	391	402	427
Other service	2,398	2,607	2,540	2,646	217	230	239	251
Precision production[4]	9,180	10,026	9,973	10,125	387	408	418	431
Mechanics and repairers	3,418	3,752	3,588	3,681	377	400	413	423
Construction trades	2,966	3,308	3,413	3,548	375	394	401	416
Other	2,796	2,966	2,973	2,896	408	433	448	463
Operators, fabricators and laborers	9,833	10,585	10,784	10,926	308	325	332	344
Machine operators, assemblers, and inspectors	4,138	4,403	4,401	4,423	319	341	354	353
Transportation and material moving	3,199	3,459	3,494	3,612	335	369	372	386
Handlers, equipment cleaners, helpers, and laborers	2,496	2,724	2,890	2,890	251	261	271	289
Farming, forestry, fishing	1,137	1,150	1,178	1,171	200	216	220	219
Occupation, female:								
Managerial and professional	7,139	8,302	8,762	9,339	357	399	414	441
Exec., admin., managerial	2,772	3,492	3,797	4,099	339	383	395	416
Professional specialty	4,367	4,810	4,965	5,240	367	408	428	458
Tech. sales, and admin. support	13,517	14,622	15,083	15,439	247	269	282	293
Tech. and related support	1,146	1,200	1,224	1,264	299	331	343	368
Sales	2,460	2,929	3,021	3,077	204	226	239	246
Admin. support, incl. clerical	9,911	10,494	10,838	11,098	248	270	284	294
Service	3,598	3,963	4,074	4,171	173	185	191	199
Private household	267	330	320	305	116	130	119	130
Protective	139	156	156	186	250	278	292	314
Other service	3,193	3,477	3,598	3,680	176	188	195	201
Precision production[4]	784	906	878	867	256	268	277	302
Mechanics and repairers	120	144	136	131	337	392	431	456
Construction trades	45	53	56	38	(B)	265	333	(B)
Other	619	709	686	699	244	253	258	286
Operators, fabricators, and laborers	3,486	3,482	3,558	3,716	204	216	225	231
Machine operators, assemblers, and inspectors	2,853	2,778	2,853	2,962	202	216	223	227
Transportation and material moving	159	189	190	186	253	252	287	299
Handlers, equipment cleaners, helpers and laborers	474	514	515	568	211	209	226	233
Farming, forestry, fishing	143	138	140	142	169	185	187	191

In current dollars of usual weekly earnings. Data represent annual averages of quarterly data.

NA: Not available. B: Base less than 50,000.

[1] Includes other races, not shown separately.

[2] Persons of Hispanic origin may be of any race.

[3] The majority of these persons are living alone or with nonrelatives. Also included are persons in families where the husband, wife or other person maintaining the family is in the Armed Forces, and persons of unrelated subfamilies.

[4] Includes craft and repair.

Source: U.S. Bureau of Labor Statistics, Bulletin 2307, and *Employment and Earnings*, January issues.

Table 6.2 ■ Employed Persons, by Sex and Occupation: 1986

Occupation	Total Employed (1,000)	Female Percent of Total
Total	109,597	44.4
Managerial and professional specialty	26,554	43.4
Executive, administrative, and managerial	12,642	36.8
Officials and administrators, public	467	42.0
Financial managers	409	38.4
Personnel and labor relations managers	114	48.8
Purchasing managers	100	29.4
Managers, marketing, advertising and public relations	440	24.9
Administrators, education and related fields	500	47.7
Managers, properties and real estate	362	44.2
Management-related occupations	3,449	46.3
Accountants and auditors	1,257	44.9
Professional specialty	13,911	49.4
Architects	132	9.7
Engineers	1,749	6.0
Mathematical and computer scientists	631	36.2
Natural scientists	384	22.5
Health diagnosing occupations	728	15.0
Physicians	489	17.6
Dentists	132	4.4
Health assessment and treating occupations	2,026	85.3
Registered nurses	1,488	94.3
Therapists	257	74.2
Teachers, college and university	639	36.0
Teachers, except college and university	3,559	73.4
Prekindergarten and kindergarten	359	98.3
Elementary school	1,340	85.2
Secondary school	1,195	54.9
Counselors, educational and vocational	173	53.9
Librarians, archivists, and curators	212	82.9
Social scientists and urban planners	312	46.0
Social, recreation, and religious workers	911	46.9
Social workers	480	65.0
Lawyers and judges	650	18.1
Writers, artists, entertainers, and athletes	1,781	45.0
Technical, sales, and administrative support	34,354	64.7
Technicians and related support	3,364	47.0
Health technologists and technicians	1,124	84.1
Licensed practical nurses	417	97.5
Engineering and related technologists and technicians	937	17.7
Science technicians	208	27.9
Technicians, except health, engineering and science	1,095	37.6
Computer programmers	549	34.0
Sales occupations	13,245	48.2
Supervisors and proprietors	3,493	30.5
Sales representatives, finance and business services	2,255	41.5
Insurance sales	562	28.7

Occupation	Total Employed (1,000)	Female Percent of Total
Real estate sales	737	50.6
Securities and financial services sales	283	24.5
Sales representatives, commodities, except retail	1,505	18.3
Sales workers, retail and personal services	5,927	68.6
Cashiers	2,310	82.9
Administrative support, including clerical	17,745	80.4
Supervisors	727	59.3
Computer equipment operators	859	68.5
Secretaries, stenographers, and typists	4,940	98.2
Information clerks	1,326	89.7
Receptionists	724	97.1
Records processing occupations, except financial	845	81.4
File clerks	311	84.5
Financial records processing	2,473	90.8
Bookkeepers, accounting, and auditing clerks	2,007	91.8
Technical, sales, and administrative support—Con		
Administrative support, including clerical—Con		
Duplicating, mail and other office machine operators	77	61.9
Communications equipment operators	230	87.4
Telephone operators	220	87.9
Mail and message distributing occupations	903	34.4
Adjusters and investigators	824	72.3
Miscellaneous administrative support	2,902	84.9
General office clerks	740	80.5
Bank tellers	482	91.8
Data entry keyers	343	91.1
Teachers' aides	381	94.2
Service occupations	14,680	60.7
Private household	981	96.0
Child care workers	400	97.4
Cleaners and servants	527	95.3
Protective service	1,787	12.4
Firefighting and fire prevention	218	2.2
Police and detectives	666	10.9
Guards	741	18.4
Service except private household and protective	11,913	65.0
Food preparation and service occupations	5,127	62.8
Bartenders	322	48.8
Waiters and waitresses	1,403	85.1
Cooks, except short order	1,563	50.6
Short order cooks	111	36.8
Food counter, fountain, and related occupations	340	78.5
Kitchen workers, food preparation	126	76.3
Waiters' and waitresses' assistants	332	39.2
Health service occupations	1,823	89.9
Dental assistants	167	99.0
Health aides, except nursing	357	83.4

Continued

Table 6.2 (continued) ■ Employed Persons, by Sex and Occupation: 1986

Occupation	Total Employed (1,000)	Female Percent of Total
Nursing aides, orderlies, and attendants	1,299	90.5
Cleaning and building service occupations	2,861	41.5
Maids and housemen	583	84.8
Janitors and cleaners	2,075	30.9
Personal service occupations	2,101	80.0
Barbers	92	16.6
Hairdressers and cosmetologists	719	88.8
Attendants, amusement and recreation facilities	121	43.1
Public transportation attendants	71	77.1
Welfare service aides	87	91.7
Child care workers, except private household	762	96.5
Precision production, craft, and repair	13,405	8.6
Mechanics and repairers	4,374	3.5
Mechanics and repairers, except supervisors	4,127	3.2
Vehicle and mobile equipment mechanics and repairers	1,787	1.0
Electrical and electronic equipment repairers	710	9.0
Telephone installers and repairers	228	13.3
Construction trades	4,924	2.0
Extractive occupations	171	2.4
Precision production occupations	3,936	22.8
Operators, fabricators, and laborers	17,160	25.4
Machine operators, assemblers, and inspectors	7,911	40.3
Textile, apparel, and furnishings machine operators	1,323	79.8
Textile sewing machine operators	737	90.6
Pressing machine operators	136	71.9
Fabricators, assemblers, and hand working occupations	1,849	32.4
Production inspectors, testers, samplers, and weighers	817	49.6
Transportation and material moving occupations	4,564	8.9
Motor vehicle operators	3,380	10.8
Trucks, heavy and light	2,452	4.3
Transportation occupations, except motor vehicles	203	2.1
Material moving equipment operators	981	3.6
Industrial truck and tractor operators	386	5.0
Handlers, equipment cleaners, helpers, and laborers	4,685	16.3
Freight, stock, and material handlers	1,713	15.8
Laborers, except construction	1,128	17.7
Farming, forestry, and fishing	3,444	15.9
Farm operators and managers	1,337	14.1
Other agricultural and related occupations	1,917	18.1
Farm workers	940	23.6
Forestry and logging occupations	112	4.4
Fishers, hunters, and trappers	77	9.0

Source: U.S. Bureau of Labor Statistics, 1987; *Employment and Earnings*, January. Washington, DC: U.S. Government Printing Office.

BOX 6-2

Comparable Worth

Since the chance for full integregation of men and women into all positions in the labor market is unlikely to occur in the near future, some social scientists believe payment on the basis of *comparable worth* is the only practical solution to the problem of differential earnings by sex (71). Comparable worth is the principle of paying men and women equal wages for work requiring equal or comparable levels of skill. Under this system all jobs would need to be assessed for levels of skill and knowledge (education, experience), mental demands (judgment, initiative, originality), accountability (responsibility for operations, equipment, and the safety of others) and working conditions (hazards), with comparable jobs being paid equally.

This principle is definitely not in operation now. Current wages reflect a past view in society in which it was thought that men needed to be paid more than women because men, but not women, had families to support. Typically secretaries make less money than janitors, nurses less than electricians, and public health workers less than sanitation workers. It is even the case that, within university settings, professors of nursing make less money than other professors.

To date, courts have failed to uphold the principle of comparable worth. Those who do not support the principle of comparable worth argue that many married women choose low-paying "pink collar" jobs so their jobs will be compatible with child rearing and moving with the husband's job requirements. The supporters of comparable worth respond that the underlying economic and family factors derive from a system that devalues women and that it should no longer be supported. ∎

labor force (67). Forty-eight percent of women with babies under one year old were in the labor force in 1985. One out of five families with children is maintained by a woman, and 34.5 percent of such families live in poverty. Women are almost twice as likely as men to fall below the poverty level. In the past, poor women were typically the wives of poor men. Today, however, they are likely to be the heads of their own households; in 1985, 48 percent of poor families in the United States were female-headed.

In addition, women are involved in their work.

A recent analysis suggests that women allocate more effort to work than men, when effort is measured by energy demands of the job and energy expenditure on the job (68).

Job segregation. A second reason for the sex difference in wages is that women are clustered into a small number of low-paying white-collar jobs such as secretary, nurse, and childcare worker. As can be seen in Table 6-2, women comprised 99 percent of secretaries, 97 percent of receptionists, and 98 percent of kindergarten and preschool teachers, but only 6 percent of engineers, 4 percent of dentists, and 18 percent of lawyers and judges. Women are often excluded both from high-paying white-collar jobs and from higher-paying blue-collar jobs (69). Women are rarely given opportunities to train in blue-collar jobs requiring job training.

Even more barriers exist for women in professional jobs (70). First, candidates are judged on their abilities to fit into the group, with similar statuses (male, white, Protestant) thought to be important indicators. Second, many professions have a protégé or mentor system in which an established professional informally supports and trains selected young recruits. Females are less likely than males to be selected as protégés by these (usually male) professionals. Third, the older professionals are often instrumental in seeing their protégés advance in the professional world. Finally, within the profession, decisions are often made in informal contests from which women are excluded, such as over lunch with "the guys" or on the basketball court after work.

If women are crowded into the jobs men don't want, the female occupations will be overcrowded. Based on the principle of supply and demand, oversupply produces lowered wages. Other researchers believe the problem is not sex segregation, but the fact that female-dominated jobs typically are dead end jobs, with few chances of promotion (72).

Family socialization. A third answer to the question of wage differences by sex involves family socialization. As we have seen previously, the family is the source of much socialization into traditional gender roles (73). Such traditional socialization leads women to lower their occupational goals (74). This happens because traditional gender-role socialization teaches women their major goal in life is marriage.

This socialization also teaches women that men disapprove of women who achieve in nontraditional ways. Women take these attitudes about women's work achievement into consideration when they are making decisions about occupational plans (75). They accurately perceive that men's aspirations for women's careers are more limited and more traditional than are women's aspirations for themselves. This makes women less likely than men to consider any occupation that requires a high degree of

commitment or training because they do not want to make occupational plans that might interfere with their chances for marriage or create marital conflict.

Consistent with this argument, research findings show that much more than young men, young women believe they will have to modify their work roles and commitment for their families (76). The result of this process is that females exclude from consideration most high-status, high-paying careers because they believe they must do so (77). Here too, gender-role socialization promotes inequality; it supports the male's privileged position in the family relative to the female's through the encouragement of high aspirations in males and the discouragement of high aspirations in females.

Women, work, and health It appears that the current gender-role system has physical and emotional costs for women who conform to it. If one compares the physical and mental health of men and women, it appears traditional marriage makes men healthier and women less healthy (78). Married men are physically and emotionally healthier than unmarried men. In contrast, employed unmarried women and employed married women are physically and emotionally healthier than married women who do not work outside the home (79).

Why should traditional marriage create emotional problems for women? Some researchers believe the problem lies in the traditional female gender role (80). Since most men have two major sources of satisfaction, family and work, they can compensate with one source if the other proves disappointing. Since many housewives have only one major source of gratification, the family, they cannot compensate for unsatisfying experiences in this realm. Second, keeping house and raising children are low-status jobs that are thought to require little skill, probably because these jobs are unpaid. The low status and respect afforded these important roles force many housewives to acquire status and esteem in the outside world vicariously—through their husbands or their children.

This analysis of women's roles in traditional marriage is consistent with other data on women's emotional health. Women who do not work outside the home suffer from depression to a greater degree than women in the labor force (81). In contrast, women who are not married or who work outside the home are comparable to men in rates of depression.

In a study of marriage patterns and depression, both husbands and wives were less depressed when the wife's employment was consistent with their own preferences (82). Wives who preferred to work outside the home, but did not, were more depressed than wives in the labor force and wives who chose to stay home. Among husbands, those whose wives were employed and who were opposed to this work were most depressed, while husbands whose wives were employed and who were supportive of this work were least depressed. The amount of housework the husband contributed also influenced the wives' levels of depression. Regardless of the wives' work status, the more housework the husbands did, the less depressed were the wives. Interestingly, the husbands' levels of depression were not increased by performing housework.

Another observer of gender roles and mental health, Phyllis Chesler, alleges that any deviation from traditional gender-role socialization is defined as mental illness by mental health professionals (83). She believes a lack of acceptance of the female (or male) gender role is viewed by mental health professionals as a symptom of severe illness, and the "cure" is always acceptance of the traditional role. She feels psychiatry and the related mental health fields thereby contribute to women's subordinate status in the society.

The Male Gender Role and Its Negative Consequences

Recently social scientists have written about the costs to men of rigid definitions of gender roles. The male gender role is said to have four dimensions: *No Sissy Stuff*—the stigma of feminine characteristics; *The Big Wheel*—the need for status and success; *The Sturdy Oak*—the need to be manly and self-reliant; and *Give 'Em Hell*—the need to be aggressive and daring (84). Others argue that the male gender role

includes a fifth component, the need to be a sexual virtuoso (85).

What are the costs of these dimensions of the male gender role? The stigma associated with anything feminine means men must studiously avoid any feminine interests or characteristics. Men involved in the men's liberation movement believe that men are not allowed the release of showing emotion and of having real emotional intimacy with friends and family. They are forced to hide their emotions in order not to appear wimpy or unmanly. Never allowed to admit any weaknesses, men live with the continual necessity of having to prove their worth and toughness. Some observers feel men's inability to show emotion, plus the pressure to be competitive, can make them incompetent in interpersonal relationships (86). Often, they are unable to feel emotionally close to their children, wives, or male friends.

Men who write about the costs of the male gender role argue that the success element means that men feel compelled to be competitive in all things. Men are placed into competition with other men, creating yet another problem in male friendships. They live in a world in which "nice guys finish last" is a motto. The belief that men should show competitive, selfish motives, plus the inhibition against showing tender emotion, can turn the male world into a harsh, cold, and lonely one. Even in marital relations, many men feel they must be in command, the head of the family running a regiment of subordinates. One problem with this system is that unequal power does not foster love, but dominance and resentment.

The predominant success expectation is that the man be a good provider. In the traditional gender-role division of labor, men have the onus of being the primary or sole support of a family and are often forced to be away from their families as a part of the breadwinner role. This single breadwinning role, taken to its extreme, can cause the man to be viewed as an outsider by his family and to be valued primarily for his paycheck.

Many men spend their lives working in jobs they hate because they earn a good living at it. Men seldom feel they can succumb to the desire to practice an interesting but low-paying career. In the last decade, some men have dropped out of their boring, distasteful first jobs and taken up a second, more enjoyable one out of a need for self-fulfillment. The labels for this practice, male midlife crisis and male menopause, show the contempt with which men who violate the traditional masculine role are often held.

The aggressiveness component of the male role means that men are encouraged to act aggressively in order to be thought manly. While we officially decry violence in this society, in fact we often condone or ignore men's acts of aggression against other men and against women. The incidence of violence against women—at least 30 percent of married women beaten by their husbands (87); a woman battered every 18 seconds (88); a 25 percent chance of being a victim of rape and a 40 to 50 percent change of being a victim of attempted rape (89)—suggests this element has been learned all too well.

"I know you expect something in return for the movie, the flowers, and the dinner. Wait here and I'll get you a receipt."

The sexual element suggests that the most manly of men should be a sexual performer of the highest rank, with scores of admiring female partners who have been loved well and left. Many men believe their failure to live up to this expectation is shared by none but them, and they lie about their sexual prowess and adventures. Sexual relations as one part of a loving relationship has no role in the pursuit of this element of masculinity; here women are truly only objects to be "taken" and dropped in pursuit of the next.

Men associated with the men's liberation movement argue that the extremity as well as rigidity of the male role creates feelings of inadequacy and concerns about masculinity. Judged against the impossible standards of the stereotypic male gender role in which individual men are taught they ought to have the combination of Dirty Harry's aggressiveness, Evel Knievel's daring, Arnold Schwartzeneger's body, and Mike Tyson's money and Bo Jackson's athletic ability and money, no mortal man ever measures up to the ideal. Some men argue that the successes men do achieve in these arenas actually constitute failures, since it is the image of masculine success, and not one's own internal standards, that governs such successful men's lives (90).

■

HOW IS RESTRICTIVE GENDER-ROLE SOCIALIZATION MAINTAINED?

We have seen that sex stereotypes are largely inaccurate and that traditional gender-role socialization can be costly to men and women alike. Why then does rigid gender-role socialization continue to exist? Inaccurate sex stereotypes survive because the gender-role socialization through which they are enacted is an important part of the fabric of the society. Gender roles are intertwined with two powerful institutions: the family and the economy. Without changes in these institutions, gender-role socialization will not radically change.

BOX 6-3

The Ten Commandments of Masculinity

Warren Farrell believes the rigid masculine gender role entails definite costs for men (91). He sets out these costs in a humorous way, by stating them as commandments for men. According to Farrell, the ten commandments of masculinity are:

1. Thou shalt not cry or in other ways display fear, weakness, sympathy, empathy, or involvement before thy neighbor.

2. Thou shalt not be vulnerable but shalt honor and respect the "logical," "practical," or "intellectual"—as thou definest them.

3. Thou shalt not listen for the sake of listening—it is a waste of time.

4. Thou shalt not commit introspection.

5. Thou shalt be condescending to women in every way.

6. Thou shalt control thy wife's body and all its relations.

7. Thou shalt have no other breadwinners before thee.

8. Thou shalt not be responsible for housework or children.

9. Thou shalt honor and obey the straight and narrow path to success: job specialization.

10. Thou shalt have an answer to all problems at all times. ■

Motherhood

Many feminists argue that the *patriarchal* or male-dominated family is the primary vehicle for maintaining women's lack of power. Women's positions as wives and mothers lock them into subordinate structures (92). The ideology of motherhood is particularly powerful. Rather than being a biological process it has been designated a lifelong career through cultural beliefs that children will be irreparably damaged if their mothers work outside the home.

Data regarding the influence of maternal employment on children suggest, if anything, the reality is the reverse of the cultural ideology. No known associations of maternal employment with juvenile delinquency, neglect, nor academic difficulties exist. Even if we confine our examination only to infants and preschoolers, no differences regarding attachment to parents, intellectual development, or social and emotional development are found between children with full-time maternal care and those with employed mothers (93). Surprisingly, mothers who do not work outside the home spend no more time in positive interaction with their children than working mothers. Much of the time these mothers and their children spend in the home together apparently is spent without interaction taking place or in negative interaction.

Maternal employment seems to have some benefits for children (94). When the mother works outside the home, the father's role in child care increases. Children from dual earner families thus have greater exposure to nontraditional behaviors exhibited by both parents. As a result, both sons and daughters of mothers who work for wages have more positive and less stereotypic views of women than children of mothers who do not work outside the home (95). In addition, employed mothers provide positive role models for adolescent daughters. Daughters of mothers in the paid labor market are more likely to name their mothers as role models than daughters of mothers who are not employed (96). Independence training is also stressed in dual earner families, with the consequence that parents have fewer difficulties "letting go" of their children at appropriate times.

Is maternal employment a benefit to all children? Apparently not. The most important factor in determining whether maternal employment benefits or hinders good parents is whether the woman is doing what she wants to do. Mothers who do not work for wages but who wish to do so score lower on measures of quality of mothering than mothers in any other category (97).

Women's Two Jobs

Many women hold two jobs: their paid job in the labor force and the unpaid job of houseworker (98). These two jobs have consequences both for women's position in the labor force and the family.

Labor market consequences Husbands of wives who work for wages do no more housework than husbands of wives who do not work outside the home (99). Women who work outside the home spend an average of 33 hours per week on housework; their husbands spend an average of 11 hours per week. The work husbands contribute consists of typical male-sex-typed jobs of yard work and home repairs (100). The author of one study feels "husbands may require more housework than they contribute."

Although many husbands feel free to put in long work weeks and work on weekends, their female coworkers often work 8-hour days, then return home to cook dinner, care for the children, and do housework in the evenings and on weekends. Of course, not all women wish to work 80-hour weeks, and it probably is not physically or emotionally healthy for men to do so. But the essential point is this: Many occupations do require professionals to spend long hours at work to receive promotions, and most married men have this opportunity, but few married women can choose to do so.

Family consequences Some theorists argue that the division of household labor creates gender roles—that as housework and child care is done, gender roles are also "done" (101). The division of labor in housework produces two products—household labor and gender roles. During the process of doing housework and child care, men and women pay homage to the cultural conceptions of proper gender roles. Traditional gender roles are merged with the necessity for an efficient system of household labor.

Some economists have argued that women's labor market position leads to overall devaluation of women's time with the result that yet another link between work and the family is forged (102). The devaluation of women's time reinforces the household division of labor, since men's time is too important to spend on such menial chores.

Women's earnings also affect their power in the family. Relative power in the marriage relationship is associated with the wife's employment status (103). If the wife works, she has more power in the marriage than if she does not. Wives who contribute a relatively higher percentage of the family income have more power than wives who contribute a lower percentage of the family income. Due to the wage difference between men and women, even women with occupations of the same status as their husbands are likely to earn less than their husbands and thus to have less power in the family.

In summary, the economy and the patriarchal family system perpetuate outmoded gender-role socialization. This is accomplished through the interconnections of gender with motherhood, childcare, housework, and family power, in which women's subordinate economic and family roles are reaffirmed.

IN SEARCH OF EQUALITY

In this section we ask our last question: What can be done to achieve equality between the sexes? Many sociologists and psychologists argue that economics is the most critical element in social relations. They believe women will achieve complete equality with men only when economic equality can be achieved. These sociologists feel equality can be attained through legal and social reforms that influence the labor market and through changes in gender-role socialization.

Other sociologists trace inequality of the sexes to the patriarchal family, in which husbands have had power over their wives and children or to both patriarchy and our economic system. These sociologists believe far-reaching changes must be made in our family and economic systems before equality of the sexes can be obtained.

Because men benefit from women's social and economic devaluation, the impetus for change is not likely to come from them. (If women were in the position of greater power and authority, they would not be likely to give up their advantages voluntarily either.) Unfortunately, one consequence of stigmatization and devaluation is a damaged self-concept. Women and men are taught that women are less important or worthy than men. Women who learn this lesson well accept their lowered life chances as fair. These women may view their best strategy for success and happiness as being an appendage of a man who has a greater chance of achieving wealth, power, and status than they do.

Whatever the ultimate solutions may be, it is clear that gender role norms are currently changing in this society. In the last thirty years, the traditional nuclear family has become a form practiced only by a small minority of families. It was economic need, rather than feminist ideology, that drove most women into the labor force during this time. But as we will see in Chapter 10, when behaviors change, changes in attitudes soon follow. Thus, one clear change is in young people's beliefs that they will be part of a two-earner family when they marry.

Although discouragingly small, corresponding changes have followed wives' entry into the labor force. Some husbands of wives who work outside the home are doing more childcare and a little more housework. Husbands are coming under increasing pressure from wives employed in the labor force to do more housework and childcare, and they can be expected to slowly respond to this pressure. In addition, many children now see their mothers working for wages rather than working solely inside the home. These children will grow up with a nontraditional view of women in the realm of work. Further, if their parents seemed happy with their lives, they are likely themselves to prefer the family structure in which they were raised (105).

Society is never stagnant; year after year more women and men seek equality for all humankind, and the position of women gradually improves. But until men and women see themselves as kindred humans, with common goals and common problems, rather than as dissimilar adversaries, complete equality and understanding cannot be achieved.

SUMMARY

Sex is the division of people into male and female, while gender roles consist of the abilities and personality traits expected of males and females.

In this chapter we have explored five questions regarding sex and gender. What are society's gender-role stereotypes? Do these stereotypes reflect actual sex differences? What is the cause of sex differences? Why do inaccurate gender-role stereotypes persist?

What are the negative consequences of these stereotypes?

In most cultures, people believe males and females have different abilities and personality characteristics. Some of these gender-role stereotypes are accurate, but most are not. No sex differences exist in overall intellectual abilities, creativity, or most motor skills. Overall, males have greater quantitative abilities than females, and females have greater verbal abilities than males. While it has been thought males have greater spatial abilities, this appears not to be true. Sex differences also exist in some personality traits. Males are more aggressive and more helpful than females, while females are sometimes more subject to social influence than males. Men typically attribute their outcomes more to skill than do women, and women typically attribute their outcomes more to luck than do men.

Four primary biological explanations have been offered for these sex differences: chromosomes, hormones, differential hemispheric processing in the brain, and maturation. Little evidence supports any of these biological explanations, except for the sex difference in aggressiveness. However, considerable evidence supports socialization as a primary explanation for sex differences. Family, peers, schools, and the mass media all teach boys and girls that they should be different from each other.

Social learning theory, cognitive developmental theory, and psychoanalytic theory give competing, environmental explanations for gender-role differences. Their explanations are, respectively, gender roles are learned though observation, cognitive maturation, and identification with the same-sex parent.

Why are inaccurate gender-role stereotypes believed? One reason may be that men and women inhibit behaviors inconsistent with their gender role if they believe the behaviors will not be accepted by others. In addition, differences in behaviors between men and women stemming from status differences are perceived to be the result of true sex differences.

Restrictive gender roles have many negative consequences. Negative beliefs about women are one harmful consequence for females. In addition, women earn less money than men, and traditional marriage can lead women who do not work outside the home to become unhappy, ill, and depressed in middle age, relative to other women and to men.

Negative consequences of gender-role stereotyping exist for males as well as for females. Men feel pressured to seek status and money, to be self-reliant and inhibit their feelings, to be aggressive, and to perform impossible sexual feats.

Restrictive gender-role socialization is maintained because gender roles are intertwined with two important institutions: the family and the economic system. The concept of motherhood, women's role in child care and housework, and the distribution of power in the family must be changed for gender-role socialization to change radically.

How can equality be achieved between the sexes? Opinions vary; some social psychologists believe economic equality is the key. Others believe patriarchy, or both patriarchy and the economic system are to blame for inequities. The increased number of wives who work outside the home has already lead to some changes in gender roles, and can be expected to lead to more such changes.

■

REFERENCES

1. Mead, M., 1935, *Sex and Temperament in Three Primitive Societies*, New York: William Morrow.
2. Mason, K. O. and Y. Lu, 1988, "Attitudes Towards Women's Familial Roles: Changes in the United States, 1977–1985," *Gender and Society* 2:39–57; W. H. McBrown, 1987, "Longitudinal Change in Sex Role Orientations: Difference Between Men and Women," *Sex Roles* 16:439–452; S. E. Tallichet and F. K. Willits, 1986, "Gender-role Attitude Change of Young Women: Influential Factors from a Panel Study," *Social Psychology Quarterly* 49:219–227.
3. U.S. Bureau of the Census, 1987, *Current Population Reports, Population Characteristics*, Series P-20, No. 424, "Household and Family." Washington, DC.: U.S. Government Printing Office.
4. Fagot, B. I., 1981, "Stereotypes versus Behavioral Judgments of Sex Differences in Young Children," *Sex Roles* 7:1093–1096; J. E. Parsons, T. F. Adler, and C. M. Kaczala, 1982, "Socialization of Achievement Attitudes and Beliefs: Parental Influences," *Child Development* 53:310–321.
5. Huston, A. C., 1983, "Sex-typing," in P. H. Mussen and E. M. Hetherington (Eds.), *Handbook of Child Psychology, Socialization, Personality, and Social Development*, Vol. 4, 4th ed. New York: John Wiley.

6. Huston, 1983, ibid.

7. Medrich, E. A., J. A. Roizen, V. Rubin, and S. Buckley, 1982, *The Serious Business of Growing Up,* Berkeley: University of California Press.

8. Munroe, R. H., R. L. Munroe, C. Michelson, A. Koel, R. Bolton, and C. Bolton, 1983, "Time Allocation in Four Societies," *Ethnology* 22:355–370; F. L. Cogle and G. E. Tasker, 1982, "Children and Housework," *Family Relations* 31:395–399.

9. Huston, 1983, op. cit.

10. Best, R., 1983, *We've All Got Scars,* Bloomington: Indiana University Press.

11. Huston, 1983, op. cit.; P. P. Minuchin and E. K. Shapiro, 1983, "The School as a Context for Social Development," in P. H. Mussen and E. M. Hetherington (Eds.), op. cit.

12. Minuchin and Shapiro, 1983, ibid.

13. Minuchin and Shapiro, 1983, ibid.

14. Eccles, J. and L. W. Hoffman, 1984, "Sex Roles, Socialization, and Occupational Behavior," in H. W. Stevenson and A. E. Siegel (Eds.), *Research in Child Development and Social Policy,* Vol. 1, Chicago: University of Chicago Press.

15. Hartup, W. W., 1983, "Peer Relations," in P. H. Mussen and E. M. Hetherington (Eds.), op. cit.

16. Bloch, M. N., 1987, "The Development of Sex Differences in Young Children's Activities at Home: The Effect of Social Context," *Sex Roles* 16:279–301.

17. Fagot, B. I., 1982, "Adults as Socializing Agents," in T. Field, A. Huston, H. Quay, L. Troll, and G. Finley (Eds.), *Review of Human Development,* New York: Wiley.

18. Cantor, M. G., 1987, "Popular Culture and the Portrayal of Women: Content and Control," in B. B. Hess and M. M. Ferree (Eds.), *Analyzing Gender: A Handbook of Social Science Research,* Newbury Park, CA: Sage.

19. Durkin, L., 1985, "Television and Sex Role Acquisition I. Content," *British Journal of Social Psychology* 24:101–113.

20. Brown, J. D., 1985, "Race and Gender in Rock Videos," *Social Science Newsletter* 70:82–86.

21. Cooper, V. W., 1985, "Women in Popular Music: A Quantitative Analysis of Feminine Images," *Sex Roles* 13:499–506.

22. Compare L. J. Weitzman, D. Eifler, E. Hokada, and C. Ross, 1972, "Sex Role Socialization in Picture Books for Preschool Children," *American Journal of Sociology* 77:1125–1150; R. Kolbe and J. C. LaVoie, 1982, "Sex-role Stereotyping in Preschool Children's Picture Books," *Social Psychology Quarterly* 44:369–374; and A. J. Davis, 1984, "Sex-differentiated Behaviors in Non-sexist Picture Books," *Sex Roles* 11:1–15.

23. Ruggerio, J. A. and L. C. Weston, 1985, "Work Options for Women in Women's Magazines: The Medium and the Message," *Sex Roles* 12:535–548.

24. Ware, M. C. and M. F. Stuck, 1985, "Sex Role Messages vis-a-vis Microcomputer Use: A Look at the Pictures," *Sex Roles* 13:205–214.

25. Brabant, S. and L. Mooney, 1986, "Sex-role Stereotyping in the Sunday Comics: Ten Years Later," *Sex Roles* 14:141–148.

26. Maccoby, E. E. and C. N. Jacklin, 1974, *The Psychology of Sex Differences,* Stanford, CA: Stanford University Press; L. J.

Harris, 1977, "Sex Differences in the Growth and Use of Language," in E. Donelson and J. E. Gullahorn (Eds.), *Women: A Psychological Perspective,* New York: Wiley, pp. 79–94.

27. Thomas, J. R. and K. E. French, 1985, "Gender Differences Across Age in Motor Performance: A Meta-Analysis," *Psychological Bulletin* 98:260–282.

28. Benbow, C. P. and J. C. Stanley, 1980, "Sex Differences in Mathematical Ability: Fact or Artifact?" *Science* 210:1262–1264.

29. Hyde, J. S., 1981, "How Large Are Cognitive Gender Differences?" *American Psychologist* 36:892–901.

30. Maccoby and Jacklin, 1974, op. cit.; J. H. Block, 1976, "Issues, Problems, and Pitfalls in Assessing Sex Differences," *Merrill-Palmer Quarterly* 22:283–308.

31. Maccoby and Jacklin, 1974, ibid; Block, 1976, ibid.

32. Caplan, P. J., G. M. MacPherson, and P. Tobin, 1985, "Do Sex-related Differences in Spatial Abilities Exist?" *American Psychologist* 40:786–799.

33. Maccoby and Jacklin, 1974, op. cit.; K. Deaux, 1976, *The Behavior of Women and Men,* Monterey, CA: Brooks/Cole.

34. Maccoby and Jacklin. 1974, ibid.; Deaux, 1976, ibid.

35. Maccoby and Jacklin, 1974, ibid.; Deaux, 1976, ibid; Eagly, A. H., 1987, *Sex Differences in Social Behavior: A Social-Role Interpretation,* Hillsdale, NJ: Erlbaum.

36. Hyde, J. S., 1986, "Gender Differences in Aggression," in J. S. Hyde and M. C. Linn (Eds.), *The Psychology of Gender: Advances through Meta-Analysis,* Baltimore: Johns Hopkins University Press.

37. Becker, B. J., 1986, "Influence Again: An Examination of Reviews and Studies of Gender Differences in Social Influence," in J. S. Hyde and M. C. Linn, ibid.

38. Eagly, 1987, op. cit.

39. Maccoby and Jacklin, 1974, op. cit.; Deaux, 1976, op. cit.

40. Whitley, B. E., Jr., M. C. McHugh, and I. H. Frieze, 1986, "Assessing the Theoretical Models for Sex Differences in Causal Attributions of Success and Failure," in J. S. Hyde and M. C. Linn, op. cit.

41. Eagly, 1987, op. cit.

42. Deaux, K. and B. Major, 1987, "Putting Gender into Context: An Interactive Model of Gender-related Behavior," *Psychological Review* 94:369–389.

43. Basow, S. A., 1980, *Sex-role Stereotypes: Traditions and Alternatives,* Monterey, CA: Brooks/Cole; K. B. Hoyenga and K. T. Hoyenga, 1979, *The Question of Sex Differences,* Boston: Little, Brown.

44. Hoyenga and Hoyenga, 1979, ibid.

45. Basow, 1980, op. cit.; Hoyenga and Hoyenga, 1979, ibid.

46. Basow, 1980, ibid.

47. Hoyenga and Hoyenga, 1979, op. cit.

48. Basow, 1980, op. cit.

49. Basow, 1980, op. cit.

50. e.g., J. Money, and A. A. Ehrhardt, 1972, *Man and Woman, Boy and Girl,* Baltimore: Johns Hopkins University Press.

51. For a critique of these theories and a review of empirical tests of them, see J. H. Pleck, 1982, *The Myth of Masculinity,* Cambridge, MA.: MIT Press.

52. Mischel, W., 1966, "A Social-Learning View of Sex Differences in Behavior," in E. Maccoby (Ed.), *The Development of Sex Differences*, Stanford, CA: Stanford University Press; A. Bandura and R. H. Walters, 1963, *Social Learning and Personality Development*, New York: Holt, Rinehart & Winston.

53. Schwartz, L. A. and W. T. Markham, 1985, "Sex Stereotyping in Children's Toy Advertisements," *Sex Roles* 12:157–170.

54. Rabban, M., 1950, "Sex Role Identification in Young Children in Two Diverse Social Groups," *Genetic Psychology Monographs* 42:81–158.

55. Hyde, 1986, op. cit.

56. Kohlberg, L., 1969, "Stage and Sequence: The Cognitive Developmental Approach to Socialization," in D. A. Goslin (Ed.), *Handbook of Socialization Theory and Research*, Chicago: Rand McNally, pp. 347–480.

57. Lynn, D. B., 1969, *Parental and Sex-role Identification: A Theoretical Formulation*, Berkeley, CA: McCutchan.

58. Chodorow, N., 1978, *The Reproduction of Mothering*, Berkeley: University of California Press.

59. Eisenberg, N. and R. Lennon, 1983, "Sex Differences in Empathy and Related Capacities," *Psychological Bulletin* 94:100–131.

60. Eagly, 1987, op. cit.; A. H. Eagly, 1983, "Gender and Social Influence: A Social Psychological Analysis," *American Psychologist* 38:971–981; J. A. Howard, 1988, "Gender Differences in Sexual Attitudes: Conservatism or Powerlessness?" *Gender and Society* 2:103–114.

61. Kollock, P., P. Blumstein, and P. Schwartz, 1985, "Sex and Power in Interaction: Conversational Privileges and Duties," *American Sociological Review* 50:34–46.

62. Kollock et al, 1985, ibid.

63. Schur, E. M., 1984, *Labeling Women Deviant: Gender, Stigma, and Social Control*, New York: Random House.

64. Sheffield, C. J., 1987, "Sexual Terrorism: The Social Control of Women," in B. B. Hess and M. M. Ferree, op. cit.

65. Treiman, D. J. and P. A. Roos, 1983, "Sex and Earnings in Industrial Society: A Nine-nation Comparison," *American Journal of Sociology* 89:612–650.

66. Dobbins, G. H. and S. J. Platz, 1986, "Sex Differences in Leadership: How Real Are They?" *Academy of Management Review* 11:118–127.

67. Current Population Reports, "Characteristics of the Population Below the Poverty Level, 1984," Consumer Income Series P-60, No. 152, August, 1986, Washington, DC: U. S. Government Printing Office.

68. Bielby, D. D. and W. T. Bielby, 1988, "She Works Hard for the Money: Household Responsibilities and the Allocation of Work Effort," *American Journal of Sociology* 93:1031–1059.

69. Current Population Reports, "Women in the American Economy," Special Study Series P-23, No. 146, November, 1986, Washington, DC: U. S. Government Printing Office; B. F. Reskin and H. I. Hartmann (Eds.), 1986, *Women's Work, Men's Work: Sex Segregation in the Job*, Washington, DC: National Academy Press.

70. Epstein, C. F., 1970, *Woman's Place: Options and Limits in Professional Careers*, Berkeley: University of California Press.

71. Blum, L. M., 1987, "Possibilities and Limits of the Comparable Worth Movement," *Gender and Society* 1:380–399; H. I. Hartmann (Ed.), 1985, *Comparable Worth: New Directions for Research*, Washington: National Academy Press; H. Remick (Ed.), 1984, *Comparable Worth and Wage Discrimination*, Philadelphia: Temple University Press.

72. DiPrete, T. A. and W. T. Soule, 1988, "Gender and Promotion in Segmented Job Ladder Systems," *American Sociological Review* 53:26–40.

73. Glenn, E. K., 1987, "Gender and the Family," in B. B. Hess and M. M. Ferree, op. cit.

74. Baruch, G., R. Barnett, and C. Rivers, 1983, *Life Prints*, New York: McGraw-Hill; L. A. Leslie, 1986, "The Impact of Adolescent Females' Assessments of Parenthood and Employment on Plans for the Future," *Journal of Youth and Adolescence* 15:29–50; M. A. Paludi and J. Fankell-Hauser, 1986, "An Idiographic Approach to the Study of Women's Achievement Strivings," *Psychology of Women Quarterly* 10:89–100.

75. e.g., E. S. Aneshensel and B. C. Rosen, 1980, "Domestic Roles and Sex Differences in Occupational Expectations," *Journal of Marriage and the Family* 42:121–139; J. Corder-Bolz and C. W. Stephan, 1984, "Females' Combination of Work and Family Roles: Adolescents' Aspirations," *Journal of Marriage and the Family* 46:391–402.

76. Herzog, A. R. and J. C. Bachman, 1982, *Sex Role Attitudes Among High School Seniors*, Ann Arbor: Institute for Social Research, University of Michigan; C. K. Tittle, 1981, *Careers and Family: Sex Roles and Adolescent Life Plans*, Beverly Hills: Sage.

77. Eccles, J. S., 1987, "Gender Roles and Women's Achievement-related Decisions," *Psychology of Women Quarterly* 11:135–172; K. Gerson, 1986, *Hard Choices: How Women Decide about Work, Career, and Motherhood*, Berkeley: University of California Press.

78. Bernard, J., 1972, *The Future of Marriage*, New York: Bantam; R. C. Kessler and J. A. McRae, 1982, "The Effect of Wives' Employment on the Mental Health of Married Men and Women," *American Sociological Review* 47:216–227; L. M. Verbrugge, 1982, "Women's Social Roles and Health," in P. W. Berman and E. R. Ramsey (Eds.), *Women: A Development Perspective*, Bethesda, MD: National Institute of Mental Health.

79. Cleary, P. D. and D. Mechanic, 1983, "Sex Differences in Psychological Distress Among Married People," *Journal of Health and Social Behavior* 24:111–121; C. Nathanson, 1980, "Social Roles and Health Status among Women: The Significance of Employment," *Social Science and Medicine* 14A:463–471.

80. Bernard, 1972, op. cit.; W. R. Gove and M. R. Geerken, 1977, "The Effect of Children and Employment on the Mental Health of Married Men and Women," *Social Forces* 56:66–76.

81. Pearlin, L. I., M. A. Lieberman, E. G. Menaghan, and J. T. Mullan, 1981, "The Stress Process," *Journal of Health and Social Behavior* 22:337–356.

82. Ross, C. E., J. Mirowsky, and J. Huber, 1983, "Dividing Work, Sharing Work, and In-between: Marriage Patterns and Depression," *American Sociological Review* 48:809–823.

83. Chelser, P., 1972, *Women and Madness*, New York: Doubleday.

84. David, D. S. and R. Brannon, 1976, "The Male Sex Role: Our Culture's Blueprint of Manhood, and What It's Done for Us Lately," in D. S. David and R. Brannon, *The Forty-nine Percent Majority: The Male Sex Role*, Reading, MA: Addison-Wesley.

85. This section draws on J. A. Doyle, 1983, *The Male Experience*, Dubuque, IA: Wm. C. Brown.

86. Fasteau, M. F., 1974, *The Male Machine*, New York: McGraw-Hill.

87. Straus, M. A., R. Gelles, and S. Steinmetz, 1980, *Behind Closed Doors*, Garden City, NY: Doubleday-Anchor.

88. Roy, M., 1977, *Battered Women: A Psychological Study*, New York: Van Nostrand.

89. Russell, D. E. H., 1984, *Sexual Exploitation*, Newbury Park, CA: Sage.

90. Malcolmson, W., 1976, *Success Is a Failure Experience*, Nashville: Abingdon Press.

91. Farrell, W., 1974, *The Liberated Man*, New York: Random House.

92. Glenn, 1987, op. cit.

93. Chase-Lansdale, P. L. and M. T. Owen, 1987, "Maternal Employment in a Family Context: Effects on Infant-Mother and Infant-Father Attachment," *Child Development* 58:1505–1512.

94. Etaugh, C., 1980, "Effects of Nonmaternal Care on Children: Research Evidence and Popular Views," *American Psychologist* 35:309–319; L. W. Hoffman, 1979, "Maternal Employment: 1979," *American Psychologist* 34:859–865; K. Moore, D. Spain, and S. Bianchi, 1984, "Working Wives and Mothers," in B. B. Hess and M. B. Sussman (Eds.). *Women and the Family: Two Decades of Change*, New York: Haworth.

95. For reviews see Hoffman, 1979, ibid.; L. W. Hoffman, 1977, "Changes in Family Roles, Socialization, and Sex Differences," *American Psychologist* 32:644–657; and S. Bloom-Feshbach, J. Bloom-Feshbach, and K. A. Heller, 1982, "Work, Family, and Children's Perception of the World" in S. B. Kammerman and C. D. Hayes (Eds.), *Families that Work*, Washington, DC: National Academy Press.

96. Houston, 1983, op. cit.

97. Lamb, M. E., 1982, "Maternal Employment and Child Development: A Review," in M. E. Lamb (Ed.), *Nontraditional Families: Parenting and Child Development*, Hillsdale, NJ: Lawrence Erlbaum; C. S. Piotrkowski and M. H. Katz, 1982, "Women's Work and Personal Relations in the Family," in P. W. Berman and E. R. Ramsey, op. cit.

98. Coverman, S., 1983, "Gender, Domestic Labor Time, and Wage Inequality," *American Sociological Review* 48:623–637; N. Glazer, 1980, "Everyone Needs Three Hands: Doing Unpaid and Paid Work," in S. F. Berk (Ed.), *Women and Household Labor*, Beverly Hills, CA: Sage, pp. 249–273.

99. Hartmann, H., 1981, "The Family as the Locus of Gender, Class, and Political Struggle," *Signs* 6:366–394.

100. Hartmann, 1981, ibid; C. Schooler, J. Miller, K. A. Miller, and C. N. Richtand, 1984, "Work for the Household: Its Nature and Consequences for Husbands and Wives," *American Journal of Sociology* 90:97–124.

101. Berk, S. F., 1985, *The Gender Factory,* New York: Plenum.

102. Bergmann, B. R., 1986, *The Economic Emergence of Women*, New York: Basic Books.

103. Scanzoni, J. H., 1972, *Sexual Bargaining*, Englewood Cliffs, NJ: Prentice-Hall; J. H. Scanzoni, 1978, *Sex Roles, Women's Work, and Marital Conflict: A Study of Family Change*, Lexington, MA: Lexington.

104. For an excellent discussion of these perspectives, see M. L. Andersen, 1983, *Thinking About Women: Sociological and Feminist Perspectives,* New York: Macmillan.

105. Stephan, C. W. and J. Corder, 1985, "The Effects of Dual-Career Families on Adolescents' Sex-Role Attitudes, Work and Family Plans, and Choices of Important Others," *Journal of Marriage and the Family* 47:921–929.

CHAPTER 7

Conformity and Society

Conformity to the Norms of Society

Consensus Is Never Total

Consensus Is Negotiated

Conformity to Group or Individual Norms

Reference Groups and Pressures to Conform

Types of Social Influence Producing Conformity

Pressures Toward Conformity

Overobedience to Authority

Deindividuation

Conformity can result in extremely negative behaviors. Consider this account, given by a participant of the 1967 My Lai massacre in Vietnam (1). The interviewer is Mike Wallace of CBS News.

Q: How many people did you round up?
A: Well, there was about 40, 50 people that we gathered in the center of the village. . . .
Q: What kind of people—men, women, children?
A: Men, women, children.
Q: Babies?
A: Babies. And we huddled them up. We made them squat down and Lieutenant Calley came over and said, "You know what to do with them, don't you?" And I said yes. So I took it for granted that he just wanted us to watch them. And he left, and came back about 10 or 15 minutes later and said, "How come you ain't killed them yet?" And I told him that I didn't think you wanted us to kill them, that you just wanted us to guard them. He said, "No, I want them dead." So—. . . .
Q: And you killed how many? At that time?
A: Well, I fired them automatic, so you can't— You just spray the area on them and so you can't know how many you killed 'cause they were going fast. So I might have killed 10 or 15 of them.
Q: Men, women, and children?
A: Men, women, and children.
Q: And babies?
A: And babies.
Q: Okay, then what? . . .
A: There was a ditch. And so we started pushing them off, and we started shooting them, so all together we just pushed them all off, and just started using automatics on them. . . .
Q: Again—men, women, and children?
A: Men, women, and children.
Q: And babies?
A: And babies. And so we started shooting them and somebody told us to switch off to single shot so that we could save ammo. So we switched off to single shot, and shot a few more rounds. . . .
Q: Why did you do it?
A: Why did I do it? Because I felt like I was

ordered to do it, and it seemed like that, at the time I felt like I was doing the right thing, because, like I said, I lost a lot of buddies. . . . So after I done it, I felt good, but later on that day, it was getting to me.
Q: You're married?
A: Right.
Q: Children?
A: Two. . . .
Q: Obviously, the question comes to my mind . . . the father of two little kids like that . . . how can he shoot babies?
A: I didn't have the little girl. I just had the little boy at the time.
Q: Uh-huh. . . . How do you shoot babies?
A: I don't know. It's just one of those things.

Conformity consists of behavior or beliefs consistent with social expectations that result from real or imagined pressure from individuals or groups. These pressures can result in actions that surprise and horrify us, like the My Lai massacre. Conformity can also result in the following, less negative acts:

- High school students write Ann Landers, asking her to tell their parents it's okay to have a punk haircut like the other kids in their clique.

- Junior high school students roam the shopping malls of America looking for the same jeans and tennis shoes worn by their friends.

Finally, the following examples demonstrate that conformity can also result in positive behavior:

- Witnesses to a car accident work together to free a victim from the wreck.

- In the performance of their duties, police and firefighters sometimes risk their lives to save those of endangered citizens.

So how should conformity be evaluated? Is conformity destructive? . . . A little silly? Heroic? It can be all of these. Acts of conformity must be evaluated within their social contexts.

In this chapter we will consider conformity in two contexts. First we will discuss conformity to the norms of society. Next we will consider conformity to individual or group pressures.

CONFORMITY TO THE NORMS OF SOCIETY

There is a deep basic need in all of us to conform
... Preface, The New Emily Post Etiquette

When in Rome, do as the Romans do.—Anonymous

Sociologists are particularly interested in the macro-level study of the establishment and maintenance of social order. One important component of the social order consists of society's *norms*. Norms are societal expectations regarding conduct in a particular social situation. Evaluations of the conduct accompany these societal expectations. That is, not only do we expect people to keep appointments they have made, but we evaluate their failure to do so negatively, and react to this failure with disappointment or anger. Norms may be *prescriptions*, guides to behavior that should be enacted (Love they neighbor.), or *proscriptions*, guides to behavior that should not be enacted (Thou shalt not kill.).

Norms vary in importance. *Folkways* specify customary conduct. They are literally ways of the folk, customs handed down from past generations. Setting off fireworks on the Fourth of July and blowing out candles on birthday cakes are folkways. While folkways are followed, they are not mandated by law or moral imperative. Although in the past they may have served an important purpose, currently they are simply behaviors that occur as a matter of custom.

The word *mores* is derived from the Latin word for morals. Mores are those norms believed important to the welfare of the society. They may or may not be mandated by law. Mores (Do unto others as you would have them do unto you.) are thought to be important because they specify aspects of fair treatment in our society, but they are not codified into law. Other mores, such as prohibitions against theft and slander, have been incorporated into our body of law.

Laws are those norms which the society formally specifies shall be observed. These norms are formalized into law because informal negative sanctions for disregarding them have proved ineffective in ensuring compliance. While many norms become law due to their importance to our welfare, others become law even though their lack of observance may not result in direct harm to anyone. We typically regard bribery as both unlawful and a breach of important societal mores. Driving a little over the speed limit, while illegal, is an issue of lesser moral concern.

Negative sanctions or *punishments* are applied to those who break norms. Violation of a folkway is likely to gain one the reputation of being odd or ignorant, and may provoke minor negative sanctions. For example, if some people applaud between movements of a symphony the audience response is likely to range from minor amusement to downright annoyance. Violation of mores might be thought rude or selfish, and will bring stronger negative sanctions, such as public rebuke or avoidance. People who talk continuously throughout the symphony are likely to be told to be quiet or asked to leave. Violations of laws may raise questions of moral character, and will bring the negative sanctions specified in the law. In the unlikely event that two people got into a fight during the symphony, they would be forcibly removed from the concert hall and then arrested. Sanctions for violations of the law range from small fines to the death penalty. Figure 7-1 shows the negative sanctions applied to violations of various types of norms in our society.

Norms make it possible for societies to exist. Without conformity to the norms and laws of society, we would live in chaos or anarchy. Our basic social institutions—education, law, family, religion, and work—could not survive because there would be no rules to define them or allow them to function. Our social environment would be completely unpredictable, and we could count on each other for nothing. For example, without norms nothing would prevent members of the society from victimizing you by committing theft, murder, rape, and other crimes. No police force or other group would protect you and your property from others in society. No court system would exist to which you could appeal for justice or redress if you were harmed by another.

Figure 7.1 ■

"Let the Punishment Fit the Crime"

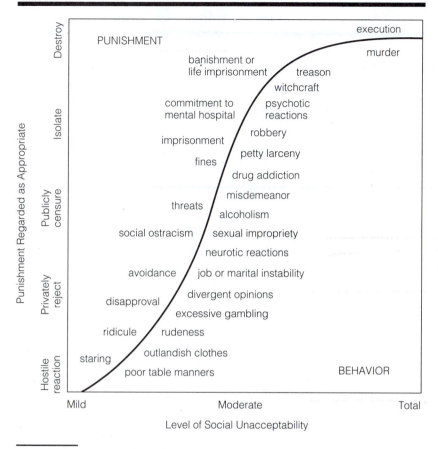

Adapted from Haas, K., 1965, *Understanding Ourselves and Others*, Englewood Cliffs, NJ: Prentice-Hall.

Why do we conform to the norms of our society? In part we conform because we support the norms. Our norms are based on common *values* or ethical principles shared by people in the culture. Much childhood socialization involves learning these values and norms so they will continue to guide us and future generations. As we saw in Chapter 4, we are continually socialized throughout life into the values and norms of the institutions of the society.

We also conform to our society's norms because we wish to avoid negative sanctions and to receive positive sanctions or rewards. Even the trivial negative sanctions applied to violations of folkways can seem quite powerful to the violator. To be laughed at by one's friends, or avoided by those with whom one wishes interaction, are actually quite powerful sanctions. No one wants to be disapproved of by people he or she likes or respects.

In addition, we often conform because we know no other way of behaving. To illustrate, we conform to our society's notions of time and space because we have no alternative concepts. Many of us conform

■ *Waiting one's turn: A societal norm in action. (WGS)*

to the norm of speaking English because we speak no other language. We speak grammatically because, once having learned the rules of grammar, they are applied naturally. It is only with conscious effort that we can break them.

Consensus Is Never Total

Some social psychologists argue that the consensus regarding norms is more imagined than real. There are virtually no norms for which complete agreement exists. In addition, the degree of acceptance of norms is constantly changing, and as a result, norms themselves change over time. In the last two decades norms regarding the behaviors appropriate for men and women have changed rapidly. During this time, little consensus has existed regarding the proper gender-role behaviors of men and women.

Subcultural variations also exist; each group has its own set of norms. Any large society is composed of a variety of groups, each with its own norms.

Honolulu, where your authors prepared this book, is a multi-cultural city. While at this moment some people are eating eggs and bacon for breakfast, a substantial minority are having dim sum, and even more are enjoying rice and seaweed.

In addition, the norms of some groups are imposed on other groups. People low in power are likely to find themselves subject to rules made by more powerful groups in the society. For instance, tax laws may benefit the wealthy more than the poor, but all people are under equal obligation to obey them.

Finally, in any society some norms are undergoing change. In the process of changing norms, uncertainties inevitably arise when some people adhere to the older norm while others adopt the new. Sexual norms have become increasingly more liberal in the last few decades, especially for women. During these decades of change, some people readily embraced the new norms, while others changed more slowly, and still others clung to the sexual

■ *Actions that are deviant in one context are conforming in another. Here, a participant awaits the beginning of a parade. (WGS)*

norms of prior generations. Recently, however, the advent of a deadly sexually transmitted disease, AIDS, has reversed this trend toward sexual freedom. Currently, many people report changing their sexual behavior considerably as a response to the AIDS epidemic (2). This change can readily be seen on most college campuses, where students have both begun to practice safe sex and voluntarily limit their number of sexual partners. On many campuses, college administrators have shown support for these changing sexual practices by supplying students with condoms or placing vending machines with condoms in dorms and campus restrooms.

Due to imperfect consensus, subcultural differences, the imposition of norms, and changing norms it may be better to think in terms of the extent to which behaviors are associated with collectively shared expectations, evaluations, and reactions rather than to think in terms of norms (3). Instead of declaring the rule, "One should be on time," as a societal norm, we can examine the extent to which people believe others should be on time, the varied conceptions among groups as to what constitutes "being on time" or "being late," and the degree to which the norm of being on time is imposed, even on groups who do not feel the norm is important.

Consensus Is Negotiated

Not only is consensus regarding norms never total, it is also under a continual process of negotiation. The symbolic interactionists remind us that reality has a subjective component. Norms are not objective phenomena, but instead are negotiated in the process of interaction with others (4). Of course, not every norm is negotiable, and certainly not at all times. Mass murder of innocent people simply is not accepted in most societies. But more is negotiable than we often recognize. The meaning of first-degree murder must be negotiated each time the issue arises. When a person is charged with first-degree murder, a legal process determines whether the defendant's behaviors fit the criteria of first-degree murder. In a criminal trial, a judge and jury struggle to decide whether the defendant's behavior fits the charge.

Negotiations regarding norms take place within small groups, organizations, institutions, communities, and societies. Their form is determined by the group structure and its existing lines of communication. Thus, disagreements regarding law take place in courts with lawyers arguing opposing sides. The debate over agreement regarding mores not yet codified into law may take place in state legislatures and new laws may be enacted.

Negotiations are temporal; regardless of the outcome of a negotiation, it will ultimately need renegotiation. The length of time an agreement lasts also is determined by group structure and lines of communication. A small cohesive group in which everyone has ample opportunity to communicate with other group members will be able to maintain a negotiated agreement longer than a large competitive group in which most people cannot easily communicate with other group members. In some instances a negotiated agreement lasts until the next relevant Supreme Court decision; in others, the agreement lasts until members of a society come to have a sense of common concern about the inappropriateness of a particular law.

In summary, norms play an important part in the maintenance of the social order. However, we must remember that consensus is never total and norms are not objective, stable phenomena but are constructed and reconstructed through a process of negotiation.

■

CONFORMITY TO GROUP OR INDIVIDUAL NORMS

Peer pressure seems to Miss Manners to be an affliction that strikes only the ignoble.—Judith Martin, "Miss Manners"

If you want to get along, go along.—Sam Rayburn

In this section, we will examine the causes of conformity to group or individual norms, the types of conformity, the characteristics of groups and individuals that facilitate conformity, and individual differences in conformity. Psychological social psychology has led the way in the micro-level study of factors that influence people's conformity to individual or group pressures.

Conformity to group norms involves processes similar to conformity to society's norms. In groups, decisions are often a product of shared group norms (5). In addition, group decisions are made through

■ *Policemen use other policemen as a reference group to evaluate their behavior. (Cookie Stephan)*

a process of negotiation. The influence process preceding group decisions is nothing more than a negotiation among group members.

Reference Groups and Pressures to Conform

We will begin our explanation of the causes of conformity to group or individual norms by examining reference groups and the role they play in conformity.

Reference groups *Reference groups* are groups with which people identify (6). Reference groups help determine our sense of who we are—our personal values, beliefs, and norms. People's reference groups are the groups whose opinions they respect (a political group, an activist organization), groups to which they wish to belong (physicians, politicians), or groups to which they are committed (family groups, close friendship groups). People may also use groups to which they will never belong to evaluate their own behavior. For instance, the blind often use sighted people as a reference group in

judging their own learning abilities, appearance, and character (7). Reference groups are relevant to the topic of conformity because we attempt to conform to the standards of these groups.

Reference groups can furnish either positive or negative standards of evaluation. The groups to which we wish to belong serve as positive reference groups. As children, we all wanted to be like adults, and we frequently used their standards to judge our behavior. Groups we reject or dislike may serve as negative reference groups. People may compare themselves to negative reference groups to emphasize the differences between themselves and the members of these groups (8). For example, adolescents reject the standards and behavior of young children and are often offended if others accuse them of behaving childishly.

In a study of negative reference groups, it was found that many Cuban-Americans use the views of the Castro government as a negative reference group (9). One group of Cuban-Americans was presented with the positions of the Castro government toward an American economic blockade, Cuba's offshore fishing limit, and diplomatic relations with the United States. When subsequently asked their own positions on these issues, these Cuban-Americans were more extreme in opposing the views of the Castro government than a group of Cuban-Americans who had not been exposed to those views.

A related set of studies showed that a comparison between a positive and a negative reference group can influence behavior (10). In one study, subjects were told that one of their positive reference groups was not as good as a relevant negative reference group. For instance, one set of subjects was told that Americans could not tolerate pain as well as Russians. These subjects later withstood higher pain levels than they had withstood before the negative comparison was made. Other studies indicate that making positive reference groups salient leads to greater fidelity to the norms of the group (11).

The choice of reference group depends on the situation. People choose a reference group relevant to a comparison they wish to make or one that furnishes norms relevant to the situation they wish to evaluate. Therefore, a parishioner will use other churchgoers to evaluate his or her behavior in church rather than using the members of his or her bowling team. In some circumstances, a person may have little choice about which group to use as a reference group. For example, members of a submarine crew must use the norms of the rest of the crew to judge some of their behaviors or risk social rejection.

The concept of reference groups explains some surprising findings regarding the relative deprivation experienced by American soldiers in World War II (12). *Relative deprivation* consists of people's feelings that their life situations are less positive, relative to the situations of others with whom they compare themselves. Researchers studying American soldiers in World War II found a number of instances in which the soldier's actual levels of deprivation and their perceived levels of deprivation differed. For example, in a comparison of noncombat soldiers, it was found that soldiers stationed in the United States were less satisfied with their lot than foreign-based soldiers stationed just beyond the combat areas. This finding was surprising because the foreign-based soldiers suffered conditions of much greater absolute

deprivation: They contended with much greater breaks in personal ties from home than soldiers stationed in the United States, and they also suffered conditions of physical deprivation unknown at home.

The answer to this riddle lies in the reference groups of each type of soldier. The soldiers based in the United States compared their lives with those of the civilians around them, and by comparison found their lives very hard. In contrast, the foreign-based noncombat soldiers compared their lives with those of the combat soldiers around them, and found their lives were actually quite easy. Thus, deprivation is experienced *relative* to one's reference group, rather than being experienced in an absolute sense.

Functions of reference groups Because reference groups are important to us, their members have influence over us, and can cause us to conform to their standards. Reference groups have two functions (13).

First, the reference group serves a *normative function* if it sets and enforces standards for the individual members. A group functions as a normative reference group to the extent that it evaluates a person on the basis of conformity to group standards and delivers rewards and punishments based on these evaluations. If you have ever paused to think, "What will my friends or my parents think of this?" you have used them as a normative reference group. A study of drug use among high school students illustrates the normative function of reference groups (14). In this study, frequency of marijuana use rose with frequency of being around marijuana users. The authors believe that this association is based on normative pressures to do as one's friends are doing.

Second, the reference group serves a *comparative function* if the group members use it as a standard for making judgments about the self and others. A group functions as a comparative reference group to the extent that it is used to evaluate the behaviors, attitudes, or characteristics of oneself or others. If you have ever said to yourself, "How smart or attractive am I compared to my friends?" you have used them as a comparative reference group.

Recent research suggests that we prefer to com-

■ *Atten*-shun! *The use of strong negative sanctions for deviance maintains high levels of compliance in the military. (WGS)*

pare ourselves to similar others—for example, to same-sex or same-job others when comparing wages or jobs (15)—and to others with "allegedly similar" perceptual styles when comparing social perceptiveness (16). Similar others presumably provide a better standard for social comparison. However, this tendency may have negative consequences when the group is disadvantaged (women comparing their wages to those of other women) (17).

Happiness is typically associated with comparing favorably with others, particularly with similar others (18). Under some circumstances, however, one's evaluation of self can be bolstered by comparison with a successful close other. If the performance is important to the individual's self-definition, his or her self-esteem will suffer if the comparison with a close other is negative. However, if the performance is not important to the individual, he or she will experience enhanced self-esteem (19). As we discussed in Chapter 4, this increased self-esteem is derived by basking in the reflected glory of the close other.

Similarly, in his theory of social comparison processes, Leon Festinger proposed that people will refer to the opinion of others if physical means of

verifying an opinion are unavailable (20). In the absence of information regarding others' opinions, we may even fabricate a consensus that does not in fact exist. For example, people are known to fall prey to the *false consensus effect,* believing that others agree with one more than they in fact do (21). (This is one of the perceptual biases we will discuss in Chapter 9 on person perception.) For example, in the absence of opinion information, individuals assumed that similar others agreed with their recommendation regarding the treatment of a juvenile delinquent (22). In addition, these individuals avoided making the comparison of their ratings with dissimilar others, in an attempt to avoid disconformation of their opinions.

Often a single reference group will serve both functions. One study of the appraisals of high school students' academic ability and performance demonstrated both normative and comparative functions of a reference group composed of their classmates (23). The normative function was shown by the students' attribution of greater ability to themselves when their classmates had favorable self-appraisals than when their classmates had less favorable self-appraisals. The group was being used for a normative purpose because the students complied with the norm of their group, which was to appraise themselves favorably.

The comparative function was demonstrated by the finding that students whose classmates had better grades had more negative evaluations of their own abilities than students whose grades were equal to or better than those of their classmates. Here the group was being used for a comparative purpose, since it allowed the students to evaluate their abilities by comparing them to those of their classmates.

Reference groups can exert different types of social influence, all of which can lead to conformity. We will now examine three types of social influence that produce conformity.

Types of Social Influence Producing Conformity

Change that is not based on one's true beliefs, or *compliance,* has often been distinguished from true changes or beliefs, or *convergence* (24). However, it is possible to differentiate types of convergence into *identification* (actual belief change based on one's desires to have a relationship with another person or group) and *internalization* (actual belief changes based on acceptance of the person's or group's values). For this reason, three types of social influence are distinguished: compliance, identification, and internalization (25). These types of social influence vary in the process through which influence occurs, the type of change induced in the conformer, and the source of the influencer's power over the conformer. *Power* here means the extent to which the conformer is dependent upon the influencer to achieve his or her goals.

Compliance *Compliance* is social influence induced by expectations of gaining rewards or avoiding punishments by conforming. In this type of conformity, public attitude and behavioral change are not accompanied by private attitude change. People comply for social reasons—to achieve a positive reaction or to avoid a negative reaction from another person or group. When the influencer's power is based on control of rewards and punishments, compliance is operating. For example, if you pretend to agree with your employer's business decisions because you want to be promoted, you are engaging in an act of compliance.

The Asch experiments. Solomon Asch conducted a number of classic experiments on compliance (26). In these experiments, a college student arrived at an experimental laboratory to find six to eight other students, who were introduced as other experimental subjects. The experimenter asked each of them to make discrimination judgments about the length of lines. They were shown three lines of varying lengths and were asked to make a judgment about which of these lines was equal in length to a fourth, standard line. The discrimination task was an easy one—the lines were rather different in length. The subjects were asked to call out their judgments, one after another.

However, all was not as it seemed to the college student. In actuality, he or she was the only *real* subject in each experimental session. The other six to eight people were confederates of the experimenter, each of whom gave a predetermined series of responses, some of which were incorrect. The real subject was always seated so his or her judgment was given last. On the first two trials, all the confederates gave correct responses. Thereafter, on some trials, the confederates unanimously gave responses that seemed obviously incorrect to the real subject.

What were the subjects' reactions to this situation? About 40 percent of the subjects remained independent of the group, giving the correct judgments on all trials, even when the confederates unanimously gave an incorrect answer. The remainder of the subjects complied with the confederates' incorrect judgments at least some of the time. Some of these compliant subjects agreed with the confederates on all of their incorrect judgments. Others complied with the incorrect majority on some trials but gave correct answers on others.

How do we know this situation is one of compliance, rather than one of true belief in the judgments? A control condition was conducted, in which only real subjects gave their judgments on the discrimination task. The results from the control condition verify the fact that the task was an easy one; subjects gave almost all correct responses. Thus, we can infer that the incorrect judgments of the previous subjects were due to compliance, rather than beliefs about the length of lines.

In addition, post-experimental interviews were conducted with the subjects. Many told the experimenter they knew they were making incorrect judgments, but felt uncomfortable disagreeing with the group consensus. Some subjects felt disagreeing with the group would be embarrassing or rude; others did not want to call special attention to themselves; and still others were concerned that they would be disliked if they disagreed with others' judgments. Agreement thus provided the subjects with rewards and allowed them to avoid negative sanctions from their peers.

In other versions of this experiment, Asch varied the number of unanimous confederates. Table 7-1 shows the results of this variation in the size of the incorrect majority. When only one confederate was present, he had little influence on the subject. When two confederates agreed, a small tendency to agree with the incorrect majority appears. When the majority is increased to three, the full false agreement effect appears; increasing the number of unanimous confederates above three does not increase the magnitude of the false agreement.

But what if the incorrect consensus is not unanimous? Asch also tried versions of this experiment in which the majority of confederates gave incorrect responses to the discrimination task on some trials,

but in which one confederate consistently gave correct responses. In this situation, the real subject's compliance dropped to virtually zero. The presence of one independent person allowed the subject to resist implicit pressure from the group to comply.

Next we will explore four techniques for inducing compliance, the foot-in-the-door and the door-in-the-face techniques, low-balling, and legitimizing paltry contributions.

The foot-in-the-door and the door-in-the-face techniques. Have you ever been asked to grant a small request and then subsequently found yourself granting a larger request to someone else? Have you ever been asked to do someone a large favor and refused, only to wind up doing a small favor for the person instead? Have you ever been offered a deal you couldn't refuse, only to have it changed at the last minute? If so, did you still take the deal? Have you ever heard a charity appeal stressing that any donation, even a penny, would help? These are all techniques of inducing compliance.

As we mentioned in Chapter 3, a person is more likely to agree to a large request if he or she has previously agreed to a smaller one (27). This effect is known as the *foot-in-the-door technique.* It occurs even when the issue involved is not the same for both requests.

The foot-in-the-door technique works with children as young as 7 (28). In a study of second graders, half were induced to give coupons redeemable for toys to "poor children who don't have any toys at all," and they were then labeled as being helpful.

Table 7.1 ■

Errors of Critical Subjects with Unanimous Majorities of Different Sizes

Size of Majority	Control	1	2	3	4	8	10–15
Mean number of errors	0.08	0.33	1.53	4.0	4.20	3.84	3.75
Range of errors	0–2	0–1	0–5	1–12	0–11	0–11	0–10

From Asch, S.E., 1952, "Effect of Group Pressure Upon the Modification and Distortion of Judgments," in H. Guetzkow (Ed.), *Groups, Leadership, and Men,* Pittsburgh: Carnegie Press.

Juliet Jones

■ *The door-in-the-face compliance technique in action.*

The other half of the students were allowed to keep the coupons and were not labeled in any way. Those who had donated coupons and been labeled helpful were subsequently more likely to choose to perform a task for sick children rather than play with toys, than the students who had not been induced to give some of their coupons to poor children.

What happens if the two requests are reversed (29)? Does making a large request first and following it with a smaller request lead to greater compliance with the smaller request than simply making the small request alone? It does. This technique is called the *door-in-the-face technique*. The door-in-the-face technique works only when the two requests are made by the same person. If you asked a friend to loan you $1,000 and were refused, your friend would be more likely to lend you $10, but no more likely to agree to another person's request for $10 than if you had not made the initial $1,000 request.

Why does compliance with a small initial request lead to later compliance with a large request, whereas rejection of a large initial request leads to later compliance with a small request? There is no real contradiction between these findings. They employ different mechanisms to induce compliance. The foot-in-the-door technique works because, on the basis of the first request, people decide that they are helpful people who cooperate with good causes (30). This perception makes it more likely that they will comply with requests for future help for a good

cause, even if these requests are larger and come from a different source.

The mechanism underlying the increased agreement found in the door-in-the-face technique appears to be reciprocal concession (31). The person perceives the requester to have made a concession by lowering the request. He or she believes a similar concession, compliance with the second request, is now demanded from him or her. This explanation stems from exchange theory, which suggests that all exchanges, including concessions, are governed by the norm of reciprocity. Thus, concessions are reciprocated, just as favors are reciprocated. This interpretation is strengthened by the finding that the door-in-the-face effect does not occur when the two requests are made by different persons.

However, the door-in-the-face effect is only found when the person feels some sense of obligation to the source of the request (32). In a study demonstrating the importance of a sense of obligation, the legitimacy of the request was varied. In the experimental condition, a person answering a phone call from the experimenter was asked to keep a journal of all the television programs watched by his or her family for two weeks and then be interviewed about these choices. No one agreed to this large request. The interviewer then asked if the person would be willing to answer a 50-item questionnaire about television viewing. In the control group, only the second request was made.

The interviewer identified herself as being from a high legitimacy organization (Parents for Good Television Programming) or a low legitimacy organization (a consultant group for commercial television). The rejection of the large initial request led to greater compliance with the small request when the organization was high in legitimacy (90 percent in the experimental condition to 60 percent in the control condition). The large initial request had no effect when the organization was low in legitimacy (35 percent in the experimental condition to 45 percent in the control condition). Similarly, compliance to the second request is much greater when individuals are made to think in terms of a continuous involvement with a charitable organization than when they are made to feel their obligation had been fulfilled by compliance with the first request (33).

Low-balling. People who sell new cars make considerable use of a technique they call *low-balling* or "throwing the low ball" (34). First, a salesperson commits a buyer to a sale by offering an extremely good deal. Later, the deal is retracted by another person, usually the manager, who says the agency will lose money on the sale. A new, higher price is then offered. Surprisingly, many people still buy the car, even though the deal is no longer a good one. The initial decision to buy seems to commit people to the deal, regardless of its terms.

Applied more broadly to conformity, individuals who initially commit themselves to comply with a request, and then find there is a "catch" to the commitment, are more likely to comply than individuals who are exposed to the full terms of the request at once. Whether the issue involves a favor you promised to do for a friend or the "five minute" telephone interview you agreed to do, low-balling occurs with some frequency.

Legitimizing paltry contributions. A charity appeal stating that "even a penny will help" can increase donations (35). Legitimizing a paltry contribution makes it difficult for people to refuse to donate money for a worthy cause because almost everyone can afford a very small donation. In an experiment designed to test this idea, experimenters canvassed a middle-class neighborhood for the American Can-

cer Society (36). In the control condition the experimenter asked for money to continue the Society's research, education, and service programs. In the experimental condition (legitimizing paltry contributions), the experimenter added, "Even a penny will help," to the request for money.

Legitimizing paltry contributions was effective in eliciting more donations and donations of greater amounts. Only 37 percent of the persons in the control condition donated, but 57 percent of the persons in the experimental condition donated money to the American Cancer Society. The average amount of money donated per person in the two groups was $.85 in the standard request condition and $1.45 in the legitimizing condition.

However, legitimizing paltry contributions may only occur when strong situational constraints exist. In a study in which contributions were made either immediately or were mailed in, legitimizing paltry contributions increased contributions only when the donation was made on the spot (37).

Identification Identification is the second type of social influence. *Identification* is social influence brought about by desires to establish or maintain a satisfying relationship with another person or group (39). In identification, people derive satisfaction from the act of conformity because their conformity is associated with the desired relationship. When the influencer's power is based on his or her attractiveness, identification is operating. For example, if you join a political group because you believe the leader of this group is a great humanitarian with whom you wish to be associated, you join because of identification.

Many theories of identification exist. Freud felt feelings of ambivalence always exist toward the person with whom one identifies (40). This ambivalence occurs because the more powerful the affection a person feels toward the other, the more sensitive he or she is to the inevitable disappointments and frustrations that occur in a relationship with the other. Because the negative components of this ambivalence are at variance with the desire to maintain the relationship with the other person, they

BOX 7-1

Salespersons as Social Psychologists of Necessity

Robert Cialdini spent three years training in a variety of sales organizations (encyclopedias, used cars) to learn the techniques used by people who make their living by getting people to comply with their wishes. He found the techniques used most widely by salespersons could be summarized in six principles (38):

1. *The commitment principle.* After committing oneself to a position, a person is more likely to comply with requests for behaviors consistent with that position. Encyclopedia salespersons use this technique by first getting people to agree that education is important for their children and that reference books can help students do well in school. Once having agreed with these statements, the customers are more likely to agree to listen to the salesperson's pitch about the set of encyclopedias.

2. *The reciprocity principle.* As we mentioned in Chapter 3, people feel obligated to reciprocate favors, gifts, and such. The Hare Krishna use this principle by giving

---

are repressed. The remaining positive components become the foundation for identification.

Sociologists have long noted the association of charismatic leadership and identification. Many investigations have linked the success of some religions to the charisma of their leaders (41), and it has been noted that cults very often have charismatic leaders. The success of the Children of God, one sect of Jesus People, has been attributed to the charisma of its leader, David Berg (42). This leader (who later renamed himself Moses Davis, and even later had his followers call him "Dad") exerted almost total control over the members of the group. Members were isolated from their families and from most contact with noncult members. They engaged in acts of kidnapping, brainwashing, imprisonment, en-

slavement, prostitution, polygamy, incest, sexual abuse, and rape, all in the name of religion. How could young religious people commit such acts and allow such acts to be committed against them? Because they accepted Berg as a savior and prophet. As Berg stated, and as the cult members believed, "If I told you to go blow up a bank, you'd do it, because the Lord is speaking through me."

Earlier in the chapter, we reported the results of a study in which frequency of marijuana use among high school students rose with their frequency of association with peers who used marijuana. The investigators assume that identification is in part responsible for these results (43). To the extent that high school students wished to establish a relationship with peers they admired, the students

unsolicited gifts to passersby and then requesting donations. The Amway Corporation also uses this principle, leaving samples of products for customers to try, and then soliciting orders when the unused portions of the generous samples are retrieved.

3. *The social validation principle*. As we mentioned earlier in this chapter, people use others as standards of comparison. If similar others are performing some behavior, this may increase our willingness to do the same. This principle is used by some evangelists, who plant "ringers" in their audiences to give donations and provide witness on cue.

4. *The authority principle*. People follow the suggestions of high status authority figures. In one scam, a con artist dressed expensively and conservatively appears at the home of a victim and identifies himself as an officer of the victim's bank. He tells the victim a teller is suspected of irregularities in transactions. He asks the victim to withdraw all his or her savings from the bank, and then give it to a bank guard who will return the money to the victim's account. An accomplice dressed as a bank guard waits outside the bank, takes the money, and the victim never sees it again.

5. *The scarcity principle*. People will seize rare opportunities. Salespersons sometimes tell customers the store has just sold the last of an advertised sale item to increase a mildly interested customer's desire for it. The salesperson then offers to call other stores to locate one for the customer. When the item is invariably located at "another" store, the customer is happy to be able to buy it.

6. *The liking principle*. We are willing to comply with the requests of friends or others we like. The Tupperware Corporation makes use of this principle by having women invite their friends over for a showing of their products. ■

would derive satisfaction from conforming to their peers' behaviors.

Internalization   The third type of social influence is internalization. *Internalization* is social influence created when the ideas or actions in a group's or individual's message are rewarding (44). In this instance, people believe in what they are doing; conforming is consistent with their values. When the influencer's power is based on credibility of beliefs, internalization is operating. For example, if you actively support a political group because you believe it will implement your values, you do so because of internalization.

The autokinetic effect. In the 1930s, Muzafer Sherif conducted a series of classic demonstrations of internalization using the autokinetic effect (45). The *autokinetic effect* is a visual illusion in which a single point of light appears to move in a darkened room. Subjects participated individually in a discrimination task in a darkened room. Each time the light came on, the subjects guessed the distance that it "moved." Sherif found that subjects established a small range within which their judgments of movement fell. Some thought the light moved several feet and others thought it moved only inches, but each subject perceived relatively consistent movement across trials.

In one demonstration, Sherif asked groups of college students to report their judgments regarding the distance the light moved. The subjects' judgments, while initially rather divergent, converged over time (see the first four panels of Figure 7-2). At the end of a set of trials, each member of the group reported about the same amount of movement. Is this convergence a result of compliance or internalization? The situation does not allow us to identify the type of conformity in operation. To do so, Sherif conducted another demonstration.

In this demonstration, Sherif placed college students together and asked them to make judgments aloud in each others' presence. As in the first demonstration, subjects' individual judgments converged over time. To determine if subjects were merely complying with each other or if they had internalized the group norm regarding amount of movement, Sherif tested the subjects alone for a second time. The results showed their conformity to be a product of internalization: Subjects continued to give judgments consistent with the group norm even when they were alone (see the second four panels of Figure 7-2). Thus, it appears the subjects used each other as guides to reality and actually altered their perceptions regarding the movement of the light.

Sherif's study provides a demonstration of internalization because subjects internalized or privately accepted the group norm. In contrast, Asch's study provides a demonstration of compliance, since subjects did not privately accept the false group judgments.

Pressures Toward Conformity

In the following section we will list the characteristics of groups and individuals that produce pressures toward conformity. We will then ask if some types of people are more likely than others to yield to pressures to conform.

Characteristics of groups What characteristics of groups promote conformity? First, the extent of agreement within the group—unanimous groups elicit more conformity than groups that are mixed in their attitudes or behaviors (46). Unanimous groups induce more conformity both because they seem more likely to be correct in their attitudes or behaviors and because they can exert more pressure

on individual members than divided groups. As we saw in our discussion of the Asch experiments, even a small amount of social support makes it possible for the individual to resist group pressures.

Second, higher status groups exact more conformity than lower status groups (47). People are more willing to forego independence for association with a higher status (the local country club) than a lower status group (the local gardening club).

Third, groups containing individuals who are expert on the issue at hand exert more conformity pressure on their members than groups containing less expert members (48). Here the motive for conforming appears to be the need to be correct. Groups with high expertise are more likely to be correct than groups with low expertise. On the topic of history, we would accept the word of a prominent historian over that of a high school history student.

Fourth, highly attractive groups can induce more conformity than groups less attractive to the members (49). Members are more willing to incur costs for a group with which they desire association than for a less desirable group.

Bulimia is a psychological disorder defined as uncontrollable eating alternating with periods of fasting, strict dieting, or purging. Because it seems to be found among individuals in social groups, such as among cheerleading squads and athletic teams, some observers have argued that the social influence of attractive groups creates shared bulimia (50). In an investigation of two sororities, each evidenced clear norms regarding the appropriate level of binge eating. In one sorority, popularity was associated with moderate binging and in another, the more the binging, the greater the popularity of the member. However, in each sorority, type of binge eating could be predicted by that of the other members.

Finally, groups that are cohesive elicit more conformity than less cohesive groups (51). (See Chapter 14 for a detailed discussion of group cohesiveness.) The feeling of closeness and camaraderie inherent in cohesive groups makes deviation from the group difficult. In the study of binge eating in sororities, as friendships within the sorority created more cohesion, the members' binging grew more similar (52).

Figure 7.2 ■

Formation of Norms and Attitudes

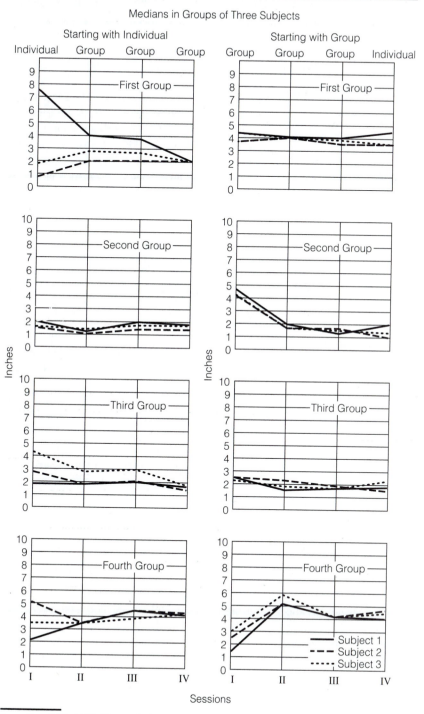

Medians in Groups of Three Subjects

From Sherif, M., 1936, *The Psychology of Social Norms*, New York: Harper & Row.

In very cohesive groups the pressure toward conformity can actually result in poor decision making (53). The type of thinking that occurs in such groups is called *groupthink*. Groupthink leads to the adoption of very poor decision strategies, which the group members strongly believe to be excellent ones. Groupthink results from the following conditions:

1. The group members have an illusion of invulnerability that encourages them to take risks.

2. The members rationalize their actions to discount the warnings of others.

3. The members so believe in the morality of the group that they ignore the ethical and moral consequences of their actions.

4. The members view their enemies as too stupid to defend themselves or as too evil to negotiate with.

5. The members apply pressure on each other to stifle any dissent they feel because they equate dissent with disloyalty.

6. The members censor their own feelings to minimize their dissent.

7. The members share an illusion of unanimity, in part because they stifle dissent and censor their own dissent.

8. Some members protect the others from any information that is contrary to their actions.

It has been argued that many United States foreign policy blunders can be attributed to groupthink. Governmental advisors tend to be an inbred group, linked by mutual friendships and loyalty, and sheltered from outside opinion. These conditions lead to the high cohesiveness conducive to groupthink. When they discuss an important policy issue, such as aiding a revolutionary movement in another country, they do not consider and weigh all the options. While this failure to consider other options is successful in reducing the controversy and distress of disagreements within the group, it results in another type of failure: ill-considered policy deci-

sions. Several poor political decisions made by a small group of close-knit advisers during the Reagan presidency, such as selling arms to Iran, illegally funding the Nicaraguan political group, the Contras, and as part of this aid, allowing illegal drugs to be brought to this country for sale, seem to provide examples of groupthink.

In an experimental demonstration of groupthink, groups of college students were led to believe they were high or low in cohesion by being given false feedback about the similarity or likely compatibility (or dissimilarity and likely incompatibility) of the members of the group. They then were (or were not) given guidelines to effective problem-solving processes. The guidelines stressed such factors as the importance of considering all options when making decisions (54). As predicted, decision making was poorest, confidence in the decision was strongest, and disagreement was lowest in the high cohesion/no problem-solving processes (groupthink) condition.

We end this discussion of the characteristics of groups that induce conformity with a look at one variable that is not a factor: Group size is not an important predictor of conformity. As reported earlier, Asch obtained about the same amount of conformity in his experiments with three confederates as with twelve (55). Other researchers have reported similar results.

Characteristics of individuals. Expectation states theory provides a framework for understanding the influence of individuals in task-oriented groups (56). People's status characteristics are associated with expectations about their abilities, with higher status characteristics being associated with expectations of greater competence. Two types of status characteristics influence the power and prestige of individuals in groups: *diffuse status characteristics,* such as sex, race, and age, and *specific status characteristics,* such as abilities relevant to a group's task.

If a diffuse status characteristic differentiates group members and the members have no other basis for discrimination among themselves, that characteristic will assume importance regardless of its relevance to the situation at hand. Thus, people with higher education, men, older people, and whites are likely to have greater status and thus be thought more competent, than people with less education, women, younger people, and minority group members, even in situations in which these characteristics are irrelevant. Physical attractiveness can also function as a diffuse status characteristic: Expectations for the task performance of an attractive person are higher than expectations for the performance of an unattractive person (57).

The influence of diffuse status characteristics helps explain why the inclusion of women and minorities in political and business arenas has not led to immediate change in these arenas. These new members now have voices, but they are not as powerful as the voices of the longstanding members.

Specific status characteristics can override the effects of diffuse status characteristics. If you were a young lawyer meeting about a case with the senior partners in your law firm you would clearly be at a disadvantage in influencing the group's decisions because your diffuse status characteristic (age) indicates low status. However, you could overcome the effects of low diffuse status by demonstrating your greater degree of competence in the specific aspects of law relevant to the case. It is nice to know the disadvantages conferred by low diffuse status can be overcome by specific competencies.

Further, the specific competency generalizes to other tasks. For instance, black students who demonstrate high task ability (high specific status) are then expected to perform competently at other unrelated tasks (high diffuse status) by the white students who have interacted with them on the first task (58). However, these findings sound a discouraging note as well because they indicate that in the absence of specific status characteristics, the contributions of low diffuse status group members will not be given their due weight.

Individual differences in conformity. Common sense tells us that people with low self-esteem conform more than people with high self-esteem; those with a high need for social approval conform more than those with a low need for social approval; and people with an external locus of control (those who believe they do not control their lives) conform more than people with an internal locus of control

(those who believe they do control their lives). In these instances, common sense is incorrect. Personality variables are weak predictors of conformity (60). People's responses to conformity pressures depend more upon characteristics of the situation than upon personality traits.

This emphasis on the situation is consistent with the views of the famous behaviorist, B. F. Skinner, regarding the causes of behavior (61). According to Skinner, we attribute too much responsibility to individuals for their positive or negative acts and too little responsibility to the situation for inducing the individuals' actions. He believes most of us do not want to admit the power of situations to influence behavior, for we feel that acknowledgement of the power of situations takes away from the accomplishments of individuals and robs them of their feelings of worth. Skinner believes the assignment of individual rather than situational responsibility results in considerable injustice (46). For instance, we often blame lower class minorities for deviant behaviors while not giving consideration to these individuals' underprivileged backgrounds—their lack of educational and occupational opportunities, the discrimination such individuals experience, and the unavailability of successful role models. At the same time we may overpraise and admire an individual born to wealth and success who simply takes advantage of his or her privileged status at birth to assume inherited wealth or power.

A similar criticism might be made by social psychologists from the social structure and personality perspective, but they would attribute behavior to structural factors, rather than the immediate situation. Individual praise or blame may be given when factors associated with the social structure (race, social class) have placed the person in a position of advantage or disadvantage.

This influence of the social structure on individual behavior often goes unrecognized, even though many aspects of our life chances are largely dependent upon social class. Role theorists from all schools of social psychology would agree with this analysis and place special emphasis on the influence of expectations on people's behavior. Factors affected by social class include the quality and amount of

BOX 7-2

Sex and Group Participation

In a test of a model derived from expectation states theory, the participation rates of male and female college students in group discussions were measured (59). The group members were asked to work as a group to complete a task. The task was to devise a problem suitable for solution by a task-oriented discussion group. This task was selected because it was sex-neutral: The skills required for its solution were not dependent on stereotypically masculine or feminine abilities. The groups were given information regarding the characteristics of a suitable problem, and were then given 20 minutes to devise one problem and show how it met the criteria given.

Expectation states theory predicts that, in the absence of task-relevant differences, the diffuse status of sex will influence performance expectations, even though sex is irrelevant to skill in devising a solution. The higher status of males relative to females in the society should result in differential expectations regarding their performance. Since higher expectations are associated with more active participation in groups, men were expected to have higher participation rates in the groups relative to women. This hypothesis was supported; the male group members participated more in the group discussions than the female members. ∎

education we receive; the types of occupations which will be available to us; the quality of our housing, food, and clothing; our health status and the availability of health care, even our life expectancy; and our lifestyles, including family forms, childrearing practices, religion, political and civic behaviors, personal values, consumer behavior, and leisure activities.

In the last two sections of this chapter, we will consider two types of overconformity to group pressures that are potentially destructive: overobedience to authority and deindividuation. Both situations can also be viewed as demonstrations of the power of the situation or the social structure or of role expectations on behavior.

Overobedience to Authority

When you think of the long and gloomy history of man, you will find more hideous crimes have been committed in the name of obedience than have ever been committed in the name of rebellion.—C. P. Snow

Human history began with an act of disobedience, and it is not unlikely that it will be terminated by an act of obedience.—Erich Fromm

Some investigators have found people to be amazingly willing to obey people in authority, even when the requests of the person in authority are immoral or unethical (63). Pretend you are a subject in the following study. You respond to a newspaper advertisement offering to pay people for participating in a study of human learning. You arrive at a laboratory at Yale University, along with another subject. The experimenter informs you that he is studying the effects of punishment on learning. He then tosses a coin to determine which roles you and the other subject will play in the study. The toss of the coin assigns the other subject to learn sets of paired words, while you are assigned to be the teacher. You will deliver electric shocks to the learner when he makes an error at his task.

The experimenter takes you and the learner into a room with electric shock equipment. After you receive a sample 45-volt shock (It stings; that machine really works!), the electrodes are attached to the learner, a man in his late 40s who is slightly overweight. He says he hopes the shocks won't be too harmful because he has a heart condition. The experimenter tells him the shocks can be extremely painful, but will cause no permanent tissue damage. Next, you are taken to an adjoining room and seated before a shock machine with a panel of switches marked in 15-volt increments, from 15–450 volts. Those over 420 volts are labeled *Danger: Severe Shock* and finally only with *XXXXXXXX*. The learner is strapped to the shock machine and you and the experimenter leave the room. You now cannot see the learner but you can hear any sound he makes.

You read a list of word pairs (for example, blue–boy) to the learner and then test him to determine if he has memorized them. His answers are communicated to you through lights on the shock panel. You must depress one of the shock switches each time the learner makes a mistake. You are to start with the 15-volt switch and move to successively higher shock levels. As the study progresses, the learner continues to make errors and you are asked to deliver increasingly higher levels of shock. If you are reluctant to administer the shock, the experimenter requests that you continue. Additional resistance on your part elicits the comment, "The experiment requires that you continue," then "It is absolutely essential that you continue," and finally, "You have no other choice, you must go on."

As the shocks increase in intensity, the learner begins to respond with groans and then cries of pain that increase in intensity. From 150 volts on, he demands to be released from the experiment. At 270 volts, the learner's response is an agonizing scream. At 300 volts, the learner shouts that he will no longer provide answers to the task. After 330 volts, an ominous silence follows all attempts to communicate with him. The experimenter tells you these nonresponses are to be counted as errors and requests you to continue administering the shocks until you have administered 450 volts three times.

At what point do you think you would have disobeyed the experimenter's orders and stopped administering the shock? A group of psychiatrists predicted that less than 2 percent of the population would deliver the full range of shocks. The actual results of Stanley Milgram's studies of obedience to authority shocked the entire scientific community. Surprisingly, although most teachers were upset by the learner's pain, his demands to be released, and his silence, they continued to administer the shocks. Despite their hesitation and protests, nearly two /65% thirds of the teachers delivered every one of the shocks to the learner!

In reality, the learner was a confederate of the experimenter. While no shocks were actually delivered to the learner, the subjects did not know this. Thus, this study shows a great proportion of people will submit to authoritarian pressure to continue a behavior that may be injurious to another person. How did the subjects feel about their actions? Many denied responsibility for their actions, stating that they would not have continued with the shocks had it been up to them. They felt the responsibility for the consequences to the learner lay solely with the experimenter. These subjects felt responsible to the authority in the situation, the experimenter, but not for the consequences of their actions.

Milgram next varied situational factors in an attempt to influence disobedience to the experimenter. He believed the Yale University setting added to the authority of the experimenter. He moved his experiment to somewhat shabby offices in downtown Bridgeport, Connecticut, where the study was said to be conducted by a private research group. While obedience was somewhat reduced in this setting, it was not significantly different from the level of obedience obtained at Yale.

Milgram also varied the spatial proximity of the learner to the teacher. Spatial proximity dramatically influenced obedience. When the teacher could not hear the learner's distress, obedience in administering the shocks increased. When the learner was placed in the same room with the teacher, increasing the teacher's knowledge of the learner's distress, obedience declined. Obedience declined even further when the teacher was required to place the learner's hand on a shock plate for the learner to receive the shock.

The proximity of the experimenter to the teacher also influenced obedience. When the experimenter described the experiment and then left the laboratory, giving instructions regarding the shock levels by telephone, obedience dropped. When the experimenter was never seen, but gave instructions only by means of a tape recording activated when the subject entered the laboratory, obedience declined still further. In these latter two conditions, the learners often pretended to administer increasing shock levels, but in fact repeatedly administered the lowest levels of shock. The teachers were disobedient, but pretended obedience.

In another version of the study, two experimenters gave conflicting orders—one to continue the shocks and one to terminate the shocks. In this situation, virtually all subjects stopped administering shocks at the point of disagreement. Finally, in a version in which the experimenter elected to be the learner, all teachers terminated the shocks at the experimenter's first complaint.

Why do individuals obey an authority despite obvious pain to another? Is it because people are sadistic animals who like to hurt others? Three pieces of information suggest this explanation is inaccurate. First, the teachers experienced real anguish at hurting the learner and expressed genuine concern for him. Second, the results of yet another version of this experiment show people do not want to hurt others in this setting. When teachers were allowed to set their own shock levels, the teachers gave very low levels of shock. Third, we have seen that teachers pretended to obey the authority, but actually gave the lowest levels of shock when they thought they would not be detected.

Why, then, was there so much obedience? The social structure and personality perspective provides insight into this situation. Social psychologists using this perspective would argue that people's behavior is a function of their position in the social structure. The position of experimenter has considerably more power and respect than that of subject, and so the experimenter's wishes were carried out.

Role theorists would remind us that individuals entered the Milgram experiment in a specific role, that of the experimental subject. In fulfilling the demands of this role, individuals are expected to be cooperative and obedient. Also, many individuals play this role because they wish to contribute to scientific knowledge, which is highly valued in our society. Since most individuals are not scientists, they do not expect to understand fully the projects in which they participate nor the reasons behind the requests that are made of them. With this idea of being a cooperative subject for the good of science in mind, it may have seemed appropriate to be unquestioningly obedient, to trust the scientists who were conducting the experiment, and to suspend ordinary judgment.

Milgram's answer to the question regarding obedience was that this and many other societies overtrain their members in obedience to authority. He felt following orders is presented as synonymous with moral behavior. An authority is viewed as having more importance than an ordinary person. According to Milgram, this overtraining in obedience occurs because, during childhood socialization, the socialization lessons (for example, treat others in a manner you would wish to be treated) are not separated from requests to obey the socializing agent. An unintended message of each socialization lesson is "and you must obey me, the authority." For instance, when parents tell their young children not to cross busy streets alone, the children understand this message, but also the implicit message, "And you'd better obey me." Milgram felt individuals are trained to feel responsible to an authority, but are not trained to feel responsible for their actions. Thus, the teachers felt it was the authority figure, not they, who was responsible for any harm to the learner.

The actual situation Milgram's subjects experienced is not likely to occur in real life, yet he believed his analysis of obedience in this experimental situation was applicable to real life situations involving obedience. His analysis has been applied to many historical events, such as to Nazi Germany and to the My Lai massacre in Vietnam. As the interview at the beginning of this chapter illustrates, at least some of the participants in the massacre at My Lai felt responsible only to their leader, Lieutenant Calley. They had no thoughts of responsibility for their own behaviors, and thus they easily violated religious and ethical tenants of respect for human life as well as international rules of warfare.

Researchers have attempted to link a variety of personality traits to obedience to authority but, as with conformity, there seem to be no strong links between personality and obedience. Most people, men or women, highly educated or barely educated, religious or nonreligious, will perform acts of destructive obedience if they are placed in a situation where obedience is demanded of them.

Deindividuation

Deindividuation theory is also based on abdication of personal responsibility (64). *Deindividuation* is a state of relative anonymity, in which a member of a group does not feel identifiable. The larger the group, the more deindividuated a person can become. When deindividuated, individuals will perform acts that they would not perform when they are capable of being singled out. As members of groups, people do not feel accountable for their actions because they are not personally identifiable. Screaming fans at a football game and shouting protesters at an anti-nuke march are both deindividuated. People in both situations are probably engaging in behavior that they would not perform if they were more identifiable.

Deindividuation was dramatically demonstrated by Philip Zimbardo in a simulated prison study (65). Widespread dissatisfaction with our prison system exists in this society. The problems of prisons are typically thought to be the fault either of the people who administer prisons or of the people who inhabit them. Zimbardo feels these personalistic explanations are incorrect. He believes the prison situation is not a result of pathological personalities, but of a pathological, deindividuating situation. This view is consistent with the dramaturgical school's analysis of prisons as total institutions (see Chapter 4).

Zimbardo stresses the fact that both prisoners and guards lose their personal identities in prisons. Prisoners are often required to wear uniforms, and they are assigned numbers. Their personal possessions are drastically limited, and, most important, their freedom is markedly curtailed. Movement outside cells is limited. Time of awakening, meals, and exercise are determined by others, and these activities are always performed with other prisoners. The guards are similarly regimented within the prison, losing personal identity through their uniforms and paraphernalia. The guards' behavior, too, is circumscribed. Prison rules restrict their behaviors, and their mistrust of the prisoners limits their abilities to relate to the prisoners as fellow human beings. Each group conforms to the role in which it is placed.

Importantly, both groups are put in a position where each sees the other as the enemy. The prisoners see the guards as unfeeling sadists, while the guards view the prisoners as pathological and dangerous animals. This situation does not facilitate communication between individual guards and prisoners. Instead, it facilitates mistrust and lack of communication between the groups.

To show that the prison environment is deindividuating, Zimbardo performed a study in which college students were randomly assigned to be either guards or prisoners. The students were recruited from newspaper ads and were selected on the basis of psychological tests, which identified them as emotionally healthy. Prisoners were "arrested" in their homes, booked and fingerprinted at the local

BOX 7-3

Shame and Conformity

Thomas Scheff argues that the emotion of shame can explain conformity, both normal levels of conformity and overconformity (66). Scheff believes we experience shame when we are negatively evaluated by others and pride when we are positively evaluated by others. People conform so they will not be evaluated negatively by others and thus will not experience shame. We fulfill social obligations to avoid shame. We also comply to avoid shame. Scheff argues that subjects in the Asch experiment who complied did so to avoid the shame or embarrassment of standing out or of being seen as misfits. In contrast, subjects who did not comply were able to manage the shame or embarrassment their deviant judgments caused.

Scheff believes that in modern societies, people are uncomfortable experiencing either pride or shame. For this reason, feeling shame induces more shame. The result of this cyclical relationship is that people overconform in order to avoid experiencing shame. Applying Scheff's analysis to the Milgram study would suggest that the teachers obeyed the authority to avoid the shame of being negatively evaluated by him. Applied to the Zimbardo study, this analysis implies that the guards were brutal to avoid the negative evaluations of other guards, who had established a norm of brutal treatment of prisoners. Prisoners were passive to avoid the negative evaluations of other prisoners, who believed passivity led to less brutal treatment, and the guards, who wanted no trouble from the prisoners. ■

police station, and then dressed in uniforms and placed in makeshift cells in the basement of the Stanford University psychology building. They were always referred to by number, rather than by name. Guards were also given uniforms, clubs, and sunglasses to hide their eyes. They were told little about how to be guards, except that guarding prisoners was serious business.

Almost immediately the guards began to harass the prisoners. First, the punishments were mild (awakening prisoners in the middle of the night for a "count"—asking them to call out their prison numbers). Later the punishments were more and more severe (making prisoners do large numbers

of pushups, verbally abusing them, refusing to allow them to use the toilet). The guards spontaneously used tactics used in real prisons to break the solidarity of prisoners. The prisoners reacted first with an organized revolt, which was put down. Almost immediately thereafter some of the prisoners started showing signs of personal disintegration, such as psychosomatic illnesses and crying.

The situation became so severe that the study, which was supposed to continue for two weeks, was terminated on the sixth day. By that time it was clear to Zimbardo that both groups were so absorbed by their roles as prisoners or guards they had ceased to behave as individuals. The members of both groups had forgotten they were subjects in an experiment. They acted as if they were real prisoners and real guards, conforming totally to these roles.

The post-experiment comments of the subjects reinforced Zimbardo's belief that he had created a state of deindividuation. The subjects who had been prisoners felt completely deprived of all identity and all freedoms. They felt the guards were a uniform mass representing power and oppression. The subjects who had been guards also felt deprived of personal identity. They had identified instead with the job of guard and had focused all their attention on controlling a group of people they felt to be dangerous and worthless.

Like Milgram's obedience studies, the Zimbardo prison experiment can also be interpreted from the social structure and personality perspective. Social psychologists from the personality and social structure perspective would note the differential power and status of the prisoners and guards, and stress the influence of these social structural variables on the subjects' behaviors. Role theorists would emphasize the overidentification of the subjects with their respective roles.

■ SUMMARY

Conformity is a change to behavior or beliefs consistent with social expectations that result from real or imagined individual or group pressure. Conformity to the norms of society allows society to exist; without this type of behavior we would live in chaos. We conform because we believe in our society's norms, to avoid punishments, and because we know no other behaviors. We should remember, however, consensus regarding norms is never total—subcultural variations exist, some consensus is forced, and some norms are in the process of change. Further, norms and their application are under continual negotiation.

Reference groups, groups with which we identify, induce conformity. Serving both normative and comparative functions, reference groups serve a normative function when they set or enforce norms for the individual, and a comparative function when they provide a standard of comparison against which the person can evaluate the self and others.

Three types of social influence exist: compliance, internalization, and identification. Compliance is social influence induced by expectations of gaining rewards or avoiding punishments. Asch's classic experiments of judgments of the length of lines provide examples of compliance. A number of ways to induce compliance were discussed, including the foot-in-the-door and the door-in-the-face techniques, low-balling, and the legitimization of paltry contributions.

Identification is social influence brought about by desires to establish or maintain a satisfying relationship with another person or group. Freud believed identification first occurs as a resolution of children's sexual attraction to their parents. Charismatic leadership typically leads to identification. This type of identification is often seen in religious cults.

Internalization is social influence created when the ideas or actions embodied in a group's or individual's message are rewarding. The Sherif demonstrations of the autokinetic effect provide an example of internalization.

Several characteristics of groups promote conformity, including group unanimity, high status, expertise, attractiveness, and cohesion. Group size, however, is unrelated to conformity. Very cohesive groups can exert strong pressures to conform to the decisions of the group that result in poor decision making. The result of these pressures is called groupthink.

Status characteristics are important determinants of the influence people have in task-oriented groups. Both diffuse and specific status characteristics are associated with expectations about people's abilities, with higher status characteristics being associated with expectations of competence.

Personality traits are weak predictors of conformity. The pressures of the situation are stronger predictors of conformity than individual personality variables. Those pressures sometimes lead to two potentially destructive types of overconformity: overobedience to authority and deindividuation.

The Milgram shock studies exemplify overobedience to authority. Milgram found an amazing willingness on the part of individuals to obey an authority, even though the request of the authority was unethical. Subjects in these studies felt it was the experimenter, not they, who was responsible for any harm to the learner. Milgram thinks this belief is symptomatic of the fact that individuals are overtrained in obedience to authority.

Zimbardo's prison simulation provides a second example of overconformity. In his simulation, college students assigned the roles of prisoner or guard became deindividuated—less accountable for their behavior than under normal conditions—because they felt anonymous. This deindividuation led to total conformity to their roles, resulting in brutal or overly passive behaviors the students would not have enacted under conditions in which they were more identifiable.

■

REFERENCES

1. *New York Times,* December 5, 1969.
2. *Gallup Reports,* 1987, Number 261, June.
3. Gibbs, J.P., 1981, *Norms, Deviance, and Social Control,* New York: Elsevier.
4. Strauss, A., L. Schatzman, R. Bucher, D. Erlich, and M. Sabshin, 1964, *Psychiatric Ideologies and Institutions,* New York: Free Press; A. Strauss, 1978, *Negotiations,* New York: Jossey-Bass; G. A. Fine, 1984, "Negotiated Orders and Organizational Cultures," in R. H. Turner and J. F. Short, Jr. (Eds.), *Annual Review of Sociology,* Vol. 10, Palo Alto: Annual Reviews, pp. 239–262.
5. Moscovici, S., 1985, "Social Influence and Conformity," in G. Lindzey and E. Aronson (Eds.), *Handbook of Social Psychology,* Vol. 2, 3d ed., Reading, MA: Addison-Wesley, pp. 347–412.
6. Singer, E., 1981, "Reference Groups and Social Evaluations," in M. Rosenberg and R. H. Turner (Eds.), *Social Psychology: Sociological Perspectives,* New York: Basic Books, pp. 66–93.
7. Strauss, H. M., 1968, "Reference Group and Social Comparison Processes among the Totally Blind," in H. Hyman and E. Singer (Eds.), *Readings in Reference Group Theory and Research,* New York: The Free Press.
8. Newcomb, T. M., 1950, *Social Psychology,* New York: Dryden.

9. Carver, C. S. and C. Humphries, 1981, "Havana Daydreaming: A Study of Self-consciousness and the Negative Reference Group Among Cuban-Americans," *Journal of Personality and Social Psychology* 40:545–552.
10. Buss, A. H. and N. W. Portnoy, 1967, "Pain Tolerance and Group Identification," *Journal of Personality and Social Psychology* 6:106–108; W. E. Lambert, E. Libman, and E. G. Poser, 1960, "The Effect of Increased Salience of a Membership Group on Pain Tolerance," *Journal of Personality* 28:350–357.
11. Charters, W. and T. M. Newcomb, 1958, "Some Attitudinal Effects of Experimentally Induced Salience of a Membership Group," in E. E. Maccoby, T. M. Newcomb, and E. L. Hartley (Eds.), *Readings in Social Psychology,* 3d ed, New York: Holt, Rinehart & Winston; H. M. Lefcourt and G. W. Ladwig, 1965, "The Effect of Reference Groups Upon Negroes's Task Persistence in a Biracial Competitive Game," *Journal of Personality and Social Psychology* 1:668–671.
12. Stouffer, S. A., E. A. Suchman, L. C. DeVinney, S. A. Star, and R. M. Williams, Jr., 1949, *The American Soldier: Adjustment during Army Life,* Vol 1, Princeton: University of Princeton Press.
13. Kelley, H. H., 1952, "The Two Functions of Reference Groups," in G. E. Swanson, T. M. Newcomb, and E. L. Hartley (Eds.), *Readings in Social Psychology,* 2d ed, New York: Holt, Rinehart & Winston, pp. 410–414.
14. Humphrey, R. H., P. M. O'Malley, L. D. Johnston, and J. G. Bachman, 1988, "Bases of Power, Facilitation Effects, and Attitudes and Behavior: Direct, Indirect, and Interactive Determinants of Drug Use," *Social Psychology Quarterly* 51:329–345.
15. Crosby, F., 1982, *Relative Deprivation and Working Women.* New York: Oxford; B. Majors and M. Testa, 1989, "Social Comparison Processes and Judgments of Entitlement and Satisfaction," *Journal of Experimental Social Psychology* 25:101–120; B. Majors and B. Forcey, 1985, "Social Comparisons and Pay Evaluations: Preferences for Same-Sex and Same-Job Wage Comparisons," *Journal of Experimental Social Psychology* 21:393–405.
16. Miller, G. T., W. Turnbull, and C. McFarland, 1988, "Particularistic and Universalistic Evaluation in the Social Comparison Process," *Journal of Personality and Social Psychology* 55:908–917.
17. Majors and Forcey, 1985, ibid.
18. Emmons, R. A. and E. Diener, 1985, "Factors Predicting Satisfaction Judgments: A Comparative Examination," *Social Indicators Research* 16:157–167; R. H. Smith, E. Diener, and D. H. Wedell, 1989, "Interpersonal and Social Comparison Determinants of Happiness: A Range-Frequency Analysis," *Journal of Personality and Social Psychology* 56:317–325; R. H. Smith and C. A. Insko, 1987, "Social Comparison Choices During Ability Evaluation: The Effects of Comparison Publicity, Performance Feedback, and Self-Esteem," *Personality and Social Psychology Bulletin* 13:111–112; 14:36–51.
19. Tesser, A., M. Millar, and J. Moore, "Some Affective Con-

sequences of Social Comparison and Reflection Processes: The Pain and Pleasure of Being Close," *Journal of Personality and Social Psychology* 54:49–61.

20. Festinger, L., 1954, "A Theory of Social Comparison Processes," *Human Relations* 7:114–140.

21. Ross, L., D. Greene, and P. House, 1977, "The 'False Consensus' Effect: An Egocentric Bias in Social Perception and Attribution Processes," *Journal of Experimental Social Psychology* 13:279–301.

22. Orive, R., 1988, "Social Projection and Social Comparison of Others," *Journal of Personality and Social Psychology* 54:953–964.

23. Felson, R. B., and M. D. Reed, 1986, "Reference Groups and Self-appraisals of Academic Ability and Performance," *Social Psychology Quarterly* 49:103–109.

24. See P. R. Nail, 1986, "Toward an Integration of Some Models and Theories of Social Response," *Psychological Bulletin* 100:190–206 for a review of these conformity models and the presentation of an integrative model.

25. Kelman, H. C., 1958, "Compliance, Identification, and Internalization," *Journal of Conflict Resolution* 2:51–60.

26. Asch, S. E., 1952, *Social Psychology,* Englewood Cliffs, NJ: Prentice-Hall.

27. Freedman, J. L. and S. C. Fraser, 1966, "Compliance Without Pressure: The Foot-in-the-Door Technique," *Journal of Personality and Social Psychology* 4:195–202.

28. Eisenberg, N., R. B. Cialdini, H. McCreath, and R. Shell, 1987, "Consistency-based Compliance: When and Why Do Children Become Vulnerable?" *Journal of Personality and Social Psychology* 52:1174–1181.

29. Cialdini, R. B., J. E. Vincent, S. K. Lewis, J. Catalan, D. Wheeler, and B. L. Darby, 1975, "Reciprocal Concessions Procedure for Inducing Compliance: The Door-in-the-face Technique," *Journal of Personality and Social Psychology* 31:206–215.

30. Freedman and Fraser, 1966, op. cit.

31. Cialdini et al., 1975, op. cit.

32. Patch, M. E., 1986, "The Role of Source Legitimacy in Sequential Request Strategies of Compliance," *Personality and Social Psychology Bulletin* 12:199–205.

33. Hornik, J., 1988, "Cognitive Thoughts Mediating Compliance in Multiple Request Situations," *Journal of Economic Psychology* 9: 69–79.

34. Cialdini, R. B., J. T. Cacioppo, R. Bassett, and A. Miller, 1978, "Low-ball Procedure for Producing Compliance: Commitment Then Cost," *Journal of Personality and Social Psychology* 36: 463—476.

35. Cialdini, R. B. and D. A. Schroeder, 1976, "Increasing Compliance by Legitimizing Paltry Contributions: When Even a Penny Helps," *Journal of Personality and Social Psychology* 36:463–476.

36. Weyant, J. M., 1984, "Applying Social Psychology to Induce Charitable Contributions," *Journal of Applied Social Psychology* 14:441–447.

37. Reeves, R. A., R. M. Macolini, and R. C. Martin, 1987, "Legitimizing Paltry Contributions: On-the-Spot vs. Mail-In Requests," *Journal of Applied Social Psychology* 17:731–738.

38. Cialdini, R. B., 1987, "Compliance Principles of Compliance Professionals: Psychologists of Necessity," in M. P. Zanna, J. M. Olson, and C. P. Herman (Eds.), *Social Influence: The Ontario Symposium,* Vol. 5, Hillsdale, NJ: Lawrence Erlbaum, pp. 165–184.

39. Jones, E. E. and H. B. Gerard, 1967, *Foundations of Social Psychology,* New York: Wiley.

40. Freud, S., 1940, *An Outline of Psychoanalysis,* New York: W. W. Norton.

41. Weber, M., 1964, *The Sociology of Religion,* Boston: Beacon.

42. Pritchett, W. D., 1980, "The Role of Charisma in the Evolution of New Religious Groups," Ann Arbor: University Microfilms International.

43. Humphrey et al., 1988, ibid.

44. Aronfreed, J., 1968, *Conduct and Conscience,* New York: Academic Press.

45. Sherif, M. A., 1935, "A Study of Some Social Factors in Perception," *Archives of Psychology* 27:187.

46. Allen, V. L., 1965, "Situational Factors in Conformity," in L. Berkowitz (Ed.), *Advances in Experimental Social Psychology,* Vol. 2, New York: Academic Press, pp. 133–176; for a review of the literature on the influence of a deviant minority, see Moscovici, 1985, op. cit.

47. Allen, 1965, ibid; C. L. Ridgeway, 1978, "Conformity, Group-oriented Motivation, and Status Attainment in Small Groups," *Social Psychology* 41:175–188; F. L. Strodtbeck and R. D. Mann, 1956, "Sex Role Differentiation in Jury Deliberations," *Sociometry* 19:3–11; R. Wahrman and M. D. Pugh, 1974, "Sex, Nonconformity, and Influence," *Sociometry* 37:137–147.

48. Allen, 1965, ibid; J. R. P. French, Jr. and R. Snyder, 1959, "The Bases of Social Power," in D. Cartwright (Ed.), *Studies in Social Power,* Ann Arbor: University of Michigan Press, pp. 118–149.

49. Allen, 1965, ibid; H. H. Kelley and M. M. Shapiro, 1954, "An Experiment on Conformity to Group Norms Where Conformity Is Detrimental to Group Achievement," *American Sociological Review* 19:667–677; H. H. Kelley and E. H. Volkart, 1952, "The Resistance to Change of Group-anchored Attitudes," *American Sociological Review* 17:453–465.

50. Crandall, C. S., 1988, "Social Contagion of Binge Eating," *Journal of Personality and Social Psychology* 55:588–598.

51. Allen, 1965, ibid; K. W. Back, 1951, "Influence Through Social Cohesion," *Journal of Abnormal and Social Psychology* 46:9–23; M. M. Sakauri, 1975, "Small Group Cohesiveness and Detrimental Conformity," *Sociometry* 38:340–357.

52. Crandall, 1988, ibid.

53. Janis, I. L., 1967, *Victims of Groupthink,* Boston: Houghton Mifflin.

54. Callaway, M. R. and J. K. Esser, 1984, "Groupthink: Effects of Cohesiveness and Problem-solving on Group Decision Making," *Social Behavior and Personality* 12:157–164.

55. Asch, 1952, op. cit.

56. e.g., J. Berger, M. H. Fisek, R. Z. Norman, and M. Zelditch, Jr., *Status Characteristics and Social Interaction: An Expectation States Approach,* New York: Elsevier; J. Berger, D. G. Wagner, and M. Zelditch, Jr., 1985, "Expectation States Theory: The Status of a Research Program," in J. Berger and M. Zelditch, Jr. (Eds.), *Status, Rewards, and Influence,* San Francisco: Jossey-Bass, pp. 215–261.

57. Webster, M., Jr. and J. E. Driskell, 1983, "Beauty as Status," *American Journal of Sociology* 89:140–165.

58. Cohen, E.G., 1982, "Expectation States and Interracial Interaction in School Settings," *Annual Review of Sociology* 8:209–235.

59. Smith-Lovin, L., J. V. Skvoretz, and C. G. Hudson, 1986, "Status and Participation in Six-person Groups: A Test of Skvoretz's Comparative Status Model," *Social Forces* 64:992–1005.

60. Mischel, W., 1968, *Personality and Assessment,* New York: Wiley; D. Marlowe and K. Gergen, 1968, "Personality and Social Interaction," in G. Lindzey and E. Aronson (Eds.), *Handbook of Social Psychology,* Vol. 3, 2d ed. Reading, MA: Addison-Wesley, pp. 590–665.

61. Skinner, B. F., 1971, *Beyond Freedom and Dignity,* New York: Knopf.

62. See also L. Ross, 1977, "The Intuitive Psychologist and His Shortcomings: Distortions in the Attribution Process," in L. Berkowitz (Ed.), *Advances in Experimental Social Psychology,* Vol. 10, New York: Academic Press, pp. 174–221.

63. Milgram, S., 1974, *Obedience to Authority,* New York: Harper & Row.

64. Zimbardo, P. G., 1969, "The Human Choice: Individuation, Reason, and Order Versus Deindividuation, Impulse, and Chaos," in W. J. Arnold and D. Levine (Eds.), *Nebraska Symposium on Motivation,* Lincoln: University of Nebraska, pp. 237–307.

65. Haney, C., C. Banks, and P. G. Zimbardo, 1973, "Interpersonal Dynamics in a Simulated Prison," *International Journal of Criminology and Penology* 1:69–97; Zimbardo, P. G., 1971, "The Psychological Power and Pathology of Imprisonment," statement prepared for the U. S. House of Representatives Committee on the Judiciary, Stanford: Stanford University.

66. Scheff, T. J., 1988, "Shame and Conformity: The Deference-Emotion System," *American Sociological Review* 53:395–406.

CHAPTER 8

Deviance

Deviance as Problematic Behavior

Strain Theories

Differential Association Theory

Control Theory

A Self Theory of Deviance

Assessing the Perspectives on Deviance as Objective

Labeling Theory

Self-Fulfilling Prophecy

Blaming the Victim

The Labeling Theory Perspective on Mental Illness

General Critique of Labeling Theory

Is Deviance Objective or Subjective?

In his high school in Atlanta, Georgia, young Mark Chapman seemed like a typical adolescent. He played in a rock band and worshiped the Beatles, a rock group and cultural influence of the 1960s. After graduating from high school in 1973, he became a counselor at the YMCA. In 1975 Chapman went to Lebanon as a missionary, and later worked at a Vietnamese resettlement center, where he was said to be good with children. But after entering college in the late 1970s, his behavior began to deteriorate. He dropped out of college. Depressed over an unhappy love affair and his parents' divorce, he attempted suicide. He then seemed to recover from his depression. He traveled around the world and, in 1979, married an Asian-American woman. But after a short time, difficulties returned. One day he quit his job, signing out with the name, John Lennon, a former member of the Beatles. In early December, 1980, Chapman went to New York to be near Lennon, the person with whom he most strongly identified, and succeeded one evening in getting Lennon's autograph. Hours later, on December 8, 1980, Mark David Chapman returned to Lennon's apartment house where he shot and killed his idol (1).

What is it that turned Chapman from a young man devoted to helping others to a man who murdered the person he most admired? When did his admiration for Lennon become pathological? At what point did admiration turn to destruction?

In this instance, virtually everyone would agree that Mark David Chapman committed an extremely deviant act. But considerable disagreement exists regarding what constitutes deviance in other instances. When a group of people was asked what type of people they thought were deviant, 180 people gave 252 different answers (2). The responses included the following: prostitutes, alcoholics, homosexuals, drug addicts, perverts, communists, atheists, and liars. The responses also included these more surprising answers: Democrats, self-pitiers, the retired, career women, divorcees, Christians, suburbanites, movie stars, perpetual bridge players, prudes, pacifists, psychiatrists, priests, liberals, conservatives, junior executives, and girls who wear makeup. It seems as though just about everyone is viewed as deviant by someone! Disagreement also exists among sociologists as to what constitutes deviance.

In addition, different cultures have different definitions of deviance. An act that is legally approved (abortion) or even required by one culture (avenging a family member's rape by murder of the perpetrator) may be extremely deviant behavior in another. Even within a single society, conceptions of deviance vary from time to time and place to place. For instance, in the United States, witchcraft was once thought to be an important form of deviance, and led to large-scale attempts to eradicate it. The behaviors thought to be deviant in the American South have always been slightly different from those of the rest of the country, as for example, in the southern emphasis on courtesy and being a perfect gentleman or lady. Behaviors that would be acceptable in other parts of the country are viewed as deviant—rude or ungentlemanly and unladylike—in the South because they violate these norms. We will examine the two differing definitions of the concept of deviance, explore the theory and research deriving from these definitions, and critique both positions. First, we present the traditional position regarding deviance as problematic behavior and explore four sociological theories of deviance that stem from this position: strain, differential association, control, and a self theory of deviance. We then present the second position regarding deviance, labeling theory, in which deviance is viewed as merely that which is labeled as deviance.

Deviance is a topic studied largely by sociologists, whether social psychologists or other sociologists. Unfortunately, the sociological study of deviance has not been integrated with the largely psychological study of conformity, to the detriment of both fields of understanding (3). While much of the study of conformity stems from concerns regarding group pressure and influence, the study of deviance springs from concerns regarding social control and crime causation.

DEVIANCE AS PROBLEMATIC BEHAVIOR

The traditional position regarding deviance is that it is *problematic behavior*. It is behavior that differs from generally accepted values and norms (4). The beliefs that society's values and norms are by and large good and proper and they should be supported underlie this view. To disregard these values and norms is to be deviant. Thus deviance is seen as working against the best interests of the society as a whole. Deviance is embodied in the acts of criminals, people with nonnormative sexual preferences or behaviors, the mentally ill, substance abusers, and other nonconformists. Sociologists who hold this view feel deviance is best studied by identifying the factors that cause individuals to behave in ways that are strongly disapproved of by society.

We consider four theories that share this perspective of deviance as problematic behavior departing from shared norms and values. Each of these theories addresses the question: What makes people behave in deviant ways? In each of these theories, crime has been the major focus of attention, although each of these theories has also been applied to other types of deviance.

Strain Theories

We will present two strain theories, each of which argues that socially induced strain causes people to behave in deviant ways.

Goal-means gap According to Robert Merton's *goal-means gap theory*, success is valued highly in our society (5). Virtually all of us accept the cultural value of success as a personal goal. However, not all members of our society have an equal chance to achieve success through legitimate channels. People in the lower social classes, compared with people in the upper social classes, have fewer opportunities to fulfill their ambitions for wealth, status, and power

through the legitimate channels of educational and occupational achievement. Some people accept the cultural goal of success, but have a low likelihood of achieving it through legitimate means. A gap exists between their goals and their means of fulfilling these goals in socially approved ways, creating strain or pressure to find alternative means or goals.

Merton believes that people with high aspirations, but low means of achieving them through legitimate means, experience *anomie*, or a state of normlessness induced by society's failure to provide an appropriate structure for people's goals and aspirations. Anomie always leads to stress. In this instance, anomie is a feeling of stress that derives from a society's inability to properly provide approved means necessary for achieving people's goals. The structure of the society thus promotes deviance because opportunities are not equal among its members. The concept of anomie was one of Durkheim's great insights, which he used to explain suicide rates (see Chapter 1 for a brief desription of this work).

When applied to adolescent subcultures, the theory assumes that lower-class adolescents hold the same goal of success as adolescents from other social classes. However, their chances for achieving these goals are comparatively low. They have high aspirations but low likelihood of achieving their means legitimately. Lower-class adolescents' low economic status limits their access to the educational system. Lower-class adolescents may also lack middle-class skills, such as verbal fluency, that would allow them to take full advantage of the educational opportunities they do have.

Some lower-class adolescents perceive that they do not have the means to achieve their goals for success through legitimate channels. This perception creates strain produced by feelings of anomie, and delinquent subcultures provide one alternative means to relieve it. Goods that cannot be purchased can be stolen. Money that cannot be earned in the legitimate job market can be earned in the underground job market of illicit drugs, stolen merchandise, and so on.

Status frustration Albert Cohen has proposed a similar theory focusing specifically on delinquency, *status frustration theory*, with status rather than economic success as the predominant goal (6). This theory argues that adolescents attempt to meet their needs for status in the schools. However, lower-class adolescents often encounter difficulties in meeting their status needs because the schools are run by predominantly middle-class people, and they promote middle-class values. Lower-class adolescents have difficulty achieving status in the schools because they are not socialized to behave in the middle-class ways the schools reward (courtesy, physical nonviolence, motivation, ability to delay gratification, verbal fluency). The result is that many lower-class adolescents fail in their attempts to achieve status in the schools. Their high aspirations for status through legitimate academic means are met with failure.

Because lower-class adolescents have been frustrated in their recognition for status in one domain, they attempt to resolve the resulting strain by achieving status in another. They create their own arenas for the achievement of status by developing delinquent subcultures. In these subcultures, the adolescents can themselves set the criteria for status in accordance with their own values. This greatly increases their chances of meeting their status needs. The values accepted in this subculture (toughness, taking extreme risks) are considered to be delinquent by others in the society. These values are selected, in part, because they oppose those of the middle-class society that has frustrated the adolescents' initial attempts to achieve status.

Revised strain theory A recent revision of the strain theory of delinquency argues that the data do not support the position that crime is most likely when aspirations are high but expectations of achieving them are low (7). Instead, the data show that deviance is highest when both aspirations and expectations are very low and deviance is lowest when both aspirations and expectations are high. Rather than the frustration of goal-seeking behavior, it is argued that inability to avoid painful situations is the cause of delinquency.

Figure 8.1 ■

The Revised Strain Theory of Delinquency

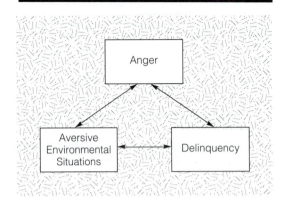

Adapted from Agnew, R., 1985, "A Revised Strain Theory of Delinquency," *Social Forces* 64: 151–167.

As learning theorists have shown (see Chapter 3), people are motivated to avoid painful situations, as well as to achieve success. Anger resulting in delinquent acts occurs when people are blocked from avoiding painful situations. As can be seen in Figure 8-1, aversive environmental situations are hypothesized to lead to acts of delinquency, both directly and indirectly through the effect of the environment on anger. For example, students who experience difficulties in school are blocked from escaping the school environment until age 16. Due to these unavoidable problems, many of these students will develop low aspirations as well as low expectations for success. If so, the strain resulting from inability to escape the school situation might lead to deviance directed at the school, resulting in truancy or school vandalism. It might also lead to anger causing the student to strike out against conventional society and its rules in general.

Data supporting these ideas show that, among junior high students, deviance is high when avoidance of painful situations is blocked. Students who experienced severe difficulties at home or at school, two environments from which minors cannot escape,

BOX 8-1

Adaptations to Strain

M-(Gap)

Merton's theory is actually a general theory of deviance, designed to explain much more than crime. According to Merton, attempts to achieve society's goals through illegitimate means constitute only one of five ways people adapt to low opportunities to achieve goals through legitimate means (11). Using illegitimate means toward culturally approved goals implies acceptance of the cultural goals but rejection of the culturally prescribed means of obtaining them. Merton terms this type of adaptation *innovation* because the individual finds nonnormative ways of meeting his or her needs as, for example, in criminal acts.

A second means of adaptation is the reverse: to lower one's goals so they can be met through legitimate means. Called *ritualism*, such an adaptation is made by people who conform to society's rules, but no longer hold hopeful expectations. Many lower-level white collar workers would fall in this category. They continue to work to survive, but not to achieve. They are disillusioned about the possibility of a significant return on their work investment.

Retreatism represents a third mode of adaptation to strain. Here the individual rejects both the cultural goals and the legitimate means to reach them, and thereby retreats from the struggle. Vagrants and substance abusers are classic examples of retreatists. Their behaviors allow them to escape both the goals and attempts to achieve them.

A fourth mode of adaptation, *rebellion*, represents a genuine recasting of values. Conventional goals and means of reaching them are rejected for different goals and means that are perceived to be better than those of society. The individual who devotes his or her life to political or social reform exhibits rebellion as defined by Merton.

Finally, we come to the most common adaptation, *conformity*. Socialization ensures that most of us accept society's goals and means, even if we are unlikely to experience success. Most individuals simply use the conventional means at their disposal to reach whatever level of success they can attain, without rejecting society's definition of success or using illegitimate means to reach it. ■

were much more likely than other students to attempt to escape the situation or commit acts of physical aggression and delinquency, such as theft, arson, and robbery.

Criticisms of strain theory The strain theories have been criticized on the grounds that they attribute deviant behavior primarily to lower-class people. Yet we know that middle-class and upper-class people also engage in deviant behaviors. Some deviant behaviors, such as the white-collar crimes of embezzlement and fraud, are by definition middle- and upper-class behaviors.

Recent studies show surprisingly little evidence of an association between crime and social class. For instance, an analysis of data from 35 studies examining offenses ranging from minor youth offenses to violent crimes shows only a very weak negative correlation between crime and social class (8). In fact, some data show a positive relationship between crime and social class for less serious offenses, such as drunken driving, simple assault, tax cheating, and theft (9). Even if an association could be shown between social class and serious crimes, the strain theories still would not explain why only some lower-class adolescents and adults commit deviant acts, while most do not.

The success and status versions of strain theory have also been criticized for their assumption that everyone uniformly accepts a single cultural goal of success or status. These theories do not acknowledge the individual variations that seem to exist in the acceptance of cultural goals. In addition, considerable data suggest that lower-class people hold substantially lower levels of aspirations than people from the upper- and middle-classes (10).

Differential Association Theory

Edwin Sutherland's *differential association theory* was developed to explain involvement in crime. He argued that people have differing levels of involvement in crime because they have learned different group norms (12). Some people are exposed primarily to reference groups (parents, lovers, other close friends) that define crime favorably, while others are exposed predominantly to reference groups that define it unfavorably. Favorable definitions of crime are manifested in the commitment of illegal acts or the holding of values that support illegal acts. Those surrounded by favorable definitions of crime are likely to become lawbreakers, while those surrounded by unfavorable definitions of crime are likely to become law-abiders. Thus, criminal behavior is learned through a process of socialization just like other behaviors are learned.

Differential association theory can be viewed as a social learning theory of deviant behavior (see Chapter 3). It states that deviance is learned through a combined process of observation and reinforcement (13). Individuals are differentially rewarded for criminal and noncriminal acts. To the extent that individuals receive rewards or avoid punishments for criminal acts, or observe this pattern of rewards and punishments in reference group members, they will engage in them. For example, if a ghetto teen or an upper-class businessman can garner desired goods through criminal means without facing punishments—whether the goods be money and drugs for the teen or multimillion-dollar contracts achieved through bribery for the businessman—they will continue to commit criminal acts. If the children of the businessman or the younger siblings of the ghetto teen see their loved ones profit from crime, they too will form favorable definitions of crime. Similarly, to the extent that individuals receive punishments or are denied rewards for criminal acts, they will avoid them. Thus, differential association is based upon differential reinforcement.

Differential association theory has also been applied to the crimes of higher status members of society—to white-collar crimes and crimes committed by government officials, such as domestic spying, political corruption, and election improprieties (14). In these cases, individuals become a part of a rather tight organization of insiders who may regard some illegal practices as "business as usual." The positive definition of illegal activity goes unchallenged from the individuals' occupational reference group. Differential association theory has also been applied to substance abuse (15) and adolescent cigarette smoking (16).

In a recent test of differential association theory, favorable definitions of criminal behavior (positive evaluations of crime, association with law-breakers) were associated with increased criminal behavior for five acts—assault, two types of theft, tax cheating, and illegal gambling (17). The association was indirect: Favorable definitions of criminal behavior were associated with increased criminal motivation, which was associated with increased criminal behavior.

Criticisms of differential association theory Some critics have argued that differential association theory is merely a truism; since crime is not genetically determined, it must therefore be learned. Other critics have called the theory untestable. Not only are terms such as "favorable definition" and "unfavorable definition" difficult to define, their measurement throughout the course of a person's lifetime would be impossible (18). It has also been noted that differential association theory does not explain the conforming behavior of those exposed primarily to favorable definitions of crime (the "straight" children of lawbreakers who were consistently exposed to favorable definitions of crime) or the deviant behavior of those exposed primarily to unfavorable definitions of crime (the delinquent child of law-abiding parents who continually modeled unfavorable definitions of crime).

Control Theory

Travis Hirschi's *control theory of delinquency* begins with Freud's notion that all people have an innate urge to seek pleasure without regard to social cost (see Chapter 4 for a discussion of Freud's concept of the id) (19). People are thus naturally inclined to commit deviant acts. The important question therefore is, "What causes conformity?" His answer is social control. Since deviance is the absence of the causes of conformity, deviance must be caused by the absence of social control.

Hirschi argues that those who have strong bonds to society are prevented from breaking its rules. Those whose bonds to society are weak are not bound by its norms and are free to deviate. He argues that bonds to society can be measured through four types of commitment:

1. attachment to conventional people and institutions, such as a close relationship with parents or conventional peers or a strong interest in school.

2. commitment to conformity. By this Hirschi means investment of time and energy in conventional activities, such as getting an education and succeeding at a job. Individuals receive rewards (prestige, wealth, power) which commit them to the conventional order.

3. involvement in conventional activities. People whose lives are filled with conventional activities simply do not have the time to commit or even think about deviant acts.

4. belief in the moral validity of the rules, such as strong moral or religious beliefs or respect for the law.

Strong religious ties should thus bond individuals to the society and protect them from deviance. A recent study measured the impact of one type of social bond, church attendance and the influence of religion, on adolescents' participation in a variety of antisocial behaviors, such as vandalism and theft (20). The investigators found that both church attendance and religious influence on daily life were strongly and negatively associated with antisocial behaviors. The adolescents who attended church frequently, and those who said that religion exerted a considerable influence on their lives were less likely to have committed delinquent acts than adolescents who attended church rarely, and those who said religion exerted little influence on their lives.

Control theory has been applied to substance abuse (21) as well as to adolescent cigarette smoking (22). Bonds to conventional society have been shown to constrain individuals from using these substances.

The deterrence doctrine The deterrence doctrine is an older version of control theory, in which it is presumed that people rationally calculate the costs and benefits of committing a crime. This theory is thus an exchange theory view of crime (see Chapter 3). If the benefits (financial, status) outweigh the costs (the possibility of legal punishment), the person will commit the crime. The argument is therefore that legal punishment for crime should be severe, swift, and certain. While the deterrence doctrine has been supported in some studies (23), it has not been supported in others (24). The effect of deterrence on deviant activity is currently unclear.

Criticisms of control theories A number of studies have failed to find support for control theory (25). In addition, it is possible that control theory has confused cause with effect. It is not clear if lack of bonds to the society promotes deviance, or if deviance causes individuals to lose their bonds to the society (26). Control theory has also been criticized for assuming a single conventional moral order in society, something that is unlikely in our complex, multicultural society. Similarly, the assumption that the motivation for delinquency is constant across individuals has been questioned.

A Self Theory of Deviance

Howard Kaplan argues that deviant behavior is associated with negative attitudes toward the self (27). Kaplan assumes that all people strive to maintain positive self-attitudes and to eliminate negative self-attitudes. However, some people do develop negative self-attitudes due to their experiences in important groups, such as their families or peer groups. Because of these negative experiences with important groups, these individuals reject themselves and lose motivation to conform to the norms of the society, since conformity has been ineffective in providing acceptance. In addition, this association of negative self-attitudes with one's reference groups leads the person to associate the conventional norms of society with distress. Deviant patterns represent alternative actions through which the person can attempt to gain self-esteem. As a result, people with negative self-images are likely to adopt deviant behavior patterns.

Support was found for this theory in a study of junior high school students in which self-rejection (self-derogation, perceived rejection by teachers, and perceived rejection by parents), disposition to deviance (motivation to deviate from conventional group norms) and deviance (self-reports of activities such as stealing, vandalism, and participation in gang fights) were measured over a 3-year period (28).

Deviance was measured in year 1 and year 3, self-rejection in year 1, and disposition to deviance in year 2. As can be seen in Figure 8-2, both early deviance and self-rejection affected disposition to deviance in year 2, and disposition to deviance in year 2 affected deviance in year 3. Thus, both self-rejection and initial deviance led to dispositions to deviance, which led to further deviance.

Criticisms of self theory The self theory of deviance has been criticized by researchers who have found little association between self-rejection and deviant behavior (29). In fact, deviant behavior and high self-esteem are often found together (30). In some subcultures deviance is associated with the acquisition of power, status, and money. Where this positive association exists, deviant behavior should increase self-esteem when it aids individuals in obtaining these rewards.

In addition, even where a positive relationship between self-esteem and deviance has been found, self theory is an incomplete explanation for deviant behavior, for few adolescents with low self-esteem commit deviant acts. This theory does not explain why only some adolescents with low self-esteem become deviant.

Assessing the Perspectives on Deviance as Objective

Which of the above theories is correct? Is deviance created by strain resulting from frustration, learned positive associations with criminal behavior, lack of attachment to conventional society, or a low level of self-esteem? Each of the theories described has been supported by some research, but not supported by other research. It is likely that each theory is valid to some extent.

The strain theories apply best to deviance committed by lower-class people. Differential association theory applies primarily to crimes in which skills must be learned and to those who commit crimes in groups. Both control theory and self theory apply best to juvenile delinquency. Neither seems applicable to the deviant acts that adults, particularly high status adults, commit.

Figure 8.2 ■

Self-rejection and Deviance

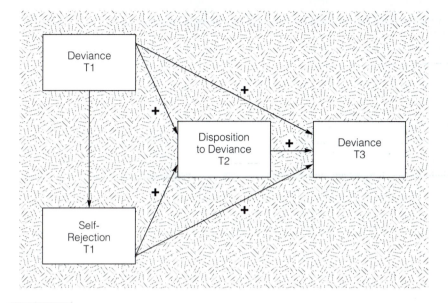

H. B. Kaplan, R. J. Johnson, and O. A. Bailey, 1986, "Self-Rejection and the Explanation of Deviance: Refinement and Elaboration of a Latent Construct, *Social Psychology Quarterly* 49: 110–128.

Each theory probably applies to some types of deviants in some instances. Doubtless there are many instances of deviance being caused by a gap between goals and means, learning in intimate groups, lack of bonds to society, and a low self-esteem. Deviance is too complex to have a single cause.

■
LABELING THEORY

The second major approach to deviance, the *labeling theory,* holds that deviants can best be identified simply as those persons in the society who are perceived to be deviant (31). From this perspective, deviance is not defined by a specific set of acts, but rather by the *reaction of some people to others.* For sociologists who hold this view, what is important in understanding deviance is the process by which an act or an individual is defined as deviant.

We sometimes think of deviance or deviant behavior as being confined to a few "abnormal" individuals. According to labeling theory, this perception is inaccurate. It does not acknowledge the range of deviation existing in a society. No one is completely deviant nor completely conforming. All of us break some norms and laws. In fact, obedience to some norms, such as speed limits, may be more unusual than violation of them. Labeling theorists believe the violation of norms is widespread, and not sufficient to label someone deviant.

According to this view, deviance is nothing more than a label applied to some individuals by other

■ *According to the labeling theory of deviance, deviance is created by groups that make the rules and then apply them to other groups. (Reuters/Bettmann Newsphotos)*

individuals (32). The people providing the labels are as important in the determination of "deviance" as is the behavior of the labeled person. In general, people who do the labeling judge behavior supporting their own values and norms as normal. Similarly, they judge behavior that diverges from their values and norms as deviant.

Thus, deviance is socially constructed, and does not exist independently from the people who define it. What is viewed as "normal" and "abnormal" and "deviant" and "nondeviant" is a function of who applies the labels. What is deviant from the perspective of some people in the society is considered proper from the perspective of others. For example, most of us would consider members of extremist political groups to be deviant. But to the members of these groups, nonmembers are the deviants. In contrast to the deviance-as-problematic-behavior emphasis on the characteristics of deviants, labeling theorists focus on the society's reactions to people's acts.

Who applies the labels? Those in power tend to apply the labels that are generally accepted in society. Less powerful people in the society tend to be those who are labeled. This means that the upper- and middle-classes and the racial majority are able to apply deviant labels to lower-class and minority people whose behaviors do not conform to the rules of the people applying the labels. Deviance is thus created by the social groups that make the rules and then apply the rules to other groups. Labeling theorists believe an individual who has broken a specific law is most likely to be labeled as a criminal if that person is poor or a minority group member, or both, than if the person is wealthy and white. Also, the type of crime that a wealthy town leader is likely to commit (industrial pollution) has a lower probability of prosecution than the type of crime committed by lower-class persons (theft), even though the former may be more damaging to society as a whole.

One primary area of study in labeling theory is the consequence of being labeled deviant. Labeling theorists believe that being labeled as deviant often makes it more likely an individual will continue to perform deviant acts. First, they believe labeling people as deviant raises a barrier between the labeled individuals and the rest of society. The deviant label is a *master status,* a status powerful enough to play a central role in evaluations of these individuals. Society is likely to treat those individuals as though they are generally deviant, not just deviant at one time and in one respect, and as though they are likely to commit other deviant acts. For instance, once labeled as a thief an individual may be distrusted. Former friends may avoid the individual after his or her arrest, both because they do not want to be associated with a person labeled as a deviant, and because they now perceive the individual as a thief who might steal from them.

In Goffman's terms, the labeled person has been stigmatized and will be treated in ways that damage his or her life chances (33). The effect of being shunned by "normals" may be to draw the labeled person away from a conventional lifestyle and into a deviant lifestyle or *deviant career.* The labeled individuals may be fully accepted only by those who share a similar negative label. Drug dealers, members of motorcycle gangs, gays, pimps, and cult members may find that only others of their kind understand them and welcome interaction with them. The self-conception of the person labeled as deviant may come to mirror the evaluation of the community. Shunned by friends for having been caught stealing, a person may come to accept their labels of him or her as "untrustworthy," "bad," or "dangerous" and the person's deviant behavior may increase.

Deviant behavior may be used by a labeled person as a defense ("They think I'm bad now; I'll show them what's really bad") or as an adjustment to the problems created by the label ("Who cares if my old friends don't like me any more; I'll hang out with the guys in the motorcycle gang who do like

me"). Deviant behavior that is a consequence of problems created by labeling is called *secondary deviation* (34), in contrast to the original deviant act, the *primary deviance.* Most of us commit acts of primary deviance, but few of us are labeled deviant, resulting in our going on to commit acts of secondary deviance.

The labeling theory differs from the other theories of deviance we have discussed in its attempt to study the world from the perspective of the people thought to be deviant. A second difference is that other theories of deviance take a correctional perspective (35). They study deviance with the ultimate aim of eliminating it. In contrast, labeling theorists accept deviance as normal and as inevitable as conformity.

While labeling theory is unlike the other theories of deviance in a number of respects, it does share a number of assumptions with symbolic interactionism. Both labeling theory and symbolic interactionism attempt to view reality from the perspective of the acting individual, assume that meaning is created through the process of interaction, and argue that others' appraisals are important determinants of the self.

In examining delinquent subcultures, labeling theorists attempt to understand the process of interaction among the members of the subculture and the people who label them as deviants. An understanding of this process may help to explain how members of delinquent subcultures come to view themselves as delinquent and to commit themselves to lifestyles involving criminal acts. The labeling theorists assume that, when a person is labeled delinquent, this label predisposes them to view themselves as delinquent and to continue the behavior that resulted in the label.

Labeling theorists argue that many, perhaps most, adolescents engage in behaviors that might cause them to be labeled as delinquent, such as underage drinking, reckless driving, and shoplifting. However, most adolescents are not labeled as delinquent. The adolescents who avoid this label are likely to have parents who had the power to prevent their children from being classified as deviants. For example,

BOX 8-2

Labeling and Delinquency

The results from a study of boys who had participated in a 5-year treatment program in the 1940s, beginning at ages 5 to 13, support the labeling viewpoint (36). Some of the boys were labeled by welfare and police officials as "difficult" and others were labeled as "average." Some boys from each group were placed in the experimental condition. Other boys from each group were placed in the control condition. The boys in the experimental and control conditions were matched in age, family background, and delinquency proneness.

Each boy in the experimental group received one of the following treatments, five years of bimonthly medical and psychiatric treatment, follow counseling, placement in summer camps, academic tutoring, or placement in community programs. As a result, the boys in the experimental group received the label, "in need of treatment." The boys in the control group received no treatment and thus avoided negative labeling.

Thirty years after the termination of the program, when these boys were men of 35 to 43, they were compared on a variety of measures of criminal behavior. It was members of the *experimental* group who were more likely to be alcoholic, to have committed more than one crime, to have a severe mental illness, and to occupy low-prestige jobs, relative to members of the control group. Both those who had been judged "difficult" as children and those who had been judged "average" seem to have been harmed by the intervention program. The investigator's conclusion was: "Intervention programs risk damaging the individuals they are designed to assist." ■

middle-class adolescents who commit a minor act of vandalism are apt to be returned to their parents without real punishment. The most extreme consequence of their behavior may be a scolding by the police. But lower-class adolescents who commit acts of minor vandalism are more likely to be taken to a police station and turned over to juvenile authorities. Their cases may proceed to juvenile court. There they may be labeled as delinquent by juvenile authorities. Thus, it is the label, rather than just the behavior, that may predict future behavior.

This differential treatment has several effects.

The middle-class adolescents continue to receive the trust of members of their community, while lower-class adolescents are assumed to be potential law-breakers. The lower-class adolescents are likely to be watched, questioned, and treated with less respect by the police and school authorities. Friends and neighbors will continue their social relationships with the middle-class adolescents, but may not with the newly labeled, lower-class adolescents. Because of these factors, the lower-class adolescents may come to accept the label of "delinquent" that adults have applied to them.

For different reasons, then, labeling theorists come to the same conclusions about crime and poverty or minority status as strain theorists. As we saw in our evaluation of strain theory, most data do not support the labeling and strain theory view that social class and ethnicity are related to crime. When prior record and seriousness of offense are taken into account, in most studies the lower classes and minorities do not appear to be labeled more frequently than the upper classes and majority group members for similar acts (37). Similarly, the data show the official response to acts of delinquency by juveniles is based predominantly on their behaviors, although nonwhites and lower-class adolescents may receive greater scrutiny in some instances (38).

However, the data are mixed. It is still true that the criminal justice system focuses on crimes committed by lower-class rather than upper- or middle-class persons. The poor and minorities are greatly overrepresented in the prison population, and they are less satisfied with our system of justice than the nonpoor and whites (39).

The response of the criminal justice system may be more complex than previously thought. Recent data indicate the sentencing of defendants of different races may vary not by race of defendant or victim, but by the current perceptions of the type of person most responsible for the crime and the type of perceived victims of the crime (40). For example, during a portion of the 1960s and 1970s, criminal justice officials believed whites were the big drug dealers, and minorities were their victims. During this time period, whites were sentenced to harsher penalties for drug offenses than minorities (41). Similarly, the Watergate burglary ordered by officials in President Nixon's campaign committee sensitized people to white-collar crime. For the period immediately after but not before Watergate, managers were more likely than workers to be prosecuted for securities violations (42).

Self-Fulfilling Prophecy

According to labeling theorists secondary deviations may be created through *self-fulfilling prophecies,* others' convictions about the future behavior of an

■ *Teachers' positive expectations about poor or minority students can also become self-fulfilling prophecies. (© Richard S. Orton 1989)*

individual (43). The best known demonstration of the self-fulfilling prophecy is Robert Rosenthal's school study (44). Rosenthal believes a primary reason why poor and minority students do not perform well in school is because of teachers' negative expectations concerning the students' capabilities. He feels some teachers of poor and minority students expect them to be slow learners and to exhibit problem behaviors. Expecting this type of student behavior, teachers treat the students as though they are slow and as though they will create problems. In this way, says Rosenthal, they produce exactly the behavior they expect.

Since it would be unethical to experimentally create negative images of students, Rosenthal tested his suspicions by experimentally creating positive images of students. In an inner city elementary school, Rosenthal randomly selected 20 percent of the students to be labeled. He told their teachers that test results had shown these students to be "late bloomers" who would show dramatic intellectual improvements in the next year. At the end of the year the school records indicated the predictions had proven to be accurate. Children who had been labeled as late bloomers increased both in grade point average and IQ more than the nonlabeled students. They were also rated as more intellectually curious and happier by their teachers than students who had not been labeled late bloomers.

Since these children were really no different from their classmates, how did these positive results occur? Rosenthal believes the teachers, who were expecting positive behaviors from the "late bloomers," may have encouraged them more than their other students. They also may have given them more attention or selectively remembered behaviors consistent with their positive expectations, and discounted inconsistent behaviors. Their positive treatment of the children resulted in actual improvements on the part of the children.

Rosenthal believes negative expectations held by teachers often become self-fulfilling prophecies, producing deviant behavior in the children. If some teachers of poor children assume their students are unmotivated to learn, they will spend more time controlling the classroom than teaching. The result will be that the students do not progress normally, not because they are unmotivated but because they have been controlled rather than taught.

Rosenthal also thinks some teachers of minority children are prejudiced against them. These teachers think minority children are intellectually inferior to majority children and, because of this bias, are less attentive and persistent in their teaching of minority children. He believes the teachers are also less likely to notice and remember their creativity and industry, and are less willing to give them the benefit of the doubt in an ambiguous situation. The result of this process is that the minority children are labeled as dumb, unmotivated, and unmanageable, regardless of their actual behaviors. Children so labeled may, in time, take on behaviors associated with the negative labels given to them.

Blaming the Victim

Blaming the victim may be involved in the process of labeling people and creating self-fulfilling prophecies about them. Victims (the poor, minorities) are blamed as follows:

1. A problem is identified.

2. Those affected by the problem, the deviants, are shown to differ from the rest of us. These differences are attributed to characteristics of the sufferers themselves.

3. The differences between the deviants and the rest of us are defined as the cause of the current problems (45).

To illustrate, poor and minority children are thought to perform poorly in school because they are "culturally deprived." However, the schools these children attend are often shabby, overcrowded facilities that leave them ill-equipped to learn. As we have seen, teachers may have negative expectations for the children. In blaming the victim, these factors are overlooked. Rather, the children themselves are viewed as the problem—as being incapable of learning.

A dramatic piece of data supports the view that such children are victims of blame. When poor and minority children enter the school system their achievement test scores are slightly lower than those of their white middle-class peers. This difference presumably occurs because middle-class children have had more exposure to aspects of intellectual culture such as books, educational toys, travel, and the arts, with the result that they are better prepared for achievement tests devised by middle-class test designers to tap the knowledge of middle-class students. However, this difference does not disappear throughout the course of schooling. On the contrary, the difference in knowledge increases. Thus, something the schools themselves are doing—or not doing—contributes to the increased gap between poor and nonpoor, white and minority students.

Schools in poor or minority areas often are underfunded. In addition, where ability tracking is used—separating children into different classes on the basis of perceived academic promise or ability—poor and minority students predominate in the lower tracks (46). Further, lower-track classes tend to stress nonacademic values, such as being cooperative and following directions, while higher-track classes stress academic values, such as independence and active involvement in learning (47).

Statistics on minorities and education demonstrate our society's failure. In 1986, over 20 percent of whites, but only 11 percent of blacks and 8 percent of Hispanics in the United States had completed at least four years of college (48). This record is not improving; between 1975 and 1985 the proportion of black high school graduates enrolling in college dropped 45 percent.

Another example of blaming the victim can be found in the *culture of poverty* hypothesis (49). The poor are said to be victims of the culture of poverty, a lifestyle that includes illicit sex and drugs, inability to delay gratification, avoidance of work, pathological family relationships, apathy, poor impulse control, and irresponsibility. This description contains no indication that poverty results directly from a lack of money. Rather, it is presumed to result from characteristics of the poor themselves.

The behaviors of the poor indeed differ from those of the nonpoor. However, the poor typically have the same values and aspirations as the nonpoor (50); they simply are unable to achieve them. Further, many of the behaviors of the poor labeled as deviant and maladjusted are, in fact, imaginative solutions to difficult life situations. For example, the poor often emphasize "street smarts." Rather than viewing this emphasis as a willful disregard for middle-class norms, one might better view it as a demonstration of flexibility in coping with difficult life circumstances. Rather than berating the poor for spending money instead of saving it, one should remember that their physical needs are likely to require the full use of their incomes. Savings accounts are a luxury of the well-to-do.

The *just world hypothesis* provides an explanation for why victims are often blamed for their problems (51). (See Chapter 2 for a related discussion of the just world hypothesis.) As you may remember from our earlier discussion, people want to believe the world is just, because only in a just world will they get what they deserve. This need to believe in a just world motivates people to attribute instances of injustice to characteristics of the victims of the injustices, and thus to blame the victims for their misfortunes. In this way, our belief in a just world can be maintained.

The situations in which victims are not blamed for their misfortunes provide further support for the argument that the goal of the belief in a just world is self-protection. Victims are unlikely to be blamed if they are similar to the person making the judgments (52), or if they were involved in circumstances in which the person making the judgments might find himself or herself (53). For example, you might be unlikely to blame a college student who accidentally caused great personal harm to another in a car accident, for all of us have had close calls while driving as a result of our inattention. The unconscious thought is, "If bad things have happened to people like me, surely it can't be their fault!"

In summary, it may be the label of deviant, rather than a specific behavior, that produces continued deviant behavior. Once applied, a deviant label may come to be accepted by the labeled individual. Labeling may be facilitated by making prophecies about people that become self-fulfilling (the proph-

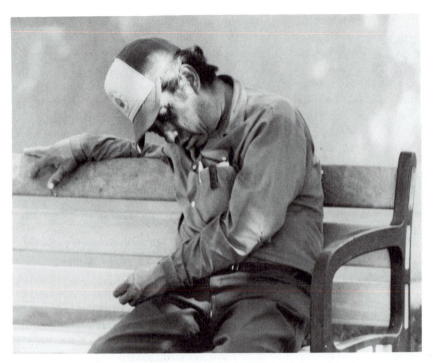

■ *Sleeping in public is a residual norm violation.* (WGS)

ecy that poor children can't learn in school), by blaming the victim for his or her misfortunes (the belief that poor families have values that prevent their children from learning), and by the belief that the world is just (the belief that poor children do not deserve better facilities and treatment than they get).

The Labeling Theory Perspective on Mental Illness

In this section, we will apply labeling theory and other related theories to a topic commonly studied from the perspective of deviance, mental illness. We then examine data relevant to the conflicting claims of labeling theorists and others about mental illness.

Labeling theorists ask whether mental illness actually exists or if it is merely a label applied to some persons by others. Some labeling theorists argue people labeled as mentally ill are simply those who violate *residual social norms* (54). Residual social norms are unwritten and unspoken rules regarding interaction. Obedience to them is so taken for granted that their violation is viewed as strange and bizarre. An example of a residual social norm is that one should not talk aloud to oneself. Another is when in public, one must be involved in or doing something. It is not appropriate to appear entirely withdrawn from one's social setting, as though in a world apart. Unlike violations of other norms (being drunk or stealing), no specific labels exist for people who break this type of norm. These violations are lumped in a residual category, and the violators are thought of and labeled as the mentally ill.

Labeling theorists argue that many causes of residual rule-breaking exist, and "mental illness" is not a good overall explanation for them. Individuals who talk to themselves may be practicing a speech or unusually preoccupied with a problem. Uninvolved people may be daydreaming or thinking through some intellectual issue. The use of mental illness as an explanation of people's behaviors often results in errors. To illustrate, early French Impressionism was thought to be the work of mad artists because it violated the rules of what was then defined as art. Today we evaluate this early work as remarkably innovative and creative.

In addition, residual rule-breaking is extremely common. Most people display such behavior occasionally, particularly when under stress, and it is simply rationalized or accepted. Many people consistently engage in residual rule-breaking and are not labeled as mentally ill. That is, they have power and status in the community, and their behavior fits a stereotype, as in the absent-minded professor, the distracted corporate official, and the withdrawn novelist who is presumed to be ruminating over his or her next work.

Labeling theorists believe our culture presents us with a stereotyped view of mental illness learned early in life, which may predispose us to "see" mental illness even though it does not exist. For example, newspapers commonly print information like "Ex-Mental Patient Kills Three," but do not typically report such news as "Ex-Mental Patient Elected Head of Garden Club." References to mental disorder occur routinely in our media and in our speech (you're crazy, that's insane, he's nuts), but only with regard to negative behaviors. This imagery becomes accepted as real.

From this perspective, mental illness can be viewed as just another social role, rather than as a disease. Why is the role accepted by some people to whom it is applied? We have all been taught to believe in mental illness. When an individual's residual rule-breaking is made public, the person may be ashamed and confused and be likely to accept others' labels. This label casts the person in the social role of the mentally ill, in which he or she will be expected to produce behaviors in conformity with the label. People may also find acceptance of the label has benefits or *secondary gains*, such as relieving them from difficult financial or social situations and providing them with excuses for negative past behaviors. The label will eventually become a part of the individual's self-concept, thus

making full acceptance of the label of mentally ill more likely. The process is exactly that detailed by symbolic interreactionists in their treatment of the development of the self.

Others treat the labeled individual as a mentally ill person and interpret that person's behaviors in light of the label. For example, when a "mentally ill" person is angry, the anger is viewed as an expression of his or her emotional problems. In contrast, when "sane" people are angry they are presumed to have a "real" reason for their feelings.

Labeling theorists argue that mental health professionals contribute to the problem because they assume the people who come to them must be mentally ill. They interpret any problems presented to them in terms of the medical model they bring to the situation, regardless of the appropriateness of this model to the case at hand. The medical model dictates that the doctor is there to detect illness, in this case mental illness, and to treat and cure it. The medical model contributes to the tendency to create "mental illness" through the belief that it is worse to dismiss a sick patient than to treat a well one and that illness will not improve without treatment.

In a 1962 study, commitment decisions in a midwestern state were scrutinized (56). People can be involuntarily committed to a mental institution if they are judged to be incompetent to administer their own affairs. This decision not only involves involuntary placement in an institution, but the suspension of most individual rights (to vote, to drive). All psychiatrists who performed admission examinations for the three large hospitals in the state completed questionnaires about the first ten patients they saw in a selected month. In addition, official records were examined, court officials and psychiatrists were interviewed, and psychiatric examinations in four courts were observed.

A number of questionable procedures were found. In many instances, patients were committed who did not meet the local requirements of incompetence. It appears that the mental health professionals assumed insanity whenever they were uncertain about the individual's competence. The professionals spent little time with the patients, only about 10 minutes on the average. Very stringent tests

BOX 8-3

The Moral Career
of the Mental Patient

Erving Goffman has examined the process by which an individual comes to accept the role of a mental patient (55). Goffman refers to the *moral career* of the mental patient. By this he means the stages through which people pass as they gradually accept the label of mental patient. He writes of two phases: the prepatient and the inpatient.

The *prepatient phase* is marked by the individual's refusal to accept the fact of institutionalization. Few mental patients willingly enter mental institutions for treatment, but are convinced to enter by family or friends. Once in the hospital, the new patients typically feel betrayed by those who pressured them to accept help. The patients usually find the view of the hospital that was presented by these others to be rather different from the reality confronting them. While the hospital was portrayed as being in the best interests of the patients, the patients suddenly change from a status in which they have rights and privileges to one where they have few of either. Often, patients state that they would not have agreed to enter the hospital had they understood more about life inside. They feel deprived and abandoned by the friends and relatives who urged them to enter. The new patients are likely to beg the people who helped put them in the hospital for release, even though they feel deeply bitter toward them. They feel they cannot trust their family and friends, and that they are being unjustly held.

During the inpatient phase, new patients gradually accept the fact of their hospitalization. They do not become happy about being hospitalized; but they realize that, for the time being, they cannot change the situation. In the beginning of their stays, new patients typically withdraw from the activity of the hospital. This withdrawal helps them to maintain the fiction that they cannot really be confined

of competency were employed. In one case a patient was asked in what ways a banana, an orange, and an apple are alike. The patient replied they are all something to eat. This answer was used against the patient at the hearing because she had not stated that they are all fruits. Furthermore, at the competency hearings, individuals typically were not informed of their rights to legal counsel.

In response to research such as the above, in recent years many states have revised their mental health codes to provide more protection for patients. While not ideal, the current situation has improved considerably over that described in the 1962 study.

A similar view asserts that mental illness is a myth (57). According to some critics, our concept of mental illness parallels the concept of witchcraft

without their consent. As the patients come to accept the fact of hospitalization, they tend to join the social life of the hospital ward.

In the *inpatient phase*, the hospital personnel use a variety of techniques to alter the patients' behaviors and attitudes. Patients' behavior is controlled, in part, by means of the ward system where they learn that their living conditions will improve when their emotional health is viewed as improved by the hospital staff. They will be transferred to a ward in which control over the patients' behavior is lower, where more activities are available, and where the other patients are functioning better. Thus, patients are motivated to move to better wards.

Behavior problems are interpreted as signs of mental disorder and lead to demotions in wards. "Good" and "bad" behaviors are consistently interpreted by the staff as "well" and "sick" behaviors. The patients are encouraged to succeed in their performances of good behaviors as a demonstration of their improved emotional health. Fellow patients who become the patients' friends will also be moving from ward to ward, further encouraging the patient to move ahead in the ward system.

At the same time, a struggle ensues between the patients and the staff over the interpretation of the patients' prehospitalization behaviors. The patients wish to excuse their past behaviors, minimizing unusual occurrences and blaming others for their problems. The staff members, who feel that the patients' stories must be discredited if they are to get well, have a two-part goal. First, they want the patients to perceive themselves as the cause of their past problems. Second, they want the patients to change their conceptions of themselves and others and of the ways in which they deal with the world.

The staff members reinterpret the patients' stories, showing how their versions of the events seem much more reasonable than the patients' own. One instrument used to convince patients is their own recorded past. The patients' past behaviors are pointed up to show the patients that they are, indeed, sick and that they should be committed until they can exhibit different behaviors. Since the staff makes and enforces the rules, patients must accept these definitions of self and reality, or at least pretend to accept them, to secure their freedom. ∎

held in earlier times: Both are imprecise, can be applied to almost anyone, and can be adapted to the labeler's purposes. Most people are cast in the role of mental patient involuntarily. These critics argue that the people most likely to be so labeled are poor persons who are in some kind of trouble. The label of mental illness may thus provide a means of intimidating and harassing nonconformists without power or isolating people who are unwanted by their families and communities, much as the label of witchcraft once did.

While it is easy to label a person as insane, it is *STIGMATA* almost impossible to remove the label and its consequences from a person's life. No pardon exists from the diagnosis of mental illness, one of the most stigmatizing labels in modern society. A person who bears this diagnosis lives under an entirely different set of rules from the rest of us. Those of us who are not labeled may marry, divorce, stand trial for a crime, drive a car, and practice our professions. Persons labeled as mentally ill often cannot do these things. Critics argue that the label victimizes disadvantaged groups of people by confirming their status as "defective objects" and by making them society's scapegoats.

According to this view, additional problems have been created by this society's inappropriate combination of the concept of crime and the concept of mental illness through the verdict of "not guilty by reason of insanity." Being labeled as insane actually puts people at a disadvantage relative to people labeled as criminals. Criminals have rights that mental patients do not have—to bail, to due process, to testify on their own behalf, and, in most states, to a determinant sentence. The mentally ill have no such rights, and their confinement is for an indeterminate period.

Some critics argue that the only benefit of the mental illness over the criminal label is that it makes the people applying the labels feel benevolent about their actions. Confinement in a mental hospital can be as powerful a punishment as confinement in a prison. These critics obviously would disagree with John Hinckley's verdict of not guilty by reason of insanity on the charges of attempting to assassinate President Reagan in 1981. (See Box 8-4.)

Mental illness: An examination of data Researchers have examined a number of more recent studies, with mixed results. One researcher reports that studies both of the screening procedures for persons suspected of mental illness and of the consequences of hospitalization have provided little support for labeling theory (59). The studies of screening procedures show that only a small proportion of people suspected of mental illness are actually committed. Further, those committed have exhibited very deviant behaviors that were generally ignored for an extremely long period before commitment was ever considered. In addition, the negative consequences of the label of mental patient may have been overestimated. Some studies show only about one half

of former mental patients and only about one quarter of their relatives feel stigmatized by the label of ex-mental patient. High rates of rehospitalization also occur, which may suggest that it is the ex-patients' behaviors, not the labels, that create problems for them.

It has also been argued that people often label their own behavior as deviant and, as a result of the label, seek treatment (60). Emotional deviance—feelings at variance with cultural norms prescribing appropriate feelings—if persistent, may cause individuals to feel they are "going crazy." At such a time, people seek social support. This social support may increase the likelihood of self-labeling because supportive others may be asked to validate the person's feeling of emotional disturbance.

In a reply to criticisms of the labeling theory of mental illness, another investigator reviewed 18 additional studies relating to the labeling of mental illness (61). All but five of these supported the labeling theory. Several studies indicated that social characteristics of patients influenced the societal reaction to their illnesses (62). Two studies, one the Rosenhan study of pseudopatients discussed in Chapter 3, suggested that psychiatric diagnoses are dependent upon the expectations of the professional making the diagnosis (63).

A recent study examined the life and feelings of five groups: new patients—those whose first visit to a psychiatrist took place less than one year previously; older patients—those who had been in treatment over a year; formerly treated patients; untreated patients—community members who scored high on diagnostic tests of psychiatric problems; and nonpatients—community members who scored low on diagnostic tests of psychiatric problems (64).

All five groups believed the label of "mental patient" has serious negative consequences for people's standings in their communities (see Table 8-1). Relative to untreated people in the community and former patients, patients currently being treated for mental illness felt demoralized and discriminated against. Further, patients and former patients who felt most demoralized and discriminated against also had lower incomes and were more likely to have experienced some period of unemployment com-

BOX 8-4

Hinckley's Defense of the Insanity Defense

John Hinckley wrote a defense of the insanity defense in a letter to *Newsweek* (58). His remarks included the following:

I don't feel guilty for being found not guilty by reason of insanity. It was the proper verdict and, although I was surprised by it, my fragile conscience is clear of useless guilt. The American people are angry with me, my parents' money, and my fame. They are jealous and just drooled at the thought of me spending the rest of my life in some wretched prison in the backwoods of North Carolina. But here I am, in this insane asylum in southeast Washington, D.C., surrounded by the criminally insane, and everyone on the outside can't stand the thought of my innocence.

Those people who wish to abolish the insanity defense are a little nuts themselves. I wish they would move to Iran or Turkey, where defendants are shot in record time. America has the insanity defense because it is a compassionate and fair country. The passions of the mind separate the mental case from the criminal, and thank God we make such a distinction in this country.

. . . Let's leave the insanity defense alone and accept the fact that, every once in a while, someone is going to use this "defense of last resort" and win with it. I was acquitted not because of my parents' money, or my attorneys, or the black jury; I was found not guilty by reason of insanity because I shot the president and three other people in order to impress a girl.

While those opposed to the insanity defense would certainly agree with Hinckley that impressing a woman is not a good reason for shooting four people, they might also note that many murders and attempted murders are committed for equally trivial reasons. They would feel no greater reason existed to define Hinckley's actions as acts of insanity than those of many other people who attempt murder.

They might also point out the fact that Hinckley's indeterminate sentence as an insane person is not really an advantage over a determinant sentence as a lawbreaker. Hinckley may well be institutionalized longer in a mental hospital than he would have been in a prison. ■

Table 8.1 ■

Dependent Measures of Patient/Non-Patient Groups

	Devaluation Beliefs	Demoralization Score	Earned Income	Weeks Unemployed
New patients	4.03	2.87	$ 7,263	24.52
Continuing patients	4.15	3.14	$ 6,312	30.44
Former patients	4.33	2.48	$11,406	13.55
Untreated patients	4.13	2.55	$10,664	17.31
Nonpatients	4.08	1.84	$14,390	9.97

High number = very demoralized

Data from Link, B. G., 1987, "Understanding Labeling Effects in the Area of Mental Disorders: An Assessment of the Effects of Expectations of Rejection," *American Sociological Review* 52: 96–112.

pared to less demoralized patients, effects that were not attributable to their illnesses. These data thus suggest mental patients are devalued by society and this devaluation can have additional, negative effects on the patients' life chances.

General Critique of Labeling Theory

Other more general critiques have been made of the labeling theory of deviance. Some critics of labeling theory have charged that the theory is so vague as to be untestable, and the concept of deviance is never defined. Others believe the theory neglects the initial causes of deviance. Still others note that the theory's emphasis on others' reactions to the label of deviant implies the individuals themselves completely lack control over their own conduct, an unlikely state of affairs (67).

In order to fully evaluate the labeling theory of deviance, its component parts must be disentangled. The labeling theory encompasses three ideas, each of which is separable from the others. These ideas are:

1. An act is deviant only if labeled as deviant.

2. A person is labeled deviant primarily on the basis of his or her power and resources.

3. Once labeled deviant, social reactions increase the likelihood of further deviant acts being committed (68).

More sophisticated examination of the labeling perspective requires that each of these assertions be assessed independently.

Is Deviance Objective or Subjective?

Which view of deviance is correct? Is deviance objective, as strain, differential association, control, and self theorists believe, or is it subjective, as labeling theorists believe? The data that each perspective can amass suggests there is truth in both perspectives (69).

The understanding of deviance is facilitated by perceiving deviance as both objective and subjective. Deviance begins with some nonnormative act. For some, it may be the result of a gap between goals and legitimate means to achieve them, as strain theory suggests. For others, the act may stem from lengthy learning of criminal definitions and behaviors in intimate groups, as differential association theory hypothesizes. For still others, the act may be the result of lack of bonds to society, as suggested in control theory. For another group, it may be designed to promote the perpetrator's self-esteem.

This initial act may be serious enough that it is unlikely to be overlooked, regardless of the social characteristics of the perpetrator. At the same time, labeling processes are likely to be at work. The outcome for the perpetrator will certainly be influenced by whether he or she is labeled as a lawbreaker. If so, a self-fulfilling prophecy may be set in motion, aided by tendencies to blame the victim, so that a deviant status is constructed for and accepted by the individual.

While the perspectives appear contradictory, it is not necessary to deny the reality of one side by accepting the other. Theorists who believe deviance is objective believe labeling processes are at work in deviance, but feel they are trivial, relative to the objective nature of deviance. Similarly, labeling theorists recognize that the deviance-as-objective argument has some validity, but feel the subjectivity of deviance plays a greater role than objective factors.

An inclusive theoretical framework of deviance and social control must combine the objective perspective of deviance, with all its competing theories, and the subjective perspective. Such a framework would specify the relative importance of the objective and subjective viewpoints, as well as the relative importance of goal-means gap, differential association, control, self-esteem, and labeling for different types of persons in differing types of situations.

■ SUMMARY

Considerable disagreement exists about what constitutes deviance. Some social scientists think deviance is anything that differs from generally accepted values and norms. Other social scientists believe deviance is simply what is perceived to be deviant.

We examined four theories that share the first perspective: strain theory, differential association theory, control theory, and a theory of deviance and the self. According to strain theory, some people cannot achieve their goals in legitimate ways. This problem creates strain that may be resolved by turning to illegitimate means to achieve goals.

Differential association theory assumes that individuals are responsive to the norms to which they have been exposed. Individuals who are exposed to definitions favorable to crime will accept these definitions, just as individuals who are exposed to definitions unfavorable to crime will accept those definitions.

Control theory assumes that most people are naturally inclined to commit deviant acts. They are prevented from doing so by their bonds to society, which act to control or restrain them from deviance.

The self theory of deviance suggests low self-esteem in adolescents is associated with deviance. These adolescents turn to deviance as a way of raising their self-esteem.

The labeling theory provides a different perspective on deviance. The labeling theory is concerned with how an act becomes defined as deviant. Labeling theorists believe deviance is quite common, but that most people who commit deviant acts are not defined as deviant. They feel powerful people apply the label of deviant to less powerful people in the society. Labeling theorists believe the process of labeling promotes deviant behavior. In other words, labels may create self-fulfilling prophecies, where individuals may come to believe the label and enact the behavior that characterizes the label. Labeling may also involve blaming the victim, in part due to the belief in a just world.

From the perspective of the labeling theory, "juvenile delinquent" is a label attached to some juveniles but not others, not on the basis of delinquent behaviors, but because their parents lack power to prevent the label. Labeling theorists also believe the label of mental patient is similarly subjective, being applied to residual rule violators who are not protected from the label by their family and friends. Some data support, while other data refute, the labeling theory explanation of mental illness.

Since considerable data support both the deviance-as-objective and deviance-as-subjective points of view, it is inappropriate to attempt to determine which view of deviance is "correct." Doubtless, truth exists in both viewpoints.

REFERENCES

1. *Time,* December 22, 1980.
2. Simmons, J. L., 1965, "Public Stereotypes of Deviants," *Social Problems* 13:223–224.
3. Gibbs, J. P., 1981, "The Sociology of Deviance and Social Control," in M. Rosenberg and R. H. Turner (Eds.), *Social Psychology: Sociological Perspectives,* New York: Basic Books.
4. Schur, E. M., 1979, *Interpreting Deviance,* New York: Harper & Row.
5. Merton, R. K., 1957, *Social Theory and Social Structure,* New York: The Free Press.
6. Cohen, A. K., 1966, *Deviance and Control,* Englewood Cliffs, NJ: Prentice-Hall.
7. Agnew, R., 1985, "A Revised Strain Theory of Delinquency," *Social Forces* 64:151–167.
8. Tittle, C. R., W. J. Villemez, and D. A. Smith, 1978, "The Myth of Social Class and Criminality," *American Sociological Review* 43:643–656; see also C. R. Tittle, 1983, "Social Class and Criminal Behavior: A Critique of the Theoretical Foundation," *Social Forces* 62:334–358.
9. Grasmick, H. G., D. Jacobs, and C. B. McCollom, 1983, "Social Class and Social Control: An Application of Deterrence Theory," *Social Forces* 62:359–374; C. R. Tittle, 1982, "One Step Forward, Two Steps Back: More on the Class-Criminality Controversy," *American Sociological Review* 47:435–438.
10. Thio, A., 1975, "A Critical Look at Merton's Theory," *Pacific Sociological Review* 18:139–158.
11. Merton, 1957, op. cit.
12. Sutherland, E. H. and D. R. Cressey, 1974, *Criminology,* 9th ed., Philadelphia: Lippincott.
13. Akers, R. L., 1966, "A Differential Association-reinforcement Theory of Criminal Behavior," *Social Problems* 14:128–147.
14. Ermann, M. D. and R. J. Lundman (Eds.), 1982, *Corporate and Governmental Deviance: Problems of Organizational Behavior in Contemporary Society,* 2d ed, New York: Oxford University Press; E. H. Sutherland, 1949, *White-collar Crime,* New York: Holt, Rinehart, & Winston.
15. Elliot, D. S., D. Huzinga, and S. S. Ageton, 1985, *Explaining Delinquency and Drug Use,* Beverly Hills: Sage; A. C. Marcos, S. J. Bahr, and R. E. Johnson, 1986, "Test of a Bonding-Association Theory of Adolescent Drug Use," *Social Forces* 65:135–161.
16. Krohn, M. D., W. F. Skinner, J. L. Massey, and R. L. Akers, 1985, "Social Learning Theory and Adolescent Cigarette Smoking: A Longitudinal Study," *Social Problems* 32:454–471.
17. Tittle, C. R., M. J. Burke, and E. F. Jackson, 1986, "Modeling Sutherland's Theory of Differential Association: Toward Empirical Clarification," *Social Forces* 65:405–432.
18. Gibbs, 1981, op. cit.
19. Hirschi, T., 1969, *Causes of Delinquency,* Berkeley: University of California Press.
20. Sloane, D. M. and R. H. Potvin, 1986, "Religion and Delinquency: Cutting Through the Maze," *Social Forces* 65:87–105.
21. Elliot et al., 1985, op. cit.
22. Krohn, M. D., J. L. Massey, W. F. Skinner, and R. M. Lauer, 1983, "Social Bonding Theory and Adolescent Cigarette Smoking: A Longitudinal Analysis," *Journal of Health and Social Behavior* 24:337–349.
23. e.g., R. A. Berk and P. J. Newton, 1985, "Does Arrest Really Deter Wife Battery? An Effort to Replicate the Findings of the Minneapolis Spouse Abuse Experiment," *American Sociological Review* 50:253–262; C. A. Murray and L. A. Cox, Jr., 1979, *Beyond Probation,* Beverly Hills: Sage.
24. e.g., R. Paternoster, L. Saltzman, T. G. Chiricos, and G. P. Waldo, 1983, "Perceived Risk and Social Control: Do Sanctions Really Deter?" *Law and Society Review* 17:459–479; I. Piliavin, R. Gartner, C. Thornton, and R. L. Matsueda, 1986, "Crime, Deterrence, and Rational Choice," *American Sociological Review* 51:101–119.
25. Agnew, R., 1985, "A Revised Strain Theory of Delinquency," *Social Forces* 64:151–167; R. L. Matsueda and K. Heimer, 1987, "Race, Family Structure, and Delinquency," *American Sociological Review* 52:826–840.
26. Liska, A. E. and M. D. Reed, 1985, "Ties to Conventional Institutions and Delinquency: Estimating Reciprocal Effects," *American Sociological Review* 50:547–560.
27. Kaplan, H. B., 1984, *Patterns of Juvenile Delinquency,* Beverly Hills, CA: Sage; H. B. Kaplan, 1980, *Deviant Behavior in Defense of Self,* New York: Academic Press.
28. Kaplan, H. B., S. S. Martin, and R. J. Johnson, 1986, "Self-rejection and the Explanation of Deviance: Specification of the Structure among Latent Constructs," *American Journal of Sociology* 92:384–411; see also H. B. Kaplan, R. J. Johnson, and C. A. Bailey, 1986, "Self-rejection and the Explanation of Deviance: Refinement and Elaboration of a Latent Structure," *Social Psychology Quarterly* 49:110–128.
29. e.g., J. D. McCarthy and D. R. Hoge, 1984, "The Dynamics of Self-esteem and Deviance," *American Journal of Sociology* 90:396–410; L. E. Wells and J. H. Rankin, 1983, "Self-concept as a Mediating Factor in Delinquency," *Social Psychology Quarterly* 41:189–204.
30. Covington, J., 1986, "Self-esteem and Delinquency: The Effects of Race and Gender," *Criminology* 24:105–138.
31. This section draws from Schur, 1979, op. cit.
32. Becker, H. S., 1963, *Outsiders,* New York: The Free Press.
33. Goffman, E., 1963, *Stigma,* Englewood Cliffs, NJ: Prentice-Hall.
34. Lemert, E. M., 1951, *Social Pathology,* New York: McGraw-Hill.
35. Matza, D., 1969, *Becoming Deviant,* Englewood Cliffs, NJ: Prentice-Hall.
36. McCord, J., 1978, "A Thirty-year Follow-up of Treatment Effects," *American Psychologist* 33:284–289.
37. Tittle, C. R., 1980, "Labelling and Crime: An Empirical Evaluation," in W. R. Gove (Ed.), *The Labelling of Deviance,* 2d ed, Beverly Hills: Sage.

38. Hagan, J. and K. Bumiller, 1983, "Making Sense of Sentencing: A Review and Critique of Sentencing Research," in A. Blumstein, J. Cohen, S. Martin, and M. Tonry (Eds.), *Research on Sentencing: The Search for Reform,* Vol. 2, Washington, DC: National Academy Press; T. Hirschi, 1980, "Labelling Theory and Juvenile Delinquency: An Assessment of Evidence" and "Postscript," in W. R. Gove, ibid.; G. Kleck, 1981, "Racial Discrimination in Criminal Sentencing: A Critical Evaluation of the Evidence on the Death Penalty," *American Sociological Review* 46:783–804.

39. Peterson, R. D. and J. Hagan, 1984, "Changing Conceptions of Race and Sentencing Outcomes," *American Sociological Review* 49:56–70.

40. Peterson and Hagan, 1984, ibid.; J. Hagan and P. Parker, 1985, "White-collar Crime and Punishment: The Class Structure and Legal Sanctioning of Securities," *American Sociological Review* 50:302–316.

41. Peterson and Hagan, 1984, ibid.

42. Hagan and Parker, 1985, op. cit.

43. Merton, 1957, op. cit.

44. Rosenthal, R. and L. Jacobson, 1968, *Pygmalion in the Classroom,* New York: Holt, Rinehart & Winston.

45. Ryan, W., 1971, *Blaming the Victim,* New York: Vintage.

46. Apple, M. W., 1982, *Education and Power: Reproduction and Contradiction in Education,* London: Routledge & Kegan Paul; R. A. Berk, W. P. Bridges, and A. Shih, 1981, "Does IQ Really Matter? A Study of the Use of IQ Scores for the Tracking of the Mentally Retarded," *American Sociological Review* 46:58–71.

47. Goodlad, J. I., 1984, *A Place Called School: Prospects for the Future,* New York: McGraw-Hill.

48. *Chronical of Higher Education,* December 9, 1987, p. 26.

49. Lewis, O., 1961, *The Children of Sanchez,* New York: Random House.

50. See, for example, J. R. Feagin, 1975, *Subordinating the Poor,* Ch. 4, Englewood Cliffs, NJ: Prentice-Hall; and H. Rodman, 1971, *Lower-class Families,* New York: Oxford University Press.

51. Lerner, M. J., D. T. Miller, and J. G. Holmes, 1976, "Deserving and the Emergence of Forms of Justice," in L. Berkowitz and E. Walster (Eds.), *Advances in Experimental Social Psychology,* Vol. 9, New York: Academic Press.

52. Stokols, D. and J. Schopler, 1973, "Reactions to Victims under Conditions of Situational Detachment: The Effects of Responsibility, Severity, and Expected Future Interaction," *Journal of Personality and Social Psychology* 25:199–209.

53. Chaiken, A. L. and J. M. Darley, 1973, "Victim or Perpetrator: Defensive Attribution and the Need for Order and Justice," *Journal of Personality and Social Psychology* 25:268–276.

54. This section draws from T. J. Scheff, 1966, *Being Mentally Ill,* Chicago: Aldine.

55. Goffman, E., 1961, *Asylums: Essays on the Social Situation of Mental Patients and Other Inmates,* Chicago: Aldine.

56. Scheff, 1966, op. cit.

57. Szasz, T. S., 1970, *The Manufacture of Madness,* New York: Delta; T. S. Szasz, 1961, *The Myth of Mental Illness,* New York: Hoeber-Harper.

58. *Newsweek,* September 20, 1982.

59. Gove, W. R., 1970, "Societal Reaction as an Explanation of Mental Illness: An Evaluation," *American Sociological Review* 35:873–884; see also H. P. White and R. L. Meile, 1985, "Alignment, Magnification, and Snowballing Processes in the Definition of 'Symptoms of Mental Illness,'" *Social Forces* 63:682–697.

60. Thoits, P. A., 1985, "Self-labeling Processes in Mental Illness: The Role of Emotional Deviance," *American Journal of Sociology* 91:221–249.

61. Scheff, T. J., 1974, "The Labeling Theory of Mental Illness," *American Sociological Review* 39:444–452.

62. e.g., D. L. Wegner and C. R. Fletcher, 1969, "The Effect of Legal Counsel on Admissions to a State Mental Hospital: A Confrontation of Professions," *Journal of Health and Social Behavior* 10:66–72; W. A. Wilde, 1968, "Decision-making in a Psychiatric Screening Agency," *Journal of Health and Social Behavior* 9:215–221.

63. Rosenhan, D. L., 1973, "On Being Sane in Insane Places," *Science* 179:250–258; M. K. Temerlin, 1968, "Suggestion Effects in Psychiatric Diagnosis," *Journal of Nervous and Mental Disease* 147:349–353.

64. Link, B. G., 1987, "Understanding Labeling Effects in the Area of Mental Disorders: An Assessment of the Effects of Expectations of Rejection," *American Sociological Review* 52:96–112.

65. Farina, A., 1980, "Social Attitudes and Beliefs and Their Role in Mental Disorders," in J. G. Rabkin, L. Gelb, and J. B. Lazor (Eds.), *Attitudes toward the Mentally Ill: Research Perspectives,* Rockville, MD: NIMH; A. Farina, D. Gliha, L. A. Boudreau, J. G. Allen, and M. Sherman, 1971, "Mental Illness and the Impact of Believing Others Know about It," *Journal of Abnormal Psychology* 77:1–5.

66. Page, S., 1977, "Effects of the Mental Illness Label in Attempts to Obtain Accommodation," *Canadian Journal of Behavioral Science* 9:84–90.

67. e.g., J. P. Gibbs, 1966, "Conceptions of Deviant Behavior: The Old and the New," *Pacific Sociological Review* 9:9–14; E. Goode, 1975, "On Behalf of Labeling Theory," *Social Problems* 22:570–583.

68. Gibbs, 1981, op. cit.

69. Gove, W. R., 1980, "The Labelling Perspective: An Overview," in W. R. Gove, op. cit.

CHAPTER 9

Person Perception

Impression Formation

Establishing Identities

Definitions of the Situation

Situated Identities

Negotiating Identities

Correspondent Inference Theory

Trait Inferences

Confirmation and Disconfirmation of Expectancies

Actor-Observer Differences in Attributions

Cognitive Information Processing and Person Perception

Biases in Information Processing

Attention

Encoding

Storage

Retrieval

The personnel manager of a large corporation is on campus interviewing students for jobs. Imagine yourself as the manager. You watch a student enter the personnel office. The first thing you notice about her is her appearance. She is slender, of average height, and appears to be Asian-American. She is wearing a light blue patterned blouse, a pair of off-white slacks, and dilapidated running shoes. She is wearing a minimum of makeup. Her dark, straight hair is worn shoulder length. It appears as if she did not go out of her way to present herself at her best. She is surprisingly relaxed. All this you take in before she is seated and the interview begins. You ask her about her major and her career interests. She's majoring in psychology and would like to work in the personnel division of a well-established company such as the one you represent.

You ask some more penetrating questions about her qualifications for the job and goals in life. She replies that she works hard at the courses she likes, but when she doesn't like a course her grades usually show it. She says if she finds the right job she'll work really hard at it. She tells you she gets along well with other people and that her former employers liked her, except for the one boss she hated. She's not sure of her long-range career interests at the moment, but the thought of working for a while and then going for a MBA has occurred to her. Right now she just wants to get some experience and start earning enough money to buy a fast car and live someplace nice. She wants to live in a big city because that's where all the action is.

Do you think your company should hire her? What is your impression of this interviewee? How did you arrive at this impression? When you record your impressions of her on your rating form at the end of the interview, what aspects of her character are you most likely to remember?

Now put yourself in the role of a student being interviewed. How would you present yourself? What type of impression would you try to create? How would you react to these questions? Given your behavior, do you think the interviewer would want to hire you?

This example introduces the concept of impression formation. Every day each of us spends a considerable amount of time interacting with other people. During these interactions we form impressions of others which influence our future relations with them. We seek out or avoid people largely on the basis of our impressions of them (1). The processes by which these impressions are formed are thus a matter of great importance in understanding interpersonal relations.

Both sociologists and psychologists study person perception, focusing their attention on different aspects of the topic. This chapter begins with a discussion of impression formation, an area of study dominated by psychological social psychology. The second topic we will consider is a mainstay of sociological social psychology, the process of establishing identities in social interaction. Next, the processes by which traits are attributed to others will be discussed. In the final sections of the chapter, the cognitive information processing approach to person perception will be presented. This approach, which derives largely from psychological social psychology, will be used to explore biases that enter into the process of imputing meaning to the behavior of others.

■

IMPRESSION FORMATION

Our impressions of others consist of information about their traits, behavior, abilities, attitudes, and backgrounds. First impressions are based primarily on appearance. For instance, studies reveal that appearance is used to infer personality traits, intellectual and social skills, mental health, as well as the person's age, sex, social class, and ethnicity (2). In addition, nonverbal behaviors, such as speaking style and facial expressions, are used to infer the emotional state of the other person (3). Even a person's handwriting may be used to infer personality characteristics (4). If you wish to be thought of as dominant and high in self-esteem you should use a large signature, as John Hancock did when he signed the Declaration of Independence (5).

■ *Write down your impressions of this person on a piece of paper. (Try it; it will only take a minute.) (WGS)*

The impressions college students formed of their classmates were analyzed in one study. Four categories of descriptors emerged: traits (65 percent), behaviors (23 percent), attitudes (6 percent), and demographic information (3 percent) (6). Similarly, when asked to describe one person to another, students relied heavily on personality traits and attitudes (7). Thus, it appears that naturalistically created impressions are composed largely of traits. This is one reason why researchers have studied traits so extensively.

One fascinating finding in recent studies is that people do not agree on their impressions of others (8). One study found that the descriptions any two members of a group gave of a third group member overlapped in only about 25 percent of the descriptors used (9). It appears that each of us has unique impressions of the people with whom we are acquainted (10).

In the initial phases of interaction we form impressions, but to actually interact with others, we must establish the roles we will play with respect to each other. Each of us will adopt an identity in the interaction. For instance, if you meet one of your professors at a basketball game, you will relate to one another either as student and professor or as two basketball fans. It is the process by which identities are established that we turn to next.

■

ESTABLISHING IDENTITIES

Although we carry some roles with us from situation to situation (gender roles), during a typical day we flow easily through a series of transitory roles. If you lived in a dormitory you might start the day enacting the role of friend as you say good morning to your roommate, then become a runner as you do your morning exercise, followed by the role of cafeteria diner as you eat breakfast, student as you attend class, aspiring actor as you practice for an upcoming play, driver as you go shopping, customer as you shop, son (daughter) when you call home, cashier at your part-time job, and audience member when you attend a rock concert to finish your busy day.

In each of these roles you interact with others who are enacting complementary roles (student-teacher, cashier-customer). Each one of these interactions occurs in a different social situation and each calls on you to behave in a different fashion. Likewise,

A

Wide World Photos, Inc..

B

AP/Wide World Photos

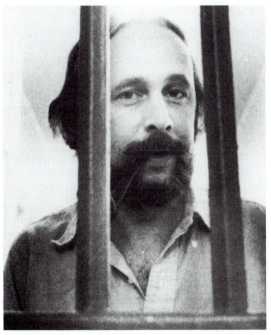

C

Wide World Photos, Inc.

D

Mike Tappin

■ *What cues do you use in forming impressions of these people? Our impressions are often wrong. Persons A and B were responsible for mass murder, person C is a journalist, and person D is a transvestite.*

each of the people with whom you interact is going through his or her own day enacting various roles. This complicated ballet of roles is performed according to a set of rules of which we typically are only vaguely aware. Our focus in this section is not on the roles the actors enact, but on the processes we use in assigning roles to others.

Definitions of the Situation

Every social interaction begins with each actor holding a preliminary *definition of the situation*—the actors' beliefs concerning the type of interaction that will take place in this setting (11). This definition is based on the actors' knowledge of the roles relevant in the situation, the information the actors have about the other participants, and the setting where the interaction occurs. Parties, courtrooms, classrooms, funerals, doctors' offices, and job interviews all call for different roles and behaviors. The definition of the situation sets up expectancies concerning who will do what during the interaction. The questions each actor must answer are, "What role do I play?" "What role is the other playing?" and "What do people in these roles do in this type of situation?"

In one investigation of definitions of social situations students were asked to form images of situations such as a museum tour, an anti-war demonstration, a job interview, or a first date and then write down everything in their images (12). The traits and behaviors of people in these situations composed 51 percent of the descriptors, the physical setting and atmosphere composed 36 percent of the descriptors, and the roles and types of people found in such situations composed 13 percent of the descriptors. The authors of the study note that people seem to emphasize social aspects of situations, and that definitions of the situation provide the actors with "information and expectations about the most likely and/or socially appropriate behavior."

Actors also consider the goals of the interaction, and each actor is likely to have a plan for achieving these goals. A young male lawyer telephoning a female friend to set up a date must first establish that the conversation concerns a date and not some other matter so she will adopt the desired role and respond accordingly. In most interactions, definitions of the situation are easily arrived at and require little thought. When you pay the cashier at the checkout stand, you automatically adopt the customer role and define the situation as a transaction involving the purchase of goods.

Situated Identities

Earlier we discussed situated identities as a component of self-identity arising during social interactions (Chapter 4). In addition to his or her own situated identity, every actor in an interaction assigns each of the other participants a *situated identity* (13). This identity consists of the roles you expect the other participants to occupy in this situation. The conceptions of the other participants' roles are generally stereotyped ones, consisting of the normative expectancies associated with the roles. In a doctor's office an incoming patient quickly sizes up the situation, decides who the other patients are and who the nurses are and then proceeds to report to a nurse. In addition, the patient may also have some expectations concerning the nurse's personality. The expectation that the nurse will be a warm, caring, and efficient person could turn out to be wrong, but these are the stereotyped expectations that are likely to be associated with the nurse's situated identity. By assigning others to roles, the actors can use their own *role-taking* abilities to analyze the interaction from the perspectives of the other participants. The actors can then use this information in deciding how to interact with the other participants.

An actor's subsequent perception of the other participants is greatly influenced by the situated identities the others are assigned. When a situated identity is assigned to a person, assumptions may be made about the person's prior history, personality traits, and abilities, as well as what behaviors are expected of him or her. For example, if you are interacting with an accountant, you are likely to make assumptions about his or her educational and

■ *For an amateur, the role of chess player is a situated identity. (WGS)*

social class background, personality traits, and abilities, as well as how he or she should handle your taxes.

Although situated identities apply only to specific contexts, the impressions actors form on the basis of situated identities tend to carry over to other situations where they may or may not be applicable. You would probably expect an accountant to possess the characteristic traits of someone in this profession (orderly, precise, mathematically skilled) regardless of the context, even if you have only interacted with this person in his or her professional capacity and have no knowledge of how he or she actually behaves in other contexts.

Negotiating Identities

For interactions to proceed smoothly, a *consensus* concerning the situated identities of the participants must be implicitly or explicitly achieved. Each actor's expectations should fit the behavior and roles of the others. Smooth interactions are likely to occur only when the roles the actors are enacting and the relationships between the roles are clear. This clarity often occurs in institutional settings, such as the military or in bureaucracies, where roles tend to be rather rigid. It can occur in other interactions, if the participants have evolved a well-defined system of roles they customarily enact.

However, not all interactions proceed smoothly. If the participants are confused about the roles each is enacting, then the interaction may break down and little will be accomplished. Consider the initial confusion that would be likely to occur if a nurse from one doctor's office makes a professional call on the office of another doctor in her street clothes. She is likely to be mistaken for a patient. Suppose she finds a male seated behind the counter in the other office. She may not be sure if this person is a nurse, the doctor, or a laboratory technician. Until the roles are clarified, she will have difficulty accomplishing her task.

When actors are competing for the same role, such as the role of foreman in a jury, the interaction probably will not proceed smoothly until it is decided who will enact the contested role. If others do not accept the situated identities assigned to them, the actor is apt to disapprove of them or dislike them. The loser in the jury leadership battle will probably resent the winner.

Also, actors occasionally have difficulty balancing the roles they must enact in an interaction, and this difficulty can be disruptive. One study found that doctors examining infants in the presence of the infants' mothers sometimes had difficulty switching between the roles of examining physician (one who examines the child) and consulting physician (one who discusses the child's case with the mother) (14). The former role calls on the physician's diagnostic skills while the latter calls on communication skills. Apparently it is difficult to use both skills simultaneously.

In many social interactions, the fit between one actor's role expectations and goals and those of other participants is imperfect. In general, each participant attempts to assign others to the situated identity most beneficial to himself or herself (15). When a lack of fit between the role expectations and goals of the parties in an interaction occurs, the actors *negotiate* their identities to arrive at a mutually acceptable definition of their roles (16).

A working consensus is usually generated through this process of negotiation. The negotiation may or may not be carried out as an open discussion. In many cases an agreement on situated identities will be arrived at tacitly, through the use of subtle communications. For instance, imagine you have a longstanding platonic relationship with a friend of the opposite sex. Should you wish to make the relationship a romantic one, your expectations and goals for the other person will change. You may state your intentions directly, but more than likely you will communicate them indirectly by expressing a desire to spend your time together differently or through the use of nonverbal gestures of intimacy, such as touch, closeness, eye-gaze, and tone of voice. This will open up a "negotiation" during which the two of you will determine whether your roles will

be changed from friends to lovers. The working consensus in any relationship may continue to change during the course of the interaction or over time. Therefore, the negotiation of identities is often an ongoing process.

Negotiating situated identities allows actors to impute attributes (traits, abilities, values) to the other participants in the interaction. The attributes and expectations associated with the others' roles are used by the actor to guide his or her conduct and to interpret the conduct of the other participants.

The processes of impression formation and the negotiation of identities have much in common. Both processes deal with the manner in which meaning is extracted from social interaction. The domain of meaning in both cases is similar: conceptions of other people. Both processes serve to create expectations concerning the behavior of others. These expectations lay the groundwork on which social interaction is built. Expectations also reduce the actors' uncertainty about how they should behave and about how others will behave.

The two processes also differ in some respects. Impression formation is primarily concerned with the personality traits imputed to others while the negotiation of identities is primarily concerned with assigning roles to others. Thus, impression formation provides us with unique information about the personalities of other people. The negotiation of identities provides us with information that locates other people in the social structure.

■

CORRESPONDENT INFERENCE THEORY

When we interact with other people we seek to understand their behavior. We ask ourselves why did she do that? What did she mean by that? What kind of person is she? To answer these questions we observe the behavior of other people and make inferences about their personality traits. In this section we will first consider the processes by which people make such trait inferences. Following this discussion, we will explore the effects of behavior that confirms or disconfirms our expectancies on trait inferences.

Trait Inferences

Correspondent inference theory concerns the processes observers use to make inferences about other people (17). The initial premise is that observers assume other people are attempting to achieve the consequences they receive. Relying on this assumption, observers use the consequences of others' behavior as a basis for making personality trait inferences about them. The inferences the observers make correspond to the perceived consequences of the behavior (I saw him hit a defenseless child so he must be a cruel person). Hence, this theory is known as *correspondent* inference theory.

When a person chooses a behavior, only one action is selected and all others are rejected. For instance, a student may consider several different universities, but ultimately he or she can attend only one. Most behaviors have multiple consequences, and this multiplicity complicates the inference process. When a student chooses which university to attend, this decision will have a number of consequences for the student, including where the student will live, with whom the student will associate, how much it will cost, and the types of degrees the student will be able to pursue.

A person's choice of behaviors provides information to observers about the consequences the person intended to bring about through the decision. Any decision involves selecting one action while rejecting others. Both the chosen and the nonchosen actions may share some of the same consequences, but each potential choice will have unique consequences as well. For instance, a student's chosen and nonchosen universities may be similar in that all offer the same degrees and require about the same number of credits to graduate. However, the universities may differ in other respects. The chosen university may be far from home whereas the rejected universities might be closer to home.

The consequences the chosen and nonchosen options share in common do not provide observers with much useful information about the person, since they would occur in any case. However, the unique consequences of the chosen and nonchosen actions provide valuable information about the consequences the person wanted to achieve—or to avoid. An observer might infer that the student who chose the university far from home wished to get away from home.

The smaller the number of unique consequences an action has, the easier it is for observers to infer the person's intentions. If there are several unique consequences of a choice, any of them might be the reason for the choice. If the distant university has a unique degree program, better athletic facilities, and a superior reputation, it would be difficult to infer the exact reason for the student's choice. If there is only one unique consequence of the choice, then only this consequence can explain the person's behavior. Thus, if the close and distant universities were similar in all respects *except* the distance factor, the student must be trying to get away from home.

The unique consequences of a person's *chosen* option are especially informative when they are *negative*. When a decision has unique negative consequences of which the person was aware, the observer can confidently draw an inference about the person. For instance, if a soldier faces enemy fire to rescue an injured comrade, an observer would infer that the soldier is a brave person. Likewise, *not choosing* an option that has very *positive* consequences is informative because it suggests that the chosen option is even more important to the actor. A man who sacrifices a good career to move to a city where he can be with a particular woman will probably be thought of as being deeply in love.

In summary, the smaller the number of unique consequences of an actor's freely chosen behavior, the more negative the consequences of the chosen alternative, and the more positive the consequences of the nonchosen alternative, the more informative an action is in drawing inferences about the actor. In spite of the apparent complexity of this process, it appears that people make trait inferences and other attributions spontaneously during the course of interaction (18).

BOX 9-1

Category-based Expectancies in Correspondent Inference Theory

A number of studies have examined the effects of confirmation and disconfirmation of role expectations on trait inferences (20). In a classic study, students listened to tape recordings of people applying for a job on a submarine or for a job as an astronaut on a one-person spacecraft. The subjects were told the submarine job required people who were cooperative, friendly, and obedient, whereas the astronaut job required people who relied on inner resources and did not need other people. Half of the subjects heard interviewees who acted in ways that would be expected if they wanted one of the jobs. For instance, one interviewee for the submarine job acted outgoing and was very cooperative. The other half of the subjects heard interviewees who acted in ways that would be unexpected in this situation. For instance, some subjects heard an applicant for the submarine job who was reserved and independent.

After listening to the interview, the subjects were asked what they thought the applicant was really like as a person. As shown in Table 9-1, strong personality inferences were made only when the applicant violated the role expectations in the situation. The submarine job applicant who behaved in a reserved and independent manner was seen as more independent than the astronaut applicant who behaved in exactly the same reserved and independent manner. Role expec-

Confirmation and Disconfirmation of Expectancies

Observers often have prior expectancies concerning the actor's behavior (19). When these expectancies are based on social roles, group membership, or appearance, they are labeled *category-based expectancies*. For instance, an expectation that social workers will be compassionate is a category-based expectancy.

Behavior that *confirms* category-based expectan-

cies provides observers with little unique information about the characteristics of the actor. However, it may reinforce the observer's stereotypes concerning the social category. If you saw a social worker expressing concern toward a client, you probably would not draw any strong conclusions about the social worker as an individual, but your stereotype of social workers as compassionate might be strengthened.

In contrast, behavior that *disconfirms* category-based expectancies is often used as a basis for

tations provide an explanation for why an applicant for the job of astronaut would behave in a reserved and independent manner: The person wants the job. Role expectations cannot explain why someone applying to be a submariner would behave in this way.

The subjects inferred that the person who applied for the submariner job, and who behaved in ways that would disqualify him for the job (acted reserved and independent), must be so independent he could not act in any other way, even when he was expected to do so (see Table 9-1). The applicant's behavior led the observers to make a personality inference that corresponded to his behavior. The researchers concluded that violations of category-based expectancies (role expectations in this study) provide observers with more information about actors' personalities than behaviors that conform to category-based expectations. ■

Table 9.1 ■

Perceptions of the Independence Level of the Interviewee

Behavior Observed	Job Interviewee Applied For	
	Astronaut	Submariner
Reserved and independent	6.91	10.59
Outgoing and cooperative	5.09	7.42

Note: High numbers indicate that the interviewee was rated as more independent.
Adapted from Jones, E.E., K.E. Davis, and K. J. Gergen, 1961, "Role Playing Variations and Their Informational Value for Person Perception," *Journal of Abnormal and Social Psychology* 63:302–310.

drawing inferences about the actor's traits (see Box 9-1). If you encountered a social worker who was rude and thoughtless in dealing with a client, you would probably think of him or her as an unkind person, but you probably would not change your stereotype of social workers as compassionate people.

When expectancies are based on prior experience with the actor, they are labeled *target-based expectancies*. Confirmation of a target-based expectancy leads observers to continue believing that the actor possesses the trait on which the expectancy was based. To illustrate, suppose your prior experience leads you to believe Greg is manipulative. If you then see Greg taking advantage of Steve, this behavior simply confirms your expectancy, and you will continue to think of him as manipulative.

A disconfirmed target-based expectancy leads either to a search for external causes of the behavior or to a reevaluation of the basis for the expectancy. If you saw Steve taking advantage of Greg, you would either try to determine what external forces could cause this unexpected turn of events ("Steve is smarter than Greg"), or you would change your opinion of Greg ("Greg is not such an effective manipulator").

People are more likely to search for external causes for behaviors that disconfirm target-based expectancies than they are to change their evaluations of the other person. Support for this idea comes from a study in which subjects read about a very likable person who had displayed a positive or negative behavior (21). The subjects explained the positive behavior in terms of the positive traits of the actor, but they explained the negative behavior in terms of external pressures.

To recapitulate our discussion so far, during social interactions we assign others to social roles, and we impute personality traits to them. Roles are assigned to others as a function of their situated identities and of any negotiations that have taken place over identity. Personality traits are imputed to others as a function of the attributions that are made to explain their behavior. Through prior experience, we often enter interactions with expectations concerning the behavior of others. When our expectancies are category-based (based on social roles or stereotypes of social groups), disconfirmation leads to trait inferences. For target-based expectancies (personality traits that lead to expectancies), confirmation substantiates the trait inferences.

■

ACTOR-OBSERVER DIFFERENCES IN ATTRIBUTIONS

As the foregoing discussion indicates, observers use a set of implicit rules to decide when the causes of an actor's behavior should be attributed to internal traits or to external causes. As a general rule, observers make internal trait attributions to explain the behavior of actors, while the actors themselves make *external* attributions for the same behavior.

There are four reasons for this difference between actors and observers (22):

1. Actors and observers have different *perspectives* on the actor's behavior. Actors see themselves as reacting to the situation, and their attention is focused outward. When asked to explain their behavior, they are apt to cite external factors in the situation to which they were reacting. For instance, mothers who abuse their children often explain their behavior in terms of the child's persistent crying and other pressures they feel.

In contrast, the focus of attention of observers is on the actors. Observers are likely to see actors as the causes of behavior because observers are not as attuned to other factors in the situation as actors are. People who observe or hear about the actions of mothers who abuse their children tend to attribute child abuse to personality defects in the mothers.

In most instances, attributions follow the focus of attention. Experimentally, this has been demonstrated in a study in which a conversation between two men was videotaped using two cameras (23). One camera focused on one participant and the other on the second participant. The subjects who later viewed only one of these tapes regarded the person on whom they were focusing as the one who had set the tone, chosen the topics for the conversation, and caused his partner to behave as he did. In other words, the person on whom the subjects focused was regarded as the primary causal agent in the interaction, but this was true *regardless* of which of the two people the subjects had watched.

2. Actors typically know their own *intentions,* but observers rarely do. An actor who hurts one of her friend's feelings with a thoughtless remark knows she did not intend to do so. An observer is likely to conclude the actor did intend the slight and infer that the actor is an insensitive person.

3. Actors have more *information* about their own prior behavior than observers do. Actors are aware of the variability in their behavior, but observers have to use the limited information available to draw inferences about the actor. The actor who unintentionally hurt her friend knows

how infrequently she has done this type of thing in the past, but the observer is likely to assume that the actor's behavior is typical of the way she usually behaves.

4. Actors know what they are feeling when they do something, while observers can only guess the actor's internal *feelings*. The actor who hurt her friend's feelings konws she was feeling playful when she made the remark, but an observer might not guess this. Lacking this information, the observer would be more likely to infer that the actor intended the consequences of her behavior.

All four of these actor-observer differences work in the same direction: The observers' focus of attention on the actor and the observers' lack of knowledge concerning the actors' intentions, prior history, and feelings all lead observers, more than actors, to emphasize internal causes as explanations for actors' behavior. This tendency for observers to explain the behavior of others in terms of internal attributes has been labeled the *fundamental attribution error* (24) because observers so often underestimate the importance of the situation.

One important implication of this error is that other people will frequently infer that your behavior reflects your personality traits, whereas you will see the same behavior as a reaction to the situation. Therefore, other people may not see you as you see yourself. One recent study found that people saw themselves as physically active, dynamic beings who covertly react emotionally, but they saw other people as static, social beings who covertly react cognitively (25). It appears that we think of ourselves as being more active and emotionally sensitive than others.

There are circumstances when observers do not fall prey to the fundamental attribution error. Observers who successfully influence actors are likely to attribute the actors' subsequent behavior to a situational factor—their own persuasion attempts (26). Observers who lose to actors in competitive situations are likely to attribute the actors' success to situational factors in order to save face (27). In a similar vein, couples with marital difficulties tend to attribute the causes of their partner's positive be-haviors to situational factors, while in nondistressed couples such behaviors are attributed to positive traits (28). In all of these situations the observer is actively involved with the actor, and factors other than those leading to the fundamental attribution error become operative. If there is no active involvement between observer and actor, the fundamental attribution error is likely to prevail.

The fundamental attribution error is compounded by a series of other biases that influence our perceptions of people. We will consider some of these biases next.

COGNITIVE INFORMATION PROCESSING AND PERSON PERCEPTION

Over the course of the last decade there has been increasing interest in psychological theories of cognitive information processing. These theories examine the ways in which people attend to information, interpret its meaning, and store it for subsequent retrieval (33). To get a feel for the cognitive approach, imagine you have just been transported to a distant planet. Alien beings are doing incomprehensible things, making unintelligible sounds, and feeding you food with totally new tastes and textures. All of this is occurring in an environment that visually and tactilely is like nothing in your previous experience.

How would you go about making sense of this new environment? What you can learn about this environment will be limited by your sensory and cognitive capacities. To learn anything at all you must choose what to attend to: Since virtually everything is new, you must decide which of the visual, auditory, and tactile stimuli are important. Then you can search for patterns among the stimuli in an attempt to form concepts about the nature of this world. You will probably use your prior knowledge of other worlds to do this, both because it may be useful and because you will not be able to avoid doing so. Of necessity, you will process much of

BOX 9-2

Labeling
and
Attribution

Labeling theory and attribution theory have much in common, even though the former was developed in sociological social psychology and the latter in psychological social psychology. As we saw in Chapter 8, labeling theory is concerned with the processes by which people come to be labeled as deviant and the effects of the label of deviant on behavior. Attribution theory is concerned with ascribing causes for behavior. It appears that attributions play a crucial role in the labeling process.

According to Harold Kelley, when people attempt to explain the behavior of others they act as naive scientists (29). They seek information on the *consistency*, degree of *consensus* or normativeness, and *distinctiveness* of the person's behavior. Ordinarily, people apply labels to others who consistently display a behavior (burglary) that is low in consensus (burglary is deviant) toward a variety of different targets (homes, businesses, and cars are robbed). Labels are applied when the behavior of others is attributed to internal causes (traits, needs, or moods). Thus, when a person consistently engages in a variety of related deviant acts for reasons that are internal, it is likely he or she will be labeled (he or she is a thief). However,

this new information within the context of your prior experiences. As you acquire knowledge about this planet, you will begin to develop a conceptual framework that may enable you to adapt to this new world.

This example illustrates four stages of cognitive information processing: attention, encoding, storage, and retrieval. The function of *attention* is to aid us in managing the environment. We selectively attend to certain stimuli in the environment because we are incapable of actively processing all of them, and only some of them are likely to be relevant to us. Choosing what to attend to limits the information

available to us for drawing inferences and forming expectations.

During *encoding*, information that has been attended to is organized in meaningful ways. As you encode information about your new environment you will need to *store* this information in memory. Storing information in a structured form will allow you to conveniently access it when you need this information in the future. When you bring this previously acquired information to bear on a current situation, you must *retrieve* it from storage. The amount of information available for retrieval is constantly being expanded by the addition of new

a person is not labeled if on one occasion he or she is coerced into engaging in a deviant act against his or her will. Studies show that a person is most likely to be labeled an alcoholic if the person's excessive drinking causes social or medical problems (nonnormative drinking), and if it occurs frequently over a long period of time (consistently) (30).

Because being labeled as deviant has negative consequences, people generally wish to avoid it. Labeling theorists argue that it is largely people who are unable to fight the imposition of such labels who are most likely to be labeled deviant (the poor, the mentally incompetent) (31). The label of deviant is frequently applied to persons during formal proceedings, such as a trial, a commitment proceeding, or a diagnostic interview. In these cases a possible identity is being negotiated, but the negotiation is being conducted formally and often without the consent of the person who may be labeled deviant. Given the fundamental attribution error, observers in official settings may be predisposed to use internal trait explanations to account for behavior, especially nonnormative behaviors that occur frequently.

The idea that an attributional analysis sets the stage for labeling a person deviant has been studied in a simulated jury setting. Participants in this study saw a videotape of a trial and deliberated in groups of six until they reached a verdict. Verdicts of guilty were most likely when the juries discussed the degree to which the behavior was nonnormative. The jurors also took into consideration whether or not the situation made it difficult to commit the crime (theft). If the crime was difficult to commit they apparently inferred a greater intention on the part of the suspect. When the jurors could convince themselves the defendant committed the crime for internal reasons, they found him guilty, an act that would lead a defendant in a real trial to be publicly labeled a criminal (32). ∎

pieces of information that have been attended to, encoded, and stored. Also, due to forgetting, some information gradually becomes less accessible over time.

The cognitive approach helps us understand who we are likely to attend to in social interactions, the effects of attention on the attributions or inferences we make about others, and our evaluations of them. The cognitive approach also aids us in understanding how meaning is imputed to the behavior of others during encoding, and how information about others is combined and organized during encoding. Finally, it reveals the

ways information about others is stored and retrieved.

Although we will be discussing attention, encoding, storage, and retrieval separately, it is important to keep in mind that each of these four facets of information processing is part of an interactive system. Thus, while only information that is attended to and encoded can be stored for later retrieval, information retrieved from memory can influence attention and encoding (see Figure 9-1). The cognitive approach applies to our moment-to-moment reactions to and evaluations of others, as well as to our more enduring impressions.

Figure 9.1 ■

Stages of Information Processing

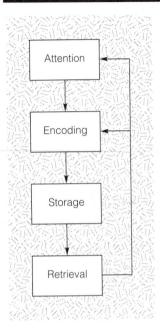

BIASES IN INFORMATION PROCESSING

Ordinarily, our cognitive systems process information accurately and efficiently. However, a number of biases can enter the system and create inaccuracies. Most of us wish to predict and explain the behavior of others—we do not want to think the world we live in is incomprehensible or uncontrollable. To attain an orderly understanding of the behavior of others, we often simplify and reduce the complexities and ambiguities of the information available to us. These simplification tendencies can result in a number of biases in the processing of social information. These biases are important because they are likely to have negative effects on our interpersonal relations, as well as on our perceptions.

We will begin our discussion of biases by considering those affecting attention. Then we will turn to biases in encoding, storage, and retrieval.

Attention

The focus of attention determines the information that will be processed. What will be attended to depends on aspects of the situation and aspects of the perceiver.

Situational factors The most important aspect of the situation in determining the focus of attention is the *salience* of the stimuli that are present. Salience is a function of such variables as the novelty, size, brightness, color, and complexity of stimuli (34). You would certainly notice and attend to a large, gaily painted person wearing a tuxedo top and running shorts in any social situation (Mardi Gras excluded, of course!). Also, stimuli that move or change, or are otherwise easily discriminated from the other stimuli in the situation, are likely to be attended to.

The stimuli attended to are *figural* against the *background* of the situation. That is, the attended stimuli seem to stand out while the other stimuli fade into the background. In social situations, people who have unusual appearances or who behave in deviant ways will be figural. In a study supporting this idea, people spent more time staring at others who were physically handicapped and at pregnant women than at others who were less unusual (35). This attention bias explains why, as children, some of us had to be reminded by our mothers not to stare at precisely those stimuli that seemed most interesting to us.

Salience can introduce bias into social perception because, as we have already noted when discussing actor-observer differences, attributions tend to follow the focus of attention. This attributional tendency helps to explain why internal explanations are frequently used to explain the behavior of people who behave in negative or deviant ways. In an investigation of this phenomenon, students watched a videotape of a bridge game in which one player frequently insulted another (36). When the videotape was shown in color, it was apparent the victim of the aggressive attack had red hair, but when the videotape was shown in black and white, her hair color was not discernable. Thus, the victim was more salient in the color videotape condition than in the black and white videotape because of her unusual hair color. The subjects attributed the aggressive attack more to the victim's internal personality traits when she was salient (in the color version) than when she was not. As this study suggests, people attribute causality to salient actors (37).

Salience can also bias social perception by influencing evaluations. Evaluations of salient others tend to be more *extreme* than evaluations of nonsalient others. To demonstrate this effect, students listened to a tape recording of a group of teachers talking in a teachers' lounge (38). The experimenters systematically re-recorded the tape so that on different versions of the tape a male or a female read each teacher's lines. Next, they spliced together twelve tapes, in which the proportion of males to females varied from 1:5 to 5:1. They hypothesized that the smaller the proportion of males or females, the more salient members of that sex would be and the more extreme would be the subjects' evaluations of them. They found both males and females were rated as more negative and as less pleasant and warm when fewer members of their sex were in the group of teachers. These results provide evidence for the propensity to give extreme evaluations to people who are salient in social interactions.

The effects of salience on attributions and evaluations apparently occur automatically. Salient stimuli draw attention like ice cream trucks draw children. Little conscious control is exerted by the perceiver, and the perceiver may not even be aware that he or she is attending to a salient stimulus. The lack of conscious awareness makes these biases difficult to overcome.

Person factors Two aspects of the perceiver that can influence the focus of attention are the perceiver's needs and expectancies. In contrast to the relatively automatic processing of the aspects of the situation

we have just discussed, the perceiver may be conscious of his or her needs and expectancies. When information processing takes place in conscious awareness, it is referred to as *controlled processing*. We engage in controlled processing any time we are consciously aware of the stimuli to which we are attending. We are especially likely to engage in controlled processing when we know we will have to discuss our judgments with others (39). Not surprisingly, knowing we will be discussing our judgments with others leads to more complex impressions of others and greater accuracy in judging their future behavior than when we do not anticipate a discussion (40).

Needs often influence the focus of attention. We are more likely to attend to need-related stimuli than to stimuli irrelevant to need fulfillment. For example, liquids take on special significance for a person who is thirsty. Needs can also distort the perception of persons, as illustrated in a study showing that sexually aroused males perceived prospective dates as more attractive than did unaroused males (41).

Another study of the biasing effects of needs examined the desire to reduce anxiety about interacting with unfamiliar others (42). The investigators asked college students to allow them to determine their dating lives for a five-week period. Some of the students were told they would date the same person for five weeks and others were told they would date a different person each week. These instructions were intended to manipulate how dependent the subjects would be on the other person and, thus, how important it would be to reduce anxiety about interacting with this person.

The students then watched a videotape of their prospective dates and two other people whom they would not be dating. After viewing the videotape, the students rated the three people they had watched. The more dependent the students were on their prospective dates (when they would be dating them exclusively), the more time they spent watching this person and the more positively this person was rated (see Figure 9-2). This study shows that when people are dependent on unfamiliar others, they

■ *Salient stimuli attract attention. (WGS)*

may reduce their anxiety by attending to them closely and by evaluating them favorably. The general conclusion emerging from research in this area is that people are prone to distort their perceptions of others in ways that satisfy their own needs.

Like needs, people's *expectancies* guide their attention. Expectancies usually have their origins in the traits others possess or the roles they occupy. Expectancies bias the gathering, perception, retention, and evaluation of social information. During the initial phases of an interaction, people with expectancies tend to actively *seek out* information that will confirm them (43). For instance, in one study, subjects were asked to interview a person and

determine if he was an extrovert (44). In selecting questions to ask this person, the subjects acted as if they expected the interviewee to be an extrovert, and they chose questions that would provide evidence supporting their expectancies. For example, the subjects chose such questions as, "What would you do if you wanted to liven things up at a party?" and "In what situations are you most talkative?" rather than questions like "What factors make it hard for you to really open up to people?" or "What things do you dislike about loud parties?"

This bias toward gathering expectancy-confirming evidence disappears when people are carefully deciding to which of *two* social categories a person

Figure 9.2 ■

The Effects of Dependency on Rating Dates

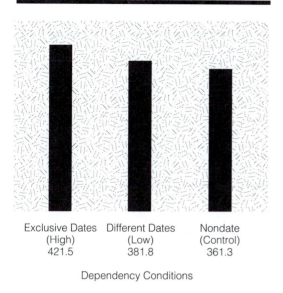

Exclusive Dates (High)	Different Dates (Low)	Nondate (Control)
421.5	381.8	361.3

Dependency Conditions

Note: High numbers indicate the stimulus person was rated more favorably across a variety of personality traits. Adapted from Berscheid, E., W. Graziano, M. Munson, and M. Dermer, 1976, "Outcome Dependency: Attention, Attribution, and Attraction," *Journal of Personality and Social Psychology,* 34: 978–989.

belongs (45). For instance, if the subjects in the preceding experiment had been asked to decide whether the person was an extrovert *or* an introvert they would probably have chosen questions in a more unbiased manner.

People are not generally so careful about collecting information, however, and it has been found that they usually *attend to* expectancy-confirming information and ignore expectancy-disconfirming information (46). In a demonstration of this selective attention bias, subjects viewed videotapes of an interview (47). The sound was eliminated and subjects were asked to evaluate the emotional state of the interviewee by using only nonverbal behavior cues. The subjects were then given different definitions of the situation. Some were told the interview

topic was the female interviewee's sex life, while others were told the interview concerned her political beliefs. The investigators assumed the subjects would expect an interview about sex to be more anxiety-provoking than an interview about politics. The subjects who thought they were seeing the interview about sex rated the interviewee as more uncomfortable, upset, and anxious than those who thought they were seeing the interview about politics. The videotape the subjects saw was actually the same; thus, the subjects "saw" what they expected to see.

Even when expectancy-disconfirming evidence is attended to, it tends to be *discounted* in impressions of other people because unexpected behavior is attributed to situational factors—unless it is quite deviant (48). We expect lawyers to be well-spoken so if we notice a famous lawyer make a few verbal blunders, we are likely to attribute it to a situational factor, such as stress. But if a lawyer is convicted of bribing a judge, we are likely to believe this reflects upon his or her character.

Not only do expectancies bias what information is attended to, they also bias the *retention* of social information. It is expectancy-confirming information that is most likely to be remembered. In one study of this phenomenon, subjects were led to believe they were viewing a videotape of two people committing a burglary or of two people trying to find a friend's drugs before the police raided his room (49). The subjects later recalled theft-related incidents (picking up a diamond ring) if they thought the tape was of a burglary, but they recalled drug-related incidents (picking up a water pipe) if they thought the tape was of a drug search. The tape was, of course, the same. In this study, the subjects remembered expectancy-confirming information better than irrelevant information (50).

In our discussion of salience effects, we suggested that *unexpected* behavior dominates attention. In our discussion of expectancies we have suggested that *expectancy-confirming* information dominates attention. Whether the focus of attention is determined by unexpected or expectancy-confirming events appears to depend on a number of factors. These factors include the strength, clarity, and number of expectancies, and the benefits and costs to the perceiver of confirmed or disconfirmed expectancies. A clear violation of a strongly held expectancy that has negative consequences for the perceiver is likely to be attended to and remembered. In contrast, a slight violation of an ambiguous expectancy that involves little cost to the perceiver probably would not be attended to or remembered. To illustrate, a person who was counting on his lover to accompany him on a vacation may never forget that she failed to appear at the airport, but he may not remember that she did not show up at a bar for a drink one night when she said she was not sure she could make it.

Expectancies also influence our *attraction* to others. People who confirm our expectancies tend to be liked better than those who disconfirm our expectancies. Several studies have shown that men and women who deviate from gender-role norms are evaluated less favorably than those who behave normatively (51). In one study, male and female confederates were trained to behave in either an aggressive or a passive manner in group problem-solving discussions. The males who behaved passively and the females who behaved aggressively were evaluated less favorably by observers than aggressive males and passive females (52).

Taken together, these studies demonstrate the central role of expectancies in the processing of social information. People tend to seek out, attend to, and recall expectancy-confirming evidence. They also tend to like people who confirm their expectancies better than those who do not (see Figure 9-3).

Encoding

The focus of attention determines what information will be processed. The process by which meaning is then attached to information is called *encoding*. In this section we will examine the ways in which incoming information is combined in forming impressions of others, the importance of the order in which we receive information about others, the relative importance of information about individual behavior versus information about group member-

Figure 9.3 ■

The Expectancy-Confirmation Syndrome

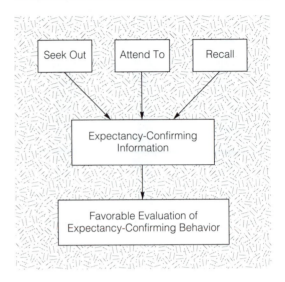

ship in forming impressions, and our tendency to perceive stronger relationships among traits than may actually exist.

Additive versus averaging models People often receive several pieces of information about another person at a time. For instance, if a friend describes another person to you or if you read in a pamphlet that a politician is honest, conservative, and devoted to family life, you are receiving information on several traits at once. It is also common to gradually build an impression of another person piece by piece. How are these pieces of information combined? (See Box 9-3 before going on.)

There are two ways in which information could be combined to form impressions. The first possibility, *the additive model*, suggests that each new piece of information adds to or subtracts from the current impression. The second possibility is the *averaging model*, in which the values of all the pieces of available information are averaged together (53).

BOX 9-3

An Attempt to Influence Impressions

The following letter is a political endorsement the authors received. How favorable is your impression of the politician described in it? How did you combine or weight the pieces of information you used to form this impression? This is a difficult question for most people to answer. The combining of information to form impressions seems to flow naturally from the information, but like so much of our information processing, this process is guided by subtle rules.

Dear Voter:

There are times when a message of truth needs to be delivered from public officials on behalf of those with whom they work. I feel I should speak out, to let the citizens of District 36 know that Sally Jackson has truly represented them and the entire state of New Mexico in the Legislature. Sally is honest, diligent, and effective in her efforts. She has gained the respect of all of her colleagues and has added to the credibility of the delegation from District 36. . . . Credibility and experience are vital to the citizens of any Legislative District in which good representation is achieved. Sally Jackson has these credentials and more. District 36 will benefit as a result of her reelection.

Sincerely,

In an interesting study comparing additive and averaging models, subjects read biographical information about past American presidents and then evaluated them (54). Subjects in one condition read four paragraphs of highly favorable information, while subjects in a second condition read four paragraphs of highly unfavorable information. These two groups formed very favorable and unfavorable impressions of the presidents, respectively. In a third condition, subjects read two of the highly favorable paragraphs, one moderately favorable paragraph, and one moderately unfavorable paragraph. In the fourth condition, two highly unfavorable paragraphs were combined with the moderately favorable and unfavorable paragraphs.

The additive model would predict that the moderately favorable and unfavorable paragraphs would cancel each other out, so only highly favorable or unfavorable evaluations would be expressed. The averaging model would predict a lowering of the

Figure 9.4 ■

Additive versus Averaging Models: Evaluations of American Presidents

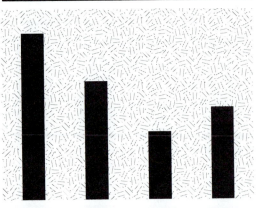

| All positive information 7.72 | Half positive, half moderate information 5.48 | All negative information 3.14 | Half negative, half moderate information 4.26 |

Note: The higher the numbers, the more favorable the evaluation.
Adapted from Anderson, N.H., 1973, "Information Integration Theory Applied to Attitudes About U.S. Presidents," *Journal of Educational Psychology* 64: 18–27.

evaluation when the moderate information was combined with the highly favorable information, and a rise in evaluation when the moderate and highly unfavorable information were combined. As you can see in Figure 9-4, the averaging model was supported—an outcome characteristic of research in this area.

The process of averaging seems to suggest that each piece of information we receive about someone has equal weight in our impressions of that person. However, other studies indicate that differential emphasis may be given to information received early or late in the impression formation process.

Primacy versus recency Would your impression of a person be different if you learned the person was honest before you learned the person was lazy, rather than learning the person was honest after you

learned he or she was lazy? This question concerns how the order in which trait information is encoded influences impressions. Is information presented first more influential (a *primacy* effect) or is information presented last more influential (a *recency* effect)? For example, if you were a lawyer defending someone in a jury trial, would you rather present your final summary of the case first or last? Do you think the jury is more likely to remember and be influenced by the first summary it hears or the last? If you guessed that the information presented first is generally more influential, you are right (55). Information presented later tends not to be closely attended to because attention usually decreases over time. Also, later information is often discounted in impression formation, particularly if it is discrepant from information presented earlier.

Primacy effects can be eliminated in some cases. Asking people to attend equally to all of the information presented to them, or warning them against forming premature impressions, eliminates primacy effects (56). Likewise, telling people they will have to justify their later judgments eliminates primacy effects (57).

In rare instances, recency effects prevail over primacy effects. When there is a long separation in time between the presentation of the initial information and the presentation of later information, recency effects can overcome primacy effects (58). A voter who has a negative impression of a presidential candidate on the basis of his convention speech may ignore the campaign until the candidate makes his last political speech the week before the election. If the voter likes the last speech, this more recent positive information is very likely to dominate the voter's final impression of the candidate. Thus, a long separation between initial and final information favors the final information.

Individuating information The next encoding bias we will discuss occurs when people's evaluations of groups are biased by information about a particular individual from that group (59). For instance, prison guards are regarded by most people as being relatively inhumane. Subjects in one study read about a very humane prison guard and were then asked about their impressions of prison guards in general (60). These subjects rated prison guards as being more humane than subjects who had not read about the humane guard. This study suggests our evaluations of *groups* may be dominated by our knowledge of particular members of the group (individuating information), rather than by social stereotypes. This bias toward relying on individuating information disappears if the source is unreliable, such as someone who is obviously prejudiced, or the information concerns a randomly selected group member (61).

Individuating information can also lead us to ignore information about group membership in our evaluations of *individuals*. When the group stereotype is weak, almost any individuating information will exert a greater impact on impressions of the individual than will the group stereotype. To illustrate this process, subjects read about the traits of an individual who was reported to be either a "day person" or a "night person" (62). In the absence of individuating information, day people were stereotyped as responsible, dependable, healthy, and self-controlled. Night people were stereotyped as rebellious, unpredictable, unconventional, and depressed. When the subjects read information about a particular day or night person, even when this information was unrelated to the stereotype (information about the occupations of the individual's parents), they did not attribute the stereotypic traits to this person. Thus, even irrelevant individuating information was more important than group stereotypic information in impressions of this individual.

Information about specific individuals does not always override the stereotype. If the stereotype is a very strong one, such as some ethnic stereotypes, individuating information that is not associated with the stereotype does not affect the degree to which stereotyped traits are attributed to the individual (63). However, even with fairly strong stereotypes, individuating information explicitly contradicting the stereotype can dominate impressions.

A study using sex stereotypes illustrates this latter phenomenon (64). Subjects who were provided with information on an individual's assertiveness used this information to predict the individual's competitiveness, decisiveness, and insensitivity to others. Information on the person's sex was ignored in making these predictions. Thus, when the information on the person's sex contradicted the individuating information (a female who was assertive), the subjects relied only on the individuating information (65). In sum, it appears that when individuating information and stereotypic information conflict, people's impressions of both the individuals and the groups to which they belong may be substantially influenced by the individuating information.

Emphasizing individuating over stereotypic information is usually identified as a bias because the impressions that result are different from those that would exist in the absence of the individuating information. However, such "bias" makes it likely that, as we gather information about others, we will treat them more as individuals, rather than as group members. So, unlike many of the biases we have discussed, the effects of this "bias" tend to be beneficial, not harmful.

Illusory correlation When encoding information about others people often fall prey to *illusory correlations*—the perception that two traits or behaviors are related to a greater degree than they actually are. In an experiment designed to demonstrate illusory correlation, subjects read about the standing of each member of a group of eight students on two traits (66). The two traits used (understanding and tolerance) are commonly thought to be positively correlated. The standings showed that in this group of eight there was no correlation between the two traits. When the subjects were later asked to recall the standings of the group members on these traits, they falsely remembered that the traits were correlated (students who were high on understanding were ranked high on tolerance, and students who were low on understanding were ranked low on tolerance). This study indicates that traits expected to occur together may be perceived as occurring together, even if they do not (67).

A similar bias occurs in the perception of the

relationship between social roles and traits associated with the roles. People tend to overestimate the degree to which people occupying a role possess traits expected of people in that role (68).

In short, when encoding information about others we tend to average the information we have to arrive at an impression. However, in forming impressions we may be unduly influenced by the initial pieces of information we receive. Also, our impressions tend to be based more on individuating trait or behavior information than on group memberships. Due to illusory correlation, we may attribute surplus traits to others because these traits are correlated with those we know they possess.

Storage

In order to facilitate later retrieval, social knowledge stored in memory is typically organized into structures such as prototypes, schemata, scripts, and implicit personality theories. As we acquire information about others we store it in long-term memory. In general, this incoming information is either assimilated into our preexisting knowledge structures, or it causes changes in our knowledge structures so we can accommodate it.

Prototypes When we assign situated identities to others, we fit them into social categories, such as roles or personality types. When we are trying to determine if a person can be placed in a given social category, we compare this person to other members of the category to determine their similarity. We do not use just any category member when performing this comparison. Instead, we compare this person to a prototypical category member (69). A *prototype* consists of information about the characteristics of the typical member of a social category. There is a subtle distinction between prototypes and stereotypes. Stereotypes are concerned with the characteristics most group members are thought to possess, while prototypes are concerned with the characteristics that the typical group member does possess. Do you have an image of a prototypical doctor tucked away in your memory? In addition to having

a medical degree and wearing a lab coat, is your prototypical doctor middle-aged, kindly, and rather serious? Did you picture the doctor as a male? If you did, this indicates your prototype includes information on sex.

Although people are capable of forming accurate prototypes on the basis of their experiences with others (70), prototypes can lead to distortions in impressions. When a person has been categorized as a member of a group, the characteristics of the prototype may be attributed to the person whether they fit or not. To illustrate this idea, subjects in one study were asked to read descriptions of another person (71). This person was either described as a prototypical extrovert ("Alice was boisterous at the movie"; "Alice danced for hours at the party") or was not prototypical, possessing a mixture of the extroverted traits and some introverted traits ("Diane showed enthusiasm"; "Diane was hesitant in class").

Two days later the subjects were asked to write their own descriptions of this person. The descriptions written by the subjects who had read about prototypical extroverts were more elaborate than the descriptions written by subjects who read about nonprototypical people. The subjects' descriptions of the extroverts also contained many new extrovert-related traits not contained in the original descriptions. Additionally, the subjects who read about prototypical extroverts were able to recall more of the original traits attributed to them than those who read about nonprototypical people. Apparently, categorizing the person as an extrovert made it easier for the subjects to remember the person's traits, and also resulted in the addition of new traits to the subjects' impressions.

Constructing impressions of others on the basis of categorization may not be a serious problem if they are actually prototypical group members, but it is likely to lead to misunderstandings if they do not closely fit the prototype. Another bias that can arise when a prototype is used is that the way we feel about this other person may be determined by how we feel about prototypical members of the category (72). For instance, if you dislike the prototypical doctor, categorizing someone as a doctor may lead you to dislike that person.

■ *Prototypes are often used to categorize people. What features of this woman enable you to categorize her as a beauty queen? (WGS)*

Schemata Social schemata are more complex than prototypes. *Schemata* consist of knowledge structures containing all the information an individual possesses about a social category (ethnic groups, social roles, personality types). This information is organized hierarchically into a kind of knowledge pyramid. At the base of the pyramid are all the separate pieces of concrete information the individ- ual possesses about the category (73). At the lowest level, a schema for extroverts might contain infor- mation on specific behaviors (likes parties, acts without thinking, speaks fast). At higher levels in the pyramid, the information is less concrete and more abstract. For extroverts, the intermediate level in the pyramid might include personality traits (sociable, impulsive, lively). The highest level of information

Figure 9.5 ■

Schematic Knowledge Pyramid for Extrovert

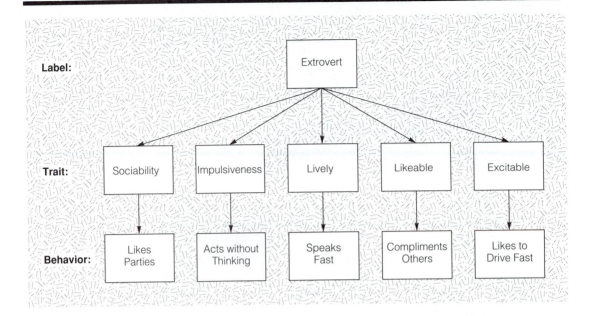

is the most abstract and often consists of the label for the social category. In our example it would be extrovert (see Figure 9-5).

As with prototypes, schemata-relevant information is more readily encoded and remembered than schemata-irrelevant information. Also, when schemata are used to encode information, schemata-consistent information may be added and subsequently remembered (74).

One particularly important schema consists of all the information a person possesses about himself or herself. We have written about this schema in Chapter 4. Here our concern is the effect of self-schemata on processing information about other people. In research on schemata, people are categorized as schematic for a trait if they believe they possess the trait and regard it as important. People are categorized as aschematic if they believe they do not possess the trait and regard it as unimportant. Using this technique, it has been found that females

who were schematic for femininity described other women by using more feminine traits than did aschematic females (75). Thus, self-schemata can lead people to judge others in terms of the traits they themselves possess, a type of egocentrism (see Box 9-4). The use of self-schematic traits appears to be automatic and may occur even when other traits are more applicable. A woman who is schematic for femininity may watch a women's gymnastic event and focus on the beauty of the contestants, not their athletic prowess.

When people use self-schemata to judge others, their judgments tend to be extreme (82). In a study of these *extremity* effects, subjects who were schematic or aschematic with respect to independence were asked to read stories about people who varied in independence (83). Schematic subjects had more polarized views of these people than did the aschematic subjects. The schematic subjects judged the independent people to be higher on traits related

BOX 9-4

Egocentrism and Ego-enhancing Biases in Perception

Egocentrism is the tendency to use the self as a frame of reference for viewing others. One form of egocentrism is known as the *false consensus effect* (76). In one experiment, students were asked to wear a sign and walk around campus for 30 minutes. The sign read "Eat at Joe's." The pretext for wearing the sign was that the students might learn something interesting in the process. Afterwards, the students were asked to estimate the percentage of other students who would have worn the sign if asked to do so. Those who agreed to wear the sign believed most other students would also do so (62 percent). Similarly, the students who refused to wear the sign felt most other students would also refuse (67 percent). The students assumed other students were like them; they generated a false consensus consistent with their behavior.

Another interesting example of false consensus occurred in a survey in which it was found that, although only 3 percent of the sample disapproved of children playing together in interracial groups, they believed their opinions were shared by a majority of others (77). The false consensus effect seems to occur when the perception of others as similar to oneself provides social support for one's own position.

However, a contrasting tendency occurs when comparing the self to others in order to bolster one's self-esteem. On a wide variety of socially desirable dimensions, people consider themselves to be different from others because they believe they are *better than average*. For instance, the majority of people consider themselves to be more intelligent than average, which is clearly impossible (78). In one study, students reported they expected to live longer, to have higher salaries, to be more likely to own their own homes and to have a mentally gifted child than other students (79). These students also said they were less likely than other students to have a heart attack, lung cancer, venereal disease, to be fired from their jobs, commit suicide, or get divorced within five years after being married. Sixty percent of a national sample of high school students who were taking the College Board test indicated they believed they were in the top 10 percent of people their age in ability to get along with others, and 25 percent rated themselves in the top 1 percent (80)! Students are not the only people who engage in ego-enhancing distortions of themselves; 94 percent of college professors rate themselves as above average (81).

Both the false consensus effect and the ego-enhancing tendency to perceive oneself as better than average help people maintain a positive self-image. But they do so at the cost of misperceiving the attitudes, behaviors, and traits of others. ■

to independence than did aschematic subjects, and they judged the less independent people to be higher on traits related to dependence than did aschematic subjects. Thus, when a trait is important to you, you are likely to make extreme judgments of others on that trait.

Scripts Scripts are another type of schemata important in social perception. *Scripts* consist of information about the normative sequence of events in a given social interaction. For instance, the script for eating in a restaurant involves entering the restaurant, being seated, receiving a menu, ordering from the menu, being served food, eating, paying, and leaving. Scripts are important in social perception because they set up expectancies concerning the course of the interaction. Violations of these expectancies can result in misunderstandings and hostility.

Consider this example of a misunderstanding discovered in a study of school desegregation (84). The white students in this school occasionally offered to help the black students with their schoolwork. In the normative script for helping, one would expect the recipient to be thankful. However, the investigator found that "black students often see such offers of help as yet another indication of white feelings of superiority and conceit. White students who do not think of themselves as conceited feel mystified and angry when, what to them seem to be friendly and helpful overtures, are rejected."

A study of scripts for sexual encounters provides another illustration of the role of scripts in social interaction. In this study, the investigators first determined the typical sequence of events in a sexual encounter between students at their university (85). The investigators then wrote stories of sexual encounters that either followed the normative script or had some behaviors occurring outside the normative sequence (petting before kissing). Students were then asked to rate how sexually arousing the stories were. The students found the stories that followed the normative script to be more sexually arousing than the stories violating the normative sequence. This study and the previous one suggest that when an interaction does not follow the normative script, people react negatively.

Implicit personality theories Take a couple of seconds and answer the following question before going on. In your view what traits do dominant people share in common? Your answer to this question is an example of an implicit personality theory. Sets of traits thought to occur together are known as *implicit personality theories* (86). Implicit personality theories are similar to illusory correlations between two traits, but they are more complex because they involve a number of traits that are thought to occur together. They introduce bias into perception because the observers relying on implicit personality theories may ignore the actual behavior of the people they are observing (87). A person using an implicit personality theory based on dominance might believe her domineering boss is cold and arrogant without ever observing her boss behave in these ways, simply because she thinks dominant people are cold and arrogant. In this case knowledge about the boss's standing on one trait leads to the perception that he possesses other traits (see Box 9-5).

The traits which lead to inferences regarding the possession of correlated traits are considered to be *central* traits. A classic experiment by Solomon Asch illustrates the important role of central traits in impression formation (88). In this study, subjects were given one of two lists of traits that were said to characterize another student. One list contained these traits: intelligent, industrious, cautious, skillful, determined, practical, and warm. The second list was the same as the first, except the word "cold" was substituted for the word "warm." The subjects were later asked to describe this person in their own words and to rate him on a number of dimensions. Their descriptions and ratings were greatly affected by the replacement of this one word. A similar replacement using the words "polite" and "blunt" had little effect on the later ratings. In this study, "warm" and "cold" proved to be central traits having a substantial impact on impressions.

Other studies indicate central traits only influence the perception of closely related traits (89). For instance, knowing a person is warm has a greater effect on perceptions of popularity than on perceptions of artistic ability. Thus, only the other traits

BOX 9-5

Implicit Personality Theory

Personality psychologists have also studied implicit theories of personality. One personality theorist proposed the diagram displayed here (Figure 9-6) as a way of arranging eight key personality traits (93). The two central trait dimensions concern warmth and dominance (contained on the horizontal and vertical axes). The closer two traits appear on this diagram, the more highly correlated they are perceived to be. Thus, this diagram represents an implicit personality theory. For example, arrogance and coldness are thought to be more highly correlated than arrogance and gregariousness.

This diagram can also be used to generate personality types. A business executive might fit in the upper right part of the diagram, being high in dominance, somewhat gregarious, and rather arrogant. Studies using this circular diagram have found that not only do people perceive these traits to be related in this way, the actual correlations of behavior to these traits fit the diagram (94). Can you fit yourself into this diagram? ■

Figure 9.6 ■

Implicit Personality Theory

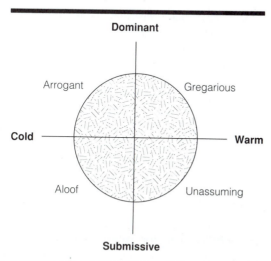

■ *List everything you can remember from your previous impression of this person. Compare what you remembered to what you originally wrote down. What did you remember correctly? What did you forget? What did you add? (WGS)*

pertinent to the observer's implicit personality theory are affected by the presence of a central trait.

Some traits, particularly strongly evaluative ones, such as vicious or sincere, may create a *halo effect* by leading to a uniformly negative or uniformly positive impression (90). The operation of halo effects is potentially important to anyone who may be evaluated by a supervisor. Supervisors often have little information about their employees, and yet they must rate them for salary increases and promotion. Under these circumstances, an employee may be rated largely on the basis of one very unfavorable or favorable event that provides information on only one trait. Be forewarned: One excellent or terrible report you write may greatly influence your career!

Unfortunately, negative information appears to be more memorable than positive information, with the result that as the interval between the behaviors to be rated and the actual rating increases, negative information has a greater impact on impressions (91). Generally, the more limited and extreme the information, the more likely it is that biases due to implicit personality theories, central traits, and halo effects will enter into impression formation (92).

Our final section deals with biases in the retrieval of information that has been encoded and stored in memory.

Retrieval

The information we store in memory and have available for later retrieval is limited in a variety of ways. Initially, the operation of selective attention eliminates the majority of unattended stimuli from being stored. Of the stimuli attended to, many will not pass from short-term memory into long-term memory. For instance, right now you can probably recall the last few words in this sentence. Within 30 seconds you will find it almost impossible to do so (unless you rehearse the sentence over and over to keep it in short-term memory). When information is transferred into long-term memory, it is the meaning of the information or inferences based on this information, rather than the exact details, that are stored in memory. You will probably remember the general principle that information is stored in summary form in memory, but it is unlikely you will remember the exact words we used to convey this idea.

The social information retained in memory is organized in such structures as prototypes, schemata, scripts, and implicit personality theories. The exact nature of the processes by which information is retrieved from these structures is a matter of much debate. This controversy largely concerns the ways in which information is structured in memory and how we search through these structures during retrieval. This much is clear: These retrieval processes are not free from bias.

The consistency bias The consistency bias is the most thoroughly studied of the retrieval biases. We have reviewed studies showing that information consistent with schemata, prototypes, and expectancies is more likely to be retained in memory than inconsistent information. Even when information was not originally encoded in schemata or similar structures, retrieval may be biased by a tendency to make the information retrieved from memory consistent with our current beliefs.

In one study illustrating this idea, subjects read a detailed fictional story about the life of Betty K., including information on her home, school, and social life (95). One week later the subjects were given some additional information about Betty, indicating she was either a lesbian or a heterosexual. At this point, the subjects were asked to recall everything they had learned about Betty. The subjects who thought Betty was a lesbian recalled more information consistent with this label (Betty never went out with men in high school) than subjects who thought Betty was a heterosexual. This study indicates that current beliefs can bias the retrieval of social information (96).

People also seem to find it easier to recall the categories they used in encoding information about someone (Wenda is a professor) than all the separate pieces of information that made this categorization possible (She teaches at a university; She has a Ph.D; She's a little absentminded) (97). They may then use traits consistently associated with the category (intelligent) to make later judgments about the person (Wenda would make a good PTA president), even though they do not possess any information about these other traits.

There is also a bias toward affective consistency in the memory of information about individuals. In a study of this bias, white students who were prejudiced toward blacks read a description of a white person or a black person (98). One week later they were asked to recall the information they had read. More negative than positive traits were recalled from the description of the black person, but there were no similar distortions of the white person. Several additional studies show that people tend to remember information about others that is consistent with their feelings toward them (99).

It seems people also remember information about others that is affectively consistent with their current moods (100). If they are feeling good they remember others' positive traits, but when they are feeling bad they recall others' negative traits. Causing others to feel good may remind them of your good qualities, on the other hand, causing them to feel bad . . .

To recapitulate briefly, retrieval biases can cause us to recall expectancy-confirming information and traits associated with the social categories to which people belong. We also tend to recall information that is consistent with our evaluations of others and our current moods.

If "to err is human," then the research on information processing stands as testimony to our humanity.

■

SUMMARY

Our impressions of others consist primarily of information about these others' traits, behaviors, attitudes, and demographic characteristics. These impressions may be formed prior to interacting with others, but they can also emerge during social interactions. In social interactions, not only are impressions formed and modified, but situated identities consisting of social roles are established and negotiated. These situated identities are typically derived from the actors' definitions of the situation. The role expectations derived from situated identities are used by actors to guide their behavior and interpret the behavior of others.

During social interactions people observe the behavior of others and may make trait attributions to explain their behavior. Observers make inferences about the actors' traits when actors freely choose to behave in deviant ways or in ways that are unexpected, given the social categories to which they belong.

In general, observers are more likely than actors to attribute the behavior of actors to internal causes. Observers tend to make this fundamental attribution error because the actor, rather than the situation, is the focus of their attention, and they err because they lack information on the actors' past history, intentions, and feelings.

The cognitive approach to social interaction demonstrates that people are susceptible to a number of biases in attending to, encoding, storing, and retrieving social information. Attentional biases due to the salience of social stimuli include an increased probability of attributing the behavior of others to internal causes and extreme evaluations of salient others. Observers' needs can influence their perceptions of others in ways that tend to satisfy these needs. Observers' expectations can bias the information they gather about others, what they attend to, how much they like others, and what they remember about them.

During encoding, positive and negative traits are averaged to arrive at an overall impression. Information received early in the impression formation process has a greater impact on impressions than information received later (the primacy effect). In forming impressions, people are typically influenced more by the specific trait or behavioral information they have about another individual than they are by information about the individual's group membership. When people expect two traits to be correlated, they often perceive that the traits have occurred together, even when the actual evidence indicates they are unrelated (illusory correlation).

Information is stored in memory in structures, such as prototypes, schemata, scripts, and implicit personality theories. Prototypes of typical members of social categories are used to categorize others. This process can lead to attributing the traits of prototypical group members to individuals who have been categorized as group members and to remembering more prototype-consistent than prototype-inconsistent information. Schemata consisting of hierarchically organized information about a given topic have similar biasing effects on encoding. Self-schemata can lead observers to make extreme judgments of others on schema-related traits. Scripts for social interactions set up expectancies which lead to negative reactions when these scripts are violated. An impression that an actor possesses a central trait can lead to the belief that the actor possesses other traits thought to be correlated with it (implicit personality theory). The belief that an actor possesses a single very positive or negative trait can lead to a halo effect, in which the actor is thought to rank high or low on other evaluative traits.

When an impression is retrieved from memory it tends to be more consistent than the original information on which it was based. Information consistent with prototypes, schemata, and scripts is more likely to be remembered than inconsistent information. Also, the initial evaluative tone of the impression will result in evaluatively consistent information being retained. People are also more likely to recall information about others that is consistent with their current moods than mood-inconsistent information.

■

REFERENCES

1. Herr, P. M., 1986, "Consequences of Priming: Judgment and Behavior," *Journal of Personality and Social Psychology* 51: 1106–1115.

2. Warner, R. M. and D. B. Sugarman, 1986, "Attributions of Personality Based on Physical Appearance, Speech, and Handwriting," *Journal of Personality and Social Psychology* 50: 792–799.

3. Riggio, R. E. and H. S. Friedman, 1986, "Impression Formation: The Role of Expressive Behavior," *Journal of Personality and Social Psychology* 50: 421–427; P. T. Hertel and A. Narvaez, 1986, "Confusing Memories for Verbal and Nonverbal Communication," *Journal of Personality and Social Psychology* 50: 474–481; K. R. Sherer, 1974, "Acoustic Concomitants of Emotional Dimensions: Judging Affect from Synthesized Tone Sequences," in S. Weitz (Ed.), *Nonverbal Communication:*

Readings with Commentary, New York: Oxford University Press; C. E. Williams and K. N. Stevens, 1972, "Emotions and Speech: Some Acoustical Correlates," *Journal of the Acoustical Society of America* 52: 1238–1250; M. Zuckerman, M. Amidon, S. Bishop, and S. Pomerantz, 1982, "Face and Tone of Voice in the Communication of Deception," *Journal of Personality and Social Psychology* 43: 347–357.

4. Zwiegenhaft, R. L., 1977, "The Empirical Study of Signature Size," *Social Behavior and Personality* 5: 177–185.

5. Zwiegenhaft, 1977, ibid.

6. Park, B., 1986, "A Method for Studying the Development of Impressions of Real People," *Journal of Personality and Social Psychology* 51: 907–917.

7. Fiske, S. T. and M. G. Cox, 1979, "Person Concepts: The Effect of Target Familiarity and Descriptive Purpose on Describing Others," *Journal of Personality* 47: 136–161.

8. Bourne, E., 1977, "Can We Describe an Individual's Personality? Agreement on Stereotype versus Individual Attributes," *Journal of Personality and Social Psychology* 35: 863–872; Park, 1986, op. cit.

9. Park, 1986, ibid.

10. DePaulo, B. M., D. A. Kenny, C. W. Hoover, W. Webb, and P. V. Oliver, 1987, "Accuracy of Person Perception: Do People Know What Kinds of Impressions They Convey?," *Journal of Personality and Social Psychology* 52: 303–315.

11. Hiess, J., 1981, *The Social Psychology of Social Interaction,* Englewood Cliffs, NJ: Prentice-Hall; S. Stryker, 1980, *Symbolic Interactionism,* Menlo Park, CA: Benjamin/Cummings.

12. Cantor, N., W. Mischel, and J. C. Schwartz, 1982, "A Prototype Analysis of Psychological Situations," *Cognitive Psychology* 14: 45–77.

13. Alexander, C. N. and J. Rudd, "Predicting Behavior from Situated Identities," *Social Psychology Quarterly* 47: 172–177; Stryker, 1980, op. cit.

14. Tannen, D. and C. Wallat, 1987, "Interactive Frames and Knowledge of Schemas in Interaction: Examples from a Medical Examination-Interview," *Social Psychology Quarterly* 50: 205–216.

15. Alexander, C. N. and M. G. Wiley, 1981, "Situated Activity and Identity Formation," in M. Rosenberg and R. H. Turner (Eds.), *Social Psychology,* New York: Basic Books.

16. Spencer, J. W., 1987, "Self-work in Social Interaction: Negotiating Role Identities," *Social Psychology Quarterly* 50: 131–159.

17. Jones, E. E. and K. E. Davis, 1965, "From Acts to Dispositions," in L. Berkowitz (Ed.), *Advances in Experimental Social Psychology,* Vol. 2, New York: Academic Press.

18. Read, S. J., 1987, "Constructing Causal Scenarios: A Knowledge Structure Approach to Causal Reasoning," *Journal of Personality and Social Psychology* 52: 288–302.

19. Jones, E. E. and D. McGillis, 1976, "Correspondent Inferences and the Attribution Cube: A Comparative Reappraisal," in J. Harvey, W. Ickes, and R. Kidd, *New Directions in Attribution Theory,* Vol. 1, Hillsdale, NJ: Lawrence Erlbaum.

20. Jones, E. E., K. E. Davis, and K. J. Gergen, 1961, "Role Playing Variations and Their Informational Value for Person Perception," *Journal of Abnormal and Social Psychology* 63: 302–310.

21. Bell, L., R. A. Wicklund, G. Manko, and C. Larkin, 1976, "When Unexpected Behavior Is Attributed to the Environment," *Journal of Research in Personality* 10:316–327.

22. Jones, E. E. and R. E. Nisbett, 1971, "The Actor and the Observer: Divergent Perceptions of the Causes of Behavior," in E. Jones, D. Kanouse, H. Kelley, R. Nisbett, S. Valins, and B. Weiner (Eds.), *Attribution: Perceiving the Causes of Behavior,* Morristown, NJ: General Learning Press.

23. Taylor, S. E. and S. T. Fiske, 1975, "Point of View and Perception of Causality," *Journal of Personality and Social Psychology* 32: 439–445.

24. Ross, L., 1978, "The Intuitive Psychologist and His Shortcomings: Distortions in the Attribution Process," in L. Berkowitz (Ed.), *Cognitive Theories in Social Psychology,* New York: Academic Press.

25. McGuire, W. J. and C. V. McGuire, 1986, "Differences in Conceptualizing Self versus Conceptualizing Other People as Manifested in Contrasting Verb Types Used in Natural Speech," *Journal of Personality and Social Psychology* 51: 1135–1143.

26. Gilbert, D. T., E. E. Jones, and B. W. Pelham, 1987, "Influence and Inference: What the Active Perceiver Overlooks," *Journal of Personality and Social Psychology* 52: 861–870.

27. Snyder, M. L., W. G. Stephan, and D. Rosenfield, 1978, "Attributional Egotism," in J. Harvey, J. Ickes, and R. Kidd (Eds.), *New Directions in Attribution Research,* Vol. 2, Hillsdale, NJ: Lawrence Erlbaum.

28. Fincham, F. D., S. R. Beach, and D. H. Baucom, 1987, "Attribution Process in Distressed and Nondistressed Couples: 4. Self-Partner Attribution Differences," *Journal of Personality and Social Psychology* 52: 739–748.

29. Kelley, H. H., 1967, "Attribution Theory in Social Psychology," in D. Levine (Ed.), *Nebraska Symposium on Motivation.* Lincoln: University of Nebraska Press.

30. Robins, L. N., 1980, "Alcoholism and Labeling Theory," in W. R. Gove (Ed.), *The Labeling of Deviance,* 2d ed., Beverly Hills, CA: Sage.

31. W. R. Gove, ibid.

32. Howard, J. A. and R. Levinson, 1985, "The Overdue Courtship of Attribution and Labeling," *Social Psychology Quarterly* 48: 192–202.

33. Anderson, J. R., 1980, *Cognitive Psychology and Its Implications,* San Francisco: Freeman; U. Neisser, 1967, *Cognitive Psychology,* New York: Appleton-Century-Crofts.

34. Berlyne, D. E., 1970, "Attention as a Problem in Behavior Theory," in D. I. Mostofsky (Ed.), *Attention: Contemporary Theory and Analysis,* New York: Appleton-Century-Crofts.

35. Langer, E. J., S. I. Fiske, S. E. Taylor, and B. Chanowitz, 1976, "Stigma, Staring and Discomfort: A Novel Stimulus Hypothesis," *Journal of Experimental Social Psychology* 12: 451–463.

36. McArthur, L. Z. and L. I. Solomon, 1978, "Perceptions of an Aggressive Encounter as a Function of the Victim's Salience and the Perceiver's Arousal," *Journal of Personality and Social Psychology* 36: 929–940.

37. Fiske, S. T., D. A. Kenny, and S. E. Taylor, 1982, "Structural Models for the Mediation of Salience Effects on Attribution," *Journal of Experimental Social Psychology* 18: 105–127.

38. Taylor, S. E., S. T. Fiske, N. L. Etcoff, and J. J. Ruderman, 1978, "Categorical and Contextual Bases of Person Memory and Stereotyping," *Journal of Personality and Social Psychology* 36: 778–793.

39. Tetlock, P. E. and J. I. Kim, 1987, "Accountability and Judgment Processes in a Personality Prediction Task," *Journal of Personality and Social Psychology* 52: 700–709.

40. Tetlock and Kim, 1987, ibid.

41. Stephan, W. G., E. Berscheid, and E. Walster, 1971, "Sexual Arousal and Heterosexual Attraction," *Journal of Personality and Social Psychology* 20: 93–101.

42. Berscheid, E., W. Graziano, M. Munson, and M. Dermer, 1976, "Outcome Dependency: Attention, Attribution, and Attraction," *Journal of Personality and Social Psychology* 34: 978–989.

43. Skov, R. B. and S. J. Sherman, 1986, "Information-gathering Processes: Diagnosticity, Hypothesis-confirmatory Strategies, and Perceived Hypothesis Confirmation," *Journal of Experimental Social Psychology* 22: 93–121.

44. Snyder, M. and W. B. Swann, Jr., 1978, "Hypothesis Testing Processes in Social Interaction," *Journal of Personality and Social Psychology* 36: 1202–1212; M. Snyder and S. Gangestad, 1981, "Hypothesis Testing Processes," in J. Harvey, W. Ickes, and R. Kidd, *New Directions in Attribution Research*, Vol. 3, Hillsdale, NJ: Lawrence Erlbaum.

45. Trope, Y. and D. M. Mackie, 1987, "Sensitivity to Alternatives in Social Hypothesis-testing," *Journal of Experimental Social Psychology* 23: 445–459.

46. Stephan, W. G., 1989, "A Cognitive Approach to Stereotyping," in D. Bar-Tal, C. F. Graumann, A. W. Kruglanski, and W. Stroebe (Eds.), *Stereotyping and Prejudice: Changing Conceptions*, New York: Springer Verlag.

47. Snyder, M. L. and A. Frankel, 1976, "Observer Bias: A Stringent Test of Behavior Engulfing the Field," *Journal of Personality and Social Psychology* 34: 857–864.

48. Crocker, J., D. B. Hannah, and R. Weber, 1983, "Person Memory and Causal Attributions," *Journal of Personality and Social Psychology* 44: 55–66.

49. Zadny, J. and H. B. Gerard, 1974, "Attribution Intentions and Informational Selectivity," *Journal of Experimental Social Psychology* 10: 34–52.

50. For an exception, see R. Hastie and P. A. Kumar, 1979, "Personal Memory: Personality Traits as Organizing Principles in Memory for Behavior," *Journal of Personality and Social Psychology* 37: 25–38.

51. Costrich, N., J. Feinstein, L. Kidder, J. Maracek, and L. Pascale, 1975, "When Stereotypes Hurt: Three Studies of Penalties for Sex-role Reversals," *Journal of Experimental Social Psychology* 11: 520–530; L. A. Jackson and T. F. Cash, 1985, "Components of Gender Stereotypes: Their Implications for Inferences on Stereotypic and Nonstereotypic Dimensions," *Personality and Social Psychology Bulletin* 11: 326–344.

52. Costrich et al., 1975, ibid.

53. Anderson, N. H., 1978, "Progress in Cognitive Algebra," in L. Berkowitz (Ed.), *Cognitive Theories in Social Psychology*, New York: Academic Press.

54. Anderson, N. H., 1973, "Information Integration Theory Applied to Attitudes about U.S. Presidents," *Journal of Educational Psychology* 64: 18–27.

55. Jones, E. E. and G. R. Goethals, 1971, "Order Effects in Impression Formation: Attribution Context and the Nature of the Entity," in E. Jones, D. Kanouse, H. Kelley, R. Nisbett, S. Valins, and B. Weiner (Eds.), *Attribution: Perceiving the Causes of Behavior*, Morristown, NJ: General Learning Press.

56. Hendrick, C. and A. F. Constantini, 1970, "Effects of Varying Trait Inconsistency and Response Requirements of the Primacy Effect in Impression Formation," *Journal of Personality and Social Psychology* 15: 158–164.

57. Tetlock, P. E., 1983, "Accountability and the Perseverance of First Impressions," *Social Psychology Quarterly* 46: 285–292.

58. Miller, N. and D. T. Campbell, 1959, "Recency and Primacy in Persuasion as a Function of the Timing of Speeches and Measurements," *Journal of Abnormal and Social Psychology* 59: 19–29.

59. Kahneman, D. and A. Tversky, 1973, "On the Psychology of Prediction," *Psychological Review* 80: 237–251.

60. Hamill, R., T. E. Wilson, and R. E. Nisbett, 1980, "Insensitivity to Sample Bias: Generalizing from Atypical Cases," *Journal of Personality and Social Psychology* 39: 578–589.

61. Ginossar, Z. and Y. Trope, 1987, "Problem Solving in Judgment Under Uncertainty," *Journal of Personality and Social Psychology* 52: 464–474.

62. Locksley, A., C. Hepburn, C. Ortiz, and V. Ortiz, 1982, "Social Stereotypes and Judgments of Individuals: An Instance of the Base Rate Fallacy," *Journal of Experimental Social Psychology* 18: 23–42.

63. Grant, P. R. and J. G. Holmes, 1981, "The Integration of Implicit Personality Theory, Schemas and Stereotype Images," *Social Psychology Quarterly* 44: 107–115.

64. Locksley, A., E. Borgida, N. Brekke, and C. Hepburn, 1980, "Sex Stereotypes and Social Judgment," *Journal of Personality and Social Psychology* 39: 821–831.

65. Berndt, T. J. and K. A. Keller, 1986, "Gender Stereotypes and Social Inferences: A Developmental Study," *Journal of Personality and Social Psychology* 50: 889–898.

66. Berman, J. S. and D. A. Kenny, 1976, "Correlational Bias in Observer Ratings," *Journal of Personality and Social Psychology* 34: 263–273.

67. Troiler, T. K. and D. L. Hamilton, 1986, "Variables Influencing Judgments of Correlational Relations," *Journal of Personality and Social Psychology* 50: 879–888.

68. Slusher, M. P. and C. A. Anderson, 1987, "When Reality

Monitoring Fails: The Role of Imagination in Stereotype Maintenance," *Journal of Personality and Social Psychology* 52: 653–662.

69. Rosch, E., 1978, "Principles of Categorization," in E. Rosch and B. B. Lloyd (Eds.), *Cognition and Categorization*, Hillsdale, NJ: Lawrence Erlbaum.

70. Epstein, S. and L. Terapulsky, 1986, "Perception of Cross-situational Consistency," *Journal of Personality and Social Psychology* 50: 1153–1160; J. D. Mayer and G. H. Bower, 1986, "Learning and Memory for Personality Prototypes," *Journal of Personality and Social Psychology* 51: 473–492; D. S. Weiss and G. A. Mendolsohn, 1986, "An Empirical Demonstration of the Implausibility of the Semantic Similarity Explanation of How Trait Ratings are Made and What They Mean," *Journal of Personality and Social Psychology* 50: 595–601.

71. Cantor, N. and W. Mischel, 1979, "Prototypicality and Personality: Effects on Recall and Personality-Impressions," *Journal of Research in Personality* 13: 187–205.

72. Fiske, S. T., 1982, "Schema Triggered Affect: Applications to Social Perception," in M. S. Clark and S. T. Fiske (Eds.), *Affect and Cognition: The 17th Annual Carnegie Symposium on Cognition*, Hillsdale, NJ: Lawrence Erlbaum.

73. Bond, C. F., Jr. and D. R. Brockett, 1987, "A Social Context-Personality Index Theory of Memory for Acquaintances," *Journal of Personality and Social Psychology* 52: 1110–1121.

74. Stephan, W. G., 1985, "Intergroup Relations," in G. Lindzey and E. Aronson (Eds.), *Handbook of Social Psychology*, 3d ed., Cambridge, MA: Addison-Wesley.

75. Tunnell, G., 1981, "Sex Role and Cognitive Schemata: Person Perception in Feminine and Androgynous Women," *Journal of Personality and Social Psychology* 40: 1126–1136.

76. Ross, 1978, op. cit.; L. Ross, S. Greene, and P. House, 1977, "The False Consensus Effect: An Egocentric Bias in Social Perception and Attribution Processes," *Journal of Experimental and Social Psychology* 13: 279–301.

77. Shields, J. M. and H. Schuman, 1976, "Public Beliefs about the Beliefs of the Public," *Social Psychology Quarterly* 40: 427–448.

78. Wylie, R., 1979, *The Self Concept*, Vol. 2, Lincoln: University of Nebraska Press.

79. Weinstein, N. D. and E. Lachendro, 1982, "Egocentrism as a Source of Unrealistic Optimism," *Personality and Social Psychology Bulletin* 8: 195–200; N. D. Weinstein, 1980, "Unrealistic Optimism about Future Events," *Journal of Personality and Social Psychology* 39: 806–820.

80. College Board, 1977, "Student Descriptive Questionnaire," Princeton, NJ: Educational Testing Service, cited in D. G. Myers, 1983, *Social Psychology*, New York: McGraw-Hill.

81. Cross, P., 1977, "Not Can but Will College Teaching Be Improved?" *New Directions in Higher Education* 17: 115.

82. Bargh, J. A., R. N. Bond, W. J. Lombardi, and M. E. Tota, 1986, "The Additive Nature of Chronic and Temporary Sources of Construct Accessibility," *Journal of Personality and Social Psychology* 50: 869–878.

83. Markus, H. and G. Long, cited in H. Markus and J. Smith, 1982, "The Influence of Self Schemas on the Perception of Others," in N. Cantor and J. Kihlstrom (Eds.), *Personality, Cognition, and Social Interaction*, Hillsdale, NJ: Lawrence Erlbaum.

84. Schofield, J. W., 1981, "Complementary and Conflicting Identities: Images and Interaction in an Interracial School," in S. Asher and J. Gottman (Eds.), *The Development of Friendship: Description and Intervention*, Cambridge, MA: Cambridge University Press.

85. Jemail, J. A. and J. Geer, 1976, "Sexual Scripts," in R. Gemme and C. Wheeler (Eds.), *Progress in Sexology*, New York: Plenum.

86. Bruner, J. S. and R. Taguiri, 1954, "The Perception of People," in G. Lindzey (Ed.), *Handbook of Social Psychology*, Vol. 2, 1st ed., Cambridge, MA: Addison-Wesley; D. J. Schneider, 1973, "Implicit Personality Theory: A Review," *Psychological Bulletin* 79: 294–309; T. Newcomb, 1931, "An Experiment Designed to Test the Validity of a Rating System," *Journal of Educational Psychology* 22: 279–289.

87. Shweder, R. A., 1982, "Fact and Artifact in Trait Perception: The Systematic Distortion Hypothesis," in B. Maher (Ed.), *Progress in Experimental Personality Research*, Vol. 2, New York: Academic Press.

88. Asch, S. E., 1946, "Forming Impressions of Personalities," *Journal of Abnormal and Social Psychology* 41: 258–290.

89. Wishner, T., 1960, "Reanalysis of Impressions of Personality," *Psychological Review* 67: 96–112.

90. Thorndike, E. L., 1920, "A Constant Error in Psychological Ratings," *Journal of Applied Psychology* 4: 25–29.

91. Skowronski, J. J. and D. E. Carlston, 1987, "Social Judgment and Social Memory: The Role of Cue Diagnosticity in Negativity, Positivity, and Extremity Biases," *Journal of Personality and Social Psychology* 52: 689–699; D. E. Carlston, 1980, "The Recall and Use of Traits and Events in Social Inference Processes," *Journal of Experimental Social Psychology* 16: 303–329.

92. Skowronski and Carlston, 1987, ibid.

93. Wiggins, J. S., 1980, "Circumplex Models of Interpersonal Behavior," in L. Wheeler (Ed.), *Review of Personality and Social Psychology*, Vol. 1, Beverly Hills, CA: Sage.

94. Gifford, R. and B. O'Connor, 1987, "The Interpersonal Circumplex as a Behavior Map," *Journal of Personality and Social Psychology* 52: 1019–1026.

95. Snyder, M. and S. W. Uranowitz, 1978, "Reconstructing the Past: Some Cognitive Consequences of Person Perception," *Journal of Personality and Social Psychology* 36: 941–950.

96. Two studies have failed to replicate this finding for reasons that remain unclear. They are F. S. Belleza and G. H. Bower, 1981, "Person Stereotypes and Memory for People," *Journal of Personality and Social Psychology* 41: 856–865, and L. F. Clark and S. B. Woll, 1981, "Stereotype Biases: A Reconstructive Analysis of Their Role in Reconstructive Memory," *Journal of Personality and Social Psychology* 41: 1061–1072.

97. Lingle, J. H. and T. M. Ostrom, 1979, "Retrieval Selectivity in Memory-based Impression Judgments," *Journal of Personality and Social Psychology* 37: 180–194.

98. Higgins, E. T. and G. King, 1981, "Accessibility of Social Constructs: Information Processing Consequences of Individual and Contextual Variability," in N. Cantor and J. Kihlstrom (Eds.), *Personality, Cognition, and Social Interaction,* Hillsdale, NJ: Lawrence Erlbaum.

99. Dutta, S., R. N. Kanungo, and V. Friebergs, 1972, "Retention of Affective Material: Effects of Intensity of Affect on Retrieval," *Journal of Personality and Social Psychology* 23: 64–80.

100. Isen, A. M., T. W. Shalker, M. Clark, and L. Karp, 1978, "Affect, Accessibility of Material in Memory, and Behavior: A Cognitive Loop," *Journal of Personality and Social Psychology* 36: 1–12.

CHAPTER 10

Attitudes and Attitude Change

Defining Attitudes

The Functions of Attitudes

The Measurement of Attitudes

Attitude-Behavior Consistency

Reasons for Inconsistencies

LaPiere's Classic Study

Attitude Change Based on Cognitive Factors

Cognitive Dissonance Theory

Self-Perception Theory

Attitude Change Induced by Persuasive Communications

Type of Communicator

Type of Communication

Type of Audience

Problems with the Communicator/Message/Audience Approach

The Elaboration Likelihood Model

In the last few years, a new and deadly disease has shaken the world—AIDS (Acquired Immune Deficiency Syndrome). In this country, between one and two million people are AIDS virus carriers. Of those carrying the virus, all may eventually contract the disease. AIDS is probably fatal in 100% of its cases.

In the United States, most of those who have contracted AIDS have been exposed to the AIDS virus through sexual contact or intravenous drug use. Sexual partners can protect themselves against AIDS by using condoms, and drug users can protect themselves by using clean needles.

Although some homosexuals and heterosexuals have eagerly embraced "safe sex," others have not. In a recent news interview, one of your authors heard students from Stanford University interviewed regarding their current sexual practices. While all the students interviewed were aware of the severity of the AIDS problem and believed any sexually active person in a nonmonogamous relationship is at risk for AIDS, none of them were planning to take precautions against AIDS. As one student said, "I only sleep with my friends. They'd tell me if they were sick."

In a second set of California interviews, several intravenous drug users said they still share needles with other users. Most of the drug users interviewed understand that they are greatly increasing their changes of contracting AIDS by this practice. Some said they now only share needles with people they know. Why does their behavior not better reflect the concern these drug users have about AIDS? How can the attitudes and behaviors of the students and drug users be so discrepant in this life or death matter? How could one persuade them to bring their behavior in line with their attitudes?

In December 1978, a U.S. congressman investigated a religious cult called the Peoples Temple at Jonestown, Guyana. As they attempted to leave Jonestown, the congressman, three newsmen, and one cult defector were murdered. After these murders, the leader of the cult, the Reverend Jim Jones, delivered a speech instructing his followers to commit suicide. He told them outside forces were coming to destroy their community, and they must commit "revolutionary suicide" to show their devotion to the cult. Jones expounded on the "beauty of dying" and the tortures that would await cult members by the Guyanese army if they did not commit suicide. Although some of Jones's followers appeared to have been murdered by others, nearly 90 percent of his followers voluntarily drank cyanide mixed with a fruit drink. Nurses and parents first squirted the liquid into the mouths of infants and then drank it themselves. How could any speech—no matter how emotional—convince people that life was no longer worth living?

In this chapter we will take up the issues that these incidents raise—attitude-behavior consistency, attitude measurement, and attitude change—as well as others. The individual-level study of attitudes and attitude change has fascinated social psychologists from sociology and psychology, and both disciplines have contributed to our knowledge of the role of attitudes in our lives.

Social psychologists believe attitudes play a pivotal role in people's lives. Stop for a moment and think about the importance of attitudes in your own life. They determine your choice of friends and dates, your leisure activities, your decision to enter college, your choice of major, and your ultimate life goals.

In the first section of this chapter, we will define attitudes, examine the functions attitudes serve, the ways attitudes are measured, and discuss the extent to which attitudes can be used to predict behavior. The remainder of the chapter is devoted to an examination of conditions under which attitude change occurs.

■

DEFINING ATTITUDES

In 1928, one of the first attitude theorists defined attitudes as general evaluations held by people about themselves, others, objects, and issues (1). Of what are attitudes composed? Many social psychologists believe attitudes have three components: cognitive, affective, and behavioral.

The *cognitive component* of an attitude concerns ideas and beliefs about the object or person in question. The *affective component* of an attitude involves feelings and emotions about the object or person. The *behavioral component* consists of tendencies toward action involving the attitude object or person. For example, let's take the attitude, "I love hot fudge sundaes," and examine its various components. The cognitive component of this attitude might consist of ideas such as, "Hot fudge sundaes are a pleasant combination of hot and cold." The affective component includes liking the taste and textures of hot fudge sundaes. Finally, the behavioral component consists of the person's inclinations to eat hot fudge sundaes.

■
THE FUNCTIONS
OF ATTITUDES

Attitudes fulfill the functions of understanding, need satisfaction, ego defense, and value expression (2). By *understanding* we mean that attitudes help us comprehend our world and make sense of what is happening around us. Our attitudes provide a consistent framework for interpreting day-to-day events. For example, without attitudes about how the political process works, even a single political occurrence (Senator Saenz opposes the president's tax bill) would be unintelligible. Since people's attitudes about politics differ, their understanding of such a single political event also differs. For instance, supporters and detractors of the president will interpret opposition to his or her tax bill differently. Whatever the individual's attitudes are, they help them organize and interpret incoming information.

The second function of attitudes, *need satisfaction,* occurs because our attitudes help us to fulfill important goals. Our attitudes have often been formed from past experiences with rewards and punishments. We develop positive attitudes toward ideas and events associated with past rewards and negative attitudes toward ideas and events associated with past punishments. These attitudes help us meet our goals of gaining rewards and avoiding punish-

■ *One function of attitudes is need satisfaction. Here, maintaining the right to bear arms is an important goal. (WGS)*

■ *Another function of attitudes is value expression. (WGS)*

ments. For example, individuals who have always excelled at sports and have received benefits from playing sports, such as praise, high status with their peers, and scholarship support, are likely to have positive attitudes toward sports participation. These positive attitudes will occur not only because of past rewards, but also because the individuals anticipate that further sports participation will continue to bring them rewards.

The third function of attitudes is *ego defense*. All of us use our attitudes to bolster our self-esteem and defend our egos against criticism. For instance, we may hold the attitude that mathematical abilities are important because we have skills in that area, and holding this attitude makes us feel good about ourselves. Or we may defend ourselves against our boss' criticism of our job performance by telling ourselves that our performance is fine, but that the boss is a creep who is impossible to please. While these attitudes may reflect reality—we may really be good at math and the boss may actually be a creep—they may also deviate from reality. We might believe that our mathematical abilities are much greater than they really are, and we might excuse our poor job performances by blaming our bosses.

The fourth function of attitudes is *value expression*. Attitudes help us convey the type of person we are—what we like and dislike, what we support and oppose, and how we define ourselves. Our attitudes toward politics, what goals are important in life, and even leisure activities and clothes are means by which we present ourselves to others. A person who supports conservative politics, believes that all abortions should be illegal, and supports school prayer is displaying very different values and presents himself or herself as a very different person from one who believes in a liberal ideology, thinks that abortion should be legal, and strongly believes that school prayer is a violation of the separation of church and state.

■

THE MEASUREMENT OF ATTITUDES

Attitudes are commonly measured in one of two ways, by Likert scales or semantic differential scales. Likert scales measure the extent of agreement with a statement of opinion (3). One example of such a statement is, "I believe marijuana should be legalized." The extent of agreement would be measured by a scale such as the following: strongly agree, slightly agree, neither agree nor disagree, slightly disagree, strongly disagree.

Semantic differential scales measure a concept on a series of items designed to tap three attitude dimensions: evaluation, measuring the dimension of positivity vs. negativity; potency, measuring the dimension of strength vs. weakness; and activity, measuring the dimension of activity vs. passivity (4). Each dimension is measured by at least two items. Evaluation is measured by bipolar scales such as good-bad and positive-negative. Potency is measured by scales such as weak-strong and light-heavy. Activity is measured by scales such as exciting-boring and fast-slow. All three attitude dimensions are usually applied to a concept (the President). However, in some cases not all the dimensions are relevant to a concept (potency and activity to describe the issue of legalizing marijuana). In such a case, only the dimensions relevant to the concept are measured.

While these methods work well for attitudes that people will admit to holding, not all attitudes are of this nature. Many people hold attitudes they are reluctant to divulge because they are unpopular (I think communism is a good thing), socially undesirable (I think foreign immigrants should go back to their home countries), or deal with private matters (I like to engage in sex with multiple partners). Box 10-1 illustrates one solution to the problem of measuring attitudes to which people are reluctant to admit.

■

ATTITUDE-BEHAVIOR CONSISTENCY

If we know a person's attitudes does this mean we can predict his or her behaviors? If attitudes do not predict behaviors, then their importance in understanding people has been overestimated. Social psychologists have attempted to answer this question for decades, amid considerable controversy. On the basis of the most recent findings, the answer to this question is a qualified yes, to a certain extent attitudes do predict behavior. Many studies show correlations of $+.30$ to $+.50$ between attitudes and behavior (remember that a correlation of $+1.00$ represents a perfect positive correlation) (7). Thus, attitudes do not perfectly predict behavior, but they predict it well enough to be quite useful in understanding people's behaviors.

Reasons for Inconsistencies

Why are attitudes and behaviors imperfectly correlated? Social psychologists have suggested a number of different reasons for this inconsistency (8):

1. Situational constraints on individuals' behaviors may make it difficult for them to behave in ways that reflect their attitudes. In many situations our behaviors are more a reflection of others' behaviors and expectations than of our own attitudes. You may dislike formal gatherings, but agree to attend a family reunion to avoid disagreements with your relatives.

   The consistency of individuals' attitudes and behaviors is also determined by the extent to which their behaviors are public. Your attendance at the reunion will be determined in large part by whether your absence will be noticed.

2. Cultural and historical constraints also exist. In another culture, you may engage in behaviors that are at variance with your attitudes; for example, eating beef intestines, even though you are sure you will not like them, because these behaviors are expected in that culture.

3. Behaviors are multi-determined—determined by more than a single attitude. Jim, who dislikes roses, may buy them for Marti because she likes them, or because they are inexpensive relative to many other suitable gifts, or because Jim simply needs a present and the roses are readily available. An individual who is not very religious may attend church for the opportunities to meet people, to satisfy family demands, or because of the lovely music played there.

4. The attitudes in question may not have been assessed adequately, so the individual's actual

BOX 10-1

The Bogus Pipeline as a Measure of "True" Attitudes

Social psychologists have long known that experimental subjects are reluctant to reveal their true feelings on some issues. On sensitive issues people are tempted to give socially desirable responses they do not actually feel (expressing positive attitudes regarding groups different from one's own, denying deviant thoughts and actions). The *bogus pipeline* is a technique developed to measure attitudes on such socially sensitive issues (5).

In this technique, experimenters convince people they have physiological equipment that can measure their inner feelings. It is called the bogus pipeline because subjects believe the experimenters have a "pipeline" to their true feelings, but in fact, the equipment is bogus. In such a situation, people give less socially desirable (and presumably more accurate) responses because they believe their physiological responses will expose any lies.

In a study demonstrating the use of this technique, subjects were asked to complete a test. The experimenter said he had selected the test because no one could have seen or heard of it before, and thus the responses to it would be completely unbiased (6). Just before entering the experimental setting, all subjects were approached by a confederate, who presented himself as the previous subject. The confederate told each subject he had just taken a test and done poorly on it, and most of the correct options were the B options.

The way in which the test was administered provided the independent variable. One third of the subjects were led to believe the experimenters made physiological readings of their emotions (bogus pipeline condition) while they took the written test; one third of the subjects completed the written test alone; and one third of the subjects gave oral responses to the experimenter.

The dependent variable consisted of questions regarding whether the subject had previous information about the test and, if so, the source of this information. As predicted, more subjects in the bogus pipeline condition confessed to prior knowledge of the test and to the source of this knowledge (58 percent) than did subjects in either the written (9 percent) or oral response (10 percent) conditions. That is, subjects who believed the bogus pipeline would show they were lying told the truth more than those who believed they could get away with lying about their prior information regarding the test.

Other types of sensitive attitudes have been measured with the bogus pipeline, including attitudes toward women's rights and minorities. ■

attitudes are at variance with what they are thought to be. If you conduct a poll and ask Jennifer if she favors candidate Johnson or candidate Chung for the mayor's race, you will probably expect her to vote for the candidate she names. However, she may actually vote for a write-in candidate whom you did not mention.

Similarly, a behavior may be atypical of the individual's usual behaviors and thus may be a poor indicator of his or her overall behaviors. You may find that a friend of yours, who believes it is important to exercise one's right to vote, failed to vote in the last election. If you conclude that her attitudes regarding voting are inconsistent with her behavior, you may be wrong. She may have voted in 15 of the last 16 elections, whereas you examined her behavior on only the last one. Multiple measures should be taken of both attitudes and behaviors because a single measure of either may not be a good indicator of the "true" attitude or typical behavior.

5. If attitudes and behaviors are not measured closely in time, changes in attitudes may occur, leading to a seeming discrepancy between the two. Polls taken six months before elections are much less reliable than polls taken immediately before elections because voters frequently change their minds about candidates during political campaigns.

6. Attitudes and behaviors need to be measured at the same level of specificity. If I ask you, "Do you like rock music?" and then determine whether you attend the next rock concert in your city, I should not expect too much consistency between your attitude and your behavior. In this example, the attitude is measured at a much broader and more general level than the behavior. However, if I determined whether you ever went to rock concerts, I should find much more attitude-behavior consistency.

In a study of students' attitudes and behaviors toward the environment, the researchers found no relationship between a measure of attitudes toward preservation of the environment and three specific behaviors: recycling reusable materials and signing two petitions about the environment (9). The researchers had expected no relationship between the global attitude measure and the specific behavioral measures.

7. Attitude-behavior consistency is dependent in part on the accessibility of the attitude in memory. An accessible attitude is more likely to guide behavior than an inaccessible attitude (10). In a study of the 1984 presidential elections, attitudes toward the candidates and subsequent votes in the election were measured (11). Accessibility was measured by latency of response to an inquiry regarding attitudes. Subjects were asked to press one of five buttons expressing extent of agreement or disagreement with the attitude object as quickly as possible. The shorter the time before response to the item, "A good president for the next 4 years would be Ronald Reagan (Walter Mondale)," the more likely the respondent's subsequent vote was consistent with the expressed attitude. That is, the more accessible the attitude, the more consistent it was with the behavior.

Attitudes formed on the basis of behavioral experience with the object of the attitude are more accessible than those that are not because behaviors strengthen the association of the object or issue in question and the attitude (12). Thus, attitudes based on past behaviors are more closely related to future behaviors than attitudes based on nonbehavioral experience.

The study of attitudes regarding preservation of the environment mentioned above also demonstrated this effect (13). A week after the global measure of environmental attitudes was completed students were asked to list past behaviors they had engaged in and their beliefs about environmental preservation. Students were divided into three groups on the basis of the number of past behaviors and beliefs they listed. For students with the greatest number of past behaviors and beliefs relevant to environmental preservation, past beliefs and behaviors strongly predicted current behaviors. These students were the most likely to perform preservation behaviors. In contrast, for students with the fewest number of past behaviors and beliefs relevant to environmental preservation, past beliefs and current behaviors were unrelated to their preservation behaviors.

Individual differences exist in the influence of behavioral experience on attitude-behavior consistency. The current attitudes of individuals who have been consistent in their past behaviors on the issue in question are better predictors of their future behaviors than the attitudes of individuals whose behavior has been inconsistent on this issue in the past. An explanation for this finding is that we infer our attitudes from our behaviors, as hypothesized by the self-perception theory (see Chapter 4 and the next section of this chapter for discussions of self-perception theory). In this explanation, then, behaviors cause attitudes, rather than attitudes causing behaviors.

People who are high in self-awareness and low in self-monitoring (see Chapter 4 for discussions of these topics) also show high consistency between their attitudes and behaviors (14). Highly self-aware people think about the implications of their actions; low self-monitors try always to behave in accordance with their beliefs.

8. In Chapter 1, we discussed the *theory of reasoned action,* which is the most complete explanation for attitude-behavior inconsistencies. The theory of reasoned action allows us to understand the associations of behaviors, behavioral intentions

Figure 10.1 ■

The Theory of Reasoned Action

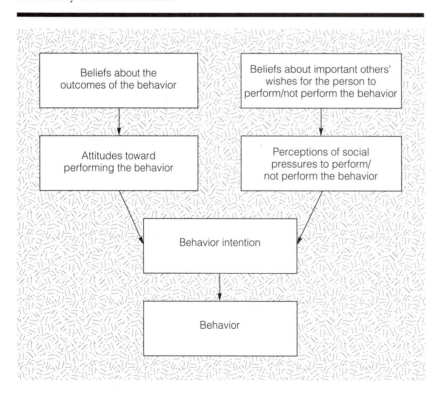

■ *Up in smoke. Most smokers believe smoking is a health hazard. But, our behaviors are not always consistent with our attitudes. (WGS)*

(intentions to engage in a certain behavior), attitudes (positive or negative evaluations toward a person or object), and beliefs (feelings of certainty about an issue or event) (15). According to this theory, beliefs about the outcomes of a given behavior determine attitudes toward the behavior, while beliefs about important others' wishes with respect to the behavior determine perceptions of social pressures to perform the behavior. Attitudes toward the behavior and perceptions of social pressures to perform the behavior determine behavioral intentions. Behavioral intentions are the immediate determinants of behaviors (see Figure 10-1).

This theory was supported in a study of women smokers (16). First, beliefs influenced attitudes and perceptions. Women who believed smoking had only mildly negative consequences and many positive consequences had more positive attitudes toward smoking than women who believed smoking had only strong, negative consequences. Women who believed they were

under strong normative pressure not to smoke were more likely to hold the attitude that they should respect these pressures than were women who believed they were under less strong normative pressure not to smoke.

Second, attitudes and perception of social pressures influenced behavioral intentions. Those women holding more negative attitudes toward smoking and firmer attitudes toward respecting normative pressures not to smoke were less likely to intend to smoke in the next month.

Third, behavioral intentions influenced behaviors; 93 percent of the women behaved in the manner they intended with respect to smoking.

LaPiere's Classic Study

A study conducted by Richard T. LaPiere in 1934 was the first to try to measure attitude-behavior discrepancy (17). Considerable prejudice against Asian-Americans existed in the United States in the 1930s. In the study, a Caucasian investigator traveled cross-country with an Asian-American couple. The trio received service in virtually all hotels and restaurants where they stopped. After the trip, the investigator wrote to each establishment asking if reservations for Asian-Americans were accepted. Most replied that they would not accept Asian-Americans.

For 30 years this study was thought to be a classic demonstration of attitude-behavior discrepancy, but more recently researchers have argued that there are other explanations for these findings.

First, this is not a study of attitudes and behaviors, but rather of *behavior* and *behavioral intentions*. Therefore, this study does not show an attitude-behavior discrepancy, but a behavior-behavior intention discrepancy.

Second, many of the above explanations for attitude-behavior inconsistency apply to this case of behavior-behavioral intention:

1. The behavior and the behavioral intention were not measured at the same level of specificity. Because the behavioral intention was measured toward the general category of Asian-Americans at a time when the stereotype of Asian-Americans

was very negative, it is likely the establishments had an image of undesirable individuals when they responded to the letters. But the behavior involved specific Asian-Americans, a couple who spoke excellent English, who, on the basis of clothing, luggage, and transportation, appeared to be wealthy, and who, futhermore, were traveling with a Caucasian. This specific Asian-American couple obviously did not fit the negative stereotype of the Asian-American.

2. The managers may have had little direct experience with Asian-Americans and thus their behavioral intentions may not have been based on experience.

3. The behavior and the behavior intention were not measured closely in time.

4. Behaviors are multi-determined. Serving the couple may have had more to do with the owners' goal of making business profits than with their acceptance of Asian-Americans.

5. The behavior may have reflected situational constraints, such as avoiding an unpleasant confrontation with the couple in the presence of other patrons.

For the remainder of this chapter we will explore the topic of attitude change. We commonly alter our attitudes, either as a result of our own thinking or in response to persuasive communications. We will examine several types of attitude change.

■

ATTITUDE CHANGE BASED ON COGNITIVE FACTORS

In this section we will discuss two theories regarding attitude change that results from the individual's own cognitions or thoughts. While we usually think that our behaviors stem from our attitudes, both these theories reverse the causal sequence and argue

that our attitudes stem from our behaviors. These two theories are cognitive dissonance theory and self-perception theory.

Cognitive Dissonance Theory

Cognitive consistency theories make the assumption that people try to appear consistent in their attitudes and behaviors both to themselves and to others. One such theory, Leon Festinger's theory of cognitive dissonance, applies to any situation in which people experience inconsistency among their attitudes, beliefs, or behaviors (18). According to this theory, three relationships can exist between any two cognitions (attitudes, beliefs, or thoughts about behaviors):

1. Cognitions may be irrelevant to each other. Cognitions are irrelevant if they have no implications for each other (I like orchids and I consider myself to be a good driver).

2. Cognitions may be consistent or consonant. Cognitions are consonant if they are logically consistent or consistent with the person's past experience or his or her self-perceptions (I consider myself to be a good driver and I have never had a traffic accident).

3. Cognitions may be inconsistent or dissonant (I consider myself to be a good driver and I was just given a ticket for reckless driving). Cognitions are dissonant when they are logically inconsistent or when they are incompatible with the person's past experience or his or her self-perceptions.

People wish to appear consistent to themselves and others. As a result, cognitive dissonance is an unpleasant state of tension that people are motivated to reduce. The more important the dissonant cognitions are to the individual, the greater is the magnitude of dissonance experienced. Dissonance can be lessened by reducing the number or importance of dissonant cognitions or increasing the number or importance of consonant cognitions. A common way of eliminating dissonant cognitions is to change one of the dissonant elements, either by attitudinal or behavioral change. I can reduce the dissonance I feel about my driving record by not driving recklessly or by coming to view myself as a bad driver.

A person only experiences cognitive dissonance when the person perceives himself or herself to have *freely taken* an action that produces or has the possibility of producing a *foreseeable negative consequence* (19). If you tell a white lie to a friend (Yes, I like your new shoes), you are unlikely to experience dissonance because the lie has no likely negative consequences. However, if you tell an important lie to a friend (No, I didn't tell your secret to anyone), you are likely to experience dissonance because the lie has several likely negative consequences—you will feel bad about the indiscretion and the lie, and if your friend finds out you lied, you may lose a valued friend.

Insufficient justification   If we can find sufficient external reasons for our dissonant cognitions (My boss might fire me if I told him what I really thought about his idea; Even though I'm a pacifist, I was paid a lot of money for working in the defense industry) we should experience no cognitive dissonance. In the absence of sufficient external justifications for dissonant cognitions (no punitive boss, no huge salary) we have *insufficient justification* for dissonant cognitions. Insufficient justification frequently leads to cognitive dissonance. In such a case, we attempt to resolve this dissonance by finding internal justifications for their behaviors. Often this entails changing our attitudes to be consonant with our behavior. (I must have liked the idea a little; I must somewhat support the concept of national defense).

Dissonance studies examining insufficient justifications have found surprising results. For instance, if you told a lie for a small reward, you will come to believe the lie more than if you told the lie for a large reward. Similarly, if you choose to fast even though your justification for doing so is weak, you will experience less hunger and eat less at the end of the fast than if you have a strong justification for the fast. Why should these effects occur?

Dissonance theorists reason that individuals who perform attitude-discrepant behaviors with sufficient justification (a large reward) have a ready-made reason for this behavior: They did it for the reward. The high level of reward keeps the dissonance about the inconsistency at a minimum. But individuals who perform attitude-discrepant behaviors for an insufficient justification (a small reward) have no such ready-made reason for the discrepancy. Thus, they experience high levels of dissonance. Since it is difficult to deny one's behavior, these individuals typically reduce dissonance by changing their attitudes to be consonant with their behaviors.

In a classic study demonstrating the insufficient justification effect, subjects were asked to work on an extremely boring task for one hour (20). Afterward, the experimenter told the subjects he was studying task perception as a function of the type of introduction to the tasks. The experimenter then asked the subjects if each would tell the subject waiting in the next room the task was very interesting. Half of the subjects were offered $1 (insufficient justification condition) for telling the lie, and the other half were offered $20 (sufficient justification condition). All subjects agreed to tell the lie, even though they had just completed the task and knew that it was very boring.

Finally, all subjects were asked to rate their enjoyment of the task. Who do you think liked the task more, the subjects paid $1 or those paid $20? The results showed that subjects who were paid $1 for telling the lie rated the task as more interesting than subjects who were paid $20 for telling the lie! The study was originally interpreted as follows: Subjects who were paid $20 to tell the lie had sufficient justification for, and thus little dissonance associated with, the lie. They might have been thinking something like "I told a lie but I had two good reasons for doing so. I was paid $20 and I helped science." Since they had little dissonance to reduce, these subjects were able to perceive the task accurately—as extremely boring. However, those who were paid $1 to tell the lie had insufficient justification for, and thus considerable dissonance associated with, the lie. They were probably thinking something like "I told a lie and it was for only $1. Am I really the kind of person who can be bought for a mere dollar?" To reduce this dissonance, they perceived the task to be much less boring than the other subjects, thus creating consonance by turning the "lie" into the truth.

However, subsequent research has shown that this interpretation is itself insufficient. In a replication and extension of the original insufficient justification study, students were paid $1 for telling a lie (21). Half of the students liked the other person to whom they told a lie, and half did not like the person. Half of the other persons in each liking condition acted as though they were convinced by the student's lie and half were not. Students who believed they had convinced the person they liked experienced dissonance, which they resolved by increasing their liking for the task. However, students who convinced a person they did not like, and students who did not convince a person (liked or disliked) did not experience dissonance, and thus did not change their liking for the task. Thus, it is not telling a lie that produces dissonance, but telling a lie to a *liked person* who *believed* the lie.

This study shows that only when a freely taken action produces, or has the possibility of producing, a foreseeable negative consequence is dissonance created. If the person does not believe the lie, little harm has been done by it. If a disliked person believed the lie, the liar is not troubled by it. Only when a liked person has successfully been deceived does the liar feel a potential negative consequence will ensue (My friend will be angry with me for the lie; My friend will be confused by my lie; My friend will think I'm an idiot excited by dull tasks).

The insufficient justification effect has also been shown in a series of studies in which subjects were induced to write counterattitudinal essays—essays that argued against the subjects' true beliefs. The less money the subjects were given for writing the essay, the *more* they came to believe in the counterattitudinal position (22).

The importance of free choice in creating dissonance has also been demonstrated using this design. When subjects were not given a choice about writing the essay, but were told to do so, dissonance

was not produced (23). Under these latter circumstances the results demonstrated the effect of reward: the more money given, the *greater* the attitude change in favor of the counterattitudinal position.

The insufficient justification effect is most striking when it involves physiological states, specifically, hunger (24) and thirst. Subjects asked to go without water for insufficient justification (This is just a pretest and we don't know if anything will come of it) feel less thirst and drink less water when allowed to do so than subjects for whom sufficient justification exists (This study is a part of important scientific work) (25). The insufficient justification effect has even been found in situations in which individuals experience pain, where insufficient justification results in the denial of pain (26).

Another type of justification effect has been found when effort is expended. In one study, female subjects were told they would be admitted to a discussion group dealing with the psychology of sex, but only if they passed a screening test (27). Half of the subjects were required to pass a mild test requiring little effort, while the other subjects were required to pass a severe test requiring great effort. The subjects then listened to an extremely boring discussion, which they were told was the first group discussion. Finally all the subjects were asked to rate the discussion and the participants on a variety of measures.

The investigators anticipated that subjects who had expended low effort would have little reason to perceive the discussions in a distorted manner; engaging in low effort for a negative outcome should produce only a low level of dissonance. In contrast, they expected that subjects who had expended high effort would experience dissonance between the cognition that they had expended considerable effort to get into the discussion group and the cognition that the group was not worth the effort.

The subjects in the high-dissonance condition were expected to reduce dissonance by perceiving the discussion and the participants more positively than the discussion warranted. These expected results were obtained; subjects in the high-effort condition rated the discussion and the participants more positively than subjects in the low-effort condition.

Recent interpretations of these findings suggest that the dissonance was not created simply by the two inconsistent cognitions, but by the fact that they had created negative consequences. In this case, the subject thought she would have to attend a very boring set of group discussions she had expended great effort to join.

Post-decisional dissonance Dissonance is also produced when an individual must make a decision between two desired alternatives (which of two cars you will buy). Dissonance is greater, the greater the similarity in the attractiveness of the alternatives. Once the decision is made, thinking about the negative aspects of the chosen alternative and the positive aspects of the nonchosen alternative produce dissonance. Dissonance is resolved in this situation by reevaluating the alternatives, coming to see the chosen alternative as much better than the nonchosen alternative.

In the first demonstration of this effect, women were told they could take home one small appliance if they would help rate a number of appliances for a market research company (28). After the women had made their ratings, they were given a choice between two appliances. In the low-dissonance condition, the subject had rated one of these appliances much higher than the other. In the high-dissonance condition, the subject had rated both the appliances highly. The women then made their selections, and were asked to re-rate the appliances. As expected, the women in the high-dissonance condition rated the chosen appliance higher and rated the nonchosen appliance lower than in the first ratings. In contrast, the ratings given by the women in the low-dissonance condition differed only slightly from the previous ratings.

Self-Perception Theory

Daryl Bem's self-perception theory offers an alternative to the dissonance explanation concerning why behaviors cause attitudes (29). As we saw in Chapter 4, self-perception theory states that individuals infer their own attitudes in the same way they infer others' attitudes: by observing their own behaviors. This effect occurs when internal cues (strong emotional reactions, reminders of one's attitude) regarding the attitude are weak. Under these conditions people observe their own behaviors and make inferences about their attitudes on the basis of these observed behaviors. Self-perception theorists believe it is unnecessary to posit a negative arousal state, such as dissonance, to account for the behaviors of subjects in the insufficient justification experiments. They believe subjects merely observe their behaviors during these experiments and make inferences about their attitudes on the basis of them, just as they do in other situations.

Self-perception theory has been used to reinterpret the results of the insufficient justification studies. Self-perception theorists argue that subjects in the sufficient justification condition have sufficient reason to engage in the action: receiving a large reward or avoiding a large punishment. In this situation subjects thus infer that their behaviors are designed to gain the rewards or to avoid the punishments. For subjects in the insufficient justification condition, however, a small reward or a small punishment is not sufficient reason for the action; thus, subjects infer they engaged in the behaviors because they believed in them.

When applied to the $1/$20 lie experiment, the self-perception explanation says that subjects in the insufficient reward condition observed themselves making a statement for $1 and inferred that the statement must be true, since $1 is not sufficient reason for lying. In contrast, subjects in the sufficient reward conditions observed themselves making a statement for $20 and believed that the statement was a lie since $20 is sufficient justification for telling a little white lie for science.

Since people infer that they perform acts for the rewards they receive for doing so, the self-perception theory thus suggests that people who are rewarded for acts they enjoy will lose interest in them. As we saw in Chapter 4, considerable evidence supports the proposition that overjustification undermines intrinsic motivation (30), *except when* the reward is a recognition of excellence at the task (31).

In a study showing the importance of lack of internal cues in the overjustification effect, children

Do Attitudes Influence Behavior or Does Behavior Influence Attitudes?

As we have just seen, cognitive dissonance theory and self-perception theory reverse the traditional position that attitudes influence behavior, stating instead that behavior influences attitudes. Which of these positions is correct? Based on statistical analyses that allow for the simultaneous measurement of the influence of attitudes on behaviors and of behaviors on attitudes, both views appear to be valid.

The direction of attitude-behavior influence has been investigated using the attitudes of high school males regarding aggression toward teachers and the actual aggressive behaviors they directed toward their teachers (36). The aggression included minor but common occurrences, such as being rude and argumentative with teachers. The mutual influence of the students' attitudes toward self-control and aggressive behaviors directed at teachers was also examined. The results varied by type of attitude (attitudes regarding self-control or aggression). The effect of aggressive behaviors on attitudes toward self-control was as strong as the effect of attitudes toward self-control on aggressive behaviors. However, the effect of aggressive attitudes on aggressive behaviors was stronger than the effect of aggressive behaviors on aggressive attitudes. (See Figure 10-2).

Further analyses suggested that people infer their attitudes from their behavior to the extent that the behavior is deviant. That is, if the males behaved in a conventionally nonaggressive manner toward teachers, they were less likely to infer attitudes from this behavior than if they behaved in an atypically aggressive manner toward teachers. This finding is consistent with the correspondent inference theory's

were asked to draw a picture with magic markers (32). Half the children were offered candy for doing so (the overjustification condition), and the other half were not (the intrinsic motivation condition). Half of the children in the reward and nonreward conditions were reminded they liked to draw with magic markers by being shown a photograph of

themselves drawing with magic markers that had been taken a week or two before (strong internal cues condition), while half were not shown a photograph (weak internal cues condition).

The self-perception effect should only occur when internal cues are weak. The investigator thus hypothesized that the rewarded children reminded

analysis of the importance of unique events in attributional inferences, discussed in Chapter 9. That is, actions are more informative if most people would not have performed them. Thus, an unusually aggressive manner yields more information about the student than a typically nonaggressive manner. ■

Figure 10.2 ■

Strength of Attitude-Behavior Associations for Attitudes toward Aggression and Self-Control and Aggressive Behaviors

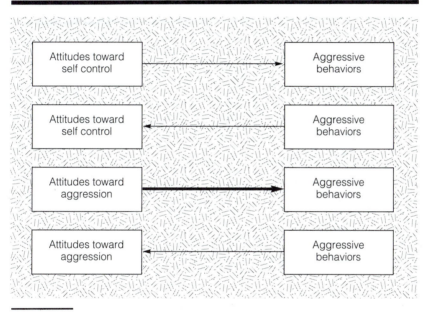

The width of the line connotes the strength of the relationship.

of their interest in drawing should not need to use self-perception to infer their attitudes: The drawing should remind them. However, the rewarded children not shown their photographs were expected to turn to self-perception of their behaviors to interpret their attitudes. These children should infer they were drawing the picture for the reward.

After the children all drew a picture they were then observed at play for 15 minutes to see how much of the time they drew with magic markers and how much of the time they played with other available toys. As expected, the reward decreased intrinsic interest only when the children had not been reminded of their liking for drawing. As can

Table 10.1 ■

Mean Proportion of Free-play Time Spent
Drawing with Magic Markers

Salience of initial attitude	Given reward	Not given reward
High (photograph)	.338	.160
Low (no photograph)	.058	.262

Data from Fazio, R. H. 1981, "On the Self-perception Explanation of the Overjustification Effect: The Role of Salience of Initial Attitude," *Journal of Experimental Social Psychology* 17:417–426.

be seen in Table 10-1, the children in the rewarded/not reminded condition played with the magic markers in the free play time significantly less than children in the other three conditions.

Attempts to choose between the cognitive dissonance and the self-perception explanations of attitude formation have produced considerable research, but ambiguous results. Recent findings support the dissonance theory contention that individuals who act without sufficient justification experience negative arousal (33). This negative or dissonant state leads to attitude change. Further, when this negative state is misattributed to a factor other than the attitude-behavior inconsistency (the effects of a drug), attitude change does not occur (34).

At present, it seems likely that both theories are useful, but that each applies to a separate domain of behavior. It appears that cognitive dissonance is aroused when individuals act without sufficient justification in a manner *opposed* to their prior opinions, as in the insufficient justification studies cited above (telling a lie for only $1). However, self-perception theory better accounts for behaviors occurring when individuals act without sufficient justification in a manner *consistent* with their prior opinions, as in the intrinsic motivation studies discussed previously (drawing pictures when drawing is a pleasant activity).

ATTITUDE CHANGE INDUCED BY PERSUASIVE COMMUNICATIONS

Attitude change can also be induced by persuasion, as well as being provoked by one's own thoughts and actions. How can we use persuasive communications most effectively to change people's attitudes? Advertising agents on Madison Avenue, politicians, and attorneys wish to know the answer to this question. So do ordinary people who want to change society in some way, such as those who wish to change people's attitudes regarding race, and others who simply want to change some small aspect of their social environments, such as their roommates' disapproval of their friends. All of us engage in many attempts to change other people's attitudes. Social psychologists have examined a variety of factors that make influence attempts more or less successful. In this section we will examine some of these factors.

When social psychology was in its infancy after

"We need something catchy that mentions ball bearings six or eight times."

(The Wall Street Journal.)

World War II, a great deal of research on persuasion was devoted to examining factors associated with the communicator, the type of communication, and the type of audience. We will briefly consider the current research on such factors, discuss some problems with this body of research, and present a theory of persuasive communication that reconciles many conflicting results regarding attitude change.

Type of Communicator

Credibility of the communicator A credible communicator is one who is both expert and trustworthy. Credible communicators are typically more persuasive than communicators who are not credible (37). In one study, subjects who had no direct experience with two brands of peanut butter agreed more with a persuasive communication favoring one of the brands given by a market research "taster" who had himself tasted the product than the taster who had only studied the ingredients and other characteristics (shelf life) of the products (38). Speech rate provides another indication of expertise. Rapidly spoken communications are more persuasive than slowly spoken communications, apparently because fast speakers are judged as more credible than slow speakers (39).

One cue that makes a communicator seem trustworthy is arguing against his or her own interests (40). When arguing against one's own interests, the communicator violates the subject's expectancies regarding his or her position. In a persuasive communication setting, a speaker with a strong pro-business commitment was more persuasive and viewed as more unbiased after giving a pro-environmental speech than a speaker with strong pro-environmental interests who gave the same speech (41). Similarly, a speaker giving a pro-environmental speech was more persuasive and viewed as more

■ *Well-known politicians are credible communicators to their followers.* (WGS)

■ *Similar communicators are very persuasive. (WGS)*

unbiased when he was speaking before a pro-business group than when he was speaking before a pro-environmental group.

For persons highly involved with an issue, communicators appear more trustworthy if they do not seem to be trying to persuade (42). Thus, an overheard conversation may be more persuasive than a deliberate advertising pitch.

Sometimes the advantage of the high-credibility source dissipates over time, as people forget the source of the messages they have heard (43). Called the *sleeper effect,* this dissipation occurs because memory for the message is better than memory for the credibility of the speaker (44).

Attractiveness Communicators who are likable are generally more persuasive than those who are not (45). Parallel to the effects of likability, physically attractive communicators are typically more persuasive than physically unattractive communicators (46).

Similarity Communicators who are similar to the audience are often more persuasive than dissimilar ones (47). Similarity of race (48) and level of expertise (49) have resulted in greater attitude change than dissimilarity when the topic of the communication involved values. The attitudes of similar persons often seem more relevant to our attitudes, since we assume that similar others share our values. However, when the topic involves facts, dissimilar others are more persuasive (50). For issues of fact, similar others may share your view of a subject only because they see the world as you do. But you know that dissimilar others do not generally share your view of reality. Thus, a dissimilar other's views may seem more likely to be due to objective facts about the topic than a similar other's views.

Type of Communication

Distraction Distraction when hearing a persuasive communication (asking subjects to complete another task while listening) tends to be associated with increased persuasion (51). Distraction makes it more difficult for subjects to formulate counterarguments to the persuasive communication.

Drawing conclusions Most studies find that attitude change is greater when the communicator draws conclusions for the audience (52). However, people who are involved in the topic are more persuaded by a communication if they must work to draw their own conclusions from it (53).

One-sided versus two-sided arguments If the audience is unaware of viable arguments counter to the position being presented, it weakens the communicator's case to point them out (54). But if the audience knows that other viable arguments exist, failing to present them may lower the communicator's credibility and lead to a negative reaction on the part of the audience.

Inoculation In attitude change research, inoculation involves giving individuals weak arguments that oppose their views in order to strengthen the original views. The name derives from its medical parallel. Just as medical patients are vaccinated with small amounts of disease viruses, such as smallpox, to protect them from contracting the disease, individuals can be inoculated with weak "dosages" of arguments, with which they disagree, to "protect" them from more persuasive arguments (55). The weak arguments spur the subjects to formulate stronger counterarguments that support their original position.

Fear appeals Fear appeals lead to a considerable amount of attitude change (56), but they may or may not lead to behavior change (57). Behavior change appears to be based on three variables: the effectiveness of suggested coping responses in reducing the danger, the probability of the negative consequence, and whether or not the person feels capable of performing the needed defensive behavior (58).

In a study in which essays on the health consequences of cigarette smoking were given to smokers, when any two of the three variables were high, behavioral intentions to quit smoking were highest (59). For example, if subjects read an essay stating the probability of negative health consequences of cigarette smoking was low, their intentions of quitting were higher if the essay also stated that quitting was effective *and* if they believed they could quit.

Type of Audience

Involvement in the issue Some studies have found that involvement in an issue leads to increased resistance to persuasion (60). Involvement is usually measured by the importance of the issue to the audience. But, since knowledge of the issue was associated with involvement in these studies, it is unclear whether it is knowledge or involvement that leads to increased resistance (61).

Discrepancy from the audience's position Many researchers have found an inverted U-shaped effect between discrepancy and attitude change: A communication only slightly discrepant from the audience's position can only produce a small amount of attitude change; a moderately discrepant communication can produce more attitude change; and a highly discrepant communication often backfires, or produces a *boomerang effect,* in which the audience changes in the *opposite* of the intended direction (62).

Other studies have found that the greater the discrepancy, the greater is the attitude change (63). One cause of these differing results appears to be the credibility of the communicator (64). The inverted U-shaped relationship between discrepancy and attitude change is usually found when the communicator has only moderate credibility. Greater attitude change stemming from greater discrepancies is usually found when the communicator is highly credible. Involvement in the issue is also important. When involvement is high, most opinions are unacceptable, so little attitude change is produced. When involvement is low, most opinions are acceptable, and attitude change can be great (65).

An *information integration model* has been proposed that accounts for many conflicting results regarding audience discrepancy (66). It assumes that the impact of persuasive communication generally decreases as discrepancy from the audience's position increases. However, several factors can affect the impact of persuasive communications. One component of impact is the credibility of the communicator, and another is number of messages. Thus, where the communicator is credible and the number of messages is high, more discrepancy produces greater *immediate* attitude change.

The model also predicts that discrepant communications will be forgotten quickly because they are unpleasant. This means that the discrepant communications that produced the greatest short-term attitude change will produce the lowest long-term attitude change because the most unpleasant messages will not be remembered. These predictions were supported in a study of college students' responses to communications advocating a tuition increase (67). Subjects received either one or two communications. Subjects receiving one communication read a recommendation for either a 15 percent or a 50 percent increase. Subjects receiving two communications read one of four sets of communications: two advocating a 50 percent increase; two advocating a 15 percent increase; the first advocating a 50 percent increase and the second, a 15 percent increase; or the first advocating a 15 percent increase and the second, a 50 percent increase.

As can be seen in Figure 10-3, students who received two communications advocating a 50 percent tuition increase showed the most attitude change immediately after the communication, and those who received one communication advocating a 15 percent increase showed the least attitude change. However, by four to eight days after the communication, the conditions in which the subjects were exposed to one or more communication advocating a 15 percent increase showed the greatest attitude change, and those exposed to one or more of the 50 percent arguments showed the least attitude change.

Figure 10.3 ■

Mean Tuition Increase Advocated, Time 1 and Time 2

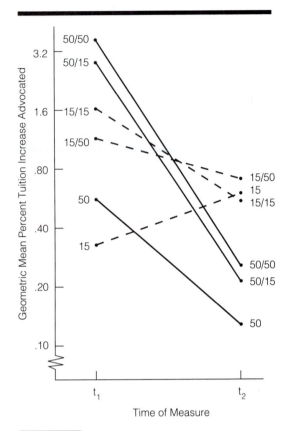

Geometric mean of percentage tuition increase advocated by subjects, by position(s) advocated in experimental message(s) and by time. The *y* axis is logarithmic; equal distance intervals represent equal ratios.

S. A. Kaplowitz, E. L. Fink, G. B. Armstrong, and C. L. Bauer, 1986, "Message Discrepancy and the Persistence of Attitude Change: Implications of an Information Integration Model," *Journal of Experimental and Social Psychology* 22:507–530.

Problems with the Communicator/Message/Audience Approach

We have just presented the information on attitude change based on persuasive communications in the traditional manner: by examining communicator, message, and audience variables. While we have made many generalizations based on these variables, none of the data regarding any given variable are completely consistent (68). Even the best documented relationships (for example, the effect of expertise on persuasibility) are not always found (69). Sometimes communicator expertise has been found to have no effect on persuasion, and sometimes its effect has been negative. In addition, a different explanation has been given for every effect. One goal of science is stated in the *law of parsimony:* A minimum number of variables should explain a maximum number of effects. Thus, the theories explaining the effects of persuasive communication fail to meet the ideals of science in two respects: They are only moderately accurate, and they are not parsimonious.

A recent theory, the elaboration likelihood model, seems to resolve many of the discrepancies in the persuasion literature and to explain a number of the above effects with one causal model (70). Since this model both increases accuracy of prediction and is parsimonious, it appears to be an important improvement in our understanding of persuasive communications.

The Elaboration Likelihood Model

The *elaboration likelihood model* attempts to explain the conditions under which people will elaborate or scrutinize the arguments in a message and think about them. This model argues that the amount and nature of issue-relevant elaboration varies with individual and situational factors.

According to the elaboration likelihood model, attitude change takes place through either a central or a peripheral route. Persuasion takes place through the *central route* if the person is motivated and capable of thinking through arguments. In this situation, where elaboration likelihood is high, the quality of the persuasive communications is a primary determinant of persuasion.

However, if the person is unmotivated or incapable of thinking through arguments, persuasion takes place through the *peripheral route*. In this route, elaboration likelihood is low. Peripheral cues trigger positive or negative emotions, and these emotions become attached to the attitude object. Peripheral cues may include such factors as the communicator's expertise, trustworthiness, attractiveness, or similarity.

A number of factors, such as distraction and the intelligibility of the arguments, influence a person's ability to elaborate or think through the arguments. These factors can either increase and decrease attitude change, depending on whether the individual uses the central or peripheral route.

Personal relevance increases motivation to elaborate the arguments. Assume you hear a speaker argue that a certain make of car is dangerously defective and should be recalled. If you or someone close to you owns one of these cars, you will be motivated to think about the arguments. You are likely to be persuaded or not on the basis of the quality of the arguments. Now assume you know no one who owns one of the allegedly defective cars. In this case your motivation to evaluate them is much lower. You are less likely to go to the trouble of assessing the arguments, and more likely to take a cognitive "short cut" and quickly form your attitude on the basis of factors such as the speaker's likability or credibility. Subjects hearing an argument that a new graduation requirement should be immediately instituted at their university were influenced by the quality of the arguments (71). Subjects hearing an argument that a new graduation requirement should be instituted at their university in ten years were influenced by peripheral cues such as the expertise of the speaker.

Variables such as distraction and the intelligibility of the message influence persuasion by enhancing or reducing the ability to think about issue-relevant arguments. If you are not willing to think about a message, distraction will not interfere with your

■ *Is attitude change in this busy airport based on argument quality or peripheral cues such as fear appeals? (WGS)*

thoughts. If you are able or willing to process information, the effect of distraction is dependent upon message strength. Distraction increases attitude change when the messages are weak, but decreases it when they are strong. When arguments are weak, distraction inhibits the ability to generate the counterarguments that would typically be made, so attitude change will increase. When arguments are strong, distraction inhibits the ability to process the favorable arguments, so attitude change is inhibited.

In one study, subjects heard an argument that tuition should be increased on their campus. The argument contained several weak messages (more trees need to be planted on campus) or several strong messages (the library needs more books) while they were distracted by a task that required them to monitor a screen and record on which quadrant of the screen a series of Xs appeared. The

distraction led to *increased* acceptance of the weak argument because it was difficult for the subjects to think of opposing arguments (72). However, the distraction led to *decreased* acceptance of the strong argument because the task made it more difficult for the subjects to consider the positive aspects of the argument. Thus, distraction inhibits the ability to process arguments, with the result that stronger arguments are less effective and weaker ones are more effective than if distraction were not present.

People are sometimes motivated to engage in biased processing of arguments. This desire often stems from a person's knowledge regarding the topic: People are typically motivated to defend their own initial attitudes. Forewarning of the message content or of the persuasive intent of the communication increases the motivation to defend an attitude, and thus increases the likelihood of biased processing for people with initial attitudes on the topic.

When people are forewarned of the content of a persuasive communication concerning a topic about which they are knowledgeable, this forewarning allows them to begin considering information that would support their beliefs. Thus, the likelihood of biased elaboration is enhanced. In a study demonstrating this effect, subjects were exposed to a communication in favor of requiring all freshmen and sophomores to live on campus (73). Half of the subjects were warned of the topic several minutes before the lecture, while the other half were not. The results showed that the forewarned subjects were not persuaded by the message, while the other subjects were influenced by it.

Attitudes reached through the central route are more resistant to change than those reached through the peripheral route because the former are based on careful consideration of the issues. Attitudes reached through the central route are also more likely to be consistent with behaviors than those reached through the peripheral route.

The two routes to attitude persuasion are shown in Figure 10-4. To summarize the model, any communication variable can have multiple outcomes:

1. When elaboration is highly likely, attitudes are affected mostly by the quality of the persuasive arguments. For example, when elaboration is highly likely, the expertise of the communicator should be unimportant to attitude change. Here, good arguments should produce more attitude change than poor arguments.

2. When elaboration is unlikely, attitudes are influenced mostly by peripheral cues. If a variable acts as a peripheral cue, the stronger the variable, the greater the attitude change.

Figure 10.4 ■

Central and Peripheral Routes to Persuasion

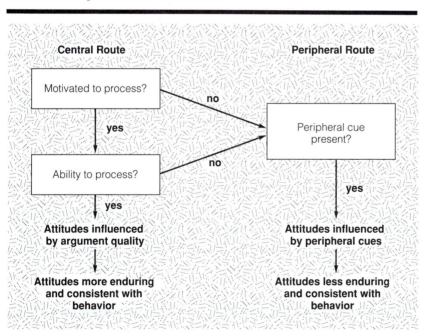

Adapted from R.E. Petty and J.T. Cacioppo, 1986, "The Elaboration Likelihood Model of Persuasion," in L. Berkowitz (Ed.), *Advances in Experimental Social Psychology*, Vol. 19, New York: Academic Press.

Cults and Persuasive Communications

By the end of the 1970s, more than three million Americans had joined one of over 1,000 religious cults operating in the United States. Sociologists are particularly interested in the means by which young people are persuaded to join them. Consider one ex-member's description of the Love Family, one religious cult:

There was no possibility of seeing or understanding what was really happening . . . the propaganda was always being drummed into us. Their beliefs and information came at us from outside, and there was never any time to sift through it. There was never any time to step back and look at it and see if any of it fit together. The Family would always say, "What's inside your mind is lies. We are your mind. The group is your mind" (74).

Cults typically seek to isolate new recruits from the world at large. Once the recruit has been cut off from the outside world, the cult members take a variety of steps to ensure that the recruit will not return to it. Initiation into the cult usually involves a change of appearance that sets the recruit apart from those in the outside world. The recruit's clothes and money may be taken. In many cults, the recruit receives a new name, and new definitions of "love" and "family" are taught so that care, concern, and communication are confined only to those who are cult members. Parents may be viewed as Satan's agents.

While some people claim that cults use hypnosis or brainwashing, many cult researchers believe their methods are the simple techniques of persuasive com-

3. Message processing can be relatively objective or biased. Biased information processing favors the retention of the original attitude.

The elaboration likelihood model thus provides a single explanatory theory for the persuasive communication literature and resolves inconsistencies in research findings. It explains why quality of persuasive arguments is important in determining attitude change in some situations and unimportant in others. It also explains why peripheral cues

(experimenter expertise, attractiveness, similarity, trustworthiness) sometimes are important in promoting attitude change and other times have no effects.

The model points out the importance of the ability and motivation to think through arguments and makes it clear why variables such as personal relevance of the issue and distraction influence attitude change. Also, by explaining that thinking about persuasive arguments can be done in either a relatively objective or biased manner, the model

munication that all of us use (75). In a situation where many communicators seek to influence only one audience member, it is not surprising that the results should be more dramatic than in more ordinary communication situations where one communicator seeks to influence many audience members. New recruits are bombarded from all sides with appeals to join the group. This type of communication assault is distracting, making it difficult to think through issues. In addition, the recruit is given little actual information about the group's beliefs. Commitment is often made in the absence of relevant information.

Because cognitive information processing is not allowed to take place, peripheral cues take on importance. The cult leader is high in status and viewed as an expert. Initially, cults often appeal to the similarity of the cult members to the recruit, and to common values. Conclusions are drawn and redrawn in a situation where the recruit has no opportunity for independent thought. No chance for inoculation exists: Recruits are presented with strong arguments against beliefs they have always taken for granted (one should love one's parents). Fear appeals are used; recruits are told the world is destroying itself and the cult can save it. The suggested means of coping with the problem is joining the work of the cult. Most important, the members are subjected to an unending barrage of forceful and one-sided persuasion attempts in a situation where opposing information is not available. The result is that cognitive information processing is minimal.

Many of these factors were probably involved in the decision by members of the People's Temple at Jonestown to commit suicide at the command of their leader, Jim Jones. Jones was a high status, attractive, and expert person, relative to his followers. The followers were in Guyana, cut off from their family and friends in California. Jones persuaded them to commit suicide by telling them that their community was being destroyed, and their lives would only gain meaning from their suicides. In his speech, Jones drew conclusions for the members, used one-sided arguments, and fear appeals. In this situation, cognitive information processing was largely peripheral. Without other sources of information, and rushed into the decision, most followers chose to take their lives. ∎

makes clear the process through which such variables as forewarning can have their effect. Box 10-3 demonstrates an extreme example of peripheral route persuasion.

■
SUMMARY

Attitudes consist of our likes and dislikes. They contain three components: cognitive, affective, and behavioral. Attitudes imperfectly predict behavior; the two are not perfectly correlated for many reasons. These include situational, cultural, and historical constraints on behavior, the multiple causes of behavior, imperfect measurement of attitudes or behaviors, change over time in attitudes, differences between reactions to general classes of objects and specific objects, and inaccessibility of the attitude in memory.

The theory of reasoned actions specifies the relationships between beliefs, attitudes, behavior intentions, and behaviors. According to this theory, beliefs influence attitudes, attitudes influence behavior intentions, and behavior intentions influence behaviors.

Attitude change can be produced through one's own thoughts or cognitions. According to the cognitive dissonance theory, dissonance is an unpleasant state leading to activity that will reduce the dissonance. Dissonance is produced when a person perceives having freely taken an action that produces, or has the possibility of producing, forseeable negative consequences. Insufficient justification for the actions or being forced to make a decision between two attractive alternatives causes dissonance. It can be reduced by eliminating or reducing the importance of dissonant cognitions or by adding or increasing the importance of consonant cognitions.

Self-perception theory provides an alternative explanation to dissonance theory for the effects of insufficient justification. According to the self-perception theory, the consequences of insufficient justification can be explained without reference to a negative state such as dissonance. Self-perception theorists believe that subjects merely observe their behaviors and make inferences about their attitudes on the basis of them. Subjects who engage in a behavior for insufficient justification infer that they must believe in what they are doing. Subjects who engage in a behavior for sufficient justification infer that they are doing so for the extrinsic reward.

We examined various factors that induce attitude change through persuasive communications, including factors related to the type of communicator, the type of communication, and the type of audience. Three factors associated with the type of communicator were discussed: the credibility of the communicator, his or her attractiveness, and the similarity of the communicator and the audience. Four issues involving the type of communication were discussed: distraction, one-sided versus two-sided communications, inoculation, and fear appeals. The influence of the type of audience has been studied by examining two issues: the audience's involvement in an issue, and the discrepancy of the persuasive communication from the audience's position.

Unfortunately, none of the data are as clear as they might be. While the above effects tend to occur, none of the data are completely consistent. Even the best documented relationships are not always found. A recent theory may prove to resolve many of the discrepancies in the persuasion literature and explain a number of the above effects in one causal model.

According to the elaboration likelihood model, attitude change takes place through one of two routes, a central or a peripheral route. Persuasion takes place through the central route if the person is motivated to elaborate on or think through arguments, in which case the quality of the persuasive communications is a primary determinant of persuasion. However, if the person is not motivated to think through arguments, persuasion takes place through the peripheral route. In this route, peripheral cues trigger positive or negative emotions.

Attitudes reached through the central route are more resistant to change than those reached through the peripheral route because they have been based on careful consideration of the issues. Attitudes reached through the central route are also more likely to be consistent with behaviors than attitudes reached through the peripheral route.

As motivation or ability to elaborate on arguments decreases, peripheral cues become relatively more important determinants of persuasion. Personal relevance enhances motivation to elaborate on arguments. Enhancing motivation to process a message in an objective manner can lead to either increased or decreased scrutiny of the persuasive arguments. Biased processing often results from a person's initial attitude because people are typically motivated to defend their initial attitudes.

■

REFERENCES

1. Thurstone, L. L., 1928, "Attitudes Can Be Measured," *American Journal of Sociology* 33:529–544.
2. Katz, D., 1960, "The Functional Approach to the Study of Attitudes," *Public Opinion Quarterly* 24:163–204.
3. Likert, R., 1932, "A Technique for the Measurement of Attitudes," *Archives of Psychology,* whole no. 142.
4. Osgood, C. E., G. J. Suci, and P. H. Tannenbaum, 1957, *The Measurement of Meaning,* Urbana, IL: University of Illinois Press.

5. Jones, E. E. and H. Sigall, 1971, "The Bogus Pipeline: A New Paradigm for Measuring Affect and Attitude," *Psychological Bulletin* 76:349–364.

6. Quigley-Fernandez, B. and J. T. Tedeschi, 1978, "The Bogus Pipeline as Lie Detector: Two Validity Studies," *Journal of Personality and Social Psychology* 36:247–256.

7. Hill, R. J., 1981, "Attitudes and Behavior," in M. Rosenberg and R. H. Turner (Eds.), *Social Psychology: Sociological Perspectives,* New York: Basic Books; H. Schuman and M. P. Johnson, 1976, "Attitudes and Behavior," *Annual Review of Sociology* 2:161–208.

8. Ajzen, I. and M. Fishbein, 1977, "Attitude-Behavior Relations: A Theoretical Analysis and Review of Empirical Research," *Psychological Bulletin* 84:888–918; S. Chaiken and C. Stagnor, 1986, "Attitudes and Attitude Change," in L. Berkowitz (Ed.), *Advances in Experimental Social Psychology,* Vol. 19, New York: Academic Press; I. Deutscher, 1966, *What We Say/What We Do,* Glenview, IL: Scott, Foresman; Schuman and Johnson, 1976, ibid.; A. W. Wicker, 1969, "Attitudes versus Actions: The Relationship of Verbal and Overt Behavioral Responses to Attitude Objects," *Journal of Social Issues* 25:755–765.

9. Kallgren, C. A. and W. Wood, 1986, "Access to Attitude-relevant Information in Memory as a Determinant of Attitude-Behavior Consistency," *Journal of Experimental Social Psychology* 22:328–338.

10. Fazio, R. H., 1986, "How Do Attitudes Guide Behavior?" in R. M. Sorrentino and E. T. Higgins (Eds.), *The Handbook of Motivation and Cognition: Foundations of Social Behavior,* New York: Guilford; R. H. Fazio, M. C. Powell, and P. M. Herr, 1983, "Toward a Process Model of the Attitude-Behavior Relations: Accessing One's Attitude upon Mere Observation of the Attitude Object," *Journal of Personality and Social Psychology* 44:723–735.

11. Fazio, R. H. and C. J. Williams, 1986, "Attitude Accessibility as a Moderator of the Attitude-Perception and Attitude-Behavior Relations: An Investigation of the 1984 Presidential Election," *Journal of Personality and Social Psychology* 51:505–514.

12. Fazio, 1986, op. cit.; R. H. Fazio and M. P. Zanna, 1981, "Direct Experience and Attitude-Behavior Consistency," in L. Berkowitz (Ed.), *Advances in Experimental Social Psychology,* Vol. 14, New York: Academic Press.

13. Kallgren and Wood, 1986, op. cit.

14. Fazio, R. H., D. M. Sanbonmatsu, M. C. Powell, and F. R. Kardes, 1986, "On the Automatic Activation of Attitudes," *Journal of Personality and Social Psychology* 50:229–238; Fazio and Williams, 1986, op. cit.; T. D. Wilson and D. S. Dunn, 1986, "Effects of Introspection on Attitude-Behavior Consistency: Analyzing Reasons versus Focusing on Feelings," *Journal of Experimental Social Psychology* 22:249–263.

15. Fishbein, M. and I. Ajzen, 1975, *Belief, Attitude, Intention, and Behavior: An Introduction to Theory and Research,* Reading, MA: Addison-Wesley.

16. Fishbein, M., 1982, "Social Psychological Analysis of Smoking Behavior," in J. R. Eiser (Ed.), *Social Psychology and Behavioral Medicine,* Chichester: John Wiley.

17. LaPiere, R. T., 1934, "Attitudes vs. Actions," *Social Forces* 13:230–237.

18. Festinger, L., 1957, *A Theory of Cognitive Dissonance,* Stanford, CA: Stanford University Press.

19. Cooper, J. and R. H. Fazio, 1984, "A New Look At Dissonance Theory," in L. Berkowitz (Ed.), *Advances in Experimental Social Psychology,* Vol. 17, New York: Academic Press.

20. Festinger, L. and J. M. Carlsmith, 1959, "Cognitive Consequences of Forced Compliance," *Journal of Abnormal and Social Psychology* 58:203–210.

21. Cooper, J., M. P. Zanna, and G. R. Goethals, 1974, "Mistreatment of an Esteemed Other As a Consequence Affecting Dissonance Reduction," *Journal of Experimental Social Psychology* 10:224–233.

22. Cohen, A. R., 1962, "An Experiment on Small Rewards for Discrepant Compliance and Attitude Change," in J. W. Brehm and A. R. Cohen (Eds.), *Explorations in Cognitive Dissonance,* New York: Wiley; J. M. Rabbie, J. W. Brehm, and A. R. Cohen, 1959, "Verbalization and Reactions to Cognitive Dissonance," *Journal of Personality* 27:407–417.

23. Linder, D. E., J. Cooper, and E. E. Jones, 1967, "Decision Freedom as a Determinant of the Role of Incentive Magnitude in Attitude Change," *Journal of Personality and Social Psychology* 6:245–254.

24. Brehm, M. L., K. W. Back, and M. D. Bogdonoff, 1964, "A Physiological Effect of Cognitive Dissonance under Stress and Deprivation," *Journal of Abnormal and Social Psychology* 69:303–310.

25. Brehm, J. W., 1962, "Motivational Effects of Cognitive Dissonance," in M. R. Jones (Ed.), *Nebraska Symposium on Motivation,* Lincoln: University of Nebraska Press; H. H. Mansson, 1969, "The Relation of Dissonance Reduction to Cognitive, Perceptual, Consummatory, and Learning Measures of Thirst," in P. G. Zimbardo (Ed.), *The Cognitive Control of Motivation,* Glenview, IL: Scott, Foresman.

26. Zimbardo, P. G., A. R. Cohen, M. Weisenberg, L. Dworkin, and I. Firestone, 1969, "The Control of Experimental Pain," in P. G. Zimbardo, ibid.

27. Aronson, E. and J. Mills, 1959, "The Effects of Severity of Initiation on Liking for a Group," *Journal of Abnormal and Social Psychology* 59:177–181.

28. Brehm, J. W., 1956, "Post-decision Changes in Desirability of Alternatives," *Journal of Abnormal and Social Psychology* 52:384–389.

29. Bem, D. J., 1967, "Self Perception: An Alternative Interpretation of Cognitive Dissonance Phenomena," *Psychological Review* 74:183–200; R. H. Fazio, 1986, "Self-perception Theory: A Current Perspective," in M. P. Zanna, E. T. Higgins, and C. P. Herman (Eds.), *Social Influence: The Ontario Symposium,* Vol. 5, Hillsdale, NJ: Erlbaum.

30. Deci, E. L., 1975, *Intrinsic Motivation,* New York: Plenum; E. L. Deci and R. M. Ryan, 1985, *Intrinsic Motivation and Self-determination in Human Behavior,* New York: Plenum.

31. Boggiano, A. K. and D. S. Main, 1986, "Enhancing Children's Interest in Activities Used as Rewards: The Bonus Effect,"

Journal of Personality and Social Psychology 51:1116–1126; W. D. Crano, D. W. Gorenflo, and S. L. Shackelford, 1988, "Overjustification, Assumed Consensus, and Attitude Change: Further Investigation of the Incentive-aroused Ambivalence Hypothesis," *Journal of Personality and Social Psychology* 55:12–22.

32. Fazio, R. H., 1981, "On the Self-perception Explanation of the Overjustification Effect: The Role of Salience of Initial Attitude," *Journal of Experimental Social Psychology* 17:417–426.

33. Croyle, R. and J. Cooper, 1983, "Dissonance Arousal: Physiological Evidence," *Journal of Personality and Social Psychology* 45:782–792; R. H. Fazio and J. Cooper, 1983, "Arousal in the Dissonance Process," in J. T. Cacioppo and R. E. Petty (Eds.), *Social Psychophysiology,* New York: Guilford.

34. Higgins, E. T., F. Rhodewalt, and M. P. Zanna, 1979, "Dissonance Motivation: Its Nature, Persistence, and Reinstatement," *Journal of Experimental Social Psychology* 15:16–34; F. Rhodewalt and R. Comer, 1979, "Induced Compliance Attitude Change: Once More with Feeling," *Journal of Experimental Social Psychology* 15:35–47.

35. Fazio, R. H., M. P. Zanna, and J. Cooper, 1977, "Dissonance and Self-perception: An Integrative View of Each Theory's Proper Domain of Application," *Journal of Experimental Social Psychology* 13:464–479.

36. Liska, A. E., R. B. Felson, M. Chamlin, and W. Baccaglini, 1984, "Estimating Attitude-Behavior Reciprocal Effects within a Theoretical Specification," *Social Psychology Quarterly* 47:15–23.

37. Hass, C. I., 1981, "Effects of Source Characteristics on Cognitive Responses and Persuasion," in R. E. Petty, T. M. Ostrom, and T. C. Brock (Eds.), *Cognitive Responses in Persuasion,* Hillsdale, NJ: Erlbaum; C. I. Hovland, I. L. Janis, and H. H. Kelley, 1953, *Communication and Persuasion,* New Haven, CT: Yale University Press; W. J. McGuire, 1985, "Attitudes and Attitude Change," in G. Lindzey and E. Aronson (Eds.), *The Handbook of Social Psychology,* 3d ed, Cambridge, MA: Addison-Wesley.

38. Wu, C. and D. R. Shaffer, 1987, "Susceptibility to Persuasive Appeals as a Function of Source Credibility and Prior Experience with the Attitude Object," *Journal of Personality and Social Psychology* 52:677–688.

39. Miller, N., G. Maruyama, R. J. Beaber, and K. Valone, 1976, "Speed of Speech and Persuasion," *Journal of Personality and Social Psychology* 34:615–624.

40. Eagly, A. H., W. Wood, and S. Chaiken, 1978, "Causal Inferences about Communicators and Their Effect on Attitude Change," *Journal of Personality and Social Psychology* 36:424–435; E. Walster, E. Aronson, and D. Abrahams, 1966, "On Increasing the Persuasiveness of a Low Prestige Communicator," *Journal of Experimental Social Psychology* 2:325–342.

41. Eagly, Wood, and Chaiken, 1978, ibid.

42. Papageorgis, D., 1968, "Warning and Persuasion," *Psychological Bulletin* 70:271–282.

43. Gruder, C. L., T. D. Cook, K. M. Hennigan, B. R. Flay, C. Alessis, and J. Halamaj, 1978, "Empirical Tests of the Absolute Sleeper Effect Predicted from the Discounting Cue Hypothesis," *Journal of Personality and Social Psychology* 36:1061–1074; C. I. Hovland, A. A. Lumsdaine, and F. D. Sheffield, 1949, *Experiments on Mass Communication,* Princeton, NJ: Princeton University Press.

44. Pratkanis, A. R., A. G. Greenwald, M. R. Leippe, and M. H. Baumgardner, 1988, "In Search of Reliable Persuasion Effects: III. The Sleeper Effect is Dead, Long Live the Sleeper Effect," *Journal of Personality and Social Psychology* 54:203–218.

45. McGuire, 1985, op. cit.

46. Chaiken, S., 1979, "Communicator Physical Attractiveness and Persuasion," *Journal of Personality and Social Psychology* 37:752–766; K. K. Dion and S. Stein, 1978, "Physical Attractiveness and Interpersonal Influence," *Journal of Experimental Social Psychology* 14:97–108.

47. Simons, H. W., N. N. Berkowitz, and R. J. Moyer, 1970, "Similarity, Credibility, and Attitude Change: A Review and a Theory," *Psychological Bulletin* 73:1–16.

48. Aronson, E. and B. Golden, 1962, "The Effect of Relevant and Irrelevant Aspects of Communicator Credibility on Opinion Change," *Journal of Personality* 30:135–146; T. M. Dembroski, T. M. Lasater, and A. Ramirez, 1978, "Communicator Similarity, Fear Arousing Communications, and Compliance with Health Care Recommendations," *Journal of Applied Social Psychology* 8:254–269.

49. Brock, T. C., 1965, "Communicator-Recipient Similarity and Decision Change," *Journal of Personality and Social Psychology* 1:650–654.

50. Goethals, G. R. and E. R. Nelson, 1973, "Similarity in the Influence Process: The Belief-Value Distinction," *Journal of Personality and Social Psychology* 25:117–122.

51. Allyn, J. and L. Festinger, 1961, "The Effectiveness of Unanticipated Persuasive Communications," *Journal of Abnormal and Social Psychology* 9:162–166; J. L. Freedman and D. O. Sears, 1965, "Warning, Distraction, and Resistance to Influence," *Journal of Personality and Social Psychology* 1:262–266.

52. Hovland, C. I. and W. Mandell, 1952, "An Experimental Comparison of Conclusion-drawing by the Communicator and by the Audience," *Journal of Abnormal and Social Psychology* 47:581–588; J. T. Klapper, 1960, *The Effects of Mass Communication,* Glencoe, IL: The Free Press.

53. Linder, D. E. and S. Worchel, 1970, "Opinion Change as a Result of Effortfully Drawing a Counterattitudinal Conclusion," *Journal of Experimental Social Psychology* 6:432–448.

54. Hovland et al., 1949, op. cit.; R. A. Jones and J. W. Brehm, 1970, "Persuasiveness of One-sided and Two-sided Communications As a Function of Awareness There Are Two Sides," *Journal of Experimental Social Psychology* 6:47–56.

55. McGuire, W. J., 1964, "Inducing Resistance to Persuasion: Some Contemporary Approaches," in L. Berkowitz (Ed.), *Advances in Experimental Social Psychology,* Vol. 1, New York:

Academic Press; W. J. McGuire and D. Papageorgis, 1961, "The Relative Efficacy of Various Types of Prior-belief Defense in Producing Immunity against Persuasion," *Journal of Abnormal and Social Psychology* 62:327–337.

56. McGuire, 1985, op. cit.; S. R. Sutton, 1982, "Fear Arousal and Communication: A Critical Examination of Theories and Research," in J. Eiser (Ed.), *Social Psychology and Behavioral Medicine,* London: Wiley.

57. Janis, I. L. and S. Feshbach, 1953, "Effects of Fear-arousing Communications," *Journal of Abnormal and Social Psychology* 48:78–92; H. Leventhal, 1970, "Findings and Theory in the Study of Fear Communications," in L. Berkowitz (Ed.), *Advances in Experimental Social Psychology,* Vol. 5, New York: Academic Press.

58. Rogers, R. W., 1983, "Cognitive and Physiological Processes in Fear Appeals and Attitude Change: A Revised Theory of Protection Motivation," in J. Cacioppo and R. E. Petty (Eds.), *Social Psychophysiology,* New York: Guilford; R. W. Rogers, 1975, "A Protection Motivation Theory of Fear Appeals and Attitude Change," *Journal of Personality* 91:93–114; R. W. Rogers and C. R. Mewborn, 1976, "Fear Appeals and Attitude Change: Effects of a Threat's Noxiousness, Probability of Occurrence, and the Efficacy of Coping Responses," *Journal of Personality and Social Psychology* 34:54–61.

59. Rogers and Mewborn, 1976, ibid.

60. Krosnick, J. A., 1988, "Attitude Importance and Attitude Change," *Journal of Experimental Social Psychology* 24:240–255; J. A. Krosnick, 1988, "The Role of Attitude Involvement in Social Evaluation: A Study of Policy Preferences, Presidential Candidate Evaluations, and Voting Behavior," *Journal of Personality and Social Psychology* 55:196–210; N. Miller, 1965, "Involvement and Dogmatism as Inhibitors of Attitude Change," *Journal of Experimental Social Psychology* 1:121–132; M. Sherif and C. I. Hovland, 1961, *Social Judgment: Assimilation and Contrast Effects in Communication and Attitude Change,* New Haven: Yale University Press.

61. Petty, R. E. and J. T. Cacioppo, 1979, "Issue-involvement Can Increase or Decrease Persuasion by Enhancing Message-relevant Responses and Persuasion," *Journal of Personality and Social Psychology* 37:1915–1926.

62. Aronson, E., J. A. Turner, and J. M. Carlsmith, 1963, "Communicator Credibility and Communicator Discrepancy as Determinants of Attitude Change," *Journal of Abnormal and Social Psychology* 67:31–36; S. Bochner and C. Insko, 1966, "Communicator Discrepancy, Source Credibility, and Opinion Change," *Journal of Personality and Social Psychology* 4:614–

621; J. L. Freedman, 1964, "Involvement, Discrepancy, and Opinion Change," *Journal of Abnormal and Social Psychology* 69:290–295.

63. Aronson et al., 1963, ibid.; A. Bergin, 1962, "The Effect of Dissonant Persuasive Communications Upon Changes in a Self-referring Attitude," *Journal of Personality* 30:423–438; Bochner and Insko, 1966, ibid.; Freedman, 1964, ibid.

64. Himmelfarb, S. and A. H. Eagly, 1974, "Orientations to the Study of Attitudes and Their Change," in S. Himmelfarb and A. H. Eagly (Eds.), *Readings in Attitude Change,* New York: Wiley; M. Sherif, 1977, "Crisis in Social Psychology," *Personality and Social Psychology Bulletin* 3:368–382.

65. Leippe, M. R. and R. A. Elkin, 1987, "When Motives Clash: Issue Involvement and Response Involvement as Determinants of Persuasion," *Journal of Personality and Social Psychology* 52:269–278.

66. Kaplowitz, S. A., E. L. Fink, G. B. Armstrong, and C. L. Bauer, 1986, "Message Discrepancy and the Persistence of Attitude Change: Implications of an Information Integration Model," *Journal of Experimental and Social Psychology* 22:507–530.

67. Kaplowitz et al., 1986, ibid.

68. Himmelfarb and Eagly, 1974, op. cit.

69. Himmelfarb and Eagly, 1974, ibid.

70. Petty, R. E. and J. T. Cacioppo, 1986, "The Elaboration Likelihood Model of Persuasion," in L. Berkowitz (Ed.), *Advances in Experimental Social Psychology,* Vol. 19, New York: Academic Press.

71. Petty, R. E., J. T. Cacioppo, and R. Goldman, 1981, "Personal Involvement as a Determinant of Argument-based Persuasion," *Journal of Personality and Social Psychology* 41:847–855.

72. Petty, R. E., G. L. Wells, and R. C. Brock, 1976, "Distraction Can Enhance or Reduce Yielding to Propaganda: Thought Disruption versus Effort Justification," *Journal of Personality and Social Psychology* 34:874–884.

73. Petty, R. E. and J. T. Cacioppo, 1977, "Forewarning, Cognitive Responding, and Resistance to Persuasion," *Journal of Personality and Social Psychology* 35:645–655.

74. Conway, F. and J. Siegelman, 1979, *Snapping: America's Epidemic of Sudden Personality Change,* Philadelphia: Lippincott.

75. Long, T. E. and J. K. Hadden, 1983, "Religious Conversion and the Concept of Socialization: Integrating the Brainwashing and Drift Models," *Journal for the Scientific Study of Religion* 22:1–14.

CHAPTER 11

Attraction

Predispositions to Attraction

Attraction Is Functional

Spatial Proximity

Familiarity

Theories of Attraction

Reinforcement Theories

Balance Theory

Misattribution of Arousal

Being in Love

The Relationship of Liking and Romantic Loving

How Do I Love Thee? Let Me Count the Stages

A Multi-Stage Theory of Love

Relationships' End: Is Breaking Up Really Hard to Do?

Critique of Theories of Romantic Attraction

■ The young couple seemed a perfect match. Both were physically attractive. They had been raised in the same city in similar privileged circumstances. Each had many suitors but perferred only the other. His gallant and daring manner attracted her; her beauty and demureness attracted him. Unfortunately, their parents opposed the match, for he was a Montague and she was a Capulet—families that had been enemies for generations. This opposition only strengthened their love. When the woman's family tried to force her to marry another, she took a sleeping potion to make her intended groom believe she was dead. When her true love saw her in this drugged sleep, he believed she was indeed dead, and he killed himself out of grief. Awakening, the woman found her suitor dead and she, too, killed herself from grief.

■ Tom and Huck shared a number of similarities—they were adventuresome young boys who would rather have fished, swam, and gotten into trouble than go to school. They were thrown into close contact with each other because they were about the same age, and they lived in a small town. As they became more familiar with each other through shared adventures, they became closer friends and they grew even more similar. At Tom's request, Huck even made a second try at living a respectable life as the adopted son of the Widow Douglas. The relationship between the boys was rewarding to both of them, because each provided the other with a spirited partner who knew some things about the world the other did not know. Tom appreciated Huck because he was streetwise; Huck admired Tom's booklearning.

Social psychologists have identified a number of factors that influence our attraction to others. Many of these factors are contained in the classic stories of the love between Romeo Montague and Juliet Capulet and of the friendship between Tom Sawyer and Huckleberry Finn. In this chapter we will examine the factors influencing attraction in these classic fictional stories, include similarity, spatial proximity, familiarity, rewards associated with relationships, competence, physical attractiveness, and parental interference.

Both sociologists and psychologists have been involved in the search at the microsocial level of analysis (see Chapter 2 for a discussion of level of analysis) for the factors that create attraction. As we will see from the theories that follow, social psychologists from virtually every theoretical persuasion believe they understand some of the conditions under which attraction occurs. Social psychologists often take research clues from folk wisdom. In the case of attraction, however, folk wisdom gives contradictory clues. Do birds of a feather flock together or do opposites attract? Does absence make the heart grow fonder or is it really correct to say, "Out of sight, out of mind?"

In this chapter we will discuss three theories that explain why we are attracted to some people but not to others. Then we will turn our focus of attention exclusively to love. We will explore the distinction between liking and loving, examine the development of romantic relationships, and discuss a theory in which the factors influencing attraction are thought to vary across the duration of the relationship. Finally we will discuss factors that cause relationships to end and critique theories of romantic attraction.

Your initial reaction to this focus may be, "This is silly. I like my friends because they are great people. The reason that I have a boyfriend/girlfriend/spouse is that I fell in love with him or her." While we *do* think our friends are great, and mate selection *is* based on love, these facts do not fully explain liking and loving. Our friends and lovers are hardly random choices. All of us "happen" to fall in love with people with certain identifiable characteristics, and we like being around certain types of people more than others.

■
PREDISPOSITIONS TO ATTRACTION

Before we examine the factors that create attraction between people, we will first discuss the benefits of interpersonal attraction and then explore two predisposing conditions of attraction: spatial proximity and familiarity.

Attraction Is Functional

Not only is it fun to like and love others, feeling attracted to others is good for you! As we saw in Chapter 1, one of the founders of sociology, Emile Durkheim, demonstrated the importance of *social integration,* being part of a larger group or community, as protection against suicide. Social integration also protects against divorce. In a study of counties with high and low divorce rates, those counties in which social integration was high had lower rates of divorce than those counties in which social integration was low (1).

Similarly, people with large and/or intimate social networks are healthier, both emotionally and physically (2). A recent study also found that high school students who listed more friends, and students who were listed as friends, more often were found to like school better, were less likely to leave the school at the end of the year, and were thought by the school principals to function better, compared with students who had fewer friendship choices (3).

Close ties with others have a number of other benefits. Friends lessen feelings of isolation and loneliness and provide sources of knowledge about appropriate feelings and actions. They also provide access to people, inside information, and jobs that help to increase our prestige and social status in society.

In summary, attraction is functional. Social integration based on personal ties to others provides a number of benefits, including protection from suicide, divorce, and loneliness, as well as happiness and ease in making life adjustments, and increased social status.

Spatial Proximity

Where did you meet your best friend? . . . your boyfriend/girlfriend/spouse? Spatial proximity, or geographic closeness, is a factor in attraction because we cannot like or love people we never meet. You are unlikely to have close friends in Hong Kong or Budapest because you probably have not met many people from those cities. Many studies demonstrate that spatial proximity is a factor in friendship formation and in romantic pairing (4).

A classic study of friendship formation among married students living in campus housing showed that spatial proximity is important in determining friendships, even within a small area (5). Friendships were more likely to occur among next door neighbors than among people separated by greater distances in the building. Also, the most popular couples in the housing project were those with apartments located where other residents frequently met (near stairs or mailboxes). The principle is simple: The more people you meet, the more people with whom you are likely to make friends. You might want to remember this fact the next time you are asked to select a dorm room, an apartment, or an office.

Spatial proximity is also important in a broader sense. The friends we make, the hobbies we pursue, the work skills we develop, and in fact, much of our sense of self, come into being as a result of spatial proximity to particular others. While we would make friends, pursue hobbies, and develop skills no matter where we lived and worked, many of the specific people that inhabit our lives and the special interests and skills on which we focus are the result of spatial proximity with others in our neighborhoods, work settings, schools, and communities. To provide one of many possible examples, most people meet their future spouses at work, at school, or in the neighborhood, and certainly within the city in which they reside.

Spatial proximity is in part a function of social proximity, and who we meet is in large part a matter of where we are located in the social structure. The social structure serves to bring some people together and to keep others apart. For example, because we meet mostly others of our own race or ethnicity and social class, we are likely to form friendship and love relationships with others that our family and friends consider to be acceptable: those who are like them.

■ *Spatial proximity is a precondition for friendship. We can't like those we don't meet. (WGS)*

Familiarity

Do you usually like your acquaintances better over time? Merely being exposed to people can lead to attraction, even if the exposure does not include social interaction (6). This phenomenon is called the *mere exposure effect*. The more we are around other people, the more we come to like them. One's attraction to others can be increased even by frequent exposure to their photographs or names (7).

In one study demonstrating this effect, male and female college students were shown photographs of an unknown male college student once a week for five weeks. Some were shown the same photograph every week, while others were shown photographs of different persons. At the end of each viewing, the subjects tried to imagine what the person in the photograph was like and then they rated their liking for him. Those who were repeatedly shown the same photograph increased their attraction for the person shown, while the liking ratings of subjects who were shown a different photograph each week remained constant over time.

A clever demonstration of the mere exposure effect used photographs of subjects' own mirror images (the image they saw in a mirror) and photographs of their true images (the image others saw of them). The experimenters reasoned that people would prefer their mirror images to their true images because their mirror images are more familiar to them. They also hypothesized that their friends and dates would prefer their true images to their mirror images because true images are more familiar to the friends (8). Subjects had their photographs taken and then returned to view them with either a same-sex friend or a person they were dating. Both the subject and the friend were asked which of two photos they preferred. One was the subject's true image, while the other showed the mirror image. As predicted, subjects selected their mirror images, while same-sex friends and dates selected the subjects' true images. That is, both the subjects and the friends were more attracted to the familiar image of the subject—the one they were used to seeing.

People regard familiar others as more likable and as more similar to themselves than unfamiliar others (9). Familiarity leads to liking, which in turn leads to perceived similarity. In a study showing the influence of familiarity on perceived similarity, subjects rated strangers whom they thought resembled close friends as more similar in personality to the friends than strangers they did not think resembled close friends (10).

THEORIES OF ATTRACTION

You may be surprised that we are exploring theories of attraction, particularly theories that pertain to those in romantic relationships. We take for granted that the basis for mate selection in this society is love. But while love is said to be a passionate feeling that strikes without premeditation or intent, it does not strike randomly.

If you are somewhat cynical about love, you may also have noticed that while people say they marry for love, it sometimes appears that they marry for other reasons—money, good looks, or to get away from home, to name only a few reasons. In any society, only a limited number of motives are judged appropriate for behavior. We use this accepted *vocabulary of motives* to explain our actions, despite what our real motives may be (11).

The following theories will examine the causal factors that seem to underlie our "falling in love," as well as our liking for others. The many factors associated with attraction can be gathered under three theoretical umbrellas: reinforcement, consistency, and misattribution of arousal.

Reinforcement Theories

Several theoretical perspectives link attraction to the reinforcements—the rewards and punishments—associated with other people. We will examine three such theories: exchange, reinforcement-affect, and a symbolic interactionist reward theory of attraction.

Exchange theory Many theorists feel friendship formation and mate selection provide examples of exchange relationships. (See Chapter 2 for a discussion of exchange theory.) Let's see if you agree. What is your idea of a perfect love relationship? One in which one partner gives 100 percent and the other partner takes 100 percent? Of course not! It is one in which each partner both gives and receives, in which a true exchange of rewards and costs occurs. But deciding what consititutes a fair exchange is somewhat complex, as we shall see.

We will first use marital selection to illustrate exchange. In the past, mates were selected by the couple's families to cement political or economic ties. Today, most young people have freedom of choice in mate selection, and the selection is typically based on love (12). The process of mate selection by the couple involves exchange just as surely as marital selection by the families did. However, the nature of the bargain changed when marital selection passed from family control to control by the couple. From a lifetime exchange, the exchange became an ongoing one in which couples bargain during courtship, over the decision to marry, and throughout the duration of the marriage.

The goal of the exchange remains the same: to strike the best bargain possible (13). Individuals continually assess the rewards and costs they receive in the relationship and compare them with those of their spouses. They may attempt to change the relationship or withdraw from it if they believe the exchange is not fair.

How strongly do individuals in unfair exchange relationships strive for change and consider leaving if attempts at change fail? This depends upon the individuals' perceived alternatives to the current relationship (14). If they have alternatives to the current relationship that are more desirable, they are more likely to leave it than if they believe their alternatives are as undesirable or more undesirable than their current unfair exchange relationship. To complicate matters, because individuals have different needs, the same alternative (leaving the relationship for no relationship) can be perceived as more desirable than the unfair relationship by one individual and as less desirable by another.

Imagine an ideal couple. One person has a great personality, is very physically attractive, and talented. Do you think the other person is likely to be unattractive, untalented, and have a rotten personality? Certainly not! We exchange our positive characteristics for those of others. We tend to like and to fall in love with people with attributes we perceive as positive, and we are liked and loved by those who view our attributes as similarly positive. In addition, we exchange goods and services, such as emotional support, sympathetic advice, and financial help with our friends and lovers.

Perhaps the most eloquent—and cynical!—statement of marriage as an exchange comes from Erving Goffman, who says, "A proposal of marriage in our society tends to be a way in which a man sums up his social attributes and suggests to a woman that hers are not so much better as to preclude a merger or partnership in these matters" (15). The traditional twentieth century marital exchange involves the male's exchange of social status and economic sup-

port for the female's beauty, emotional support, and nurturance. In less traditional exchanges, each partner exchanges attractiveness, social status, and economic and emotional support with the other. This latter type of exchange has become increasingly common as women have entered the labor market, and it will probably continue to increase in popularity in the foreseeable future.

Exchange is also important in the continuation of friendships. For example, an individual's rewards and alternatives to the relationship are important in determining liking between roommates (16) and whether same-sex acquaintances become friends (17).

As we discussed in Chapter 2, power may be unequally distributed in relationships. In our society, men typically have more power in love relationships than women. First, women are more likely than men to have been socialized to equate self-worth with being in a romantic relationship, so the relationship is more valuable to the woman. Second, men's

■ *A woman may exchange beauty for a man's financial security, or both partners may exchange attractiveness, social status, and economic and emotional support with each other. (WGS)*

power in love relationships derives from their greater status, relative to women, in the society. Unromantically, research suggests that the wife's power in a marriage is associated with the proportion of family income she earns (18). Thus, women who work in the labor force typically have more power than housewives.

The effect of unequal power is specified in *the principle of least interest:* The person with the most power has the least to lose if the relationship should end (19). Consequently, the more powerful person can assume more control of the relationship.

Equity. Equity theory is a variant of exchange theory which stresses judgments of fairness in exchange relationships (see Chapter 2 for a discussion of equity theory). Remember that an equitable relationship is one in which each person's input/output ratio is proportional. Each person gets from the relationship what he or she puts into it (20). The relationship does not have to be 50-50. An individual who incurs more costs, but also receives more rewards from the marriage relative to his or her spouse, is likely to find the exchange equitable. But an individual who incurs more costs without receiving more rewards in the relationship is likely to find the exchange inequitable.

Interestingly, people prefer equitable relationships not only to those in which they are underbenefited, but to those in which they are overbenefited. Being overbenefited may sound good at first thought, but it entails costs. It is often accompanied by guilt feelings and by relationship instability—you know at any moment your partner may decide to leave the relationship to seek another one fairer to him or her. If you were taking advantage of a classmate by only pretending to like her because she helped you with your calculus homework, and doing nothing for her in exchange, you would have reason to fear losing her friendship.

Inequity is associated with marital discord and personal unhappiness (21). For example, one study examined the relation of equity to depression. Husbands and wives who perceived equity in the marriage with respect to family roles (the division of housework, cooking, and parenting) were less depressed than those who believed they were over-benefited (did less than their share of the work) or underbenefited (did more than their share of the work) in these roles (22). In another study, perceived inequity in a love relationship was associated with negative emotions such as anger and hurt and with the absence of positive emotions such as respect and confidence (23).

Similarity as exchange: I like me so I like you. The well-known association of attraction and similarity provides one example of exchange. Birds of a feather really do flock together! Does any type of similarity lead to attraction, or do we only prefer individuals who are similar to us in specific ways? You can easily answer this question yourself. Are your friends all your height? Were they all born in the same month as you or in the same town? Do your friends have attitudes and values that are similar to yours? Do they also have personalities similar to yours? While similarity of some characteristics is important to liking, similarity of others may be irrelevant.

Both field studies of acquainted people and laboratory studies of the first impressions of strangers demonstrate that we like others whose attitudes and values are similar to ours (24). One study found that junior high school girls select as friends other junior high school girls whose sexual behavior is similar to their own (25). This similarity does not exist for boys. For girls, similarity in sexual behavior is a better predictor of friendship than year in school or the shared experience of visible deviant behaviors. It is not clear from the data if sexual standards influence friendships or if friends influence sexual standards.

It has also been found that college women prefer roommates similar in values to those who are dissimilar (26). In this study value similarity was assessed by asking the women to rank order seven values: political, theoretical, economic, aesthetic, social, religious, and physical-athletic. Even young children are attuned to similarity. Elementary school children prefer peers who perform at about their level on such dimensions as academics and sports, rather than those with much greater or lesser skills (27).

A number of laboratory studies show we like

■ *Birds of a feather flock together. Similarity breeds attraction. (WGS)*

individuals even if we only *think* they are similar to us (28). Prior to each study, and in a different setting, subjects' attitudes were measured on a variety of topics. In these studies, the investigators used this background information to create a stimulus person who appeared to be rather similar or rather dissimilar in attitudes to the subject. Subjects were given information about the stimulus person's "attitudes" and then asked to rate how much they liked the person and how much they would enjoy working with him or her. In these studies a person said to be similar was liked more and was preferred more as a work partner than a person said to be dissimilar.

However, some studies suggest the similarity-attraction relationship is mediated by people's attributions of others' evaluations of them. That is, it may be that we like similar others only because we think similar others will evaluate us favorably (29). Thus, similarity may be merely an indirect indicator of the probability of a mutually rewarding relationship based on shared positive regard.

Other researchers believe that dissimilarity leads to disliking, but that similarity does not lead to liking. They have found support for this position in a laboratory study of similarity of attitudes on ten issues and in a field study measuring similarity of political attitudes among participants at a political caucus (30). In the latter study, participants at Democratic caucuses and Republican rallies were asked to rate a stimulus person from a description that did or did not include political party affiliation. Compared to the stimulus person whose party affiliation was not given, subjects from both political parties liked the stimulus person from another party less, but did not like the stimulus person from their own party more.

Assortative mating. The principle of assortative mating states that like marries like. That is, like species mate with like species—greylag geese with greylag geese, red foxes with red foxes. Interestingly, *Homo sapiens* follow this principle, just as foxes and fish do. For humans, however, this principle means

■ *Mating is assortative. We typically date others who are similar in age, social class, physical attractiveness, and ethnicity. (WGS)*

that we tend to mate with others who are similar to us in social characteristics. We tend to form romantic relationships with others who are about our age, and who are from the same ethnic group, religion, and social class (31). People also tend to marry others who live a short distance from them. However, it is not clear that these data demonstrate a preference for similar others. Most individuals do not have much opportunity to meet, much less marry, individuals who are extremely different from themselves.

How similar are you to your boyfriend/girlfriend/ spouse? To the extent that we select mates similar to us in attitudes or personality, we are exhibiting a preference for similarity. Unlike the research findings for liking, the data for loving lead to mixed conclusions. Some findings show people love others whose attitudes, values, and personality are similar

to theirs (32). For instance, in one study demonstrating a similarity effect, married couples were found to be similar in a variety of personality traits, including sensation-seeking, field dependence, reasoning accuracy, and impulsivity (33). However, other findings suggest that similarity and love are not related (34).

Some research suggests that similarity benefits the couple. Studies of married and dating couples have found that similarity in needs, personality, and attitudes is associated with marital and dating happiness, while dissimilarity is associated with marital unhappiness and breakups of romantic relationships (35). A study of over 100 couples who had been in love, but had broken up, found dissimilarity of interests, background characteristics, sexual attitudes, and attitudes regarding marriage were commonly cited as reasons for the end of the relationship (36). In another study, not only did a significant correlation exist between marital satisfaction and perceived similarity of attitudes toward marital roles, but happily married people believed their attitudes regarding marital roles were more similar to those of their spouse than did unhappily married people (37). For happily married couples, assumed similarity was even greater than actual similarity.

The opposite hypothesis has also been proposed with respect to mate selection. This hypothesis states that individuals select others with complementary needs (38). *Complementarity* sometimes implies differing levels of the same need, in which case the complementary needs hypothesis and the similarity hypothesis make opposing predictions. For example, a male with a high need for dominance might select a female with a low need for dominance so each could exhibit the desired level of dominance in the marital relationship, whereas according to the similarity hypothesis, both should have the same level of need.

Complementarity can also imply high levels of two different needs that can only be satisfied together. A female who is highly dependent might select a male who is high in nurturance, so each can gratify his or her need. Although some research has supported this theory, much has not (39). Most researchers have found that dating and mating couples have similar, rather than complementary, needs (40). For example, males high on needs for dependence or nurturance tend to date and marry females with similarly high needs for dependence or nurturance, not females with low needs in these domains.

Reinforcement-affect theory Reinforcement-affect theory is a theory of attraction derived directly from psychology's learning theory. As you may remember from our discussion in Chapters 1 and 2, the underlying principle of learning theory is the *law of effect:* A response closely followed by satisfaction will be more likely to reoccur, while a response closely followed by discomfort will be less likely to reoccur (41). For instance, a child rewarded for looking both ways before crossing a street will be more likely to look both ways in the future than a child who has not been rewarded for this behavior.

According to reinforcement-affect theory, rewarding events generate positive affects or feelings, while punishing events generate negative affects or feelings (42). Therefore, people who are associated with rewarding and punishing events evoke positive and negative feelings. Thus, we come to like people who are associated with rewards and to dislike people who are associated with punishments. Reinforcement-affect theorists hypothesize that attraction toward a person is a function of the number and magnitude of positive associations with that person divided by the number and magnitude of positive and negative associations with that person. The more the positive associations outweigh the negative associations, the more liking will exist.

What are these rewards and punishments? Friends and lovers commonly offer each other assistance, companionship, and good times. They have positive personality attributes that make association with them pleasant (rewarding). However, they may also be unreliable or unkind at times or have other negative personality attributes that may sometimes make them unpleasant to be around (punishing).

Most research has supported this theory. For instance, one study has shown the level of rewards received to be the best predictor of satisfaction in dating relationships (43). In this study reward level was measured by the subjects' indication of how much the outcomes from their current relationships were above or below what they thought they would receive from a relationship of that type. In fact, subjects' beliefs that their outcomes in their current relationships were above what they would be able to receive in another relationship were a better indicator of satisfaction than feelings of equity or equality.

People do not have to be the cause of rewards or punishments to be liked or disliked; their mere presence when rewards and punishments are given is sufficient (44). To illustrate, subjects in one experiment liked their partner more when they received an unexpected reward in his or her presence than when they did not (45).

A number of variables associated with attraction

■ *Rewards and punishments associated with others influence liking. (Miss Peach by Mell Lazarus. Courtesy of Mell Lazarus and Field Newspaper Syndicate.)*

can be subsumed under reinforcement-affect theory. We will discuss two such variables: physical attractiveness and competence.

Competence. We prefer individuals who are competent to those who are incompetent (46). Competent people not only give us better information about reality, but their competence may also reflect favorably on us. If we associate with competent people, others may believe we are also competent. At least, others will think we show good judgment in selecting friends. Interestingly, however, we seem to prefer competent persons who are slightly flawed to competent people who appear to be perfect.

In a test of this idea, subjects in one study listened to a taped interview of another student who they were told was a candidate for the university College Quiz Bowl team (47). Some of the subjects heard a candidate who performed extraordinarily well, while others heard a candidate who performed poorly. When asked how much they liked the candidate, the subjects liked the competent candidate better than the incompetent candidate.

Another set of subjects heard the same interviews with either the competent or incompetent candidate, but in addition heard the tape end with the candidate spilling a cup of coffee on his new suit. What was the effect of this blunder on the subjects' liking for the candidates? Those who had heard the incom-

petent student blunder liked him less than those who had heard the incompetent student who did not blunder. However, those who heard the competent student blunder liked him *more* than those who heard the competent student who did not blunder. It appears that a blunder on the part of a competent person makes him or her appear more human (like the rest of us) and thus more endearing, but a blunder on the part of an incompetent person only makes him or her less appealing.

Physical attractiveness. Physical attractiveness is an extremely strong predictor of liking and loving (48). It is so important that even children as young as three or four prefer physically attractive to unattractive people. For example, physically unattractive nursery school children are less popular than more attractive children. Their peers also believe the unattractive children to be antisocial, particularly if the unattractive children are males (49). In a study of a tri-ethnic (black, white, and Mexican-American) sample of 6- and 10-year-olds, one of your authors and a colleague found physical attractiveness to be a more important predictor of liking than ethnicity (50). We also found a single standard of physical attractiveness: The physical attractiveness ratings of children from these three ethnic groups did not vary significantly by the ethnic group of the raters.

Physically attractive adults are also rated higher on most dimensions than physically unattractive adults (51). In one study, physically attractive men and women were rated as being more sexually warm and responsive, sensitive, kind, outgoing, nurturant, interesting, strong, poised, modest, and sociable than less physically attractive men and women. The physically attractive individuals were also thought to be more exciting as dates and to have better characters than less physically attractive individuals (52).

Why do we prefer physically attractive people to physically unattractive people? Our "folk wisdom" says that we can tell what people are like by looking at them (53). For example, we say that fat people are jolly and that redheads have hot tempers. The idea that inner qualities are reflected in an individual's outward appearance can be found in the Bible, in Greek and Hebrew literature, in descriptions of witches, and even in our fairy tales (remember Cinderella and her ugly stepsisters?).

To a certain extent, the physical attractiveness stereotype may be self-fulfilling (see Chapter 8 for a discussion of self-fulfilling prophecies) (54). Because physically unattractive people are thought to possess negative qualities, others expect negative behaviors from them. Since people expect negative behaviors from unattractive people, they may treat them less well than they treat attractive people. For example, when a physically attractive child approaches a stranger, he or she is likely to be rewarded for being outgoing by the stranger's attention and admiration; but a physically unattractive child may be punished for the same behavior by the stranger's curtness and rejection.

Due to this differential treatment, physically attractive and physically unattractive individuals may come to exhibit differing behaviors. In our example, attractive children may become outgoing, whereas unattractive children may become shy and aloof. While no differences in intelligence exist between physically attractive and unattractive people, physically attractive people are probably more likely than unattractive people to be given credit for their intelligence, to be given special attention by their teachers, and to be selected for awards and fellowships.

In one study demonstrating a self-fulfilling prophecy, college men were incorrectly led to believe a woman with whom they talked over the phone was physically very attractive or very unattractive (55). Despite its inaccuracy, the belief the men had concerning the physical attractiveness of these women dramatically influenced their conversations. College students who knew nothing of the circumstances of the conversations listened to the women's or men's part of the conversation and rated the speakers. The men who believed they were talking with a physically attractive woman were rated as more sociable, interesting, sexually warm, and humorous than the men who believed they were talking with a physically unattractive woman. How do you suppose the women reacted to this attention? The judges found that the women who were thought to be physically attractive were more poised, sociable, animated, and confident than the women thought to be physically unattractive. Thus, the men's behaviors influenced the women's responses.

While most students seem unaware of (or unwilling to admit) the importance of physical attractiveness in their dating choices (56), research data suggests an enduring attraction to the handsome hunk and the gorgeous coed. For example, in a study of blind dates during freshmen Welcome Week at the University of Minnesota, physical attractiveness was the only significant determinant of how much each partner liked his or her date (57). In addition, the woman's physical attractiveness was the only factor determining whether the man asked the woman out for another date.

The importance of physical attractiveness may vary by sex. In one study of preferences in mate selection, men were more likely than women to prefer mates high in physical attractiveness, while women were more likely than men to prefer college educated mates, and those with good earning potential (58). In another study, decreases in physical attractiveness due to aging influenced husbands' responses to their wives more than wives' responses to their husbands. Wives' loss of beauty was associated with husbands' declining sexual interest, unhappiness in the sexual relationship, and unfaithfulness (59). These data demonstrate that the traditional

■ *The mating game: The matching hypothesis holds for couples of all ages. (WGS)*

exchange of beauty for earnings power is not yet dead, even in this age of changing gender roles.

Does our preference for beauty mean that only highly physically attractive people date and marry? Of course not! Even though highly physically attractive people are preferred, there are not enough of them to go around. Thus, it cannot be the case that very physically attractive people are the only ones involved in romantic relationships. However, it does appear that people tend to become romantically involved with as physically attractive a person as they can.

In fact, most of the data examining the physical attractiveness of people who are romantically linked support the *matching hypothesis* (60). The matching hypothesis is one variant of the principle of assortative mating that like mates with like. Thus, people tend to date and mate with people who are similar to them in level of physical attractiveness—highly attractive people with other highly attractive people, mediums with mediums, lows with lows. While everyone prefers the highly physically attractive person, dating involves selection by both partners. The most physically attractive person who returns your interest is likely to be someone at about your level of physical attractiveness.

One study demonstrates both interest in physically attractive people and realistic choices in date selection (61). Male college students were asked to select a blind date from among six photographs. The photographs were of six women: two highly attractive, two of medium attraction, and two of low attraction. In one condition, the men were assured of a date with the woman they selected. In this condition, virtually all the men selected the most physically attractive women. However, in another condition, the men were told that the woman would look at a photograph of the man who selected her and then determine if she would accept the date. In this condition, the tendency to select the most physically attractive women was much less pronounced. The men's beliefs about whether they would be accepted varied with their own levels of physical attractiveness: More attractive men (60 percent) than unattractive men (45 percent) thought the woman they selected would accept the date.

Studies of actual dating couples have also shown support for the matching hypothesis. For example, in a study of college student couples, the more serious the relationship, the higher was the correlation between the partners' levels of physical attractiveness (62). The couples who broke up within the next nine months were less similar in level of physical attractiveness than those who were still dating. However, among engaged or cohabiting couples, breakups were not related to level of physical attractiveness. Therefore, physical attractiveness may play a stronger role in earlier than later stages of love.

A recent study suggests an even more surprising type of matching: Married couples eventually begin to look alike (63)! Couples who originally bore no physical resemblance to each other came to resemble each other over the course of 25 years of marriage. Further, the more happily married the couple, the stronger the physical resemblance. The authors of the study believe that habitual use of certain facial muscles permanently affects the physical features of the face. Based on empathy, repeated mimicry of the spouse's expressions should occur, particularly in happily married couples. Over time, this mimicry should result in physically similar facial features.

Gain-loss theory *Gain-loss theory* is an application of one premise of learning theory: Reinforcements lose their value over time. According to this theory, an increase in rewards from an individual has a more positive impact than consistent rewards from the same individual (65). Similarly, an increase in punishments from an individual has a more negative impact than consistent punishments from the same individual. Consistent responses come to be expected and thus do not have the same impact as changing responses. This means that the influence of reward on attraction weakens over time, as the same person repeatedly confers the same rewards. For example, the first time your boyfriend or girlfriend told you that he or she loved you, the statement was more reinforcing than the 50th time he or she made the same statement because you had come to expect such statements. Using the same principle, an unexpected punishment has a much greater

BOX 11-1

Physical Attractiveness in Singles Ads

One measure of the importance of physical attractiveness in attraction is the frequency with which it is mentioned in singles ads. One of your authors examined the singles ads in one issue of a biweekly magazine devoted to book reviews on literature, politics, and history (64). Despite the intellectual content of the magazine, it runs two pages of singles ads per issue. People advertising in this magazine are presumably looking for well-educated, intellectual dates.

The issue contained 84 singles ads. As is common with singles ads, most of the advertisers were women (70 percent women to 30 percent men). Most advertisers were heterosexual. Despite the advertisers' presumed interest in attracting intellectual others, they commonly fail to mention their intelligence, but instead advertise their physical attractiveness. Fully 63 percent of the women mentioned they were attractive, great-looking, beautiful, or even very beautiful; in addition, 7 percent of the remaining women mentioned other positive physical attributes, such as slender, tall, and ash blond. Only two women mentioned monetary success.

Surprisingly, the self attribute most commonly mentioned by men was not financial security (mentioned by 32 percent), but physical attractiveness (handsome, good-looking, mentioned by 40 percent). Only one man admitted to average looks. Sixteen percent of the remaining men mentioned other positive physical attributes (tall, slender, fit).

As might be expected, men typically wanted the people answering their ads to be physically attractive and intelligent. Women wished to hear from others who were intelligent, financially secure, and—you guessed it—physically attractive.

If physical attractiveness plays this large a role in the singles ads of the intelligentsia of our society, what role do you think it plays in the romantic pairing in the larger society? ■

influence on attraction than an expected punishment. If, on the 50th time you expected a declaration of love, your boyfriend or girlfriend told you that he or she now disliked you, this statement would be more punishing than if someone who has always disliked you said the same thing because the information is so unexpected.

A symbolic interactionist theory of reward In George McCall's symbolic interactionist reward theory, we become attached to others who provide us opportunities to enact role identities that are rewarding to us. Attachments to others are thus determined by a combination of our desire for social rewards and our opportunities to obtain those rewards (66). If you have many means of obtaining a desired reward, you will be less attached to another person who provides that reward than if you are dependent on that person alone to provide the reward.

In addition, people are more attached to persons who are associated with salient and important roles. A particular role identity becomes salient if we have a high need or desire for the rewards associated with the enactment of this role identity. Since role salience varies with one's current needs, attachment to others varies with the salience of a particular need. In other words, we appraise others on the basis of whether we can have our current needs met through association with them. For instance, if you love to dance, and only one of your friends likes to go dancing with you, he or she will offer you more rewards and, thus, will be better liked than if you have many friends who like to go dancing with you. If you have been out dancing a lot recently, this friend's power to reward you is lower than if you have not.

Now that we have discussed the various reinforcement theories of attraction, we turn to two other theories: balance and misattribution of arousal.

Balance Theory

Have you ever had two close friends who disliked each other? Have you ever dated someone your parents or friends disliked? Balance theory can explain the discomfort you may have felt in these situations. *Balance theory* is a theory dealing with feelings that result when an individual realizes that inconsistencies exist among his or her beliefs. Like cognitive dissonance theory (see Chapter 10), balance theory assumes that consistency among beliefs is pleasing and inconsistency is displeasing.

Balance theory applies to relationships among a person (P), another person (O), and an object or third person (X) (67). Relationships associated with liking (+) and disliking (−) are called *sentiment relationships*. Sarah likes Jonathan and Clarisse dislikes Jordan are statements of sentiment relationships. Balance theory deals with *unit relationships,* relationships characterized by association with or lack of association with an individual or object.

Joshua owns a Ferrari and Cassie doesn't know Jackson provide examples of unit relationships. Let us examine some examples of triadic relationships involving sentiment relationships (see Figure 11-1).

Let's say that you (P) like Nina (O), and that Nina likes John (X), and that you also like John. Thus, the relationships among P, O, and X are all positive (+). This example shows a balanced triad: There is agreement among all three components (persons) in the triad.

Let us look at some of your other relationships. Assume that you (P) like Jennifer (O), that Jennifer dislikes Susan (X), and that you also dislike Susan. Here, there is only one positive relationship (you-Jennifer) and two negative relationships (Jennifer-Susan, you-Susan). However, this triad is also balanced, since the negative relationships also point up a type of harmony: The person you like dislikes someone you dislike. Since we expect our enemies to be associated with negative people and objects, two negative relationships and a positive relationship also yield a balanced triad.

The situation is different when we examine

Figure 11.1 ■

Balanced and Imbalanced Triads

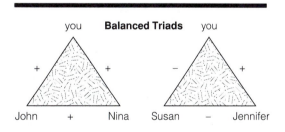

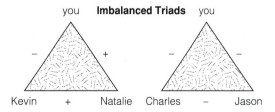

another relationship. You (P) like Natalie (O), Natalie likes Kevin (X), and you dislike Kevin. Here we have two positive relationships (you-Natalie and Natalie-Kevin) and one negative relationship (you-Kevin). Such a triad is imbalanced. This triad is not harmonious, because someone whom you like is attracted to a person whom you dislike, whereas we expect our friends to like those we like and dislike those we dislike. Any triad consisting of two positive relationships and one negative one is imbalanced.

A final type of triad is created by your (P) dislike of Jason (O), Jason's dislike of Charles (X), and your dislike of Charles. This triad has three negative relationships. Triads with three negative relationships are also imbalanced. This triad is imbalanced because you share a common dislike with a person whom you dislike. We expect our enemies to have preferences for objects and people that differ from our own. My enemy's enemy should be my friend!

When a triad is balanced, there is no strong motivation to change the relationships. It may be unpleasant to dislike someone; but if your friend dislikes him too, then at least you agree with the person you like. We apparently do not expect all of our relationships with others to be positive. On the other hand, when a triad is imbalanced, this imbalance is experienced as unpleasant, and the individual is motivated to change one of the relationships to make the triad balanced. For example, in the triad consisting of you, Natalie, and Kevin, you may attempt to convince Natalie that Kevin really isn't a very good person, thus hoping to restore balance by making the (+ + −) imbalanced relationship into a (+ − −) balanced relationship, where two friends agree that a third person is dislikable. With respect to you, Jason, and Charles, you may attempt to persuade yourself that Jason really isn't so bad, thus making the (− − −) imbalanced relationship into a (+ − −) balanced one.

Balance is important because it is associated with pleasantness and stability in relationships. It is a force in attraction because our friends often know one another. It is very difficult to maintain a close romantic or friendship relationship with someone that our friends dislike, because the resulting imbalance is unpleasant and destabilizing to the relationship.

Misattribution of Arousal

Have you ever found yourself attracted to someone with whom you've shared an exciting or physically energizing experience? Have you ever fallen in love with someone your parents disliked? We will explore three types of arousal we can misattribute or misinterpret as attraction: fear, physical arousal, and parental interference. These theories argue that some feelings that people think are love in fact are only physical arousal that is caused not by love but by some other source.

Several theories of emotion argue that emotion is a function of physiological arousal and cognitions or thoughts about the source of the arousal (68). Physiological arousal determines the intensity of the emotion, whereas one's cognitions determine the particular emotion felt. However, in some instances, we experience arousal but do not have a ready explanation for it. In such situations, we look to the immediate environment for explanations of our arousal, and we may then misattribute our arousal to current environmental conditions.

Misattribution of arousal may explain some instances of romantic love (69). A person who is physiologically aroused, but who does not have a good explanation for it, might decide the feeling of arousal is love if an attractive and available person happens to be present at the right moment.

Fear In a study of the effect of fear on attraction, a physically attractive female or male interviewer approached males as they were crossing either a swaying, 450-foot-long suspension bridge 230 feet above a rocky river gorge or a solid bridge 10 feet above the ground (70). The interviewer asked a few questions and then offered each subject his or her telephone number so the subject could call the interviewer if he wished to know the results of the survey. When the interviewer was male, his phone number was taken by few subjects and he received few calls. When the interviewer was female and the context of the interview was nonarousing (the bridge was low and stable), she also received few calls. But when the experimenter was female and the context of the interview was associated with physiological arousal (the bridge was high and unstable) many of the male subjects called the attractive female experimenter.

This study demonstrates the facilitating effect of an ambiguous but arousing situation upon attraction. The investigators interpreted the inquiries about the study as an excuse for the men in the high-arousal condition to contact the attractive female interviewer. Apparently the men who had been exposed to this experimenter during a fear-arousing experience—crossing a high suspension bridge—interpreted their arousal as attraction to her.

Physical arousal Misattribution of arousal can also occur with general physical arousal. We can be either more or less attracted to others when we are physically aroused than when we are not. It appears that we sometimes misattribute our physical arousal to feelings of attraction to or revulsion toward another person. In a test of this idea, male subjects were either asked to run in place for 120 seconds (arousal condition) or for 15 seconds (nonarousal condition) (71). Half of the men in each arousal condition saw a physically attractive female confederate, while the other half saw a physically unattractive one. Following the exercise, the men rated the woman on a number of dimensions, including her sexiness, and rated their liking for her and their desire to date and kiss her. Overall, the physically attractive woman was viewed more positively than the unattractive woman on measures of personality traits, romantic attraction, and liking. More importantly, aroused men liked the attractive woman more and liked the unattractive woman less than did the unaroused men (see Table 11-1). Thus, when physically aroused, the men attributed their arousal to attraction to a physically attractive woman or to revulsion toward an unattractive woman.

A similar effect was found for both positive and negative stimuli in a second study (72). Men exposed to portions of the sound track of a comic movie or a horror movie liked a physically attractive partner more than men who had listened to the sound track

Table 11.1 ■

Mean Attraction Scores as a Function of Arousal and Physical Attractiveness

Condition	Trait	Romantic Attraction	Liking
		Variable	
High arousal–high attractiveness	98.15	32.38	28.54
Low arousal–high attractiveness	86.63	26.06	25.13
High arousal–low attractiveness	58.69	9.38	12.62
Low arousal–low attractiveness	68.50	15.08	17.42

Note: A high score indicates a more favorable response to the confederate.
From G.L. White, S. Fishbein, and J. Rutstein, 1981, "Passionate Love and the Misattribution of Arousal," *Journal of Personality and Social Psychology* 41:56–62.

of a nonarousing tape about the frog's circulatory system. When the partner was unattractive, she was liked less by men who had listened to the comic movie or the horror movie than men who had listened to the tape about the circulatory system.

Parental interference Misattribution of arousal may also occur as a consequence of parental interference. Researchers have labeled the positive influence parental interference can have on romantic relationships the *Romeo and Juliet effect* (73). In studies of dating and married couples, researchers found positive correlations between romantic love and parental opposition. They also found that romantic love intensifies following parental interference.

A popular play, *The Fantasticks,* draws on this theme. In the play, the fathers of a young male and female forbid them to see each other. In this way, the fathers create a romance between the pair, who defy their fathers and seek each other out. At the end of the play, the audience finds that this result was intentional. The fathers were sure their children would do the opposite of their wishes. For this reason, they hid their desires for their children to wed, instead presenting the children with obstacles to overcome in the secret hope that they would fall in love.

Why does parental opposition intensify love? If the misattribution of arousal explanation is correct, parental interference leads to arousal, which is misinterpreted as love. Reinforcement theorists have offered another answer to this question. They have shown that frustration increases the desirability of a goal (74). Frustration created by parental opposition could thus increase the desirability of the relationship.

■ BEING IN LOVE

Finally, we turn our attention exclusively to romantic love. We will explore the relationship between liking and loving, examine the stages of development of a romantic relationship, and consider reasons for its dissolution. We then end this chapter with a critique of the theories of romantic love.

The Relationship of Liking and Romantic Loving

Measurement scales have been devised to determine if liking and loving are distinct emotions or if love is merely a stronger version of liking (see Box 11-2) (75). What do you think? Research findings suggest feelings of liking and love are not the same. Loving consists of feelings of attachment, caring, and intimacy, while liking consists of favorable evaluations of another person and feelings of similarity to him or her.

Studies using these scales have found that ratings by women of their boyfriends and by men of their

■ *Romance comes early. (WGS)*

In the Love Scale and the Liking Scale, all items are scored on nine-point scales ranging from strong agreement to strong disagreement with the statement. Here are examples of items from each of these scales (76).

Items from the Love Scale:

1. I would do almost anything for _____.
2. One of my primary concerns is _____'s welfare.
3. It would be hard for me to get along without _____.

Items from the Liking Scale:

1. Most people would react very favorably to _____after a brief acquaintance.
2. _____ is one of the most likeable people I know.
3. _____ is the sort of person whom I would like to be like. ■

girlfriends are extremely similar. However, women seem to like their boyfriends more than men like their girlfriends. This difference is probably related to gender role stereotypes. In this society, such characteristics as intelligence, maturity, and good judgment, which are important in the liking score, are thought to be more characteristic of men than women. Thus, it is not surprising that women rate their boyfriends higher on these dimensions than men rate their girlfriends, even though the ratings of the men as more intelligent, mature, and better in judgment are probably inaccurate.

Love and friendship (liking) relationships seem to share a number of characteristics. Both relationships include enjoyment of each other's company, acceptance of each other as you truly are, feelings of trust and respect, assistance and emotional sup-port, understanding of each other's values and behaviors, the freedom to be oneself, and being a champion and advocate for the other.

However, love includes aspects not found in liking (77). Unlike friendships, love relationships also include a fascination with the other, often to the detriment of one's own actions; the placement of a priority on this relationship above all others; and giving the utmost to the other, even to the point of self-sacrifice. Love has both an up side and a down side: Relative to friendship, love is the source of greater satisfaction, but is also the source of greater frustration. Love relationships also have a greater potential for distress, ambivalence, conflict, and mutual criticism than friendships.

What do you mean when you say you are in love? Do you mean the same thing your loved one

BOX 11-3

The Styles of Love

The styles of love are measured by agreement with the following items (79). Answer each question on a five-point scale ranging from 1—strongly agree to 5—strongly disagree. The lower the score, the higher the agreement with the style of love.

Everyone is presumed to have elements of each style of love, but for each person, typically only one or two styles predominate.

Eros

1. My lover and I were attracted to each other immediately after we first met.
2. My lover and I have the right physical "chemistry" between us.
3. Our lovemaking is very intense and satisfying.
4. I feel that my lover and I were meant for each other.
5. My lover and I became physically involved very quickly.
6. My lover and I really understand each other.
7. My lover fits my ideal standards of physical beauty/handsomeness.

Ludus

1. I try to keep my lover a little uncertain about my commitment to him/her.
2. I believe that what my lover doesn't know about me won't hurt him/her.
3. I have sometimes had to keep two of my lovers from finding out about each other.
4. I get over love affairs pretty easily and quickly.
5. My lover would get upset if he/she knew of some of the things I've done with other people.
6. When my lover gets too dependent on me, I want to back off a little.
7. I enjoy playing the "game of love" with a number of different partners.

Storage

1. I did not realize that I was in love until I actually had been for some time.
2. I cannot love unless I first had *caring* for awhile.
3. I still have good friendships with almost everyone with whom I have ever been involved in a love relationship.

4. The best kind of love grows out of long friendship.

5. It is hard to say exactly when my lover and I fell in love.

6. Love is really a deep friendship, not a mysterious, mystical emotion.

7. My most satisfying love relationships have developed from good friendships.

Pragma

1. I consider what a person is going to become in life before I commit myself to him/her.

2. I try to plan my life carefully before choosing a lover.

3. It is best to love someone with a similar background.

4. A main consideration in choosing a lover is how he/she reflects on my family.

5. An important factor in choosing a partner is whether or not he/she will be a good parent.

6. One consideration in choosing a partner is how he/she will reflect on my career.

7. Before getting very involved with anyone, I try to figure out how compatible his/her hereditary background is with mine in case we ever have children.

Mania

1. When things aren't right with my lover and me, my stomach gets upset.

2. When my love affairs break up, I get so depressed that I have even thought of suicide.

3. Sometimes I get so excited about being in love that I can't sleep.

4. When my lover doesn't pay attention to me, I feel sick all over.

5. When I am in love, I have trouble concentrating on anything else.

6. I cannot relax if I suspect that my lover is with someone else.

7. If my lover ignores me for a while, I sometimes do stupid things to get his/her attention back.

Agape

1. I try to use my own strength to help my lover through difficult times.

2. I would rather suffer myself than let my lover suffer.

3. I cannot be happy unless I place my lover's happiness before my own.

4. I am usually willing to sacrifice my own wishes to let my lover achieve his/hers.

5. Whatever I own is my lover's to use as he/she chooses.

6. When my lover gets angry with me, I still love him/her fully and unconditionally.

7. I would endure all things for the sake of my lover. ∎

means? People differ in their *styles of love* or characteristic ways of loving (78). Six love styles are thought to exist:

1. *eros,* passionate love characterized by a strong erotic attachment

2. *ludus,* in which love is viewed as a game to be played with many partners

3. *storage,* friendship love, where love and friendship are merged

4. *pragma,* logical or rational love, based on careful calculation of the other's attributes

5. *mania,* possessive, dependent love, in which love is based on uncertainty concerning the self and the other

6. *agape,* altruistic love, an all-giving, nondemanding love.

Which type of lover are you? If your love is characterized by strong physical preferences, strong commitment to the partner, and great intensity of love, your primary love style is eros. If love to you is a game to be played with many partners, a game of low intensity and no great depth of feeling, your primary love style is ludus. If you typically merge love and friendship in a down-to-earth, non-erotic blend, your primary love style is storage. If you rationally calculate the desired attributes in a lover and then systematically set about finding someone who matches your criteria, your primary love style is pragma. If your love feels like symptoms of the flu, and you are often jealous and uncertain of your lover or in such ecstasy you can't concentrate on anything else, your primary love style is mania. If your love is a devoted, all-giving, nondemanding love, then your primary love style is agape.

Men are more likely to be ludic, and women are more likely to be storgic, pragmatic, and manic. Erotics tend always to be in love, while ludics are most likely to say they have never been in love or have been in love three or more times. Erotics are high in self-esteem, while manics are low in self-esteem.

How Do I Love Thee? Let Me Count the Stages

Next we consider the development of romantic relationships. Like all other relationships, romantic relationships become less superficial over time. They involve progressively more interaction, self-disclosure, trust, involvement, and less inhibition (80). In recognition of the changes that take place during romantic relationships, several social psychologists have attempted to specify the stages through which an ongoing relationship passes. The events occurring in the relationship at each stage determine if it will progress to the next stage or be dissolved.

It has been proposed that relationships develop in four stages (81):

1. *The early stage:* Here, the individuals explore the potential rewards of developing a relationship. A couple who are just getting to know one another and who have no real commitment to the relationship are in the early stage.

2. *The bargaining stage:* In this stage the individuals negotiate the terms of the relationship. A couple who are just beginning to determine what types of relationship are and aren't acceptable to each individual, and whether these types are compatible, are in the bargaining stage.

3. *The commitment stage:* During this stage the individuals reduce their involvement in and exploration of alternative relations and become more dependent on the one relationship. A couple who are beginning to become involved, and begin to be thought of as a couple are in the commitment stage.

4. *The institutionalization stage:* In this stage shared expectations emerge, and the couple, as well as other people, recognize the exclusivity of the relationship. A couple who are widely recognized as a couple and known to be dating only each other are in the institutionalization stage.

A Multi-Stage Theory of Love

Which theories of attraction are most accurate when applied to romantic relationships? We have just seen that relationships pass through various stages. Recently theorists have sought to develop theories of attraction that take into consideration the fact that different stages of a relationship may be guided by different factors.

Filtering theory The *filtering theory* of attraction incorporates factors from several earlier theories (82). According to this theory, the concept of exchange governs the overall process. Three different sets of variables act as the filters through which the relationship must pass if it is to progress from earlier to later stages. Further, while exchange is involved in each stage of the relationship, it is more important in the earlier stages than in the last stage.

Stimulus stage. In the first stage of the relationship, *the stimulus stage,* we form initial impressions such as those based upon physical attractiveness, information about the person's reputation, and the person's social status. These impressions are most important in determining attraction to another. For example, you might be initially attracted to someone who is good-looking, has a reputation for wit, and grew up in the same kind of neighborhood as you did.

Value comparison stage. If the stimuli the couple present represent a fair enough exchange (both are highly physically attractive but low in social status, or one is very beautiful but low in status while the other is unattractive but wealthy), they may progress to the second or *value comparison stage.* In this stage, the couple compare their interests, attitudes, beliefs, and needs to determine if they are compatible. While the stimulus variables are still somewhat influential in this stage, their influence has waned. In this stage, you and your partner would determine if your attitudes toward life, your overall values, and your life goals are similar enough to sustain the relationship. If you find yourself too dissimilar in attitudes, values, and goals, the relationship will probably fade.

Role stage. In the third, or *role stage,* the couple determine if they are sufficiently compatible in their role needs to warrant marriage. That is, each individual considers whether the other can satisfy his or her needs for a friend, lover, teacher, and critic. This stage is the most intimate and the most difficult to assess. Here, complementarity of roles may be critical in determining compatibility. During this stage, stimuli and values remain somewhat influential in the outcome of the relationship, but have lessened in importance. If individuals believe they could function well in a marital relationship with each other, taking into consideration the roles they desire for themselves and for the other, then the courtship may lead to marriage.

In this final stage, you and your partner would be looking to see if your similarity is only superficial or if you really want the same things from life, and if the other seems to be able to fulfill your most important needs.

In a study of several groups of college students, filtering theory was generally supported (83). It was found that exchange was an important principle in determining whether or not relationships progressed. Further, relationships did seem to progress from stimulus through value to role stages. As hypothesized, variables such as equal physical attractiveness were of prime importance in the initial stage of dating. As we reported earlier in this chapter, other research also shows physical attractiveness to be most important at the beginning of relationships. While the correlation between the couple's values was low in the initial stage, couples who continued their relationships beyond a few dates were those who were matched in values and beliefs. Those whose courtship lasted the longest rated their partners higher on the ideal-spouse dimension than those who terminated their courtship. They also were better matched than other couples in levels of self-acceptance, acceptance of the other, sex drive, and marital expectations.

It is not always the case, however, that couples are in the same stage of a relationship. Relationships are frequently assymetrical (one member of a couple is still bargaining while another has fully committed), with resulting disharmony.

These two theories of the development of love provide complementary analyses. The first theory describes the changing focus of the couple's interactions, while the second theory describes the change

Figure 11.2 ■

The Four Stage Theory of Relationship Development and the Filtering Theory of Love

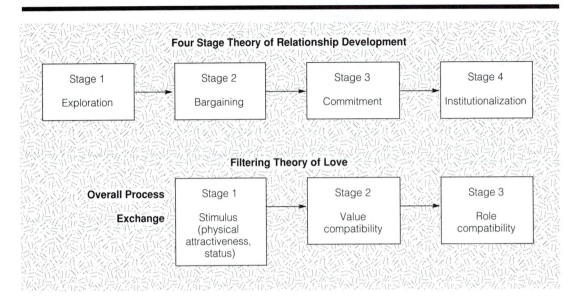

in variables that are foremost in the ongoing process of exchange. See Figure 11-2 for a comparison of the relationship stages and the filtering theory of love.

What do we know about attraction throughout a marriage? Studies of marital happiness have consistently shown a curvilinear relationship with length of marriage. Marriages are happier at the beginning and end than in the period in which the oldest child is in school (84). Why should this be the case? In a study of 129 couples in this middle period of marriage, marital dissatisfaction was highest in families with negative father-son or mother-son relationships and in which the wives were experiencing some form of midlife crisis (85). The authors suggest that the decline in marital satisfaction during the children's school years may be somewhat inevitable. During this time of life children do become more distant from parents, and midlife concerns are common.

Relationships' End: Is Breaking Up Really Hard to Do?

Theories of attraction can also help us understand the end of relationships. Using exchange theory to explain marital disruption, three factors which interact to produce marital breakdown can be cited: declining attraction within the relationship, few barriers to terminating the relationship, and alternative attractions outside the relationship (88).

The rewards and costs of marital relationships constantly change. The first factor, declining attraction within the relationship, is one possible outcome of this changing reward structure. For a variety of reasons, the rewards associated with the relationship (sexual fulfillment, companionship, status, material rewards) can decline and the costs associated with the relationship (boredom, social and financial obligations) can increase. Second, the barriers to marital dissolution, such as religious prohibitions, finan-

Is Marital Happiness Declining?

Survey data show a steady decline, from 1972 to 1986, in the association of being married and reported happiness in life (86). This weakened association is due to the increase in happiness of never married men and the decrease in happiness of married women. The investigators suggest the reason for these changes is that, in the last two decades, the circumstances of the married and unmarried have become more similar. By the late 1980s, unmarried persons could engage in regular sexual relations without great stigma. In addition, with the increased acceptance and ease of divorce, marriage no longer provides the security, financial or otherwise, that it once did.

While early data suggested a relationship between wives' employment and marital dissatisfaction, more recent and reliable data suggest no such relationship exists (87). Wives' employment, high occupational commitment on the part of wives, and the higher occupational status of wives than husbands are all unrelated to the marital satisfaction of husbands or wives. While wives' employment is related to marital dissolution, this relationship appears to be based on economics: Unhappily married women who are employed in the labor force are more able financially to divorce than unhappily married women who do not work outside the home. ■

cial loss, family and community pressure, and feelings of responsibility toward minor children, may be low. Third, alternative attractions may undermine marital stability. These attractions can be not only other individuals, but material rewards and opportunities for self-actualization. Where attraction within the relationship is low, barriers to marital dissolution are low, and alternative attractions outside the relationship are high, marital breakups become likely.

Imagine you know two couples who are unhappily married. One couple is nonreligious, have no minor children, are in a social setting that condones divorce, and one or both partners view the marriage as a barrier to greatly desired experiences. The other couple are religious, have several small children,

their church and community disapprove of divorce, and no outside attractions add to the couple's marital problems. It is easy to see that, given the same level of marital unhappiness, the former couple are more likely to divorce than the latter.

Another way to learn about marital dissolution is to study the characteristics of people who divorce (89). It has long been known that age at marriage is associated with marital disruption: The younger the couple at marriage, the more likely the marriage is to end in divorce. Why do you think age is such an important factor? Social psychologists argue that couples who marry young are less emotionally mature than older couples and less successful at selecting a compatible partner. In addition, younger people have more life cycle transitions left to experience. These include completing an education, selecting a career, developing adult interests, and establishing a life apart from one's parents. Thus, younger people have more dramatic adjustments to make than older people, adjustments calling for changes that could result in marital incompatibility later.

Parenthood reduces the risk of marital disruption, but only if the birth occurs after the couple are married. Parenthood does not appear to increase marital satisfaction, but it does increase legal, financial, and emotional ties to the relationship. Children born to the mother prior to the current marriage, however, do not provide the same barrier to marital disruption. The husband is less likely to be the biological father of children born prior to the marriage. He, thus, may feel fewer legal, financial, and emotional commitments to the child.

Critique of Theories of Romantic Attraction

It has been argued that most theories of attraction, particularly those addressed to romantic love, rely too strongly on individual factors and ignore the effects of the social setting (90). The social setting is important for three reasons.

First, social structure determines which people will actually have contact with each other. As mentioned before, there is less chance of meeting someone outside one's own age group, social class, religion, ethnic group and geographic area than of meeting someone from within one's own groups. The association of attraction and similarity may not be due to our preference for similar others, but only to the fact that they are the ones we typically meet.

Second, the social setting determines the individual's definition of a desirable spouse. Value and attitude similarity may be important only in middle-class styles of marriage, in which high levels of interaction and companionship are anticipated. In another pattern of marriage, more typical of working-class marriages, low levels of interaction and low companionship are anticipated. In this form of

marriage, value consensus is largely irrelevant and adherence to the traditionally distinct roles of husband and wife is stressed. Inattention to this pattern of marriage has led to a middle-class bias in much of the research on marital selection.

Third, regardless of the definition of a desirable spouse, people are not held responsible to the same degree for selecting a spouse who meets this definition. People who marry unusually late are less tied to their group's norms concerning appropriate mate selection than others. These individuals are not only less likely to follow these norms, but they are also held less responsible for doing so. Thus, the theories of attraction we have described may apply most clearly to only a subset of American society: young, middle-class people who are most strongly expected to follow social norms regarding marriage.

■

SUMMARY

In this chapter, we attempted to understand attraction and the factors that influence liking and loving. Liking and loving have benefits for the individual. Close associations with others protect us from loneliness and provide cultural information and economic resources. Proximity and familiarity provide preconditions for attraction. Attraction is associated with spatial proximity because we cannot be attracted to those we have not met. In addition, we prefer familiar to unfamiliar others.

The theories of attraction can be subsumed under three theoretical umbrellas: reinforcement, balance or consistency, and misattribution of arousal. Three reinforcement theories were presented: exchange theory, reinforcement-affect theory, and a symbolic interactionist reward theory of attraction. Exchange theory suggests the goal in interpersonal relations is to strike the best bargain possible. Equitable relationships are those in which the individuals' rewards and costs are proportional. Equitable relationships are associated with marital happiness and friendship endurance and strength.

The association with similarity and attraction provides one example of exchange. Similarity of attitudes and values have been related to friendship selections and sometimes to positive marital relations. The opposite hypothesis, that complementarity of traits is associated with attraction, has received relatively little support.

According to reinforcement-affect theory, attraction toward a person is a function of the number and magnitude of positive and negative associations with that person. We prefer others who provide us with rewards. The known associations of attraction with competence and with physical attractiveness provide examples of reinforcement-affect. Although we prefer competent to incompetent others, we seem to prefer competent persons whose small blunders make them appear more human to perfect competent persons. While we prefer highly physically attractive dates and mates, we must often settle for what we can get, typically people of about our own physical attractiveness level. Gain-loss theory also is a variant of reinforcement-affect. It states that an increase in rewards from an individual has a more positive impact on liking than consistent rewards from the same individual.

The symbolic interactionist reward perspective argues that attachment is determined by a combination of the individual's desire for social rewards and his or her opportunities for obtaining those rewards.

Balance theory suggests that we wish to maintain consistency among our liking relationships. In any triad of liking relationships, inconsistency among them is perceived as unpleasant. Attempts will be made to make the triad consistent by changing one of the liking relationships.

According to the misattribution of arousal hypothesis, a person who feels physiological arousal without appropriate cognitions to explain this arousal may misinterpret it as attraction when in the presence of an attractive person. The arousal can be created by fear, general physical arousal, or parental interference.

Liking and loving appear to be separate emotions; loving is not just strong liking. Liking consists of favorable evaluations of the other person and of feelings of similarity to the other; loving consists of feelings of attachment, caring, and intimacy. Friend-

ship and love relationships share many characteristics, although love contains components not found in liking. Research on styles of love suggests people differ in their characteristic ways of loving.

Romantic relationships become more intimate over time. A four stage theory of relationship development was presented. It posits that couples go through exploration, bargaining, commitment, and institutionalization as the relationship develops.

We presented a multi-factor theory of love that takes into consideration the fact that different stages of a relationship may be guided by different factors. Filtering theory, an exchange theory, suggests that, in the first or stimulus stage, such initial impressions as those based upon physical attractiveness are most important to the continuation of the relationship. In the middle or value comparison stage, similarity of values best predicts intensification of the relationship. In the final or role stage, role compatibility governs the fate of the relationship.

An exchange theory was proposed to explain the dissolution of relationships. Where attractions within the relationship are low, barriers to marital dissolution are low, and alternative attractions to the relationship are high, marital breakups become likely.

Theories of attraction, particularly of mate selection, rely too strongly on individual factors and overlook the larger social setting. The social setting is important because it determines which spouse-candidates will actually have contact with each other. Further, the social setting determines the individual's definition of what is desirable in a spouse.

■

REFERENCES

1. Breault, K. D. and A. J. Kposowa, 1987, "Explaining Divorce in the United States: A Study of 3,111 Counties, 1980," *Journal of Marriage and the Family* 49:549–588.
2. Seeman, M., T. Seeman, and Marnie Sayles, 1985, "Social Networks and Health Status: A Longitudinal Analysis," *Social Psychology Quarterly* 48:237–248; P. A. Thoits, 1983, "Multiple Identities and Psychological Well-being," *American Sociological Review* 48:174–187.
3. Hansell, S., 1985, "Adolescent Friendship Networks and Distress in School," *Social Forces* 63:698–715.

4. Kerckhoff, A. C., 1974, "The Social Context of Attraction," in T. L. Huston (Ed.), *Foundations of Interpersonal Attraction,* New York: Academic Press.

5. Festinger, L., S. Schachter, and K. Back, 1950, *Social Pressures in Informal Groups: A Study of Human Factors in Housing,* New York: Harper & Row.

6. Swap, W. C., 1977, "Interpersonal Attraction and Repeated Exposure to Rewarders and Punishers," *Personality and Social Psychology Bulletin* 3:248–251; R. B. Zajonc, 1968, "Attitudinal Effects of Mere Exposure," *Journal of Personality and Social Psychology Monographs Supplement* 9:1–27.

7. Harrison, A. A., R. M. Tutone, and D. G. McFadgen, 1971, "Effects of Frequency of Exposure of Changing and Unchanging Stimulus Pairs on Affective Ratings," *Journal of Personality and Social Psychology* 20:102–111; R. B. Zajonc, H. Markus, and W. R. Wilson, 1974, "Exposure Effects and Associative Learning," *Journal of Experimental Social Psychology* 10:248–263.

8. Mita, T. H., M. Dermer, and J. Knight, 1977, "Reversed Facial Images and the Mere-exposure Hypothesis," *Journal of Personality and Social Psychology* 35:597–601.

9. Moreland, R. L. and R. B. Zanonc, 1982, "Exposure Effects in Person Perception: Familiarity, Similarity, and Attraction," *Journal of Experimental Social Psychology* 18:395–415.

10. White, G. L. and D. Shapiro, 1987, "Don't I Know You? Antecedents and Social Consequences of Perceived Familiarity," *Journal of Experimental Social Psychology* 23:75–92.

11. Mills, C. W., 1940, "Situated Actions and Vocabularies of Motive," *American Sociological Review* 5:904–913.

12. Goode, W. J., 1970, *World Revolution and Family Patterns,* 2d ed, New York: The Free Press.

13. Scanzoni, J., 1972, *Sexual Bargaining,* Englewood Cliffs, NJ: Prentice-Hall.

14. Thibault, J. W. and H. H. Kelley, 1959, *The Social Psychology of Groups,* New York: Wiley; see also H. H. Kelley and J. W. Thibault, 1978, *Interpersonal Relations: A Theory of Interdependence,* New York: Wiley Interscience; and H. H. Kelley, 1982, "Love and Commitment," in H. H. Kelley, E. Berscheid, A. Christensen, J. Harvey, T. L. Huston, G. Levinger, E. Mc-Clintock, A. Peplau, and D. R. Peterson, *Close Relationships,* San Francisco: Freeman.

15. Goffman, E., 1952, "On Cooling the Mark Out: Some Aspects of Adaptation to Failure," *Psychiatry* 15:451–463.

16. Berg, J. H., 1984, "Development of Friendship between Roommates," *Journal of Personality and Social Psychology* 46:346–356; J. H. Berg and R. D. McQuinn, 1986, "Attraction and Exchange in Continuing and Noncontinuing Dating," *Journal of Personality and Social Psychology* 50:942–952.

17. Hays, R. B., 1985, "A Longitudinal Study of Friendship Development," *Journal of Personality and Social Psychology* 48:909–924; R. B. Hays, 1984, "The Development and Maintenance of Friendship," *Journal of Social and Personal Relationships* 1:75–97.

18. Scanzoni, 1972, op. cit.

19. Eslinger, K. N., A. C. Clarke, and R. R. Dynes, 1972, "The Principle of Least Interest: Dating Behavior and Family Integration Settings," *Journal of Marriage and the Family* 34:269–272.

20. Hatfield, E., J. Traupmann, S. Sprecher, M. Utne, and J. Hay, 1985, "Equity and Intimate Relations: Recent Research," in W. Ickes (Ed.), *Compatible and Incompatible Relationships,* New York: Springer-Verlag; E. Walster, G. W. Walster, and E. Berscheid, 1978, *Equity: Theory and Research,* Boston: Allyn and Bacon.

21. Davidson, B., 1984, "A Test of Equity Theory for Marital Adjustment," *Social Psychology Quarterly* 47:36–41; B. Davidson, J. Balswick, and C. Halverson, 1983, "Affective Self-disclosure and Marital Adjustment: A Test of Equity Theory," *Journal of Marriage and the Family* 45:93–102; J. Mirowsky, 1985, "Depression and Marital Power: An Equity Model," *American Journal of Sociology* 91:557–592.

22. Schafer, R. B. and P. M. Keith, 1980, "Equity and Depression among Married Couples," *Social Psychology Quarterly* 43:430–435.

23. Sprecher, S., 1986, "The Relation between Inequity and Emotions in Close Relationships," *Social Psychology Quarterly* 49:309–321.

24. Byrne, D., 1971, *The Attraction Paradigm,* New York: Academic Press; M. H. Gonzales, J. M. Davis, G. L. Loney, C. K. Lukens, and C. M. Jughans, 1983, "Interactional Approach to Interpersonal Attraction," *Journal of Personality and Social Psychology* 44:1192–1197; C. Hendrick and H. A. Page, 1970, "Self-esteem, Attitude Similarity, and Attraction," *Journal of Personality* 38:588–601.

25. Billy, J. O. G., J. L. Rodgers, and J. R. Udry, 1983, "Adolescent Sexual Behavior and Friendship Choice," *Social Forces* 62:653–678.

26. Hill, C. T. and D. E. Stull, 1981, "Sex Differences in Effects of Social and Value Similarity in Same-sex Friendships," *Journal of Personality and Social Psychology* 41:488–502.

27. Tesser, A., J. Campbell, and M. Smith, 1984, "Friendship Choice and Performance: Self-evaluation Maintenance in Children," *Journal of Personality and Social Psychology* 46:561–574.

28. Byrne, 1971, op. cit.; W. Griffitt, 1974, "Attitude Similarity and Attraction," in T. L. Huston, op. cit.

29. Condon, J. W. and W. D. Crano, 1988, "Inferred Evaluation and the Relation between Attitude Similarity and Interpersonal Attraction," *Journal of Personality and Social Psychology* 54:789–797.

30. Rosenbaum, M. E., 1986, "The Revulsion Hypothesis: On the Nondevelopment of Relationships," *Journal of Personality and Social Psychology* 51:1156–1166; M. E. Rosenbaum, 1986, "Comment on a Proposed Two-stage Theory of Relationship Formation: First Repulsion, Then, Attraction," *Journal of Personality and Social Psychology* 51:1171–1172.

31. Kerckhoff, 1974, ibid.

32. Antill, J. K., 1983, "Sex Role Complementarity versus

Similarity in Married Couples," *Journal of Personality and Social Psychology* 45:145–155; S. A. Pursell and P. G. Banikiotes, 1978, "Androgyny and Initial Interpersonal Attraction," *Personality and Social Psychology Bulletin* 4:235–243.

33. Lesnik-Oberstein, M. and L. Cohen, 1984, "Cognitive Style, Sensation-seeking, and Assortative Mating," *Journal of Personality and Social Psychology* 46:112–117.

34. Berscheid, E., 1985, "Interpersonal Attraction," in G. Lindzey and E. Aronson (Eds.), *Handbook of Social Psychology,* 3d ed, New York: Random House.

35. Byrne, D. and S. Murnen, 1988, "Maintaining Love Relationships," in R. J. Sternberg and M. L. Barnes (Eds.), *The Psychology of Love,* New Haven: Yale University Press; S. S. Hendrick, C. Hendrick, and N. L. Adler, 1988, "Romantic Relationships: Love, Satisfaction, and Staying Together," *Journal of Personality and Social Psychology* 54:980–988; J. H. Pickford, E. I. Signori, and H. Rempel, 1966, "Similar or Related Personality Traits as a Factor in Marital Happiness," *Journal of Marriage and the Family* 28:190–192; J. H. Pickford, E. I. Signori, and H. Rempel, 1966, "The Intensity of Personality Traits in Relation to Marital Happiness," *Journal of Marriage and the Family* 28:458–459.

36. Hill, C. T., Z. Rubin, and L. A. Peplau, 1976, "Breakups before Marriage: The End of 103 Affairs," *Journal of Social Issues* 32:147–168.

37. Levinger, G. and J. Breedlove, 1966, "Interpersonal Attraction and Agreement: A Study of Marriage Partners," *Journal of Personality and Social Psychology* 3:367–372.

38. Winch, R. F., 1967, "Another Look at the Theory of Complementary Needs in Mate-selection," *Journal of Marriage and the Family* 29:756–762; R. F. Winch, 1958, *Mate-selection: A Theory of Complementary Needs,* New York: Harper & Row.

39. Levinger, G., 1983, "Development and Change," in H. H. Kelley et al., op. cit.; B. I. Murstein, 1976, *Who Will Marry Whom?* New York: Springer.

40. Murstein, 1976, ibid.

41. Thorndike, E. L., 1898, *Animal Intelligence,* New York: Macmillan.

42. Clore, G. L. and D. Byrne, 1974, "A Reinforcement-Affect Model of Attraction," in T. L. Huston, op. cit.

43. Michaels, J. W., J. N. Edwards, and A. Acock, 1984, "Satisfaction in Intimate Relationships as a Function of Inequality, Inequity, and Outcomes," *Social Psychology Quarterly* 47:347–357.

44. Clore and Byrne, 1974, op. cit.

45. Griffitt, W., 1968, "Attraction toward a Stranger as a Function of Direct and Associated Reinforcement," *Psychonomic Science* 11:147–148.

46. Rosenblatt, P. C., 1974, "Cross-cultural Perspective on Attraction," in T. L. Huston, op. cit.

47. Aronson, E., B. Willerman, and J. Floyd, 1966, "The Effect of a Pratfall on Increasing Interpersonal Attractiveness," *Psychonomic Science* 4:227–228.

48. Langlois, J. H. and C. W. Stephan, 1981, "Beauty and the Beast: The Role of Physical Attractiveness in the Development of Peer Relations and Social Behavior," in S. S. Brehm, S. M. Kassin, and F. X. Gibbons, *Developmental Social Psychology,* New York: Oxford University Press.

49. Dion, K. K. and E. Berscheid, 1974, "Physical Attractiveness and Peer Perception among Children," *Sociometry* 37:1–12.

50. Langlois, J. H. and C. Stephan, 1977, "The Effects of Physical Attractiveness and Ethnicity on Children's Behavioral Attributions and Peer Preferences," *Child Development* 48:1694–1698.

51. Berscheid, E. and E. Walster, 1974, "Physical Attractiveness," in L. Berkowitz (Ed.), *Advances in Experimental Social Psychology,* Vol. 7, New York: Academic Press; G. R. Adams, 1982, "Physical Attractiveness," in A. G. Miller (Ed.), *In the Eye of the Beholder,* New York: Praeger.

52. Dion, K. K., E. Berscheid, and E. Walster, 1972, "What Is Beautiful Is Good," *Journal of Personality and Social Psychology* 24:285–290.

53. Berscheid and Walster, 1974, op. cit.

54. Langlois and Stephan, 1981, op. cit.

55. Snyder, M., E. D. Tanke, and E. Berscheid, 1977, "Social Perception and Interpersonal Behavior: On the Self-fulfilling Nature of Social Stereotypes," *Journal of Personality and Social Psychology* 35:656–666.

56. Miller, H. L. and W. H. Rivenbark III, 1970, "Sexual Differences in Physical Attractiveness as a Determinant of Heterosexual Likings," *Psychological Reports* 27:701–702; A. Tesser and M. Brodie, 1971, "A Note on the Evaluation of a 'Computer Date,'" *Psychonomic Science* 23:300.

57. Walster, E., V. Aronson, D. Abrahams, and L. Rottman, 1966, "The Importance of Physical Attractiveness in Dating Behavior," *Journal of Personality and Social Psychology* 4:508–516.

58. Buss, D. M. and M. Barnes, 1986, "Preferences in Human Mate Selection," *Journal of Personality and Social Psychology* 50:559–570.

59. Margolin, L. and L. White, 1987, "The Continuing Role of Physical Attractiveness in Marriage," *Journal of Marriage and the Family* 49:21–27.

60. Berscheid and Walster, 1974, op. cit.

61. Huston, T. L., 1973, "Ambiguity of Acceptance, Social Desirability, and Dating Choice," *Journal of Experimental Social Psychology* 9:32–42.

62. White, G. L., 1980, "Physical Attractiveness and Courtship Progress," *Journal of Personality and Social Psychology* 39:660–669.

63. Zajonc, R. B., P. K. Adelmann, S. T. Murphy, and P. M. Niedenthal, 1987, "Convergence in the Physical Appearance of Spouses," *Motivation and Emotion* 11:335–346.

64. *New York Review of Books,* December 17, 1987.

65. Mettee, D. R. and E. Aronson, 1974, "Affective Reactions to Appraisal from Others," in T. L. Huston, op. cit.

66. McCall, G. J., 1974, "A Symbolic Interactionist Approach to Attraction," in T. L. Huston, op. cit.

67. Heider, F., 1958, *The Psychology of Interpersonal Relations,*

New York: Wiley; T. Newcomb, 1961, *The Acquaintance Process,* New York: Holt, Rinehart & Winston.

68. Schachter, S. and J. E. Singer, 1962, "Cognitive, Social, and Physiological Determinants of Emotional State," *Psychological Review* 69:379–399.

69. Berscheid and Walster, 1974, op. cit.

70. Dutton, D. and A. Aron, 1974, "Some Evidence for Heightened Sexual Attraction under Conditions of High Anxiety," *Journal of Personality and Social Psychology* 30:510–517.

71. White, G. L., S. Fishbein, and J. Rutstein, 1981, "Passionate Love and the Misattribution of Arousal," *Journal of Personality and Social Psychology* 41:56–62.

72. White, Fishbein, and Rutstein, 1981, ibid.

73. Driscoll, R., K. E. Davis, and M. E. Lipetz, 1972, "Parental Interference and Romantic Love: The Romeo and Juliet Effect," *Journal of Personality and Social Psychology* 24:1–10.

74. e.g., A. Bandura and R. Walters, 1963, *Social Learning and Personality Development,* New York: Holt, Rinehart & Winston.

75. Rubin, Z., 1970, "Measurement of Romantic Love," *Journal of Personality and Social Psychology* 16:265–273.

76. Rubin, 1970, ibid.

77. Davis, K., 1985, "Near and Dear: Friendship and Love Compared," *Psychology Today,* February, 22–30.

78. Hendrick, C. and S. Hendrick, 1986, "A Theory and Method of Love," *Journal of Personality and Social Psychology* 50:392–402.

79. Hendrick and Hendrick, 1986, ibid.

80. Burgess, R. L. and T. L. Huston (Eds.), 1979, *Social Exchange in Developing Relationships,* New York: Academic Press.

81. Secord, P. F. and C. W. Backman, 1974, *Social Psychology,* 2d ed, New York: McGraw-Hill; C. W. Backman, 1981, "Attraction in Interpersonal Relationships," in M. Rosenberg and R. H. Turner (Eds.), *Social Psychology: Sociological Perspectives,* New York: Basic Books.

82. Murstein, 1976, op. cit.

83. Murstein, 1976, ibid.

84. Steinberg, L. and S. B. Silverberg, 1987, "Influences on Marital Satisfaction during the Middle Stages of the Family Life Cycle," *Journal of Marriage and the Family* 49:751–760.

85. Steinberg and Silverberg, 1987, ibid.

86. Glenn, N. D. and C. N. Weaver, 1988, "The Changing Relationship of Marital Status to Reported Happiness," *Journal of Marriage and the Family* 50:317–324.

87. Spitze, G., 1988, "Women's Employment and Family Relations: A Review," *Journal of Marriage and the Family* 50:595–618.

88. Levinger, G., 1979, "A Social Psychological Perspective on Marital Dissolution," in G. Levinger and O. C. Moles (Eds.), *Divorce and Separation,* New York: Basic Books.

89. Morgan, S. P. and R. R. Rindfuss, 1985, "Marital Disruption: Structural and Temporal Dimensions," *American Journal of Sociology* 90:1055–1077.

90. Kerckhoff, 1974, op. cit.

CHAPTER 12

Prosocial Behavior

Sociobiology

Biological Evolution

Social Evolution

Bystander Intervention

Stage I

Stage II

Stage III

Stage IV

Helper/Situation/Recipient Approach

The Helper

The Situation

The Recipient

In a single day our local newspaper carried the following contrasting stories:

NEW YORK (UPI)—*At least 30 people watched a vagrant beaten and stabbed to death in a mid-morning attack in Central Park but no one went to the victim's aid.... "Nobody came near," said Transit Authority Police Officer Charles Irving. "I can half understand it—it was so awful they had to be frightened. But there's strength in numbers. They could have thrown a rock or something. They did nothing to stop it."*

Irving said 30 to 40 people were standing along Central Park West about 90 feet away from where a man identified as Jimmy Lee Jones attacked another man who had been sleeping on a rock in the park, beating him with a wire litterbasket. Jones then took a piece of wire from his pocket and tried to sever the victim's head, Irving said, and stabbed him in the face, neck, and back of the head with a 28-inch piece of wood. The assailant tried to decapitate his victim while the crowd watched, Irving said. "It's the worst thing I've seen in 23 years on the job," he said. "There was blood running off the rocks, across the grass and into the bushes."

CALUMET CITY, ILL. (UPI)—*Neighbors begged James Stigall to flee his blazing ramshackle home. "I'm not coming down unless I can save my children first," the father of seven screamed. Moments later the house's roof collapsed in flames Sunday, trapping and killing Stigall and five of his daughters. His body was found atop his 15-month-old daughter Samantha in the second floor of the house that his neighbors called a firetrap.*

Two other daughters, one of them seven months pregnant, escaped the blaze in a south Chicago suburb. The pregnant daughter, Ila, 17, was pushed from a second-floor window by a neighbor and landed on an awning that broke her fall.... The unidentified neighbor who helped Ila escape said he had Samantha in his arms but dropped her "because I couldn't breathe. I

did my best," he said. Another daughter, Lisa, 9, was rescued by two men who pulled a ladder up to the attic windows and helped her climb down. (1)

These two incidents raise the primary question we will address in this chapter: Why are people willing to be helpful in some situations, even to the point of giving their lives, and yet unwilling to help in others? Before we can begin to answer this question, we should clarify what we mean by helping.

We can probably agree that donating blood, helping a blind person cross the street, and rescuing a drowning person are helpful behaviors. But what about a student who helps another with her homework with the idea of starting up a relationship in the process; an alumnus who gives money to her alma mater in hopes that they will name a building after her; or a person who donates a kidney so his beloved sister can live? Definitions of help are very much linked to issues of motivation and the relative costs and benefits of the behavior for the giver and the recipient. It is clear that behaviors that are intended to benefit the recipient and which involve considerable costs and few rewards for the giver are helping. When the motive is less purely altruistic and the giver receives benefits, as well as bestowing them, it is less clear that the behavior is an instance of helping. We will use a definition which says that helping behaviors are intended to benefit the recipient and entail greater costs than rewards for the giver. The complexity of applying this definition is apparent in considering the motives of volunteerism (see Box 12-1 and Figure 12-1).

One attempt to understand the causes of helping has been made by sociobiologists and social psychologists concerned with the influence of biology on behavior. These theorists have sought to determine if there is a biological basis for altruistic behavior. Other social psychologists have examined the decision-making processes involved when bystanders decide whether or not to help someone in need. A third approach has focused on factors in the person, the situation, and the recipient that influence helping. We will explore each of these

BOX 12-1

Charitable Giving and Volunteerism

Americans are a generous people. The vast majority (86 percent) give money to charities every year (2). In 1985, they donated 66 billion dollars to nonprofit charitable, religious, and educational organizations (3). On the average, this amounted to about 2 percent of our incomes, the highest rate in over 15 years.

When we attempt to profile those who are most generous, some interesting findings emerge. People who are middle-aged are more likely to give than younger or older people. Those who are better educated are somewhat more generous than those with less education (4). However, the percentage of employed people who give is not very different from the percentage of unemployed people who give (88 percent vs. 83 percent). And, if we look at the percentage of their incomes they contribute to charity, the poor are more generous than the rich. Internal Revenue Service figures show that people with incomes of less than $15,000 contribute a greater percentage of their incomes to charity than those whose incomes are above $15,000 (see Figure 12-1). The lowest rates of giving are for people earning $30,000 to $75,000 per year (5). During the 1980s the contributions of the wealthy steadily declined, while those of people with incomes of $5,000 to $50,000 increased (6).

When interviewed, people say they give primarily out of a sense of moral obligation, although many acknowledge the importance of personal satisfaction (7). But, when asked why others give, people say that others do it for reasons of status, prestige, respect, and acclaim (8). It seems that charitable people are not so charitable when it comes to describing the motives of others.

Every year millions of Americans also volunteer their time and energy to help others. The amount of time Americans volunteer to help charities is worth almost as much as their monetary contributions. The typical volunteers are women, young to middle-aged people, people who have gone to college, and those earning more than $20,000 (9). When asked why they volunteer their time, people say it is primarily for reasons of personal satisfaction, but for many people moral obligations also play a role (10).

These people hardly seem selfish, but a number of them appear to be seeking some sort of self-satisfaction by giving of themselves. Thus, they derive some benefits from serving as volunteers. Does this mean that their considerable efforts should not be considered helpful? No. Here, the costs to the individuals in terms of their own time and money seem to be great, the benefits to them are probably not the primary reason they make these donations, and the donations are enormously beneficial to the recipients. ■

Figure 12.1 ■

Charitable Deductions for People Who Itemize Their Deductions

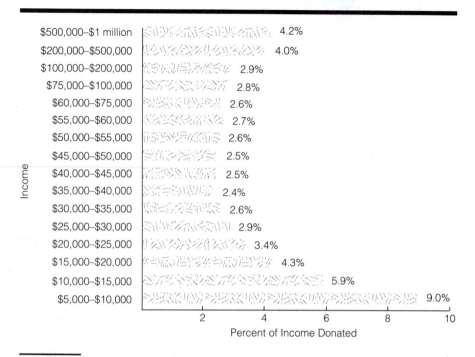

Income	Percent of Income Donated
$500,000–$1 million	4.2%
$200,000–$500,000	4.0%
$100,000–$200,000	2.9%
$75,000–$100,000	2.8%
$60,000–$75,000	2.6%
$55,000–$60,000	2.7%
$50,000–$55,000	2.6%
$45,000–$50,000	2.5%
$40,000–$45,000	2.5%
$35,000–$40,000	2.4%
$30,000–$35,000	2.6%
$25,000–$30,000	2.9%
$20,000–$25,000	3.4%
$15,000–$20,000	4.3%
$10,000–$15,000	5.9%
$5,000–$10,000	9.0%

Note: The numbers represent percent of income donated.

Adapted from *Individual Income Tax Returns,* 1984. Internal Revenue Service. Washington DC: U.S. Government Printing Office.

approaches. Although the majority of the research that forms the basis for this chapter was done within psychological social psychology, sociological social psychologists have made significant contributions to every topic discussed.

■
SOCIOBIOLOGY

Is human behavior genetically determined and if so to what degree? The debate has raged for more than a century. The question concerns the very roots of human nature. Are we selfish or are we altruistic? A pessimistic sociologist recently wrote, "Most of us most of the time are nasty, brutish, and self seeking" (11). Do you agree?

Biological Evolution

Sociobiology is the study of the biological origins of social behavior. It is based on the theory of evolution, formulated by Charles Darwin more than a century ago. This quote from Darwin gives the essence of the theory:

> *As many more individuals of each species are born than can possibly survive; and as, consequently, there is a frequently recurring struggle for existence, it follows that any being, if it vary however slightly in any manner profitable to itself . . . will have a better chance of surviving, and thus be naturally selected. From the strong principle of inheritance, any selected variety will tend to propagate its new and modified form. (12)*

Three concepts are central to the theory of evolution: variation, selection, and retention. In biological evolution, *variations* in physiology and behavior occur as a result of random mutations in the genes. The variations in physiology and behavior that enable organisms to reproduce more effectively are *selected*. The variations that are ultimately selected are said to be adaptive because they enable the organisms to adapt more effectively to their environments. Adaptive mutations are *retained* through inheritance, which allows them to be passed from one generation to the next.

Evolutionary changes in species are usually painstakingly slow, taking place over an enormous number of generations. However, occasionally rapid changes occur when an adaptive mutation spreads quickly within a species. It is important to keep in mind that evolution is a random process—there is no plan. It is not predestined nor is there a goal toward which it is headed—it just happens. Most mutations are fatal. For example, being born without a stomach would doom most animals. Only a small proportion of mutations are adaptive. For example, a mutation that enabled an animal to digest a readily available food source such as fibrous plants would be adaptive. When mutations make it possible for an animal to survive and reproduce more effectively than other animals, these adaptive mutations become more prevalent in the next generation due to inheritance.

Both physiological and behavioral characteristics can be inherited. Nest building in birds and dam building in beavers are examples of inherited behaviors in animals, while the sucking reflex and the pain-withdrawal reflex are examples of adaptive inherited behaviors in humans.

The question that sociobiologists ask about altruistic behavior is, "Is it adaptive?" since, if it is not adaptive, it is unlikely to be biologically determined. Altruism involves giving aid to another member of one's species without receiving anything in return. If giving assistance involves some danger to the giver, or if it involves considerable costs to the giver in terms of time or energy, it does not seem likely that it would be adaptive. For instance, if a bird that gives a warning call increases the chances it will be eaten by the hawk circling overhead, then it would seem to be maladaptive to give the warning. Biologically, it would seem to be more adaptive to be selfish, to look after one's own welfare, rather than that of others. However, sociobiologists argue there are two conditions under which the genetic bias toward selfishness is overcome.

When Darwin discussed the survival of the fittest, he was referring to the individual organism's ability to survive and reproduce. Recently, sociobiologists have expanded this concept. If an organism's behavior increases the chances that its relatives will survive and reproduce, then the probability that the organism's genes will survive also increases. This is called *inclusive fitness*. If a parent sacrifices itself so its offspring can survive, it has improved its inclusive fitness—its genes will survive, even if it does not. Sociobiologists refer to this type of altruism as *self-sacrificial altruism* (13). A mother seal who dies successfully defending her offspring from predation is engaging in this type of altruism.

Since genes are passed down from one generation to the next, anything increasing the chances that an individual's genes will survive is adaptive. As one theorist put it: "The animal can be regarded as a machine designed to preserve copies of the genes" (14). In some cases, preserving one's genes can best be accomplished by sacrificing oneself so one's offspring can survive.

The second type of adaptive altruistic behavior occurs when one animal gives assistance to another with the expectation it will receive similar assistance in return. This is called *reciprocal altruism* (15). A monkey grooming another monkey to remove lice and other parasites does not improve its own chances of survival by doing so—unless it receives a similar benefit in return. Reciprocal altruism occurs when the ultimate benefits received by both animals, in terms of survival and reproduction, are greater than their costs. This type of altruism fits the Biological Golden Rule—do unto others as you would have them do unto you—if the costs are low and the benefits are high (16). Reciprocal altruism is most likely to evolve in intelligent, highly social species in which the members are capable of recognizing and remembering one another. Thus, human beings should display this type of altruism.

Just how much of human behavior is governed by biologically determined tendencies and how much is culturally determined is hotly disputed among sociobiologists. One leading sociobiologist, Edward O. Wilson, argues that genes hold culture on a "very long leash." He means that a great deal of human behavior is culturally determined, but that the essence of human nature is biologically determined. Thus, the form and intensity of behavioral acts may be culturally determined, but the tendency to engage in certain types of behavior could be biologically determined (17). The father's self-sacrificial altruism during the fire included many culturally learned behaviors, but was the desire to save his children biologically determined? Sociobiology tells us how such behaviors could have evolved, but at present we do not know for certain whether altruistic behaviors in humans are among the acts that are genetically influenced.

One suggestive piece of evidence comes from a recent study of 573 pairs of twins (18). The identical twins (those whose genes are identical) were more similar to one another on a measure of altruism than the fraternal twins (those who are no more similar genetically than other brothers and sisters). The higher similarity in altruism of the identical twins is most likely due to their greater genetic similarity, thus indicating that tendencies toward altruism may be inherited. The researchers estimated that 50 percent of altruism in the twins was biologically determined and 50 percent was culturally determined. These results support the sociobiological position that altruistic tendencies can be inherited, but they also show that culture plays a major role.

Social Evolution

Social evolutionists believe the biological theory of evolution has a cultural counterpart (19). According to the social evolutionists, societies also evolve through the processes of variation, selection, and retention. In social evolution, these processes op-erate on whole societies, not on individuals as they do in biological evolution. Thus, social evolution is concerned with the survival of societies more than the survival of individuals. In social evolution, social structure and customs are analogous to the physiology and behavior studied in biological evolution.

Variations in customs can occur intentionally or haphazardly. In some cases, members of one society consciously adopt a practice they have observed in another society. This process is called *cultural diffusion,* and it accounts for the spread of important innovations, such as the use of pottery, writing, and more recently, the spread of modern technology. All societies are constantly changing, but only some of the changes are selected and endure.

The ultimate selection criterion for societies, as for individuals, is whether they survive. As we know, some societies, such as the Greek, Roman, and Mayan civilizations, did not survive. Typically, the variations that are *selected* improve the society's chances of survival. For example, the Ten Commandments have survived for more than 20 centuries because these rules apparently help societies to survive by prohibiting socially destructive behaviors. The primary mechanism through which a society *retains* the selected variations is the socialization of the young. Socialization is very serious business; without it no society could survive, because children would not learn the customs, norms, and roles that constitute their society.

From the social evolutionary perspective, one of the goals of society is to oppose biological tendencies toward selfishness. To do so, nearly all societies have evolved norms that promote altruism. Altruism is preached by all the great religions of the world. For example, the followers of Nibbanic Buddhism are instructed to base their behavior on love. For Nibbanic Buddhists, love has three components: one stresses pity for those who suffer; another stresses friendliness for all creatures; and the third stresses feeling pleasure in the happiness of others. Only when one's actions show these kinds of love can one achieve the emotional detachment required for salvation. Giving to others is the primary way one acquires merit in this type of Buddhism (20).

■ *Tying one on. Children learn the norm of altruism at an early age. (WGS)*

From the social evolutionary perspective, norms of altruism have evolved because they are adaptive for the survival of the society, not the individual. Such norms lead to the sharing of scarce resources, as occurs in hunting and gathering societies when a hunter distributes the meat from a kill. They also contribute to social cohesion and integration by binding people together and fostering concern about the welfare of others.

As evidence for the social evolution of altruism, social evolutionists cite a type of altruism human beings display that is never seen in other animals—altruism that benefits nonfamily members. Human beings will help others who are not related to them at considerable cost to themselves and without any thought of receiving future benefits for themselves. The behavior of the nonfamily members who tried

to save the children in the burning house, in the example we cited above, illustrates altruism that does not benefit one's kin. Less dramatic examples of altruism toward nonfamily members, including giving to charities, helping in emergencies, and simple generosity, occur frequently.

While the social evolutionists argue that social evolution is analogous to biological evolution in important ways, there are also differences between them. Biological evolution is principally concerned with individual fitness, is usually slow, and is random. Social evolution is concerned with societal fitness, is relatively fast, and can take place in planned, as well as unplanned, ways. One of the most fascinating facts about these two types of evolution is that they occur simultaneously and are interdependent. Social evolution depends in part on fundamental aspects

Table 12.1 ■

A Comparison between Biological and Cultural Evolution

	Biological Evolution	Cultural Evolution
Mechanisms	Variation (random mutation in the genes)	Planned and haphazard change
	Selection (adaptive changes increase reproduction)	Adaptive changes aid societal survival
	Retention (genetic variations transmitted through inheritance)	Socialization
Causes of Variation	Changes always random (but genetic engineering is changing this)	Changes often planned
Criterion of Fitness	Individual fitness emphasized	Societal fitness emphasized
Rate of Change	Usually slow, but rapid changes do occur	Usually faster than in biological evolution

of human nature created through biological evolution. However, biological evolution continues to occur at the same time that culture evolves. What is biologically adaptive at one point in cultural evolution, such as in hunting and gathering societies, may be different from what is adaptive in modern industrial societies. Biological evolution therefore depends on cultural evolution to some extent. In the case of altruism, cultural evolution appears to have expanded the limited range of altruistic behaviors humans are biologically predisposed to display. Table 12-1 summarizes the main points of social and biological evolution.

Despite whatever biological and cultural tendencies may favor helping and altruism, in many instances people do not help when help is needed. In the next approach to helping that we will discuss, some of the reasons why people do not help in emergency situations will be considered.

■ BYSTANDER INTERVENTION

Why did the people in the first example we cited in our introduction to this chapter stand and do nothing while they watched someone being beaten to death? John Darley and Bibb Latané have studied reasons why people do not offer help (21). They suggest that in making a decision about whether to help in an emergency, people progress through a series of four stages (see Figure 12-2).

Stage I

In the *first stage,* the crucial issue is whether people notice that someone needs help. People sometimes fail to notice others who need help because they

Figure 12.2 ■

Decision Tree for Bystander Intervention

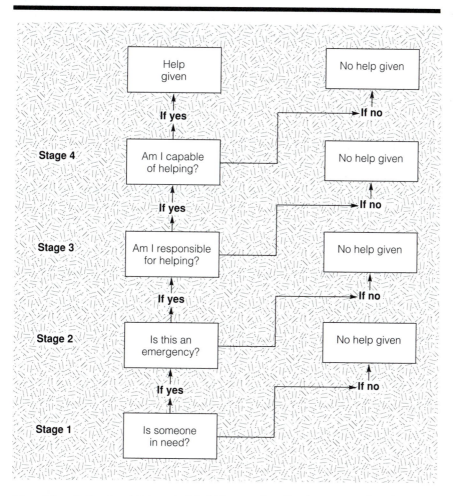

Adapted from Darley, J. and B. Latané, 1968, "When People Will Help in a Crisis," *Psychology Today* 2:54–57.

think it is impolite to look too closely at others. Most of us were taught to respect the privacy of others and to avoid staring at them. Following this norm can mean we will fail to notice another person who needs our help.

In other cases, people fail to notice someone in need because they are distracted by other things. In

a study demonstrating the effects of distraction, the investigators devised a situation in which a person with a cast on his arm appeared to need assistance (22). The person began unloading boxes from his car when a lone male approached. As the lone male came nearer, the person with the boxes stumbled and dropped them. If someone was mowing an adjacent yard with a noisy mower, only 15 percent of the passersby stopped to help. When the mower was a quiet one, 80 percent of the passersby stopped to help. The authors suggest that the noisy mower acted as a distraction and made it less likely the passersby would notice that someone needed their help.

People are also less likely to notice someone who needs help if they are very involved in what they are doing or if there are too many things to attend to at one time. Students doing a complex task under crowded conditions and people in crowded urban areas have been found to be less helpful than those in less demanding situations (23).

Stage II

The *second stage* concerns whether an individual defines the situation as an emergency, once he or she has noticed it. If the situation is not defined as an emergency, the individual is unlikely to help. People sometimes misinterpret what they see. For instance, people may pass by a heart attack victim if they believe they are seeing a drunk who has passed out.

In attempting to decide if a given situation is an emergency, the individual may use social comparison information. The person may ask, "Are others responding to this situation as if it were an emergency?" If other people are not acting like the situation is an emergency, then the person may decide there is no problem. The person may also do nothing in an attempt to stay cool or to avoid the embarrassment of responding to an "emergency" only to find it is not really an emergency. The problem is that other people in the situation may also be playing it cool and acting like they are unconcerned. Thus, no one will respond until someone else takes the initiative, and as a result, no help is given.

In a classic experiment dealing with this process, students were asked to participate in a study of their reactions to urban living (24). A solitary student or a group of three students then started to complete a questionnaire. While the students were completing the questionnaire, smoke began to seep through a vent into the room. When the students were alone, they typically noticed the smoke immediately, looked for its source, and then left the room to find the experimenter. Seventy-five percent of the students who were alone quickly reported this emergency.

The students who were in groups of three responded much differently. These students were slower to notice the smoke and, after they did notice it, they furtively looked at the other students to see how they were responding. Less than 15 percent of these students reported the smoke to the experimenter. When they were asked why they had not reported the smoke, these students gave answers indicating they had not defined the situation as an emergency. One student said he thought the smoke came from steam pipes used to heat the building, while another said he thought the smoke came from the chemistry labs located in the building.

Misinterpretations of an emergency situation can only occur when there is some ambiguity about what is happening. Generally, the more ambiguous a situation is, the less likely bystanders are to help, especially if they are in a group (25).

Stage III

If a situation is defined as an emergency, people enter the *third stage,* in which they must decide who is responsible for responding to the emergency. In any emergency situation where more than one bystander is present, each person may feel the others are at least as responsible as he or she is. This phenomenon is known as *diffusion of responsibility.* The larger the group, the more each person's sense of responsibility is diluted, and the less likely it is that help will be given.

To test this idea, an experiment was conducted in which there was no ambiguity about whether an emergency existed (26). Each subject in this study believed he was participating in a discussion of the problems of urban living. He was led to believe there were two, three, or six people in the group. The subject was placed in an enclosed cubicle to "insure anonymity." The first "person" to respond mentioned various difficulties he was having in adjusting to New York and finished by saying he sometimes had nervous seizures. The other "people" in the group then discussed their problems in turn. All of these comments were prerecorded, including those of the first person. The real subject always spoke last. When it was the first person's turn to talk again, he started out hesitatingly and gradually became more and more incomprehensible. The last words the subject heard were "I could really er use er some h-help s-so if somebody would er give me a little h-help uh er-er-er-er c-could somebody er er help er uh uh uh I'm gonna die er er I'm gonna die er help er er seizure er er."

Among the subjects who believed they were alone with this person, 85 percent responded by leaving their cubicles to help him. When the subjects thought three people were in their group, 62 percent responded; and when the subjects thought six people were in their group, only 31 percent responded by helping. This study shows that as the size of a group increases, the responsibility for helping is diffused among a greater number of people and each person feels less responsible for helping.

The reduced helping among bystanders brought about by diffusion of responsibility does not occur when people in a group are acquainted with one another (27), or when the bystanders anticipate future interaction with each other (28). Also, when the help is easily rendered, the size of the group of bystanders does not affect helping (29). Thus, diffusion of responsibility is greatest and help is least likely when the bystanders are strangers and when helping involves some costs to the helpers. An example might help to clarify this point. One cold day in January 1982, a plane crashed over the Potomac River in Washington, D.C. Witnesses watched in horror as the icy waters claimed the survivors of the crash. One of the passengers was saved when a bystander jumped into the water and helped a helicopter lift her to safety. The witnesses were strangers and the costs of plunging into the frozen waters were great which explains why so few people helped. The exception to the rule, Lenny Skutnik, was given a heroism award by the president for his unusual bravery.

Stage IV

In *stage four* the person must formulate a plan to help and decide if he or she is capable of carrying out the plan. As in the earlier stages in this decision sequence, if a negative decision is made, no help will be given. For example, if you saw a person who was drowning and you were the only person available to help, you probably would not enter the water if you did not know how to swim. Studies have found that people with specialized training, such as Red Cross training, are more likely to help in emergencies than people who lack these skills (30). One study of people who intervened in actual emergency situations found that, in comparison to noninterveners, they had more training in lifesaving and medical techniques, and they were taller and heavier than noninterveners (31). The thread running through these studies is that competence promotes helping in emergencies.

When other people are available to help someone in need, each person may wonder if one of the others is more capable of giving help than he or she is. In a study done in the subways of New York, people were less likely to help a person in need if another bystander was wearing a doctor's coat than if the same bystander was dressed differently (32). The potential competence of other bystanders is another reason why the more people there are to help, the less likely someone who needs help will receive it.

One final example from our own experience will serve to illustrate these stages. While we were writing this chapter, we took a weekend off to do some skiing. After driving all evening, we arrived at a large city and found a motel. Just as we were going to sleep, we heard a knock on the door of the room above us. This knock was followed moments later by what sounded like a fight. We heard bodies crashing against the walls and floor. The struggle lasted no more than a minute. Then we heard someone leave. This person walked a few steps and faintly cried, "Help. Help." Then all was silent. What were we to do? We lay in the darkness for a minute or two waiting for something to happen—and think-

Are There Urban-Rural Differences in Helping?

People who live in cities are often viewed as unfriendly, brusque, untrusting, and unhelpful by people who do not live in cities. If this characterization is correct, research should show that people living in cities are less altruistic than people living in small towns or rural areas. Indeed, this is what many studies of this issue have found (34). However, other studies have failed to find rural-urban differences or have found that people from urban backgrounds are actually more helpful than people from rural backgrounds (35). Obviously, the problem is more complex than it seems.

What could account for the discrepancies in these findings? A study done in the Netherlands provides one clue (36). Although the investigators found no differences in the helpfulness of people living in large cities or small towns, they did find that when stimulus input was high (noisy, crowded streets), people were less helpful in both cities and towns. This result suggests that environmental factors, such as the aversiveness of the situation, may be more important than population size or personality factors in understanding helping in cities and towns.

A second clue comes from a study which found that people in cities were less

ing. Was this any of our business? Was it a fight between a couple of friends who had been drinking? What had happened to the victim? Why was the cry so weak? Was this a joke? Was the assailant gone or was he or she still in the room above us? Finally, one of us got up and looked out the window. There, slumped on the stairs was a young man, apparently unconscious. A moment later a person came to his aid. He immediately called to a second person to phone the police and an ambulance. The victim was a pizza delivery boy who had been attacked when he brought a pizza to the man in the room above us. He died shortly thereafter from four knife wounds he received during the attack.

Obviously, we noticed the fight (stage 1); but was someone in need (stage 2)? The situation was somewhat ambiguous, although it clearly needed

looking into. When we looked, it was apparent that help was needed. Were we responsible for helping this young man (stage 3)? Would we be attacked for doing so? We heard the person who responded first say that the victim's throat had been slit. Unfortunately, neither of us has any training in first aid, so we were poorly equipped to help (stage 4). Although we found the experience of being bystanders deeply distressing, it appears that there was little we could have done that had not already been done (stage 4).

Darley and Latané's four stages in decision making apply primarily to bystander intervention in emergency situations. They suggest that a bias exists toward not helping in emergencies. Intervention in emergencies is low because people fail to notice or misinterpret emergencies and do not regard themselves as responsible or feel competent to help. In

likely to let an interviewer into their homes than people who live in rural areas (37). This was especially true of older cities (for example, Pittsburgh) regardless of size, and of large new cities (for example, Phoenix). When they probed more deeply, they found the cause of these differences was that people in older cities and large new ones have a higher fear of crime than people in rural areas or newer small cities. Again, it was not the personality characteristics of city dwellers that influenced helping, but a perceived aspect of the environment. This conclusion is reinforced by a third study, which found that the strongest predictor of people's unwillingness to help someone who comes to their home is a concern for their own personal safety and vulnerability (38).

Another set of studies indicates that the density of the population within cities affects helping (39). As density increases, helping decreases. The lack of helping in these studies was not due to people not noticing the problem because the need for help was very obvious in most of these studies (a lost child asking for assistance). Instead, it appears that density makes people less sensitive to the needs of others. Although these studies did not examine urban-rural differences, they again show variations in helping in cities are due to environmental factors.

Considered together, these studies suggest that when people in cities are less helpful than people in towns or rural areas it is because of environmental factors, such as the complexity and aversiveness of the stimulus environment or a fear of negative consequences, rather than the negative personality characteristics of city dwellers. Thus, for helping in cities, it appears that environmental factors (E factors, in Lewin's terminology) may be more important than personality factors (P factors). ■

addition, emergencies are unexpected and people cannot plan how to respond ahead of time. Reasoned action is also inhibited by the fact that emergencies typically require an immediate response. Finally, fear of getting involved or being injured may inhibit helping in some emergency situations (33). To counteract the tendency to avoid helping, some states have Good Samaritan laws, making a failure to help in an emergency a punishable offense and protecting those who do help from being sued.

However, there are many other situations where help is needed and there is time for reasoned action. In these nonemergency situations, additional factors enter into the decision to help. The third approach we will present to helping, the helper/situation/recipient approach, applies to such nonemergency situations.

■
HELPER/SITUATION/ RECIPIENT APPROACH

As you may remember from Chapter 1, one of the founding fathers of social psychology, Kurt Lewin, used the following formula to represent the causes of human behavior $B = f(P + E)$. In this formula, the B stands for behavior, the f means "is a function of," the P stands for the person, and E represents the environment. Lewin viewed behavior as a product of an interaction between the person and the environment (see Box 12-2). We will use this approach, with one small addition, as a framework to guide this portion of our discussion of the causes of helping. A very important component of any situation in which a person is in need of help consists of the characteristics of the potential recipient. For this reason, we will separate the characteristics of the person who needs help from the other aspects of the situation in our discussion. Thus, in our approach we will give separate consideration to characteristics of the helper, of the situation, and of the recipient that affect helping.

The Helper

Although sociobiologists argue that certain types of altruism have a genetic base, their arguments are based largely on observations of animals. The challenge of establishing the existence of altruism as a fundamental element of human nature has attracted the attention of a number of psychological social psychologists. The issue is a difficult one to resolve. Pessimists have long held that all human behavior is ultimately selfish. Even behavior that appears not to be selfish, such as helping, may involve ulterior selfish motives. People may help because of the rewards they expect to receive, or they may help to avoid punishments or the disapproval of others. Even when no external rewards or punishments exist, they may help just to reduce the distress that someone else's suffering is causing them. In all of these cases the ultimate goal being satisfied by helping is selfish, so none of them is an example of pure altruism.

To show that pure altruism exists it is necessary to demonstrate that helping occurs with the ultimate goal of relieving the suffering of the person in need, not benefiting the self. In attempting to address this issue, social psychologists have devised situations in which students listen to a tape of a person who has a major problem, such as needing blood of a certain type to cure a disease from which she suffers. The students then have an opportunity to help this person, for instance, by calling people who have this blood type to solicit donations. In a large number of studies it has been found that if the students are asked to take the role of the person who needs help as they listen to the tape, they are likely to help (40). If the students listen to the tape, but are not asked to take the other person's role, helping is much

lower. Taking the other's role presumably leads the students to empathize with her plight, and they help her to reduce her distress. But how can we be sure they are not helping in order to reduce the distress that the other person's suffering is causing them? If they were only helping to reduce their own distress their motivation to help would be selfish, not altruistic.

Empathic concern and egoistic self-concern   Researchers believe people generally experience one of two distinct emotions when they see someone else who is suffering. One common reaction is *empathic concern,* in which the observer feels sympathy for the other person's suffering (see Box 12-3). The other common reaction is *egoistic self-concern,* in which the observer reacts to someone else's suffering with feelings of alarm or disgust. When people who are feeling empathic concern help a person in need, they do so to reduce the suffering of the victim. Helping in this situation is altruistic. When people who are feeling egoistic self-concern help a person in need, they do so to reduce their own distress. In this case, helping someone else is selfish (see Figure 12-3).

Let's say you come across a car accident and see a badly injured person. She is hanging out of the car, bloodied and bruised, and her mangled arm is twisted in a grotesque position. One reaction you might have is compassion for the victim's suffering. This empathic concern would cause you to want to help. Alternately, you might respond with horror and revulsion. You may still help, but it will be to reduce your own distress, as well as hers. However, another way to reduce this egoistic self-concern would be to escape from the situation if you could justify doing so.

When students in laboratory studies of helping are given an easy way to avoid helping the person in need (or a good justification for not helping), they take advantage of it. However, they do not avoid helping if they have empathized with the other person's suffering. Students who empathize with the other person's plight continue to help because escaping would not relieve the other's distress. Thus, it appears that empathic concern for the distress of

A Measure of Empathy

The following items were taken from a well-established empathy scale by Mark Davis (41). These items are designed to tap into two dimensions of empathy: perspective taking and empathic concern. Perspective taking allows individuals to anticipate the behavior and reactions of others by enabling them to view the world from their perspectives (items 1–4). It stresses the cognitive element of empathy. Empathic concern leads to feelings of sympathy and concern for unfortunate others (items 5–8). It stresses the emotional element of empathy. Empathy is a potent cause of helping because the sympathy and distress caused by taking the role of others who are suffering can be relieved by helping. How do you score on these items?

Response Scale

A   Does not describe me

B   Describes me a little

C   Describes me somewhat

D   Describes me well

E   Describes me very well

1. I sometimes try to understand my friends better by imagining how things look from their perspective.

2. When I'm upset with someone, I usually try to "put myself in their shoes" for a while.

3. Before criticizing somebody, I try to imagine how I would feel if I were in his/her place.

4. I try to look at everybody's side of a disagreement before I make a decision.

5. I am often quite touched by things I see happen.

6. When I see someone being taken advantage of, I feel kind of protective towards them.

7. I would describe myself as a pretty soft-hearted person.

8. I often have tender, concerned feelings for people less fortunate than me. ■

Figure 12.3 ■

Flowchart for Empathic and Egoistic Self-concern

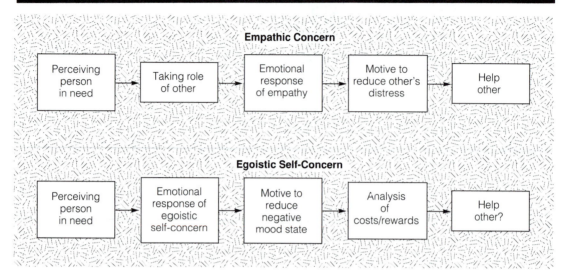

Adapted from Batson, D., 1987, "Prosocial Motivation: Is It Ever Truly Altruistic?" in L. Berkowitz (Ed.), *Advances in Experimental Social Psychology,* Vol. 20, New York: Academic Press.

another leads to pure altruism. Another study showed that students help less when their helping cannot relieve the other's distress than when it can. This study also supports the existence of pure altruism because altruism has as its goal relieving the other's distress. If the other's distress cannot be relieved there is little reason to help.

Mood Numerous studies have found that people who are in a good mood are more likely to be helpful than people whose mood is neutral. In one demonstration of this effect, people who found money left in a pay telephone were more likely afterwards to help someone who dropped some papers than were people who did not find money (42). Other studies show that succeeding on a test, feeling self-confident, fantasizing about pleasant experiences, hearing pleasant music, and being mildly sexually aroused can increase helping. It has even been found that people are more likely to be helpful on sunny days than on shady ones (43).

Equity theory (Chapter 2) provides one explanation for the finding that good moods lead to helping: Feeling good makes people feel advantaged compared with others who are less fortunate. In this view, helping results from a desire to restore equity by increasing the benefits of others. In support of this interpretation, one study found that subjects who focused on their own joy were more helpful than a control group, but subjects who focused on another person's joy were less helpful than the control group (44). Subjects focusing on another's joy most likely felt disadvantaged rather than advantaged and thus helped less. In addition, good moods may increase attentiveness to others, create feelings of competence, and engender a feeling of closeness to others and thus facilitate helping (45).

If positive moods increase helping it seems logical that negative moods would decrease helping, but the situation is not that simple. Some negative moods, like guilt, shame, and sadness, have been found to increase helping (46). As with egoistic self-concern, if the negative affect can be reduced by helping others, then negative affect leads to helping. In one interesting demonstration of this effect, it was found that people were more likely to make donations to their church before they had been to confession than they were after they had confessed (47). Presumably going to confession reduced their negative feelings of guilt, so they had less negative affect to reduce by donating to the church afterward than they did beforehand.

However, even with these negative mood states, if the negative mood cannot be reduced by helping others, then helping is unlikely (48). It is easy to see that helping due to feelings of sadness or guilt is selfish because it leads to improvements in the helper's mood, but we should not be so cynical as to ignore the fact that people in need are being helped in the process.

In contrast to the negative moods we have just discussed, negative moods produced by failure and rejection often reduce helping. When one experiences a negative mood because of what is happening to someone else, the negative mood often can be counteracted by helping. However, when one experiences a negative mood that is not due to what is happening to someone else (due to one's own failure), helping others may not relieve this mood. One reason why failure and rejection produce low levels of helping is that preoccupation with oneself makes it difficult to take the role of people in need (49).

In a study illustrating the effects of self-focused versus other-focused negative moods, subjects were asked to imagine that a close friend was terminally ill. Some of the subjects were asked to attend to their own reactions and some were asked to attend to the reactions of the dying friend. In a control condition, subjects were not asked to imagine a dying friend. Next, the subjects were asked to volunteer to help another student on a study he was doing. As you can see in Table 12-2, the subjects who had focused on their friend's reactions helped two and a half times as much as both the subjects who had focused on themselves and those in the control condition (50).

Even negative moods that focus attention inward

Table 12.2 ■

Effects of Self- versus Other-Focused Attention on Helping

Attention to Other	Attention to Self	Control
657.33	254.25	244.58

Note: The numbers indicate the time, in seconds, that the subjects spent helping the other student.
Adapted from Thompson, W.C., C.L. Cowan, and D.L. Rosenhan, 1980, "Focus of Attention Mediates the Impact of Negative Affect on Altruism," *Journal of Personality and Social Psychology* 38:291–300.

can lead to helping, but only under special circumstances. Several studies have shown that if the needs of others are especially salient (if the helper can be made aware of the fact that the other person really needs help), then people whose attention has been focused on their own negative moods will be helpful (51). To summarize, negative moods caused by others' distress lead to helping when helping relieves the negative mood, while negative moods that focus attention inward lead to helping only when the other person's needs are highly apparent.

Motivation to help The degree to which an individual feels motivated to help someone in need is a function of four factors:

1. the proximity of the person who is suffering

2. the similarity of the person needing help to the helper

3. the responsibility the potential helper feels for the suffering of the other person and

4. the severity of the other person's suffering (52).

The closer the observer is to the person who is suffering, the greater the observer's motivation to help. In support of this idea, one study found that students donated more money to the needy families of Lancaster County when they believed the county was located in the same state than when they believed it was located out of state (53). In another study subjects who saw a person collapse were twice as likely to help when the person collapsed 40 feet, as opposed to 40 yards, away from them (54).

Similarity to the person in need increases the motivation to help because it is easier to empathize with a similar than a dissimilar other (55). Greater empathy creates more empathic concern, and this concern increases the motivation to help. A study demonstrating this effect provided subjects with information concerning the similarity between themselves and a person about whom they were asked to form an impression. The subjects then saw this person react with considerable pain to a series of electric shocks given to her as she performed a number-recall task. The subjects were asked if they would be willing to change places with the other person. Subjects who thought they were similar to the other person were more willing to change places with her than the subjects who thought they were dissimilar to her (56).

People who feel responsible for another person's suffering are more motivated to help the other person than people who do not feel responsible. Feeling responsible for another's suffering is likely to lead to guilt feelings that can be reduced by helping that person. If you were the cause of a car accident in which someone was injured, you would feel more responsible for helping and would be more apt to help the person, than if you merely witnessed the accident.

The greater the victim's need or the greater the victim's suffering, the greater the individual's motivation to help the victim. University students were much more likely to give another student a ride if the person said he needed to get back to a roommate who had just taken too many sleeping pills than if he needed to get back to a roommate who was depressed (57).

However, in some situations, the greater a person's suffering, the greater the danger involved in helping that person. For instance, when a fire is out of control, the dangers involved in helping may be very substantial. Under these circumstances, the motivation to help may be great, but the costs of helping may be so high that no help is offered.

In general, close distances, similarity, responsibility, and severity create high levels of motivation to help, but whether or not helping actually occurs depends on situational factors. It is to these factors that we turn next.

The Situation

A wide variety of situational factors affect helping. We will focus on two: the costs and rewards of helping and the norms that influence helping.

Costs and rewards The majority of everyday helping does not involve emergencies nor does the other person's need arouse strong emotional responses or powerful motives to help. In these types of everyday helping situations, people often adopt a *minimax* strategy. This strategy consists of minimizing one's costs and maximizing one's rewards. In making helping decisions, people analyze four factors: the costs and rewards of helping and the costs and rewards of not helping.

The costs of helping include the time and effort involved, the potential danger involved, feelings of inadequacy if one does not succeed, the experience of unpleasant events, and potential embarrassment if help is not needed. A study of people's intentions to donate blood provides an example of how costs affect helping. People who did not intend to give blood cited the pain, the time, and the fact that it would make them feel tired and faint more frequently than people who intended to donate blood (58).

The benefits of helping also influence decisions to help. These benefits include praise from others, thanks from the recipient of the help, self-approval, and feelings of self-efficacy. When a female "subject" thanked a male for taking shocks in her place, the males were much more likely to take her shocks on subsequent trials than if she did not thank them (59). In situations where some of these potential rewards are absent, helping becomes less attractive. For instance, if the help is offered anonymously, approval from others and thanks from the recipient are not likely to be forthcoming. This is one reason

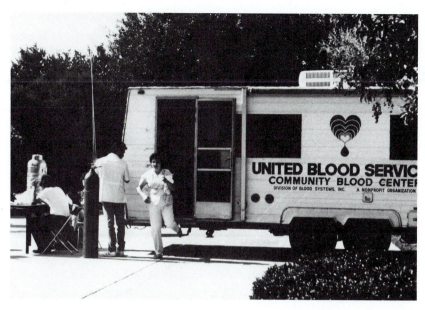

■ *For some people, the benefits of donating blood outweigh the costs; for others, the reverse is true. (WGS)*

why strangers are generally less likely to be helped than acquaintances.

The potential costs of not helping include the disapproval by the person who needs the help, the censure of other people, and self-criticism or feelings of guilt.

The benefits of not helping include being able to continue doing whatever one was doing and avoiding the costs of helping.

The extensive research using this approach (minimizing costs, maximizing rewards) has yielded four general conclusions (60):

1. As the costs of helping increase, helping decreases.

2. As the rewards of helping increase, helping increases.

3. The costs of helping are more important determinants of decisions to help than the rewards.

4. Costs to oneself are more heavily weighed than costs to the person in need.

In making decisions about whether or not to help a person in need, both the costs of not helping and the costs of helping are weighed heavily (61). There are four combinations of costs outlined in Figure 12-4, and we will consider each one.

When the costs of helping are low and the costs of not helping are high, people are the most likely to help. In a simple field study, a customer in a supermarket came up 30 cents short at the checkout counter. The customer was more likely to be helped if the item being purchased was antiseptic ointment for a burned child than if the item was beer (62). Not helping the person with the burned child would have made people feel more guilty (high cost of not helping) than not helping the person buy beer and since the cost of helping was low, people helped the customer with the burned child.

When the costs of not helping are low and the costs of helping are high, people are least likely to help and most likely to flee the situation. In one of our opening examples a person who was attacked in Central Park was not aided by any of the witnesses

Figure 12.4 ■

Responses to Someone in Need as a Function of the Costs Involved

		Costs of Helping	
		Low	High
Costs of not helping	High	Helping	Justifications for not helping
	Low	Social norms determine response	Fleeing

Adapted from Walster (Hatfield), E. and J. Piliavin, 1972, "Equity and the Innocent Bystander," *Journal of Social Issues* 28:165–189.

to the assault in part because each person could deny that he or she was responsible for helping (low cost of not helping) and the consequences of helping might have been to be assaulted oneself (high costs of helping). This set of costs characterizes many bystander situations, in which it is easy to pass by without helping and in which offering help may be costly in terms of time, effort, or danger.

When both the costs of helping and not helping are high, people are placed in a difficult conflict situation because whatever they do will be costly. If you were the only person in your group who possessed technical rock climbing skills and one of your friends had fallen in an especially dangerous place on the mountain, you would either have to face the danger associated with helping or the disapproval of your friends for not trying to help.

There are several possible resolutions to this high cost conflict. One solution is to find a justification for not helping. In one study the investigators had a confederate fall to the floor of a Philadelphia

subway while blood trickled from his mouth (63). Since the bleeding person presumably was in great need of help, the costs of not helping were high, but helping would also have entailed considerable costs. During one trial of this study two of the observers got up when the person fell, then one said, "Oh, he's bleeding," and they both sat down again. They probably justified not helping by telling themselves it was none of their business or they were not competent to help a person whose needs were so great. This study also supports the idea that costs to oneself may be more influential in helping decisions than costs to the person in need.

A second solution is to offer help indirectly by seeking the assistance of others who are highly qualified to help. For instance, you might tell your friends that you shouldn't undertake such a dangerous rescue without additional help.

A third solution to the high cost of helping/not helping dilemma is to redefine the situation so that the costs of not helping are perceived to be small. To do this, the victim can be denigrated (he's just a bum), the victim's suffering can be minimized (he's not that badly hurt, he'll be okay), or responsibility can be diffused (why should I be the one to help, someone else should intervene).

When the costs of helping and not helping are both low, social norms play a major role in determining the person's behavior. If there are norms that clearly indicate that helping is appropriate then help is likely, but in the absence of supportive norms little help is likely (see Box 12-4). The next section considers social norms that affect helping.

Norms Many of the factors we have discussed so far seem to imply that people rarely help others. Yet we all know from our own experience that people often help others. The next set of factors we will discuss provides some understanding of why people give money to charities, risk their lives for causes they believe in, donate blood, stop for stranded motorists, rescue people in danger, volunteer to help service organizations, and so on.

Why should norms for helping exist? The social evolutionists say such norms increase the chances a

BOX 12-4

The Good Samaritan

There was once a man who was going down from Jerusalem to Jericho when robbers attacked him, stripped him, and beat him up, leaving him half dead. It so happened that a priest was going down that road; but when he saw the man, he walked on by on the other side. In the same way a Levite also came there, went over and looked at the man, and then walked on by on the other side. But a Samaritan who was traveling that way came upon the man, and when he saw him, his heart was filled with pity. He went over to him, poured oil and wine on his wounds and bandaged them; then he put the man on his own animal and took him to an inn, where he took care of him. The next day he took out two silver coins and gave them to the innkeeper. "Take care of him," he told the innkeeper, "and when I come back this way I will pay you whatever else you spend on him." (Luke 10:30–35)

The story of the Good Samaritan has had an enduring fascination. Why? After reading this chapter you should be able to answer this question. The Good Samaritan's behavior is extraordinary for several reasons. First, consider the factors that influence the motivation to help. On the one hand, the severity of the person's need was great, and the Samaritan had to pass fairly close to the person who had been assaulted. These factors would lead to a high motivation to help.

On the other hand, there is no reason to think the Samaritan was particularly similar to the person in need, nor was the Samaritan responsible for the other person's suffering. These factors would reduce the motivation to help. Thus, the overall motivation to help this person was not high.

The costs of helping were great in terms of time, effort, inconvenience, and money. The benefits would appear to have been low, since no one seems to have known of the Samaritan's good deed, and there is no indication that he was thanked for his efforts. The costs of not helping were low. Others had passed by without helping, and the Samaritan could easily have done likewise. Finally, there were probably some rewards for not helping. For instance, the Samaritan could continue on his way.

Despite all these reasons for not helping, the Samaritan chose to help the person in need. According to attribution theory, when a person engages in a costly behavior such as this for no obvious benefit, people will infer that the cause was an internal trait. Throughout history people have made the inference that the Samaritan was indeed an exceptionally kind person (64). ■

■ *You rub my back and I'll rub yours. The norm of reciprocity at work. (WGS)*

society will survive. If the individual members of a society are concerned with the welfare of the group, they will engage in actions that increase the chances of survival of other members of the group. Although helping may not be adaptive for the individual, it is adaptive for the group.

Most societies have norms that promote helping. Some societies' helping norms are virtually identical to the concept of reciprocal altruism. Consider the Golden Rule, which enjoins us to do unto others as we would have them do unto us. When applied to helping, this norm indicates that if we wish to receive help from others, we should help them.

Other norms also promote helping. The norm of *distributive justice* (equity) suggests that a relationship is fair when the ratio of one person's inputs and outputs equals that of the other people in the relationship. This norm can lead people to assist others who are receiving less than they deserve. Although the U.S. Social Security system contains elements of distributive justice (compensation varies in proportion to the amount people have contributed), some people are not adequately compensated by the system. When other social agencies help these

deserving people, the norm of distributive justice is at work. In a related vein, the norm of *social responsibility* specifies that we should help those who are dependent on us. The social responsibility norm is a form of true altruism since it calls on people to act on the behalf of others, without a concern for material gain or social approval. The helping norms characterizing most societies dictate that people should give to others, be willing to accept help from others, and recognize an obligation to repay others (65).

Alvin Gouldner has offered a detailed treatment of this last general norm—the norm of *reciprocity* (66). In his view the norm of reciprocity consists of two interrelated injunctions. First, people should help those who have helped them. Second, people should not harm those who have helped them (see Box 12-5 for other recipient reactions to help). The size of the obligation to help others depends on the value of help one has received. The value of the help received depends on the recipient's need and the costs to the donor of giving the help. The recipient may also consider the donor's motives and the constraints on the donor in deciding how in-

BOX 12-5

Recipient Reactions to Helping

Have you ever given a gift to someone or done someone a favor only to find yourself disappointed in his or her reaction? We expect people to be thankful for our gifts and they usually are, but sometimes people react in unexpected ways. Why do recipients sometimes respond negatively to receiving help? One problem is that help can reduce the recipient's self-esteem or imply the recipient is incompetent (67). As the exchange theorist George Homans put it, "Anyone who accepts from another a service he cannot repay in kind incurs inferiority as a cost of receiving the service." (68). When you help someone with his homework, he may resent it if it implies he is incapable of doing the work himself or if he cannot repay you.

Many helping situations make the recipients feel indebted. If they cannot repay the debt, the giver of the gift or the gift may be devalued (69). Another reaction to potential feelings of indebtedness is to redefine the situation as a rightful obligation on the part of the donor. Recipients of U.S. foreign aid display both responses. They often resent the United States because of the feeling of indebtedness that accompanies such aid and react by adopting negative attitudes toward the United States (70). Other countries see U.S. aid as the rightful obligation of the undeserving rich to the deserving poor.

Help may also seem less burdensome if it has been freely offered rather than being requested. Requested help creates greater feelings of indebtedness and the greater the feeling of indebtedness, the greater the negative reaction. It follows that help that is seen as manipulative also elicits negative reactions. If a country feels we are offering them aid solely to gain their support in world politics or to secure a military base, the help may be resented. Similarly, a woman who perceives that a man is offering to fix her car at a reduced price so that she will go out with him may not react kindly to the offer.

Too little help may be worse than no help at all. The recipient of too little help is still obliged to the donor, the recipient's feelings of incompetence may be heightened, and the need remains unmet. Aid that severely restricts people's freedoms, such as that offered in total institutions like hospitals or homes for the elderly, or help given to welfare recipients, can elicit negative reactions and feelings of helplessness.

In general, recipients do not wish to feel inferior, indebted, dependent, or have their freedoms restricted, and receiving help often entails such negative consequences. ■

debted he or she is. For example, you would probably feel very indebted to a person who stopped and fixed your car if you were in the middle of nowhere and the person who stopped had other obligations to meet. This feeling of indebtedness would be tempered, however, if you suspected that he was sizing you up to see if you were worth robbing.

In practice, the norm of reciprocity is followed most precisely among people who are equal in status and among people whose relationships are not intimate. People feel less of an obligation to reciprocate help when they are lower or higher in status than the person who has helped them (71). In close relationships, precise reciprocity over short periods of time is not considered necessary, although a lack of overall reciprocity over the long run can ruin a relationship (72).

An interesting example of the norm of reciprocity, and the exceptions to it, is furnished by family gift giving at Christmas (73). Family members expect to get gifts from those to whom they give them, except for gifts given to young children. But, the gifts need not be of equal value, especially if the givers are not of equal status in the family. The gift of a child to a parent need not be as expensive as the gift of the parent to the child. A parent can give a child money, but a child cannot give a parent money. Gifts are distributed at gatherings where every person is expected to receive at least one gift. The gifts should be wrapped. The ideal gift demonstrates the giver's familiarity with the recipient's preferences, surprises the recipient, and is scaled in value according to the emotional value of the relationship. For instance, a father should not give his son a more expensive gift than he gives his wife.

Social norms specify how we should behave. Our fidelity to the norms of our social group often depends on whether other members of our group witness our behavior or will find out about it. The more salient the presence of others, the more likely it is that norms influence our behavior. An intriguing study in Israel demonstrated the powerful effect of social norms on helping in groups (74). There is a norm in Israel that encourages people to report suspicious objects to the authorities as a means of reducing terrorism. In the study it was found that a planted "package" was more frequently reported to the police if it was noticed by passersby in a group than by a solitary passerby. The group was more helpful because failure to comply with the social norm would have been more obvious in this context.

Another study illustrating the importance of norm salience employed a variant of the seizure scenario in which subjects in groups of varying sizes overhear a person experiencing a "seizure" (75). The subjects were either members of a campus social service organization or fraternity members. Some of the subjects' memberships in these groups were made salient by having them comment on the effects of group membership on the problems posed by college life. The subjects who subsequently were most likely to help the person experiencing the "seizure" were the service group members whose group membership had been made salient, and who thought there were three other people in the discussion. Thus, the salience of a group whose primary norm is to help others was sufficient to overcome the usual tendency not to help when there are other bystanders.

Helping norms will also be salient if ingroup members model helping (76), if the victim's need is unusually great (77), or if the potential helper has prior experience with similar situations. Factors such as stress reduce the salience of helping norms, as illustrated in the following study (78). Half of a group of students at a theological seminary read the story of the Good Samaritan (see Box 12-4), while the other half did not. The students were then told that they needed to go to another building to complete the study. To create stress, half the students were told that they were late and must hurry. On their way to the other building, the students passed a person who was slumped in an alleyway. This person was not moving and he was coughing and groaning. Subjects who were in a hurry helped less frequently than those who were not (10 percent versus 63 percent), while subjects who had read about the Good Samaritan helped somewhat more than those who had not (53 percent versus 29 percent). These seminary students aspired to a vocation with a helping norm. Making this norm salient increased helping—but only when the students were not under stress.

Through the process of socialization many social norms become internalized. If the socialization agents model helping norms and reinforce them in children, these social norms will be internalized as *personal norms* by the children. Personal norms can affect behavior even when others are not present or will not know about the behavior. The reason is that once a social norm has been internalized as a personal norm, the rewards for obeying the norm and the sanctions for disobeying the norm are self-administered (see Chapter 7 for a longer discussion of internalization). If you help someone when your values tell you that you should, you will feel proud of yourself; if you do not help when you think you should, you will probably feel guilty.

In a study designed to examine the relationship between personal norms and helping the blind, a questionnaire was used to measure students' feelings of moral obligation to help others (79). Later, the investigators asked the students if they would contribute their time to tape record children's texts that were unavailable in Braille. For those students who reported in the earlier questionnaire that they rarely denied their responsibility to help, there was a high correlation between personal norms of moral obligation and willingness to help the blind ($r = .72$). However, for students who tended to deny their feelings of personal responsibility, there was no relationship between personal norms and helping the blind ($r = .03$). It appears that a relationship between personal norms and helping exists only when people have strong personal helping norms and feel a responsibility to help others (80).

When a person repeatedly engages in a particular type of helping, such as donating blood or volunteering time to help dying people, the person may merge with this helping role in a role-person merger (a concept discussed in Chapter 4). They come to view themselves as "blood donors" or "hospice volunteers," and these views of the self lead them to continue being helpful. Their helpful behavior may be consistent with social and personal norms, but these norms are no longer the cause of the behavior. Such a person would continue helping

even in the absence of social and personal norms favoring helping. For example a person who had always volunteered time to help drug addicts would continue doing so even if many of the addicts were infected with AIDS, despite the social disapproval received from friends and despite personal norms of avoiding risky situations. Indeed, one study found that identification with the role of blood donor was a better predictor of future blood donations than either social or personal norms (81). Role-person mergers produce some of the most dedicated and persistent forms of helping. A person who dedicates his or her life to helping the poor, such as Mother Teresa in India, provides an example of this type of role-person merger.

The Recipient

Characteristics of the recipient and the relationship between the benefactor and the recipient influence the amount of help the recipient receives. We will discuss five such influences on helping: the equity of the relationship between the recipient and the benefactor; the similarity between them; how much the benefactor likes the potential recipient; attributions for the causes of the potential recipient's need for help; and group membership.

Equity   Considerations of equity arise only when there is a relationship between a benefactor and a potential recipient. If no relationship exists, the benefactor cannot be overbenefited or underbenefited with respect to the potential recipient. If an inequitable relationship does exist, the overbenefited member will feel distress—a distress that can often be relieved by helping the underbenefited person. For instance, a business owner who underpays her employees may experience pangs of conscience at Christmas time and surprise her employees with a bonus. She would be unlikely to give the same money to people she does not employ because no inequality exists concerning such people.

A benefactor may also be concerned that helping another person will create an inequality between them that may not be repaid. This may lead the benefactor to be reluctant to help. Indeed, people are more likely to help those who can repay them than those who cannot. Likewise, potential recipients are more likely to accept aid if they can reciprocate it than if they cannot (83) (see Box 12-5). However, in some cases, the benefactor may wish to create an inequality with respect to a recipient (82). For example, a friend of yours might help you study for your social psychology exam so you will help him later with his calculus.

The belief that the world is just can undercut helping based on considerations of equity. If others are perceived as deserving their unfortunate fates, then even the underbenefited may not be helped. When equity is difficult to restore to a relationship, people often resort to blaming the victim as a way of relieving their distress. The belief in a just world and the tendency to blame victims can hinder efforts to aid the poor, the disabled, the sick, and the elderly if potential benefactors do not believe these people deserve to be helped.

Liking and similarity   People are more apt to help a person whom they like or who likes them than they are to help someone with whom they have a negative relationship (84). In one study, subjects who were led to believe that another subject liked them were more willing to comply with a request from the other subject to return some books to the library than were subjects who thought the other subject did not like them (85).

As we mentioned previously when discussing helping motivation, people are also more apt to help others who are similar to them than others who are dissimilar (86). The effect of similarity on helping is so strong that it occurs even when little suffering is involved (when empathic concern is low). An interesting study of this phenomenon was conducted during the 1972 presidential election (87). When a voter approached the polling place, a campaign worker with a large Nixon or McGovern placard dropped a bundle of campaign literature. The campaign worker then recorded whether the voter helped to pick up the literature. Later, the voters were asked for whom they had voted. When the voter and the campaigner had similar political pref-

erences, the voters helped 71 percent of the time. When they had different preferences, the voters helped pick up the literature in only 46 percent of the cases.

Causal attributions   Under some conditions, the amount of help a benefactor offers depends on the perceived causes of the recipient's need for help (88). When we see another person who needs help, we may ask ourselves why this person is in need. Is the other person to blame for his or her predicament, or was it brought on by forces outside of his or her control? Suppose another student asked you to lend him your social psychology notes. Would you be more likely to do so if he had cut class to party or if he had filled in for a sick friend at work and missed class?

When the potential recipient's need is due to controllable personal factors, potential benefactors often respond with anger or annoyance; but if the need is caused by uncontrollable external factors, potential benefactors are more likely to experience empathic concern. As we have shown earlier, empathic concern generally leads to helping. Annoyance is more likely to lead to avoidance of the person in need. In one study, students were asked if they would be willing to lend an acquaintance money to pay his rent (89). Empathic concern was very high when the acquaintance was unable to pay his rent because he "was permanently disabled by an injury on the job and did not receive adequate compensation." In contrast, annoyance was very high when the rent was not paid because he "did not like to work." Consistent with their feelings, the students were much more likely to help the former than the latter acquaintance.

Attributions are important primarily when the need is not grave. Students said they would be as likely to help a person *severely* injured in a car accident whether the accident had been caused by a tire blowout or by the driver's negligence (90). When the injuries were not serious, the students said they would help the victim of the uncontrollable accident more than the victim who was driving recklessly. Thus, in emergency situations, helping norms may be more important than attributions.

Figure 12.5 ■

Attributional Model of Helping in Nonemergencies

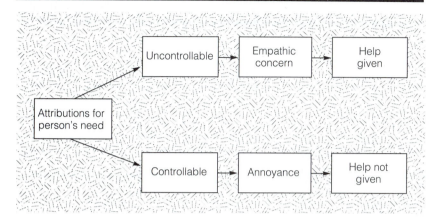

Adapted from Weiner, B., 1980, "A Cognition (Attribution)-Emotion-Action Model of Motivated Behavior: An Analysis of Judgments of Help-giving," *Journal of Personality and Social Psychology* 39:186–200.

The attributional approach can be integrated with the empathic concern model. The attributional approach suggests that in nonemergency situations people ask why an individual needs help. The answer to this question determines whether the potential benefactor's emotional reaction is one of annoyance or of empathic concern. The amount of help offered is a result of the benefactor's emotional reaction (see Figure 12-5). In this model, as in the model of empathic concern, emotional reactions are the primary determinants of helping. The difference between the two approaches to helping is that attributional theorists believe a causal analysis by the benefactor precedes the benefactor's emotional reaction.

Group membership Members of one's own group tend to be helped more than outgroup members, particularly members of stigmatized outgroups. Several studies have found that whites are more likely to help whites than blacks (91), although other studies indicate this is not always the case (92). When prejudicial treatment would be obvious, whites

do not help whites more than blacks (93). A study using a different set of ingroups and outgroups found that students maintained a greater distance between themselves and a person soliciting donations to the United Way if the person was handicapped than if the person was not handicapped (94).

In another study, people approached in a mall were less likely to help a student dressed in a punk style than a student in ordinary dress, especially when the punker approached very close to make the request (95). The decreased helping in this study was caused by the anxiety the subjects experienced. In this instance, it was not egoistic distress caused by the other person's need that reduced helping, but anxiety caused by the other's appearance. It may be that members of stigmatized outgroups, such as the handicapped, make people anxious and this anxiety leads to avoidance, not to helping (96).

An exception to the general rule that ingroup members are helped more than outgroup members occurs for gender. Males tend to help females more than they help males. Females tend to be equally helpful to females and males (97). These findings can be interpreted in terms of sterotypical gender roles. Males view females as being dependent and, thus, females are seen as likely to need and accept help. This interpretation is supported by a study in which females were helped more than males only when they were placed in dependent roles (98). When the females were not dependent on the subjects (when their behavior was inconsistent with traditional gender role stereotypes) they were helped less than males. Both males and females helped the dependent females most, suggesting that when a dependency relationship exists, females are helped more than males by members of both sexes. Another finding that shows a relationship between helping and dependency is that older people tend to be helped more than young people (99). It appears that, consistent with the norm of social responsibility, people generally help others who are dependent (100).

■

SUMMARY

In this chapter, we have considered factors that influence helping. We began by discussing the sociobiological approach to altruism. Based on the evolutionary concepts of variation, selection, and retention, this approach suggests that two types of altruistic behavior may be adaptive: behaviors that increase the chances of survival of one's kin and altruistic behaviors that will be reciprocated. Social evolutionists take this argument one step further and suggest that altruistic behaviors increasing the group's chances of survival are also adaptive. In particular, they suggest that human beings, unlike lower animals, engage in self-sacrificial altruism for the benefit of the group.

In the second section of this chapter, we discussed bystander intervention. According to this approach, people go through four stages in making decisions about whether to help someone in need: noticing that someone is in need, defining a situation as an emergency, deciding if they are responsibile for helping the person who is in need, and deciding if they are competent to help. A negative decision

at any one of these stages means that the person in need will not be helped. Among the reasons why people do not help in emergencies are that the responsibility for helping may be diffused among all the bystanders who are present, bystanders may feel that others are more competent than they are, people may not be prepared to meet the demands that the emergency will make on them, and people may fear getting involved in emergencies.

In the third section of the chapter, the influence of helper, situation, and recipient factors on helping were presented. Altruism occurs when a person's empathic concern for the suffering of others leads to helping. When a person experiences egoistic distress in response to the suffering of others, this produces helping that is selfish. Good moods tend to increase helping. In contrast, bad moods may either increase or decrease helping, depending on the cause of the bad mood. If the bad mood can be alleviated through helping or if the person focuses on the other's need, helping is likely. If a person in a bad mood is inwardly focused, help is unlikely.

A person's motivation to help depends on the severity of the victim's suffering, the proximity of the person who is suffering, the responsibility the potential helper feels for the suffering of the victim, and the similarity to the potential helper of the person who needs help.

The first situational factor discussed was the costs and rewards of helping and not helping. Generally, people try to minimize their costs and maximize their rewards in helping situations. When the costs of helping are low and the costs of not helping are high, people are likely to help. When the costs of both helping and not helping are high, people may attempt to justify not helping. When the costs of helping are high and the costs of not helping are low, people may flee the situation. Finally, when the costs of helping and of not helping are both low, social norms determine whether or not help is given.

Social norms constitute a second situational factor that affects helping. Most societies have norms that promote helping, such as injunctions that one should give to others, that one should accept help from others, and that one should repay others. The norm of reciprocity encourages us to help those who have helped us and to not hurt those who have helped us. Norms that promote helping affect our behavior to the degree that they are salient in a given situation. The presence of ingroup members, people who model helping, prior experience, and a great need for help tend to make norms salient, while stress may reduce the salience of helping norms. When social norms become internalized through socialization, they become personal norms. Personal norms that promote helping can influence behavior even in the absence of social norms promoting helping. Role-person mergers result from repeated helping in given roles and lead to persistent helping in the future.

If the donor and the recipient have a relationship, considerations of equity may affect helping. People are less likely to give or receive help that cannot be reciprocated than to give or receive help that can be reciprocated. Liking and similarity increase helping. If the causes of a person's need are perceived to be under their control and preventable, the potential donor is likely to feel annoyed and reduce the amount of help that is offered; if the causes of the person's need are beyond his or her control, a feeling of empathic concern is created and more help is likely to be offered. People are more likely to help ingroup members or those who are dependent on them than outgroup members or those who are not dependent on them.

■

REFERENCES

1. *Las Cruces Sun News,* August 25, 1980.
2. Hodgkinson, V. A. and M. S. Weitzman, 1984, *Dimensions of the Independent Sector,* Washington, DC: Independent Sector.
3. *Giving USA,* 1986, New York: American Association of Fund-Raising Council, Inc.
4. Hodgkinson and Weitzman, 1984, op. cit.
5. *Giving USA,* 1986, op. cit.
6. *Giving USA,* 1986, ibid.
7. *Giving USA,* 1986, ibid.
8. Bakal, C., 1979, *Charity U.S.A.,* New York: Times Books.
9. Hodgkinson and Weitzman, 1984, op. cit.
10. Bakal, 1979, op. cit.
11. Lopreato, J., 1984, *Human Nature and Biological Evolution,* Boston: Allen & Unwin.

12. Darwin, C. R., 1859, *On the Origin of Species by Means of Natural Selection, or the Preservation of Favoured Races in the Struggle for Life,* 1st ed., London: John Murray.
13. Wilson, E. O., 1978, *On Human Nature,* Cambridge, MA: Harvard University Press; E. O. Wilson, 1975, *Sociobiology: The New Synthesis,* Cambridge MA: Belknap Press of Harvard University Press.
14. Ridley, M. and R. Dawkins, 1981, "The Natural Selection of Altruism," in J. P. Rushton and R. M. Sorrentino (Eds.), *Altruism and Helping Behavior: Social Personality and Developmental Perspectives,* Hillsdale, NJ: Lawrence Erlbaum.
15. Trivers, R., 1971, "The Evolution of Reciprocal Altruism," *Quarterly Review of Biology* 46: 3557.
16. Barash, D. P., 1977, *Sociobiology and Behavior,* New York: Elsevier North Holland.
17. Wilson, 1978, op. cit.
18. Rushton, J. P., D. W. Fulker, M. C. Neale, D. K. B. Nias, and H. J. Eysenck, 1986, "Aggression and Altruism: The Heritability of Individual Differences," *Journal of Personality and Social Psychology* 50: 1192–1198.
19. Campbell, D., 1965, "Ethnocentrism and Other Altruistic Motives," in D. Levine (Ed.), *Nebraska Symposium on Motivation,* Lincoln: University of Nebraska Press; D. T. Campbell, 1975, "On the Conflicts between Biological and Social Evolution and between Psychology and Moral Tradition," *American Psychologist* 30: 1103–1126; D. T. Campbell, 1978, "On the Genetics of Altruism and the Counter-hedonic Components in Human Culture," in L. Wispe (Ed.), *Altruism, Sympathy, and Helping,* New York: Academic Press.
20. Cohen, R., 1978, "Altruism: Human, Cultural or What?" in L. Wispe, ibid.
21. Darley, J. and B. Latané, 1968a, "When People Will Help in a Crisis," *Psychology Today* 2: 54–57.
22. Mathews, K. E., Jr. and L. K. Canon, 1975, "Environment Noise Level as a Determinant of Helping Behavior," *Journal of Personality and Social Psychology* 32: 571–577.
23. Bickman, L., A. Teger, T. Gabriele, C. McLaughlin, M. Berger, and E. Sunaday, 1973, "Dormitory Density and Helping Behavior," *Environment and Behavior* 5: 465–490; C. Korte and N. Kerr, 1975, "Response to Altruistic Opportunities in Urban and Non-urban Settings," *Journal of Social Psychology* 95: 183–184; J. A. Piliavin, J. F. Dovidio, S. L. Gaertner, and R. D. Clark III, 1981, *Emergency Intervention,* New York: Academic Press.
24. Darley, J. and B. Latané, 1968b, "Bystander Intervention in Emergencies: Diffusion of Responsibility," *Journal of Personality and Social Psychology* 8: 377–383; B. Latané, S. E. Nida, and D. W. Wilson 1981, "The Effects of Group Size on Helping Behavior," in J. P. Rushton and R. M. Sorrentino, op. cit.
25. Clark, R. D., III and L. E. Word, 1972, "Why Don't Bystanders Help? Because of Ambiguity?" *Journal of Personality and Social Psychology* 24: 392–400; L. R. Shotland and W. D. Heinhold, 1985, "Bystander Response to Arterial Bleeding: Helping Skills, the Decision Making Process and Differentiating the Helping Response," *Journal of Personality and Social*

Psychology 49: 347–356; L. Z. Soloman, H. Soloman, and R. Stone, 1978, "Helping as a Function of Number of Bystanders and Ambiguity of Emergency," *Personality and Social Psychology Bulletin* 4: 318–321.

26. Darley and Latané, 1968b, op. cit.

27. Rutkowski, G. K., C. L. Gruder, and D. Romer, 1983, "Group Cohesiveness, Social Norms, and Bystander Intervention," *Journal of Personality and Social Psychology* 44: 545–552.

28. Gottlieb, J. and C. S. Carver, 1980, "Anticipation of Future Interaction and the Bystander Effect," *Journal of Experimental Social Psychology* 16: 253–560.

29. Morgan, C. J., 1978, "Bystander Intervention: Experimental Test of a Formal Model," *Journal of Personality and Social Psychology* 36: 43–55.

30. Pantin, H. M. and C. S. Carver, 1982, "Induced Competence and the Bystander Effect," *Journal of Applied Social Psychology* 12: 100–111; Shotland and Heinhold, 1985, op. cit.

31. Huston, T. L., M. Ruggiero, R. Connor, and G. Geiss, 1981, "Bystander Intervention into Crime: A Study Based on Naturally Occurring Episodes," *Social Psychology Quarterly* 44: 14–23.

32. Piliavin, I. M., J. A. Piliavin, and J. Rodin, 1975, "Costs, Diffusion, and the Stigmatized Victim," *Journal of Personality and Social Psychology* 32: 429–438.

33. Takooshian, H. and H. Bodinger, 1982, "Bystander Indifference to Street Crime," in L. Savitz and N. Johnston (Eds.), *Contemporary Criminology,* New York: Wiley.

34. Korte, C. and N. Kerr, 1975, op. cit.; S. Milgram, 1970, "The Experience of Living in Cities," *Science* 167: 1461–1468; M. Smithson, P. R. Amato, and P. Pearce, 1983, *Dimensions of Helping Behavior,* Oxford: Pergamon.

35. Korte, C., I. Ympa, and A. Toppen, 1975, "Helpfulness in Dutch Society as a Function of Urbanization and Environmental Input Level," *Journal of Personality and Social Psychology* 32: 996–1003; M. Merrens, 1973, "Nonemergency Helping Behavior in Various Sized Communities," *Journal of Social Psychology* 90: 327–328; F. H. Weiner, 1976, "Altruism, Ambience, and Action: The Effects of Rural and Urban Rearing on Helping Behavior," *Journal of Personality and Social Psychology* 34: 112–124; F. W. Schneider and Z. Mockus, 1974, "Failure to Find a Rural-Urban Difference in Incidence of Altruistic Behavior," *Psychological Reports* 35: 294.

36. Korte et al., 1975, op. cit.

37. House, J. and S. Wolf, 1978, "Effects of Urban Residence on Interpersonal Trust and Helping Behavior," *Journal of Personality and Social Psychology* 36: 1029–1043.

38. Holahan, C. J., 1977, "Effects of Urban Size and Heterogeneity on Judged Appropriateness of Altruistic Responses: Situation vs. Subject Variables," *Sociometry* 40: 378–382.

39. Bickman et al., 1973, op. cit.; Piliavin et al., 1981, op. cit.; H Takooshian, S. Haber, and D. J. Lucido, 1976, "Helping Responses to a Lost Child in a City and Town," paper presented at the American Psychological Association Convention, Washington, DC.

40. Batson, D., 1987, "Prosocial Motivation: Is It Ever Truly Altruistic?" in L. Berkowitz (Ed.), *Advances in Experimental Social Psychology,* Vol. 20, New York: Academic Press.

41. Davis, M. H., 1980, "A Multidimensional Approach to Individual Differences in Empathy," *JSAS Catalogue of Selected Documents in Psychology* 10: 85.

42. Isen, A. M. and P. F. Levin, 1972, "The Effect of Feeling Good on Helping," *Journal of Personality and Social Psychology* 21: 384–388.

43. Cunningham, M. R., 1979, "Weather, Mood, and Helping Behavior: Quasi Experiments with the Sunshine Samaritan," *Journal of Personality and Social Psychology* 37: 1947–1956; M. R. Cunningham, J. Steinberg, and R. Grev, 1980, "Wanting to and Having to Help: Separate Motivations for Positive Mood and Guilt-induced Helping," *Journal of Personality and Social Psychology* 38: 181–192; D. L. Rosenhan, 1978, "Toward Resolving the Altruism Paradox: Affect, Self-reinforcement, and Cognition," in L. Wispe, op. cit.; R. Fried and L. Berkowitz, 1979, "Music Hath Charms . . . and Can Influence Helpfulness," *Journal of Applied Social Psychology* 9: 199–208; A. M. Isen, and P. F. Levin, 1972, "Effect of Feeling Good on Helping: Cookies and Kindness," *Journal of Personality and Social Psychology* 21: 384–388; C. W. Mueller and E. Donnerstein, 1981, "Film Facilitated Arousal and Prosocial Behavior," *Journal of Experimental Social Psychology* 17: 31–41; D. P. J. Przybyla, 1986, "The Facilitating Effects of Erotica on Prosocial Behavior," doctoral dissertation, State University of New York at Albany.

44. Rosenhan, D. L., P. Salovey, J. Karylowski, and K. Hargis, 1981, "Emotion and Altruism," in J. P. Rushton and R. M. Sorrentino, op. cit.

45. Dovidio, J. H., 1984, "Helping Behavior and Altruism: An Empirical and Conceptual Overview," in L. Berkowitz (Ed.), *Advances in Experimental Social Psychology,* Vol. 17, New York: Academic Press.

46. Rosenhan et al., 1981, op. cit.

47. Harris, M. B., S. M. Benson, and C. Hall, 1975, "The Effects of Confession on Altruism," *Journal of Social Psychology* 96: 187–192.

48. Cialdini, R. B., M. Schaller, D. Houlihan, K. Arps, J. Fultz, and A. L. Beaman, 1987, "Empathy-based Helping: Is It Selflessly or Selfishly Motivated," *Journal of Personality and Social Psychology* 52: 749–758.

49. Aderman, D. and L. Berkowitz, 1983, "Self-concern and the Unwillingness to be Helpful," *Social Psychology Quarterly* 46: 176–179; L. Berkowitz, 1987, "Mood, Self-awareness, and Willingness to Help," *Journal of Personality and Social Psychology* 52: 721–729.

50. Thompson, W. C., C. L. Cowan, and D. L. Rosenhan, 1980, "Focus of Attention Mediates the Impact of Negative Affect on Altruism," *Journal of Personality and Social Psychology* 38: 291–300.

51. Gibbons, F. X. and R. Wicklund, 1982, "Self-focused Attention and Helping," *Journal of Personality and Social Psychology* 43: 462–474; M. Rogers, N. Miller, S. Meyer, and S. Duval, 1982, "Personal Responsibility and Salience of the Request for Help:

Determinants of the Relation between Negative Affect and Helping Behavior," *Journal of Personality and Social Psychology* 43: 956–970.

52. Walster, E. and J. Piliavin, 1972, "Equity and the Innocent Bystander," *Journal of Social Issues* 28: 165–189; E. Walster, G. W. Walster, and J. A. Piliavin, 1978, "Equity Theory and Helping Relationships," in L. Wispe, op. cit.

53. Piliavin, J. A. and I. M. Piliavin, 1969, "Distance and Donations," unpublished manuscript, University of Pennsylvania.

54. Staub, E. and R. S. Baer, 1974, "Stimulus Characteristics of a Sufferer and Difficulty of Escape as Determinants of Helping," *Journal of Personality and Social Psychology* 30: 279–284.

55. Krebs, D., 1975, "Empathy and Altruism," *Journal of Personality and Social Psychology* 32: 1134–1146.

56. Batson, D. C., B. D. Duncan, P. Ackerman, T. Buckley, and K. Birch, 1981, "Is Empathic Emotion a Source of Altruistic Motivation?" *Journal of Personality and Social Psychology* 40: 290–302.

57. Shotland, L. and T. L. Huston, 1976, "Emergencies: What They Are and Do They Influence Bystanders to Intervene?" *Journal of Personality and Social Psychology* 37: 1822–1834.

58. Pomazal, R. J. and J. J. Jaccard, 1976, "An Informal Approach to Altruistic Behavior," *Journal of Personality and Social Psychology* 33: 317–326.

59. McGovern, L. P., J. L. Ditzian, and S. P. Taylor, 1975, "Sex and Perceptions of Dependency in a Helping Situation," *Bulletin of the Psychonomic Society* 5: 336–338.

60. Dovidio, 1984, op. cit.; Piliavin et al., 1981, op. cit.

61. Walster and Piliavin, 1972, op. cit.

62. Field, M., 1974, "Power and Dependency: Legitimation of Dependency Conditions," *Journal of Social Psychology* 92: 31–37.

63. Piliavin, J. A. and I. M. Piliavin, 1972, "The Effects of Blood on Reactions to a Victim," *Journal of Personality and Social Psychology* 23: 253–261.

64. Walster and Piliavin, 1972, op. cit.

65. Walster, E., G. W. Walster, and E. Berscheid, 1978, *Equity: Theory and Research,* Boston: Allyn & Bacon.

66. Gouldner, A. W., 1960, "The Norms of Reciprocity: A Preliminary Statement," *American Sociological Review* 25: 161–179.

67. Fisher, J. D., A. Nadler, and S. Whitcher-Alagna, 1983, "Four Theoretical Approaches for Conceptualizing Reactions to Aid," in J. D. Fisher, A. Nadler, and B. M. DePaulo, *New Directions in Helping,* Vol. 1, New York: Academic Press.

68. Homans, G. C., 1961, *Social Behavior: Its Elementary Forms,* New York: Harcourt.

69. Hatfield, E. and S. Sprecher, 1983, "Equity Theory and Recipient Reactions to Aid," in J. D. Fisher, A. Nadler, and B. M. DePaulo, op. cit.

70. Gergen, K. J. and M. Gergen, 1974, "Foreign Aid That Works," *Psychology Today,* June, 53–58.

71. Carnevale, P. J. D., D. G. Pruitt, and P. J. Carrington, 1982,

"Effects of Future Dependence," *Social Psychology Quarterly* 45: 9–14.

72. Hatfield and Sprecher, 1983, op. cit.

73. Caplow, T., 1984, "Rule Enforcement without Visible Means: Christmas Giving in Middletown," *American Journal of Sociology* 89: 1306–1323.

74. Yinon, Y., I. Sharon, Y. Gonen, and R. Adam, "Escape from Responsibility and Help in Emergencies among Persons Alone or within Groups," *European Journal of Social Psychology* 12: 305–310.

75. Horowitz, I., 1971, "The Effect of Group Norms on Bystander Intervention," *Journal of Social Psychology* 83: 265–273.

76. Darley and Latané, 1968a, op. cit.

77. Rutkowski et al., 1983, op. cit.

78. Batson, C. D., J. M. Darley, and J. S. Coke, 1978, "Altruism and Human Kindness: Internal and External Determinants of Helping Behavior," in L. Pervin and M. Lewis (Eds.), *Perspectives in Interactional Psychology,* New York: Plenum.

79. Schwartz, S. H. and J. A. Howard, 1980, "Explanations of the Moderating Effect of Responsibility Denial on the Personal Norm-Behavior Relationship," *Social Psychology Quarterly* 43: 441–446.

80. Underwood, B. and B. Moore, 1982, "Perspective-taking and Altruism," *Psychological Bulletin* 91: 143–173.

81. Callero, P. L., J. A. Howard, and J. A. Piliavin, 1987, "Helping Behavior as Role Behavior: Disclosing Social Structure and History in the Analysis of Prosocial Behavior," *Social Psychology Quarterly* 50: 247–256.

82. Walster et al., 1978, op. cit.

83. Goranson, R. E. and L. Berkowitz, 1966, "Reciprocity and Responsibility Reactions to Prior Help," *Journal of Personality and Social Psychology* 3: 227–232; S. A. Shumaker and J. S. Jackson, 1979, "The Aversive Effects of Nonreciprocated Benefits," *Social Psychology Quarterly* 42: 148–158; E. Staub, 1978, *Positive Social Behavior and Morality: Social and Personal Influences,* Vol. 1, New York: Academic Press; M. S. Greenberg and S. P. Shapiro, 1971, "Indebtedness: An Adverse Aspect of Asking for and Receiving Help," *Sociometry* 34: 290–301.

84. Gross, A. E., B. S. Wallston, and I. M. Piliavin, 1975, "Beneficiary Attractiveness and Cost as Determinants of Help," *Sociometry* 38: 131–140; K. Kelley and D. Byrne, 1976, "Attraction and Altruism: With a Little Help from My Friends," *Journal of Research in Personality* 10: 59–68.

85. Baron, R. A., 1971, "Behavioral Effects of Interpersonal Attraction: Compliance with Requests from Liked and Disliked Others," *Psychonomic Science* 25: 325–326.

86. Piliavin et al., 1981, op. cit.; Krebs, 1975, op. cit.

87. Karabenick, S. A., R. M. Lerner, and M. D. Beecher, 1972, "Relation of Political Affiliation to Helping Behavior on Election Day, November 7, 1972," *Journal of Social Psychology* 91: 223–227.

88. Weiner, B., 1980, "A Cognition (Attribution)-Emotion-Action Model of Motivated Behavior: An Analysis of Judgments of Help-giving," *Journal of Personality and Social Psychology* 39: 186–200.

89. Meyer, J. P. and A. Mulherin, 1980, "From Attribution to Helping: An Analysis of the Mediating Effects of Affect and Expectancy," *Journal of Personality and Social Psychology* 3: 201–210.

90. Smithson et al., 1983, op. cit.

91. Bryan, J. H. and M. A. Test, 1967, "Models and Helping," *Journal of Personality and Social Psychology* 6: 400–407; J. F. Dovidio and S. I. Gaertner, 1981, "The Effects of Race, Status and Ability on Helping Behavior," *Social Psychology Quarterly* 44: 192–203; S. L. Gaertner, 1973, "Helping Behavior and Racial Discrimination among Liberals and Conservatives," *Journal of Personality and Social Psychology* 25: 335–341; Piliavin and Piliavin, 1969, op. cit.; Piliavin and Piliavin, 1972, op. cit.

92. Gaertner, S. L. and J. F. Dovidio, 1977, "The Subtlety of White Racism, Arousal, and Helping Behavior," *Journal of Personality and Social Psychology* 35: 691–707; L. G. Wispe and H. B. Freshly, 1971, "Race, Sex, and Sympathetic Helping Behavior: The Broken Bag Caper," *Journal of Personality and Social Psychology* 17: 59–65.

93. Dovidio, 1984, op. cit.

94. Pancer, S. M., L. M. McMullen, R. A. Kabatoff, K. G. Johnson, and C. A. Pond, 1979, "Conflict and Avoidance in the Helping Situation," *Journal of Personality and Social Psychology* 37: 1406–1411.

95. Glick, P., J. E. Abbott, and C. A. Hotze, 1988, "Keeping Your Distance: Similarity, Personal Space, and Requests for Small Favors," *Journal of Applied Social Psychology* 18: 315–330.

96. Stephan, W. G. and C. W. Stephan, 1985, "Intergroup Anxiety," *Journal of Social Issues* 41: 157–175.

97. Eagly, A. H. and M. Crowley, in press, "Gender and Helping Behavior," *Psychological Bulletin;* A. M. Isen, 1970, "Success, Failure, Attention, and Reaction to Others: The Warm Glow of Success," *Journal of Personality and Social Psychology* 15: 294–301; R. J. Pomazal, 1974, "Attitudes, Normative Beliefs, and Altruism: Help for Helping Behavior," unpublished doctoral dissertation, University of Illinois; S. G. West, G. Whitney, and R. Schnedler, 1975, "Helping a Motorist in Distress: The Effects of Sex, Race and Neighborhood," *Journal of Personality and Social Psychology* 31: 691–698.

98. Gruder, C. L. and T. D. Cook, 1971, "Sex, Dependency, and Helping," *Journal of Personality and Social Psychology* 19: 290–294.

99. Tipton, R. M. and S. Browning, 1972, "The Influence of Age and Obesity on Helping Behavior," *British Journal of Social and Clinical Psychology* 11: 404–409.

100. Berkowitz, L., 1972, "Social Norms, Feelings, and Other Factors Affecting Helping Behavior and Altruism," in L. Berkowitz (Ed.), *Advances in Experimental Social Psychology*, Vol. 6, New York: Academic Press, pp. 63–108.

CHAPTER 13

Aggression

■

Family Violence and Rape

Wife Battering

Child Abuse

Rape

Aggressor/Situation/Target Model

The Aggressor

The Situation

The Target

In the summer of 1987 an epidemic of violence broke out on the freeways of California. By Labor Day 24 people were dead or wounded as a result of 119 separate shooting incidents. Most of the aggression was aimed at strangers who had committed minor acts of discourtesy while driving on the freeways. In one incident Sandra Tait did not move aside quickly enough to suit a driver who had flashed his lights. When the other car pulled alongside, the driver began shooting. A passenger in Ms. Tait's car was killed.

What do you think caused this wave of violence? Here are some facts to consider. The incidents all occurred during the summer. It appears that all of the assailants were men. In most of the incidents a pistol was used. Nearly all of the incidents occurred between 1 p.m. and 10 p.m. The majority of incidents occurred on weekends when traffic was lightest. All of the incidents came as a surprise to those who were attacked (1).

Various explanations were offered in the media for this wave of aggression. One explanation was that the arousal produced by high speed driving, combined with the feeling of invincibility people experience while driving a car, and the reduction of normal restraints on aggression caused by the anonymity of the drivers, were the causes. Another explanation was that drivers are more competitive today and treat the road as a kind of gladiator contest—your vehicle against mine. The stress and frustration caused by recurring traffic jams on a road system designed for another era were also cited. Some people blamed the easy availability of guns and suggested that traffic violence is a logical extension of the increase in violence seen throughout our society. Still others suggested a copycat syndrome was involved in which one person's violent act set the stage for others to imitate it. It was also noted that July was an unusually hot month in 1987. Issues of territoriality were invoked as an explana-

■ *Most freeway driving does not lead to violence. What triggers freeway violence when it does occur? (WGS)*

■ *Is this aggression or is it play? How you make this decision tells a lot about your own definition of aggression. (WGS)*

tion; people view their cars as extensions of themselves and they protect them with the same vigor. One police officer said simply, "People who get caught up in these incidents are nuts."

Why were so many explanations proposed? As you will see in this chapter, aggression is a complex behavior with many contributing causes. Like helping, some of the causes lie within the person (P), some are associated with aspects of the situation (S), and some concern the target (T) of the aggression (when discussing helping we referred to the person receiving help as the *recipient*). You can see that each of these categories of causes is represented in the explanations given above. In this chapter we will discuss the P + S + T model as it applies to aggression, but first we will consider three specific types of aggression in our society: wife battering, child abuse, and rape.

Due to their interests in the structure and functioning of society, sociological social psycholo-

gists have typically focused on particular types of aggression such as wife battering, child abuse, and rape. They examine the frequency of these types of aggression, and the characteristics of the perpetrators and the victims, as well as the causes of these behaviors. Adherents of psychological social psychology have focused less on specific types of aggression and more on general causes of aggression. Psychological social psychology focuses on person, situation, and target factors common to many aggressive behaviors. Ultimately, the two approaches are complementary. Sociological social psychology provides a rich description of particular types of aggression and specific causal factors unique to each type of aggression, while psychological social psychology gives us general models of the causes of aggression that can be applied to many situations.

Before delving into the nature of aggression and its causes we must first consider some issues of definition. How would you define aggression? Consider the following behaviors: assault, first-degree murder, wife battering, and rape. You probably have no difficulty labeling these behaviors as examples of aggression. Now consider some more ambiguous behaviors: corporal punishment of children, negligent manslaughter, participation in a firing squad, and fighting in response to a provocation. It's not so easy to decide about these examples, is it?

What all of these behaviors have in common is that one person causes another to suffer. Clearly, this constitutes one component of aggression. The first set of behaviors cited above differs from the second primarily because in assault, first-degree murder, wife battering, and rape, the harm is unjustified in the eyes of society. In most of the second set of examples, one person intends to harm another, but there is a justification offered for doing the harm. The justification makes it difficult to label these behaviors as aggression. Most Americans believe physically punishing children is justifiable, and duty is the reason given to justify participation in a firing squad. Also, people often feel justified in fighting in response to provocation. Negligent manslaughter is different. Although it involves obvious harm, an intent to do harm is absent. The term aggression is best reserved for behaviors *intended* to cause suffering to others that are *not justifiable* in terms of the laws and norms of society. Thus, a man who plans to kill his business partner in a dark alley, but who shoots and misses has still committed an act of aggression. This is an act of aggression because he intended to cause harm even though he was unsuccessful.

■
FAMILY VIOLENCE AND RAPE

Our families provide us with love, affection, support, and esteem. Tragically for many people, the family is also a source of conflict and violence. Wife battering and child abuse are examples of violence within the family. Only recently has the prevalence of these types of familial violence come to light.

Because the family is considered to be private, and people who experience violence in the family often experience love there as well, studying family violence has proved to be difficult. Many acts of violence go unreported and people are reluctant to discuss those they do report.

Nonetheless, growing evidence shows just how common family violence is. One set of early researchers, appalled by their findings, were prompted to comment, "It would be hard to find a group or an institution in American society in which violence is more of an everyday occurrence than it is within the family" (2). Gradually we are starting to understand more about the causes of family violence.

In our discussions of wife battering, child abuse, and rape we will first discuss the prevalence of each of these forms of aggression, describe the typical perpetrators, and profile the victims, and then conclude with a discussion of theories that have been used to explain these types of violence.

Wife Battering

Because wife battering so often goes unreported (perhaps as few as 2 percent of the cases come to the attention of the police) we can only estimate its frequency (3). However, the estimates are staggering. It is believed that 20 to 35 percent of all wives are battered by their husbands (4). One researcher believes 50 percent of all women will be beaten by someone they love at some time during their lives (5).

Although a small number of husbands are beaten by their wives, women are overwhelmingly the targets of violence and men are overrepresented as aggressors. Women are often severely injured when violence occurs, due to the greater physical strength of men (6). One study found that a shocking number of the women (60 percent) are beaten when they are pregnant (7). At its worst, wife beating can be lethal. Domestic quarrels are a factor in about 25 percent of all homicides (8). Violence directed at women by men occurs both before and after marriage, but seems to be more frequent after marriage, and for some victims it becomes progressively more severe as the marriage goes on.

Many abused wives experience a consistent cycle of violence. It starts with a *tension building stage* during which a few discrete incidents of abuse occur, but they do not get out of control. As tensions between the couple build, the *acute battering stage* is ultimately reached and an incident of serious uncontrolled abuse occurs. The abusive incident is then followed by the *loving contrition stage* in which the husband begs for forgiveness and acts in a loving and caring way—until the tension starts to build again and the cycle repeats (9).

The perpetrators Abusive husbands come from all social classes, but among reported abusers more come from the lower class and their education levels also tend to be lower than nonabusive husbands (10). Many, but by no means all, abusive husbands are unemployed (11). Abusive husbands are generally also aggressive in their nonfamilial behavior (12). Many were brought up in violent families where they witnessed wife battering or were themselves abused (13). In the majority of cases, abusive husbands are heavy drinkers (14). Other characteristics of abusive husbands include: beliefs in traditional gender roles (15), lack of assertiveness and self-esteem, high levels of sexual jealousy (16), and social isolation (17).

The victims Abused wives are no more likely to have come from abusive families than nonabused wives (18). Also, no psychological differences have been found between abused and nonabused wives (19). However, several studies suggest abused wives often come from higher social class backgrounds and have more education than their husbands (20). Thus, the study of abusive husbands and abused wives suggests that while almost any type of woman can become the victim of an abusive relationship, abusive husbands share more characteristics in common.

In addition to the physical suffering they experience, battered wives suffer from fear and anxiety, depression, feelings of helplessness and guilt, and psychologically related physical complaints such as sleeplessness and nightmares (21). Children of wife batterers are often abused by the fathers as well,

and they may suffer in other ways including being fearful, having low self-esteem, and attaining low academic achievement (22). A variety of explanations has been offered for wife battering including feminist theories, sociocultural theories, and psychological theories.

Feminist theory The *feminist* perspective suggests that men batter women to gain or maintain power over them. It is argued that the patriarchal nature of our society leads men to expect to dominate and control women. Historically, women have often been treated as if they were the property of men, for men to do with as they pleased. For centuries wife battering was not illegal. In fact, the term "rule of thumb" originally referred to the English common law idea that a man could beat his wife as long as the stick he used was not wider than his thumb (23). Until recently wife rape was not a crime in many states.

In support of the feminist approach, research indicates battering is most likely when men's power or dominance in the family is threatened. The research findings showing that battered women often come from higher social class and educational backgrounds than their husbands is consistent with feminist theory, especially if the husbands interpret these differences in relative status as a threat to their dominance or superiority (24). Also, the extreme sexual jealousy of abusive husbands suggests that they think of their wives as possessions.

Traditional gender role socialization encouraging aggressiveness, competitiveness, and male superiority is also thought to promote wife battering. The research finding that abusive husbands have traditional gender role attitudes is consistent with this idea.

Sociocultural theory This theory stresses the high levels of acceptance of aggression in our society. It argues that aggression is used as a technique of resolving conflicts and controlling the behavior of others—a technique that is employed when other methods fail. As a society, we do commit high levels of aggression as the statistics in Figure 13-1 so amply illustrate. We also condone aggression in sports, on

Figure 13.1 ■

Rates of Violent and Property Crime in the United States in 1987

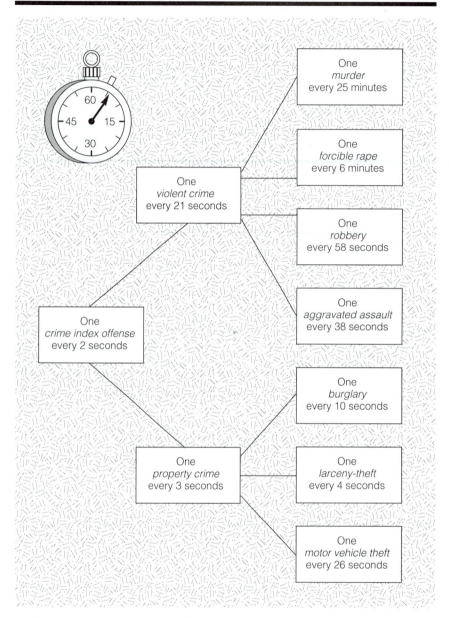

Uniform Crime Reports for the United States: 1987, Washington, DC: U.S. Department of Justice.

television, and in interpersonal relations (the use of corporal punishment on children) (25). This theory suggests the culture's *laissez faire* attitudes toward violence promote wife battering by reducing inhibitions against aggression. Recent survey findings indicating that Americans do not approve of violence within the family stand as evidence against this theory (26).

These negative attitudes toward family violence and the recent upsurge of interest in battered wives— as evidenced by greater enforcement of laws against battering and the provision of hotlines and shelters for battered women in many communities—suggest that tolerance for this type of aggressive behavior is rapidly decreasing. If the earlier *laissez faire* attitudes toward aggression did foster wife battering, perhaps we can hope that condemnation will decrease it.

Psychological theories Early psychological theories stressed pathological defects, such as masochism, in the victims of battering. These defects allegedly led these women to allow themselves to be abused. Such blame-the-victim theories have received no support. Similarly, theories stressing pathological defects in abusive husbands have received little support. Abusive husbands are not "crazy," although they are often jealous, aggressive men and many of them are alcoholics.

Other psychological theories emphasize the stress and frustration abusive husbands experience as the causes of abuse. For instance, pregnancy often introduces considerable stress into a family. The finding that many battered wives are pregnant at the time they are beaten tends to support the stress theory, as does the finding that many of the men were unemployed at the time of the beatings.

Social learning theory suggests that wife battering may be learned through modeling. The finding that many abusive husbands witnessed similar abuse or were the victims of abuse themselves suggests these individuals may be imitating the abusive behavior they witnessed or experienced as children.

Although the different types of theories have typically been proposed by different researchers, they are not incompatible. The existence of a patriarchal society, a factor favored by the feminist theorists, is consistent with the sociocultural theorists' emphasis on societal support for aggression. Both of these factors may culminate in abuse only when high levels of stress are present or when individuals have a predisposition to be aggressive due to their backgrounds; as psychological theorists stress. Thus, these three theories provide us with complementary perspectives on the causes of wife battering.

Child Abuse

The vast majority of American parents approve of the use of corporal punishment to discipline children. The use of corporal punishment does not ordinarily constitute abuse, but physical punishment which harms or injures the child does constitute *child abuse*. When failing to provide for children's basic physical needs results in harm to the child this constitutes *child neglect*. Using these definitions, the National Center on Child Neglect and Abuse estimates that about 2 million children a year are abused or neglected by their parents (27). Some 50,000 of these children suffer a major physical injury and each year 1,000 to 2,000 children die from abuse (28). A child in an abusive home is beaten an average of six times a year.

The perpetrators Both men and women are perpetrators of child abuse and neglect. More males than females commit physical abuse, but more females than males are neglectful (29). Parents who are young, lower class, high school dropouts, or who are experiencing marital conflicts, unemployment (30), or financial problems are the most typical abusers (31). The parents of abused children commonly lack good parenting skills, especially empathy, and they often have low self-esteem (32). Many abusive parents were themselves abused as children (33). It is common for abusive parents to justify their behavior as a legitimate form of discipline and to "scapegoat" or blame their victims (34).

Abusive parents tend to have unrealistic expectations regarding their children's conduct and are rigid in their beliefs about what constitutes appropriate behavior (35). Since younger children are the least able to comply with their parents' expectations, they often suffer the most. Abusive parents are more easily angered by their children's disruptive behavior than nonabusive parents (36), and they react with aggression when they cannot control their children's behavior (37). Social isolation due to frequent moves or low participation in the community is also associated with child abuse (38).

The victims The victims of child abuse are about evenly split between males and females. Child abuse tends to decrease as children get older, but one study reported an increase in the 16–18-year-old group (39). The victims are disproportionately from minority groups and the majority live in lower-class families. Children who were born prematurely or who are physically handicapped, ill, unwanted, difficult to care for, or disruptive are more likely than normal, healthy children to be the victims of abuse (40).

Multi-factor theory Most explanations of child abuse draw on four sets of causal factors, rather than emphasizing just one (see Figure 13-2) (41). The first constellation of factors consists of cultural beliefs and norms concerning parental use of discipline (the widespread support for corporal punishment in our society). A second constellation of factors consists of the characteristics of children that increase the chances they will become targets of abuse (the child is difficult to care for). A third constellation of factors concerns the characteristics of the abusive parents that predispose them to the use of excessive force (socially isolated, easily angered). These background factors trigger abuse when a fourth constellation of factors is present: high levels of real or perceived stress (unemployment, marital difficulties) (42).

Multi-factor models help us to understand why most premature, handicapped, or "difficult" children are not abused, and why most lower-class, unemployed parents do not abuse their children. According to this theory, abuse is likely only when a conjunction occurs between predisposing factors and a stressful situation. The presence of one or two of

Figure 13.2 ■

Multiple Factor Model of Child Abuse

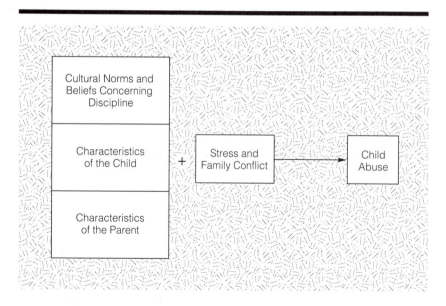

these factors, for instance a young parent with poor parenting skills who is experiencing marital and financial difficulties, might not lead to abuse if the child is easy to care for.

The multi-factor model fits the data we have cited on child abuse quite well. Particular characteristics of children and parents are associated with abuse. And, stress inside and outside of the home frequently triggers the most severe episodes of abuse. In addition, it has been found that child abuse is more common in cultures that approve of corporal punishment than in those, such as China and Japan, that do not (43).

Rape

In terms of reported offenses, rape is one of the fastest growing crimes in America: The number of reported rapes increased 42 percent from 1977 to 1986 (44). According to the FBI, in 1987 a rape was reported every six minutes in this country. However, relying only on reported rates grossly underestimates the actual number of rapes that are committed. It is estimated that 50 percent to 95 percent of all rapes are not reported to the police (45). The divergence among these estimates is an indication of how little we know about the actual incidence of rape. In one study of a random sample of women in San Fransisco, 24 percent reported they had been the victim of at least one rape and 31 percent reported someone had attempted to rape them (46). A 1987 study of over 3,000 college women found that 15 percent had been the victims of rape and 12 percent of attempted rape (47). The same study found that 25 percent of the 3,000 men in the sample reported engaging in some type of sexual aggression. These figures reflect much higher rates of sexual assault than police records indicate. The underreporting of rape makes it difficult to form an accurate picture of the characteristics of rapists and their victims because the rapes that are reported may not be representative of those that are committed (see Box 13-1).

The perpetrators Rapists are nearly all men. Most of the men are young and a considerable number (30

percent to 60 percent) are married (53). Like wife beaters and child abusers, rapists can be found in all social classes, but those who are apprehended are disproportionately lower class, unemployed, and low in educational achievement (54). Also, like wife beaters and child abusers, a significant number of rapists (20 percent to 25 percent) were victims of child abuse (55). Rapists reported to the police are disporportionately from minority groups (56).

Few differences in personality traits have been found between rapists and nonrapists (57), and extreme forms of mental disorder are rare among rapists (58). However, as many as half of all rapists are heavy drinkers (59), and more than half were drinking at the time of the assault (60). Rapists are sexually aroused by depictions of rape to a greater degree than nonrapists (61). Sexual aggressiveness (a term that includes rape as well as other forms of sexual aggression) in men is associated with callous and hostile attitudes toward women, a belief in myths concerning rape (see Box 13-2), a variety of delinquent behaviors, and unstable home environments (62).

Several investigators have suggested there are three types of rapists (63). The categories are based on the relative importance of anger, power, and sex as motives. The most common type is the *power* rapist, who asserts his masculinity by coercing his victim into sex. Force is used as a means of obtaining sexual gratification. The second most common type is the *anger* rapist, who uses more force than would be necessary to coerce his victim into sex. He is acting out of rage and anger in an attempt to hurt and debase his victim. The anger is impulsive and sexual motives are secondary to aggressive ones. The third type, the *sadistic* rapist, torments, maims, or murders his victim. The assault is premeditated, not impulsive. This type is relatively rare.

The victims Although the victims of rape are mostly female, males are the victims in about 5 percent of the cases (in these cases the perpetrators are generally male as well) (65). Women of all ages are raped, but the highest percentage of rape victims are between the ages of 15 and 25. Minority and poor women are the most likely to report being

BOX 13-1

Date Rape

One of the most underreported types of rapes is date rape. These rapes are no less devastating in their consequences than rapes by strangers, but the victims often cannot bring themselves to report them. The causes of these rapes differ in some ways from the causes of rape among strangers. Dating is typically associated with voluntary sexual behavior. In date rape sexual behavior becomes coercive, goes against the woman's wishes, and ends in intercourse.

One factor that contributes to date rape is that males do not interpret sexual interactions in the same way as females. Men often see a sexual invitation where none was intended (48). For instance, they may interpret a "no" as a "yes," or feel that if they are "allowed" to engage in one form of sexual foreplay, they are being "led on" to others. One study found that 30 percent of male students felt that a date fondling a male's sex organ was an invitation to intercourse, but only 7 percent of the female students felt this way (49).

Exchange theory sheds some light on the date rape problem. Viewed as an exchange, the traditional date in which the male initiates the invitation, picks up his date, and pays for the entertainment puts the female in a position where she may implicitly feel pressured to provide sex as her part of the bargain. A study of over 400 male and female teenagers in California found that two thirds of them said a boy would be justified in holding down a girl and forcing her to have sexual intercourse if she's led him on or she gets him sexually excited (50). One third of

raped. Although most reported rape victims are unmarried, married women are also victims. Recent studies of marital rape indicate that 3 percent to 14 percent of wives are raped by their husbands (66). The most frequently reported occupation of rape victims is student, a fact that is probably due largely to the age of the victims (67). In contrast to the relatively high frequency with which the rapists had been drinking prior to the assault, the victims were intoxicated in less than 10 percent of the cases (68). Only a very small percentage of rape victims were experiencing psychiatric problems at the time of the rape (69).

Psychopathology theory In the psychopathology theory of rape it is argued that rapists have had pathological socialization experiences, such as parental rejection, sexual seduction, or overstimulation, that cause them to be maladjusted. As adults, the rapists then use rape as a defense against feelings of sexual inadequacy or homosexuality, as a reaction against feelings of dependency, or as a form of

the teenagers said a boy would be justified in doing this if "he had spent a lot of money on her."

In addition to viewing sexual foreplay as an invitation to sex and expecting sex as part of an exchange, date rapists expect sex sooner in a dating relationship than their partners do and interpret resistance as an instance of women playing the feminine role by denying their interest in sex (51). Even with these predisposing factors, a point is reached when misunderstanding of the woman's resistance would no longer be possible.

Would you define the following situation as rape? Lee and and Diane had dated occasionally for a couple of months. One night, after attending a movie, they went to his apartment. They started kissing and things progressed to the point where Diane's dress was unbuttoned to her waist. When Lee tried to go further Diane objected, but Lee continued. Diane told him again to stop, then slapped him and tried twisting away from him. Lee attempted to reassure her, and then he held her arms behind her back. When she continued resisting, Lee pressed his forearm against her neck. Although she continued to struggle vigorously, he eventually undressed her and intercourse occurred.

In a study of college students, using this and similar vignettes, it was found that whether the situation was defined as rape depended on how far the sexual interaction had proceeded and on how much force the male used (52). When the level of force was low and the interaction had proceeded to the point where both people were undressed, two thirds of the students in the study did not define the ensuing sexual intercourse as rape. In the above interaction, where the woman's dress was unbuttoned and the male used considerable force, one-fifth of the students did not define this as rape. Legally, however, "no" at any stage means "no," and sexual intercourse after verbal resistance or any other kind of resistance constitutes rape. ■

displaced aggression where the original target was a female who had mistreated them (70). Thus, in this theory rape is regarded as a means of resolving internal conflicts created by pathological socialization experiences.

The findings indicating there are few personality differences between rapists and nonrapists, and that rates of psychopathology are low among rapists, stand as evidence against this approach (71). The high number of men who admit using force or would be willing to use it to obtain sex also argues against the psychopathology theory. However, the fact that a number of rapists were abused as children and that sexual aggressiveness in young men is associated with unstable home environments indicates some rapists have had abnormal socialization experiences.

Symbolic interactionist theory At the microsociological level, the symbolic interactionists see rape as a breakdown of the role-taking process; rapists do not take the perspectives of women into account during

BOX 13-2

Rape Myth Acceptance Scale

Responses to the following scale have been found to correlate with sexual aggressiveness, conservative gender role attitudes, and low educational and occupational achievement.

1. A woman who goes to the home or apartment of a man on their first date implies that she is willing to have sex.

2. Any female can get raped.

3. One reason that women falsely report a rape is that they frequently have a need to call attention to themselves.

4. Any healthy woman can successfully resist a rapist if she really wants to.

5. When women go around braless or wearing short skirts and tight tops, they are just asking for trouble.

6. In the majority of rapes, the victim is promiscuous or has a bad reputation.

7. If a girl engages in necking or petting and she lets things get out of hand, it is her own fault if her partner forces sex on her.

8. Women who get raped while hitchhiking get what they deserve.

a sexual interaction. As a result, rapists are not dissuaded by the resistance or suffering of their victims. By ignoring or redefining his victim's resistance and suffering, the rapist can avoid defining his own behavior as rape.

Rapists also look for ways in which they can justify their behavior. For instance, rapists use the fact that they have been drinking as an excuse to diminish their responsibility for their behavior. In support of this view, a study of convicted rapists found those who *did* define their behavior as rape frequently tried to excuse it by citing their use of alcohol. In contrast, rapists who *did not define* their behavior as rape offered other justifications for their

behavior and typically blamed the victims (72). The latter group denied they were drunk, but they often claimed the victim was.

In criticizing the psychopathology model, symbolic interactionists have pointed out that if rape is viewed as the act of a person suffering from a psychological disorder, the rapist's responsibility for the act is diminished (73). Also, blaming the victim by citing her use of alcohol, sexual history, or provocative clothing focuses attention on the victim's motives and diverts attention from the cultural context in which rape takes place (see Box 13-3) (74). Focusing on the motives of the perpetrator and the victim does not so much explain rape as

9. A woman who is stuck up and thinks she is too good to talk to guys on the street deserves to be taught a lesson.

10. Many women have an unconscious wish to be raped and may then unconsciously set up a situation in which they are likely to be attacked.

11. If a woman gets drunk at a party and has intercourse with a man she's just met there, she should be considered "fair game" to other males at the party who want to have sex with her too, whether she wants to or not.

12. What percentage of women who report a rape would you say are lying because they are angry and want to get back at the men they accuse?

13. What percentage of reported rapes would you guess were merely invented by women who discovered they were pregnant and wanted to protect their own reputations?

14. A person comes to you and claims he or she was raped. How likely would you be to believe his/her statement if the person were:
   A. Your best friend
   B. An Indian woman
   C. A neighborhood woman
   D. A young boy
   E. A black woman
   F. A white woman

Scoring: Use a 7-point scale running from *agree strongly* to *disagree strongly* for the first 11 items. For items 12–13 use a 5-point scale in which the response options are: *almost all, 75, 50, 25, almost none*. For A–F on item 14 use the following 5-point scale: *always, frequently, sometimes, rarely, never*. Low scores mean a higher acceptance of rape myths. The average score is 49 (64). ■

---

explain it away. In fact, symbolic interactionists would argue these "explanations" form one part of the society's belief system that makes rape possible.

Symbolic interactionists with a feminist orientation argue that the causes of rape are found in society's attitudes toward women. One element of this belief system is the widespread belief in rape myths. Studies indicate that acceptance of rape myths and negative attitudes toward women are associated with sexual aggression (76). In addition, men in this society are commonly socialized to believe that to be masculine is to be dominant, strong, and aggressive. In this view, rape is an outcome of typical socialization, not of atypical socialization (77). This view is buttressed by the common finding that among college males, 35 percent report they would commit rape if they were sure they could get away with it (78).

Historically, in our society women have been subordinated and treated as inferior. In some societies, and in our society at an earlier time, women are (were) regarded as the property of men. Viewed from this cultural perspective, rape may be seen as simply an extreme manifestation of a society's norms and values. The basic message in many societies has been that men can use their power to obtain sex through the use of force. Lesser forms of sexual aggression are so common as to be the norm. Several

BOX 13-3

Blaming the Victim

Rape victims are often blamed for being raped by the courts, their husbands or lovers, and even themselves. They often wonder what they did to have brought such a terrible calamity upon themselves. In the courts, questions are often asked about the behavior of the victim that may have provoked the attack. The absurdity of asking such questions is nicely captured in the following parody.

Prosecutor: Mr. Mann, can you tell the jury what time the alleged robbery took place?
Victim: Late at night, about 11:30 p.m.

Prosecutor: And where were you at the time of the assault?
Victim: I had been having a drink at a downtown bar and was on my way to my car.

Prosecutor: Were you alone?
Victim: Yes.

Prosecutor: And what were you wearing?
Victim: A three piece suit.

Prosecutor: An expensive suit?
Victim: Yes, I pride myself on my appearance.

Prosecutor: What else were you wearing?
Victim: I had on my Rolex watch.

Prosecutor: Let me ask you this. Do you give money to charitable organizations?
Victim: Why, yes, of course.

Prosecutor: When the accused approached you and asked for your money, how did you respond?
Victim: I gave him my money and my watch. He is much bigger than I am and I knew I could not win a struggle against him.

Prosecutor: Let me get this straight Mr. Mann, you want the jury to believe you were robbed against your will, but you intentionally went downtown late at night, drank in a bar, then walked alone to your car wearing expensive clothing and accessories—it would be fair to say you were dressed provocatively, wouldn't it? You also have a prior history of willingly giving money away and on this occasion you gave your money away without a struggle. It looks to me like you were just asking to be robbed and you didn't seem to mind if you were. Why it seems to me you must have secretly wanted to be robbed, isn't that so, Mr. Mann? (75) ■

IN 1983, HANDGUNS KILLED
35 PEOPLE IN JAPAN
8 IN GREAT BRITAIN
27 IN SWITZERLAND
6 IN CANADA
7 IN SWEDEN
10 IN AUSTRALIA
AND 9,014 IN THE UNITED STATES.

GOD BLESS AMERICA.

The pen is mightier than the gun.
Write Handgun Control, Inc. Now.
1400 K Street, N.W., Washington, D.C. 20005
Or call (202) 898-0792

STOP HANDGUNS BEFORE THEY STOP YOU.

studies of college women report that more than 50 percent were the targets of some form of sexual aggression in the last year (79). The finding that sexual aggression is the second most frequently shown type of sexual interaction on television soap operas is also consistent with this argument (80).

As indicated by the accompanying poster and Figure 13-3, the United States is an unusually aggressive country and has an unusually high rate of rapes. In societies where interpersonal violence is an accepted pattern of behavior, there is no reason not to expect that rape will be included among the common forms of aggression. The United States has many of the characteristics of rape-prone cultures

Figure 13.3 ■

Rape Rates

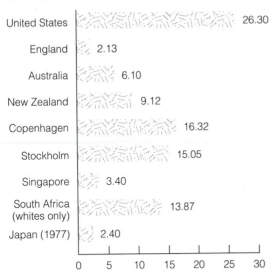

United States	26.30
England	2.13
Australia	6.10
New Zealand	9.12
Copenhagen	16.32
Stockholm	15.05
Singapore	3.40
South Africa (whites only)	13.87
Japan (1977)	2.40

Court, J.H., 1984, "Sex and Violence: A Ripple Effect," in N. M. Malamuth and E. Donnerstein (Eds.), *Pornography and Sexual Aggression*, New York: Academic Press.

(81): such cultures value toughness, aggressiveness, and competitiveness in the men, while women are demeaned, and women's work is devalued.

The diverse theories that have been offered to explain wife battering, child abuse, and rape reflect the complexity of the causes of aggression we alluded to at the outset of this chapter. In general, theories stressing the psychopathology of the perpetrators have not fared well. Similarly, theories that have tried to explain these types of aggression by citing personality characteristics of the victims have not been very successful. However, theories stressing situational, structural, and historical factors have fared somewhat better. If there is a thread that ties these topics together it is that in wife battering, child abuse, and rape, aggression is being directed at the powerless by the powerful.

■

AGGRESSOR/SITUATION/ TARGET MODEL

We move now from a consideration of specific examples of aggression to causal factors associated with many different types of aggression. In doing so, we will again employ the model that holds that factors in the person, the situation, and the target combine to influence aggression. Many of the factors we consider in this section affect wife battering, child abuse, and rape.

The Aggressor

The primary factors within the individual we will consider are emotional and cognitive states that predispose people to be aggressive. Emotional states and the manner in which they are defined are among the most important determinants of aggression. Three emotional states have received considerable attention as causes of aggression: anger, sexual arousal, and emotional responses to humor. We will also consider how misattributions concerning the causes of emotional arousal can affect aggression. In addition, we will discuss the roles of self-awareness and drugs as factors affecting the aggressor. As we discuss the factors that predispose people to aggression, bear in mind that all instances of aggression involve an aggressor, a situation in which the aggression takes place, and a target toward whom the aggression is directed. We have separated these three essential aspects of aggression only for purposes of presentation.

Anger Probably the most important cause of physical aggression is anger. We have already seen that anger can play a role in spouse abuse, child abuse, and rape. Both murder and assault frequently involve anger. Three-fourths of all murders are motivated by anger (82). The most frequent cause is an "altercation of relatively trivial origin: insult, curse, jostling, etc." (83). Anger also plays a role in collective violence, such as urban riots.

In our discussion of the role of anger as a cause of aggression, we will be guided by the *three-factor theory*. The first factor concerns the induction (creation) of anger, the second concerns the appraisal of and experience of anger, and the third concerns behavioral reactions to anger.

Induction phase. One of the earliest theories of the causes of aggression stated that frustration was its principle cause (84). In a subsequent elaboration of this theory, it was hypothesized that frustration led to aggression primarily when frustration caused anger (85). A sexually frustrated husband is unlikely to become abusive if he attributes his wife's behavior to the stress of her job. However, if he becomes angry because he feels she is intentionally witholding sex he is more likely to become abusive.

Although frustration can cause anger, it is not the only cause. Attacks or provocations that pose a danger to a person or which threaten the person's status are also a major cause of anger (86). Pain can lead to anger, as can the threat of loss of a valued person or possession. In addition, anger can be self-generated, as when you think about someone who might insult you, but who has not yet done so.

Appraisal phase. All of the situations cited above are capable of creating negative arousal that can be defined as anger. Because the same state of arousal can be interpreted in many different ways, an arousal state is not anger unless it is defined as anger by the individual. In a study illustrating this idea, subjects who believed they were participating in an investigation of the effects of visual stimuli on physiological responding were treated rudely by the experimenter (87). For instance, the experimenter said, "Apparently you don't listen to instructions very well. You were told that you had to sit still. This machine shows that you've been moving." After the study was over, the subjects had an opportunity to express aggression by negatively evaluating the experimenter on a questionnaire affecting the experimenter's chances of receiving financial aid in the future. When a second experimenter explained that the first experimenter was nervous about an exam, the subjects' evaluations were less negative than when no information about mitigating circumstances was provided.

However, mitigating information did not affect aggression if the aggressor was extremely aroused (88).

It appears the subjects who were given the mitigating information did not interpret moderate arousal as anger and, therefore, were less aggressive. If negative arousal is not defined as anger, aggression is not a likely response. However, when the subjects were extremely aroused, the cause of the provocation was not re-appraised due to the limited information processing that occurs during high arousal.

Behavior phase. When people are angry, they do not always respond with aggression. We have just seen that one factor influencing the response to anger is level of arousal. Angry people are most likely to act aggressively if their arousal level is extremely high. Under these circumstances, people may engage in impulsive aggression without giving a thought to whether their actions are right or wrong and without taking into consideration the consequences of their behavior (89). Aggression is particularly likely if the person has previously learned to respond with aggression in this type of situation. For instance, a husband who batters his wife may do so primarily when he is jealous. The jealousy causes him to feel very angry and, if he has learned to respond aggressively to being jealous, he will react by hitting his wife.

When an angered person's arousal level is moderate, an aggressive response is likely only if the aggression can be justified. A child abuser who is angry at his or her child is most likely to behave aggressively if he or she can justify the aggression as a "necessary" punishment. If aggression cannot be justified, cognitive factors such as fear of retaliation, social disapproval, or guilt can reduce the chances of aggression. An employee who is angry because she was criticized by her boss may suppress an aggressive response out of fear of retaliation. Cognitive thought processes also play an important role when the original arousing stimulus is ambiguous. If someone bumps into you and hurts you, you will probably attempt to determine if he or she intended to hurt you before responding aggressively.

When anger produces low levels of arousal,

BOX 13-4

Does Pornography Cause Rape?

Many people believe that the sexist nature of our society creates a climate that encourages violence toward women. They point to pornography as a prime example of the society's attitudes toward women. In the words of Susan Brownmiller:

The gut distaste that a majority of women feel when we look at pornography . . . comes, I think, from the gut knowledge that we and our bodies are being stripped, exposed, and contorted . . . to bolster that "masculine esteem" which gets its kick and sense of power from viewing females as anonymous, panting playthings . . . to be used, abused, broken, and discarded (93).

Is there a link between pornography and rape? This is a very difficult question to answer. Consider what the research on this topic has shown. Laboratory studies have shown that brief exposure to violent pornography (depictions of rape) increases aggressive sexual fantasies and beliefs in rape myths (94). Brief exposures to violent pornography (but not to erotica) increase aggression toward women, but not toward men. This is especially true if the pornographic depiction portrays women as ultimately deriving pleasure from the sexual assault. Aggression is most likely to increase in response to violent pornography among men with a propensity

withdrawal or no response is likely. Events that reduce an angry person's arousal level decrease the probability of aggression. The old adage about counting slowly to ten when you are angry really can reduce the chances that you will behave in an impulsively aggressive way! Watching an absorbing, but nonviolent, movie can also dissipate anger (90). Activities that raise your level of arousal, such as violent movies, stimulating physical exercise, or thinking hostile thoughts may actually increase later aggression.

Sexual arousal Certain types of sexual arousal can decrease aggression. In studies of this issue, the subjects typically are provoked in some way (someone insults them or finds fault with the work they

have done), and then they are asked to view sexually arousing materials under some pretext (the experiment is concerned with the effect of visual stimuli on physiological responses). Next, in a new context the subjects are given an opportunity to aggress against the person who provoked them.

Sexual arousal is likely to reduce subsequent aggression when the provocation is relatively mild and the arousing material consists of enjoyable erotica (depictions of mutually satisfying sex) (91). Why would this type of sexual arousal reduce aggression? Being sexually aroused after being provoked may shift the person's attention away from the annoyance and focus it on the more pleasant topic of sex. The pleasant emotions created by thinking about sex cause the annoyance to dissipate and, as

to rape (those who admit they could commit rape if they thought they would get away with it) and who already subscribe to common rape myths. The aggression is greatest when the men are angered, but it also occurs in the absence of provocation. Repeated exposure to erotica leads students to regard rape as a less offensive crime (95). Studies of the availability of erotica and pornography find that the more available the materials, the higher the incidence of rape (96). Finally, as noted previously, rapists are more sexually aroused by pornography depicting violence than are nonrapists (97).

These findings all seem to point to a causal relationship between pornography and rape, but caution must be exercised before coming to this conclusion. First, the laboratory studies are done in an atypical setting with special subject populations. The exposure to pornography is brief and the effects are measured immediately afterwards. The effects only hold for certain stimuli and for a subset of the subjects. The aggression measured is not sexual aggression. Thus, it is unclear whether these results can be generalized to the use of pornography in the natural environment. Second, it is possible that a third variable is responsible for the relationship between consumption of pornographic materials and rape. One such third variable would be an emphasis on hypermasculinity (machismo) which could cause both an interest in pornography and high rape rates. If this were true, pornography would be a part of the culture's emphasis on masculinity, but it would not be the cause of rape. Third, it is possible that rapists are aroused by violent pornography because committing rape leads rapists to find violent pornography arousing, rather than the reverse.

Thus, while the evidence consistently suggests that violent pornography promotes aggression against women among some men, we cannot yet be certain of this conclusion. ■

the arousal decreases, so does the aggression. Another explanation that has been offered for these findings is that sexual arousal interferes with aggressive behavior. However, this second explanation is rendered implausible by studies showing that high levels of sexual arousal created by exposure to violent pornography (explicit sex in which women are humiliated and degraded) leads to increases in aggression (see Box 13-4). It appears that when sexual arousal causes pleasant emotional reactions, it reduces aggression, but when it causes negative emotional reactions, it increases aggression (92).

Humor   It might seem strange to suggest that humor can affect aggression, but several studies have shown it can increase as well as decrease aggression (98).

One study found cartoons from magazines like *The New Yorker* reduced the aggression of subjects who had been provoked (99). A later study showed that only nonhostile humor reduced later aggression (100). When subjects were exposed to hostile humor, aggression increased. These results are quite similar to those for sexual arousal, in that positive (nonhostile) stimuli reduce aggression whereas negative (hostile) stimuli increase aggression.

Misattribution of arousal   The findings regarding the effects of sexual arousal and humor on aggression can both be interpreted within the framework of the *arousal transfer model* of aggression (101). This model proposes that arousal created in one situation can be transferred to a second situation in which it

Figure 13.4 ■

Arousal Transfer Model of Aggression

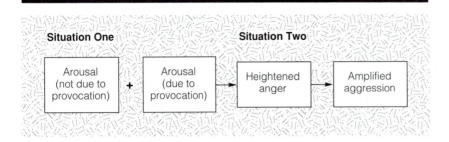

will amplify behavior (see Figure 13-4). The two assumptions underlying this model are: Many different types of stimuli produce nearly identical states of arousal; and people generally have limited insight into the causes of their arousal. Misattribution can occur when arousal created in one situation lasts long enough to be carried over into a new situation. People tend to attribute all of the arousal they are experiencing in the second situation to a single source, usually the most recent plausible cause for arousal.

In a test of the arousal transfer model, subjects first participated in a study during which they engaged in a physically arousing activity (riding an exercise bicycle) (102). Immediately after this study, some subjects were provoked by a confederate, who was the subject's opponent in a second study. The subjects then had an opportunity to thwart their opponents by administering noxious noise to them when the game continued. These provoked subjects were more aggressive than provoked subjects who had not engaged in an arousing task first or than subjects who had not been provoked. Apparently, arousal from the physical exercise transferred to the second situation and amplified the aggression that was displayed.

The transfer of arousal theory can explain the results of laboratory studies of the effects that violent pornographic materials and hostile humor have on aggression. The negative arousal created by pornographic materials or hostile humor transfers to

situations where people have an opportunity to respond to a provoker. In such situations, people are prone to misattributing the cause of their heightened arousal entirely to the provocation, ignoring the contribution of other arousing stimuli. The heightened level of anger then leads to a high level of aggression (see Fig. 13-4). In a related fashion, the stress produced by driving on crowded roads during the hot summer months can create negative arousal that augments the anger experienced when other drivers do annoying things, thus enhancing the chances of a highly aggressive outburst.

Misattribution of arousal is unlikely to occur when people are aware of the source of the original arousal. Also, misattribution is limited to the duration of the arousal from the initial arousing stimulus. For this reason, misattribution of arousal rarely occurs more than ten minutes after the original arousing stimulus.

Self-awareness Both types of self-awareness—public self-awareness (concern with the evaluations of others) and private self-awareness (concern with self-evaluations)—affect aggression (Chapter 4). When social norms or roles favor aggression, high public self-awareness will increase aggression (103). One such situation would be when people believe the norm of "an eye for an eye" is appropriate. In contrast, when social norms prohibit aggression, as they usually do, high public self-awareness will reduce aggression. Low public self-awareness often facilitates aggression. For example, the privacy of the family reduces public self-awareness and may therefore facilitate aggressive behaviors like child abuse and wife battering.

The aggression facilitating and inhibiting effects of public self-awareness are illustrated in a study in which a sample of people including ex-mental patients and ex-convicts were asked to recall real world disputes in which they had been involved (recall the last dispute that you can remember clearly where slapping or hitting with the fist was involved). The recalled incidents of aggression were more severe if third parties actively supported the aggression, but they were less severe if third parties actively discouraged aggression (104). In these situations, the aggressors were probably made publicly self-aware by the presence of others and they then behaved in accordance with the others' expectations.

When one's personal standards indicate that aggression is legitimate (to maintain self-respect), high private self-awareness increases aggression (105). When one's personal standards indicate that aggression is wrong, as they usually do, high private self-awareness decreases aggression while low self-awareness increases aggression. For instance, private self-awareness can be reduced by anger, which focuses attention on the source of irritation, rather than on the self. The resulting low levels of private self-awareness may facilitate aggression, including child abuse and wife battering because the perpetrators are not using their personal standards to evaluate their behaviors. In sum, the effects of high self-awareness depend on the standards applied to one's behavior, but low self-awareness generally facilitates aggression.

Drugs On the basis of our knowledge of the misattribution of arousal, we might expect drugs, that increase arousal to increase aggression, and drugs that decrease arousal to decrease aggression. Unfortunately, the evidence is not so clear-cut. Stimulants, such as amphetamines, have little or no effects on aggression. However, Valium, a tranquilizer, and alcohol, a depressant, lead to increased aggression (106).

In a series of studies, subjects competed in completing a task in which the winner of each round could shock the loser. Subjects who had previously drunk alcoholic beverages were more aggressive than subjects given a placebo (107). This increase in aggression occurred primarily when there was a possibility of retaliation, which would seem to be precisely the conditions under which aggression is most ill-advised (108). The explanation for this paradox is that alcohol increases aggression because it reduces private self-awareness which lowers the use of personal standards discouraging aggression (109). The role alcohol so frequently plays in rape and wife battering may be due to its capacity to lower private self-awareness.

Even alcohol, however, does not always increase aggression. If people who have been drinking can be made to feel high private self-awareness, they become less aggressive (110). A father who has had a couple of drinks too many on the way home from work may inhibit his aggression toward his small boy if he focuses his attention on how wrong it is for a grown man to beat a defenseless child. Interestingly, people who have been drinking are quite susceptible to the effects of public self-awareness. When people who have been drinking are led to feel high in public self-awareness, their aggression increases or decreases depending on whether their audience encourages or discourages aggression (111).

The complexity of the effects of drugs on aggression is also illustrated in another study (112). In this experiment, the effects of alcohol were compared to the effects of THC, the active ingredient in marijuana. Alcohol again increased aggression, but THC decreased aggression (see Table 13-1). It appears that THC induces a pleasant state of euphoria that is incompatible with aggressive behavior. Thus, the effects of THC on aggression are parallel to the effects of pleasant sexual arousal and nonhostile humor. In combination, these three findings suggest that moderate levels of positive arousal generally reduce aggression.

The Situation

Situational factors are particularly important determinants of aggression. Aspects of both the physical

Table 13.1 ■

The Effects of Alcohol and THC on Aggression

	Dosage	
	Low	High
Alcohol	2.1	5.4
THC	3.1	1.9

Note: Higher numbers indicate that more shock was given.
Adapted from Taylor, S., C. Gammon, and D. Capasso, 1976, "Aggression as a Function of the Interaction of Alcohol and Threat," *Journal of Personality and Social Psychology* 34:938–941.

and the social environment influence aggression. We will consider the role of stressors, social learning, and environmental cues as causes of aggressive behavior. For a discussion of one aspect of the physical environment that is widely, but falsely, believed to affect aggression, see Box 13-5.

Environmental stressors During the 1960s this country experienced some of the most violent race riots in our nation's history. In response to these riots, President Johnson impaneled a committee to investigate their causes. The U.S. Riot Commission cited a number of factors as contributing to the riots including perceived social injustice on the part of the rioters and provocative actions on the part of the police. In addition, the commission cited uncomfortably high temperatures as a contributory factor. Their reasoning was that high temperatures made people irritable and thus more likely to respond violently to any real or perceived provocation (115).

This idea has been carefully scrutinized in a study of 102 of the riots that occurred during this period (116). The relationship between the frequency of riots and the maximum temperature on the day of the riot was charted. As the commission had conjectured, it was found that as the temperature

increased, so did the frequency of riots. Similarly, violent crimes such as murder and assault occur more frequently during very hot weather (with no corresponding increase in nonviolent crimes like burglary and theft) (117). Does this mean that uncomfortably high temperatures cause aggression? To answer this question, social psychologists have brought this phenomena into the laboratory.

In two of these experiments, students who had been provoked by a confederate were actually less aggressive toward the confederate under uncomfortably hot conditions (94 degrees) than under cooler conditions (73 degrees) (118). Very cold temperatures produced a similar inhibition of aggression (119). These findings seem to conflict with those of the commission. One explanation is that when stressful conditions can be avoided or escaped, as is possible in a short-term laboratory experiment, people become preoccupied with leaving the situation. In these cases, heat does not increase aggression. If the stressful conditions are long-term and cannot be avoided, as is true when the weather is hot, people become irritable and respond aggressively to minor provocations. There are, of course, other important differences between laboratory settings and inner cities that may account for the differences in the findings. In inner cities heat leads people to spend more time in the streets which facilitates the rumor transmission that can ignite riots. Social interaction in laboratory settings is usually kept at a minimum.

Consistent with this general thesis, other studies have shown that aggression increases under unavoidable, stressful conditions. In one study, subjects who had been provoked were more aggressive toward their provoker if they delivered the aggression while hearing loud (97db) unavoidable noise than while hearing soft (73db) unavoidable noise (120). In a later study, angered subjects who aggressed while hearing noxious noise were less aggressive if they thought they could control the noise than if they believed they could not control it (121). Apparently, when the subjects thought they could control the noise, they experienced it as less stressful.

BOX 13-5

Lunacy: Murder Rates and the Phases of the Moon

The age-old question of whether there is a relationship between the phases of the moon and such deviant behaviors as murder has recently come under the scrutiny of social science researchers (113). A set of investigators obtained data on the time and day of occurrence of every murder occurring in the Houston area from 1957 to 1970. There were 2,613 homicides during this period. The investigators then charted these homicides against the lunar cycle (29.53 days). Their results indicated that a full moon was not associated with any increase in homicide rates. Murder rates were related to the day of the week, with the highest rate of homicides occurring on Saturday night and 53 percent of the homicides occurring during the weekend. Also, most homicides occurred during the three hours before midnight.

A review of nearly 50 studies of lunacy indicates that the full moon is not associated with homicide, criminal offenses, suicide, psychiatric disturbances, psychiatric admissions, or crisis calls (114). It may be concluded that, "Until other and more convincing evidence is presented, we believe that the effect of moon phases on homicide, suicide, and mental illness should be viewed as a myth." ■

(Bloom County. © 1988 Washington Post Co.)

Additional studies have demonstrated that the presence of moderately unpleasant odors in the environment (122) and cigarette smoke also increase aggression (123). The increase in aggression due to cigarette smoke has been found for both angered and nonangered subjects. It did not matter whether the origin of the smoke was from the target of the aggression or a third party. In addition, the increase in aggression occurred for both smokers and non-smokers. If you are a smoker, this study may help you to understand the negative reactions people have toward you. An intriguing recent study suggests that air pollution plays a role in domestic violence. A two-year study of Dayton, Ohio found that family violence rates and air pollution were correlated (124).

Taken together, these studies show that stressful environmental conditions can increase aggression. Stress is important not only in laboratory studies of aggression, but as we have seen, stress plays an important role in real world aggression including child abuse, wife battering, murder, and urban riots. These increases in aggression are most likely among people who are angry and who cannot avoid the aversive stimuli. The effects of stress on aggression fit the misattribution model rather well. Stress increases negative arousal, which can transfer to situations in which provocations occur and then amplify aggressive responses.

The consequences of aggression Social learning theory is especially useful in understanding the influence of the consequences of aggression on future behavior (125). You will recall that social learning theory is concerned with direct learning, which occurs on the basis of rewards and punishments, and with observational learning.

Aggression is not always the result of anger or provocation. In many instances, people have learned to behave aggressively because aggression pays. This is true for contract murderers, muggers, and mafioso as well as children who beat up other children to steal their toys. These types of calculated aggression are labeled *instrumental aggression* to contrast them with the more *impulsive aggression* that has been

our primary concern up to now. If people find aggression rewarding, aggression should increase in frequency.

The relevant research indicates that social approval, status, valued rewards, and monetary gain can all serve as rewards for aggression (126). For instance, a study of juvenile gangs found that the most frequent cause of fights was a threat to the social status of the gang (127). As with reinforcement in general, subsequent aggression is most likely when aggressive responses in the past have been intermittently reinforced, rather than reinforced every time they occur (128).

Punishment can reduce aggression (129). However, this is only likely to occur when the punishment is perceived as justified (130). If punishment is perceived as excessive or undeserved, it is more likely to increase aggression than to decrease it (131). Two other conditions under which punishment can reduce aggression are: when it is administered in a sure and predictable manner and, when it occurs soon after the aggression (132). Certain, swift, and severe punishment can be an effective deterrent to aggression as illustrated in a study of wife battering in Minneapolis. Arresting the perpetrator immediately following a domestic assault was more effective in preventing subsequent abuse than sending the perpetrators away or trying to counsel them (133).

Do *threats* of punishment reduce aggression? The answer to this question is: only under special conditions. Threats of punishment seem to reduce aggression when all of the following conditions are met:

1. The persons preparing to aggress are not very angry.

2. The magnitude of punishment they anticipate for such actions is great.

3. The probability of punishment is high.

4. The aggressors have relatively little to gain through their aggression (134).

Studies of *nonviolent crime* indicate that the severity of a threatened punishment, by itself, is not a very effective deterrent to crime (135). Similarly, the certainty of punishment, by itself, is not a strong deterrent to crime (136). When both severity and certainty are high, a somewhat stronger deterrence effect is sometimes found (137). One explanation for the limited effect of threats of punishment on crime is that the probability of being punished in the criminal justice system is not very high. It is estimated that only about 5 percent to 10 percent of all crimes are cleared through conviction and sentencing (138). Criminals are apparently well aware of this fact. What is true for nonviolent crime is likely to be even more true for impulsive aggression (assault), where consideration of rational factors such as the severity and certainty of punishment may be clouded by emotion. Only in cases of instrumental aggression (muggings) are the severity and certainty of punishment likely to serve as deterrents, and then only if they outweigh the anticipated rewards (139) (see Box 13-6).

Observational learning also influences aggression. In our earlier presentation of social learning theory (Chapter 2), we noted that observing models affects both the acquisition and the performance of aggressive behaviors. The behavior of models can lead to either increases or decreases in aggression (147). The circumstances under which observed aggression is most likely to result in modeling aggression are when the model has been reinforced for behaving aggressively, when the observer has been reinforced for observing the model, and when the model has high status. Also, if the observed aggression is regarded by the observer as justified, the chances that the behavior will be imitated are greater (148). For instance, boys who observe their fathers beating their mothers may later imitate these behaviors in their own marriages because they saw their fathers getting their own way by using aggression. The fathers are high in status and they may justify their actions to their sons by insisting that their mothers deserved to be beaten.

There is an additional consequence of observing aggression: Exposure to aggression desensitizes observers to the consequences of aggression for the victims. In a study illustrating this effect, boys and girls watched either a violent television show or an exciting, but nonviolent, television show while their physiological responses were monitored (149). Both sets of children found the shows emotionally arousing, as indicated by their physiological responses. Next, all the children watched a fight between two children, which they believed was real. The children who had watched the nonviolent show responded with more emotional arousal to this aggressive encounter than the children who had previously been exposed to the violent show. The reduced emotional responses of the children who had been exposed to the violent show suggests that watching the show desensitized them to a later incident of aggression. Similarly, boys who see their mothers abused may become desensitized to their mothers' suffering.

Television and aggression Does watching violent television programs lead to modeling aggression? It is certainly the case that television frequently portrays acts of violence. It has been estimated that by the age of 16, the average American child has viewed 13,000 murders on television (150). The effects of television violence have been the topic of intense public debate. The National Institute of Mental Health has investigated the effects of television on aggression. Here is their conclusion:

> Violence on television does lead to aggressive behavior in children and teenagers who watch the programs. . . . Not all children become aggressive, of course, but the correlations between violence and aggression are positive (151).

We will review three of the studies on which this conclusion was based.

The first study investigated the effects of violent movies on the behavior of juvenile delinquents in the United States and Belgium (152). The teenagers were living in minimum security institutions. Their behavior was observed for a 3-week baseline period before half of them viewed a steady 1-week diet of aggressive full-length films while the other half viewed only neutral films. In both the United States

BOX 13·6

Capital Punishment as a Deterrent to Murder

The ultimate punishment is death. For centuries people have believed the threat of capital punishment deters crime, especially murder. There has been an ongoing debate in the United States about the morality, constitutionality, and effectiveness of capital punishment. The data are not as clear as one would like them to be, but in general they suggest that capital punishment is not a very effective deterrent to murder. Here are some of the facts.

A study of the nationwide rates of execution showed that from 1951 to 1966, execution rates per year dropped steadily from 105 in 1951 to 1 in 1966 (140). One could say that more and more people were getting away with murder during this period, at least in the sense that fewer and fewer people were being executed each year. If a lack of the ultimate punishment was no longer a deterrent, then murder rates should have increased during this period, but they did not; they stayed about the same (141).

Some states have abolished and then reinstated the death penalty. If murder rates are affected by the possibility of capital punishment, then these transitions should increase or decrease murder rates, but they do not (142).

In a study of California, it was found that during the period from 1950 to 1962, the correlation between the execution rate and the murder rate was $-.08$ (143). As the execution rate went up, the murder rate went down, but to an almost trivial degree. A similar nationwide study of the period 1933 to 1969 found that the correlation between execution rates and murder rates was $+.14$ (144). In this study, as the execution rate went up so did the murder rate, but again the size of the

and Belgium, the teenagers who viewed the aggressive movies displayed more physical aggression during this week than the students who saw the neutral movies (see Table 13-2). This study provides an important demonstration of the short-term disinhibiting effects of viewing aggression on a population that is predisposed to be aggressive.

The second study followed a large group of boys from the third grade through high school (153). When the boys were in the third grade, a careful record of their television viewing habits was ob-

tained. In addition, a rating of each child's aggressiveness was obtained from classmates. Similar measures were then collected ten years later. After rating the amount of violence in the shows the children and teenagers watched, the investigators examined the correlations between the amount of aggression in the shows and the subjects' aggressiveness as rated by their peers. Figure 13-5 reveals that watching violent television in the third grade was associated with later aggressiveness; but being aggressive in the third grade was not associated with a preference

correlation was small. A study of the years 1973 to 1984 also found that execution rates had no deterrent effect (145).

Two studies have found that execution does have a deterrent effect (146). Both of these studies examined highly publicized executions. One found that murder rates dropped 2.7 percent during the month after the executions, but then returned to the usual levels, and the other found that murder rates dropped for two weeks after the executions. Thus, highly publicized executions give temporary pause to some prospective murderers, but they do not seem to have long-term deterrent effects. Since very few executions are highly publicized (3 percent), the deterrence effect of executions is quite limited.

Why isn't capital punishment an effective deterrent? For deterrence to be effective, prospective murderers must perceive that there is a reasonably high probability of getting caught, being convicted, and then executed. None of these probabilities is very high. For example, during the period covered by the California study, the execution rate varied from 0.1 percent to 4.2 percent of convicted murderers. If the probability of punishment is low, it is unlikely to be a deterrent, even if it is the ultimate punishment. Also, the punishment is distant in time from the act, while any rewards resulting from the murder are immediate. In general, the immediate consequences of an act are more influential in determining whether the act will be committed than are more remote consequences.

Deterrence due to the threat of capital punishment depends on prospective murderers knowing the possible punishment for their crimes. It seems likely that many prospective murderers do not know the laws concerning capital punishment in their states, just as you probably do not know the laws on possession of illegal drugs or theft in your state. Finally, as noted earlier in this chapter, the most common cause of murder is anger, and rational thoughts about the negative consequences of one's actions are not likely to be uppermost in the minds of angry people. The people who should be most affected by death as a deterrent would be those few who commit premeditated murder. However, these people usually believe that, by planning the murder carefully, they will not be caught. ■

for violent television shows ten years later. This study suggests that viewing aggressive shows may have a small long-term effect on aggression.

The third study examined the relationship between preference for violent TV shows and peer-rated aggression in boys and girls in the first through the third grade in the United States, Finland, Poland, and Australia (154). The average correlation was .21. The importance of this study is in its demonstration of both the consistency of the relationship and its relatively small size. After reviewing these and other studies, one group of researchers concluded: "TV violence has a large effect on a small percentage of youngsters and a small effect on a large percentage of youngsters" (155).

The weakness of the relationship between viewing television violence and subsequent aggression surprised many researchers. If we consider the conditions under which modeling occurs, perhaps we can understand why the relationship is so weak. The perpetrators of television violence are often punished for their deeds, many of them are not of

Table 13.2 ■

Effects of Viewing Violent Movies on the Physical Aggression of Juvenile Delinquents in Belgium

	Aggressive Film Group	Neutral Film Group
Before seeing the films	.013	.013
After seeing the films	.040	.002

Note: The higher the number, the higher the level of physical aggression.
Adapted from Parke, R.D., L. Berkowitz, J. P. Leyens, S.G. West, and R.J. Sebastian, 1977, "Some Effects of Violent and Nonviolent Movies on the Behavior of Juvenile Delinquents," in L. Berkowitz (Ed.), *Advances in Experimental Social Psychology,* Vol. 10, New York: Academic Press.

high status, most are not similar to the viewer, and the viewers are rarely reinforced while observing the aggression (156). This is not to argue that violence on television is positive. It does appear to have a small effect on aggression and it desensitizes viewers to the suffering of others, as well as teaching them

Figure 13.5 ■

The Relationship between Violence on Television and Aggression for Boys

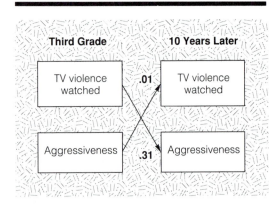

Note: The numbers are correlation coefficients.

Eron, L.D., L. R. Huesman, M. M. Lefkowitz, and L. O. Walder, 1972, "Does Television Violence Cause Aggression?" *American Psychologist* 27:253–263.

techniques of aggression they would not be exposed to otherwise.

Catharsis The premise of the researchers studying the effects of television violence, which is derived from social learning theory, is that viewing violence increases aggression. However, this premise directly contradicts one of the most venerable concepts in the study of aggression—*catharsis*—the idea that viewing, fantasizing, or engaging in aggression reduces future aggression.

There are several different versions of catharsis theory. One is associated with Aristotle's idea of catharsis. In discussing Greek drama, Aristotle suggested that members of the audience vicariously experienced the emotions portrayed on stage. Seeing others express these emotions purged them from the viewers. Catharsis is "the stillness at the center of one's being which comes after pity and fear have been burned out. The soul is purified and calmed, freed from the violent passions" (157). Thus, *viewing others* act in hostile and aggressive ways should decrease feelings of hostility and aggressiveness in the viewers (158). For Freud, catharsis occurred when people had an opportunity to *verbally express or fantasize* their hostile feelings. He thought the expression of these feelings of hostility (particularly in therapy) reduced the need to behave aggressively. Plato believed that *behaving* aggressively was cathartic and reduced the drive to behave aggressively in the future (159).

In addition to the studies already cited indicating that viewing aggression sometimes increases and rarely decreases aggression, other studies provide evidence against Aristotle's idea that viewing aggression is cathartic (160). In one study, feelings of hostility were measured before and after spectators had watched one of several different types of competitive sporting events (161). Watching aggressive events, such as wrestling matches or hockey games, led to increases in feelings of hostility, while watching nonviolent events, such as a swimming meet, did not. It appears that watching aggressive sporting events does not allow spectators to blow off steam; instead, they seem to build up steam.

Freud's idea that expressing aggression is cathartic has fared somewhat better in experimental tests (162). The majority of studies of this idea indicate that verbally expressing or imaging fantasy aggression reduces later aggression (163). However, a study of factory workers who were angry over losing their jobs found that an opportunity to express their hostile feelings increased later aggressiveness (164).

Studies of Plato's idea that behaving aggressively reduces aggression have found that behaving aggressively toward a provoker can reduce later aggression, but aggression displaced toward an innocent person often increases later aggression (165). In one sense, the finding that aggression against a provoker reduces later aggression can hardly be counted as a benefit of catharsis, since it takes aggression to reduce aggression.

The results of the studies on catharsis are complex. We can tentatively conclude that viewing realistic aggression and verbally expressing hostility are more likely to increase future aggression than to decrease it, while fantasizing aggression and behaving aggressively toward the provoker sometimes reduce aggression.

Environmental cues The frustration-aggression hypothesis states that people who are angry as a result of being frustrated are most likely to behave aggressively if cues associated with aggression are

■ *In a conflict situation, the presence of an armed police officer (an environmental cue) could actually increase the chances of aggression, according to a number of studies. (WGS)*

present in the situation (166). Research on this question has yielded mixed results. In one study, subjects who had been angered were given an opportunity to behave aggressively. If there were two guns on a table in the experimental laboratory, the subjects behaved more aggressively toward their provokers than when no guns were present (167). This study suggests that the mere presence of stimuli associated with aggression can facilitate aggression. Later studies of this phenomenon are evenly divided in their support or lack of support of the hypothesis (168). One problem with these studies is that the presence of stimuli associated with aggression in an experimental laboratory may evoke suspicion and lead subjects not to behave naturally. In the world of everyday life the presence of weapons is unlikely to evoke suspicion and thus may facilitate aggression.

In a study using a different approach, the subjects were asked to wear outer garments provided by the experimenter to "reduce individual difference characteristics that might be influential" (169). The garments were nurses' uniforms or homemade Ku Klux Klan uniforms. The subjects wearing uniforms associated with an aggressive group (the KKK) were more aggressive toward a person performing a learning task than were subjects wearing the uniforms of a nonaggressive group. This study provides additional support for the conclusion that stimuli associated with aggression can facilitate aggression.

The Target

The target's reactions to aggression, the characteristics of the target, and the target's capacity to retaliate all influence the amount of aggression directed toward the target.

Reactions of the target If you are the target of someone else's aggression and you are relatively defenseless, what should you do to get the person to stop? Should you cry out in pain and beg for mercy or should you accept the pain stoically? When the aggressor has not been provoked, showing pain typically reduces later aggression (170). Apparently, seeing someone else suffer elicits empathic concern that is then reduced by behaving less aggressively. However, when the aggressor has been severely provoked, the target's display of pain can increase aggression. In this case, the pain serves as an indication the aggressors are achieving their goal, namely retaliation for the injury they received (171).

Sex As we have seen, women are more frequently the victims of physical abuse and rape than men (172). However, more men than women are victims of murder and assault (173). For child abuse the victims are about evenly split between males and females. Laboratory studies generally show that male

targets receive more aggression than female targets (174). One study points to the greater guilt aroused by aggression against women as the explanation for the reduced aggression directed toward them in laboratory settings (175). As we noted previously (Box 13-4), an exception to this pattern of laboratory findings occurs when males are sexually aroused by violent pornography. Overall, it appears that in aggression toward strangers, males are most likely to be the victims, while in aggression toward intimates, females are most likely to be the victims.

Race Blacks and members of other minority groups are proportionately more likely to be the victims of violence than whites (176). Although the vast majority of violent crimes are intraracial, a certain percentage are interracial in nature (177). For instance, the interracial murder rate is 7 percent, for aggravated assaults it is 15 percent, and for rape it is 22 percent. Among interracial violent crimes, the proportion of white victims with black assailants is greater than that of black victims with white assailants. Does this mean that black assailants seek out white victims more than whites seek out black victims?

The answer appears to be no. The greater proportion of crimes with black assailants and white victims is due primarily to the small percentage of blacks in the population (11 percent) and to racial segregation. Blacks more frequently have contact with whites than whites do with blacks. Not only are there many more whites than blacks, whites are not likely to enter segregated black areas. Thus, many more opportunities exist for blacks to be aggressive towards whites than for whites to be aggressive toward blacks (178).

Laboratory studies of interracial aggression reveal the instability of current norms concerning race relations. When the initial studies were done in the early 1970s, the results indicated whites directed more aggression toward blacks than toward whites (179). More recent studies suggest this pattern is changing. Now whites sometimes behave more aggressively toward whites than toward blacks (180). These studies suggest the historical pattern of discrimination against blacks shifted to one of egalitarian treatment of blacks and more recently, to a norm of favoring blacks, at least among college students.

Egalitarian treatment or favoring blacks only appears to occur when white subjects are concerned with others' evaluations of their behaviors—when they are publicly self-aware. Angered white students and whites who can behave aggressively toward blacks anonymously often revert back to the older norm of discrimination against blacks (181).

A parallel phenomenon may exist among blacks (182). For blacks, the historical norm prescribed favorable treatment of whites as a means of avoiding potential retaliation (183). With the emergence of the civil rights movement and the black power movement in the 1960s and 1970s, new norms of militancy evolved, dictating that blacks treat blacks as favorably or more favorably than whites. In a study of aggression in nonangered and angered blacks it was found that nonangered blacks did not differ in the duration of shocks given to whites and blacks, but angered blacks gave *shorter* shocks to whites than to blacks (184). In this study, the new norms of egalitarian treatment prevailed when the blacks were not angered, but anger appears to have caused the black students to revert to the older norm of favorable treatment of whites.

Retaliatory capacity   The threat of retaliation usually reduces aggression (185). Consistent with the effects of punishment on aggression, the degree to which the threat of retaliation reduces aggression is directly related to the probability that the target will be able to retaliate (186). This inhibition of aggression is not found when people are angry or drunk, apparently because they do not rationally weigh the costs and benefits of their behavior—when private self-awareness is low. The low threat of immediate physical retaliation contributes to child abuse, rape, spouse abuse, date rape, and freeway violence.

■
SUMMARY

Aggression consists of behaviors intended to harm others that are not justifiable in terms of the laws and norms of society.

Wife battering is a shockingly common form of family violence. It is characterized by a three-stage progression starting with a tension building stage which leads to the acute battering stage, followed by the loving contrition stage. Abusive husbands tend to be lower-class, unemployed, aggressive, alcoholic, traditional, low in assertiveness and self-esteem, jealous, and socially isolated. Many were abused or witnessed wife battering as children. Abused wives often have higher social class backgrounds or more education than their husbands. The attacks cause fear, anxiety, depression, helplessness, guilt, and psychosomatic problems, as well as physical injury.

Feminist theory argues that the patriarchal nature of our society encourages men to seek power over women. Men are especially likely to batter their wives if their power is threatened. Historically, women have been treated as the property of men and men have been socialized to be aggressive and dominant. Wife battering is viewed as resulting from these traditional values and the socialization practices that foster them. Sociocultural theories of wife battering cite acceptance of violence in our society as a contributing cause of wife battering. Psychological theories emphasize the role of stress in triggering episodes of battering and suggest that wife battering is a behavior that may be acquired through modeling in some cases.

Child abuse may affect as many as 2 million children a year in the United States. Both men and women abuse their children. Abusers are predominantly lower class; many have employment problems; and they are often socially isolated. They lack good parenting skills, have unrealistic expectations of their children, and are easily angered. Many were abused as children. Both boys and girls are the targets of abuse; many are difficult to care for or were unwanted. Multi-factor theories suggest child abuse is due to cultural beliefs supporting corporal punishment, the characteristics of the parents, the characteristics of the child, and high levels of stress.

Rape is one of the fastest growing crimes in America. By college, one woman in six has been raped. Rapists who are reported to the police are predominantly young, lower-class, unemployed men who come from minority groups. Most were drinking at the time of the assault. They find depictions of rape to be sexually arousing. A significant number were abused as children. Three types of rapists have been identified: the *power* rapist who uses force to obtain sex, the *anger* rapist whose motive is to harm and debase his victim during sex, and the *sadistic* rapist who maims or murders his victim.

The highest percentage of rape victims fall between the ages of 15 and 25. Both married and unmarried women are raped. The women have been drinking in less than 10 percent of the cases and few were experiencing psychiatric problems before the rape.

Psychopathology theories of rape citing inner conflicts as a source of rape have received little support. Symbolic interactionist theory cites cultural belief systems as a major cause of rape. Like the feminists, they cite the socialization of men to be aggressive and dominant as predisposing factors. In addition, they note that historically women have been regarded as the property of men and that beliefs promoting the use of force to obtain sex are common in our society.

Date rape is also a growing problem. Date rapists appear to expect sex as part of the exchange relationship involved in dating and they expect sex soon in this relationship. They also tend to misinterpret their dates' behavior as indicating a greater receptiveness to sex than is intended.

Anger, sexual arousal, and humor are three emotional states that affect aggression. Anger is the most common cause of aggression. The likelihood that anger will lead to aggression depends, in part, on the level of arousal the person is experiencing. The higher the arousal, the more likely it is that anger will lead to impulsive aggression. Sexual arousal created by negative stimuli, such as degrading pornography, is also likely to increase aggression. Sexual arousal created by pleasant erotica appears to reduce aggression. Similarly, negative or hostile humor may increase aggression, while positive humor may decrease aggression. Arousal created in one situation can be transferred to a situation in which a person is provoked and thus can increase

aggression. The transfer of arousal may explain why negative sexual arousal and negative humor increase aggression.

High levels of private self-awareness increase aggression when the individual's personal standards favor aggression in a given situation, but generally they decrease aggression because most individuals' standards discourage aggression. High levels of public self-awareness increase aggression if social norms favor aggression, but generally they decrease aggression because social norms discourage most types of aggression. Alcohol, a drug that decreases private self-awareness, increases aggression, while marijuana reduces aggression.

Moderately stressful environmental conditions created by aversive noise, heat, or noxious odors can increase aggression. These increases in aggression are most likely to occur when the people under stress have also been provoked in some way and cannot avoid or control the aversive stimuli. Aggression resulting in favorable consequences, such as the acquisition of money or status, is likely to increase aggression. Swift, certain, and severe punishment that is perceived as just can decrease aggression, but in some instances punishment increases later aggression. Threats of punishment are most effective when anger levels are low, the punishment is severe and certain, and the aggressor has little to gain by behaving aggressively.

Aggression can also be influenced by observing aggressive or nonaggressive models. Modeling is most likely to occur when the model is of high status, the model is reinforced for his or her behavior, and the observer is reinforced for observing the model. Observing aggression desensitizes viewers to subsequent aggression. Television violence appears to increase aggressive behavior in young viewers who are predisposed to aggression because it teaches them how to behave aggressively and disinhibits aggressive tendencies.

Viewing fantasy aggression can have a cathartic effect and reduce aggression. However, seeing realistic aggression or expressing aggression (unless it is directed at the person who provoked the aggressor) usually increases aggression. Environmental cues, such as the presence of guns or other stimuli associated with aggression, can also increase aggressive behavior.

If an aggressor has not been severely provoked, then a target who shows pain will receive reduced aggression. However, severely provoked aggressors may react to signs of pain with increased aggression because these signs indicate the aggressor is achieving his or her goal. Females are less likely to be the targets of some types of aggression involving strangers (murder, assault, laboratory aggression) than males, but they are more likely to be the targets of domestic or sexual violence than males.

Interracial aggression more often involves white victims than black victims because there are more whites than blacks in the population. Nonangered racial ingroup members respond in ways that are consistent with current group norms, whether these norms stress whites favoring blacks or equal treatment of ingroup and outgroup members by blacks. When angered, ingroup members may regress to older norms of discrimination against blacks by whites or favorable treatment of white outgroup members by blacks. If the probability that the target of aggression will retaliate is great, aggression directed at the target is likely to be reduced, but only if the aggressor is not angry.

■

REFERENCES

1. *Albuquerque Journal,* July 30, 1987; *Associated Press,* July 28, 1987; *Newsweek,* August 10, 1987; *Time,* August 17, 1987; *UPI,* August 9, 1987.
2. Steinmetz, S. K. and M. A. Straus (Eds.), 1974, *Violence in the Family,* New York: Harper & Row.
3. Dobash, E. R. and R. P. Dobash, 1979, *Violence Against Wives,* New York: Free Press.
4. Walker, L. E., 1979, *The Battered Woman,* New York: Harper Colophon; K. Yllo and M. A. Straus, 1981, "Interpersonal Violence among Married and Cohabiting Couples," *Family Relations,* 30: 339–347.
5. Frieze, I. H., 1979, "Rape in Marriage: Rape as an Aspect of Wife-battering," cited in L. E. Walker, 1984, *The Battered Woman Syndrome,* New York: Springer.
6. Steinmetz, S. K., 1986, "The Violent Family," in M. Lystad

(Ed.), *Violence in the Home: Interdisciplinary Perspectives,* New York: Brunner-Mazel.
7. Pagelow, M. D., 1984, *Family Violence,* New York: Praeger.
8. Steinmetz, 1986, op. cit.
9. Walker, 1979, op. cit.; Walker, 1984, op. cit.; L. E. A. Walker, 1986, "Psychological Causes of Family Violence," in M. Lystad, op. cit.
10. Steinmetz, 1986, op. cit.
11. Straus, M. A., R. Gelles, and S. K. Steinmetz, 1980, *Behind Closed Doors: Violence in the American Family,* New York: Doubleday.
12. Walker, 1984, op. cit.
13. Rosenbaum, A. and K. D. O'Leary, 1980, "Marital Violence: Characteristics of Abusive Couples," *Journal of Consulting and Clinical Psychology* 49: 63–71; Steinmetz, 1986, op. cit.; Walker, 1979, op. cit.; Walker, 1984, op. cit.
14. Kaufman, G. K. and M. A. Straus, 1987, "The 'Drunken Bum' Theory of Wife Beating," *Social Problems* 34: 213–225; Steinmetz, 1986, op. cit.
15. Walker, 1979, op. cit.; Walker, 1984, op. cit.
16. Walker, 1979, ibid.; Walker, 1984, ibid.
17. Koval, J. E., J. J. Ponzetti, and R. M. Cate, 1982, "Programmatic Intervention for Men Involved in Conjugal Violence," *Family Therapy* 9: 147–152.
18. Frieze, 1979, op. cit.; Walker, 1984, op. cit.
19. Walker, L. E., 1983, "The Battered Woman Syndrome Study," in D. Finkelhor, R. J. Gelles, G. T. Hotaling, and M. A. Straus (Eds.), *The Dark Side of Families,* Beverly Hills: Sage; Walker, 1984, op. cit.
20. Walker, 1986, op. cit.
21. Walker, 1979, op. cit.; Pagelow, 1984, op. cit.
22. Walker, 1984, op. cit.
23. Walker, 1984, ibid.
24. Finkelhor, D., 1981, "Common Features of Family Abuse," in D. Finkelhor et al., op. cit.
25. Pagelow, 1984, op. cit.
26. Walker, 1986, op. cit.
27. National Center on Child Abuse and Child Neglect, 1985 *Highlights of Official Child Neglect and Child-Abuse Reporting,* Denver, CO: American Humane Association.
28. Pagelow, 1984, op. cit.
29. Pagelow, 1984, ibid.
30. Steinberg, L., R. Catalano, and D. Dooley, 1981, "Economic Antecedents of Child Abuse and Neglect," *Child Development* 52: 260–267.
31. Creighton, S. J., 1987, "Quantitative Assessment of Child Abuse," in P. Maher (Ed.), *Child Abuse,* Oxford: Blackwell; D. G. Gil, 1970, *Violence against Children,* Cambridge, MA: Harvard University Press; Pagelow, 1984, op. cit.
32. Ganley, A. L. and L. Harris, 1978, "Domestic Violence: Issues in Designing and Implementing Programs for Male Batterers," paper presented at the American Psychological Association Convention, Toronto; Pagelow, M. D., 1981, *Woman-Battering: Victims and Their Experiences,* Beverly Hills: Sage;

J. P. Kropp and O. M. Haynes, "Abusive and Nonabusive Mothers' Ability to Identify General and Specific Emotion Signals of Infants, *Child Development* 58: 187–190.

33. Straus, M. A., 1980, "Stress and Child Abuse," in C. H. Kempe and R. E. Helfer (Eds.), *The Battered Child,* 3d ed., Chicago: University of Chicago Press; Widom, C.S., 1989, "Does Violence Beget Violence: A Critical Examination of the Literature." *Psychological Bulletin* 106:3–28.

34. Parke, R. D. and C. W. Collmer, 1975, "Child Abuse: An Interdisciplinary Analysis," in E. M. Hetherington (Ed.), *Review of Child Development Research,* Vol. 5, Chicago: University of Chicago Press.

35. Larrance, D. T. and C. T. Twentyman, 1983, "Maternal Attributions and Child Abuse," *Journal of Abnormal Psychology* 92: 449–457.

36. Wolfe, D. A., A. Fairbank, J. A. Kelly, and A. S. Bradlyn, 1983, "Child Abusive Parents' Physiological Responses to Stressful and Non-stressful Behavior in Children," *Behavioral Assessment* 5: 363–371.

37. Patterson, G. R., 1985, "A Microsocial Analysis of Anger and Irritable Behavior," in M. A. Chesney and R. H. Rosenman (Eds.), *Anger and Hostility in Cardiovascular and Behavioral Disorders,* Washington, DC: Hemisphere.

38. Gil, 1970, op. cit.; J. Newson and E. Newson, 1968, *Four Years Old in an Urban Community,* Chicago: Aldine; Pagelow, 1984, op. cit.

39. Straus, Gelles, and Steinmetz, 1980, op. cit.

40. Bousha, D. M. and C. T. Twentyman, 1984, "Mother-Child Interactional Style in Abuse, Neglect, and Control Groups: Naturalistic Observations in the Home," *Journal of Abnormal Psychology* 93: 106–114; E. Vizard, 1987, "The Historical and Cultural Context of Child Abuse," in P. Maher, op. cit.

41. Belsky, J., 1980, "Child Maltreatment: An Ecological Integration," *American Psychologist* 35: 320–335; A. Bentovin, 1987, "The Breakdown of Parenting Functions in Abusing Families: How Can Professionals Think about These Issues and Be Helpful," in P. Maher, op. cit.; B. Steele, 1986, "Psychodynamic Factors in Child Abuse," in R. E. Helfer and R. S. Kempe (Eds.), *The Battered Child,* Chicago: University of Chicago Press; M. A. Straus and G. K. Kantor, 1986, "Stress and Child Abuse," in R. E. Helfer and R. E. Kempe, op. cit.

42. Wolfe, D. A., 1985, "Child Abusive Parents: An Empirical Review and Analysis," *Psychological Bulletin* 97: 462–482.

43. Parke and Collmer, 1975, op. cit.

44. *Uniform Crime Reports for the United States: 1986,* Washington, DC: U.S. Department of Justice.

45. Katz, S. and M. A. Mazur, 1979, *Understanding the Rape Victim,* New York: Wiley.

46. Russell, D. E. H., 1984, *Sexual Exploitation,* Beverly Hills: Sage.

47. Koss, M. P., C. A. Gidycz, and N. Wisniewski, 1987, "The Scope of Rape: Incidence and Prevalence of Sexual Aggression and Victimization in a National Sample of Higher Education Students," *Journal of Consulting and Clinical Psychology* 52: 162–170.

48. Abbey, A., 1982, "Sex Differences in Attributions for Friendly Behavior: Do Males Misperceive Females' Friendliness?" *Journal of Personality and Social Psychology* 52: 830–838.

49. Schultz, L. G. and J. DeSavage, 1975, "Rape and Rape Attitudes on a College Campus," in L. G. Schultz (Ed.), *Rape Victimology,* Springfield, IL: Thomas.

50. Goodchilds, J. D. and G. L. Zellman, 1984, "Sexual Signalling and Sexual Aggression in Adolescent Relationships," in N. M. Malamuth and E. Donnerstein (Eds.), *Pornography and Sexual Aggression,* New York: Academic Press.

51. Jenkins, M. J. and F. H. Dambrot, 1987, "The Attribution of Date Rape: Observer's Attitudes and Sexual Experiences and the Dating Situation," *Journal of Applied Social Psychology* 17: 875–985; D. Knox and K. Wilson, 1981, "Dating Behaviors of University Students," *Family Relations* 30: 255–258.

52. Shotland, R. L. and L. Goodstein, 1983, "Just Because She Doesn't Want to Doesn't Mean It's Rape: An Experimentally Based Causal Model of Rape in a Dating Situation," *Social Psychology Quarterly* 46: 220–232.

53. Katz and Mazur, 1979, op. cit.

54. Knight, R. A., R. Rosenberg, and B. Schneider, 1985, "Classification of Sexual Offenders: Perspectives, Methods, and Validation," in A. W. Burgess (Ed.), *Rape and Sexual Assault,* New York: Garland; R. T. Rada, 1978, *Clinical Aspects of the Rapist,* New York: Grune & Stratton.

55. Rada, 1978, ibid.

56. Katz and Mazur, 1979, op. cit.

57. Scully, D. and J. Marolla, 1985, "Rape and Vocabularies of Motive: Alternative Perspectives," in A. W. Burgess, op. cit.

58. Koss, M. K. and K. E. Leonard, 1984, "Sexually Aggressive Men: Empirical Findings and Theoretical Implications," in N. M. Malamuth and E. Donnerstein, op. cit.

59. Knight, Rosenberg, and Schneider, 1985, op. cit.

60. Ageton, S. S., 1983, *Sexual Assault among Adolescents,* Lexington, MA: Lexington.

61. Koss and Leonard, 1984, op. cit.

62. Ageton, 1983, op. cit.; Koss and Leonard, 1984, ibid.; N. M. Malamuth, 1984, "Aggression against Women: Cultural and Individual Causes, in N. M. Malamuth and E. Donnerstein, op. cit.; N. M. Malamuth, 1986, "Predictors of Naturalistic Aggression," *Journal of Personality and Social Psychology* 50: 953–962; D. L. Mosher and R. D. Anderson, 1986, "Macho Personality, Sexual Aggression, and Reactions to Guided Imagery of Realistic Rape," *Journal of Research in Personality* 20: 77–94; J. E. Stets and M. A. Pirog-Good, 1987, "Violence in Dating Relationships," *Social Psychology Quarterly* 50: 237–246.

63. Groth, A. N., 1979, *Men Who Rape: The Psychology of the Offender,* New York: Plenum; D. E. H. Russell, 1982, *Rape in Marriage,* New York: MacMillan.

64. Burt, M. R., 1980, "Cultural Myths and Support for Rape," *Journal of Personality and Social Psychology* 38: 217–230.

65. Massey, J. B., C. R. Garcia, and J. P. Emich Jr., 1971, "Management of Sexually Assaulted Females," *Obstetrics and Gynecology* 38: 29–36.

66. Russell, 1982, op. cit.

67. Katz and Mazur, 1979, op. cit.

68. Katz and Mazur, 1979, ibid.

69. Katz and Mazur, 1979, ibid.

70. Rada, 1978, op. cit.

71. Koss and Leonard, 1984, op. cit.

72. Scully, D. and J. Marolla, 1984, "Convicted Rapists' Vocabulary of Motives," *Social Forces* 31: 530–544.

73. Franks, D. D., 1985, "Role-taking, Social Power, and Imperceptiveness: The Analysis of Rape," in N. K. Denzin (Ed.), *Studies in Symbolic Interactionism,* Greenwich, CT: JAI Press; Scully and Marolla, 1985, op. cit.

74. Borgida, E. and N. Brekke, 1985, "Psycholegal Research on Rape Trials," in A. W. Burgess, op. cit.

75. Borkenhagen, C. K., 1975, "House of Delegates Redefines Death, Urges Redefinition of Rape, and Undoes the Houston Amendments," *American Bar Association Journal* 61: 464–465.

76. Burt, 1980, op. cit.; Koss and Leonard, 1984, op. cit.; Malamuth, 1986, op. cit.

77. Weis, K. and S. S. Borges, 1977, "Victimology and Rape: The Case of the Legitimate Victim," in D. R. Nass (Ed.), *The Rape Victim,* Dubuque, IA: Kendall-Hunt.

78. Malamuth, 1984, op. cit.

79. Kanin, E. and S. Parcell, 1977, "Sexual Aggression: A Second Look at the Offended Female," *Archives of Sexual Behavior* 6: 67–76; Katz and Mazur, 1979, op. cit.; Rada, 1978, op. cit.

80. Lowry, D. T., G. Love, and M. Kirby, 1981, "Sex on the Soap Operas: Patterns of Intimacy," *Journal of Communication* 31: 90–96.

81. Sanday, P. R., 1981, "The Sociocultural Context of Rape: A Cross-cultural Study," *Journal of Social Issues* 37: 5–27.

82. Zillmann, D., 1979, *Hostility and Aggression,* Hillsdale, NJ: Lawrence Erlbaum.

83. Wolfgang, M. E., 1958, *Patterns in Criminal Homicide,* Philadelphia: University of Pennsylvania.

84. Dollard, J., L. W. Doob, N. E. Miller, O. H. Mowrer, and R. R. Sears, 1939, *Frustration and Aggression,* New Haven, CT: Yale University Press.

85. Berkowitz, L., 1962, *Aggression: A Social Psychological Analysis,* New York: McGraw-Hill; Berkowitz, L., 1989, "Frustration Aggression Hypothesis: Examination and Reformulation." *Psychological Bulletin* 106:59–73.

86. Blanchard, D. C. and R. J. Blanchard, 1986, "Affect and Aggression: An Animal Model Applied to Human Behavior," in R. J. Blanchard and D. C. Blanchard (Eds.), *Advances in the Study of Aggression,* Orlando, FL: Academic Press; Zillmann, 1979, op. cit.

87. Zillmann, D. and J. R. Cantor, 1976, "Effect of Timing of Information about Mitigating Circumstances on Emotional Responses to Provocation and Retaliatory Behavior," *Journal of Experimental Social Psychology* 12: 38–55.

88. Berkowitz, L., 1978, "Whatever Happened to the Frustration-Aggression Hypothesis?" *American Behavioral Scientist* 21: 691–708; T. E. Johnson and B. G. Rule, 1986, "Mitigating Circumstance Information, Censure, and Aggression," *Journal of Personality and Social Psychology* 50: 537–542; D. Zillman,

J. Bryant, J. R. Cantor, and K. D. Day, 1975, "Irrelevance of Mitigating Circumstances in Retaliatory Behavior of High Levels of Excitation," *Journal of Research in Personality* 9: 282–293.

89. Bandura, A., 1973, *Aggression: A Social Learning Analysis,* Englewood Cliffs, NJ: Prentice-Hall; A. Bandura, 1973, "Social Learning Theory of Aggression," in J. F. Knutson (Ed.), *The Control of Aggression: Implications from Basic Research,* Chicago: Aldine; Zillmann, 1979, op. cit.

90. Bryant, J. and D. Zillmann, 1977, "The Mediating Effect of the Intervention Potential of Communications on Displaced Aggressiveness and Retaliatory Behavior," in B. D. Ruben (Ed.), *Communication Yearbook,* Vol. 1, New Brunswick, NJ: ICA Transaction Press.

91. Baron, R. A., 1977, *Human Aggression,* New York: Plenum; R. A. Baron and P. A. Bell, 1977, "Sexual Arousal and Aggression by Males: Effects of Type of Erotic Stimuli and Prior Provocation," *Journal of Personality and Social Psychology* 35: 79–87; A. Frodi, 1977, "Sexual Arousal, Situational Restrictiveness and Aggressive Behavior," *Journal of Research in Personality* 11: 48–58; J. Ramirez, J. Bryant, and D. Zillmann, 1982, "Effects of Erotica on Retaliatory Behavior as a Function of Level of Prior Provocation," *Journal of Personality and Social Psychology* 43: 971–978.

92. White, L. A., 1979, "Erotica and Aggression: The Influence of Sexual Arousal, Positive Affect, and Negative Affect on Aggressive Behavior," *Journal of Personality and Social Psychology* 37: 591–601.

93. Brownmiller, S., 1975, *Against Our Will,* New York: Bantam.

94. Donnerstein, E., 1984, "Pornography: Its Effects on Violence against Women," in N. M. Malamuth and E. Donnerstein, op. cit.; Malamuth, 1984, op. cit.

95. Zillmann, D. and J. Bryant, 1984, "Effects of Massive Exposure to Pornography," in N. M. Malamuth and E. Donnerstein, op. cit.

96. Baron, L. and M. A. Straus, 1984, "Sexual Satisfaction, Pornography, and Rape in the United States," in N. M. Malamuth and E. Donnerstein, op. cit.; Court, 1984, op. cit.

97. Abel, G. G., D. H. Barlow, E. Blanchard, and D. Guild, 1977, "The Components of Rapists' Sexual Arousal," *Archives of General Psychiatry* 34: 895–903.

98. Baron, R. A., 1978, "Aggression-inhibiting Influence of Sexual Humor," *Journal of Personality and Social Psychology* 36: 189–197.

99. Baron, R. A. and R. L. Ball, 1974, "The Aggression-inhibiting Influence of Nonhostile Humor," *Journal of Experimental Social Psychology* 10: 23–33.

100. Baron, R. A., 1978, "The Influence of Hostile Humor upon Physical Aggression," *Personality and Social Psychology Bulletin* 4: 77–80.

101. Zillmann, 1979, op. cit.

102. Zillmann, D. and J. Bryant, 1974, "Effect of Residual Excitation on the Emotional Response to Provocation and Delayed Aggressive Behavior," *Journal of Personality and Social Psychology* 30: 782–791.

103. Carver, C. S., 1975, "Physical Aggression as a Function of

Objective Self-awareness and Attitudes toward Punishment," *Journal of Experimental Social Psychology* 11: 510–519; M. F. Scheier, A. Fenigstein, and A. H. Buss, 1974, "Self-awareness and Physical Aggression," *Journal of Experimental Social Psychology* 10: 264–273; C. S. Carver, 1974, "Facilitation of Physical Aggression through Objective Self-awareness," *Journal of Experimental Social Psychology* 10: 365–370; R. D. Johnson and L. L. Downing, 1979, "Deindividuation and Valence of Cues: Effects on Prosocial and Antisocial Behavior," *Journal of Personality and Social Psychology* 37: 1532–1538; S. Taylor, 1986, "The Regulation of Aggressive Behavior," in R. J. Blanchard and D. C. Blanchard, op. cit.

104. Felson, R. B., 1982, "Impression Management and the Escalation of Aggression and Violence," *Social Psychology Quarterly* 45: 245–254.

105. Prentice-Dunn, S. and R. W. Rogers, 1982, "Effects of Public and Private Self-awareness on Deindividuation and Aggression," *Journal of Personality and Social Psychology* 43: 503–513; S. Prentice-Dunn and R. W. Rogers, 1983, "Deindividuation and Aggression," in R. Geen (Ed.), *Aggression: Theoretical and Empirical Reviews,* New York: Academic Press.

106. Taylor, 1986, op. cit., C. J. Wilkerson, 1985, "Effects of Diazepam (Valium) and Trait Anxiety on Human Physical Aggression and Emotional State," *Journal of Behavioral Medicine* 8: 101–110.

107. Schmutte, G. T. and S. P. Taylor, 1980, "Physical Aggression as a Function of Alcohol and Pain Feedback," *The Journal of Social Psychology* 110: 235–244; R. J. Shuntich and S. P. Taylor, "The Effects of Alcohol on Human Physical Aggression," *Journal of Experimental Research in Personality* 6: 34–38; S. P. Taylor and C. B. Gammon, 1975, "Effects of Type and Dose of Alcohol on Human Physical Aggression," *Journal of Personality and Social Psychology* 32: 169–175.

108. Bennett, R. M., A. H. Buss; and J. A. Carpenter, 1969, "Alcohol and Human Physical Aggression," *Journal of Studies on Alcohol Quarterly* 30: 870–876; S. P. Taylor, C. B. Gammon, and D. R. Capasso, 1976, "Aggression as a Function of the Interaction of Alcohol and Threat," *Journal of Personality and Social Psychology* 34: 938–941.

109. Hull, J. G., 1981, "A Self-awareness Model of the Causes and Effects of Alcohol Consumption," *Journal of Abnormal Psychology* 90: 586–600.

110. Bailey, D., K. Leonard, J. Cranston, and S. Taylor, 1983, "Effects of Alcohol and Self-awareness on Human Physical Aggression," *Personality and Social Psychology Bulletin* 9: 289–295.

111. Taylor, S. and C. Gammon, 1976, "Aggressive Behavior of Intoxicated Subjects: The Effect of Third-party Intervention," *Journal of Studies on Alcohol* 37: 917–930; C. Jeavons and S. Taylor, 1985, "The Control of Alcohol Related Aggression," *Aggressive Behavior* 11: 93–101.

112. Taylor, S. P., R. M. Vardaris, A. B. Rawtich, J. W. Gammon, J. W. Cranston, and A. I. Lubetkin, 1976, "The Effects of Alcohol and Delta-9-Tetrahydrocannabinol on Human Physical Aggression," *Aggressive Behavior* 2: 153–161.

113. Porkorny, A. D. and J. Jachimczyk, 1974, "The Questionable Relationship between Homicides and the Lunar Cycle," *American Journal of Psychiatry* 31: 827–829.

114. Rotton, D. and I. W. Kelly, 1985, "Much Ado about the Full Moon: A Meta-analysis of Lunar-Lunacy Research," *Psychological Bulletin* 97: 286–306.

115. U.S. Riot Commission, 1968, *Report of the National Advisory Commission on Civil Disorders,* New York: Bantam.

116. Carlsmith, J. M. and C. A. Anderson, 1979, "Ambient Temperature and the Occurrence of Collective Violence: A New Analysis," *Journal of Personality and Social Psychology* 37: 337–344.

117. Anderson, C. A., 1987, "Temperature and Aggression: Effects of Quarterly, Yearly, and City Rates of Violence and Nonviolent Crime," *Journal of Personality and Social Psychology* 52: 1161–1173; J. L. Cotton, 1986, "Ambient Temperature and Violent Crime," *Journal of Applied Social Psychology* 16: 786–801; Anderson, C.A., 1989," Temperature and Aggression: Ubiquitous Effects of Heat on Occurrence of Human Violence." *Psychological Bulletin* 106:74–96.

118. Baron, R. A., 1972, "Aggression as a Function of Ambient Temperature and Prior Anger Arousal," *Journal of Personality and Social Psychology* 21: 183–189; Baron and Bell, 1977, op. cit.

119. Bell, P. A. and R. A. Baron, 1976, "Aggression and Heat: The Mediating Role of Negative Affect," *Journal of Applied Social Psychology* 6: 18–30.

120. Konecni, V. J., 1975, "The Mediation of Anger and Cognitive Labeling," *Journal of Personality and Social Psychology* 32: 706–712.

121. Donnerstein, E. and D. W. Wilson, 1976, "Effects of Noise and Perceived Control on Ongoing and Subsequent Aggressive Behavior," *Journal of Personality and Social Psychology* 34: 774–781.

122. Rotton, J., J. Frey, T. Barry, M. Milligan, and M. Fitzpatrick, "The Air Pollution Experience and Physical Aggression," *Journal of Applied Social Psychology* 9: 397–412.

123. Jones, J. W. and G. A. Bogat, 1978, "Air Pollution and Human Aggression," *Psychological Reports* 43: 721–722; D. Zillmann, R. A. Baron, and R. Tamborini, 1981, "Social Costs of Smoking: Effects of Tobacco Smoke on Hostile Behavior," *Journal of Applied Social Psychology* 11: 548–561.

124. Londer, R., 1987, "Can Bad Air Make Bad Things Happen?" *Parade,* August 9, 7–8.

125. Bandura, 1973, op. cit.

126. Buss, A. H., 1971, "Aggression Pays," in J. L. Singer (Ed.), *The Control of Aggression and Violence: Cognitive and Physiological Factors,* New York: Academic Press; A. H. Buss, 1961, *The Psychology of Aggression,* New York: Wiley; G. R. Patterson and J. A. Cobb, 1971, "A Dyadic Analysis of 'Aggressive' Behaviors: An Additional Step toward a Theory of Aggression," in J. P. Hill (Ed.), *Minnesota Symposia on Child Psychology,* Vol. 5, Minneapolis: University of Minnesota Press.

127. Short, J. F., Jr. and F. L. Strodtbeck, 1964, "Why Gangs Fight," *Transaction* 6: 25–29.

128. Walters, R. H. and M. Brown, 1963, "Studies of Reinforcement of Aggression: III. Transfer of Responses to an Interpersonal Situation," *Child Development* 34: 563–571.

129. Deur, J. L. and R. D. Parke, 1970, "Effects of Inconsistent Punishment on Aggression in Children," *Developmental Psychology* 2: 403–411.

130. Bandura, 1973, op. cit.; Zillmann, 1979, op. cit.

131. Kimble, C. E., D. Fitz, and J. Onorad, 1977, "The Effectiveness of Counteraggression Strategies in Reducing Interactive Aggression by Males," *Journal of Personality and Social Psychology* 35: 272–278; R. Pisano and S. P. Taylor, 1971, "Reduction of Physical Aggression: The Effects of Four Strategies," *Journal of Personality and Social Psychology* 19: 237–242.

132. Baron, R. A., 1973, "Threatened Retaliation from the Victim as an Inhibitor of Physical Aggression," *Journal of Research in Personality* 7: 103–115.

133. Berk, R. A. and P. J. Newton, 1985, "Does Arrest Really Deter Wife Battery? An Effort to Replicate the Findings of the Minneapolis Spouse Abuse Experiment," *American Sociological Review* 50: 253–262; L. W. Sherman and R. A. Berk, 1984, "The Specific Deterrent Effect of Arrest for Domestic Assault," *American Sociological Review* 49: 261–272.

134. Baron, 1977, op. cit.

135. Paternoster, R. and L. Iovanni, 1986, "The Deterrent Effect of Perceived Severity: A Reexamination," *Social Forces* 64: 751–776.

136. Piliavin, I., C. Thornton, R. Gartner, and R. L. Matsueda, 1986, "Crime, Deterrence, and Rational Choice," *American Sociological Review* 51: 101–119.

137. Grasmick, H. G. and G. J. Bryjak, 1980, "The Deterrent Effect of Perceived Severity and Punishment," *Social Forces* 59: 469–491; M. C. Stafford, L. N. Gray, B. A. Menke, and D. A. Ward, 1986, "Modeling the Deterrent Effects of Punishment," *Social Psychology Quarterly* 49: 338–347.

138. Konecni, V. J. and E. B. Ebbesen, 1982, *The Criminal Justice System,* San Francisco: W. H. Freeman.

139. Piliavin et al., 1986, op. cit.; Stafford et al., 1986, op. cit.

140. Chambliss, W. J., 1981, "Does Punishment Deter Crime?" in S. Sidney Ulmer (Ed.), *Courts, Law, and Judicial Processes,* New York: The Free Press.

141. Chambliss, 1981, ibid.

142. Sellin, T., 1959, *The Death Penalty,* Tentative Draft No. 9, Model Penal Code, Philadelphia: American Law Institute.

143. Bailey, W. C., 1979, "The Deterrent Effect of the Death Penalty for Murder in California," *Southern California Law Review* 52: 743–764.

144. Ehrlich, I., 1975, "The Deterrent of Capital Punishment: A Question of Life and Death," *American Economic Review* 65: 397–416.

145. Peterson, R. D. and W. C. Bailey, 1988, "Murder and Capital Punishment in the Evolving Context of the Post *Furman* Era," *Social Forces* 66: 774–807.

146. Stack, S., 1987, "Publicized Executions and Homicide, 1950–1980," *American Sociological Review* 52: 532–540; D. P. Phillips, 1980, "The Deterrent Effect of Capital Punishment: New Evidence on an Old Controversy," *American Journal of Sociology* 86: 139–148.

147. Baron, R. A. and C. R. Kepner, 1970, "Model's Behavior and Attraction toward the Model as Determinants of Adult Aggressive Behavior," *Journal of Personality and Social Psychology* 14: 334–335; Baron, 1977, op. cit.

148. Berkowitz, L. and P. C. Powers, 1979, "Effects of Timing and Justification of Witnessed Aggression on the Observers' Punitiveness," *Journal of Research in Personality* 13: 71–80.

149. Thomas, M. H., R. W. Horton, E. C. Lippincott, and R. S. Drabman, 1977, "Desensitization to Portrayals of Real-life Aggression as a Function of Exposure to Television Violence," *Journal of Personality and Social Psychology* 35: 450–458.

150. Merriam, E., 1968, "We're Teaching Our Children That Violence Is Fun," in O. N. Larson, *Violence and the Mass Media,* New York: Harper & Row.

151. National Institute of Mental Health, 1982, *Television and Behavior: Ten Years of Science Progress and Implications for the Eighties,* Rockville, MD: National Institute of Mental Health.

152. Parke, R. D., L. Berkowitz, J. P. Leyens, S. G. West, and R. J. Sebastian, 1977, "Some Effects of Violent and Nonviolent Movies on the Behavior of Juvenile Delinquents," in L. Berkowitz (Ed.), *Advances in Experimental Social Psychology,* Vol. 10, New York: Academic Press.

153. Eron, L. D., L. R. Huesman, M. M. Lefkowitz, and L. O. Walder, 1972, "Does Television Violence Cause Aggression?" *American Psychologist* 27: 253–263.

154. Eron, L. D., 1982, "Parent-Child Interaction, Television Violence, and Aggression of Children," *American Psychologist* 37: 197–211.

155. Liebert, R. M., J. N. Sprafkin, and E. S. Davidson, 1982, *The Early Window,* Elmsford, NY: Pergamon Press.

156. Freedman, J. L., 1984, "Effect of Television on Aggressiveness," *Psychological Bulletin* 96: 227–246; J. L. Freedman, 1986, "Television Violence and Aggression: A Rejoinder," *Psychological Bulletin* 100: 372–378.

157. Scharr, J. H., 1961, *Escape from Authority: The Perspectives of Erich Fromm,* New York: Basic Books.

158. Feshbach, S., 1976, "The Role of Fantasy in the Response to Television," *Journal of Social Issues* 32: 71–85.

159. Konecni, V. J., 1982, "Aggression," in D. Sherrod (Ed.), *Social Psychology,* New York: Random House, p. 252.

160. Quanty, M. B., 1976, "Aggression Catharsis: Experimental Investigations and Implications," in R. G. Geen and E. C. O'Neal (Eds.), *Perspectives on Aggression,* New York: Academic Press.

161. Arms, R. L., G. W. Russell, and M. L. Sandilands, 1979, "Effects on the Hostility of Spectators of Viewing Aggressive Sports," *Social Psychology Quarterly* 42: 275–279.

162. Feshbach, 1976, op. cit.

163. Berkowitz, L., 1960, "Some Factors Affecting the Reduction of Overt Hostility," *Journal of Abnormal and Social Psychology* 60: 14–21; L. Berkowitz and J. T. Alioto, 1973, "The Meaning of an Observed Event as a Determinant of Its Aggressive Consequences," *Journal of Personality and Social Psychology* 28:

206–217; S. Feshbach, 1955, "The Drive-reducing Function of Fantasy Behavior," *Journal of Abnormal and Social Psychology* 50: 311–319; D. Fitz and W. G. Stephan, 1976, "Effects of Direct or Displaced Cathartic Aggression on Subsequent Aggression," *Psychological Reports* 39: 967–973; D. Landy and D. Mettee, 1969, "Evaluation of an Aggressor as a Function of Exposure to Cartoon Humor," *Journal of Personality and Social Psychology* 12: 66–71.

164. Ebbesen, E. B., B. Duncan, and V. J. Konecni, 1975, "Effects of Content of Verbal Aggression on Future Verbal Aggression: A Field Experiment," *Journal of Experimental Social Psychology* 11: 192–204.

165. Konecni, V. J. and A. N. Doob, 1972, "Catharsis through Displacement of Aggression," *Journal of Personality and Social Psychology* 23: 378–387; Quanty, 1976, op. cit.

166. Berkowitz, 1978, op. cit.

167. Berkowitz, L. and A. LePage, 1967, "Weapons as Aggression-eliciting Stimuli," *Journal of Personality and Social Psychology* 7: 202–207.

168. Buss, A., A. Booker, and E. Buss, 1972, "Firing a Weapon and Aggression," *Journal of Personality and Social Psychology* 22: 296–302; J. P. Leyens and R. E. Parke, 1975, "Aggressive Slides Can Induce a Weapons Effect," *European Journal of Social Psychology* 5: 229–236; M. M. Page and R. J. Scheidt, 1971, "The Elusive Weapons Effect: Demand Awareness, Evaluation Apprehension, and Slightly Sophisticated Subjects," *Journal of Personality and Social Psychology* 20: 304–318; C. W. Turner and L. S. Simons, 1974, "Effects of Subject Sophistication and Evaluation Apprehension on Aggressive Responses to Weapons," *Journal of Personality and Social Psychology* 30: 341–348.

169. Johnson and Downing, 1979, op. cit.

170. Baron, R. A., 1971, "Aggression as a Function of Audience Presence and Prior Anger Arousal," *Journal of Experimental Social Psychology* 7: 515–523; R. A. Baron, 1971, "Magnitude of Victim's Pain Cues and Level of Prior Anger Arousal as Determinants of Adult Aggressive Behavior," *Journal of Personality and Social Psychology* 17: 236–243; A. H. Buss, 1966a, "Instrumentality of Aggression, Feedback, and Frustration as Determinants of Physical Aggression," *Journal of Personality and Social Psychology* 3: 153–162; A. H. Buss, 1966b, "The Effect of Harm on Subsequent Aggression," *Journal of Experimental Research in Personality* 1: 249–255; R. A. Baron, 1974, "Aggression as an Indication of Victim's Pain Cues, Level of Prior Anger Arousal, and Exposure to an Aggressive Model," *Journal of Personality and Social Psychology* 29: 117–124.

171. Baron, 1974, op. cit.; R. J. Sebastian, 1978, "Immediate and Delayed Effects of Victim Suffering on the Attacker's Aggression," *Journal of Research in Personality* 12: 312–328.

172. Stets and Pirog-Good, 1987, op. cit.

173. Meithe, T. D., M. C. Stafford, and J. S. Long, 1987, "Social Differentiation in Criminal Victimizations: A Test of Routine Activities-Lifestyle Theories," *American Sociological Review* 52: 184–194.

174. Eagly, A. H. and V. J. Steffen, 1986, "Gender and Aggressive Behavior: A Meta-analytic Review of the Social Psychological Literature," *Psychological Bulletin* 100: 309–330; A. Frodi, J. Macaulay, and P. R. Thome, 1977, "Are Women Always Less Aggressive Than Men? A Review of the Experimental Literature," *Psychological Bulletin* 84: 634–660.

175. Frodi, Macaulay, and Thome, 1977, ibid.; Buss, 1966b, op. cit.

176. *Uniform Crime Reports,* 1986, op. cit.

177. O'Brien, R. M., 1987, "The Interracial Nature of Violent Crimes: A Reexamination," *American Journal of Sociology* 92: 817–835.

178. O'Brien, 1987, ibid.; S. J. South and S. F. Messner, 1986, "Structural Determinants of Intergroup Association: Interracial Marriage and Crime," *American Journal of Sociology* 91: 1409–1430.

179. Donnerstein, E. and M. Donnerstein, 1971, "Variables Affecting Black Aggression," *Journal of Social Psychology* 84: 157–158; E. Donnerstein and M. Donnerstein, 1973, "Variables in Interracial Aggression: Potential Ingroup Censure," *Journal of Personality and Social Psychology* 27: 143–150; E. Donnerstein, M. Donnerstein, S. Simon, and R. Ditrichs, 1972, "Variables in Interracial Aggression: Anonymity, Expected Retaliation, and a Riot," *Journal of Personality and Social Psychology* 22: 236–245; R. W. Genthner and S. P. Taylor, 1973, "Physical Aggression as a Function of Racial Prejudice and the Race of the Target," *Journal of Personality and Social Psychology* 27: 207–210.

180. Baron, 1979, op. cit.; Griffin and Rogers, 1977, op. cit.; R. W. Rogers and S. Prentice-Dunn, 1981, "Deindividuation and Anger-mediated Interracial Aggression: Unmasking Regressive Racism," *Journal of Personality and Social Psychology* 41: 63–73.

181. Rogers and Prentice-Dunn, 1981, ibid.; Donnerstein and Donnerstein, 1973, op. cit.; Donnerstein et al., 1972, op. cit.

182. Rogers, R. W., 1983, "Race Variables in Aggression," in R. G. Geen and D. I. Donnerstein (Eds.), *Aggression: Theoretical and Empirical Reviews,* New York: Academic Press.

183. Baughman, E. E., 1971, *Black Americans,* New York: Academic Press.

184. Wilson, L. and R. W. Rogers, 1975, "The Fire This Time: Effects of Race of Target, Insult, and Potential Retaliation on Black Aggression," *Journal of Personality and Social Psychology* 32: 857–864.

185. Baron, 1973, op. cit.; R. W. Rogers, 1980, "Expressions of Aggression-inhibiting Effects of Anonymity to Authority and Threatened Retaliation," *Personality and Social Psychology Bulletin* 6: 315–320.

186. Baron, 1973, op. cit.

CHAPTER 14

Groups

■

Types of Groups
Primary Groups
Formal Task Groups, Informal Groups, and Aggregates
Group Structure
Power Structures
Communication Structures
Interpersonal Attraction Structures
Group Performance
Additive Tasks
Disjunctive Tasks
Conjunctive Tasks
Complementary Tasks
Social Facilitation
Group Dynamics
Group Cohesion
Group Polarization
Minority Influence
Leadership
Leadership Traits
Behavioral Style
Bureaucracies
Transactional Theories of Leadership

On January 17, 1971, the Supreme Court of the United States heard oral arguments on the constitutionality of the death penalty (1). In his arguments against the death penalty, attorney Anthony Amsterdam said the death penalty constituted cruel and unusual punishment and was, therefore, in violation of the Eighth Amendment of the Constitution. He cited four reasons: The death penalty was imposed in a way that discriminated against minorities; it was imposed in an arbitrary and random fashion; it was not an effective deterrent; and the death penalty had become unacceptable to contemporary society.

Justice Marshall agreed with Amsterdam's arguments, but he worried that he was the only one on the Court who was strongly opposed to the death penalty. In the previous term, the Court had upheld a decision imposing the death penalty by a margin of 6 to 3. So strong were Marshall's convictions that he had written a long opinion against the death penalty even before the oral arguments were given in the case. Marshall hoped that Justices Brennan and Douglas, the Court's other liberals, would vote with him.

Before the oral arguments were presented, Justice Stewart was undecided. He felt the death penalty was clearly "unusual" since it was imposed in less than 20 percent of the cases in which it could be applied. Also, 700 men were waiting on death row in prisons around the country, and he felt that the Court should not condemn these men to die on a bare majority vote. Justice White believed the death penalty was not a credible deterrent, but he also felt it represented the will of the states, 38 of whom still retained it.

The members of the Court met for a preliminary discussion on the death penalty on January 21. Chief Justice Burger said he favored the death penalty. Justices Brennan, Douglas, White, and Stewart indicated they favored striking the death penalty. Thus, with Marshall's vote, there appeared to be a majority against the death penalty, even after Justices Powell, Rehnquist, and Blackmun indicated support for it.

■ *The 1971 Supreme Court. (Historical Pictures Service, Chicago)*

Justice Powell, the newest member of the Court, was concerned about the preliminary vote in the conference. He wrote an opinion he hoped would draw a majority of the members of the Court to his side. He argued that a long line of precedents upheld the death penalty, including the case from the previous term. Since the death penalty was mentioned in the Fifth Amendment to the Constitution, he felt that it was considered acceptable by the framers of the Constitution. He further argued that it was now possible for minority group members to get fair trials, although it may not have been possible in the past. Justice Powell circulated his 49-page opinion to the other members of the Court on May 12.

As the opinions of the other members of the Court were written, it became clear that Marshall's views and not Powell's had prevailed. On June 29, by a 5-to-4 vote, the death penalty laws were struck down, but the Court left it to the states to draft death penalty laws that would not be arbitrary or discriminatory (and many have done so). In a highly unusual move, the Court published nine separate opinions, totaling 243 pages. It was the longest decision in the history of the Court.

We use this example to introduce some of the characteristics and processes associated with groups that we will discuss in this chapter. The Supreme Court is the final judicial forum in the United States. The processes that affect its decisions are extremely important. Like all groups, the Supreme Court is guided by norms, some of them unwritten, that influence the conduct of its members. In many regards the Court is more formal than most groups. The Court has many explicit rules, such as those requiring preliminary conferences in which the justices state their tentative decisions. Their subsequent deliberations are generally conducted formally by exchanging written opinions, but considerable behind-the-scenes persuasion also occurs.

In this group the final decision-making rule is a vote of the majority, but this is only one type of decision-making rule that could be used. For instance, many jury decisions are decided on a unanimous basis. How could a member of the minority in a given case, like Justice Powell in the example above, successfully influence members of the majority to change sides? Was Powell's failure to do so in this case due to his recent tenure on the Court? Does the lengthy and careful deliberation process used by the Court lead it to make bolder or more conservative decisions than the members would otherwise make? Could the Chief Justice have had a greater influence on the decision of the Court? What kind of person would make a powerful Chief Justice? We will consider the answers to questions such as these in this chapter.

The behavior of people in small groups is the primary focus of this chapter. *Groups* consist of two or more people who influence one another. The study of groups was one of the first topics examined by sociologists when sociology emerged as a discipline in Europe at the end of the nineteenth century. One of these sociologists, Georg Simmel, suggested there were important differences between even the two smallest types of groups, dyads—consisting of two people—and triads—consisting of three people (2). For instance, in three person groups a member can leave and a group still exists, coalitions of two against one can occur, and a potential mediator exists in the event of disputes between two group members.

In this chapter we will discuss several different types of groups. We will also examine group structure, concentrating on power, communication, and friendship patterns. Following this, we will present some factors that affect group performance. Next, we will explore group dynamics—the processes that influence behavior and decisions in groups. In the final section, we will present several perspectives on leadership.

■

TYPES OF GROUPS

Primary Groups

One of the earliest American contributors to the theory of groups, Charles Horton Cooley, discussed the concept of *primary groups* in the second decade of this century (3). Cooley wrote that primary groups

■ *The family is a primary group. (WGS)*

are "characterized by intimate face-to-face association and cooperation . . . They are fundamental in forming the social nature and ideals of the individual. . . . They give the individual his earliest and completest sense of social unity" (4). He thought of primary groups as the "wellspring of social life" because they provide us with a source of emotional support that allows us to participate in social interaction. Primary groups tend to be small and permanent, and they are not usually oriented toward achieving a specific goal (5). Primary groups usually function as reference groups (Chapter 7), but unlike reference groups, primary groups are always membership groups.

The best example of a primary group is the family, but our closest friends also constitute a primary group. This is the type of group with which one can feel completely at home. These groups congratulate us when we succeed and support us when we need help, but they may also criticize us when we fail and reproach us when we do something wrong. Your family may comfort you in times of

need, but it also socializes you and controls your behavior to some extent. If you get out of line your family will let you know it in subtle, and sometimes not so subtle, ways.

Primary groups respond to the whole person, not just to one role the person may occupy. For instance, the members of the Supreme Court respond to one another principally as judges, so the Court is not a primary group, despite its importance in its members' lives. In contrast, the members of your family respond to you as a person, regardless of the roles you may achieve as you mature; you may become the chief justice of the Supreme Court, but you will still be pretty much the same person to your parents. The ties that bind primary groups together are affective (based on liking or love), not pragmatic or concerned with the material benefits to be derived from the group.

At the time that Cooley discussed primary groups, the concept already had a long history. In the nineteenth century the French sociologist Emile Durkheim had proposed that primary groups created the shared values that made social stability possible. In preindustrial societies primary groups were the dominant social form, but Durkheim believed the importance of primary groups would wane with the rise of industrialization. Indeed, some observers found this to be the case. In a study of American cities in 1938 one observer said of urban areas, "The bonds of kinship, of neighborliness, and the sentiments arising out of living together for generations under a common folk tradition are likely to be absent" (6).

Much to their surprise, later researchers found themselves documenting the tenacity of primary groups. Far from disappearing in modern society, primary groups seemed to flourish. It was as if the need for the intimate, sympathetic guidance provided by primary groups could not be denied (7). In modern societies primary groups simply took on new forms. In addition to the family, high school students created cliques and gangs; workers coalesced into friendship groups; young mothers formed babysitting cooperatives; people suffering from alcoholism, child abuse, cancer, or other afflictions formed support groups; and so on. Thus, primary groups are still very much a part of our lives today (see Box 14-1). Which of the groups to which you belong fit the definition of primary groups?

Formal Task Groups, Informal Groups, and Aggregates

Many of the groups to which we belong are formal task groups with established goals (15). A professional football player belongs to an organized team and probably to the players' union. The team and the union are both *formal* task groups. He is also likely to belong to a variety of *informal* groups, such as the group of players who are his friends, his former college buddies, and perhaps his neighbors. If he takes the subway home from practice or rides an elevator, he is a part of an *aggregate* of people who are in the same place at the same time. We will discuss each of these types of groups.

Formal task groups are characterized by a set of interrelated norms that are acknowledged by the members. The primary function of such norms is to accomplish specific goals, such as winning football games or making decisions, as corporation boards of directors do. Formal task groups are usually made up of interconnected roles. A football team has eleven offensive and defensive positions, each with its own responsibilities. A corporate board usually has a president, vice president, treasurer, and secretary plus other regular board members.

Formal task groups have a definable structure, often consisting of a hierarchical arrangement of positions such as those of a corporate board. Formal task groups can often exert a strong influence over the individual members because the members can be sanctioned (rewarded for conformity and punished for nonconformity). Football players who do not follow the formal rules or informal norms of the team risk sanctions running from disapproval to being removed from the team.

Informal groups are often transitory and their norms are usually not formalized. If goals exist, they may be temporary. On one occasion, a group of friends may go to a nightclub with the idea of listening to the live band, but on another occasion they may go to a movie to relax. Roles in informal groups tend to change with the situation and as the membership of the group changes. The leader for the trip to the nightclub may be different from the leader for the trip to the movie. A pickup game of basketball is an informal group, as is the group of card players who gather in the dorm each evening.

An informal group has some bond in common, while in an aggregate there is no bond among the people. The aggregate of people riding the subway home from work has nothing in common, except the fact that they are in the same place at the same time. Nonetheless, an aggregate is a type of group since people who are together can influence each other's behavior, even when there is no bond among them. To illustrate, recall the reluctance of bystanders to intervene in an emergency when others are present. No bond exists among the bystanders, yet the presence of other people inhibits them from helping the person in need. Also, unlike formal and informal groups, aggregates lack structure, the topic we will take up next.

BOX 14-1

Gangs as Primary Groups

In 1943 William F. Whyte published a now classic study of street corner gangs in Italian-American neighborhoods (8). Gangs flourished in many American cities, then as now. The gangs consisted of relatively small groups of boys or men. They tended to be stable over time, in some cases lasting for more than a decade. Although many gang members engaged in some type of criminal activity and fought with other gangs, these activities were not the primary functions of the gangs. The primary functions were social and psychological. The members frequently lacked self-confidence and found support in the gang.

Gangs typically have a strong leader as a focal point. It is he or she who plans and executes group activities, exemplifies the rules, and enforces them. One leader of the Hell's Angels, a California motorcycle gang, has been described as "the coolest head in the lot, and a tough, quick-thinking dealer when any action starts. By turns he is a fanatic, a philospher, a brawler, a shrewd compromiser, and a final arbitrator" (9).

Gangs have unwritten but generally accepted norms. One norm requires each gang member to "help his friends when he can and to refrain from doing anything to harm them" (10). This is the norm of reciprocity which we discussed more extensively in Chapter 12. Another common norm concerns lying. As one Hell's Angel put it:

The best thing about the Angels is that we don't lie to each other. Of course that don't go for outsiders because we have to fight fire with fire. Hell, most people you meet won't tell you the truth about anything (11).

GROUP STRUCTURE

Three basic types of structures are found in groups: *power* structures, *communication* structures, and *interpersonal attraction* structures (16). These structures can overlap, but they are often distinct. In some groups, the person with the most power, the leader, is also the person who receives the most communications and is liked the most; but in other groups, three separate people may occupy these positions.

Power Structures

In formal groups, a chart often outlines the group's table of organization. Such charts are usually hierarchical, listing one person at the top, then listing a

Other norms cover spending and lending of money. For instance, in the gangs Whyte studied, the leader spent more money on his followers than they spent on him, and he lent them money but did not borrow from them. A premium is placed on loyalty to the gang, even if it involves costs for the member. Similarly, the gang members loyally support one another, a sentiment captured in the following quote about the Hell's Angels.

In any argument a fellow Hell's Angel is always right. To disagree with a Hell's Angel is to be wrong—and to persist in being wrong is an open challenge (12).

The members come to be very close to one another; indeed, to be dependent on one another. Doc, the leader of one of the gangs Whyte studied, is quoted as saying:

I suppose my boys have kept me from getting ahead. . . . But if I were to start over again—If God said to me, "Look here, Doc, you're going to start over again, and you can pick out your friends in advance," still I would make sure that my boys were among them (13).

Of the Hell's Angels it has been written, "They are intensely aware of belonging, of being able to depend on one another" (14).

Gangs are hierarchically structured. The leader has one or two close lieutenants and then the rest of the gang is arrayed below them. The status of individuals can change, but the hierarchical structure tends to be quite stable. Status in the group depends in large measure on how well a gang member fulfills the norms of the group. Status also depends on possessing the skills valued by the group, such as physical strength. Thus, although we tend to think of gangs as renegades from the rest of society, they have norms and status hierarchies and fulfill the members' needs just as other less menacing groups do.

Due to their violent nature, little research has been conducted on gangs that are involved in the distribution of drugs. These gangs have added an economic function to the social psychological function studied in earlier gangs. How do you think these gangs are likely to differ from those that were studied earlier? ∎

small group of people having equal power at the next level down, and then a larger group with less power at the third level, and so on. In the judicial branch of the U.S. government, the justices of the Supreme Court occupy the top position, the judges of the appellate courts occupy the next level down, and below them come district court judges in each of the federal judicial districts.

Informal groups usually have no table of organization, although they may have a power structure.

Among a group of friends, one or two individuals may be acknowledged as exerting more control over the group than others. In both formal and informal groups power is sometimes distributed equally. This type of power distribution may characterize a group of couples that jointly decide where to go for dinner or a group of students working in a study group for their chemistry exam.

Power is the ability to control and influence others. There are six basic types of power:

■ *An aggregate of people waiting for a light displays civil inattention—they politely ignore one another. (WGS)*

■ *In contrast to aggregates, informal groups have a reason for being, even if it is only entertainment. (WGS)*

1. *reward power*—the power to reward others for compliance. Your family has this type of power.

2. *coercive power*—the power to punish others for noncompliance. Your boss has the power to fire you, a clear example of coercive power.

3. *legitimate power*—the power formally granted to acknowledged leaders by their followers. A platoon leader in the military possesses this type of power.

4. *expert power*—power that accrues to people because of their knowledge. Expert witnesses in jury trials possess this type of power.

5. *referent power*—power that derives from the attraction followers feel toward the leader. Cult leaders often possess this type of power.

6. *information power*—the power that derives from persuasiveness. A skilled legislative debater has this type of power (17).

A charismatic national leader, like the late President John F. Kennedy, may possess all six types of power. As a national leader, Kennedy had rewards to distribute and could impose punishments; he had legitimate power because he was elected to the office he occupied; others regarded him as an expert in the art of government; his followers were strongly attracted to him; and he was a very persuasive speaker.

A few studies have compared the effectiveness of different types of power on group performance. In one study, the use of reward and coercive power was compared (18). The leader of a small group could reward his subordinates or he could punish them by giving or witholding money for their performances on an anagram task. The leader either used his power or did not use it during the course of the first seven trials. On the final trial, the leader made a special request—that the subordinates work hard. On this final trial, the subordinates worked hardest for the leader who had coercive power, but had not used it. Apparently, subordinates appreciate leaders' restraint in the use of coercive power.

Communication Structures

In any group it is possible to chart who communicates with whom. For instance, the younger justices on the Supreme Court may frequently confer with one another but may confer with their older colleagues only occasionally. Some justices closely supervise their law clerks, others do not. The law clerks for the more liberal justices may talk with one another often, but they may rarely converse with the clerks of the more conservative justices. In this way any group's communication network can be charted. Typically, the table of organization in a formal group does not adequately capture the actual communication links. In informal groups, a chart of the communication network is essential to understanding the functioning of the group. One of the reasons communication networks are important is that the efficiency of the group may be influenced by these networks.

It is theoretically possible for every member of a group to be linked to every other member of the group; but in practice this rarely occurs, except in very small groups. In Figure 14-1 you will find some of the common forms of communication networks in five-person groups. In networks in which communication can be channeled through one person, such as the wheel, the Y, and the double-barred circle, centralized leadership easily emerges during group interaction. Groups with centralized leadership are generally more effective in solving simple problems than are groups with decentralized leadership, such as that depicted in the circle (19). For complex problems, decentralized groups are often superior to centralized groups because these communication networks allow a more efficient exchange of ideas (20).

Because communication is freer in decentralized networks like the circle, group members usually find participation in these groups more satisfying than participation in centralized groups (21). In one study it was found that the individuals in an organization who could most easily communicate with others in the organization were more satisfied than those whose communications with others were limited (22).

Figure 14.1 ■

Communication Networks

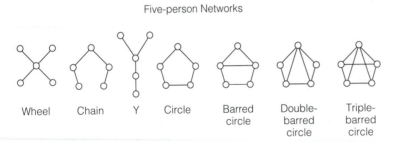

Five-person Networks

Wheel   Chain   Y   Circle   Barred   Double-   Triple-
                                  circle   barred   barred
                                            circle   circle

Adapted from Shaw, M.E., 1964, "Communication Networks," in L. Berkowitz (Ed.), *Advances in Experimental Social Psychology*, Vol. 1, pp. 111–147.

In hierarchically structured groups, information flows through the network more easily in some directions than in others (23). Overall, more communication is directed to people at the same level of the hierarchy than upward or downward in the communication network (24). Generally, more information flows upward than downward (25). Also, positive information flows upward from subordinates more frequently than negative information, especially if the subordinates think there is a chance for them to move up in the hierarchy (26). The cumulative effect of these communication tendencies is that, although individuals at the top of a hierarchy often receive more information than individuals who are lower in the hierarchy, their views of the functioning of the organization may be biased in a positive direction.

One of your authors had an opportunity to view a particularly costly example of the distorted perceptions produced by these communication biases. While working for the Agency for International Development (AID) in Vietnam during the war, one of his jobs was to write reports on the economic situation in the province where he was working. Because the United States government wanted so desperately to win the war, and because subordinates wanted to please their superiors, there was tremendous pressure to report only information that would

make it appear the war was going well. His immediate superior actually deleted negative information from the reports he wrote, such as descriptions of rampant inflation and black market activities. Later, when he and some of his colleagues in similar jobs had an opportunity to meet with the American ambassador to Vietnam, they were shocked at how limited the ambassador's understanding was of the actual conditions in the field. On the basis of the information available to him, the ambassador was predicting in 1966 that the war would end within six to twelve months. America actually left Vietnam six years later—frustrated and unvictorious. Both the American military and American civilian leaders consistently underestimated the opposition, in part because they had such an unrealistic view of how successfully the war was being waged at the local level.

Interpersonal Attraction Structures

Groups are also structured by the nature of the interpersonal relations within the group—the pattern of likes and dislikes. Charting this pattern results in a *sociogram* indicating the links between the members of a group. You could probably create a sociogram for your friends in a couple of minutes (see Box 14-2). In the Sherifs' study of intergroup relations at a boys camp (discussed in Chapter 1),

Figure 14.2 ■

Sociogram of Rattlers

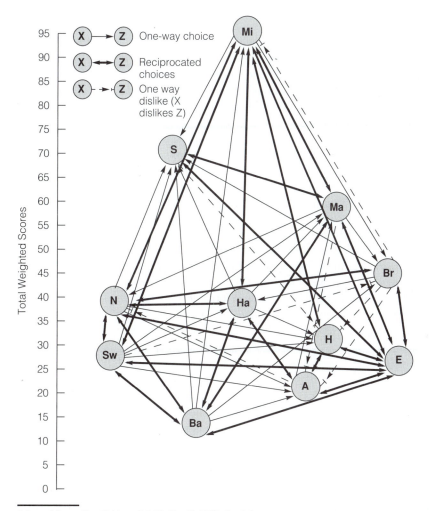

In-Group Structure
(based on sociometric with four criteria combined)

Adapted from Sherif, M. and C.W. Sherif, 1969, *Social
Psychology*, New York: Harper & Row.

sociograms were used to examine the structures of
interpersonal attraction within the "Rattlers" and the
"Eagles" (27). As you can see in Figure 14-2, the
Rattlers were a highly cohesive group, as evidenced
by the fact that most of the members of the Rattlers

liked each other. Notice also that there were some
clear differences among the boys in how much they
were liked. *E* was a sociometric star; he was liked
by everyone. On the other hand, *A* was somewhat
socially isolated; although six members liked him,

BOX 14-2

Social Support Networks

Take a minute to think about your friends. How many friends and family members could you call on for emotional or other kinds of help in case of need? If you listed all of these people, how many of *them* would know one another and be likely to help one another in time of need. The first question is the type of question researchers use to measure the *size* of a person's social support network, while the second question measures the *density* of a person's social support network. Do you have a large or a small social support network? Is it high in density (lots of interconnections among your friends) or low in density?

In social support networks we both receive and give social support. These support networks have been referred to as our "personal communities," for they consist of the interpersonal ties that link us to friends at work, at play, and at home. Social support networks help to establish and support our social identities, and they reflect our participation in various spheres of social life (32).

Having an extensive social support network has been shown to help people cope with mental and physical health problems, work problems, and negative events such as divorce or the loss of a loved one (33). One of the most dramatic effects of extensive social support networks is an increase in longevity (34). People who have very limited social support networks have mortality rates 2 to 4.5 times greater than people with strong social support networks, and this is true at all age

---

two members disliked him, and he was not selected by four members. After the conflict between the Rattlers and the Eagles had been reduced through cooperation, the boys in both groups chose many more boys from the other group as friends than they had when the two groups were in conflict.

In most groups, sociometric choices are determined by many of the same factors that determine interpersonal attraction in other settings (discussed in Chapter 11) (28). In groups, patterns of exchange among the members, especially those involving rewards and punishments, are particularly important in determining attraction. Likewise, similarity influences attraction in groups. The spatial location of other group members and their accessibility through

the communication network also affect attraction. In general, people like the members of a group with whom they can most easily communicate, and these people are likely to be those that are nearby (29).

The relative statuses of the individual members and the amount of time that group members talk during social interactions can also have an impact on sociometric choices. People tend to choose high-status members more often than low-status members (30), although these choices may not be reciprocated. Individuals who talk in the group tend to be chosen more than quieter members, but members who are perceived as talking too much are not chosen frequently (31). These studies suggest that if you wish to be a sociometric star in your group you

levels. Occupying a central role in social support networks has even been found to be associated with functioning well in school (35).

Social support networks have these beneficial effects because they help people to maintain a positive self-image, and they provide opportunities to discuss one's feelings and sound out and evaluate responses to situations. In a crisis friends may also know best how to provide help, and they can assist the professionals treating the person in understanding and helping that person. Furthermore, a strong social support network can help a person to initiate and maintain needed changes, such as seeking professional help or following a difficult medical regimen (36).

The relationship of density of social networks and responses to stressful situations may surprise you. Studies of recently divorced or widowed women and mature women returning to college indicate that the women with the *least* dense social support networks adjusted best to these difficult life transitions (37). Apparently low density networks include a greater variety of resources that can be called on in time of need. Additionally, people who have varied friends and interests may be less devastated by stressful changes in one sphere of their own lives than those with a tightly knit support network that may tie them to their former role.

But there can be a downside to social networks. Some people are primarily recipients of social support while others are primarily givers of social support. Rewards are derived from giving social support, but emotional and physical costs are also incurred. For instance, the parents and friends of children with cancer find providing support to be emotionally draining (38). It has been argued that the greater emotional demands placed on women in social support networks is one of the factors contributing to the greater incidence of some types of mental health problems in women than in men (39). Also, one study found that providing emotional support over a long period of time reduced the capacity of the immune system to fight disease and led to depression (40). ■

should act in ways that others find rewarding, stress your similarities with them, maintain lines of communication to as many members as possible, stay in close proximity to them, try to occupy positions of high status, and talk a lot, but not too much.

■
GROUP PERFORMANCE

We entrust groups with many of the most important decisions in our society. Groups in industry, government, and the military work together to make decisions that affect all of our lives. As a society we seem to assume that groups can work more effec-

tively than individuals. In this section we will discuss factors affecting performance in small groups. The old adage "two heads are better than one" clearly suggests that groups perform better than individuals. However, it has also been suggested that a camel is a mouse designed by a committee, which doesn't speak too well for group decision making. Both the optimistic and the pessimistic views of group performance have received some support.

One factor influencing group performance is the size of the group. As the size of a group increases, so do the resources of the group; but if the group cannot utilize these resources effectively, it may not perform well. Our discussion concerns the conditions under which groups typically perform better

■ *In additive tasks, groups can accomplish what individuals cannot. (WGS)*

or worse than individuals. The key to understanding these conditions is the types of tasks the groups are performing.

Additive Tasks

On *additive* tasks, such as paddling a river raft through a rapids or pushing a car to start it, individuals perform the same task jointly. For additive tasks, groups are obviously superior to individuals, since one person might not be able to perform the task alone. One interesting question about performance on such tasks is whether individuals put forth more or less effort when working in groups. In laboratory studies using an apparatus similar to a tug-of-war, the number of people pulling on a rope was varied (41). As the number of people pulling on the rope increased, the amount each person pulled on the rope decreased, a tendency termed *social loafing*. Similarly, as the number of people in an audience increases, the amount of noise they individually produce decreases, even then they are told to make as much noise as possible (42). It is easy to see that social loafing can be a major problem in any industry where people work jointly at the same task. Fortunately, social loafing can be reduced by leading people to believe that their contributions to the group can be individually monitored (43). Another

factor that eliminates social loafing is commitment to an important task, like winning a championship game (44).

Remarkably, social loafing has also been found in creative intellectual tasks, as well as purely physical tasks. You may be acquainted with a group problem-solving procedure known as *brainstorming*. In brainstorming, the group members try to create as many solutions to a problem as they can, and they do so with no discussion of the merits of the solutions and with no criticism of the solutions. An example of a problem that has been used in brainstorming research is, "What would happen if everyone born after the year 2000 had an extra thumb on each hand?" People working in brainstorming groups produce more solutions than an average individual would, but they do not produce more or better solutions than the same number of people working alone (45). Thus, on additive tasks, groups often elicit less, not more, individual effort.

Disjunctive Tasks

Disjunctive tasks consist of problems that have only one correct answer, such as math problems or scientific puzzles like the structure of DNA. For disjunctive tasks, as group size increases, so does the chance that the group will find the correct solution (46). An example of this type of problem is:

On one side of a river are three wives and three husbands. All of the men, but none of the women, can row. Get them all across the river by means of a boat carrying only three at one time. No man will allow his wife to be in the presence of another man unless he is also there. (The answer appears in reference 47 at the end of this chapter.)

For disjunctive tasks performance improves with group size because, as the size of the group increases, the probability increases that the group will contain at least one member who can solve the problem. If we compare the performance of a group to the performance of the best individual in the group, the group usually does no better than this individual. Thus, it is not the process of group decision making that leads to improved performance with increased size.

On a difficult disjunctive task, the correct answer may not be obvious, even when it is produced by one of the group members. If the majority of the group think they have the correct solution when they do not, the group's decision is likely to be worse than the performance of the best member of the group. This decrease in performance due to the ineffective processing of information by the group is called *process loss*. (A good example involving process loss is "groupthink," discussed in Chapter 7.) In groups solving difficult disjunctive problems, the typical strategy adopted by the group is "truth supported wins." The group is only likely to select the right answer if the person who has figured out the answer is supported by at least one other member of the group (48). Many a good suggestion has failed for lack of a second. If you have ever played the game "Trivial Pursuit" in teams you know how frequently this happens.

Conjunctive Tasks

On conjunctive tasks, the group's performance is limited by the performance of the worst member in the group. For conjunctive tasks, as group size increases, performance decreases (49). An example of this type of task is a team of Boy Scouts on a competitive cross-country map-reading exercise. The group's performance can only be as good as the performance of the slowest walker in the group. Many assembly lines consist of conjunctive tasks; the line can move no faster than its slowest member works.

In a study comparing conjunctive and disjunctive tasks, subjects were asked to blow as much air through a tube as they could in 30 seconds (50). On the basis of a pretest, the subjects were told they were either high or low in this ability. Next, the subjects were told a ten dollar prize would be awarded on the basis of the quality of performance of the best (disjunctive task) or the least good (conjunctive task) member of the group. As Figure 14-3 shows, high-ability individuals worked harder on the disjunctive task than on the conjunctive task

Figure 14.3 ■

The Effect of Type of Task and Ability on Performance

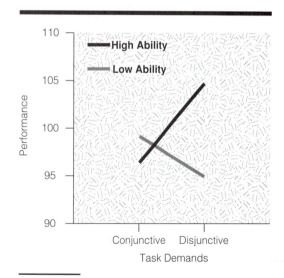

Adapted from Kerr, N.L. and S.E. Bruun, 1983, "Dispensability of Member Effort and Group Motivation Losses: Free-rider Effects," *Journal of Personality and Social Psychology* 44: 78–94.

because their contribution was crucial only on the disjunctive task. Low-ability individuals worked harder on the conjunctive task than on the disjunctive task because only on the conjunctive task was their contribution likely to matter. This study indicates people do not go out and "give it their best shot" every time out; rather, they put forward the greatest amount of effort when their contribution matters most.

Complementary Tasks

On complementary tasks, the members of a group must combine their diverse abilities to create a group product. Groups often perform better than individuals on these tasks. An example of this type of task occurs when a NASA space shuttle crew must coordinate its efforts to respond to an emergency. Groups are particularly likely to perform better than individuals when the groups are made up of individuals who are high in ability and possess diverse skills (51). Groups in which the members work together cooperatively also typically perform as well as or better than individuals working alone (52). In an old-fashioned barn-raising the members of a farming community worked cooperatively to build a barn. The result was probably a better barn than

the individual farmer could have built for himself and it was certainly faster.

Complementary tasks are the only kind of tasks in which group processes frequently cause groups to perform better than the same number of individuals working independently (see Table 14-1). From this discussion of group tasks you can see that if you were an executive charged with setting up a new division of your corporation, a knowledge of the ways in which task structure affects performance would be invaluable.

■

SOCIAL FACILITATION

We have discussed situations in which groups of people work together to perform a task. In other situations, individuals work in the presence of other people, even though they are not working together on the same task. Open-space offices provide an example. Anyone who performs in front of an audience is also in this situation. How does the mere presence of others affect performance?

The presence of others facilitates the performance of behaviors which have been well learned in a given situation (the dominant responses in the

Table 14.1 ■

Group Performance as a Function of Type of Task

Type of Task	Performance Depends on	Result
Additive	Joint effort	Groups superior to individuals, but social loafing occurs
Disjunctive	The performance of the best individual	Groups are no better than the best individual
Conjunctive	The performance of the worst individual	Groups worse than individuals, on average
Complementary	A combination of diverse abilities	Groups better than individuals

■ *Social facilitation and social loafing can occur in the same situation. Adult scrutiny encourages social facilitation in the front, but social loafing occurs on down the line. (© Richard S. Orton 1990)*

situation). This effect explains why a well-trained athlete often performs better in competition than in practice. The situation and the behaviors are exactly the same in both instances, but the size of the audience varies. This effect is known as *social facilitation*. In contrast, for novel or poorly learned behaviors, the presence of others hinders performance (53). Thus, an athlete who is not well trained might perform worse in competition than in practice.

The growth of knowledge is an evolutionary process in which competing theories often battle against one another until research indicates one is superior or that several theories can be reconciled. In the area of social facilitation the battle is at its peak. Several explanations have been offered for this pattern of effects. All of these explanations suggest that the presence of others creates arousal in the performer (54). They differ in the proposed cause of this arousal. One theory states that the mere presence of others leads to a state of alertness. A second theory suggests that arousal is created by the apprehension the performer feels about the evalu-

ations of the audience. A third theory hypothesizes that arousal is caused by distraction due to a conflict between attending to others and the task at hand (55).

Each of these theories has considerable support, and each has its limitations. The first theory has trouble explaining social facilitation when the performers are told that others will be observing them via videotape since this theory requires the presence of an audience. The second theory cannot account for social facilitation when the audience will not be evaluating the performer. Both the second and the third theories must strain to account for social facilitation in animals (yes, chickens and even cockroaches display social facilitation too).

The current ferment in this area is illustrated in an experiment. The subjects were asked to perform a simple copying task in the presence of another subject (56). The other subject either performed the exact same task or a different task. The experimenters reasoned that the presence of another subject would be most distracting when the other subject performed the same task as the subject because only

Figure 14.4 ■

Distraction and Social Facilitation

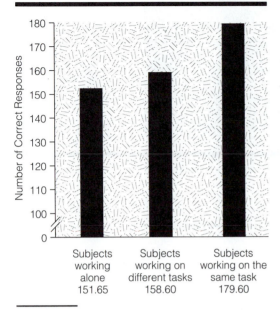

Subjects working alone	Subjects working on different tasks	Subjects working on the same task
151.65	158.60	179.60

Adapted from Sanders, G.S., R.S. Baron, and D.L. Moore, 1978, "Distraction and Social Comparison as Mediators of Social Facilitation Effects," *Journal of Experimental Social Psychology 14:* 291–303.

then could the second subject be used for social comparison purposes. The experimenters expected the arousal created by this distraction to have a positive effect on the subjects' performances.

Compared to subjects who worked alone, subjects who worked on the same task as another subject felt more competitive and performed better (see Figure 14-4). These results suggest that the presence of a distracting other increases arousal and facilitates performance, as predicted by the third (distraction) theory. The subjects who worked in the presence of another subject working on a different task did not perform significantly better than those who worked alone. These results provide some evidence against the theory suggesting that social facilitation is due to alertness caused by the mere presence of others. The final resolution of this battle between theories remains for the future.

■
GROUP DYNAMICS

Group dynamics deal with the processes that affect the outcomes of group interaction. We will examine three processes. First, we explore the causes and consequences of group cohesion. Second, we discuss the polarization of responses that occurs in groups. Third, we present the ways in which group members who are in the minority can maximize their influence.

Group Cohesion

Causes of cohesiveness *Cohesiveness* concerns the forces that bind the members of a group together (57). It is a critical feature of groups because it affects the members' willingness to stay in the group, their satisfaction with the group, and the group's motivation and efficiency. If you have ever been in a group where the members did not like each other, you know what a deadening effect the lack of cohesiveness can have. Two categories of factors affect group cohesion: the rewards offered by the group, and the types of interaction (cooperative or competitive) that characterize the group.

Exchange theory can help us understand the rewards of group membership, particularly the relative rewards offered by membership in a group. Relative rewards are the rewards and costs of membership in a particular group (the reward/cost ratio) relative to the rewards and costs of other comparable groups (the comparison level of alternatives) (58). Among the rewards offered by group membership are the fulfillment of biological needs, security, affiliation, acceptance by others, self-esteem, and achievement of individual and group goals. The costs of group membership include the time and effort required by the group, interaction with disliked others, and criticism or rejection by other group members. When the group provides rewards to its members at little cost to them, group cohesion tends to be high (59). If group members feel that they can get more rewards at less cost by belonging to another group, group cohesiveness is undermined. When times are good and they are running the government well, the members of the president's cabinet are likely to be highly cohesive; but when times are bad and criticism is raining down on them, lucrative jobs in industry may start looking more attractive and cohesion may plummet.

The cooperative or competitive nature of group interactions also affects cohesion. Cooperation within groups generally increases cohesion, but competition within groups reduces cohesion. The presence of both types of interaction in the same situation can create problems—for example, for coaches of athletic teams. Individual team members must compete with one another for positions on the team, but they must also cooperate with one another in order to play effectively. The coach's dilemma is to avoid having the competition among the players destroy the cohesiveness of the team as a whole.

Fortunately for coaches, competition between teams typically increases cohesion within teams. In general, when groups (large or small) confront outside threats or crises, cohesion increases (60). For example, in a classic study of suicide, Emile Durkheim found that suicide rates decrease during times of war (61). He attributed this decrease to the increased group cohesion that occurs during war.

Under some conditions, however, crises and outside threats to the group will not increase cohesion. When the group can neither end the crisis nor provide the members with support or comfort, cohesion is likely to decrease. Imagine the bickering and dissension that would result among the district managers of a large corporation if they were told some of them would be fired during the reorganization ordered by the new owners of their company. In this situation the managers have little control over the crisis; they are separated from one another so they cannot easily support or comfort one another, and there will be competition for the remaining jobs.

To summarize briefly, maximal cohesiveness should exist in groups that are personally rewarding and highly successful, are characterized by cooperation, and feel threatened (perhaps by competition with rival groups), and when there are no attractive alternative groups to join.

Consequences of cohesiveness Group cohesiveness affects both conformity to group norms and group productivity. As cohesiveness increases, so does conformity to group norms (62). In a demonstration of this effect, subjects were led to feel accepted or rejected by a group of their classmates (63). The subjects then performed a task in which they estimated the number of dots on a series of slides. After recording their own estimates, the subjects were informed of the average estimate of the members of their group. On half of the judgments, the group average was said to be 30 percent higher than their own estimates. Next, the subjects had an opportunity to revise their estimates. Subjects in the high-acceptance groups, where cohesiveness was high, changed their estimates more in the direction of the group average than did the subjects in the low-acceptance groups.

In cohesive groups conformity is due to the power the group has over its members (64). The power derives from the members' dependence on the group. A group member is more dependent the greater the rewards provided by the group and the less available other groups are that could provide these rewards. One might expect a highly paid, aging football player to conform more to team rules than an equally talented younger player because he has more to lose by being fired and fewer other teams would be interested in him.

Have you ever been in a cohesive group when one of the group members disagrees with the rest of the group about an issue? How did you react to this deviant member of the group? If your group was like most cohesive groups, it did not appreciate the deviant's disagreement. As a rule, deviants tend to be rejected in highly cohesive groups. In a classic study conducted over three decades ago, cohesiveness was manipulated by varying the attractiveness of the groups students could join (65). During a meeting of these groups, a confederate of the experimenter either deviated from the consensus of the group on a decision or agreed with the group. In the cohesive groups, the confederate was ranked lower if he deviated from the group consensus than if he had agreed with the group. In groups that were low in cohesiveness, the confederate was rated about the same whether he deviated or agreed with the group.

The group's power to promote conformity can have detrimental effects on the members, leading them to engage in behaviors that they would consider inappropriate if they were acting alone. This can be seen in gangs and in athletes who take steroids to improve performance.

Group cohesion typically increases productivity because group members who are highly attracted to the group want to help the group achieve its goals (66). However, under certain conditions, cohesion does not increase productivity. In some groups, productivity may not be an important goal. In industrial settings, work groups who do not feel management supports them will sometimes decide to limit their productivity (67). In this case, cohesion may help the group achieve its goals, but high productivity is not one of the goals. Another example of cohesion having negative effects on performance occurs in student groups that are actively anti-intellectual (68). This phenomenon is sometimes referred to "taking a dive," and it occurs when loyalty to the norms of a small group is more important than achieving some larger group's goals (69).

In a laboratory study of this phenomenon, groups of college students formed assembly lines to produce checkerboards (70). To create highly cohesive groups, the subjects were told pretesting indicated they were highly congenial and would like each other. In the low-cohesion groups, the subjects were told pretesting had uncovered no reason for thinking they would like each other. Halfway through the experiment, the other group members, all of whom were confederates, informed the subjects that they wanted them to slow down or speed up their work. As Table 14-2 indicates, the subjects in the highly cohesive groups were more responsive to these requests than the subjects in the low-cohesion groups. This was particularly true when the request was to slow down.

Cohesiveness also has an impact on other group processes that can influence the amount and quality of the group's work. For instance, cohesiveness increases motivation (71), leading to greater effort, thus resulting in greater productivity. Cohesiveness also improves communication (72) and cooperation

Table 14.2 ■

The Effects of Cohesiveness on Productivity

	High Cohesion	Low Cohesion
Slow down	− 1.58	− .50
Speed up	4.42	4.00

Note: Positive numbers indicate increases in productivity and negative numbers indicate decreases in productivity. Adapted from Schachter, S., N. Ellertson, D. McBride, and D. Gregory, 1951, "An Experimental Study of Cohesiveness and Productivity," *Human Relations* 4: 229–238.

(73) within the group, facilitating the functioning of the group.

Group Polarization

One of the most fascinating findings in the entire literature on groups is that groups generally make more extreme decisions than individuals (74). This effect has been found in many settings, including juries, businesses, the military, mental health facilities, gambling casinos, and in classrooms when students evaluate their professors (75). In the initial studies of this phenomenon, subjects were given problems, such as the following one, and asked to make individual decisions about what should be done.

> Henry is a writer who is said to have considerable creative talent but who so far has been earning a comfortable living by writing cheap westerns. Recently he has come up with an idea for a potentially significant novel. If it could be written and accepted it might have considerable literary impact and be a big boost to his career. On the other hand, if he is not able to work out his idea or if the novel is a flop, he will have expended considerable time and energy without remuneration.

> Imagine that you are advising Henry. Please indicate the lowest probability of success that

you would consider acceptable for Henry to attempt to write the novel (76).

When people respond to this item individually, they favor a somewhat risky (low probability of success) course of action. After discussing this problem in a group, people tend, on the average, to make even riskier decisions. This finding, known as the *risky shift,* was obtained in a number of different studies. Then something surprising happened: Some studies began to indicate that groups made more cautious decisions than individuals (77). This suggested that group discussion did not simply lead to riskier decisions, but rather to more polarized opinions. The plot of this scientific whodunit thickened. What could explain the direction of the polarization that occurs in groups?

The first hint came with the discovery that the direction of polarization was related to the initial direction of the individual decisions. If individuals favored a risky course before group discussion, then the groups favored an even riskier course; but if individuals initially favored a cautious course, groups favored an even more cautious course. Thus, cultural values appeared to affect group decision making. If people in a culture generally value a risky course of action, such as they do in Henry's case, then groups polarize in the direction of risk; but if the culture values caution in a given situation, groups will be even more cautious. The question that still remained was why groups cause opinions to polarize.

Two theories have been proposed to explain group polarization, both of which have received strong support. The first, information pooling, is based on the arguments that emerge during group discussion (78). When individuals make private decisions, they develop arguments favoring their own decisions. If individuals in a group generally favor a risky course, during group discussion they will end up pooling all of their arguments favoring risk. Each person then has even more arguments favoring his or her position than before the discussion.

Arguments that do not support the course favored by the majority of the group are either not mentioned during the discussion or are given little weight (79). In fact, people who are initially in the minority may join the majority. After group discussion, when individuals reassess their positions, they find they have more arguments favoring risk than before, and they may have dismissed some of the arguments favoring caution. The result is riskier decisions.

In a study supporting this theory, a simulated jury was created (80). Students read about a case and were asked to make a preliminary decision about the defendant's guilt. They were also asked to cite five facts they thought were relevant to the case. These facts were supposedly passed to the other members of the jury, and then each student received five facts from each of the other members in return. In one case, they received facts matching the proportion of favorable and unfavorable facts they had cited themselves. When the students reassessed their decisions after reading these facts, their decisions became more extreme because they now had more arguments favoring their decisions.

A subsequent study showed that polarization occurred only when the five facts from the other "jurors" were different from their own. This study demonstrates that it is not simply finding out that others agree with you that causes polarization, but the addition of new information.

The second theory about the causes of group polarization is based on social comparison theory (81). This theory suggests that people use similar others to assess their abilities and the correctness of their opinions. When people in group discussions discover their views are shared by others in the group, they become even more certain their views are correct. People who may have expressed tentative opinions because they did not wish to appear extreme to the group are then free to express more extreme opinions, as long as they are in the direction favored by the group (82).

In a clever demonstration of the effects of social comparison in a small group, two subjects were asked to rate the attractiveness of people in a set of photographs (83). Each of the two subjects called out his rating in turn. Half of the pictures were of attractive people and half were of unattractive people. Due to social comparison with the first person's ratings, the second person's ratings were expected

Figure 14.5 ■

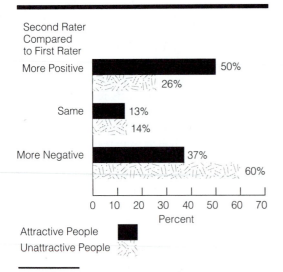

Second Rater
Compared
to First Rater

More Positive   50%

26%

Same   13%

14%

More Negative   37%

60%

0   10   20   30   40   50   60   70
Percent

Attractive People ■
Unattractive People

Adapted from Myers, D.G., 1982, "Polarizing, Effects of Social Interaction." In H. Brandstatter, J.H. Davis, and G. Stocker-Kreichgauer (Eds.), *Group Decision Making.* New York: Academic Press.

to be more extreme than the first person's in the direction favored by the first person. Thus, if the first person said the depicted individual was somewhat attractive, it was predicted the second would say the person was quite attractive. As you can see in Figure 14-5, the data support this hypothesis.

The difference between these theories of group polarization is that the pooling of information requires an exchange of ideas, whereas social comparison requires only that individuals know the positions of others, not the reasons why they have adopted those positions (84). In most real group discussions, both pooling of information and social comparison typically occur. Thus, these forces may combine to lead individuals in groups to make more extreme decisions than the individuals would make on their own. After reading about polarization the faith we place in groups as the best means of avoiding poor decisions may be somewhat shaken. Now you are in a position to decide whether or not you think group decision making leads the Supreme Court to

make more extreme decisions than would the individual judges.

Minority Influence

When groups make decisions or solve problems, they often adopt decision-making strategies, such as "majority rules." These strategies are sometimes adopted formally, but in many cases they arise spontaneously. For instance, most juries employ an implicit rule specifying that unless two thirds of the jury initially vote for a verdict of guilty, then the defendant will be acquitted. Generally, the majority rules in group decision making, but it is possible for members who are in the minority to exert some influence. If you found yourself in the minority in a group to which you belonged, how could you have the greatest impact on the majority?

In *social impact theory* it is argued that the same factors affecting the impact of the majority on a minority also affect the impact of the minority on the majority (85). In both cases, the impact depends on the *strength* (power, status, expertise, and the like), the *immediacy* (closeness in space or time), and the *number* of people holding a given position. Thus, a majority that is powerful, present, and large is likely to be very persuasive.

In groups that are making decisions, the minority is by definition smaller than the majority, and thus is numerically weak. Since in small groups the minority is usually present, its immediacy is high and cannot be increased further. Therefore, about the only way a minority can increase its influence is to increase its strength. Indeed, it has been found that a high-status minority member is more persuasive than a low-status one (86). But because one's diffuse statuses (social class, sex, age) are relatively fixed, they too cannot be altered easily. So, can a minority do anything to increase its strength and thus its influence? Yes, there appear to be two mechanisms.

The first mechanism is to present consistent and confident opposition to the majority. A consistent minority has a greater impact on the majority than an inconsistent one (87). For instance, in one study, a majority was confronted by a minority maintaining that a series of blue-green slides should be labeled as green. More members of the majority came to agree these slides should be labeled as green when the minority was consistent (called all the slides "green") than when it was inconsistent (called only two thirds of the slides "green") (88). Why does a consistent minority have a strong impact on the majority? One reason is a deviant minority threatens the cohesiveness of the group, so the group may make concessions to maintain harmony (89). In maintaining consistency, the minority should try to avoid appearing rigid or dogmatic (90).

The second mechanism a minority can use to increase its strength is to initially conform to the majority and then move away from it on the critical issue (91). Initially conforming to the majority increases the chances the minority will be taken seriously when it later deviates from the group. When the minority does deviate, this causes the majority to question its own position, and the result of this questioning may be a shift toward the minority's position. For this strategy to work, the minority must be perceived as high on the specific status characteristic of competence. Suppose two highly respected community leaders who have been elected to the school board deeply desire to introduce a new elementary school curriculum as the primary item on their agenda. They know the remaining board members are not very enthusiastic about their ideas. Their best strategy may be to go along with the majority on all of the issues of less importance to them and then to place their prestige and accumulated credit on the line as they consistently advocate their position on the new curriculum.

The members of a deviant minority are usually disliked, even when they are successful in influencing the majority (92). The threats to cohesion and the uncertainty produced by the minority apparently create negative feelings that are directed at the minority group members. As a result, greater minority influence is often purchased at the price of being disliked.

In our discussion of group performance and group dynamics, we have focused primarily on groups in which the members have equal status. In many groups, status hierarchies exist where the leader plays a particularly important role in the dynamics and productivity of the group. We turn next to a discussion of leadership. The practical importance of one type of leadership role is illustrated in Box 14-3.

LEADERSHIP

Imagine your favorite leader. Why do you think this person is effective? If you are like most people, you will respond to this question by thinking about the traits he or she possesses.

One of our favorite leaders was Mahatma Gandhi, the man who led India to independence (96). Certainly Gandhi possessed a singular personality. His self-discipline was extraordinary. He worked 18 to 20 hours a day, spent an hour a day spinning cloth, brushed his teeth for 15 minutes a day, was a strict vegetarian, possessed no worldly goods, answered every bit of his voluminous correspondence, and was celibate after the age of 35. He was a fanatic about cleanliness in a notoriously unclean country, and he was self-confident almost to the point of arrogance. Gandhi had a finely honed moral sense that guided his behavior. He could be more stubborn than anyone you can imagine; yet he was also kind, giving, creative, and funny.

Were these the traits that made Gandhi a great leader—someone who commanded the obedience of millions and the respect even of his enemies? One might well ask how these traits were translated into action. What does a great leader like Gandhi do that causes others to follow him? This question raises the issue of styles of leadership, the techniques that leaders use to exert influence over others. Here, too, we find Gandhi was unusual. He often made decisions himself, without consulting his followers. He fasted to punish his followers for disobeying him. Although Gandhi was in constant conflict with the British, he never advocated the use of aggression against his enemies. Instead, he sought suffering at

BOX 14·3

The Use of Groups to Resolve Conflicts

Can knowledge of group dynamics help solve conflicts that arise between nations? Groups of researchers from Harvard, Yale, and London have attempted to reduce international conflicts by bringing together members of the conflicting parties in a neutral setting with a third-party leader (93). In the *first* stage the participants begin by defining the conflict. In the *second* stage, they talk about the nature of conflict in general and their conflict in particular. In the *third* stage, options for resolving the conflict are discussed. In the *fourth* stage, one of four options may be pursued: create new options, attempt an actual solution, redefine the conflict, or gather more information and start through the process again. Typically, the goal is to manage the conflict, rather than to eliminate it completely.

The leader establishes the ground rules and the conditions that will lead to de-escalation of the conflict. The leader also attempts to extend the range of options being considered and to present the conflict as a problem to be solved, and not a contest to be won. The leader tries to create a norm of analytical processing of the psychological and sociological aspects of the conflict. This emphasis on analysis is balanced by a norm that permits expressiveness. The participants are free to express the full intensity of their feelings, hopes, anxieties, and definitions of national identity (94).

the hands of his enemies as a way of demonstrating the moral superiority of his cause.

Indisputably Gandhi was charismatic. His followers were willing to follow him to their deaths. He asked for, and received, commitments from them to undergo unlimited suffering. He inspired in them a vision of what could be and provided them with a pathway, the practice of nonviolent protest, of getting there. He was revered almost as a god.

Are these universal traits of leaders? Certainly not. But undeniably they were effective for Gandhi. Ask yourself if Gandhi's techniques would be effective in other situations. For instance, is this the way the chief executive officer of a large corporation should run his or her business? Could the president of your student senate employ these techniques? Obviously,

Gandhi's techniques were uniquely suited to his situation. He faced a militarily superior enemy and his "army" consisted largely of unarmed illiterate peasants. It is doubtful that Gandhi's nonviolent techniques would work against a repressive dictator like Hitler. However, against an enemy that had a long tradition of parliamentary democracy and a free press, Gandhi's techniques of moral persuasion may have been the only tactics that could have succeeded.

Gandhi's case illustrates the complexity of understanding leadership. The leader's personality, behavioral style, the nature of the followers, and the situation are all important. In our discussion of leadership, we will first discuss the research on leadership traits; we then cover research on behavioral styles; next we discuss a specific situational

The leader helps the participants engage in role-taking so they can see how the other side views itself and the issues involved. Information processing by group members often mirrors the broader conflict, pointing to ways the group members' interactions reflect intergroup perceptions and expectations. Focusing on the way each side views itself and understands its actions facilitates the discussion of realistic future courses of action because the group members must take the views of both sides into consideration. The ultimate goal is for the participants to feed new ideas, changed perceptions and attitudes, and innovative proposals to government decision makers.

In 1979, just a year before Israel and Egypt established normal diplomatic relations for the first time in their histories, a group such as those described above met to discuss the conflict between Israelis and Egyptians (95). The discussants were members of the elites of the two countries and the group was led by American leaders. The Israeli participants discovered that for the Egyptians the autonomy of the Palestinians was a central issue, while the Egyptians learned that normalization of relations was the central issue for the Israelis. The Israelis argued that if a Palestinian state were created it would reduce their security as a nation, while the Egyptians countered that security for Israel could only occur if the Arabs accepted Israel and this acceptance would hinge on autonomy for the Palestinians. Both groups agreed on the importance of ending the Arab-Israeli conflict and on the right of self-determination for the Palestinians, but they disagreed on whether the latter could be reconciled with issues of security and acceptance. Obviously, the conflict was not resolved in this one meeting, but it did provide the participants with useful information that could be used to further the cause of peace. ∎

context (bureaucracies), and finally we deal with the relationships among personality, behavioral styles, and situational factors.

Leadership Traits

The oldest approach to understanding leadership focuses on the traits of leaders. Most of the research on the personality traits of leaders has found only weak relationships between traits and effective leadership. One summary indicates that effective leaders tend to be somewhat higher in achievement needs, power needs, self-confidence, motivation, originality, and stress tolerance than less-effective leaders (97). One surprising finding in many studies is that

intelligence is not closely related to successful leadership (98). In one study the correlation between intelligence and the performance of platoon sergeants was $-.02$ (99).

The absence of a relationship between intelligence and performance can be understood by examining situations where intelligence does, or does not, make a difference (100). Under conditions of stress, such as those occurring in combat, intelligence tends to be unrelated to performance, apparently because such traits as decisiveness are more important or because under stress even intelligent people do not function well. In nonstressful situations, intelligence *is* related to performance, *if* the leader is directive *and* has the support of the group. In other words, for intelligence to matter the leader must actively use it, and the group must be willing to follow the leader.

A particularly intriguing study using the trait approach to leadership was conducted on political leaders (101). Personality tests were given to over 2,000 political officials in the United States. Overall, the officials were higher than the national average on the traits of self-confidence, dominance, and achievement orientation, just as earlier studies of leadership have found. Republican leaders were higher than Democratic leaders in personal adjustment, needs for order, and self-control. Democrats were higher than Republicans on self-assurance, independence, and needs for change. These differences between Republicans and Democrats, which have been relatively constant over a 16-year-period, seem to fit reasonably well with the respective emphasis of the two parties on conservatism and liberalism. This study shows that even for political leaders, the traits associated with successful leadership depend to some extent on the social situation in which the leaders are working.

One reason why the research on leadership has not been particularly successful in identifying the traits of leaders is that this research typically focuses on large numbers of people in leadership positions (platoon sergeants). While these people *occupy* leadership roles, that alone does not necessarily make them good leaders. A better approach to studying the traits of leaders may be to focus on leaders who are unusually successful.

Recently there has been renewed interest in studying one type of highly successful leader— *charismatic* leaders. The nineteenth century German sociologist Max Weber was among the first to discuss the characteristics of charismatic leaders. Weber used the term charismatic leader to refer to self-appointed leaders whose followers were in distress and believed the leader was extraordinarily qualified to solve their problems (102). In religious leaders these extraordinary qualities were considered to be divine in origin; in military leaders, they consisted of extraordinary strength or heroism; and in political leaders, extraordinary wisdom or vision. Weber regarded charismatic leaders as spontaneous and creative, capable of inspiring in their followers the great sacrifices required to bring about revolutions.

As the concept of charisma evolved to fit into modern contexts, its meaning has changed somewhat. Another well-known sociologist, Edward Shils, has more recently emphasized the capacity of charismatic leaders to inspire awe and reverence in followers (103). According to Shils, the charismatic leader embodies the core values of human existence and thus is less of a revolutionary figure than in Weber's conception. Shils also argued that charismatic leadership can emerge in normal times, as well as distressed times. Hence, Shils's idea of charisma can apply to strong industrial or political leaders and to leaders of small groups, not just to leaders of major social changes. Charismatic leaders provide a vision of the future to their followers that promises a better life (104). They often ask for, and receive, undivided loyalty as they inspire supreme efforts from their followers.

The traits thought to be associated with such "normal" charisma are dominance, self-confidence, need for influence, and strong convictions (note that these traits describe Gandhi quite well). The research that has been done to test for the personality traits associated with charisma is largely supportive (105). One study compared charismatic presidents of the United States (Lincoln, Roosevelt, Kennedy) with noncharismatic presidents and found the former group to be higher in needs for achievement and power (106). Similar traits characterize successful business leaders (107). A well-known example of a charismatic business leader is Lee Iacocca who almost singlehandedly brought Chrysler Corporation back from the brink of bankruptcy to become a profitable business again. Chrysler was clearly in distress so the situation was ripe for a charismatic leader. Iacocca succeeded by convincing its suppliers, employees, the U.S. government, and its shareholders to forestall their immediate self-interest in the pursuit of the higher goal of saving the company (108).

Behavioral Style

Early work by Robert Bales uncovered two basic leadership styles, one oriented toward the task and the other oriented toward socioemotional relations with their followers (109). The *task leader* contributes ideas to the group, seeks and gives information and opinions, coordinates group activity, energizes the group, and evaluates group performance. The *socioemotional leader* gives praise, mediates conflicts, encourages participation, and provides feedback to the group on group processes. In informal groups, these roles are often assumed by different people; but in formal task groups, with an elected or assigned leader, the two roles must often be performed by one person. Most studies of behavioral styles have investigated how these and other styles are combined within a given individual (see Box 14-4).

Building on the work of Bales, a group of investigators at Ohio State University examined the degree to which leaders are task oriented versus people oriented (their term for socioemotional leadership) (111). In a study of foremen at International Harvester, the foremen who were people oriented had few grievances filed by employees and had low turnover rates, while foremen who were task oriented had many grievances filed and high turnover rates (112). Although this study and others show that these two dimensions of behavioral style are related to worker satisfaction, neither style is consistently related to performance (113).

Another set of leadership styles closely related to people-oriented and task-oriented styles is *democratic* versus *autocratic* leadership. The democratic style is people oriented because it invites group participation in decision making, while the autocratic style is more task oriented because it involves the leader making decisions for the group. Not surprisingly, people tend to prefer democratic to autocratic leadership styles; but again, neither style produces consistently superior performance (114).

Studies of the personality traits and behavioral styles of effective leaders generally pay only limited attention to the situational contexts in which the leaders operate. In some situations the traits and style of the leader are clearly important, but other situations are so powerful the traits and style of the leader are not especially important. One of the earliest approaches to understanding leadership fo-

cused on a very powerful and very common type of organizational context—bureaucracies.

Bureaucracies

Max Weber was also a pioneer in the study of bureaucracies (115). Bureaucracies have existed almost since the dawn of civilization. Both the ancient Chinese and the Roman systems of government were largely bureaucratic. Bureaucracies have flourished in modern industrial societies because they are a relatively efficient means of large scale administration. Bureaucratic organizations comprise a hierarchical network of positions. The duties, responsibilities, and privileges of each position are clearly specified. People are hired on contracts for fixed salaries, and they do not own the organizations for which they work.

In bureaucratic organizations the attributes of individuals matter very little, provided they possess the skills necessary to do their jobs. People become like cogs in a large machine, and like cogs they can be easily replaced, especially if they occupy lower positions in the hierarchy. Workers are expected to owe their allegiance to the organization, not to individuals within it. Promotion is based on merit, and the criteria are objectively specified. Many government civil service jobs are essentially bureaucratic in nature.

The role of leaders in bureaucracies is extremely limited. Their duties, too, are clearly specified and their power is severely limited, particularly the power to change the organization. They have the power to hire, promote, and dismiss subordinates, but even for these administrative functions, the rules and norms must be obeyed. Like followers, leaders are expected to be loyal to the organization and not encourage loyalty to themselves among their subordinates. Bureaucratic leaders help to maintain the structure of the organization, facilitate internal communication, and design jobs and tasks. Since working conditions, standards of performance, and even grievance criteria are all standardized, little room exists for creative leadership. Formal training is likely to be required for upper level positions in a

BOX 14-4

SYMLOG (The Analysis of Group Interaction)

SYMLOG is a coding system that can be used to analyze interactions occurring in group contexts (110). SYMLOG stands for "a *System* for the *Multiple Level Observation* of *Groups*." Using this system, every behavior by the participants in a group is coded into 1 of 26 basic categories. The coding scheme contains three dimensions: friendly-unfriendly, dominant-submissive, and instrumentally controlled-emotionally expressive.

The most important behaviors related to task and socioemotional leadership are the instrumentally controlled and emotionally expressive categories. Instrumentally controlled behaviors are task oriented. They include serious efforts at problem solving such as trying to understand, assess, or diagnose the problem. Emotionally expressive behaviors are often directed away from the task. They include expressing desires to change from work to play or expressing emotions that distract the group from the task. Examples of instrumentally controlled behaviors and expressive behaviors combined with the friendly-unfriendly and dominant-submissive dimensions are found below.

Category	Example
Instrumentally controlled, Friendly, Dominant	Takes initiative in helping the group on the task confronting it
Instrumentally controlled, Friendly, Submissive	Admits responsibility for disapproved behavior
Instrumentally controlled, Unfriendly, Dominant	Tries to take control arbitrarily and shows disapproval
Instrumentally controlled, Unfriendly, Submissive	Attempts to shame others by acting overworked
Emotionally expressive, Friendly, Dominant	Gives reward
Emotionally expressive, Friendly, Submissive	Asks for special attention
Emotionally expressive, Unfriendly, Dominant	Attacks authority
Emotionally expressive, Unfriendly, Submissive	Expresses a desire to withdraw as a sign of rejection

bureaucracy. However, experience in the bureaucracy and knowledge of the organization's goals and practices are the most valuable characteristics of effective bureaucratic managers. The personality traits of bureaucratic managers are largely irrelevant. That is why you will sometimes hear people use the term "faceless bureaucrat" to describe managers in bureaucracies.

Up to this point we have considered the trait approach to leadership as exemplified by the idea of charisma, the behavioral styles of leaders as exemplified by task-oriented versus people-oriented leadership styles, and the situational approach as exemplified in bureaucracies. Each approach has strengths and weaknesses, but a general dissatisfaction with all of them has led to the emergence of approaches to leadership combining all three of these narrower approaches.

To illustrate how important the simultaneous consideration of the traits, leadership style, and situational context are, think about the difference between a tank commander and a leader of the local March of Dimes campaign. On the field of battle, an authoritarian leadership style is probably most effective. Quick decisions must be made, and they must be obeyed faithfully or the lives of the entire group will be endangered. In contrast, leaders of the March of Dimes are most likely to be effective if they are able to enlist voluntary help. They have little real power and probably will be most effective if they function democratically, involving as many people in the decision-making process as possible. Speed and obedience are less important to them than motivation. However, in both cases we might expect a touch of charisma to be useful.

Transactional Theories of Leadership

One of the best-known multifaceted approaches to leadership is called *transactional leadership* (116). Transactional theories of leadership examine the explicit and implicit exchanges or bargains leaders strike with their followers to accomplish the goals of the group. Thus, these theories trace their origins to exchange theories. Transactional theories are based on the idea that follower motivation is a product of the followers' expectations that task effort will yield intrinsic rewards (satisfaction in a job well done) and extrinsic rewards (money, recognition). The leaders' role is to structure the rewards to maximize their followers' performance. They must also provide support, direction, and motivation. In the pursuit of these goals the leaders may have to clarify the followers' roles, arrange the work setting, provide the needed resources for good performance, as well as make rewards dependent on performance. Ultimately, it is the leaders' task to help their followers fulfill their own needs, including affiliation, achievement, and power. Thus, this is a theory that recognizes the crucial role relationship between leaders and followers. There can be no leaders without followers and vice versa; the two roles are complementary.

This view of leaders requires them to be flexible and inventive. They must diagnose what is needed in a given situation and tailor their behavior to the needs of followers in that situation. For instance, *supportive* leadership is most effective in situations where followers are dissatisfied, frustrated, bored, or under stress—a common occurrence in many industrial settings (117). In these situations leaders who are helpful and provide guidance can be very effective. In situations where the followers face complex, ambiguous tasks requiring frequent problem solving, *participative* leadership is most successful. A team of lawyers working on a complicated criminal case might benefit from this approach. The leader needs to structure the situation so that the lawyers exchange information on different facets of the case in a way that enables each of them to participate. Otherwise, the team members risk being uninformed on some aspects of the case. In situations where the tasks are informal and nonroutine, and roles are nonspecialized, *directive* leadership is most successful (118). If you really want your friends to attend a particular movie, you may have to take control of the group to direct it to your goal. Transactional theories, then, propose that the type of leader behavior that is called for depends on the situation.

The complexity of putting the transactional theories into practice is obvious. It demands a proper diagnosis of what type of leadership is needed in a given situation, and that the leader possess the necessary skills to adopt the appropriate leadership style.

■
SUMMARY

Groups consist of two or more people who influence one another. We discussed four types of groups: primary, formal task, informal, and aggregates. Primary groups, such as the family, consist of close social groups that provide people with emotional support. Formal task groups have defined roles and norms, but informal groups do not. Aggregates are composed of people who are in the same place at the same time, but may have nothing else in common.

There are three basic types of structures within groups. First are structures based on the distribution of power in the group. Power may be based on reward, punishment, legitimate status, expertise, attraction, or information. Second, communication structures show who communicates with whom. For simple problems, centralized networks are more efficient than decentralized networks, but the opposite is true for complex problems. Communication tends to flow horizontally and upward in hierarchical networks. Third, attraction structures, called sociograms, outline the likes and dislikes among the members of a group. Rewards, similarity, proximity, status, and participation in the group all affect sociometric choices.

Group performance is largely determined by the nature of the group's task. On additive tasks, in which each person's effort is combined with the efforts of others, groups are superior to individuals; but, as group size increases, each member tends to contribute less (unless the members' contributions can be identified). On relatively simple disjunctive tasks, in which there is only one right answer, groups also outperform individuals. However, large groups are superior only because, as group size increases, the chances that one person will be able to solve the problem also increase. On more difficult dis-

junctive problems, groups may perform worse than the best member of the group due to process loss. On conjunctive tasks, in which the group is only as good as its worst member, low-ability people work harder than high-ability people (the converse is true for disjunctive tasks). On complementary tasks, in which the members combine their diverse abilities, groups often perform better than individuals.

People tend to perform well-learned behaviors (dominant responses) better in the presence of others than they would alone, but they perform worse on novel or poorly learned behaviors in the presence of others. The social facilitation effect of the presence of others may be due to arousal created by alertness, the association of the presence of others with rewards and punishments, or the distraction created by attending to the audience as well as to the task.

Cohesiveness consists of the forces that bind a group together. It is high in groups that meet the members' needs and have members who cooperate with one another and in groups that compete against other groups. Highly cohesive groups expect the members to conform to the group's norms, and they tend to reject deviants. They also tend to be more productive than groups that are not cohesive, unless one of the group's norms is low productivity.

Group decisions are generally more extreme than the decisions of individuals because groups pool the arguments in favor of the decision the majority of their members individually prefer. Also, when members compare their opinions to those of the other group members, they often find support for their positions and become more extreme in the direction favored by the group.

A minority can maximize its influence by consistently and confidently opposing the majority on a given issue. A competent minority can also be influential by conforming to the majority on some issues and opposing the majority only on issues of critical importance. Members of a deviant minority are often disliked, even when they are influential.

The traits associated with effective leadership include high achievement and power needs, self-confidence, motivation, originality, and stress tolerance. Charismatic leaders, those possessing extraordinary abilities and who inspire awe in their followers due to their vision of the future, are often especially effective. Socioemotional leaders are usually liked better than task leaders; but neither type of leadership style consistently leads to greater productivity. Successful bureaucratic leaders possess high levels of experience and training, but their particular personality traits do not appear to be important.

Recent theories of leadership suggest that the leader's behavior must be suited to the needs of the subordinates and the structure of the situation.

■

REFERENCES

1. Woodward, B. and S. Armstrong, 1979, *The Brethren: Inside the Supreme Court,* New York: Simon & Schuster.
2. Simmel, G., 1905, *Conflict and the Web of Group Affiliation,* K. H. Wolf and R. Bendix (Eds.), New York: The Free Press, 1955.
3. Cooley, C. H., 1909, "Primary Group and Human Nature," in J. G. Manis and B. N. Meltzer (Eds.), *Symbolic Interaction: A Reader in Social Psychology,* 2d ed., Boston: Allyn & Bacon, 1970.
4. Cooley, C. H., 1912, *Social Organization,* New York: Scribner's.
5. Bates, A. P. and N. Babchuck, 1961, "The Primary Group: A Reappraisal," *Sociological Quarterly* 2: 181–191.
6. Wirth, L., 1938, "Urbanism as a Way of Life," *American Journal of Sociology* 44: 1–24.
7. Acock, A. C., J. J. Dowd, and W. L. Roberts, 1974, *The Primary Group: Its Rediscovery in Contemporary Sociology,* Morristown, NJ: General Learning Press.
8. Whyte, W. F., 1943, *Street Corner Society,* Chicago: University of Chicago Press.
9. Thompson, H., 1966, *Hell's Angels,* New York: Ballantine, p. 20.
10. Whyte, 1943, op. cit., p. 256.
11. Thompson, 1966, op. cit., p. 35.
12. Thompson, 1966, ibid., p. 95.
13. Whyte, 1943, op. cit., p. 168.
14. Thompson, 1966, op. cit., p. 101.
15. Mitchell, J. C., 1973, "Networks, Norms, and Institutions," in J. Boisserain and J. C. Mitchell (Eds.), *Network Analysis: Studies in Human Interaction,* Paris: Mouton & Co.
16. Cartwright, D. and A. Zander, 1968, *Group Dynamics,* New York: Harper & Row.
17. French, J. R. P. and B. H. Raven, 1959, "The Bases of Social Power," in D. Cartwright (Ed.), *Studies in Social Power,* Ann Arbor: University of Michigan Press; T. Litman-Adizes, B. H. Raven, and G. Fontaine, 1978, "Consequences of Social Power and Causal Attribution for Compliance as Seen by Powerholder and Target," *Personality and Social Psychology Bulletin* 4: 260–264.
18. Sheley, K. and M. E. Shaw, 1979, "Social Power: To Use or Not to Use?" *Bulletin of the Psychonomic Society* 13: 251–260.
19. Leavitt, H. J., 1951, "Some Effects of Certain Communication Patterns on Group Performance," *Journal of Abnormal and Social Psychology* 46: 38–50; M. E. Shaw, 1964, "Communication Networks," in L. Berkowitz (Ed.), *Advances in Experimental Social Psychology,* Vol. 1, pp. 111–147.
20. Kano, S., 1977, "A Change of Effectiveness of Communication Networks under Different Amounts of Information," *Japanese Journal of Experimental Social Psychology* 17: 50–59.
21. Shaw, 1981, op. cit.
22. Rice, L. E. and T. R. Mitchell, 1973, "Structural Determinants of Individual Behavior in Organizations," *Administrative Science Quarterly* 18: 56–70.
23. Ridgeway, C. L., 1983, *The Dynamics of Small Groups,* New York: St. Martin's.
24. Blau, P. M. and W. R. Scott, 1962, *Formal Organizations: A Comparative Approach,* San Francisco: Chandler Publishing; D. C. Barnlund and C. Harland, 1963, "Propinquity and Prestige as Determinants of Communication Networks," *Sociometry* 26: 467–479; P. H. Bradley, 1978, "Power, Status, and Upward Communication in Small Decision-making Groups," *Communication Monographs* 45: 33–43.
25. Back, K. W., L. Festinger, B. Hymovitch, H. H. Kelley, S. Schachter, and J. W. Thibaut, 1950, "The Methodology of Studying Rumor Transmission," *Human Relations* 3: 307–362; P. V. Crosbie, 1975, *Interaction in Small Groups,* New York: Macmillan; M. M. Riley, R. Cohn, J. Toby, and J. W. Riley, Jr., 1954, "Interpersonal Orientations in Small Groups: A Consideration of the Questionnaire Approach," *American Sociological Review* 19: 715–724; J. I. Hurwitz, A. F. Zander, and B. Hymovitch, 1968, "Some Effects of Power on the Relations among Group Members," in D. Cartwright and A. Zander, op. cit.
26. Kelley, H. H., 1951, "Communication in Experimentally Created Hierarchies," *Human Relations* 4: 39–56; Crosbie, 1975, op. cit.
27. Sherif, M. and C. W. Sherif, 1969, *Social Psychology,* New York: Harper & Row.
28. Crosbie, 1975, op. cit.
29. Festinger, L., S. Schachter, and K. Back, 1950, *Social Pressures in Informal Groups,* New York: Harper & Row.
30. Hurwitz, Zander, and Hymovitch, 1968, op. cit.; H. H. Jennings, 1950, *Leadership and Isolation: A Study of Personality in Interpersonal Relations,* 2d ed., New York: McKay; R. H. Turner, 1964, *The Social Context of Ambition,* San Francisco: Chandler Publishing.
31. Bales, R. F., 1965, "Task Roles and Social Roles in Problem

Solving Groups," in I. D. Steiner and M. Fishbein (Eds.), *Current Studies in Social Psychology,* New York: Holt, Rinehart, & Winston; A. Bavelas, A. H. Hastorf, A. E. Gross, and W. R. Kite, 1965, "Experiments on the Alteration of Group Structure," in D. Cartwright and A. Zander, op. cit.

32. Hirsh, B. J., 1981, "Social Networks and the Coping Process," in B. H. Gottlieb, *Social Networks and Social Support,* Beverly Hills: Sage.

33. Gottlieb, B. H., 1981, "Social Networks and Social Support in Community Mental Health," in B. H. Gottlieb, op. cit.; S. Cohen and S. L. Syme (Eds.), 1985, *Social Support and Health,* Orlando, FL: Academic Press; D. Riley and J. Eckenrode, 1986, "Social Ties: Subgroup Differences in Costs and Benefits," *Journal of Personality and Social Psychology* 51: 770–778.

34. Berkman, L. F. and S. L. Syme, 1979, "Social Networks, Host Resistance, and Mortality: A Nine-year Followup Study of Alameda County Residents," *American Journal of Epidemiology* 109: 186–204; L. F. Berkman, 1985, "The Relationship of Social Support to Morbidity and Mortality," in S. Cohen and S. L. Syme, op. cit.

35. Hansell, S., "Adolescent Friendship Networks and Distress in School," *Social Forces* 63: 698–715.

36. DiMatteo, M. R. and R. Hays, 1981, "Social Support and Serious Illness," in B. H. Gottlieb, op. cit.

37. Hirsh, B. J., 1980, "Natural Support Systems and Coping with Major Life Changes," *American Journal of Community Psychology* 8: 159–172; B. L. Wilcox, "Social Support in Adjusting to Marital Disruption: A Network Analysis," in B. H. Gottlieb, op. cit.

38. Chesler, M. A. and O. A. Barbarin, 1984, "Dilemmas of Providing Help in a Crisis: The Role of Friends and Parents of Children with Cancer," *Journal of Social Issues* 40: 113–134.

39. Kessler, R. C., J. D. McLeod, and E. Wetherington, 1988, "The Costs of Caring: A Perspective on the Relationship between Sex and Psychological Distress," in I. G. Sarason and B. R. Sarason (Eds.), *Social Support: Theory, Research, and Application,* The Hague: Martinus Nijhof.

40. Kiecolt-Glaser, J. K., R. Glaser, E. Shuttlesworth, C. S. Dyer, P. Ogrocki, and C. E. Speicher, (1987), "Chronic Stress and Immunity in Family Caregivers of Alzheimer's Disease Victims," *Psychosomatic Medicine* 49: 523–535; R. Schulz, C. A. Tompkins, D. Wood, and S. Decker, 1987, "The Social Psychology of Caregiving: Physical and Psychological Costs of Providing Support for the Disabled," *Journal of Applied Social Psychology* 17: 401–428.

41. Latané, B., 1981, "The Psychology of Social Impact," *American Psychologist* 36: 343–356; W. Moede, 1927, "Die Richtlinien der Leistungs-psychologie," *Industrielle Psychotechnik* 4: 193–207.

42. Latané, 1981, op. cit.

43. Williams, K., S. Harkins, and B. Latané, 1981, "Identifiability as a Deterrent to Social Loafing: Two Cheering Experiments," *Journal of Personality and Social Psychology* 40: 303–311.

44. Zaccaro, S. J., 1984, "Social Loafing: The Role of Task Attractiveness," *Personality and Social Psychology Bulletin* 10: 269–274.

45. Hill, G. W., 1982, "Group versus Individual Performance: Are N + 1 Heads Better Than One?" *Psychological Bulletin* 94: 517–539.

46. Hill, 1982, op. cit.; Shaw, 1981, op. cit.

47. The first husband and wife cross the river and she stays while he returns to pick up the second husband and wife. The second wife is left with the first wife on the other side of the river and the two men return. The first husband drops off the second husband and then he rows the third husband and wife to the other side where the third wife is left with the other two. The first and third husbands then row back to pick up the second husband.

48. Laughlin, P. R. and J. Adamopoulos, 1982, "Social Decision Schemes on Intellective Tasks," in H. Brandstatter, J. H. Davis, and G. Stocker-Kreichgauer (Eds.), *Group Decision Making,* London: Academic Press.

49. Shaw, 1981, op. cit.

50. Kerr, N. L. and S. E. Bruun, 1983, "Dispensability of Member Effort and Group Motivation Losses: Free-rider Effects," *Journal of Personality and Social Psychology* 44: 78–94.

51. Hill, 1982, op. cit.

52. Hill, 1982, op. cit.; R. E. Slavin, 1979, "Effects of Biracial Learning Teams on Cross-racial Friendships," *Journal of Educational Psychology* 71: 381–387.

53. Zajonc, R. B., 1965, "Social Facilitation," *Science* 149: 269–274; R. B. Zajonc, 1980, "Compresence," in P. B. Paulus (Ed.), *Psychology of Group Influence,* Hillsdale, NJ: Lawrence Erlbaum.

54. Sanders, G. S., 1981, "Driven by Distraction: An Integrative Review of Social Facilitation Theory and Research," *Journal of Experimental Social Psychology* 17: 227–251.

55. Sanders, G. S., R. S. Baron, and D. L. Moore, 1978, "Distraction and Social Comparison as Mediators of Social Facilitation Effects," *Journal of Experimental Social Psychology* 14: 291–303.

56. Baron, R. S., 1986, "Distraction-Conflict Theory: Progress and Problems," in L. Berkowitz (Ed.), *Advances in Experimental Social Psychology,* Vol. 20, New York: Academic Press.

57. Ridgeway, 1983, op. cit.

58. Steiner, I. D., 1972, *Group Process and Productivity,* New York: Academic Press.

59. Dion, K. L., 1979, "Intergroup Conflict and Intragroup Cohesiveness," in W. G. Austin and S. Worchel (Eds.), *The Social Psychology of Intergroup Relations,* Monterey, CA: Brooks/Cole.

60. Stein, A. A., 1976, "Conflict and Cohesion: A Review of the Literature," *Journal of Conflict Resolution* 20: 143–172.

61. Durkheim, E., 1897, *Suicide: A Study in Sociology,* New York: The Free Press.

62. Cartwright and Zander, 1968, pp. 139–151, op. cit.; Shaw, 1981, op. cit.

63. Wyer, R. S., 1966, "Effects of Incentive to Perform Well, Group Attraction, and Group Acceptance on Conformity in a Judgmental Task," *Journal of Personality and Social Psychology* 4: 21–26.

64. Thibaut, J. W. and H. H. Kelley, 1959, *The Social Psychology of Groups,* New York: Wiley.

65. Schachter, S., 1951, "Deviation, Rejection, and Communication," *Journal of Abnormal and Social Psychology* 46: 190–207.

66. Hare, A. P., 1976, *Handbook of Small Group Research,* New York: The Free Press; Shaw, 1981, op. cit.

67. Schreisheim, J. F., 1980, "The Social Context of Leader-Subordinate Relations: An Investigation of the Effects of Group Cohesiveness," *Journal of Applied Psychology* 65: 183–194; S. Seashore, 1954, *Group Cohesiveness in the Industrial Work Group,* Ann Arbor, MI: Institute for Social Research.

68. Kett, J. F., 1977, *Rites of Passage: Adolescence in America 1790 to Present,* New York: Basic Books.

69. Williams, R. M., Jr., 1984, "Field Observations and Surveys in Combat Zones," *Social Psychology Quarterly* 47: 186–192.

70. Schachter, S., N. Ellertson, D. McBride, and D. Gregory, 1951, "An Experimental Study of Cohesiveness and Productivity," *Human Relations* 4: 229–238.

71. Grench, J. R. P., Jr., 1941, "The Disruption and Cohesion of Groups," *Journal of Abnormal and Social Psychology* 36: 361–377.

72. Lott, A. J. and B. E. Lott, 1961, "Group Cohesiveness, Communication Level, and Conformity," *Journal of Abnormal and Social Psychology* 62: 408–412.

73. Shaw, M. E. and L. M. Shaw, 1962, "Some Effects of Sociometric Grouping upon Learning in a Second Grade Classroom," *Journal of Social Psychology* 57: 453–458.

74. Myers, D. G. and H. Lamm, 1976, "The Group Polarization Phenomenon," *Psychological Bulletin* 83: 602–627.

75. Lamm, H. and D. G. Myers, 1978, "Group-induced Polarization of Attitudes and Behavior," in L. Berkowitz (Ed.), *Advances in Experimental Social Psychology,* Vol. 11, New York: Academic Press.

76. Stoner, J. A. F., 1961, "A Comparison of Individual and Group Decisions Involving Risk," unpublished M. A. thesis, Massachusetts Institute of Technology.

77. Moscovici, S. and M. Zavalloni, 1969, "The Group as a Polarizer of Attitudes," *Journal of Personality and Social Psychology* 12: 125–135.

78. Burnstein, E. and A. Vinokur, 1977, "Persuasive Argumentation and Social Comparison as Determinants of Attitude Polarization," *Journal of Experimental Social Psychology* 13: 315–332.

79. Judd, B., Jr., 1975, "Information Effects in Group Shift," unpublished M.A. thesis, University of Texas at Arlington.

80. Kaplan, M. F., 1978, "Group Discussion Effects in a Modified Jury Decision Paradigm: Informational Influences," cited in Lamm and Myers, 1976, op. cit.

81. Festinger, L., 1954, "A Theory of Social Comparison Processes," *Human Relations* 7: 117–140.

82. Sanders, G. and R. S. Baron, 1977, "Is Social Comparison Irrelevant for Producing Choice Shifts?" *Journal of Experimental Social Psychology* 13: 303–314.

83. Myers, D. G., 1982, "Polarizing Effects of Social Interaction," in H. Brandstatter, J. H. Davis, and G. Stocker-Kreichgauer (Eds.), *Group Decision Making,* New York: Academic Press.

84. Goethals, G. R. and M. P. Zanna, 1979, "The Role of Social Comparison in Choice Shifts," *Journal of Personality and Social Psychology* 37: 1469–1476; D. Isenberg, 1986, "Group Polarization: A Critical Review and Meta-analysis," *Journal of Personality and Social Psychology* 50: 1141–1151.

85. Latané, B. and S. Wolf, 1981, "The Social Impact of Majorities and Minorities," *Psychological Review* 88: 438–453.

86. Wolf, S., 1985, "Majority and Minority Influence: A Social Impact Analysis," in M. P. Zanna, J. M. Olson, and C. P. Herman (Eds.), *Social Influence: The Ontario Symposium,* Vol. 5, New York: Lawrence Erlbaum.

87. Moscovici, S. and C. Nemeth, 1974, "Social Influence II: Minority Influence," in C. Nemeth (Ed.), *Social Psychology: Classic and Contemporary Integrations,* Chicago: Rand McNally.

88. Moscovici, S., E. Lage, and M. Naffrechaux, 1969, "Influence of a Consistent Minority on the Responses of a Majority in a Color Perception Task," *Sociometry* 32: 365–379.

89. Wolf, S., 1979, "Behavioral Style and Group Cohesiveness as Sources of Minority Influence," *European Journal of Social Psychology* 9: 381–395.

90. Nemeth, C. J., 1986, "Intergroup Relations between Majority and Minority," in S. Worchel and W. G. Austin, *Psychology of Intergroup Relations,* Chicago: Nelson-Hall.

91. Bray, R., D. Johnson, and J. Chilstrom, Jr., 1982, "Social Influence by Group Members with Minority Opinions: A Comparison of Hollander and Moscovici," *Journal of Personality and Social Psychology* 43: 78–88; E. Hollander, 1958, "Conformity, Status, and Idiosyncracy Credit," *Psychological Review* 65: 393–404; J. M. Levine, L. Saxe, and H. J. Harris, 1976, "Reaction to Attitudinal Deviance: Impact of Deviate's Direction and Distance of Movement," *Sociometry* 39: 97–107.

92. Levine, J. M., 1980, "Reaction to Opinion Deviance in Small Groups," in P. B. Paulus, op. cit.; C. Nemeth, 1979, "The Role of an Active Minority in Intergroup Relations," in W. G. Austin and S. Worchel, op. cit.

93. Burton, J. W., 1972, "Resolution of Conflict," *International Studies Quarterly* 16: 41–52; L. W. Doob, 1976, "A Cyprus Workshop: Intervention Methodology during a Continuing Crisis," *Journal of Social Psychology* 98: 143–144; H. C. Kelman and S. P. Cohen, 1979, "Reduction of International Conflict: An Interactional Approach," in W. G. Austin and S. Worchel, op. cit.; H. C. Kelman and S. P. Cohen, 1986, "Resolution of International Conflict: An Interactional Approach," in W. G. Worchel and S. Austin, ibid.; B. J. Hill, 1982, "An Analysis of Conflict Resolution Techniques," *Journal of Conflict Resolution* 26: 109–138.

94. Kelman and Cohen, 1979, op. cit.

95. Cohen, S. P. and E. E. Azar, 1981, "From War to Peace: The Transition between Egypt and Israel," *Journal of Conflict Resolution* 25: 87–114.

96. Erikson, E. H., 1969, *Gandhi's Truth: On the Origins of Militant Nonviolence,* New York: W. W. Norton; L. Fischer, 1954, *Gandhi: His Life and Message for the World,* New York: New American Library.

97. Yukl, G. A., 1981, *Leadership in Organizations,* Englewood Cliffs, NJ: Prentice-Hall.

98. Stogdill, R. M., 1974, *Handbook on Leadership: A Survey of Theory and Research,* New York: The Free Press.

99. Fiedler, F. E. and J. E. Garcia, 1987, *New Approaches to Leadership,* New York: Wiley.

100. Fiedler and Garcia, 1987, op. cit.

101. Constantini, E. and K. H. Craik, 1980, "Personality and Politicians: California Party Leaders, 1960–1976," *Journal of Personality and Social Psychology* 38: 641–661.

102. Weber, M., 1947, *The Theory of Social and Economic Organization,* New York: Oxford University Press.

103. Shils, E., 1965, "Charisma, Order, and Status," *American Sociological Review* 30: 199–213.

104. Fiedler, F. E. and R. E. House, 1988, "Leadership Theory and Research: A Report of Progress," in *Reviews of Industrial Organizational Psychology,* New York: Wiley.

105. Bass, B. M., 1985, *Leadership and Performance Beyond Expectations,* New York: The Free Press; R. J. House, 1988, "Exchange and Charismatic Theories of Leadership," in G. Reber (Ed.), *Encyclopedia of Leadership;* B. J. Smith, "An Initial Test of a Theory of Charismatic Leadership Based on the Responses of Subordinates," cited in House, ibid.

106. House, 1988, ibid.; Woyck and Fodor, cited in Fiedler and House, 1988, op. cit.

107. McClelland, D. C. and R. E. Boyatzis, 1982, "Leadership Motive Pattern and Long-term Success in Management," *Journal of Applied Psychology* 67: 737–743.

108. Bass, 1985, op. cit.

109. Bales, R. F., 1950, "A Set of Categories for the Analysis of Small Group Interaction," *American Sociological Review* 15: 257–263.

110. Bales, R. F., 1979, *Symlog,* New York: The Free Press.

111. Fleishman, E. A., 1957, "A Leader Behavior Description for Industry," in R. M. Stogdill and A. E. Coons (Eds.), *Leader Behavior: Its Description and Measurement,* Columbus: Bureau of Business Research, Ohio State University; J. K. Hemphill and A. E. Coons, 1957, "Development of the Leader Behavior Description Questionnaire," in R. M. Stogdill and A. E. Coons, ibid.; Stogdill, 1974, op. cit.

112. Fleishman, E. A. and E. F. Harris, 1962, "Patterns of Leadership Behavior Related to Employee Grievances and Turnover," *Personnel Psychology* 15: 43–56; E. W. Skinner, 1969, "Relationships between Leadership Behavior Patterns and Organizational-Situational Variables," *Personnel Psychology* 22: 489–494.

113. Stogdill, 1974, op. cit.

114. Locke, E. A. and D. M. Schweiger, 1978, "Participation in Decision-making: One More Look" in B. M. Staw (Ed.), *Research in Organizational Behavior,* Greenwich, CT: J. A. I. Press; Shaw, 1981, op. cit.

115. Weber, 1947, op. cit.

116. House, R. J. and T. R. Mitchell, 1974, "A Path-Goal Theory of Leadership," *Journal of Contemporary Behavior* 3: 81–97; House, in press, op. cit.

117. House, 1988, ibid.; House and Mitchell, 1974, op. cit.

118. House, 1988, op. cit.; House and Mitchell, 1974, op. cit.

CHAPTER 15

Intergroup Relations

The Historical Approach to Intergroup Relations
Internal Colonialism
Assimilation and Acculturation
Blau's Macrosocial Theory of Structural Assimilation
Institutional Racism
Reactions to Minority Status
Cognitive Processes That Contribute to Prejudice and Stereotyping
Categorization
Perceptual Assimilation and Contrast
The Principle of Least Effort
The Norm of Ingroup-Outgroup Bias
The Ultimate Attribution Error
Ethnocentrism
Ambivalent Attitudes and Polarized Responses
Reducing Prejudice and Stereotyping
The Contact Hypothesis
The Effects of Desegregation
The Jigsaw Classroom
Reducing Intergroup Ignorance
Other Techniques

Can you identify the years when these incidents took place or the groups that were involved?

- The president of the United States orders the armed forces to be integrated.

- Two hundred thousand members of this group, many of them U.S. citizens, are shipped to a foreign country against their will by order of the U.S. government because their labor is not needed in this country.

- The U.S. Congress outlaws discrimination on the basis of race, creed, or national origin.

- In Miami a jury finds 4 white policemen innocent in the beating death of a black insurance agent, triggering a riot in which 18 people are killed and $200 million in property damage is done.

- Martin Luther King Jr. is assassinated.

- One hundred thousand members of this group, most of them U.S. citizens, are forced from their homes and placed in virtual prisons for two years without due process of law. Their property is confiscated and never returned.

- The U.S. Supreme Court rules that separate schools for blacks and whites cannot be equal and orders that America's schools be desegregated with "all deliberate speed."

- During this decade 32 blacks are lynched by mobs of angry whites.

These landmark incidents in intergroup relations in America concern the triumphs and tragedies of our complex interracial society. Over 40 years ago Gunnar Myrdal wrote that we were caught in what he called "The American Dilemma" (1). Myrdal said that there was a fundamental contradiction in American race relations—a contradiction between America's dedication to a democratic creed in which we profess that all people are created equal and the actual prejudice and discrimination directed toward minority groups. This dilemma is still with us today.

(Answers: 1948; Mexican-Americans; 1964; 1980; 1968; Japanese-Americans; 1954; 1940s)

Figure 15.1 ■

Median Income by Race and Sex (1985)

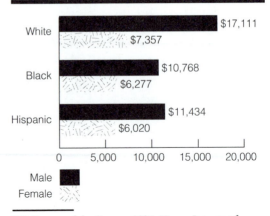

U.S. Bureau of the Census, 1987, *Money Income of Households, Families, and Persons in the United States: 1985.* Washington, DC: U.S. Department of Commerce.

As a case in point consider the situation of blacks in America (see Figure 15-1). In 1959, the average black family was earning only 52 percent of the average income of white families. Although this figure improved to 64 percent by 1970, it fell back to 56 percent by 1987. Similarly, 55 percent of blacks were below the poverty line in 1959, but this figure had been reduced to 30 percent by 1973. However, the figure rose to 33 percent in 1987 (2). Black teenagers were eight times as likely as white teenagers to be unemployed during the 1970s. In 1987, 35 percent of blacks aged 16–19 were unemployed (3). The degree of residential segregation was nearly as great in the 1970s as it was after World War II (4), although more recently there has been greater integration in some large cities such as Dallas, Jacksonville, and Richmond (5). The gap between whites and blacks in infant mortality rates changed little from the 1950s to the 1970s (6): In 1986, the infant mortality rate for blacks was almost twice as high as for whites (7). About half the percentage of blacks attend college as whites (8). These dismal statistics amply illustrate that discrimination is still with us.

In this chapter we explore the origins of prejudice and discrimination and some of the techniques that have been employed to reduce them. We begin by addressing two questions: What are prejudice and, its fellow traveler, stereotyping? What causes them? After defining prejudice and stereotyping and discussing the importance of understanding them, we will address the origins of real and perceived differences between groups.

Prejudice may be defined as a negative attitude toward a socially defined group. *Stereotypes* consist of the sets of traits attributed to socially defined groups. There are several reasons why the study of prejudice and stereotyping is important. First, prejudice and stereotypes lead to *discriminatory* behavior—unequal treatment based on group membership. Second, the prejudices and stereotypes of one person influence the attitudes of other ingroup members through socialization processes, persuasion, identification, compliance, and conformity. Third, the prejudices and stereotypes of one person may also influence the behavior of outgroup members. They may respond by acting in ways that are consistent with the stereotypes held about them, or they may feel compelled to act in ways that contradict the stereotypes. Fourth, prejudice and stereotypes affect the outgroup members' evaluations of themselves because they are an important type of reflected appraisal.

THE HISTORICAL APPROACH TO INTERGROUP RELATIONS

Prejudice and stereotyping evolve from past contact between groups. A clear example of the ways in which the historical conditions of contact have shaped relations and perceptions between groups started with the arrival of blacks in this country in 1619. Blacks were brought to America to serve as a source of cheap manual labor. The differences in physical appearance between blacks and whites made it easier for whites to maintain them in a subordinate position. The institution of slavery created a relationship characterized by only two roles: master and slave. Two inevitable consequences of these roles were whites' judgment of blacks as inferior, and their negative stereotyping of blacks.

Because slaves were forced to work under the threat of punishment and there were few incentives for hard work, slaves generally worked as little as possible. As a result, whites regarded blacks as lazy, not recognizing that the institutionalized role relationships of master and slave caused blacks to act in this way. Slave owners did little or nothing to educate their slaves. In fact, educating blacks was illegal in every state in the South before the Civil War. Because slaves were uneducated, they were regarded as unintelligent—but again the cause was slavery. Black slaves were provided with the most minimal maintenance: poor housing, poor clothes, and poor food. Whites came to regard blacks as dirty, seemingly unaware that they created the conditions that led them to this conclusion. Blacks were kept in a totally dependent condition and whites came to think of them as being in a perpetual state of childhood (this is the origin of the deep resentment the term "boy" causes in black men). Because slaves were often punished for showing anger or resentment, they learned to hide their emotions. This led white slave owners to regard blacks as being content with their lot (9).

In these and other ways the role relations between blacks and whites shaped the views that each group held of the other. The processes operating in relations between blacks and whites also explain the formation of other stereotypes. Stereotypes emerge from specific types of role relations in societies around the world (10). For instance, manual laborers are generally regarded as strong, stupid, pleasure-loving, and lacking in foresight, while businessmen are regarded as grasping, haughty, cunning, and domineering. Upper-class people are seen as intelligent, ambitious, progressive, and neat, while lower-class people are seen as ignorant, lazy, dirty, and happy-go-lucky. Thus, economic relations between groups create stereotypes. These stereotypes are usually associated with specific groups, as was the case with blacks under slavery, but they really have little to do with the actual nature of the groups. Any group occupying a given role will receive the stereotype associated with the role. Had whites been the slaves and blacks the masters, the stereotypes would have been reversed!

Internal Colonialism

Robert Blauner has offered the provocative thesis that the black experience in America is a form of colonialism. He calls it *internal colonialism* (11). He further suggests that this concept can be applied to other nonwhite groups in America, especially Native American Indians and Mexican-Americans. Internal colonialism is a variant of classic colonialism. The classic forms of colonialism had three primary characteristics.

First, there is the forced subjugation of one group by another. Typically, the dominant group comes from the outside and invades another group's territory, as was done in the United States to Native American Indians by European whites. Second, in colonial societies the subordinate group is restricted in its economic and political development and in freedom of movement. Blacks in America were deprived of their freedom through slavery. The third characteristic of colonialism is the transformation or destruction of the subordinate group's values and customs. The Africans who were brought to America as slaves were from diverse ethnic backgrounds. Upon their arrival, they were often systematically separated and forced to speak English. Thus, the experience of blacks in America was similar in two important respects to classic colonialism, but it differed in one respect because blacks were brought to America and subjugated, rather than being the resident population.

Blauner argues that the experiences of nonwhite racial groups differed markedly from the experiences of white ethnic minorities in America. Integration into the social system of the dominant group was more available to the Irish, German, Polish, Italian, Swedish, and other European ethnic groups than to nonwhites. In part this was true because once the members of these groups acquired the language and basic social customs of the dominant group, they

were no longer distinguishable. Also, the European ethnic groups were not oppressed to the same degree as the nonwhite racial groups. One reason for this was that the cultural differences between the European groups and the white majority were not as great as between African groups and the white majority. The European groups continued to practice their religions, and they retained their family systems and many of their unique cultural practices. In addition, they were free to move from place to place to better their conditions. The process of absorption into American society has been much more rapid for the European ethnic groups than it has been for nonwhite groups because the barriers have not been as great. In many cases, the former immigrants have become members of the white majority, an option that has been unavailable to nonwhites.

Assimilation and Acculturation

For many years America was viewed as a melting pot to which various countries contributed ingredients that would eventually combine into a thoroughly blended stew. While some ethnic groups have been absorbed into the core white Anglo-Saxon Protestant (WASP) culture, many continue to retain a firm sense of subcultural uniqueness. To capture these differences Milton Gordon has suggested a distinction between assimilation and acculturation. *Assimilation* occurs when a subcultural group is so totally absorbed into the core culture that it ceases to exist as a subculture (12). It participates in all aspects of national life (political, economic, recreational, and the like), does not suffer discrimination, ceases to maintain separate cultural practices, intermarries freely, identifies with the society as a whole, and adopts the cultural practices of the core group.

Acculturation is less total than assimilation. It involves adjusting to the core group's cultural practices without yielding a sense of the separate identity of one's own group. An acculturated group is likely to adopt the language of the core group and to participate in economic and political institutions. However, it retains a sense of separate identity and some, if not all, of its cultural practices (for example, religion), its members probably will not intermarry freely with members of the core culture, and it may be involved in conflict with the core group or other subcultural groups.

Acculturation occurs more rapidly than assimilation. As each new ethnic group arrived in America, it was forced to become acculturated in some degree simply to survive. Assimilation was another matter. The core group in America resisted the assimilation of nonwhite groups. Many subcultural groups, both white and nonwhite, have resisted assimilation. The fact that we still speak of groups such as Japanese-Americans, Polish-Americans, Mexican-Americans, Irish Catholics, Jews, blacks, and Native Americans indicates that these subcultural groups have not been entirely assimilated.

The term *ethnic pluralism* has been used to explain the continued existence of identifiable ethnic groups in America. Ethnic pluralism implies many groups coexisting in a pot that is sometimes gently bubbling and is sometimes boiling violently, the ingredients of which may never result in a completely blended stew. It implies that separate groups coexist and interact with one another in a process that includes not only acculturation of the minority groups to the majority, but also includes the ways in which the majority group changes as a result of contact with the minority racial and ethnic groups. For example, many ethnic foods, such as pizza, egg rolls, and tacos, have entered the national culture and are eaten by members of nearly all ethnic groups. Similarly, American English has absorbed words from many foreign languages.

Let's examine a specific example to put flesh on the abstract bones of these concepts. The nation's second largest minority consists of Hispanics. This ethnic group is diverse, containing Puerto Ricans, Cubans, Dominicans, Central Americans, Mexicans, and immigrants from other Latin American countries. We will focus primarily on the largest subgroup, Mexican-Americans. Like every other ethnic group, Mexican-Americans have a unique history that has shaped their relations to other groups. Despite this uniqueness, the experience of Mexican-Americans can be understood within the context of theories concerning internal colonialism and assimilation (13).

In 1803, the nations of Mexico and the United States became neighbors as a result of the Louisiana Purchase. At this time Mexico occupied much of what is now Texas, New Mexico, Arizona, Colorado, and California. A period of protracted conflict ensued as Americans began to settle on Mexican land. These regional conflicts culminated in a war between Mexico and the United States in 1846. As a consequence of the Treaty of Guadalupe Hidalgo (1848), Mexico ceded what is now the American Southwest to the United States. Thus, just as has often occurred in traditional colonialism, the Mexicans in this area became a subordinate ethnic group through conquest.

Beginning about 1900, Mexican nationals began to immigrate to the United States in increasing numbers. From 1920 to 1930 nearly three quarters of a million legal immigrants entered the United States from Mexico. This transformed the Mexican-American subculture. It no longer consisted primarily of people who lived on land that had become part of the United States. Now, the majority of Mexican-Americans had chosen to come to America, as had so many European ethnic groups.

In the Southwest, Mexican-Americans were often treated in ways that were more similar to the treatment of blacks than the treatment of European ethnic groups. They were generally regarded as inferior by Anglo-Americans. They were segregated in separate neighborhoods and schools, and attempts were made to limit their cultural practices. For instance, Mexican-American students were often forbidden to speak Spanish at school, even on the playground. A clear indication of the marginal status occupied by Mexican-Americans was the attempt to deport them during the Great Depression. At this time there was little need for their labor, so large numbers (200,000 during 1931) were shipped to Mexico without regard to their wishes or legal status as citizens of the United States.

Mexican-Americans have resisted assimilation more effectively than many other groups. Mexican-Americans in the Southwest have retained a strong and distinctive culture. This may be due in part to the proximity of Mexico, a close link to the mother culture that is unavailable to other immigrants. As

■ *The residues of racism. Many Mexican-Americans are still left out of the American mainstream. Most field workers are neither acculturated nor assimilated. (WGS)*

recently as 1970, over 90 percent of a sample of Mexican-Americans in San Antonio, Texas, said they were more comfortable speaking Spanish than English (14). This indicates a greater degree of independence from the Anglo-American majority than has been displayed by most other American minority groups. Perhaps the ultimate index of assimilation is intermarriage with the dominant group. The rate of outgroup marriage among Mexican-Americans has increased throughout this century, but is still rather low (under 30 percent in most cities, although there is considerable variability) (15). The independence of Mexican-Americans is consistent with the idea that many colonized peoples, while they may become acculturated, tend to resist assimilation.

On the other hand, there is considerable evidence that Mexican-Americans have been assimilated into American society, at least in some respects. Since 1950, Mexican-Americans have moved steadily out of lower-prestige occupations and into higher-

prestige white-collar and professional occupations (16). In 1960, the average income of Hispanic men was 63 percent of the income of white men, but by 1976 this figure had increased to 72 percent (17). During this same period, the educational attainment of Mexican-Americans has also increased. For instance, in 1950 Mexican-Americans born to parents who were also born in the United States averaged 7.1 years of education. By 1970 this figure had risen to 10.4 years (18). Because public education is one of the primary ways in which ethnic minority groups are socialized into the dominant culture, these increasing levels of education indicate an ever-increasing degree of assimilation during the post-World War II period. Mexican-Americans have increasingly moved into residential neighborhoods that were previously predominantly white, indicating a substantial degree of assimilation into white neighborhoods (19). However, one study found that the level of segregation in Chicago was still considerably higher for Mexican-Americans than for the Irish, Norwegians, and Swedes (20). Thus, assimilation occurred, but not to the same degree as for these European ethnic groups.

Mexican-Americans fit the colonialism model in the sense that their lands were occupied by outside forces, they were treated as inferior, and attempts were made to destroy some aspects of their cultural heritage. Mexican-Americans show some indications of acculturation and assimilation into the core group, as evidenced by upward occupational mobility, increasing educational attainment, and decreased segregation. The assimilation of Mexican-Americans, however, has not been total as shown by the high level of retention of the Spanish language and other cultural practices, as well as the low level of intermarriage and high level of segregation of Mexican-Americans, compared to European ethnic groups. Mexican-Americans appear to fit the cultural pluralism model about as well as any ethnic group in America. They are acculturated without being fully assimilated. They have retained their own cultural heritage; at the same time they have become increasingly successful in American society.

Blau's Macrosocial Theory of Structural Assimilation

As America has changed, new theories have been developed to deal with the growing complexity of our intergroup relations. One such theory has been developed by Peter Blau (21). Blau argues that for much of our history the degree of overlap among the various dimensions of social structure (social class, religion, ethnicity) in our society was fairly limited and relatively stable. For instance, there was a racial status hierarchy in which white people occupied a higher status than nonwhites and this status hierarchy corresponded pretty closely to the social class hierarchy (most whites were of a higher social class than nonwhites). Similarly, there were few nonwhites who were Catholic or Jewish; memberships in racial and religious groups did not overlap. Group boundaries including ethnicity, race,

religion, and social class were maintained by residential segregation. This meant there was relatively little contact between members of different racial, religious, and social class groups.

Over time this pattern changed so that there were members of all social classes within every ethnic group and religion. For example, by the third generation after immigration, most ethnic groups were indistinguishable from the white Anglo-Saxon majority in social class (the exceptions being Hispanics and blacks) (22). Residential segregation by religion and ethnicity, and to a limited degree by race, also began to disappear. Religious boundaries started to fade. More and more contact occurred between groups that had previously had little contact. For instance, middle class blacks interacted with middle class whites in their jobs and Eastern European Jews interacted with Norwegian Protestants and Irish Catholics in their suburban neighborhoods. The overlap between social categories increased. People therefore became less dependent on the groups to which they belonged and did not feel such strong bonds connecting them to any one of their groups.

The result of the increasing overlap between dimensions of social structure has been more intergroup friendships and marriages, not only across racial and ethnic lines, but across religious and social class lines as well (23). One reason rates of intermarriage increased is that people who differ on one dimension, say religion, may be similar on other dimensions, such as social class and race, and the similarities are strong enough to override the differences. The children of these intermarriages, including interethnic marriages (24), usually do not identify themselves as being from either of their parents' groups, which further erodes group boundaries. Viewed from the perspective of this theory, our society is becoming less rigidly defined in terms of group memberships (less pluralistic) and the groups are blending together just as the melting pot metaphor suggested they would. The principal exception to this general trend is that there continues to be a strong correspondence between race and social class—most blacks are still poor and black

BOX 15-1

Institutional Racism and Japanese-Americans

The history of Japanese-Americans during this century provides many examples of institutional racism (26). Around 1900 the news media in California ran anti-Japanese campaigns featuring headlines like, "The Japanese Invasion, The Problem of the Hour" and "The Yellow Peril—How Japanese Crowd out the White Race." Also during this period, civic organizations (for example, the Asiatic Exclusion League), labor unions, and even the American Socialist Party fought against the entry of Japanese into the United States.

In 1905, the California legislature asked Congress to restrict Japanese immigration, a movement that succeeded in 1920. Every year for the next 40 years anti-Japanese legislation was considered by the California legislature. In 1909, attempts were made by the California legislature to prevent Japanese-Americans from acquiring title to land. Japanese immigrants were ruled ineligible for citizenship in a Supreme Court decision in 1924. As these few facts make clear, Japanese-Americans suffered discrimination at the hands of a variety of institutions, including state and national governmental bodies, civic organizations, labor unions, political parties, and the media.

The low point in the treatment of Japanese-Americans came during World War II. After the attack on Pearl Harbor in 1941, Japanese-Americans were increasingly mistrusted by members of the dominant majority. In particular, the military was concerned that Japanese-Americans might engage in espionage or sabotage. In 1942,

and white interracial marriage is less common than other types of interethnic marriage.

Institutional Racism

We have demonstrated that historical processes created institutionalized relationships among racial and ethnic groups. These institutional arrangements often begin with the ethnic groups being cast in a single occupational role, such as Asian-Americans who built railroads in the West, Mexican-Americans who worked in agriculture, Vietnamese who worked as fishermen, and, of course, blacks who were forced to work the land in the South. These institutionalized occupational arrangements influenced intergroup relations in educational, religious, recreational, economic, and political institutions. One legacy of these historical relations between groups is *institutional*

over 100,000 Japanese-Americans, the majority of whom were American citizens, were forced from their homes and relocated in primitive camps in remote areas of the United States. Their property and land were confiscated, and often they were given little time to abandon their homes. They remained in these camps until the camps were declared illegal in 1944. Why was this done? An American general explained:

In the war in which we are now engaged racial affinities are not severed by migration. The Japanese race is an enemy race. . . . Along the Pacific Coast over 112,000 potential enemies, of Japanese extraction, are at large today. There are disturbing indications that these are organized and ready for concerted action at a favorable opportunity. The very fact that no sabotage has taken place to date is a disturbing indication that such action will be taken.   General John L. Dewitt (27).

Thus, a large group of Americans was arrested and imprisoned by their own government because of their race. In contrast, nothing similar happened to American citizens of German or Italian descent, although the United States was also at war with Germany and Italy. The most likely explanation is that Americans of Italian and German descent are racially and culturally similar to the rest of the white majority, whereas Japanese-Americans are racially and culturally different from the white majority.

In spite of the institutional racism that has been historically directed at them, Japanese-Americans are an American success story. Even during the dark days of World War II Japanese-American men joined the armed forces in such great numbers many had to be turned away and they fought so valiantly that their regiment was among the most decorated in the entire army (28). Earlier, we noted that by the third generation most ethnic groups were similar to the white majority in social class. By the third generation, Japanese-Americans actually exceeded the white majority in average earnings (29), although this was due partly to the fact that Japanese-Americans have been concentrated in a state (California) where high wages are paid (30). Japanese-Americans now have the highest average level of education of all the ethnic groups in the United States. (31) ■

racism—discrimination against racial groups by social institutions including economic, political, and educational institutions (see Box 15-1) (25).

Traditional institutional racism was overt and blatant. Before the presidential decree integrating the armed forces in 1948, the Supreme Court decision on school desegregation in the *Brown* v. *Board of Education* (1954) case, and the Civil Rights Act of 1964, segregation between blacks and whites was a matter of law. Blacks could not go to the same hotels as whites, nor could they go to the same restaurants or bars, or use the same toilets or drinking fountains. They could not vote and they were not even allowed to sit with whites in the gallery of the U.S. Senate. This constituted blatant institutional racism. After 1964, institutional racism was no longer backed by the force of law, and the practices that maintained it declined. In fact, over

■ *From 1942 to 1944, a large group of Americans was arrested and imprisoned by their own government because of their race. Although the U.S. was also at war with Germany and Italy, only Japanese-Americans were singled out. Why do you think this was so? (See Box 15-1.) (Special Collections Division, University of Washington Libraries. Negative No.: UW 526.)*

time the institutional racism that was overtly directed at many minority groups became more covert and subtle. In recent years the people who engage in racial discrimination often do not do so intentionally.

Even equal opportunity employers may engage in discrimination in spite of their intentions. Due to past discrimination, blacks and members of other minority groups are less able than members of more advantaged groups to acquire the credentials required for entry into the professions and other white-collar jobs. They are not rejected by employers because they are black (or Mexican-American, and so on), but because they are "unqualified." However, they are "unqualified" because they and many others of their ethnic heritage are lower class, and they are lower class because of past discrimination (32). The gatekeepers who maintain this type of institutional racism often are not racists in their own personal attitudes. Yet, these personnel directors, admissions officers, and employers sometimes act in discriminatory ways.

In some cases, discrimination is intentional, but it is subtle. A study of the real estate industry provides an example (33). As part of this study, one black couple and one white couple of similar economic background and qualifications visited 97 real estate brokers in Detroit. The black couple was less likely to be shown houses on the first visit; cheaper houses were recommended to the black couple; and the houses the black couple were shown tended to be in or near black neighborhoods. Also, the brokers spent less time with the black couple than with the white couple.

In this study, the black couple was not turned away by the brokers nor were they treated discourteously, but they were still subjected to discrimination. Another example is provided by professional sports. In spite of the changes that have occurred in sports with respect to the number of minority athletes who participate in them, minority groups are underrepresented at the managerial level—although there are a few prominent exceptions (see Box 15-2).

There are four possible relationships between prejudice and discrimination. First, people with negative attitudes toward minority groups (prejudiced people) may intentionally act in discriminatory ways. This appears to be true of some white real estate brokers. Second, people who are not prejudiced may unintentionally act in discriminatory ways. This could occur when professors who are considering applicants for medical school find that few black applicants have the qualifications they would like, so the black applicants are rejected. Third,

■ *The military was the first U.S. social institution to be integrated (1948), and it remains among the most integrated today. (WGS)*

prejudiced people sometimes do not act in discriminatory ways. This could occur when a prejudiced personnel officer hires whites and minority group members at equal rates because he or she is implementing an affirmative action program. Fourth, non-prejudiced people often act in nondiscriminatory ways.

Reactions to Minority Status

How do minority groups react to the discrimination and prejudice directed toward them? James Vander Zanden believes they react by accepting their status, working toward assimilation, avoiding the majority group, or responding aggressively (34). Every minority group displays some combination of these four reactions. Blacks in the South before World War II had little choice but to accept their subordinate status, for even the laws were stacked against them. *Acceptance* is usually accompanied by a conscious resignation or a sense of futility about changing the status of one's group. Acceptance is frequently followed by *assimilation*.

European ethnic groups characterize the reaction of assimilation. The Italians, for instance, in the first stages after immigration formed "little Italys" and created Italian-American immigrant mutual aid societies as a way of coping with their problems. But by the early 1900s they had started the upward climb into the middle class. Over time, the patriarchal Italian family gave way to more democratically oriented family interactions. Marriage ages rose, the use of birth control increased, and parents were less likely to choose their children's marital partners. These and other Italian customs gave way to American practices on the pathway to assimilation.

Avoidance can be seen in separatist movements such as Zionism, the Black Muslims, the Mormon's flight to Utah, and the ghost dance movement among Native American Indians. In the late 1800s Native Americans were confined to reservations. During the 1890s Wovoka, a Paiute Indian, had a vision that all the whites would perish and the Indians would be restored to their former glory. The movement he started centered around the ghost dance in which people danced themselves into a trance state. In

BOX 15-2

Institutional Racism in Sports Management

Sports fans: Ask yourselves how much things have changed since the following broadcast.

"Jackie Robinson broke the color barrier in baseball in 1946, and in that same year two other blacks, Bill Willis and Marion Motley, started playing football for the Cleveland Browns. Since the 1940s, the number of black athletes in professional sports has increased dramatically. By 1960, about 20 percent of the players in the NFL were black; now blacks make up almost 50 percent of professional football players, about 60 percent of professional basketball players, and 30 percent of major league baseball players.

"These are impressive numbers. It is no wonder that sports is sometimes held up as one place where blacks have overcome prejudice. But the problem goes beyond being an athlete. Blacks are overrepresented as players, but they are still underrepresented in leadership positions. You would expect that, as the number of black players and the number of good black players has increased, the number of black coaches and managers would increase, but it hasn't. It doesn't work that way for blacks; it doesn't work that way for minorities. It doesn't now and it never has. There are about 280 assistant coaches in the NFL, but in the last 20 years only about 20 blacks have been chosen as assistant coaches. Right now, there are no black head coaches, no black offensive or defensive coordinators, no black general managers, no blacks in the NFL Management Council, no blacks in policy-making positions in the NFL office, and, of course, there are no black owners. Right now, being a black player is a dead-end in football.

"There are qualified blacks. I know any number of former players who have the skill and who want to coach, but who just can't get the opportunity. The problem is racism. Some of the racism is the obvious kind. There are people who just won't promote blacks. Not everybody, but it is there. And there are more subtle barriers, also. Maybe the biggest problem is a kind of institutionalized racism in the NFL. Coaching is a fraternity. Once you get in, you stay in. The problem is that the people who are in are mostly white. There are not many black coaches and new ones can't get in. It's subtle, but discrimination in its subtle forms is still discrimination. The intent doesn't really matter." (Alan Page, former defensive tackle for the Minnesota Vikings and member of the Pro Football Hall of Fame, National Public Radio Broadcast, 1982) ■

anticipation of the coming cataclysm, Native Americans were encouraged to return to their former lifestyles and turn away from white ways—and for a time many did.

In some instances avoidance leads to a violent aggressive reaction to subordination. An *aggressive* reaction to subordination can be seen in the more violent phases of the black protest movement of the 1960s. The goal of this movement was to modify the social system that oppressed blacks, but its means sometimes became violent. In the summers of 1964 to 1968 major riots took place in New York, Los Angeles, Cleveland, Newark, Detroit, and Washington D.C. Many of those in 1968 were triggered by the assassination of Martin Luther King Jr. In the Newark, Los Angeles, and Detroit riots over 100 lives were lost and upwards of $350 million in property damage occurred.

During the course of their history in the United States many groups displayed more than one of these reactions to subordination. Currently trends toward both assimilation and separatism can be found in most groups. Only the future will tell which of these opposing trends will prevail.

■ COGNITIVE PROCESSES THAT CONTRIBUTE TO PREJUDICE AND STEREOTYPING

The historical approach to intergroup relations provides valuable insights into the origins of the status differences of various groups in the United States, the transitions through which they have passed in adapting to one another, and the views that they have of one another. The macrosocial orientation of the historical approach provides an essential backdrop for understanding the context in which intergroup interactions occur. In the following section we will adopt a more microsocial approach to intergroup relations starting with an analysis of the ways in which our interactions with other people

are affected by the groups to which they and we belong. We will pay particular attention to the cognitive thought processes that affect intergroup interactions.

Categorization

People have an almost overwhelming tendency to categorize other people. Upon meeting new people, we may place them into categories based on their race, sex, age, level of physical attractiveness, some aspects of their physical health (for example, a handicap), and social class or occupational information (quality of clothing, a uniform). When they speak, we may obtain additional information that allows us to categorize them further on the basis of ethnic background, social class, intelligence, and social skills. Why do we categorize others? One reason is that categorizing others helps to bring order out of chaos. The social world would be exceedingly complex if we did not attempt to simplify it by putting people into categories.

Categorizing others also enables us to make decisions about interacting with them. For instance, if you know that the person to whom you are talking is a member of a sorority, then you may feel you know something about the kind of people she knows and what her interests are. Categorizing others into social groups seems to provide us with information about their backgrounds and characteristics. This facilitates social interaction when the information associated with the social category is correct, but can create problems when the information is wrong. For instance, as was pointed out in Chapter 6, many stereotyped traits attributed to women such as being more nurturant, dependent, and empathic than men are wrong and basing one's behavior on these stereotypes can cause difficulties.

When people categorize others, they employ a set of criteria to define group membership. For instance, in categorizing a person as a criminal, an elderly person, a Catholic, or an Indonesian, information is needed respectively on the person's police record, age, frequency of church attendance and type of church attended, or nation of birth and

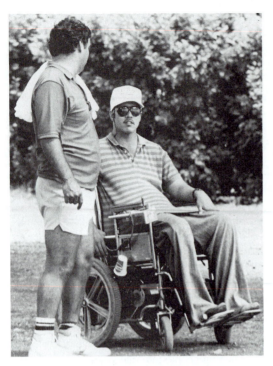

■ *Social categories affect our perception and treatment of others. (WGS)*

current citizenship. The pieces of information needed to place someone into a category are called the *defining features* of the category (35).

Nearly all social categories have additional features associated with them. Typically, these additional features consist of personality traits. We do not expect all members of the category to possess the related traits, but we expect many members to possess them. These features are called *characteristic features* and they form the basis of stereotypes. For example, the stereotype of people who are over-weight is that they are lazy, weak, talkative, warm-hearted, old-fashioned, sympathetic, good-natured, agreeable, dependent, and trusting (36). The defining features for members of this group consist of weight in relation to height, while the characteristic features consist of the set of personality traits that allegedly indicate what overweight people are like (for a diagram of one group see Figure 15-2).

When we categorize a person into a social group the associated stereotype and feelings toward the group become readily accessible to our minds. The stereotyped traits associated with the category create expectations concerning how the other person will behave. These expectations, in turn, influence our perceptions and our behavior (see Chapter 9). In a study illustrating this process, white students thought a black debater who lost a debate was less competent than a white debater who lost if another white referred to blacks with a pejorative label before the debate (37). The black debater was not negatively evaluated if no negative remark was made or if he won. The negative label apparently triggered a negative expectation concerning blacks that was then used to explain the black debater's behavior when it confirmed the expectancy.

Perceptual Assimilation and Contrast

Social categories are formed on the basis of some type of similarity among members of the categories. Consider the category of disabled people. People in this category are similar in that they are all handi-capped in some way. When this group label is used, differences among members of this group are less relevant than the fact that they are handicapped. The process of categorizing people on the basis of perceived similarity generally leads to an overesti-mation of the degree of similarity that actually exists among members of the labeled group. For instance, handicapped people are thought to be more similar to one another than they actually are. This tendency is referred to as *perceptual assimilation,* which should be distinguished from cultural assimilation, covered earlier in this chapter.

A second consequence of categorization is that differences between groups are overestimated. This phenomenon is referred to as the *contrast* effect. Evidence from several studies indicates that in the absence of information to the contrary, outgroup members are perceived to hold beliefs that are dissimilar to those held by ingroup members. Thus, nonhandicapped people think that differences be-tween themselves and the handicapped are greater than they actually are.

■ *Although there is a stereotype for people who are overweight, we do not expect all overweight people to possess the stereotyped traits. Would you be likely to attribute any of the traits mentioned in the text to this person? (WGS)*

Figure 15.2 ■

Schematic Diagram of Information Associated with the Category of Male

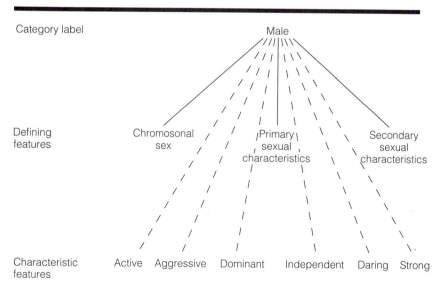

In a study of assimilation and contrast effects, students rated slides of paintings by Klee and Kandinsky without knowing which painter had done the paintings (38). Afterward, the students were told that they consistently preferred the paintings of either Klee or Kandinsky. Next, the students were asked to predict the beliefs of people who preferred Klee and Kandinsky. The students thought that other students who preferred the same painter as they did also would have beliefs similar to theirs (assimilation), but that the beliefs of people who preferred the other painter would be different from theirs (contrast). Since people tend to dislike others who are dissimilar to them (see Chapter 11), assimilation and contrast promote prejudice.

Perceptual assimilation and contrast interfere with our ability to see the differences that actually exist among group members. The operation of assimilation can be seen in a study where students were asked to view a discussion among a mixed group of blacks and whites (39). When these students were later asked to recall who said what, they were reasonably good at recalling the race of the person who made each suggestion, but they made errors in trying to recall which member of the racial group made which suggestion. Students could not recall the differences among people (due to assimilation), but instead recalled only their social group. In other studies people often have been found to have greater difficulty recognizing the faces of outgroup members than of members of their own group (40). This suggests that assimilation effects may be stronger for outgroups than for ingroups (41).

To an ingroup member, the members of an outgroup really may all look alike. In a well-publicized example of this perceptual problem, Lenell Geter, who is black, was identified by five eyewitnesses as the person who had robbed a Dallas area restaurant. Three of the eyewitnesses were Hispanic and two were white. After the case received national publicity because of a variety of procedural problems, four of the eyewitnesses changed their testimony and identified another black man as the robber. The man who was identified argued that the eyewitnesses who were unreliable in identifying Geter

should not have been believed when they identified him either. We will have more to say about the fallibility of eyewitness testimony in Chapter 17.

The Principle of Least Effort

People tend to be cognitively economical, a fact that Gordon Allport pointed out in his classic book *The Nature of Prejudice*. Allport said, "The principle of least effort inclines us to hold coarse and early formed generalizations as long as they can possibly be made to serve our purposes" (42). The principle of least effort leads people to resist attempts to modify their established perceptions of social reality and is one reason why people prefer information that is consistent with their views.

Another laboratory study illustrates this point (43). Again, students were arbitrarily divided into groups according to their alleged preferences for paintings. In this study, the students were then given an opportunity to review information about the similarity or dissimilarity of members of their group and the outgroup—that is, to people who had the same or different preferences for paintings. The students chose information regarding the similarity of ingroup members and the dissimilarity of outgroup members. Thus, the subjects made choices that provided them with information consistent with their beliefs that ingroup members are similar and outgroup members are dissimilar to them. To the extent that people seek out information consistent with their beliefs, perceptions of outgroups are difficult to modify.

The Norm of Ingroup-Outgroup Bias

Not only does categorizing people into ingroups and outgroups promote prejudice, it also leads to discrimination in favor of ingroup members. This effect has been demonstrated in a number of studies. In the best known study, British high school students were asked to indicate the number of dots they saw on slides that were projected on a screen (44). Half the students were told that they had consistently overestimated the number of dots on the slides and the other half were told that they had consistently underestimated the number of dots. This division into "overestimators" and "underestimators" is, of course, a totally meaningless distinction. Later in the study, the students were given an opportunity to allocate money to other students, who were identified as overestimators or underestimators. The students gave more money to students who were similar to them in estimation skills than to students who were different from them. This phenomena has been labeled the *generic norm of ingroup-outgroup bias,* and it has been traced to social identification processes.

Most people strongly identify with the groups to which they belong. In fact, people maintain a positive self-concept by favorably evaluating these groups. Favorable ingroup evaluations carry with them a corresponding tendency to evaluate outgroups negatively. This evaluative bias is such a basic part of self-identity that any division of people into ingroup and outgroup, however meaningless, can activate it. The evaluative bias can then lead to discrimination because treating the ingroup better than the outgroup is consistent with the view that the ingroup is superior to the outgroup.

The Ultimate Attribution Error

The tendency to make biased attributions that favor the ingroup has been labeled the *ultimate attribution error* (45). People are making the ultimate attribution error when they blame outgroup members more for negative behaviors than ingroup members or when they give more credit for positive behaviors to ingroup than to outgroup members. Ingroup members use a variety of strategies to deny credit to outgroup members. To be specific, the behavior of an outgroup member who does well may be:

1. perceived as an exception to the rule

2. attributed to some special advantage, such as affirmative action

3. perceived as an instance of overcoming the limitations of members of his or her group through hard work

4. attributed to situational factors, such as role demands (managers are supposed to be decisive so if a minority group manager is decisive his or her behavior may be attributed to the role, not the person).

In several studies people tended to explain the positive behavior of ingroup members in terms of internal characteristics but explained the same positive behaviors on the part of outgroup members in terms of external factors (Table 15-1). For instance, if white students are asked to explain why a white student did well in a course, they are likely to attribute the high grade to internal factors such as ability. However, if a black student did well, the whites may use external factors, such as the ease of the task or luck.

For negative behavior, the opposite pattern occurs. When ingroup members engage in negative behaviors, the behaviors are explained in terms of external factors that excuse the ingroup member; but when outgroup members behave in the same ways, the behaviors are explained in terms of negative internal characteristics of the outgroup. For example, whites may explain criminal behavior by whites in terms of economic factors, like poverty; but they may explain crime by blacks in terms of negative traits, like aggressiveness and antisocial tendencies.

In an interesting study of this bias, the investigators examined the attributions white students made to explain the performance of whites and blacks on an extrasensory perception (ESP) task (46). In the experiment, the subjects watched black or white students perform an ESP task. Then they were asked to explain the causes of the student's performance. The subjects who were prejudiced toward blacks attributed the white student's good performance to ability, but attributed the black's good performance to luck. They also attributed the black student's poor performance to lack of ability more than they did the white student's poor performance.

The ultimate attribution error leads to the use of positive trait labels to explain the behavior of

Table 15.1 ■

The Ultimate Attribution Error

	Group	
	Ingroup	Outgroup
Behavior		
Positive	Internal Attribution (high ability)	External Attribution (easy task)
Negative	External Attribution (hard task)	Internal Attribution (low ability)

ingroup members and negative labels to explain the behavior of outgroup members. Therefore, it enables ingroup members to maintain unfavorable stereotypes of outgroups and favorable stereotypes of ingroups.

Ethnocentrism

The tendency of ethnic ingroups to create negative stereotypes of outgroups is part of the more general behavior pattern of *ethnocentrism*—the "view of things in which one's own group is the center of everything, and all others are scaled or rated with reference to it" (47).

Ethnocentrism biases the perception of outgroups (48). In some cases, ethnic groups perceive real differences in customs, values, and beliefs between the groups. Ethnocentrism has the effect of biasing the manner in which these real differences are labeled. As an illustration, we can use the stereotypes of English people and Americans. The English consider themselves to be reserved, and they believe that they respect the rights of others. When referring to these same behaviors, Americans label the English as cold and snobbish. Americans view themselves as friendly and outgoing, but the English label these same behaviors as intrusive and forward. In each case, positive labels are used for ingroup behaviors and negative labels are used for outgroup behaviors.

Even when two groups engage in the same behavior, ethnocentrism can lead to biased labeling. One characteristic that all ethnic groups share is ethnocentrism. Within the ingroup, devotion to the ingroup is labeled positively, as loyalty or patriotism. Within the outgroup, the same behavior is labeled negatively, as clannishness or favoritism.

When ingroup members compare themselves to outgroups, they use traits on which their group can be rated favorably (49). If the outgroup is actually superior to the ingroup in some ways, these differences tend to be ignored by ingroup members. This helps ingroup members to maintain favorable impressions of the ingroup. You can probably see the operation of these ingroup biases in perception if you think about your own attitudes toward the groups to which you belong. It is probably the case that you regard members of your age group, sex, race, university, town, region, and country more favorably than members of the relevant comparison groups. These favorable impressions help you to maintain a positive self-image, but they do so at the cost of creating negative stereotypes of outgroups.

Ambivalent Attitudes and Polarized Responses

We have reviewed factors that contribute to the creation and maintenance of negative intergroup attitudes and stereotypes. But intergroup attitudes and stereotypes are not always exclusively negative. Attitudes toward disadvantaged groups are often a mixture of feelings of sympathy and feelings of aversion and hostility. This is a potentially explosive mixture. It flies in the face of the general tendency to maintain consistency among one's cognitions. The reason the inconsistencies in intergroup attitudes do not result in internal conflicts, such as cognitive dissonance, is that people are typically unaware of these inconsistencies. Instead, in any particular situation the positive or negative feelings become salient and predominate in the person's thoughts and actions. If the situation is a positive one, or if the disadvantaged individual is presented in a positive manner, feelings of sympathy predominate. Feelings of aversion or hostility are dominant in negative situations or when the disadvantaged person is presented in a negative way.

These ambivalent feelings lead to polarized responses toward disadvantaged or otherwise stigmatized people (50). In one study, female students found that their work partner was either handicapped or nonhandicapped. (The same woman served as an accomplice for both roles by using crutches in the handicapped condition) (51). The subject and the confederate were told they would be competing as a team against a team of males on an anagram task. The "team" members took turns solving the anagrams. The confederate either did very well (solving seven out of eight anagrams) or very poorly (solving zero anagrams), thereby contributing greatly to the "team's" success or failure. At the completion of the experiment, the subjects evaluated their partners on a number of personality traits.

When the subjects succeeded, they evaluated the handicapped person more favorably than the nonhandicapped person. When they failed, the subjects evaluated the handicapped person more unfavorably than the nonhandicapped person (see Table 15-2). In a related study it was found that white students reported feeling better after succeeding with a black partner than with a white partner, but they felt worse when failing with a black partner than a white partner (52). This study clearly shows the effects of ambivalent feelings on reactions to disadvantaged people. When the situation was positive, amplified positive reactions occurred, but when it was negative, amplified negative reactions occurred. Why do these polarized reactions occur? One explanation is that people feel uncomfortable or anxious when interacting with people who are disadvantaged, such as the handicapped. The arousal created by this anxiety then amplifies the normative reaction to the situation, making it more positive in positive situations and more negative in negative situations (see Box 15-3).

The microsocial processes we have just reviewed

Table 15.2 ■

Amplification of Evaluative Responses to a Handicapped Person

	Handicapped Person	Nonhandicapped Person
Success	96.47	84.13
Failure	48.27	58.00

Note: The higher the number, the more positively the person was evaluated.
Adapted from Gibbons, F. X., W. G. Stephan, B. Stephenson, and C. R. Petty, 1981, "Contact Relevance and Reactions to Stigmatized Others: Response Amplification vs. Sympathy," *Journal of Experimental Social Psychology* 16: 591–605.

BOX 15-3

Modern Forms of White Racism

White Americans no longer regard it as appropriate to hold overtly racist attitudes. Unfortunately, this does not mean that racism has disappeared. Instead, racism has become more subtle in form and content. Correspondingly, researchers have had to develop new techniques to explore the operation of modern racism. Modern racists believe that discrimination is a thing of the past and that blacks are now free to compete with whites on an equal footing. They think that overt racial discrimination is bad and that it is wrong to be prejudiced or have negative stereotypes of blacks. But they also believe that blacks are pushing too hard for equal rights and that their demands are unfair to whites (they may lead to reverse discrimination). Therefore, modern racists think that the gains blacks have made recently are undeserved and that blacks are getting too much favorable treatment and attention (53). A scale that measures modern racism contains the following items (respondents are asked to agree or disagree).

1. Blacks shouldn't push themselves where they are not wanted.

2. Blacks are getting too demanding in their push for equal rights.

3. Over the past few years, blacks have gotten more economically than they deserve.

(assimilation and contrast, the principle of least effort, the norm of ingroup-outgroup bias, the ultimate attribution error, ethnocentrism, modern racism, and ambivalent attitudes), can all operate in the service of group interests. Although the formal barriers to equality have been largely eliminated (discrimination in jobs, housing, and voter registration), informal barriers abound. Whites generally support racial justice but oppose the programs that would create it. The dominant majority uses the products of the microsocial processes to justify the economic and political inequality of the races, racial segregation, and opposition to programs that threaten the status quo (affirmative action, school and housing desegregation). The accentuation and negative in-terpretations of group differences feed opposition to social changes that threaten the interests of the majority. Similarly, the difficulty of changing entrenched stereotypes and ethnocentric or ambivalent attitudes make progress toward equality difficult.

Macrosocial and microsocial approaches to understanding intergroup relations are not mutually exclusive frameworks of analysis. Each is necessary to understand the other. The content of the microsocial processes (the specific traits attributed to ingroups and outgroups) depend on the macrosocial structural and historical context, but the macrosocial context is maintained by the microsocial processes that are used to justify and explain it (assimilation

4. Over the past few years, the government and the news media have shown more respect for blacks than they deserve.

Agreement with the items on this scale has been found to be related to favoring white over black mayoral candidates in three elections in Los Angeles (54). High scores on this scale are also related to opposition to school busing (55), and to favoring poorly qualified white job candidates over equally poorly qualified black candidates (56).

Another component of modern racism is the tendency of whites to avoid letting their negative feelings toward blacks show (57). This leads them to overreact in positive ways in some situations. However, in situations where racist behavior can be justified in nonracial terms, these individuals' underlying racist attitudes will show in their behavior. One common way these racist feelings surface is in minimizing or avoiding contact with blacks. Subtle forms of racist behavior are most likely to occur in situations where the norms are ambiguous or conflicting and ready rationalizations exist for discrimination.

For instance, white liberals (those most likely to deny they are racist) hang up on black strangers more frequently than white strangers who have called the wrong number, a situation where not listening to the caller is easy to justify (58). In another study whites were less likely to ask a black for help than a white (59). In this study the whites could easily avoid contact with blacks simply by not asking for help, even though they needed it. It appears that whites often avoid contact with blacks when they can, but are extra helpful when they cannot. In a study showing the latter effect, white subjects were more likely to help a black who had accidentally dropped a container of pencils than they were to help a white (60). In this case not helping could easily be taken as an indication of prejudice so the whites were helpful. Again, we see the ambivalence and complexity of whites' attitudes and behaviors toward blacks. ■

and contrast, ultimate attribution error, ingroup-outgroup bias, ethnocentrism).

It is against the backdrop of these entrenched macro- and microsocial processes that social psychologists attempting to improve intergroup relations have worked.

■
REDUCING PREJUDICE AND STEREOTYPING

For decades, social psychologists have attempted to find conditions that lead to improved intergroup relations. We will focus on two of the more successful techniques. The first technique is based on the contact hypothesis, and it addresses the conditions under which intergroup contact reduces prejudice and stereotyping. The second technique, the cultural assimilator, is based on the premise that ignorance and fear are major causes of prejudice and stereotyping. Such techniques are typically concerned with educating people about group differences.

The Contact Hypothesis

Social psychologists have long recognized that contact between groups does not necessarily lead to improved intergroup relations. One of the first statements of the conditions under which intergroup contact should improve intergroup relations was offered by Gordon Allport in 1954:

> *Prejudice may be reduced by equal status contact between majority and minority groups in the pursuit of common goals. The effect is greatly enhanced if this contact is sanctioned by institutional supports (by law, custom, or local atmosphere), and provided it is of a sort that leads to the perception of common interests and common humanity between members of the two groups (61).*

In that same year, the Supreme Court handed down its decision in the *Brown* v. *Board of Education* case. This decision mandated an end to segregated education. It was a crucial turning point in American race relations, and it initiated one of the great social experiments of the twentieth century—school desegregation. The decision was based, in part, on testimony given by social psychologists, some of which reflected the thinking behind the contact hypothesis. The social scientists hoped school desegregation would improve relations between blacks and whites, as well as eliminate unequal treatment of blacks by school systems.

Why did they believe school desegregation would improve race relations? The starting point for their argument was that segregation stemmed from white prejudice. Here is the way Kenneth Clark put it when he testified in the *Brown* case:

> *Segregation is prejudice concretized in the society, and in my work with Negro youth and in my interviewing them, I find this is the way they interpret it: Segregation is a mist, like a wall, which society erects, of stone and steel—psychological stone and steel—constantly telling them that they are inferior and constantly telling them that they cannot escape prejudice. Prejudice is something inside people. Segregation is the objective expression of what these people have inside (62).*

The effect of segregation was to impose on blacks the belief that they were inferior. The social scientists believed that one consequence of segregation was

lowered self-esteem of black children. As Clark testified:

> *I have reached the conclusion from the examination of the entire field that discrimination, prejudice, and segregation have definitely detrimental effects on the personality development of the Negro child. The essence of this detrimental effect is a confusion in the child's concept of his own self-esteem—basic feelings of inferiority, conflict, confusion in his self-image, resentment, hostility toward himself, and hostility toward whites (63).*

The social scientists thought that lowered self-esteem, combined with the belief by whites that blacks were intellectually inferior, led to low levels of academic expectancies and achievement among black students. Psychologist Horace English relied on the self-fulfilling prophecy to spell out this process in his testimony:

> *If we din it into a person that he is incapable of learning, then he is less likely to be able to learn. . . . There is a tendency for us to live up to—or perhaps I should say down to—social expectations and to learn what people say we can learn, and legal segregation definitely depresses the Negro's expectancy and is therefore prejudicial to his learning (64).*

The lower levels of black self-esteem and achievement were believed to cause frustration and anger toward whites. A statement written by a group of social psychologists and submitted to the Supreme Court for consideration in the 1954 decision makes this point:

> *Minority group children learn the inferior status to which they are assigned. . . . Under these conditions, the minority group child is thrown into a conflict with regard to his feelings about himself and his group. He wonders whether his group and he himself are worthy of no more respect than they receive. . . . Some children, usually of the lower socio-economic classes, may react by overt aggressions and hostility directed toward*

Figure 15.3 ■

Causal Model Derived from Social Science
Testimony in *Brown* v. *Board of Education*

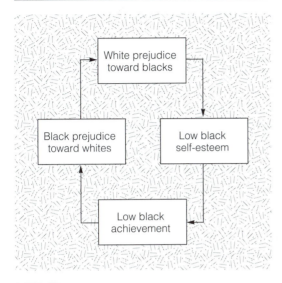

White prejudice
toward blacks

Black prejudice
toward whites

Low black
self-esteem

Low black
achievement

Adapted from Stephan, W.G., 1978, "School
Desegregation: An Evaluation of Predictions Made in
Brown v. *Board of Education*," *Psychological Bulletin*
67: 325–432.

*their own group or members of the dominant
group* (65).

The social psychologists also believed that the prejudice and anger directed toward whites tended to perpetuate and deepen white prejudice toward blacks.

To summarize, the social scientists believed that white prejudice created segregation, which caused black schoolchildren to have low self-esteem. These low levels of self-esteem, in turn, depressed the achievement of black schoolchildren. Low self-esteem and low achievement led to hostility and prejudice toward whites, which further hardened white prejudice toward blacks. This vicious circle is outlined in Figure 15-3.

Desegregation was expected to break the vicious circle by eliminating segregation, which was an important institutionalized support for white prejudice that fostered beliefs in the inferiority of blacks. In desegregated schools the self-esteem of blacks was expected to increase because they would no longer be stamped by the badge of inferiority represented by segregation. The achievement of black students was expected to increase because blacks would attend better-equipped schools and have higher expectations due to their increased self-esteem. Contact between the groups in desegregated schools was expected to decrease the prejudices of whites toward blacks and of blacks toward whites.

The Effects of Desegregation

What does the evidence on desegregation show? More than 35 years have passed since the *Brown* decision. In this time, hundreds of studies have examined the effects of desegregation on prejudice, self-esteem, and achievement. These studies have been reviewed by several social scientists, including one of your authors. His conclusion was that:

1. There is some evidence that desegregation more often increases than decreases prejudice among whites, while the opposite is true for blacks.

2. Black self-esteem sometimes decreases and rarely increases as a result of desegregation.

3. Black achievement in reading may increase a small amount as a result of desegregation, while desegregation has no effects on math. (66)

However, these conclusions are only tentative because most of the studies examined only the short-term effects of desegregation, some did not include adequate comparison groups, the types of desegregation that were studied varied tremendously from community to community (busing, pairing schools, voluntary desegregation, the use of "magnet" schools), the age of the students and the region of the country differed across studies, and the ratio of minority to majority group students was different in most studies. Despite the tentative nature of these conclusions, it does appear that desegregation has not had the

Like school desegregation, affirmative action programs are macrosocial intervention strategies designed to overcome historical discrimination against blacks, other minority groups, and women. Affirmative action arose in response to the failure of antidiscrimination laws to eliminate the disparities that exist between minority groups and the white majority. Affirmative action programs attempt to facilitate access to occupations where minority members are underrepresented due to past discrimination. Employers give preference in hiring and promotion to the members of specific groups, provided they are qualified for the jobs. The argument supporting affirmative action is that since these groups have been discriminated against in the past, discrimination in their favor is justified to redress past damage. It is argued that affirmative action is necessary as a temporary measure to create equal opportunities.

Critics responded that if it was wrong to discriminate on the basis of race, sex, or creed in the past it is just as wrong to do so today—even when the discrimination favors groups that have suffered in the past. The critics also argue that discrimination in favor of one group, means reverse discrimination against the majority group, and that it is unfair to make members of this group suffer for past discrimination they did not personally commit.

---

positive short-term effects that the social scientists who testified in the *Brown* trial anticipated.

Until recently it was impossible to study the long-term effects of desegregation because there just weren't enough students who had graduated from desegregated schools. In the last few years several large scale studies of the long-term effects of desegregation have appeared and the results are quite interesting. These studies show that:

1. Blacks who attended desegregated schools in the North are more likely to go to college than blacks who attended segregated schools. Blacks who attended desegregated schools in the South are more likely to attend formerly all white

universities than blacks who attended segregated schools.

2. Blacks who attended desegregated schools are more likely to work in integrated environments as adults than blacks who attended segregated schools.

3. Both blacks and whites who attended desegregated schools are more likely to live in integrated neighborhoods and send their children to desegregated schools than adults who attended segregated schools (67).

These findings indicate that desegregation in the schools promotes integration in adulthood, sug-

To this the proponents of affirmative action reply that it is individual members of the majority who benefit from discrimination. In particular, in the absence of affirmative action less qualified majority group members receive jobs that are denied to minority group members. One of the proponents of affirmative action, Ira Glasser, gives this example:

At the time Jackie Robinson broke the color line in baseball, there were approximately 400 major league jobs for baseball players. All were held by whites, because blacks were totally excluded. If blacks had been permitted, in a nondiscriminatory fashion, to compete for these jobs on the basis of merit, certainly some blacks would have proved better than some whites. If 100 blacks had won jobs, 100 whites would have been out of jobs. But those whites were employed only because blacks were excluded. Except for racial discrimination, they would not have been good enough to hold these jobs. The benefit of employment for those 100 white players was a direct result of discrimination. These jobs were unjustly awarded (68).

The American public is in favor of giving blacks the training required to successfully compete for jobs on an equal footing with whites (69). However, as noted in Box 15-3, many white Americans (80–90 percent) reject programs that give preferential treatment to blacks in hiring and promotion. Blacks (70 percent) generally support such practices. The authors of one recent survey conclude: "Opposition to all (affirmative action type) programs in part rests in the tendency of most Americans to deny the structural causes of poverty . . . (and) from the threat these programs present to an economic order that is believed to be just in principle and to work well in fact" (70). The Supreme Court has followed a middle road on affirmative action, holding that affirmative action programs can be constitutional, particularly when employers undertake them voluntarily. ■

gesting that the long-term effects of desegregation are somewhat more in accord with the social psychologists' original predictions—at least with respect to race relations (for a discussion of another controversial social policy see Box 15-4). But why weren't the social psychologists' predictions concerning the short-term effects of desegregation more on target?

The answer to this question lies in the circumstances under which desegregation has been implemented. Recall the conditions outlined by Allport for optimal contact between groups. Most desegregation plans fail on all counts. First, the students who are brought together are usually not of equal status. Frequently, middle-class whites and lower-class blacks are integrated in the same schools. In many cases, the inferior preparation of black students in low-quality segregated schools has made it difficult for them to compete successfully with their better-trained white counterparts. This has led to a confirmation of beliefs by whites that whites are academically superior to blacks. Another form of inequality existing in many desegregated schools is that the ratio of white to black students favors the whites. This generally means that whites are able to exercise more power and influence in the schools.

The nature of the contact that occurs in desegregated schools is more often competitive than cooperative. Outside the athletic field, students typically do not pursue common goals. In the majority of communities, support for desegregation from

■ *Segregation persists in many school systems, as illustrated by this class of children on a field trip. (WGS)*

crucial authorities is lacking. Desegregation is usually implemented amidst considerable opposition from parents, school boards, and teachers. Finally, there is little focus on the common interests of students or on their common humanity in most desegregated schools.

The social psychologists who testified in the Brown trial did not intentionally mislead the Supreme Court. They based their arguments on the best available evidence. They could not foresee the conditions under which desegregation would occur. As the initial evidence on the lack of short-term improvements in race relations began to accumulate, investigators attempted to develop programs to create the conditions under which desegregation would improve intergroup relations.

The Jigsaw Classroom

Working independently, researchers in Maryland, Colorado, Texas, Minnesota, and California developed similar techniques to improve intergroup relations (71). These techniques involve small inter-ethnic groups of students cooperating to learn academic curriculum materials. The origins of all of these techniques can be traced back to research on cooperation, such as the Robbers Cave study that was discussed in Chapter 1. One of the techniques is known as the *jigsaw classroom*. It was devised by a team of social psychologists, headed by Elliot Aronson and including one of your authors.

In the jigsaw classroom, half a dozen students from two or more ethnic groups work together on

■ *In contrast to the traditional teacher-taught classroom, students in jigsaw classrooms work together in interethnic groups to achieve joint goals. (© Richard S. Orton, 1990)*

standard curriculum materials. The material to be learned is divided into as many sections as there are students in the group. Each student is responsible for teaching his or her section to the other students. When the students in the group have covered all of the material, they are tested individually. The students in jigsaw classrooms are dependent on one another to learn the material, but they earn their grades independently. In technical terms, the students are *means* interdependent but *goals* independent. You can get a feel for what it is like to be in one of these groups from this quote by Aronson.

> *When thrown on their own resources, the children eventually learned to teach each other and to listen to each other. The children came to learn that none of them could do well without the aid of each person in the group—and that each member had a unique and essential contribution to make. Suppose you and I are children in the same group. You've been dealt Joseph*

Pulitzer as a young man; I've been dealt Joseph Pulitzer as an old man. The only way I can learn about Joseph Pulitzer as a young man is to pay close attention to what you are saying. You are a very important resource to me. The teacher is no longer the sole resource—she isn't even in the group. Instead every kid in the circle becomes important to me. I do well if I pay attention to the other kids; I do poorly if I don't (72).

In jigsaw classrooms, the students cooperate in the pursuit of common goals and they have a common interest in succeeding. They have equal status in the groups; each student is a teacher some of the time and a learner most of the time. Since teachers adopt the groups voluntarily, the intergroup contact that occurs in these groups has the support of these important authority figures. Thus, the jigsaw classroom fulfills all of Allport's criteria for creating positive intergroup relations. Research using this technique has found that the jigsaw classroom leads to increases in self-esteem, liking for other group members, and empathy.

These positive effects occur without any loss in achievement levels. When students in jigsaw classes are compared to students learning the same material in traditional teacher-taught classes, they perform as well. In fact, there is some indication that minority group students perform better in the jigsaw classes than in traditional classes (73).

Other cooperative techniques differ in small ways from the jigsaw classroom. In some of the techniques, students are goals interdependent as well as means interdependent: Their grades depend on how well the group does. In these techniques the groups compete against one another so there is a mixture of cooperation within groups and competition between groups. In another technique, the minority group members are given pretraining in the tasks on which the interethnic groups will work. This training is designed to help the minority students disconfirm the stereotype that minority group members are less competent than whites. The success of this technique has been explained in terms of expectation states theory (see Chapter 7 for a discussion of expectation states theory) (74). According to expectation states theory, people possess two types of statuses: diffuse status characteristics (race, sex, and ethnicity) and specific status characteristics (math ability or gymnastic skills). In the above technique, the specific status characteristic of high ability on a task offsets the diffuse status characteristic of race. The white students typically have low expectancies concerning the abilities of the black students in their groups; but when these expectancies are disconfirmed—because the pretrained blacks possess high task ability—the whites' behavior toward blacks becomes more favorable.

Other factors may also contribute to the positive results of cooperative interethnic groups. As the students work closely together in this relatively informal setting, they learn that outgroup members are just as diverse as ingroup members. The students also may learn that members of the other group are not as dissimilar to them as they had thought. These factors tend to undercut perceptual assimilation and

contrast effects. In addition, the students are likely to identify with their work groups. Since these groups contain both ethnic ingroup and ethnic outgroup members, the cooperative group experience reduces ingroup-outgroup bias by providing cross-cutting loyalties. Finally, to the extent that the outcomes are positive, amplified favorable evaluative responses toward outgroup members should occur.

Reducing Intergroup Ignorance

Overgeneralized stereotypes, assumed dissimilarity of outgroup members, and perceptual assimilation and contrast effects are all fostered by ignorance of outgroups. When faced with a complex social world and little information regarding outgroup members, people reduce their fear and uncertainty of outgroups by relying on stereotypes. Social psychologists and educators have long believed that overcoming ignorance of ethnic outgroups can reduce stereotyping.

Public schools throughout the country present the history of various American ethnic groups in social studies classes. These materials are sometimes discussed in class or are incorporated into "ethnic awareness" weeks. Such segments are often of short duration, lasting only one or two weeks. Investigations of the effects of multiethnic curricula indicate that, in about two thirds of the cases, these educational techniques reduce prejudice or stereotyping to some degree (75). The most successful of these programs consist of speakers, discussions, movies, role-playing, and interaction with members of the other group, as well as written materials. In addition to focusing on the history of various groups and highlighting the achievements of outstanding members of these groups, educational programs frequently stress the underlying similarities among the groups. The more these programs actively involve the students, the more effective they tend to be (76). Subsequent research suggests that these educational techniques might be even more successful if they provided students with information about other groups that reduces fear about interacting with outgroup members. The *cultural assimilator* technique provides this type of information (77).

The cultural assimilator technique was developed to help Americans who were going overseas adapt to the countries in which they would be living. The cultural assimilators were used to teach Americans about the *subjective* culture of other countries. Subjective culture consists of such things as the values, norms, and roles of a given group. These features of a cultural group are often taken for granted by members of the culture. As you may recall from our discussion of ethnomethodology (Chapter 2), members of a given cultural group often are not consciously aware of the guiding assumptions that underlie their social life. Members of the group may even have some difficulty verbalizing the values, norms, and roles that prevail in their culture. For instance, the norms for taking turns during conversation often involve a subtle combination of terminating one's hand gestures and dropping or raising the tone of one's voice, but most people would have difficulty verbalizing these norms. They simply accept them. Hence, these implicit aspects of culture cannot be easily transmitted to members of another cultural group.

When two groups differ in subjective culture, misunderstandings and conflict are lifely to occur. These difficulties may arise because of differences in what members of the two groups believe is right and wrong (values), how they think people should behave (norms), or whom they believe is supposed to do what (roles). The cultural assimilator is based on the assumption that it is the differences between cultural groups that create problems, rather than the similarities between groups. Thus, the technique attempts to teach ingroup members about the subjective culture of the outgroup.

The cultural assimilator consists of "critical incidents" concerning misunderstandings between members of two groups. These incidents usually describe common social situations that members of the two groups interpret differently. The differences in interpretation generally take one of two forms. Members of the two groups either make different attributions to explain the same behavior or they evaluate people who engage in the behavior differently (Box 15-5).

To illustrate, consider this incident. An American manager was brought into a Mexican business to improve production. Upon arriving, he called in the section heads of the plant and proceeded to tell each what was wrong with his section and what changes should be made. Much to his surprise, an hour later all of the section heads resigned. Obviously, the Mexican section heads had a very different interpretation of the manager's behavior than he did. He fully intended to shake up the section heads and motivate them to improve. But the section heads thought the manager had humiliated them publicly, and they found his behavior intolerable.

This technique has recently been adapted for use with different cultural groups within the same society. Programmed learning workbooks have been developed to teach whites about black and Hispanic culture. In a test of the effectiveness of a workbook designed to teach white college students about the subjective culture of blacks, it was found that whites who read the workbook made attributions which were more similar to those of blacks and regarded the behavior of blacks as being more under intentional control than did untrained whites. In addition, the training led whites to stereotype blacks less.

Other Techniques

A number of other techniques have also been used to improve intergroup relations (79). For instance, techniques based on principles of group therapy have been found to reduce prejudice, as have techniques based on learning theories that employ reinforcement principles or attempt to reduce negative emotional reactions to outgroup members. Some of the more promising techniques are based on attitude change theories, such as techniques that highlight people's cognitive inconsistencies. In one study, white students were led to see the inconsistencies between their attitudes toward civil rights and their beliefs in the importance of freedom and equality (80). The students were presented with their own personal version of Myrdal's American dilemma—the conflict between their beliefs in equality and their behavior toward minorities. A full year and a half later, these students were more likely to have participated in activities sponsored by the

The Cultural Assimilator

The cultural assimilator contains a number of critical incidents presented in a programmed learning format. The person reads the incident and chooses an answer from a set of explanations for the behavior in the incident. The reader then looks up the answer in the back of the book. If the reader has chosen the wrong answer, an explanation is given as to why this answer is wrong. The reader is asked to choose another answer until he or she selects the correct answer. When the reader makes the correct choice, an explanation is provided of the difference between the two groups that led to the problem. The reader then goes on to the next item. Here is an example from a cultural assimilator designed to teach whites about blacks:

John Harris, a 24-year-old black man, has just completed a training program for the hard-core unemployed at GMB. On his third day on the job, he failed to show up on time (8 A.M.). At 9 A.M. he had still not arrived, nor had he called in. His foreman went to the office, got the phone number John listed on his application, and called the number. When the phone was answered, a man said, "Deluxe

---

National Association for the Advancement of Colored People (NAACP) than students in an untreated control group.

The continuing existence of prejudice, ethnocentrism, negative stereotypes, and discrimination in our society are a tragic legacy of our past, but gradually we are developing more and more effective techniques of eliminating them. We have come a long way, but we have a long way yet to go.

■
SUMMARY

The historical approach to prejudice and stereotyping suggests that the conditions of contact between two groups influence the perceptions they have of one another. Economic factors, such as social class and the type of labor performed by members of the group, influence stereotypes. Some minority groups in the United States have undergone a form of internal colonialism, in which they were treated as members of a subjugated group. Restrictions were placed on the freedoms of these groups and attempts were made to destroy their cultures.

Some ethnic minorities, such as those of European origin, were assimilated into the culture of the dominant group. Others, such as Mexican-Americans, have only been acculturated, as indicated by a continued sense of group identity and the retention of many aspects of their cultural heritage. The current state of intergroup relations might be portrayed as an unstable state of ethnic pluralism that is tending toward assimilation, in part through intermarriage.

*Pool Hall." The foreman slammed the receiver down and went back to his work
area.*

*At 10 A.M., John showed up and walked over to where the foreman and the
other men were working.*

*"Where the hell have you been and why didn't you call in?" the foreman
said to John. "You know that one of the rules is that you have to call in if you're
not going to be here on time. You better get on the ball, or you're not going to
be here much longer."*

*"Ease off, man," John said. "My old lady was sick this morning, and I didn't
have a chance to call. It's a real hassle for me to get to a phone."*

Why didn't John call?

1. Because he couldn't get to a phone.
2. He knew that if he called from the pool hall, the boss would think he was really goofing off.
3. He was afraid to call because he thought the foreman wouldn't believe him.
4. He didn't know he was supposed to call.

Correct answer: 1

It was obvious he didn't have a phone at home. The reason he gave the pool
hall number was that he didn't have a phone, and, in case of emergency, someone
at the pool hall would take a message for him. It is sometimes difficult for those
who take a phone for granted to realize the problems of those who don't have a
home phone (78). ■

Historical relations between groups have led to institutional racism, in which minority group members are treated unequally by a variety of institutions, such as religious, educational, and political institutions. Minority groups respond to discrimination by reluctantly accepting it, assimilating into the majority group, avoiding the majority group, or aggressing against the majority.

A variety of cognitive processes influence prejudice and stereotyping. In categorization, the defining features of a category are used to decide if an individual is a member of that category. If the individual is categorized as a group member, the characteristic features of the group (the stereotype of the group) are likely to be attributed to the individual. When people are categorized into groups, the differences between the groups tend to be overestimated (a contrast effect), and the differences within the groups tend to be underestimated (an assimilation effect). Due to the principle of least effort, people tend to form and use simple categories and resist attempts to modify their conceptions of category members.

Categorization also promotes prejudice and discrimination through the generic norm of ingroup-outgroup bias. Identification with the ingroup leads to favoritism toward ingroup members and rejection of outgroup members. This evaluative bias can cause the ultimate attribution error, in which internal traits are used to explain the positive behavior of ingroup members and the negative behavior of outgroup members, while external attributions are used to account for the negative behavior of ingroup members and the positive behavior of outgroup members.

Similarly, ethnocentrism can lead to the perception that the ingroup possesses positive traits, while the outgroup possesses negative traits.

Attitudes toward disadvantaged groups tend to be a mixture of sympathy and aversion. The result of these ambivalent attitudes is often response polarization, in which behavior is more positive or more negative toward a member of a disadvantaged group than toward other people. Ambivalence characterizes modern forms of racism in which people do not betray their racist feelings unless their behavior can be justified in nonracial terms.

The contact hypothesis, which suggests that intergroup contact will reduce prejudice under certain conditions, was one of the cornerstones of social scientists' testimony in the *Brown* decision concerning school desegregation. Subsequent evidence indicated that in the short-term desegregation often did not reduce prejudice or raise black self-esteem, although it did increase black achievement on verbal tests. Studies of the long-term effects of desegregation indicate that school desegregation increases integration in adult life. The reason for the relative lack of short-term success appears to be that the intergroup contact occurring in desegregated schools does not occur under optimal circumstances. Techniques, such as the jigsaw classroom, which employ small interethnic cooperative groups, improve intergroup relations and minority self-esteem at no cost in achievement levels. These techniques provide the equal status, pursuit of common goals, and institutional support that the contact hypothesis suggests are necessary for contact to improve intergroup relations.

Techniques based on expectation states theory, in which high levels of a specific status characteristic (for example, ability) are used to offset low levels on a diffuse status characteristic (for example, race), have also been successful in improving intergroup relations. In addition, techniques that reduce intergroup ignorance, such as the cultural assimilator, have been used to improve relations between groups. Finally, multiethnic educational programs, group therapy, and techniques that rely on cognitive inconsistencies can be used to reduce prejudice and stereotyping.

■ REFERENCES

1. Myrdal, G., 1944, *An American Dilemma,* New York: Harper & Row.
2. Farley, R., 1985, "Three Steps Forward and Two Back? Recent Changes in the Social and Economic Status of Blacks," in R. D. Alba, *Ethnicity and Race in the U.S.A.,* Boston: Routledge & Kegan Paul; *Statistical Abstracts of the United States,* 1989, Washington, DC: U.S. Census Bureau.
3. U.S. Commission on Civil Rights, 1978; *Statistical Abstracts of the United States,* 1989, ibid.
4. Farley, R., 1975, "Residential Segregation and Its Implications for School Integration," *Law and Contemporary Society* 39: 164–193.
5. Farley, 1985, op. cit.
6. Christmas, J. J., 1977, "How Our Health System Fails Minorities," *Civil Rights Digest* 10: 4.
7. *Newsweek,* July 13, 1987.
8. Farley, 1985, op. cit.
9. Franklin, J. H., 1974, *From Slavery to Freedom,* 4th ed., New York: Knopf; E. T. Thompson, 1975, *Plantation Societies, Race Relations, and the South: Regimentation of Populations,* Durham, NC: Duke University Press.
10. LeVine, R. E. and D. T. Campbell, 1972, *Ethnocentrism,* New York: Wiley.
11. Blauner, R., 1972, *Racial Oppression in America,* New York: Harper & Row.
12. Gordon, M. M., 1964, *Assimilation in American Life,* New York: Oxford University Press.
13. McLemore, S. D., 1980, *Racial and Ethnic Relations in America,* Boston: Allyn & Bacon.
14. Grebler, L., J. W. Moore, and R. C. Guzman, 1970, *The Mexican American People,* New York: The Free Press.
15. Murguia, E. and W. P. Frisbee, 1977, "Trends in Mexican-American Intermarriage: Recent Findings in Perspective," *Social Science Quarterly* 58: 374–389.
16. McLemore, 1980, op. cit., p. 238.
17. Hirshman, C. and M. G. Wong, 1984, "Socioeconomic Gains of Asian Americans, Blacks, and Hispanics: 1960–1976," *American Journal of Sociology* 90: 584–607.
18. McLemore, 1980, op. cit., p. 239.
19. Massey, D. S. and B. P. Mullen, 1984, "Processes of Hispanic and Black Assimilation," *American Journal of Sociology* 89: 836–873.
20. Taeuber, K. E. and A. F. Taeuber, 1964, "The Negro as an Immigrant Group: Recent Trends in Racial and Ethnic Segregation in Chicago," *American Journal of Sociology* 69: 374–394.
21. Blau, P. M., 1977, *Inequality and Heterogeneity,* New York: The Free Press.
22. Neidert, L. J. and R. Farley, 1985, "Assimilation in the United States: An Analysis of Ethnic and Generation Differences in Status and Achievement," *American Sociological Review* 50: 840–849.

23. Blau, P. M., C. Beeker, and K. M. Fitzpatrick, 1984, "Intersecting Social Affiliations and Intermarriage," *Social Forces* 1984 62: 585–606.

24. Stephan, W. G. and C. Stephan, 1987, "After Intermarriage: Ethnic Identity among Mixed-Heritage Japanese-Americans and Hispanics," *Journal of Marriage and the Family* 51: 507–519.

25. Carmichael, S. and C. Hamilton, 1967, *Black Power,* New York: Vantage Press.

26. McLemore, 1980, op. cit., pp. 155–202.

27. Quoted in E. V. Rostow, 1945, "Our Worst Wartime Mistake," *Harper's Magazine* Sept., p. 140.

28. Daws, G., 1968, *Shoal of Time,* Honolulu: University of Hawaii Press.

29. Neidert and Farley, 1985, op. cit.

30. Nee, V. and J. Sanders, 1985, "The Road to Parity: Determinants of the Socioeconomic Achievement of Asian Americans," in R. D. Alba, *Ethnicity and Race in the U.S.A.,* Boston: Routledge & Kegan Paul.

31. U.S. Census, 1973, *Characteristics of the Population,* Washington, DC: U.S. Government Printing Office.

32. Feagin, J. R. and C. B. Feagin, 1978, *Discrimination American Style,* Englewood Cliffs, NJ: Spectrum.

33. Pearce, D. M., 1976, "Black, White, and Many Shades of Gray: Real Estate Brokers and Their Racial Practices," Ph.D. dissertation, University of Michigan.

34. Vander Zanden, J. W., 1983, *American Minority Relations,* New York: Alfred A. Knopf.

35. Smith, E. E., E. J. Shoben, and L. J. Rips, 1974, "Structure and Process in Semantic Memory: A Featural Model for Semantic Decisions," *Psychological Bulletin* 81: 214–241.

36. Wells, W. D. and B. Siegel, 1961, "Stereotyped Somatotypes," *Psychological Reports* 8: 77–78.

37. Greenberg, J. and T. Pyszczynski, 1985, "The Effect of an Overheard Ethnic Slur on Evaluations of the Target: How to Spread a Social Disease," *Journal of Experimental Social Psychology* 21: 61–72.

38. Allen, V. L. and D. A. Wilder, 1979, "Group Categorization and Attribution of Belief Similarity," *Small Group Behavior* 10: 73–80.

39. Taylor, S. E., S. T. Fiske, N. L. Etcoff, and A. J. Ruderman, 1978, "Categorical and Contextual Bases of Person Memory and Stereotyping," *Journal of Personality and Social Psychology* 36: 778–793.

40. Brigham, J. C. and P. Barkowitz, 1978, "Do 'They All Look Alike?' The Effect of Race, Sex, Experience, and Attitudes on the Ability to Recognize Faces," *Journal of Applied Social Psychology* 8: 306–318.

41. Tajfel, H., A. A. Sheikh, and R. C. Gardner, 1964, "Content of Stereotypes and the Inferences of Similarity between Members of Stereotyped Groups," *Acta Psychologica* 22: 191–201.

42. Allport, G. W., 1954, *The Nature of Prejudice,* Reading, MA: Addison-Wesley, p. 172.

43. Wilder, D. A. and V. L. Allen, 1978, "Group Membership and Preference for Information about Others," *Personality and Social Psychology Bulletin* 4: 106–110.

44. Tajfel, H., 1970, "Experiments in Intergroup Discrimination," *Scientific American* 223: 96–102.

45. Pettigrew, T. F., 1979, "The Ultimate Attribution Error: Extending Allport's Cognitive Analysis of Prejudice," *Personality and Social Psychology Bulletin* 5: 461–476.

46. Greenberg, J. and D. Rosenfield, 1979, "Whites' Ethnocentrism and Their Attributions for the Behavior of Blacks: A Motivational Bias," *Journal of Personality* 47: 643–657.

47. Sumner, W. G., 1906, *Folkways,* Boston: Ginn.

48. Campbell, D. T., 1967, "Stereotypes and the Perception of Group Differences," *American Psychologist* 22: 812–829.

49. Brewer, M. B., 1986, "The Role of Ethnocentrism in Intergroup Conflict," in S. Worchel and W. Austin (Eds.), 2d ed., *The Social Psychology of Intergroup Relations,* Monterey, CA: Brooks/Cole.

50. Katz, I., J. Wackenhut, and D. C. Glass, 1986, "An Ambivalence-Amplification Theory of Behavior toward the Stigmatized," in S. Worchel and W. Austin, ibid.

51. Gibbons, F. X., W. G. Stephan, B. Stephenson, and C. R. Petty, 1981, "Contact Relevance and Reactions to Stigmatized Others: Response Amplification vs. Sympathy," *Journal of Experimental Social Psychology* 16: 591–605.

52. Stephan, W. G. and C. W. Stephan, 1987, "Emotional Reactions to Interracial Achievement Outcomes," *Journal of Applied Social Psychology* 19: 608–621.

53. McConahay, J. B., 1986, "Modern Racism, Ambivalence, and the Modern Racism Scale," in J. F. Dovidio and S. L. Geartner (Eds.), *Prejudice, Discrimination, and Racism,* New York: Academic Press.

54. McConahay, J. B. and J. C. Hough Jr., 1976, "Symbolic Racism," *Journal of Social Issues* 32: 23–45. D. R. Kinder and D. O. Sears, 1981, "Symbolic Racism versus Racial Threats to 'The Good Life,' " *Journal of Personality and Social Psychology* 40: 414–431.

55. McConahay, J. B., 1982, "Self-interest vs. Racial Attitudes as Correlates of Anti-busing Attitudes in Louisville," *Journal of Politics* 44: 692–720; J. B. McConahay, 1984, "Its Still the Blacks and Not the Buses," unpublished paper, Duke University.

56. McConahay, 1986, op. cit.

57. Gaertner, S. L. and J. F. Dovidio, 1986, "The Aversive Form of Racism," in J. F. Dovidio and S. L. Gaertner, op. cit.

58. Gaertner, S. L., 1973, "Helping Behavior and Discrimination among Liberals and Conservatives," *Journal of Social Psychology* 25: 335–341.

59. Dovidio, J. F. and S. L. Gaertner, 1983, "Race, Normative Structure, and Help Seeking," in B. M. DePaulo, A. Nadler, and J. D. Fisher (Eds.), *New Directions in Helping,* Vol. 2, New York: Academic Press.

60. Dovidio, J. F. and S. L. Gaertner, 1981, "The Effects of Race, Status, and Ability on Helping Behavior," *Social Psychology Quarterly* 44: 192–203.

61. Allport, 1954, op. cit., p. 281.

62. Kluger, R., 1976, *Simple Justice,* New York: Holt, Rinehart & Winston, p. 495.

63. Kluger, 1976, ibid., p. 353.

64. Kluger, 1976, ibid., p. 415.

65. Allport, F. H. et al., 1953, "The Effects of Segregation and the Consequences of Desegregation: A Social Science Statement," *Minnesota Law Review* 37: 429–440.

66. Stephan, W. G., 1986, "The Effects of School Desegregation: An Evaluation 30 Years after Brown," in L. Saxe and M. Saks (Eds.), *Advances in Applied Social Psychology*, Vol. 3, New York: Lawrence Erlbaum.

67. Braddock, J. H., II, 1985, "School Desegregation and Black Assimilation," *Journal of Social Issues* 41(3): 9–22; W. G. Stephan, 1986, ibid.

68. Glasser, I., 1988, "Affirmative Action and the Legacy of Racial Injustice," in P. A. Katz and D. A. Taylor (Eds.), *Eliminating Racism: Profiles in Controversy*, New York: Plenum Press.

69. Kleugel, J. R. and E. R. Smith, 1986, *Beliefs about Inequality*, New York: Aldine De Gruyter.

70. Kluegel and Smith, 1986, ibid., pp. 209–212.

71. Aronson, E., C. Stephan, J. Sikes, N. Blaney, and M. Snapp, *The Jigsaw Classroom*, Beverly Hills, CA: Sage; E. G. Cohen, 1980, "Design and Redesign of the Desegregated Schools: Problems of Status, Power, and Conflict," in W. Stephan and J. Feagin (Eds.), *School Desegregation: Past, Present, and Future*, New York: Plenum; D. L. DeVries and R. E. Slavin, 1978, "Teams-Games-Tournament (TGT): Review of Ten Classroom Experiments," *Journal of Research and Development in Education* 12: 28–38; D. W. Johnson, R. Johnson, and L. Scott, 1978, "The Effects of Cooperative and Individualized Instruction on Student Attitudes and Achievement," *Journal of Social Psychology* 104: 207–216; R. H. Weigel, D. L. Wiser, and S. W. Cook, 1975, "The

Impact of Cooperative Learning Experience on Cross-ethnic Relations and Attitudes," *Journal of Social Issues* 31: 219–244.

72. Aronson, E., 1980, *The Social Animal*, San Francisco: W. H. Freeman, p. 230.

73. Lucker, G. W., D. Rosenfield, J. Sikes, and E. Aronson, 1977, "Performance in the Interdependent Classroom: A Field Study," *American Educational Research Journal* 13: 115–123.

74. Cohen, 1980, op. cit.

75. Stephan, W. G., 1985, "Intergroup Relations," in G. Lindzey and E. Aronson (Eds.), *The Handbook of Social Psychology*, 3d ed., Reading, MA: Addison-Wesley.

76. Stephan, W. G. and C. W. Stephan, 1985, "The Role of Ignorance in Intergroup Relations," in N. Miller and M. B. Brewer (Eds.), *Groups in Contact*, New York: Academic Press.

77. Triandis, H. C. (Ed.), 1976, *Variations in Black and White Perceptions of the Social Environment*, Urbana: University of Illinois Press.

78. Slobodin, L. F., M. I. Collins, J. L. Crayton, J. M. Feldman, J. J. Jaccard, K. Rissman, and D. E. Weldon, 1972, "Cultural Assimilator: For Interaction with the Economically Disadvantaged," mimeograph, University of Illinois.

79. Weldon, D. E., D. E. Carlston, A. K. Rissman, L. F. Slobodin, and H. C. Triandis, 1975, "A Laboratory Test of Effects of Culture Assimilator Training," *Journal of Personality and Social Psychology* 32: 300–310.

80. Rokeach, M., 1971, "Long Range Experimental Modification of Values, Attitudes, and Behavior," *American Psychologist* 26: 453–459.

CHAPTER 16

Collective Behavior

What Is Collective Behavior?

Types of Collective Behavior

Mass Behavior

Crowds

Social Movements

One day Mrs. Marian Keech began to receive messages from outer space. Mrs. Keech, about 50, received these messages in writing, in a handwriting that was not her own. The messengers told Mrs. Keech they were superior beings from the planet Clarion. While visiting the earth in their spaceships, they had observed fault lines in the earth's crust that foretold of a giant flood. This flood was to submerge virtually the entire Western Hemisphere. She was asked to warn those who were enlightened enough to receive this message.

Mrs. Keech began to talk of her experiences to people interested in outer space and soon found a small, but eager, band of followers, which included a physician and a Ph.D. scientist. Through Mrs. Keech, the beings told the group the flood would come on a specific date, but the chosen ones, the true believers, would be rescued by a flying saucer. The group members quit their jobs and quickly sold or gave away their worldly goods in anticipation of the cataclysm.

News reporters heard of the group and wrote stories about it that were carried nationwide. After this publicity the group was besieged by interested persons, but the group members ignored them; they made no attempts to convert outsiders.

The day before the flood, a message was received saying that the group would be rescued by a flying saucer at midnight. Before midnight, the followers gathered at Mrs. Keech's house. Midnight passed, but no flying saucer appeared to rescue them. The morning hours slowly passed. The group was visibly shaken. Mrs. Keech was in tears. But at 4:45 A.M. she received a message saying the faithfulness of this small group had saved the earth from the flood.

After the prophesied flood failed to materialize, the group became interested in recruiting others to join them. They gave press conferences and made tapes to be played on the radio. All visitors were seen and attempts were made to recruit them into the group (1).

Social psychologists would term this group a *cult*. A cult is a quasi-social movement, one of many forms of collective behavior, the topic we will explore in this chapter. In the sections that follow, we will define collective behavior, examine patterns of interaction that make up collective behavior, and focus on the causes of each of the major types of collective behavior.

WHAT IS COLLECTIVE BEHAVIOR?

Collective behavior is the study of group behavior governed by spontaneous or *emergent* norms, rather than the social norms of the larger society (2). In fact, the behaviors exhibited in collective behavior may conflict with the norms of the society and the beliefs of the majority of its citizens. For example, to have belonged to Mrs. Keech's group, one must have had a belief in beings from outer space and a willingness to structure much of one's life around this belief. To belong to an environmental group, one must believe that current social practices are causing irreparable damage to our natural resources and be willing to direct one's time and resources to altering those practices. Groups displaying collective behavior do not accept all of the norms of the society but instead have alternative norms. Collective behavior is displayed by people in such diverse areas as public opinion, crazes, fads, fashions, panics, mobs, riots, cults, and social movements.

Although the norms associated with collective behavior are often at variance with those of society, collective behavior does not necessarily lead to conflict. Over time, it may become conventional behavior, that which is regulated and predictable. For instance, collective behavior in Cuba has become orchestrated by the state (3). In Cuba, collective behavior has been made into a conventional way of showing support for the revolution. Instances of collective behavior are planned by established organizations and state agencies. Each city block has an organizer whose job is to see that the neighbors turn out for these events. In addition, the Cuban labor union gives merit points for participation in

■ *Strikes provide one example of collective behavior. (WGS)*

such events. This manipulation of collective behavior keeps the elite's political ideology popular, encourages participation in the revolutionary process, and provides a basis for identifying potential deviants who do not support the revolution.

Neither does collective behavior necessarily result in negative consequences for society. On the contrary, collective behavior is often the basis for positive social change—for new ways of looking at old ideas and for implementing new values whose time has come. Collective behavior is a crucial determinant of social and cultural change (4). Cultural change is important to the survival of any culture, and collective behavior can be a critical part of this process of change. You can probably think of instances of sustained collective behavior that have taken place in your own lifetime and have led to significant change in our society.

■

TYPES OF
COLLECTIVE BEHAVIOR

Collective behavior can be divided into three types: mass behavior, crowds, and social movements. *Mass behavior* occurs when individuals respond separately to a common stimulus in the same way, as occurs in public opinion, fads, fashions, crazes, and panics. *Crowds* are large numbers of people gathered together, for example, street crowds, riots, and mobs. *Social movements* are organized collective responses to issues about which people are concerned, such as protest movements.

Mass behavior and crowds can also be characterized by the dominant emotion displayed by the individuals involved (5). *Hostility* is the basis for most mobs and riots. *Fear* produces panic, as well as mass responses to social and environmental disasters. These disasters can be both actual (earthquakes, revolutions) and imagined (mass "illnesses" produced by fears of poisoned aspirin, space invasions). *Joy* is the motivating emotion for such behaviors as religious gatherings and excited crowds, crazes, fashions, and fads.

We will examine each of the major types of collective behavior in some detail. Collective behavior has been studied almost exclusively by sociologists, probably because of its natural macro-level focus. However, some attitude theorists from psychological social psychology have contributed to the study of public opinion.

Mass Behavior

Mass behavior is produced by the mass media and by communication from person to person. We will compare and contrast five different forms of mass behavior: public opinion, crazes, fads, fashions, and panics.

Public opinion   Public opinion is the set of values and beliefs that members of a society hold on some issue at a given time. Public opinion is a form of collective behavior because it is an expression of emerging norms. Public opinion is constantly changing. At times, the society becomes politically more liberal or conservative. Certain issues become "hot topics" and then are soon forgotten. Public opinion is anything but uniform. At any one time many opinions are held about any given topic. The composite public opinion is a function of the strength of these differing opinions. At times, minority groups exert a much greater influence in shaping public opinion than their numbers would suggest. At other times, minority feelings have little influence on public opinion. For instance, civil rights activists

charge that the gains made by minorities in the 1960s were eroded by the conservative political administrations of the 1980s.

Public opinion is formed, in part, through discussions among members of the society (6). The public comprises both special interest groups that have strong concerns about specific issues and other, more disinterested, citizens. Interest groups may present information or misinformation to the more disinterested public.

Propaganda is a type of misinformation; it consists of attempts to influence the public to accept a given view without giving fair treatment to opposing views. Propaganda differs from accurate information in several ways. Propaganda appeals to emotion rather than to reason. It attempts to foster an attitude as "true" or "proper." In propaganda, appeals are often made to an ingroup against an outgroup. For example, an issue is identified with democracy or freedom and America, and the opposing viewpoint is identified with communism or coercion and Russia. When the American Nazi Party tells us that the only "true" Americans are Aryan and all others are inferior people who do not belong in this country, they are using propaganda.

There are two views about the amount of information that guides public opinion. Some analysts support the *elitist participation view* of public opinion, believing that most citizens are poorly informed about public affairs (7). They think only a small well-educated, well-informed *elite* has a sophisticated understanding of public issues and well-developed, abstract belief systems. According to this view, most people's belief systems tend to be highly concrete and concerned with personal, rather than public, issues.

Other analysts cite evidence for an opposing position, the *mass participation view* of public opinion (8). According to this viewpoint, ordinary people do have well-developed political beliefs on some issues. For example, most people show consistency in their political party preference over time. While the issues that most interest ordinary citizens may differ from those of the most educated people in our society, people do learn about the issues that are important to them. Most people are more informed about public affairs when they are asked about issues that are important to them than when they are asked about an interviewer's choice of issues. The issues of interest to most people may be more local than national or international, but most individuals are concerned and informed about some aspects of public affairs (9).

It has also been suggested that a *knowledge gap* exists in our society (10). According to this hypothesis, as mass media information has increased, upper-class and middle-class people have acquired information at a more rapid rate than working-class and lower-class people. For this reason, the difference in attaining information between these segments of the population has increased, creating a large knowledge gap. A review of the literature shows that this hypothesis has been supported with respect to political behavior: People of higher social status are more informed regarding politics and more likely to participate in the political process than those of lower status (11). The findings from a recent study of election campaigns, however, show only limited support for the knowledge gap hypothesis. No gap was found in information regarding a relatively clear and straightforward issue (a political candidate's views on a new tax), but a gap did occur in information regarding an ambiguous and complex issue (the candidate's views on a tax hidden in other legislation). It is possible that the knowledge gap exists only for complex issues, but will increase overall because fundamental information is becoming more and more complex (12).

For public opinion to have influence, it must be communicated to the society's decision makers. Votes and public opinion polls are two common ways through which public opinion is expressed. Other ways are through the products people buy, the movies they attend, the music they play, and so on.

A recent study of voter preferences in national elections from 1952 to 1980 suggests that television has changed the basis for people's voting decisions (13). Before television, political party identification and attitudes toward the political parties were crucial

in determining votes. Post-television, however, the decisions have turned more on people's personal reactions to the candidates, as based on their television appearances. Even self-interest often is unimportant in determining votes, surfacing only when the issue is of prime importance to the voter (14).

Crazes, fads, and fashions Crazes, fads, and fashions are all manifested in a rush of behavior *toward* something. A *craze* is an intense and spontaneous mass action that achieves some goal or expresses some belief. A craze can have quite serious consequences for a society. *Fads* are characterized by a common interest or behavior that is of limited duration. Fads involve less intense behavior, last a shorter time, and have less serious consequences for society than crazes. The game of Trivial Pursuit provides an example of a recent, but departed, fad. A *fashion* is a clothing fad. The punk look is one such recent fashion. Fads and fashions are thought to be less intense and more superficial than crazes (see Box 16-2 for examples of fads and fashions).

Crazes can have important implications for our economic, political, and religious lives. Speculative behavior in the economic sphere, bandwagon effects for political candidates, and religious revivalism are examples of crazes that have had lasting consequences for our society.

The current fitness craze provides an example of a craze with notable social consequences (16). Why is the fitness craze important? The United States is the most overweight nation on earth, and people who are physically fit survive longer than those who are not fit. Fitness became popular during the 1970s and 1980s as more and more evidence accumulated that cardiovascular health is improved by aerobic exercise and attention to cholesterol levels. Currently, 26 million people jog and another 42 million people take brisk walks for exercise.

One indication of the magnitude of this craze is the money people expend on fitness. Ten billion dollars per year is spent on weight loss; in addition, the workout industry takes in about $8 billion per year. The newest fad in the workout craze is health camps or spas where people are exercised and fed

■ *Shorts, T-shirts, and day packs: Today's summer campus fashions. (WGS)*

healthily at an exorbitant cost per day. Even infant exercise classes are filling fast, some at the cost of $150 per week.

The fitness craze also has a down side. Many normal weight people constantly diet, and most of these nonobese dieters are teenagers or children. *Anorexia nervosa,* starving oneself to become thin out of an overconformity to society's view that thin is beautiful, and *bulimia,* a cycle of binging and purging for the same purpose, are dangerous conditions that have become common among the young. Some researchers believe eating disorders are reaching epidemic proportions on college campuses (17). Possibly 15 percent of college age women are bulimic at some time during their college years, and 1 percent of the U.S. population is anorexic (18). Minor eating disorders are even more common: In a survey of 33,000 women's magazine readers, 45 percent had fasted, 50 percent had used diet pills, 19 percent had used diuretics, 19 percent had used laxatives, and 15 percent had used self-induced vomiting to control their weight (19). These disor-

ders affect mostly women, on whom society unfortunately imposes strict standards of beauty.

Panics A panic is a spontaneous, disorganized reaction. In contrast to crazes, panics involve a rush of behavior *away* from something (20). Physical flight may or may not be involved. Panics are characterized by high levels of inappropriate anxiety, lack of preparation, and an expectation of some future calamity (21). In panics, a person's typical approach to solving problems fails to work. Hysterical beliefs prevail. When events occur to transform the diffuse anxiety of individuals into a specific fear, panic behavior results (22).

A panic occurred on Black Monday, October 29, 1987, when the stock market plunged by 22.6 percent, far more than on the worst day of the stock market crash of 1929 (23). In a single day, the market value of U. S. securities declined by $500 billion. This crash brought about similar crashes all over the world. On Tuesday, October 30, 1987, the London market lost 12.2 percent; the Tokyo market, 15

BOX 16-1

Public Opinion

Public opinion polls keep the nation informed of its citizens' changing attitudes and beliefs. These opinions often are created by, and in turn create, social change. For instance, a Gallup poll in 1987 of a national sample of adults asked the question, "Do you think there should or should not be a complete ban on cigarette advertising?" and "Would you favor or oppose a complete ban on smoking in all public places?" (15). For the first time, more respondents supported than opposed the bans, despite the fact that 30 percent of the sample smoked. The responses to the questions were as follows:

Ban Advertising		Ban Smoking in Public Places	
Should	49%	Favor	55%
Should not	47%	Oppose	43%
No opinion	4%	No opinion	2%

Women, whites, and people with more education were more likely to favor these bans than men, minorities, and people with less education.

Negative opinions regarding smoking are clearly having an impact on society. Gallup reports that many employers have introduced sharp restrictions on smoking in the work place due to the potential health risks to nonsmokers of breathing cigarette smoke. Smoking is now banned in many public places and on airline flights of under two hours. Doubtless these changes have further influenced people's opinions on these issues, and these changed opinions will lead to even greater social changes. ■

---

percent; the Paris market, 6 percent; and the Toronto market, 7 percent.

Before the crash, large U. S. spending and trade deficits led most investors to believe the market value of stock on the U. S. exchange was too high, but they were disinclined to leave the market when great profits were still being made. Knowledge of the market's inflated condition led to panicked selling once computer trading of entire stock portfolios touched off a sharp drop in prices. Chaos

reigned on the floor of the New York Stock Exchange. So many sell orders were received that brokers could not find buyers in many instances. Many investors watched their investments drain away as they helplessly telephoned their brokers and for hours heard only busy signals at the end of the line.

The panic affected a great many people, not just shareholders. The consequences of the crash included lost profits in mutual funds, pension plans, savings plans, and threats to job security. Fortunately,

Fads & Fashions

The fads and fashions of the last two decades have included the following items. How many of these do you remember? Some fads and fashions come and go so quickly that they are soon forgotten.

streaking	Spuds McKenzie	stone washed jeans
skateboarding	video pets	designer drugs
Cabbage Patch Kids	video babies	psychedelic drugs
pet rocks	walkmen	backgammon
Perrier	the safari look	polyester
Rubik cubes	"Baby on board" signs	Swatches
Reeboks	toga parties	leisure suits
designer jeans	earrings for men	discotheques
grazing	aerobic dancing	the Jennifer Beals look
wearable art	jogging	
shoulder length hair for men	distance biking	
adult roller skating	miniskirts	
tattoos for women	maxiskirts	
3-D movies	any diet you can think of	
the return of 3-D movies	health foods	

the U. S. market now has safeguards that did not exist in 1929, when the stock market crash led to the collapse of the banking system. Unlike 1929, the 1987 crash did not lead to the collapse of the entire U. S. economy.

Recent survey data suggest we may be on the verge of a national AIDS panic that threatens basic rights of privacy (24). A nationwide survey conducted in 1987 found a large percentage of U. S. citizens want to protect the country from AIDS by subjecting huge numbers of people to mandatory AIDS screen-

ing. Respondents were asked if a number of people should be tested for AIDS. The types of people to be tested, and the percentages of respondents answering "yes" were as follows: immigrants applying for personal residence in the United States, 90 percent; inmates of federal prisons, 88 percent; members of the armed forces, 83 percent; couples applying for marriage licenses, 80 percent; visitors from foreign countries, 66 percent; all American citizens, 52 percent. Most college educated respondents opposed AIDS testing for all citizens, while

■ *Jogging: One aspect of the fitness craze. (WGS)*

most respondents with less than a high school education supported testing all citizens.

Three quarters of the respondents said they currently were taking or planned to take AIDS prevention measures. Some preventative measures were appropriate, such as avoiding elective surgery requiring blood transfusions (42 percent) and donating one's blood for one's own possible future use (42 percent). Other measures appear to be totally unnecessary, such as not associating with

suspected AIDS victims (43 percent), avoiding the use of restrooms in public facilities (28 percent), and not donating blood (20 percent).

These responses to the AIDS epidemic suggest the beginnings of a panic in their overly high levels of fear and their inappropriate and strong reactions.

We have discussed public opinion, crazes, fads, fashions, and panics which are all types of collective behavior that are performed individually, rather than as a part of a group. We now turn to two types of collective behavior performed in groups, crowds and social movements.

Crowds

Crowds can be classified into several types (27). A *street crowd* is composed of passersby who stop at some common object of interest. A *mob* is a crowd of angry persons who have the potential for violence and unlawful action. A *riot* is a type of mob behavior in which violence occurs.

Before considering the question, Why do crowds form? we will first explore the physical movement and interaction that accompany crowd behavior.

Collective locomotion Whether we refer to a demonstration or a procession, or a street crowd or a riot, all involve *collective locomotion,* the movement of people from place to place (28). This movement ranges from the very simple (a small group of listeners moving closer to a speaker) to the very complex (a well-orchestrated protest march of hundreds of thousands of people).

In most instances of group collective behavior, the group interaction involves three sequential steps (29). These are milling, collective excitement, and social contagion.

■ *Milling* is the most basic type of collective group behavior. In milling, people move among one another randomly, much as excited cattle move about. As a result of milling, people in a group grow more sensitive to each other. Rapport develops within the group. The group members become more and more likely to respond to each other quickly, without thinking, and to the

Terrorism

An ominous new type of collective behavior has appeared in the last two decades: political or ideological demands made with the threat of violence (25). The 1980s have been called the decade of terrorism. From 1970 to 1984, some 23,000 domestic and international terrorist incidents occurred, with 41,000 deaths, 24,000 wounded, and over $1 billion in property damage resulting from these attacks. The number of terrorist incidents has increased about 20 percent per year since the early 1970s.

In the last few years, a new brand of terrorism has emerged: Nations use terrorist proxies they can publicly disown and privately control. Such groups are becoming increasingly more adept and more violent. Their primary goal is to show the powerlessness of governments to prevent such terrorist attacks. American experts believe all nations are put at risk by Third World and Communist countries' resistance to implementation of international anti-terrorist protective actions, and their willingness to believe some terrorist groups are legitimate "national liberationists" rather than terrorists. While ample national and international anti-terrorism statutes exist, they are not enforced.

In the last few years attention has turned to possible attacks using nuclear terrorism. The possibility of a terrorist incident for theft of nuclear weapons or fissionable material is considered to be increasing. Since much terrorism is directed against U. S. citizens or interests, U. S. nuclear plants are likely targets. Unfortunately, these plants are only designed for protection against nuclear accidents, not for protection from terrorist attacks.

---

exclusion of all else. Milling people are more apt to act together than they would be if they were not part of a group. Milling sets the stage for collective excitement.

- *Collective excitement* is an intense form of milling. In collective excitement, the milling is speeded up and may become circular. These excited behaviors focus the individuals' attention, and bring them more directly under the influence of the dominant mood of the group. People become more emotionally aroused than they

would if they were alone in the same situation. Old behavior patterns may be broken, and individuals become more likely to act sheerly on impulse and feelings. People may engage in behaviors which they would ordinarily not perform. Collective excitement leads directly to social contagion.

- *Social contagion* is the rapid spread of a mood or impulse. It is a natural result of intense and widespread collective excitement. Through social contagion, many individuals who were pre-

Although it may surprise you, many terrorists are not much different from many of you. They tend to be young, university-educated people from middle-class or professional backgrounds who are inclined to idealism and social activism (26). Few of them display evidence of psychopathology. They often start out by being active in pacifist groups. They frequently experience frustration at the lack of success of these groups and at that point they are ripe for recruitment into groups that eventually adopt violence as a means to accomplish their ends.

The road to use of violence is often a gradual one. It starts with demonstrations, and then when these fail, actions against property, then violence against others who are defined as the enemy (the police, politicians), followed by violence against unarmed supporters of the opposition, and finally against random members of the other group and innocent bystanders.

On the road toward violence, group cohesion usually increases and the group becomes more singleminded. Members of the terrorist group who are unwilling to escalate their tactics drop out of the group, facilitating the move towards more extreme forms of action. Thus, the processes of groupthink and group polarization are in operation in these groups. (See Chapters 7 and 14 for a discussion of these concepts). The group develops its own norms and morality as it becomes more and more isolated from society and as it engages in the self-justification necessary to accept its increasingly violent behavior. Killing people can eventually become an end in itself, particularly if the group suffers losses it wishes to revenge.

Terrorist groups, like all successful groups, provide important rewards for their members. Initially they provide members with an opportunity to act on their ideals and thus contribute to the members' sense of identity. In addition, the members often receive strong social support from other members; the group offers opportunities to achieve recognition both within the group and in the larger society; and when the group meets with success, it enhances the members' self-esteem and sense of self-efficacy. In addition, many members of such groups find them exciting. ■

viously merely detached bystanders or passersby may become caught up in the group. During social contagion, individuals become less self-conscious and less likely to make judgments before acting. When people have a predisposition to act in a certain way, as when they have a common grievance or concern, a pattern of behavior can spread quickly throughout the group.

The behavior of people delayed in airports demonstrates each of these group behaviors. Many

of you have been stranded in an airport waiting for a late plane. The passengers and the people waiting to meet the plane first become restless and start to mill around. While a large number of people may be waiting for the plane, they typically do not pay much attention to each other until they begin to walk around in frustration and boredom.

As the plane is later and later, the members of the crowd begin to feel angry and frustrated. The crowd members notice each other's irritation and this recognition feeds their own irritation. As they mill around more intensely, people may complain to each other loudly, slam things around, or show their anger openly in other ways. At this point, a state of collective excitement has been reached.

If the plane still does not arrive, the waiting crowd members may begin to talk among themselves about taking some action—demanding, as a group, that the local airline officials find them another plane or book them on another airline. People who have maintained calm up to this point are likely to become caught up in the collective mood of anger and indignation. The group may vent its collective frustration on any available airport official. People who would not ordinarily do so may raise their voices or use obscenities. At this point, social contagion exists.

Now we turn to the question, Why do crowds form? We will give several different answers, the first of which derives from LeBon's classic theory. Then three modern theorists will be compared with LeBon's theory: convergence, emergent norm, and value-added theories.

LeBon's crowd psychology At the turn of the century, the French sociologist Gustave LeBon argued that crowds are characterized by impulsive and uninhibited behavior (30). According to LeBon, people in a crowd cease to function and think as individuals. They function solely as members of the group, and think with a *collective mind,* in which each member of the crowd experiences the same emotions and has the same responses to the situation at hand. The collective mind is inferior to that of the individual members of the crowd. The dominant characteristics of the crowd are emotionality and irrationality.

LeBon believed that three mechanisms encourage the formation of crowd behavior. The first mechanism is *anonymity.* Individuals feel less responsible for their behavior the less likely it is that they can be identified. Crowds create relative anonymity and thus reduce individual responsibility. In this state individuals commit acts for which they believe they cannot later be held responsible. The second mechanism is *contagion.* LeBon believed that, in a crowd, emotional states spread from person to person like diseases spread. The third mechanism

is *suggestibility.* LeBon felt that crowd members completely accept all suggestions made to them, just as if they were hypnotized.

LeBon's observations capture the uniformity of purpose and belief that crowds often seem to exhibit. Individuals in crowds often commit acts such as public profanity, vandalism, or destruction of property they would not engage in if they were more identifiable. In crowds, one can often see an emotion "catch hold" in a crowd and spread, and often people in crowds take the suggestions of their leaders.

The fans at a basketball ball game seem to provide an example of contagion. First, there is some evidence of a collective mind in the fans' reactions to the referees' calls and the score of the game. The home-court fans are angry, happy, or sad in unison because their emotions are all focused on the game. Their thinking processes tend not to be highly complex, as indicated in their frequently biased perceptions of the referees' calls. Second, the fans tend to be swallowed up by the crowd so that they become almost anonymous. There is a great deal of stimulation, which induces high arousal and undercuts critical thinking and a sense of individual responsibility. One often sees behavior that the fans would not exhibit elsewhere, such as jeering or shouting obscenities at the members of the opposing team. Third, the fans' moods are clearly contagious. The joy created by a win over a highly rated opponent quickly infects everyone in the arena. Fourth, basketball crowds display some types of suggestion. For instance, when the cheerleaders call for the wave, almost everyone goes along with their request without giving it much thought. However, modern observers of crowd behavior have questioned the validity of a collective mind, a crowd's ability to act with a single purpose, and the low intelligence of a crowd.

Convergence theory *Convergence theory* provides another perspective on crowds. According to this theory, people who share similar convictions and predispositions converge because of some particular event (31). A common mood is *brought to* the crowd,

BOX 16-4

Working the Crowd

Marjoe Gortner became the youngest ordained minister in the country in 1948, at the age of four. He preached to thousands of enthusiastic listeners all over the United States, giving carefully memorized speeches that his parents claimed were given to him in his sleep by the Lord. In his teens, Marjoe decided that he could no longer practice such deception and he left the evangelical circle. He returned only once, to make the film *Marjoe*, which used his story to expose illegitimate faith healing in the United States.

When interviewed about his ability to drive crowds to religious frenzy night after night, Marjoe spoke in terms compatible with convergence theory (32). His explanation was that people came to his revivals with a problem that the medical profession had not been able to solve, with a belief that faith healing was the only remaining solution. They then saw others in the same position who appeared to have their problems solved by him. With this set of beliefs, people wanted to perceive that he could heal them.

Marjoe's view of building religious frenzy contains no mysticism, only show-manship. According to Marjoe, "It's the same as a rock-and-roll concert. You have an opening number with a strong entrance, then you go through a lot of the old standards, building up to your hit song at the end." ■

as in a protest demonstration, rather than created by the crowd. The crowd eventually acts out their similar feelings. If one were able to identify the latent tendencies and beliefs of large numbers of people, one could predict their crowd behavior.

The Cuban inmate riots of December 1987 contained elements of convergence (32). In 1980, Castro allowed a large number of Cuban refugees to enter the United States. Much to the surprise of U. S. officials, this group contained a number of "undesirable" people, such as criminals and mental patients. Approximately 2,700 refugees who arrived with a record of offenses that would have denied them access as refugees, and other Cuban refugees

who had committed crimes in the United States, were placed in federal prisons.

In late 1987, these prisoners had hopes of being released after their long imprisonment. However, in late December the inmates learned from radio and television reports that the U. S. had ruled they had no constitutional rights, and the United States and Cuban governments had reached an agreement to begin deporting the refugees back to Cuba.

The inmates believed they would be killed if they were returned to Cuba. They experienced a common mood of fear, anger, and betrayal brought about by the government's decision to deport them. In two federal prisons, the inmates converged to exchange views and their emotions intensified. Feeling they had nothing left to lose, they seized control of the prisons and took 122 hostages.

The riot continued for two weeks. In the end, the hostages were released unharmed in exchange for promises of an indefinite moratorium on deportation and an individual review of each case.

One problem with convergence theory is that it does not explain the changes that often occur in crowd behavior (34). If common beliefs and desired actions exist, no shifts of motives, behaviors, and moods should occur in crowds. Frequently, however, such shifts are observed. A peaceful demonstration against nuclear power can become violent; a volatile mob of majority group members threatening racial violence against a minority group may disperse without incident. The next theory we will explore addresses such changes in crowd behavior.

Emergent norm theory Ralph Turner and Lewis Killian formulated an *emergent norm theory* of collective behavior that applies both to crowds and social movements (35). Emergent norms are spontaneous norms that emerge in crowds. According to these theorists, all crowds share a number of common elements. Crowds form in ambiguous situations in which the participants' behaviors are unplanned. A sense of urgency characterizes the feelings of the members of the crowd. As the crowd grows, norms are communicated throughout the crowd about appropriate moods, imagery, and actions. The dominant mood, imagery, and actions come to be viewed as right, as those to which the crowd should conform. A group norm thus emerges. Individuals become highly susceptible to suggestions consistent with the emergent norm. As a result, the participants may engage in actions they would ordinarily inhibit.

Turner and Killian disagree with LeBon's and the convergence theorists' assumption of uniform crowd predispositions and thinking. According to emergent norm theory, members initially have divergent motives, attitudes, and behaviors. Some crowd participants are certain the time is ripe for actions. Others are committed to reform, but within

■ *A campaign stop: An example of a crowd. (WGS)*

institutional avenues. Others simply enjoy participating in crowds and join solely for that reason. Most crowds also contain mere spectators.

Crowd members differ initially in their levels of participation. As the emotional feelings in the crowd intensify, the members' actions may become more similar. Uniformity ultimately results from the interaction among the initially dissimilar members. Some crowds even shift leadership between earlier and later stages of development. If some crowd members lack inhibitions, this deficit can become important to the facilitation of antisocial crowd action.

Emergent norm theory is exemplified in some anti-nuclear protests. These protests may begin by looking more like Sunday outings than civil protests. There may be guitar playing and singing. Picnickers are scattered about. Committed protesters, some of whom are in costume, concerned but noncommitted protesters, amateur photographers, and spectators all mingle. There is laughter and idle talking. Passionate anti-nuke speeches can make the crowds' mood more serious. Then group chanting (NO NUKES, NO NUKES), banner waving, and marching increase the commitment to the protest and provide an outlet for the dominant mood. The crowd may become angry. Onlookers and photographers sometimes become emotionally involved and join the protesters to chant and march.

At this point, the police may react as though the group were dangerous, which can further increase solidarity and passion among the protesters. The leaders of the protests typically plan and practice lawful protest. However, other leaders sometimes emerge who lead the group to destructive acts, such as attempting to damage nuclear plants. Certainly the groups are not initially singleminded and committed. During the course of the protest, they often become so.

A study of the 1960s civil rights movement in Tallahassee, Florida, showed the importance of emergent norms (36). In the South in the early 1960s, city buses were still segregated. Blacks could sit only in the back row of the bus; the remaining seats were reserved for white patrons. One day two female students from a local black college spontaneously decided to take the only two remaining empty seats on a bus. These seats were in the "white only" section. The bus driver called the police and the students were arrested.

The following day a cross was burned at the students' off-campus residence hall. A student meeting was called. The students at the college, who had no history of activism as a group, decided to boycott the city buses. They asked the community to join them. Black leaders from the city met and decided to join the boycott. As a result of the black leaders' meeting a strong black activist organization was formed, and a successful bus boycott was begun. This unplanned boycott thus emerged from a series of spontaneous actions and reactions.

One problem with emergent norm theory is that it does not explain crowds which meet with a common mood and purpose. While some crowds experience shifts of motives, behaviors, and moods, others do not. A crowd may convene with a common mood and explicit purpose that is carried out exactly as planned. For example, in early 1989 a crowd of people met outside the prison in Starke, Florida for Ted Bundy's execution for a series of murders of young women. They came explicitly to celebrate the execution, and their celebration proceeded in a predetermined manner.

Value-added theory Neil Smelser's classic theory of crowds and social movements suggests that a breakdown in the aspects of society that channel people into conventional behavior leads to discontent and to unconventional behavior (37). His theory is called the *value-added theory* of collective behavior because each of six stages "adds its value" in a certain way before the next stage can be reached. At each stage, the range of possibilities for the final outcome narrows. The stages are:

1. *Structural conduciveness.* Collective behavior cannot occur unless social structures permit them. To illustrate, for collective behavior to occur, it must be possible for individuals to be in the same place in large numbers and to have some mechanism for exchanging grievances. Many totalitarian governments understand this concept and thus prohibit public meetings. In nontotalitarian societies, blocked opportunities

■ *The emergent norm theory and the value-added theory are different ways to explain escalations in the collective behavior of crowds, such as a protest march that begins peacably and ends up in violence. (AP/Wide World Photos)*

for expressing grievances within the normal channels of society facilitate their expression in unconventional ways such as crowd protests and social movements.

2. *Structural strain.* Some form of social strain or frustration with some aspect of the society always precedes collective behavior. The more severe the strain, the more likely it is to generate a crowd or social movement. Without the prior existence of structural conduciveness, however, structural strain could not lead to collective behavior.

3. *Generalized belief.* The generalized belief is a common belief held by the potential actors about the source of the strain, the characteristics of the source, and the appropriate responses to this strain. The growth and spread of a generalized belief could not result in collective behavior without the prior appearance of structural conduciveness and structural strain.

4. *Precipitating factors.* A precipitating factor is some event, often dramatic, which provides a concrete example of the problem. Crowds and social movements are always preceded by one or more precipitating factors.

5. *Mobilization* of participants. Once sensitized by some precipitating event, members must be mobilized to act.

6. *Operation of social control.* Social control consists of the means used in the society to ensure that people behave in ways that are expected and approved. Any incidence of collective behavior will bring about attempts at social control by those in authority to prevent or lessen the effects of the behavior.

Smelser's ideas were supported in a study of the 1980 New Mexico prison riot, the most brutal and costly prison riot in U. S. history (33 inmates killed, 400 inmates wounded, $200 million in damages) (38):

1. Structural conduciveness existed; it included such factors as the ability of inmates to move around in the prison, security lapses, and defects in the prison facility.

2. Structural strain was present in the considerably worsened prison conditions from 1975 to 1980. Under a new warden living conditions declined dramatically, chronic violence existed, community contact programs were abandoned, inmate incentives declined, and a system of inmate informants was instituted. It was, in short, a horrible, horribly run prison.

3. Generalized beliefs led a number of people to join the riot. The inmates believed the already unlivable conditions would continue to decline, and they were helpless to halt or lessen this disintegration.

4. A precipitating factor occurred when several inmates overpowered four guards. Security lapses allowed this small incident to turn into a full-fledged riot.

5. Mobilization efforts were launched to involve other inmates in the riot. The small group of inmates who overpowered the guards were able to release all prisoners from their cells through a combination of unlocked doors and physical defects which allowed them access to the control room. Inmates were encouraged by other inmates to act out their anger and frustration on the system.

6. *Social control* attempts were brought to bear on the inmates. The riots led to severe reprisals against inmates and a long period of strict "lock up" conditions. Further, significant reforms were made in the prison to prevent new riots.

One criticism that has been made of value-added theory is that, after an instance of collective behavior, these conditions typically can be identified. However, the theory has not proven to be as useful in predicting when these conditions will culminate in collective behavior and when they will not do so.

In the next section, we will consider a type of collective behavior that is less spontaneous and longer in duration than mass behavior and crowds: social movements.

Social Movements

Social movements are organized collective displays by people who have considerable concern about some issue. The purpose of the movement is to do something about the issue. Movements deliberately attempt to promote or resist change in a group, society, or world order of which they are a part. They do so through a variety of means, not excluding violence, revolution, or withdrawal into utopian communities (39).

Social movements always have continuity of action and purpose. They have a program for social change, a plan for satisfying members' needs, and they make an attempt to gain power for the beneficiaries of the movement (40). Social movements are intertwined with other types of collective behavior; a major portion of many social movements consists of repeated incidents of other types of collective behavior (41).

One current social movement is MADD (Mothers Against Drunk Drivers). Their issue of concern is drunk driving, and their purpose is to lower deaths due to drunk drivers. Their program for social change includes raising penalties for drunken driving and raising the legal drinking age to 21 in all states. The movement formally started in 1980 with the formation, in California, of the first chapter of MADD. After only a few years, the movement has gained considerable power and has begun to enact legal changes. By 1983, 40 states had strengthened their drunken-driving laws and 8 states had raised their legal drinking age. Data collected after these changes were made suggest that they have had the desired results. In New York, where the legal drinking age was raised from 18 to 19, alcohol-related accidents resulting in death or injury dropped 21 percent in the first six months after the law was changed (42).

Quasi-social movements lack one of the above defining features of true social movements (43): They make no attempt to change the world order. For example, cults, such as Mrs. Keech's group of believers in beings from the planet Clarion, are quasi-movements if they make no attempt to change the broader society.

We will examine two theories that attempt to explain the existence and fate of social movements. First, however, we examine a problem common to all social movements: recruitment of activists into the movement.

Recruitment   You have almost certainly been contacted by members of some social movement asking you to join their group. How were you approached? Few groups recruit many of their members off the street. Instead, preexisting social networks provide an important means of movement recruitment (44). People who are acquainted with someone in a social movement, like friends, relatives, work associates, or fellow members of other organizations, are prime targets for recruitment.

Not all people who are contacted become recruits. What characteristics make some individuals more susceptible to recruitment than others? For groups such as cults, the fewer social ties the individual has, the more likely he or she is to become involved in the movement. For example, a study of the typical recruits to the Nichiren Shoshu Buddhist movement found they were young, single, and either students or marginally employed (45). They had large amounts of free time and few commitments to curtail their involvement.

Recruitment is a difficult task because pursuit of a group goal is not a sufficient motivator for most people to become actively involved in a movement (46). Out of rational self-interest, most individuals will choose to ride free on the efforts of a few activists. *Free-riders* do not contribute to the movement, but benefit from others' work without having to invest individual resources. People must be offered some incentive in addition to the group goal to become activists, rather than free-riders, such as prestige or a sense of identity.

These ideas were tested with residents of communities in the vicinity of the Three Mile Island nuclear plant after the March 1979 evacuation of over 150,000 nearby residents following an accident at the plant (47). The researchers identified people who reported they were involved in issues regarding the safety and desirability of the nuclear plant and then determined if they had contributed time or

■ *Cults like the Hare Krishna are quasi-social movements.* (WGS)

money to pro- or anti-Three Mile Island groups. Consistent with the hypothesis, most concerned respondents were free-riders, contributing neither time nor money to their cause. Only 2 percent of the supporters and 13 percent of the opponents of the nuclear plant had contributed more than nominal time or money to pro- or anti-nuclear groups. The free-riders tended to give reasons for their noninvolvement that were consistent with the hypothesis of rational self-interest: The respondents thought that other people would do the job, and they would benefit just as much as the activists if they were successful.

An additional problem for recruitment into social movements is that some movement participation is high in risk and/or cost: It may be dangerous, as was participation in the early civil rights movement in the South, or it may involve considerable time, energy, or money. One researcher has found that strong ideological identification with movement values, a prior history of activism, and integration into activist social networks encourages people to act on their beliefs (48). In the 1964 Freedom Summer project, volunteers committed two months to reg-

istering black voters in Mississippi (49). This project was demanding of both time and money; volunteers not only had to forego summer employment, they were also expected to support themselves. It was also dangerous; three project members were killed, and many others were subjected to beatings, bombings, and arrests. Participants were distinguished from other volunteers who eventually withdrew by their greater number of affiliations with civil rights organizations, higher levels of prior civil rights activity, and stronger and more extensive ties to other participants.

Next we turn to two theoretical explanations for the occurrence of social movements: relative deprivation and resource mobilization.

Relative deprivation theory According to relative deprivation theorists, *relative* rather than *absolute* deprivation leads to the formation of social movements. *Relative deprivation* occurs when individuals feel they are deprived, relative to others with whom they compare themselves (50). The greater the feeling of relative deprivation, the greater the feeling of distress and frustration. These feelings lead to aggression and to attempts to change the group's status. One can feel relatively deprived in two ways, deprived relative to individuals in another group or deprived relative to one's ideal expectations.

This theory can explain the puzzling finding that social movements take place during times of rising expectations, not during the worst of times. When times are bad, people are absolutely deprived, but their expectations for the future are low. It is only when individuals see others' lives improving that they begin to have positive expectations for the future. Under these conditions, if others' fates improve, but theirs does not, people come to feel relatively deprived.

Relative deprivation theory has often been applied to the civil rights movement of the 1960s. More recently, relative deprivation predicted participation in South Boston's 1980 anti-busing protests (51). Relative deprivation was measured by asking white respondents to compare their individual economic gains over the last five years to those of several groups (whites, blacks, middle-class people, working-class people). The investigators believed deprivation results in a type of protest closely related to the type of deprivation experienced. They anticipated that relative deprivation based on class (status deprivation) would be responded to by collective protest designed to improve the status of the group, while relative deprivation based on the emotional reaction of racism (race deprivation) would lead to individual emotional reactions of hostility.

As predicted, relative deprivation based on class (the belief that one has experienced less economic gain than members of other socioeconomic classes) predicted collective protest, such as participation in anti-busing marches and rallies. Also as predicted, relative deprivation based on race (the belief that one has experienced less economic gain than members of another race) predicted individual protest, such as expressing hostility toward blacks.

In recent years, relative deprivation theory has been a topic of much dispute (52). Critics have charged that it overemphasizes personal factors and ignores social factors in considering people's commitment to social movements.

Resource mobilization theory One of the most recent perspectives on social movements is resource mobilization. *Resource mobilization* refers to the process of obtaining and organizing the resources of individual members of a group for a common goal (53). Resource mobilization theories examine the links of social movements to other groups, the dependence on external support for the movement's success, and the tactics used in the broader society to control or to incorporate movements (54).

While earlier theories emphasized ideological concerns and grievances, resource mobilization theorists argue that participation in social movements is based on exchange: Participation results from weighing the costs of participation against the benefits, taking into consideration factors such as the availability of resources to the movement.

The resource mobilization perspective and other perspectives on social movements also differ regarding a social movement's support base, strategy and tactics, and relationship to the larger society (55). We will discuss each difference in perspective in turn.

Older theories of social movements view the support base for a movement as an aggrieved population that provides resources and labor. The resource mobilization theorists think social movements may or may not be based upon an aggrieved group. Individuals and organizations who are not a part of the group may provide the major resources and labor. For example, the movement to force U.S. corporations to divest themselves of their South African holdings is largely a U.S. student movement. Groups such as MADD contain not only friends and relatives of people killed by drunk drivers but many other people as well.

From other perspectives, the study of a group's strategy and tactics focuses on the movement leaders' choice of tactics (bargaining, violence) based on their past relations with authorities, the success of previous strategies, and the group's ideology. The resource mobilization perspective directs major concern not only to relations with authorities, but also to intragroup strategies and tactics. Resource mobilization theorists study the mobilization of supporters and the dilemmas created by multiple goals that may require conflicting strategies. To illustrate, a resource mobilization theorist studying the Miami race riots of 1983 might be concerned with the involvement of nonblacks in the riots. Resource mobilization theorists might also examine the conflict that violence presented for the group: While the riots dramatized the plight of blacks in Miami, the violence also alienated a large number of potential supporters of their cause because the riots were so destructive.

With respect to a movement's relationship to society, other theories have emphasized the extent of hostility or tolerance of the group in the larger society. In contrast, resource mobilization theorists examine the movement's use of society's institutions, the degree of access of movement supporters to institutional power, and the integration of the movement's supporters into the larger society. The media play a significant role in developing a collective sense of a problem and can create a coordinated response among widely scattered people (56). For instance, resource mobilization theorists might study the extent to which Miami's black leaders were drawn from other organized groups (the ministry) and the extent to which these extra-movement ties facilitated access to the resources of other institutions (mass media) (57).

Some resource mobilization theorists believe indigenous social movements are being replaced by "professional" social movement organizations, which use little constituent labor and operate on the basis of outside donations (58). These organizations emerge from the interests of intellectuals concerned about the disadvantaged, who have time and money to contribute to the organization. Mass media publicity and direct mail fundraising are used to publicize problems and recruit other concerned citizens. Professional organizations have had a positive impact on the development of social movements (NAACP for the civil rights movement, Greenpeace for the environmental movement, MADD for the movement against drunk drivers).

Considerable data have been amassed to support the resource mobilization theory. A study of the Polish workers' union, *Solidarity,* found the mobilization of Polish engineers to be critical to the movement's success (59). *Solidarity* was formed in 1980 as an opposition political force to the state Communist party. Worker-professional alliances are atypical in social movements, due to conflicting interests and social statuses. However, in Poland all workers joined the union to protest against work policies imposed by the Soviet regime that had led to an economic crisis (for example, filling positions on the basis of Communist party affiliation).

The engineers were particularly important to the union because they constituted the largest group of highly educated workers. Engineers not in managerial positions joined *Solidarity* because they had limited opportunities for individual remedy. The economic crisis was worsening due in part to the fact that their supervisors were high school educated nonprofessionals, and the engineers' socioeconomic status was declining. Managerial engineers joined the movement because they could not continue production without good relations between themselves and this powerful union. *Solidarity* was extremely successful in organizing nationwide worker strikes. It was so successful, in fact, it was banned by the ruling Communist party, although it was reinstated after several years and is now an important political force in Poland.

Critics of resource mobilization have raised several points (60). Some analysts believe most social movements really are indigenous movements in which professionals have played a secondary role. Second, elite patronage of these movements may not stem from social justice concerns, but from a desire to channel these movements into more mainstream, institutionalized actions. Third, the professionalization of social movements may hurt rather than help them. These theorists believe a movement can be successful only when the aggrieved community of people is organized and can devise tactical innovations and supply leaders to direct their use; and the group has political opportunities it can seize to spread the protest to other similar groups operating in other areas (61).

The 1960s civil rights movement has also yielded

data supporting this viewpoint (62). The black movement was an indigenous movement in which elite patronage came late and was directed toward support of the more moderate groups in the movement. This elite patronage may have weakened the indigenous groups by diverting indigenous organizing efforts and by intensifying rivalries among groups. The weakening of indigenous groups led to decay of the movement. Since both resource mobilization and its critics have found empirical support for their positions, a final assessment must await further data specifying the conditions under which each theory is most useful.

Other critics have argued that, while resource mobilization theory pointed to overlooked structural factors in the analysis of social movements, it neglected social psychological factors that would account for movement participation. Resource mobilization theory has cogently argued that individuals participate on the basis of a cost/benefit analysis, but it gave little attention to analysis at the individual level and to the interactions among individuals that create mobilization. Thus, analysts have been trying to reconcile resource mobilization theory with social psychological factors, such as relative deprivation (63) or attribution theory (64) in an effort to combine the strengths of both.

In one reformulation, emphasis is placed on the values and expectations of potential movement members (65). Since people must decide whether to participate in a social movement at a point when they do not know whether others will participate, their decisions are based on their expectations regarding: the number of other participants, the probability of success of the movement if many people participate, and their own contribution to the probability of success. According to this theory, willingness to participate is a function of the perceived attractiveness or aversiveness of the expected consequences of participation and the possibilities of obtaining them.

People join movements when they perceive mobilization to be the means to achieve a collective good. If an individual thinks many people will participate, this individual is more likely to join than if he or she thinks few people will participate. These expectations regarding others' actions thus form a self-fulfilling prophecy with respect to the movement. Mobilization efforts attempt to foster the view that many people will participate. If this effort fails, the belief that joining the movement is useless can easily cause it to fail.

We have now explored recruitment of individuals into social movements and reviewed two theories that attempt to explain the formation of social movements and their ultimate fate. Why is it important to study social movements? All societies are in a constant process of change. Social movements constitute one major source of social change in the society.

In your own lifetimes, the civil rights movement, the women's liberation movement, the gay rights movement, the environmental movement, the pro-abortion movement, and the anti-abortion movement have already enacted considerable change in the society, and are still the cause of continuing change. More recently, the work of groups such as MADD, the anti-nuclear movement, and the South African divestment movement have begun to make important changes in the society. The study of social movements provides one critical way to accomplish the major purpose of social psychology—understanding the mutual influence of the individual and the society.

■
SUMMARY

Collective behavior is the study of groups that are governed by spontaneous or emergent norms, rather than by formal norms. Collective behavior can be divided into three types: mass behavior, crowds, and social movements. Mass behavior and crowds can be distinguished by the dominant emotion displayed by the individuals involved.

Mass behavior occurs when individuals respond separately to a common stimulus in the same way. We discussed five types of mass behavior. Public opinion includes the many opinions that are held within a society on any given topic. Some people believe that only elites are well informed about public affairs. Other researchers believe that most people have well-developed views about political affairs. A knowledge gap may exist between upper-class and middle-class individuals relative to working-class and lower-class individuals with respect to the acquisition of mass media information.

Crazes, fads, and fashions are manifested in a rush of behavior toward something. Fads are less serious and more limited in duration than crazes. A fashion is a clothing fad. In contrast, panics involve a rush of behavior away from something. They too may be relatively serious.

Crowds are large numbers of persons gathered together, such as street crowds, mobs, and riots. Crowds always include *collective locomotion,* the movement of people from place to place. The three forms of interaction characterizing crowd behavior are milling, collective excitement, and social contagion.

We discussed four explanations of crowd behavior. LeBon's theory suggests that, in a crowd, individuals act in an impulsive and uninhibited manner due to anonymity, contagion, and suggestibility. Convergence theory suggests that persons who already share the same convictions converge on an area because of some particular event. According to Killian and Turner's emergent norm theory, as a crowd grows, a group norm develops with respect to mood, imagery, and action. Smelser's value-added theory suggests that structural conduciveness, structural strain, growth and spread of a generalized belief, precipitating factors, mobilization of participants, and operation of social control must exist in crowd behavior.

Social movements are organized collective manifestations of issues for which people have considerable concern. Movements deliberately promote or resist change in the group, society, or world. Recruitment into social movements is difficult because most individuals will choose to ride free on the efforts of a few activists. People must be offered some incentive other than the success of the group to become activists.

Two explanations of social movements were considered. Relative deprivation theory suggests that social movements arise when individuals feel deprived, relative to others with whom they compare themselves.

While earlier theories emphasized ideological concerns and grievances, resource mobilization theorists argue that participation is based on an exchange model. It results from weighing costs against benefits of participation, taking into consideration structural factors such as the availability of resources. Resource mobilization theory also differs from other theories in its belief that movement members may not be members of an aggrieved group, its focus on intragroup mobilization, and its study of the group's use of and access to other groups and social institutions.

Resource mobilization refers to the process of obtaining and organizing the resources of individual members of a group for a common goal. According to resource mobilization theory, the structure of the social movement is critically important to its ability to mobilize. One concern that all social movements share is the commitment of the movement constituents' time and money to the group.

Critics of resource mobilization theory believe new social movements are merely indigenous movements in which professionals have played a secondary role; elite patronage of these movements may not stem from social justice concerns, but from a desire to channel these movements into more mainstream, institutionalized actions; and the professionalization may hurt rather than help some movements.

Recently, theorists have argued that, while resource mobilization theory points to overlooked structural factors in the analysis of social movements, it neglects social psychological factors that would account for movement participation. Thus, theorists have been trying to reconcile resource mobilization theory with social psychological factors in an effort to combine the strengths of both. In one reformulation, it is hypothesized that an individual is more likely to join if he or she thinks many, rather than few, people will participate.

It is important to study social movements, for they are the source of much social change within the society. Social movements show how the individual and the society mutually influence each other.

■

REFERENCES

1. Festinger, L., H. W. Riecken, and S. Schachter, 1956, *When Prophecy Fails,* Minneapolis: University of Minnesota Press.
2. Turner, R. H. and L. M. Killian, 1957, *Collective Behavior,* Englewood Cliffs, NJ: Prentice-Hall.
3. Aguirre, B. E., 1984, "The Conventionalization of Collective Behavior in Cuba," *American Journal of Sociology* 90:541–566.
4. Turner and Killian, 1957, op. cit.
5. Lofland, J. F., 1981, "Collective Behavior: The Elementary Forms" in M. Rosenberg and R. H. Turner (Eds.), *Social Psychology: Sociological Perspectives,* New York: Basic Books.
6. Blumer, H., 1955, "Collective Behavior," in A. M. Lee (Ed.), *Principles of Sociology,* New York: Barnes & Noble.
7. Converse, P. E., 1964, "The Nature of Belief Systems in Mass Publics," in D. Apter (Ed.), *Ideology and Discontent,* New York: The Free Press, pp. 206–261.
8. Oskamp, S., 1977, *Attitudes and Opinions,* Englewood Cliffs, NJ: Prentice-Hall.
9. Smelser, N. J., 1963, *Theory of Collective Behavior,* New York: The Free Press.
10. Tichenor, P. J., G. A. Donohue, and C. N. Olien, 1970, "Mass Media Flow and Differential Growth of Knowledge," *Public Opinion Quarterly* 34:159–170.
11. Gaziano, C., 1983, "The Knowledge Gap: An Analytical Review of Media Effects," *Communication Research* 10:447–486.
12. Moore, D. W., 1987, "Political Campaigns and the Knowledge-gap Hypothesis," *Public Opinion Quarterly* 51:186–200.
13. Keeter, S., 1987, "The Illusion of Intimacy: Television and the Role of Candidate Personal Qualities in Voter Choice," *Public Opinion Quarterly,* 51:344–358.
14. Young, J., E. Borgida, J. Sullivan, and J. Aldrich, 1987, "Personal Agendas and the Relationship between Self-interest and Voting Behavior," *Social Psychology Quarterly* 50:64–71.
15. *Gallup Reports,* Number 258, March 1987.
16. Information from this section is taken from *Life,* "A Special Report on Fitness," February 1987, pp. 22–80.
17. Squire, S., 1983, *The Slender Balance,* New York: Pinnacle.
18. Wooley, S. and A. Kearney-Cooke, 1986, "Intensive Treatment of Bulimia and Body-image Disturbance," in K. D. Brownell and J. P. Foreyt (Eds.), *Handbook of Eating Disorders,* New York: Basic Books.
19. Wooley, S. C. and O. W. Wooley, 1984, "Feeling Fat in a Thin Society," *Glamour,* February: 198–201, 251–252.
20. Smelser, 1963, op. cit.
21. Turner and Killian, 1957, op. cit.
22. Smelser, 1963, op. cit.
23. *Newsweek,* November 2, 9, 1987; *Time,* November 2, 9, 1987.
24. *Gallup Reports,* Number 261, June 1987.
25. Beckman, R. L. (for the Conference on International Terrorism), June 24–25, 1986, "Internal Terrorism: The Nuclear Dimension," *Terrorism* 8:351–378; B. L. Steward (Ed.), 1985, "State Sponsored Terrorism: The Threat and Possible Countermeasures," *Terrorism* 8:253–313.
26. McCauley, C. and M. E. Segal, 1987, "Social Psychology of Terrorist Groups," in C. Hendrick (Ed.), *Group Processes and Intergroup Relations,* Vol. 9, Beverly Hills: Sage.
27. Milgram, S. and H. Toch, 1968, "Collective Behavior: Crowds and Social Movements," in G. Lindzey and E. Aronson (Eds.), *The Handbook of Social Psychology,* Vol. 4, 2d ed., Reading, MA: Addison-Wesley.
28. McPhail, C. and R. T. Wohlstein, 1986, "Collective Locomotion as Collective Behavior," *American Sociological Review* 51:447–463.
29. Blumer, 1955, op. cit.
30. LeBon, G., 1897, *The Crowd: A Study of the Popular Mind,* London: T. F. Unwin.
31. Turner, R. H., 1964, "Collective Behavior," in R. E. L. Faris (Ed.), *Handbook of Modern Sociology,* Chicago: Rand McNally.
32. *Newsweek,* December 7, 1987; *Time,* December 7, 1987.
33. Conway, F. and J. Siegelman, 1978, *Snapping,* Philadelphia: Lippincott.
34. Turner, 1964, op. cit.
35. Turner and Killian, 1957, op. cit.; see also L. M. Killian, 1980, "Theory of Collective Behavior: The Mainstream Revisited," in H. M. Blalock Jr. (Ed.), *Sociological Theory and Research: A Critical Appraisal,* New York: The Free Press.
36. Killian, L. M., 1984, "Organization, Rationality, and Spontaneity in the Civil Rights Movement," *American Sociological Review* 49:770–783.
37. Smelser, 1963, op. cit.
38. Useem, B., 1985, "Disorganization and the New Mexico Prison Riot of 1980," *American Sociological Review* 50:677–688.
39. Zurcher, L. A. and D. A. Snow, 1981, "Collective Behavior: Social Movements," in M. Rosenberg and R. H. Turner, op. cit.
40. Turner and Killian, 1957, op. cit.
41. Marx, G. T., 1980, "Conceptual Problems in the Field of Collective Behavior," in H. M. Blalock, Jr., op. cit.
42. *Time,* January 16, 1984, p. 62.
43. Turner and Killian, 1957, op. cit.
44. Zurcher and Snow, 1981, op. cit.
45. Snow, D. A., L. A. Zurcher Jr., and S. Ekland-Olson, 1980, "Social Networks and Social Movements," *American Sociological Review* 45:787–801.
46. Olson, M., 1965, *The Logic of Collective Action: Public Goods and the Theory of Groups,* New York: Schocken.

47. Walsh, E. J. and R. H. Warland, 1983, "Social Movement Involvement in the Wake of a Nuclear Accident: Activists and Free Riders in the TMI Area," *American Sociological Review* 48:764–780.

48. McAdam, D., 1986, "Recruitment to High-risk Activism: The Case of Freedom Summer," *American Journal of Sociology* 92:64–90.

49. McAdam, 1986, ibid.

50. Davis, J. C., 1962, "Toward a Theory of Revolution," *American Sociological Review* 27:5–19; T. R. Gurr, 1970, *Why Men Rebel,* Princeton, NJ: Princeton University Press, A. Oberschall, 1978, "Theories of Social Conflict," in R. H. Turner, J. Coleman, and R. C. Fox (Eds.), *Annual Review of Sociology,* Vol. 4, pp. 291–316; C. Tilly, 1978, *From Mobilization to Revolution,* Reading, MA: Addison-Wesley.

51. Begley, T. M. and H. Alker, 1982, "Anti-busing Protest: Attitudes and Actions," *Social Psychology Quarterly* 45:187–197.

52. See M. L. Sayles, 1984, "Relative Deprivation and Collective Protest: An Impoverished Theory?" *Sociological Inquiry* 54:449–465; Useem, 1985, op. cit; S. E. Finkel and J. B. Rule, 1986, "Relative Deprivation and Related Psychological Theories of Civil Violence: A Critical Review," in K. Lang and G. E. Lang (Eds.), *Research in Social Movements, Conflicts, and Change,* Vol. 9, Greenwich, CT: JAI Press; J. C. Jenkins and C. M. Eckert, 1986, "Channeling Black Insurgency: Elite Patronage and Professional Social Movement Organizations in the Development of the Black Movement," *American Sociological Review* 51:812–829.

53. Oberschall, 1978, op. cit.

54. McCarthy, J. D. and M. N. Zald, 1977, "Resource Mobilization and Social Movements: A Partial Theory," *American Journal of Sociology* 82:1212–1241.

55. McCarthy and Zald, 1977, ibid.

56. Keilbowicz, R. B. and C. Sherer, 1986, "The Role of the Press in the Dynamics of Social Movements," in K. Lang and G. E. Lang, op. cit., pp. 71–96.

57. For such an analysis of the 1970s civil rights movement, see A. Oberschall, 1973, *Social Conflict and Social Movements,* Englewood Cliffs, NJ: Prentice-Hall.

58. McCarthy and Zald, 1977, op. cit.

59. Kennedy, M. D., 1987, "Polish Engineers' Part in the Solidarity Movement," *Social Forces* 65:661–669.

60. McAdam, D., 1983, "Tactical Innovation and the Pace of Insurgency," *American Sociological Review* 48:735–753; J. C. Jenkins, 1983, "Resource Mobilization Theory and the Study of Social Movements," *Annual Review of Sociology,* Vol. 9, pp. 527–553; Jenkins and Eckert, 1986, op. cit.

61. McAdam, D., 1982, *Political Process and the Development of Black Insurgency,* Chicago: University of Chicago Press.

62. Jenkins and Eckert, 1986, op. cit.

63. Sayles, 1984, op. cit.

64. Ferree, M. M. and F. D. Miller, 1985, "Mobilization and Meaning: Toward an Integration of Social Psychological and Resource Perspectives on Social Movements," *Sociological Inquiry* 55:38–61.

65. Klandermans, B., 1984, "Mobilization and Participation: Social-Psychological Expansions of Resource Mobilization Theory," *American Sociological Review* 49:583–600.

CHAPTER 17

Applications of Social Psychology

■

Social Psychology and the Criminal Justice System
Pretrial Influences
Jury Selection
Presentations of Evidence
Judicial Instructions
Jury Decision Making
Concluding Methodological Note
Social Psychology and Medicine
From Health to Illness
Stress
Cancer
Heart Disease
Preventing and Treating Disease

Imagine that you are arrested for a theft you did not commit. You are brought to trial. Two eyewitnesses identify you as the thief, but two of your friends testify that you were with them at the time the theft was committed. Your lawyer shows that one of the eyewitnesses has poor eyesight and, thus, should not be believed. The prosecution raises some questions about your prior conduct, but your lawyer objects and the judge tells the jury to disregard what they have heard. When you give your testimony you are scared; you hesitate and stumble as you testify. Do you think that the jury would find you innocent or guilty?

Are you achievement oriented, impatient, aggressive, or competitive? Do you react to stressful events with anger? Do you smoke, get too little exercise, or are you overweight? If the answer to any of these questions is yes, you may have a higher risk of having a heart attack than people who lack these characteristics. If you had a heart attack, how would you react? Would you change your habits? Would you follow your doctor's orders?

In this chapter we will cover two topics: social psychology and law and social psychology and medicine. These topics share a common theme: Each deals with an application of social psychology to a real world problem. Social psychologists have always tried to understand and solve the problems of society. Their concern with deviance, antisocial behavior, and intergroup relations provides examples of this involvement. Recently there has been an upsurge of interest in the application of social psychology to social problems. The two topics we will discuss are currently receiving a great deal of attention from social psychologists.

We begin by discussing the criminal justice system. In this section we focus on the contributions that social psychologists are making to our understanding of the jury trial system, with particular emphasis on potential sources of bias in trials. In the second section, we focus on social and psychological factors that contribute to disease. The subjective road from health to illness is presented, followed by a discussion of stress. Cancer and heart disease are then examined; the section ends with a discussion of a model that has been used to help prevent and treat disease.

■
SOCIAL PSYCHOLOGY AND THE CRIMINAL JUSTICE SYSTEM

In this section we discuss the various ways that social psychologists have contributed to our understanding of the criminal justice system and then present a more detailed analysis of their contributions to one aspect of the system, jury trials. The criminal justice system is an institution designed to enforce the laws of our society. In one way or another most of us participate in the system. The relevant roles include criminals, police, prison guards, parole officers, legislators and the people who elect them, judges, attorneys, jurors, victims, the people who report crimes, and, of course, law-abiding citizens.

The laws enforced by this institution consist of a body of formalized social norms intended to support the functioning of society. The laws are formal expressions of society's values in the realms of politics, economics, religion, the family, and everyday interaction. Criminal laws come into existence when ordinary sanctions, such as disapproval, are insufficient to maintain social norms. As noted in Chapter 8, many people believe laws serve the interests of those in power. Laws allow the state to coerce people into obeying social norms by using force to punish those who disobey them (1).

The criminal justice system involves a sequence of stages, starting with the causes and commission of crime and ranging through the adjudication process to incarceration and release from prison. Social psychologists have studied all of these stages. They have investigated the causes of crime at the individual level, asking why people commit crimes. They have also asked why some acts and people are judged to be criminal while others are not (see Chapter 8). They have been concerned with the detection and reporting of crime and the processes of investigation and arrest. Some attention has been devoted to understanding interrogation techniques. The process of determining the charges to be brought against a defendant, particularly the role of plea bargaining, has received considerable attention. Psychological responses to incarceration have been studied, as have various approaches to sentencing. In addition, parole procedures and reintegration into the community have been examined by social psychologists. One aspect of the criminal justice system that has been investigated very thoroughly is the jury trial; it will be our focus in this chapter (2).

Here is a dramatic example of the possible consequences of trial by jury:

The Sawyer brothers, 18-year-old Lonnie and his 20-year-old brother Sandy, came from the small town of Mint Hill, North Carolina. To their horror, they were arrested for a kidnapping that took place on May 15, 1975. Robert Hinson, assistant manager of Collins's Department Store in Monroe, North Carolina, was forced into a car by two men, one of whom pointed a gun at him and demanded that he lie down in the back of the car. He got only a glimpse of his abductors before they pulled stocking masks over their faces, preventing any further view. The men planned to drive Hinson to the store where he would open the safe for them. However, Hinson convinced them that he did not know the combination, and they took $35 from his wallet and let him go. . . .

Three days after the incident, the police stopped a 1965 white Plymouth Valiant and arrested the driver and passenger, Sandy and Lonnie Sawyer. . . . At their trial, the prosecution introduced the testimony of the victim, Robert Hinson, who positively identified the Sawyers as the men who kidnapped him at gunpoint. . . . Four witnesses testified that Sandy was at home at the time of the kidnapping, and four witnesses testified that Lonnie was at a printing plant, where he was visiting his girlfriend.

After two hours the jury was deadlocked,

nine for conviction. The judge instructed the jurors to try hard to reach a unanimous decision, and within a few minutes all twelve jurors voted to convict. The younger brother was sentenced to 28 to 32 years, and the older one received 32 to 40 years (3).

Later, another man confessed to the crime and, after two years in prison, the Sawyers were released. The case raises some important questions about trial by jury. How could the victim have made such a confident identification of the Sawyers? Why did the jury believe the victim, rather than the eight witnesses who testified that the Sawyers could not have committed the crime? What role did the judge's instructions play in the jury's decision? Why didn't the jurors who believed the Sawyers were innocent hold out and create a hung jury?

Why has the jury trial been the subject of so much attention? Only about 20 percent of all cases where a formal charge has been made actually go to trial. This would seem to imply that other aspects of the criminal justice system are more important in dealing with crime than trial by jury (Figure 17-1). Nonetheless, trial by jury is the hub around which the other aspects of the criminal justice system revolve. It is the hub because trial by jury is guaranteed by our Constitution and because trial by jury has an impact on other aspects of the criminal justice system where decisions are made. For example, plea bargaining occurs with the constant threat of a jury trial looming in the background. Similarly, decisions about arresting and charging criminals often depend on whether the responsible authorities believe they can back up the charges in court.

A trial by jury progresses through five stages that lend themselves to a social psychological analysis: pretrial influences (for example, pretrial publicity), selection of the jury, presentations of testimony, the judge's instructions regarding the law, and decision making by the jury. We will cover all five stages, examining the potential biases that exist at each stage. Much of the research on these stages deals with weaknesses in the jury trial system. Researchers concentrate on the weaknesses of the jury trial system, rather than the strengths, so that knowledge

Figure 17.1 ■

Processing of Cases by the Criminal Justice System

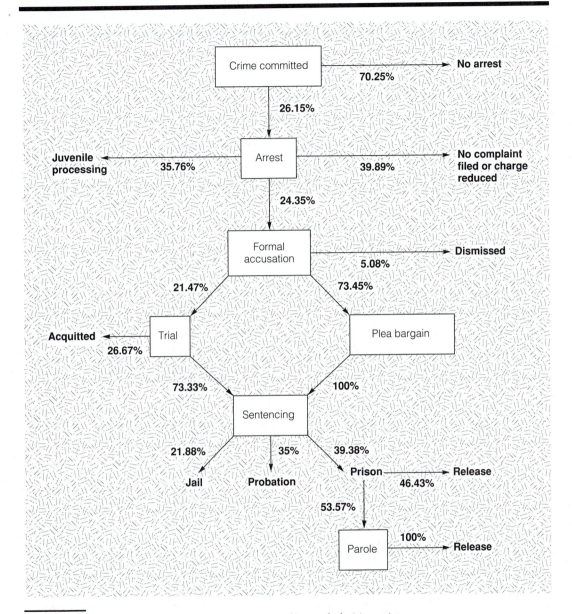

Note: The percents indicate the disposition of the cases reaching each decision point.
Adapted from The President's Commission on Law Enforcement and the Administration of Justice, 1967, *The Challenge of Crime in a Free Society*, Washington, DC: U.S. Government Printing Office.

of the system's weaknesses can be used to improve the administration of justice.

Pretrial Influences

Although the Sixth Amendment to the Constitution guarantees the right to an impartial jury that is representative of the community, pretrial publicity about a defendant may prejudice potential jurors against the defendant and make an impartial jury difficult to obtain. This issue, which pits the First Amendment right of freedom of the press against the Sixth Amendment rights of defendants, has been the subject of a number of Supreme Court decisions. It has also been examined by social psychologists.

Does adverse pretrial publicity really affect juries? One survey study examined the exposure of prospective jurors to prejudicial pretrial publicity concerning three highly publicized cases in California (4). Prospective jurors were more likely to believe the defendants were guilty the more they had been exposed to the pretrial publicity.

Another approach to addressing the effects of pretrial publicity has been to try to simulate the relevant aspects of jury trials in laboratory settings. In this, as in most jury research, the jurors are either students or people eligible to sit on juries. Groups of jurors are presented with the evidence in the case. During these presentations, the independent variable (adverse vs. no adverse publicity) is manipulated. The jurors then deliberate the case and make a decision.

In one such study of the jury system, groups of jury-eligible subjects were exposed to prejudicial newspaper clippings immediately before listening to a tape recording of the defendant's trial; they then deliberated until they reached a verdict (5). These groups were five times more likely to convict the defendant (75 percent) than groups who had not read the prejudicial clippings (15 percent). (The remaining 10 percent did not reach a verdict.) Other studies have consistently found that pretrial publicity has negative effects, although some have found that mild forms of prejudicial information do not bias simulated juries toward conviction (6).

The scrutiny of pretrial influences is still in its infancy. Many questions remain to be resolved. How much and what type of pretrial publicity leads to bias? Does it matter how recently the jurors have been exposed to prejudicial publicity? How can such biases be eliminated?

Jury Selection

Jurors are selected in a three-step process. First, lists of jury-eligible persons are drawn from voter registration lists, tax roles, driver's license registration lists, or similar lists. Second, people are chosen from these lists, usually randomly, to be called for jury duty. Third, jurors are selected through a *voir dire* process during which the attorneys or the judge questions prospective jurors concerning potential biases that could lead them not to be impartial. Some prospective jurors are dropped for "cause," meaning there is reason to question their impartiality. Others are dropped for peremptory reasons, meaning the attorneys may strike some jurors without citing a cause. Problems threatening the impartiality and representativeness of the jurors can arise during any of these steps (Box 17-1).

The composition of the master lists from which prospective jurors are drawn can threaten the representativeness of juries. Although it is illegal to exclude specific groups, such as blacks and women, from jury lists, the lists can be drawn up in ways that underrepresent some groups. Social scientists have participated in challenges to jury selection systems by analyzing the degree to which constitutionally protected groups, such as blacks, are underrepresented in a given jurisdiction. In some instances, survey data have been used to argue that an impartial or representative jury cannot be obtained in a given locale and that a change of venue, a request to try the case in another judicial district, is needed (11).

A related problem involves dropping prospective jurors because of their attitudes on a given topic. For instance, jurors who oppose the death penalty are frequently eliminated from juries in cases where capital punishment is a possible outcome (12). The problem created by excluding such people is that people favoring capital punishment are more likely to convict defendants than those opposing capital punishment, thus reducing the impartiality of the jury and increasing the chances that an innocent defendant could be convicted (13). Also, since women and blacks are more likely to oppose the death penalty than white men, eliminating people opposed to the death penalty also tends to exclude these groups from juries, thereby making the juries less representative (14).

The results of studies dealing with the effects of using only jurors who are not opposed to the death penalty were debated in a Supreme Court case *Arkansas* v. *McCree* in 1986. The majority of the justices had "serious doubts about the value of these studies in predicting the behavior of actual jurors" and therefore decided to let the practice of using only jurors who do not oppose the death penalty stand (15). In general, very compelling evidence is required for the Court to overturn an established practice. In this instance the justices did not feel that the studies done to date were sufficiently convincing. It is important to note that the Supreme Court did take the social science studies into account in making their decision, even if they were not swayed on this occasion. It appears that additional studies that more clearly establish cause and effect relationships will have to be done before the justices can be convinced to change current practices.

Presentations of Evidence

Jury trials are conducted in a manner designed to be fair to both sides. Since the burden of proof lies with the prosecution, the prosecution presents its case first. The prosecution presents documents and witnesses whom the defense may cross-examine. The defense then presents its rebuttal of the prosecution's case by presenting its own documents and witnesses. Typically these presentations of evidence are then followed by the closing statements, this time with the defense going first. One choice the defense must make is when to present its opening statement. The defense's opening statement can be given immediately after the prosecution's opening statement or the defense can wait until after the prosecution has presented its entire case and then present its opening statement just before its own case.

Opening statements Is it better for the defense to present its opening statement immediately or is there an advantage to waiting until the prosecution has completed its case? A study exploring this question found that if the defense presented its opening case at the first opportunity, its case was viewed more favorably than the prosecution's case and the jurors' decisions were more likely to favor its client (16). Although this is only one study and many other factors, such as the type of crime, strength of evidence, and delays due to recesses, might affect when the defense should present its opening statement, this study does support conventional judicial wisdom (17).

Most defense attorneys do choose to present their opening statements at the first opportunity. The success of this strategy may be due to the opportunity it gives the defense to establish a thematic framework that guides the jurors' processing of the facts in the case. Other studies on this topic suggest that if the defense attorney's opening statement promises somewhat more than the defense can deliver, it has a beneficial effect on the jury. The benefit apparently occurs because it is the favorability of the defense attorney's presentation, and not the content, that is remembered (18).

Questioning witnesses When witnesses give testimony during a trial, they do so in response to questions from the attorneys. Research suggests that attorneys can influence the testimony they elicit from the witnesses by asking suggestive or misleading questions. In one illustration of this problem, students were shown a series of slides of a car hitting a pedestrian at an intersection where there was a *stop* sign (19). Later, if they were asked the misleading question "Did you see a *yield* sign?" only 41 percent could correctly identify the slide showing the *stop* sign as the one they had seen. In contrast, 73 percent

BOX 17-1

Scientific Jury Selection

The *voir dire* process of jury selection offers attorneys an opportunity to eliminate jurors whom they believe are not impartial. In the last decade social psychologists have developed a new set of tools to help lawyers make these decisions. One technique is to conduct a community survey of people who closely match the characteristics of the potential jury pool. The respondents are asked their opinions concerning issues to be raised during the trial. Their answers are used to create a profile of the types of jurors most likely to favor the prosecution and the defense. For instance, the survey might show that young, Hispanic, working class men would be most likely to acquit the defendant. The lawyers can then use this information in questioning prospective jurors to try to eliminate people who do not fit this profile.

Another technique is to use mock juries, a group of people similar to those who might actually serve on the jury, to help the attorneys sharpen their strategies. In one case involving two corporate giants (the telecommunications companies MCI and AT&T), the attorneys for one side discovered that a mock jury would award them little in damages if they presented the precise figure for the loss in income caused by the other corporation. In the actual trial the attorneys decided not to mention this sum, and they were awarded six times as much money in damages as the mock jury had awarded (7).

of subjects asked if they had seen a *stop* sign correctly identified the slide they had seen.

In another study, the subjects viewed a film of a multiple car collision (20). Although the film did not show a broken headlight, half the subjects were asked, "Did you see *a* broken headlight?" The other half were asked the leading question "Did you see *the* broken headlight?" When presented with the first question, only 6 percent of the subjects reported seeing a broken headlight; but when asked the leading question, 20 percent reported seeing a nonexistent broken headlight. These studies demonstrate that small differences in the ways witnesses

are questioned affect the types of testimony they give.

Whether it is the prosecution or the defense attorney who asks these questions may also affect the answers given. In a study concerned with this issue, subjects viewed a slide show of an aggressive incident (21). Later, they were questioned by students acting as "attorneys" for the prosecution or the defense. During the following week, they gave their testimony to a "judge" in the case. Students interviewed by the "attorney" for the prosecution gave presentations that were more favorable to the prosecution than students interviewed by the "attorney"

Do these techniques work? Apparently many attorneys think they do, since a number of businesses are now devoted exclusively to scientific jury selection. Most of the cases in which they have been used have ended in acquittals, but it is by no means certain the scientific jury selection was responsible for these results. One experimental study provides some support for the effectiveness of these techniques. In this study, law students were trained in scientific jury selection or they were trained to select jurors in the traditional way. The students trained in scientific jury selection were more effective than the traditionally trained students in predicting mock jurors' verdicts. However, their superiority was limited to cases where prior surveys indicated that certain juror characteristics were associated with attitudes toward the offenses involved (8).

Generally, the evidence in a case is more important than the jurors' characteristics (9). But when the stakes are high and the case involves controversial issues, strongly held attitudes that differ among groups may affect verdicts. It appears that scientific jury selection is most likely to be useful in controversial cases where the evidence is ambiguous, the jury pool is highly varied, and judges permit considerable leeway in asking questions during the *voir dire* process (10).

The goal of the jury selection system is to create juries that are impartial and representative. However, the end result of scientific jury selection is to create juries that are partial and unrepresentative. This raises an ethical question: Is the use of scientific jury selection wrong because it threatens the impartiality of justice by giving those who use it an unfair advantage? Defense attorneys argue that scientific jury selection merely systematizes what they have always attempted to do anyway. The system has always permitted them to try to eliminate jurors biased against their clients. Now they believe they have a technique that allows them to do so more effectively. How do you feel about the use of scientific jury selection? ■

for the defense. Thus, the students' statements about what they saw were influenced by the attorney who interviewed them.

Does the style with which witnesses respond to questions affect their credibility? One study found that witnesses who gave their testimony in a powerful manner (no hedging, no repetition, little deference to authority) were more believable than witnesses who gave testimony in a powerless manner (22). Studies in nonjury contexts have shown that people who use a conversational tone, have a fluent delivery, speak at a moderate rate, use low pitch, vary their pitch and intonation, and are animated but not intense are the most credible (23). In addition, the more self-confident witnesses feel, the more likely their testimony will be seen as credible (24).

Eyewitness testimony Eyewitness testimony is one of the most compelling types of testimony introduced in jury trials, as the example of the Sawyer brothers illustrates. When a witness says, "That's him; that's the man who did it," juries are apt to be swayed. A study conducted in England found that for cases in which eyewitness testimony was the only evidence against the defendant, 74 percent resulted in conviction (25).

■ *Manhunt in Santa Fe, New Mexico: Apprehension is one of the most critical links in the criminal justice process. (WGS)*

Given how influential eyewitness testimony can be, there is good reason to be concerned about its accuracy. The data on this question are mixed. A large number of studies have found that eyewitnesses are not reliable. For instance, in one study a purse-snatching was staged by an NBC television crew and shown as part of a documentary on eyewitness testimony (26). Following the presentation of this 12-second incident, viewers were given an opportunity to choose the assailant from a lineup of six men who resembled the assailant. Of the 2,000 viewers who called the station, only 14 percent correctly identified the assailant. This is almost exactly the number who would have made the correct identification by chance alone. In another study, people made purchases in convenience stores (27). Two hours later, the clerks in these stores were asked to identify these customers from a set of mug shots. Correct identifications were made in only about one third of the cases. Other clerks were asked to identify these customers 24 hours later, and identification rates fell to chance levels.

In sharp contrast, a number of laboratory studies have found eyewitnesses can be accurate more than 75 percent of the time (28). The people who have the most extensive experience with eyewitnesses, attorneys, have split opinions about their accuracy. Prosecution attorneys believe eyewitnesses are accurate about 90 percent of the time, while defense attorneys believe they are accurate only about 35 percent of the time (29).

The critical question is, under what conditions are eyewitnesses most likely to be accurate? The issue of the accuracy of eyewitness testimony came before the Supreme Court in a 1977 case *Manson v. Braithwaite*. Justice Blackmun, writing for the majority, argued that the reliability of eyewitness testimony depended on five factors: "opportunity of the witness to view the criminal at the time of the crime, the witness' degree of attention, the accuracy of his prior description of the criminal, the level of certainty at the confrontation [for example, the lineup], and the time between the crime and the confrontation" (30). On the whole, research has supported Justice Blackmun, but often the role of these factors is more complex than he envisioned.

Opportunity Although most studies report that the accuracy of recall of faces does improve with increased exposure (31), as Justice Blackmun surmised, some studies have found no relationship between exposure time and accuracy (32). If disguises are used, even people who have long exposures to the criminals are unlikely to be accurate (33).

Degree of attention A witness' degree of attention depends on such factors as the stress caused by the situation and what stimuli are salient. Research generally finds that stress decreases eyewitness accuracy (34), particularly in extremely stressful situations. Aspects of a crime that attract attention away from the perpetrator can also decrease eyewitness accuracy. For instance, weapons attract attention and decrease the accuracy of eyewitness identification (35). Attention is also influenced by the importance of the perceived events. Important events tend to be better remembered than unimportant ones. In one study, eyewitnesses to a theft were more accurate when the theft involved a calculator (56 percent) than a cigarette (19 percent) (36). In actual situations involving crime, stress is often high but the situation is important, so these factors may operate in opposition to one another.

Accuracy of prior description Little research has been done on the accuracy of prior descriptions on later identification. One relevant study found that 80 percent of the subjects who gave accurate written descriptions of an accident were subsequently accurate when attempts were made to mislead them (37). Unfortunately, it has also been found that people who have made inaccurate initial identifications subsequently have difficulty recognizing the real suspect (38). It appears that initial inaccuracy interferes with people's ability to recognize the real suspect later. It is true that once people have learned to recognize a face they can often remember it accurately for long periods of time. For instance, recognition of high school classmates was found to be 90 percent accurate after 35 years in one study

(39). Thus, accurate identifications at one point in time probably do lead to later accuracy, but by the same token, inaccurate identifications may lead to later inaccuracy.

Certainty The relationship between certainty of identification and accuracy of identification has been extensively studied. Although numerous studies find that certainty and accuracy are related, an equal or larger number find no relationship (40). When the initial observation and the later identification occur under optimal circumstances (low to moderate stress, good lighting, long exposure to the individual, short interval between the crime and the identification) the relationship between certainty and accuracy tends to be highest (41). However, under conditions that most resemble those of eyewitness identifications in real trials, the relationship between certainty and accuracy is weak or nonexistent (42).

Eyewitnesses who confidently, but inaccurately, identify a defendant pose a major problem in jury trials. If they are believed, an innocent defendant could be convicted. An important question, then, is whether juries believe such witnesses. Unfortunately, studies show that eyewitnesses who have made incorrect identifications are just as convincing as accurate eyewitnesses (43). In one study, a theft was staged for a group of witnesses. The witnesses were asked to identify the "thief" from a set of mug shots and later the witnesses were cross-examined before a group of students. These students were then asked to indicate whether they believed the witnesses had correctly identified the "thief." The witnesses were believed about 80 percent of the time, regardless of whether they had correctly identified the "thief." Also, the more confident inaccurate witnesses are, the more they tend to be believed (44).

Time interval Studies of the time interval between the crime and the opportunity for identification typically show that shorter time intervals lead to higher accuracy (45). However, unusual faces may continue to be recognized, even after long periods of time (46). And, as already noted, very familiar faces are well remembered over time.

How do jurors weigh the various factors affecting

eyewitness accuracy? Mock jurors in one study paid little attention to information on any of the factors affecting eyewitness reliability, with one exception. They were influenced by one of the factors that appears to be most weakly associated with reliability—the witness' certainty (47). Justice Blackmun rightly argues that jurors should weigh several other factors in assessing the testimony of eyewitnesses. However, it appears that these subtle factors may be swept aside in the face of a confident witness, a misplaced emphasis that could be very damaging to defendants.

In order to offset the jury's reliance on eyewitness testimony, defense attorneys often try to discredit the eyewitness with evidence that the witness' testimony was not accurate. However, studies suggest this is difficult to accomplish because juries have such a strong tendency to believe eyewitnesses (48). Defense attorneys have also attempted to limit the jury's reliance on eyewitnesses by using social psychologists as expert witnesses who present evidence on the fallibility of eyewitness testimony. Laboratory studies suggest that expert witnesses can successfully reduce the impact of eyewitness testimony (49).

Judicial Instructions

After the attorneys have made their closing arguments, the judge typically instructs the jury, although in a few states these instructions are given before closing arguments. These instructions cover definitions of relevant laws, statements about the presumption of innocence, the standard of proof (beyond a reasonable doubt), the need to decide the case only on the evidence presented (for example, ignore pretrial publicity), and special instructions regarding such topics as considering each charge separately when there are multiple charges. These instructions play a crucial role in framing the jurors' task for them.

Several studies have shown that if the instructions are too complicated or if they are unclear, jurors may not focus on the relevant aspects of the case during their deliberations. Even when the instructions are completely clear, juries may have difficulty following them (50). Juries are asked to ignore

pretrial publicity, the defendant's prior criminal record, and inadmissible evidence in their deliberations. Attorneys say this is like asking the jury to unring a bell—it's a little hard to do. One Supreme Court Justice has commented, "These instructions are like exorcising phrases intended to drive out evil spirits" (51).

In addition to defining relevant laws, judicial instructions are designed to overcome problems created by the obligation to introduce all the evidence a jury may need to make its decision and to exclude all evidence that is irrelevant to this decision. For instance, evidence concerning a defendant's prior record is introduced because it may be relevant to evaluating the truthfulness of his or her testimony, but jurors are later told to ignore this evidence in making decisions concerning the defendant's guilt or innocence.

Are judicial instructions effective? Some types of prejudicial evidence are harder to ignore than others. As previously noted, jurors find it difficult to overcome the effects of negative pretrial publicity, even when told to do so (52). They also find evidence of prior convictions difficult to ignore (53). However, instructions to ignore inadmissable evidence are effective more often than not (54). One study found that inadmissible evidence favoring the defense was more difficult to ignore than evidence favoring the prosecution (55). When a defendant is tried on multiple charges, juries are instructed to make separate decisions on each charge, but studies suggest that their initial verdicts affect their later verdicts (56).

The majority of these studies support the skepticism of judges and attorneys concerning the effectiveness of judicial instructions. A solution to some of these problems is the use of videotaped testimony from which inadmissible evidence has been excluded (57). Providing juries with written copies of the judge's instructions has also been recommended (58).

Jury Decision Making

The jury represents the conscience of the community. Its mandate is to determine the guilt or innocence of the defendant based on the facts of the case. Its decision is final, except in cases of appeal on procedural matters. The judge cannot change a jury decision in criminal cases.

Trial by jury evolved to place the citizens between the prosecution (the state) and the defendant. The intent was to limit the capacity of the state to oppress its citizens by directly enforcing the same laws it created. In a trial by jury system, the state grants a group of legal novices—the jury—the right to make decisions they deny to the legal experts—the judges. Some judges are skeptical of the citizens' capacity to carry out their role. To paraphrase Supreme Court Justice Jerome Frank, juries apply laws they do not understand to facts they cannot get straight (59). Is this skepticism justified?

Judges and juries actually agree in the majority of cases (60). In a study of 3,500 verdicts it was found that the judges and juries agreed in 75 percent of the cases (61). In most of the instances of disagreement, the jury was more lenient than the judge. When judges and juries disagree, it is typically because juries take a broader view of a particular law, such as the right of self-defense. The consistent nature of these disagreements suggest that juries are not capricious in their applications of the law. Studies of jury deliberations indicate that most of their time is spent on judicially relevant issues concerning the facts, laws, and instructions in the case (62). An analysis of mock juries found they considered 85 percent of the relevant facts in the case (63).

On the other hand, we have already reviewed a number of factors that influence jury decisions when they should not. Both mock juries and real juries sometimes discuss issues that are not legally relevant to the case, such as the consequences of conviction for the defendant (64). Despite these problems, it appears that juries take their duties seriously and try to perform them conscientiously.

Most juries go through four stages in rendering a verdict. They begin with an *orientation* phase during which a foreman (sadly the term still fits; most foremen are men) is chosen, the task is discussed, and a preliminary vote may be taken (65). This stage is followed by an *open conflict* stage, unless the jury's initial vote is unanimous. Jurors take sides, present their opinions, defend their views, and attack opposing views during this stage. A *conflict resolution* stage comes next during which disagreements are settled and a mutually acceptable decision begins to emerge. When a decision is reached, or the jury concludes that it cannot reach a decision, a final *reconciliation* stage occurs. During this stage hurt feelings are soothed and support is gathered for the decision (or a truce is declared, if no decision has emerged).

The orientation and open conflict stages determine the verdict. The juror's predeliberation opinions typically foreshadow the final verdict (66). The decision initially favored by the majority prevails in over 90 percent of the cases (67). When an initial majority is overthrown, it is generally one that favored conviction. Just as juries are more lenient than judges, the internal dynamics of juries favor leniency if only a minimal majority (for example, 7 to 5) favors conviction. If the jurors are fairly evenly split for conviction and acquittal, the side that first experiences a defection is almost always the eventual loser (68).

Both *informational* and *normative* influences come into play in changing jurors' minds (informational and normative influence were discussed in Chapter 7). The importance of information is apparent in the finding that jurors are often swayed by the number of arguments formulated for conviction or acquittal. When the arguments on one side greatly outnumber those on the other side, the first side prevails. One study suggests this tipping point comes when one side has articulated seven more arguments than the other (69).

The number of people in the majority also exerts an influence—a normative one. The majority defines the normative opinion and may explicitly or implicitly communicate to other jurors what they should do. Members of the minority may be concerned with disapproval by the majority, in addition to being persuaded by its arguments (70).

In a study of informational and normative influences in a case involving multiple charges, it was found that the first charge was decided primarily on the strength of the arguments (informational factors) (71). For the ensuing charges, normative pressures to conform to the majority's view were more important. Another study found that 7 percent of the jurors voted with the majority, but privately held a different opinion, indicating that they were influenced by normative pressures (72).

We may conclude that, for the most part, when biases enter the jury trial system they do so before the deliberations begin. Once the deliberations begin, juries function as well as can be reasonably expected.

Although we have seen that jury trials are susceptible to bias at almost every stage, we should not lose sight of the fact that the jury trial system is an admirable, if fragile, social institution. Our society has chosen to place certain types of judgments of right and wrong in the hands of representative groups of ordinary citizens. Trial by jury is designed to overcome the potential biases any single individual might bring to bear on these judgments. It allows for highly structured presentations of both sides of a case. Witnesses are subject to cross examination, and the entire proceedings are open to public scrutiny. Further, jury trials are subject to review for procedural problems. In making jury deliberations private, the system recognizes the need for juries to be free from outside pressures. The use of jury trials implies that a sufficient consensus of values exists in our society so that mutually agreed on judgments of right and wrong can be made. Ultimately, jury trials represent our faith in our fellow citizens.

Concluding Methodological Note

A cautionary note: Much of the research on juries has been conducted with simulated juries of students. The use of simulations raises the issue of validity. Is it reasonable to generalize from simulations done in laboratory settings to real jury trials? Critics of these studies have raised the following points that should lead us to be cautious about generalizing the findings of these studies to real juries (73).

■ College students come from a more restricted sample of people than actual jurors do.

■ The presentations of short, written summaries or even videotapes cannot capture the complexities of real jury trials.

■ In many studies, there are no judicial instructions, no deliberation takes place, or deliberations are not conducted in secret.

■ Highlighting one aspect of a case (for example, eyewitness testimony) may lead to an overestimation of the importance of this variable.

■ The jurors are not responsible for their verdicts in simulated trials as they are in real trials.

Despite these limitations, simulations are conducted because they are the only way some problems can be studied. It would be impossible or unethical to study many of these issues in real trials. For instance, one simply could not introduce testimony that was inadmissible into a real trial in order to examine its effects. Also, the deliberations of real juries are secret; they cannot be recorded in any way. If we wish to understand what people do or say in this context our only recourse is to simulate this context as realistically as we can.

Social psychologists have made several different kinds of contributions to the study of the criminal justice system. Sociological social psychologists have formulated basic theories of the law, performed survey analyses to support change of venue challenges and challenges to the representativeness of jury selection, and conducted empirical studies of issues such as deterrence. In addition, sociologists have studied many other aspects of the criminal justice system such as juvenile delinquency, the labeling of criminals, and society's reactions to crime. Psychological social psychologists have contributed theories of judicial decision making and done laboratory and field studies of eyewitness identification, jury decision making, and other topics. Both types of social psychologists have participated in scientific jury selection, and both have served as expert witnesses on selected issues. Thus, social psychologists have contributed to theory and research on the criminal justice system, and they have played active roles in the transactions of the criminal justice system. Their participation has been nearly as extensive in the study of health and illness, as you will see in the next section.

SOCIAL PSYCHOLOGY AND MEDICINE

Our second topic in applied social psychology concerns health and illness. This is a topic of relatively recent interest to social psychologists, although there is a long history of interest in medicine among sociologists. The fascination that health and illness hold for social psychologists is due in part to the changing nature of the diseases we suffer from in our postindustrial society. Until well into the twentieth century, medicine was primarily concerned with acute diseases having lethal consequences. Plague, cholera, smallpox, tuberculosis, and pneumonia are examples of such diseases. During this century many of these diseases have been brought under control through public health measures such as better diets and improved sanitation, and through medical measures such as vaccines against smallpox and polio.

The medical profession is now more concerned with chronic degenerative diseases such as cancer and heart disease than they were in the past. These diseases are influenced by social psychological factors to a much greater extent than acute catastrophic diseases are. Voluntary behavior patterns and stress play important causal roles in these diseases. Also, the gradual onset and course of these diseases means opportunities for prevention and behavior change occur over long periods of time. Whether or not patients improve depends to some extent on whether they comply with medical regimens and alter their negative health-related behaviors (74). Thus, social psychological factors are important in the course these diseases take over time.

With the entry of sociology and psychology into the field of medicine new models of disease have emerged. The traditional *medical model* of disease

held that diseases were caused by single agents (for example, bacteria) which operated within the body at the cellular or biochemical level. Following a tradition that can be traced back at least as far as the French philosopher Descartes (1596–1650), the body and the mind were considered to be separate entities in the traditional medical model. Disease occurred within the body and mental factors were thought to play no role in disease. The recognition of the role of social factors in disease was also extremely limited.

The more recent *biopsychosocial* models emphasize psychological and social factors, as well as biological factors, as causes of disease (75). These models emerged because the medical model was inadequate in dealing with certain important aspects of disease. Medical models have difficulty accounting for why only a portion of the people exposed to a disease contract it and why treatments of disease work for some people, but not others. A consideration of psychological and social factors helps to fill this gap. In addition, the medical model does not give sufficient consideration to the subjective interpretations of symptoms and sickness that determine people's disease-related behavior. Also, it fails to adequately account for the factors influencing compliance with medical regimens. Finally, the medical model is not as oriented toward prevention and health as biopsychosocial models are.

The change from a medical to a biopsychosocial model is a profound one that is far from complete. In the section that follows we will explore the role of psychological and social factors in disease. We begin by defining health and illness and then consider the stages people pass through in defining themselves as sick. Following this discussion, we consider one of the mechanisms through which psychological and social factors influence disease—stress. The next two sections examine the contributions of social psychology to our understanding of two of the country's most lethal diseases, cancer and heart disease. We end with an analysis of the health belief model, a model that has been applied to changing health-related behaviors.

From Health to Illness

The traditional medical model conceives of health and illness as objective states. Health is the absence of disease. The presence of disease can be determined by various clinical tests plus an objective assessment of signs (temperature) and symptoms (sore throat) displayed by the patient. This is the way most physicians still think today. However, this is not a view shared by their patients. Patients are not usually confronted by full blown diseases in their daily lives. Instead, patients encounter symptoms and must decide what to do about them. The way they interpret their symptoms determines whether they go to see a physician or decide to go on with their lives. It is the patient who initially decides if he or she is feeling "ill." If the symptoms are perceived to be severe enough, the person may decide he or she is "sick," even without visiting a physician, and take himself or herself to bed. In this case, the experience of symptoms, the interpretation of the symptoms as illness, and the adoption of the sick role take place within the individual without regard for the views of the medical profession. There are several roads to illness and they do not all pass through the physician's office. Let us review them in more detail (Fig. 17-2).

Symptoms The first stage on the road to illness involves perceiving symptoms. Recent research reveals that most people are inaccurate perceivers of many of the internal sensations produced by their own bodies. Except at the extremes, people cannot tell how fast their hearts are beating, how high their blood pressure is, what their glucose levels are, or any number of other medically relevant symptoms (76). This does not mean that they do not experience symptoms, but it does mean some symptoms go unnoticed and some of the symptoms they experience have little to do with occurrences within their bodies. Symptoms are most likely to be noticed and reported when they cause pain, weakness, or an inability to function normally (77).

Illness The next stage on the road to illness is interpreting the meaning of the symptoms. Are they normal or abnormal? Some symptoms are so common people regard them as normal. Only 1 headache in 60 is regarded as important enough to consult a physician, and for backaches the ratio is 1 in 38 (78). But for stomachaches, 1 person in 11 sees a physician, and for sore throats the ratio is 1 in 9. On occasion, people ignore medically relevant symptoms because they seem unimportant. One survey found that although 40 percent of those queried said they would treat themselves for headaches that occurred more than once a week for a month, only 17 percent of physicians felt that such people should be treating themselves (79). The initial symptoms of some of the most lethal disorders, such as cancer, frequently go unnoticed (breast lumps).

Nonetheless, it is typically the person's own definition of the meaning of the symptoms, or the definitions provided by significant others, that determine whether the person feels "ill." Of course, a person may decide he or she is ill, even in the absence of symptoms, because of the gains involved. A person who is ill can expect sympathy from others and may be excused from his or her usual obligations (80). Because illness is subjectively defined, one does not have to have a disease to be ill.

Responses to illness If a person decides that the symptoms are serious, then he or she must decide how to respond. The most likely response is to seek help through self-treatment, treatment by one's family or acquaintances, or treatment by a physician. However, if the person cannot afford to feel ill because of competing social responsibilities, cannot afford to seek treatment, or fears the consequences of being certified as ill, the symptoms may be ignored. Treatment may then be delayed until the symptoms become incapacitating. There are many cases on record where women have discovered lumps in their breasts, but have delayed reporting them—a response that reduces their chances of survival. On occasion people attempt to deny the symptoms they are feeling. People suffering from heart attacks have been known to do push-ups or run up stairs to convince themselves they are not having a heart attack (81).

Figure 17.2 ■

From Health to Illness

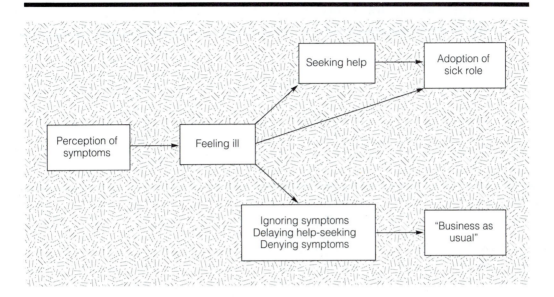

The sick role Admitting that one is ill, or being found to be ill by significant others or a physician, can lead to adopting the sick role. In a classic treatment of the sick role, Talcott Parsons outlined the rights and obligations of this role (82). To be healthy, according to Parsons, is to be functioning up to capacity in one's roles. Being sick means being unable to fulfill the requirements of one's roles. Generally, people are not held responsible for being sick so they are not negatively evaluated for failing to perform their usual duties. Sick people are expected to try to get well, unless the disease is unalterable, in which case they are expected to try to hold their own. People who are sick are also expected to seek and follow the advice of their physicians, but they do not always do so (Box 17-2).

Stress

There are two general processes by which social and psychological factors affect disease. The first is through negative health-related behaviors. The most prominent of these factors is smoking, which has been conclusively shown to be linked to a variety of diseases, particularly lung cancer. Other behaviors such as excessive drinking, a diet heavy in fats and cholesterol, lack of exercise, and poor hygienic practices have also been linked to disease.

The second process by which social and psychological factors affect disease is through the effects of stress on the body. Stress plays a major, if not fully understood, role in the development of many diseases. *Stress* may be defined as an excess of demands over coping resources. Stress increases as the costs of a failure to cope with it increase, but it decreases if people have social support systems that help them cope. Although objective levels of stress have an important impact on disease, the perception of stress may be as important as the objective level of stress in affecting disease (90).

Flight or fight syndrome To understand the role of stress in the development of disease, we must first explore how people react to stress. External threats,

The Patient-Physician Relationship

People's health care behavior has changed dramatically in the last couple of decades. People are taking a new interest in their health and investing enormous amounts of time and energy in health. They fuel a large health industry publishing self-help books on diet, stress, exercise, medication, and prevention. They buy diagnostic kits and medications with which to diagnose and cure their illnesses, and they avidly follow the latest medical advances in the mass media. For their part, physicians are now more knowledgeable than ever; they have more advanced technologies for diagnosis and treatment, and new, more effective drugs are constantly being developed. However, even with all these changes, the role relationship between the patient and the physician is still at the heart of medical practice. For all their knowledge, physicians continue to rely on patients to report their symptoms and patients continue to decide whether or not to carry out their doctor's orders.

In this relationship there is an enormous competence gap. Physicians know more about disease than patients. This difference in competence, combined with the fact that the patient is often weak and experiencing symptoms that are demeaning or degrading, places the patient in a dependent position. Add to this the fact that patients are often frightened, embarrassed, and feeling desperate, and you can see that the relationship between patient and physician faces some unique difficulties.

The patient comes to the physician with a problem. Physicians believe their role is to determine the source of the problem and relieve the patient's suffering. Their task is complicated by the inaccuracies of patients' reports of symptoms and the patients' reluctance to even admit having some symptoms. The physician is typically working under time pressure and a heavy work load. When the physician does diagnose the problem and prescribes drugs or advocates behavioral changes, the patient may not comply with them or return for checkups.

such as the possibility of being attacked, elicit the *flight or fight syndrome*. In this syndrome the sympathetic nervous system reacts by preparing the body for action. Arousal levels are increased as adrenaline floods into the blood stream, surface blood vessels constrict to prevent blood loss in case of injury, and normal bodily functions such as digestion come to a standstill. The intense activation

associated with this syndrome can cause strokes or heart attack (91).

Although the flight or fight syndrome was clearly adaptive during the evolution of our species, in modern society it has lost much of its adaptive value. This syndrome can be almost as easily elicited by an internal psychological threat, such as failure to meet a deadline, as by an external physical threat.

Patient compliance has been found to be linked to several aspects of the patient-physician relationship. The central difficulty in compliance is poor communication. In a shocking number of instances, patients fail to understand the physician's advice or the physician fails to adequately communicate what he or she desires the patient to do. One study found that in 90 percent of the cases in which a physician prescribed a drug, he or she failed to give specific advice on how to use it (83). An added problem is that physicians often use language, we might call it medspeak, that is incomprehensible to their patients (84). Because patients are placed in a passive role, they often fail to request information when they do not understand something (86). Being in a weakened condition or being anxious may make it hard to assimilate and remember advice (86). One study found that after medical visits, 56 percent of the patients could not remember the instructions they were given (87).

A second difficulty in compliance is that patients are less likely to follow the orders of a physician who does not express concern for them, answer their questions, or agree with them concerning their diagnosis. Patients are likely to comply with the orders of physicians they regard as competent, but patients often use unreliable criteria to judge physician competence, such as the physician's confidence or the speed of the diagnosis (88). In one study it was found that patients' judgments of competence were only slightly correlated with the judgments made of the physicians by their supervisors ($r = .16$) (89). Thus, some patients do not comply with the orders of the most competent physicians because they fail to recognize their competence.

A third difficulty centers around physicians' interpersonal relationships with their patients. Physicians often attempt to maintain a degree of professional detachment that makes it difficult for them to express warmth. Time pressures may make answering questions seem like a waste of time. Physicians also tend to dehumanize patients in order to treat their problems more objectively. You have probably had enough experience with physicians to know that you are more likely to follow the recommendations of the ones who treat you as a person rather than a set of symptoms.

In combination, poor communication, time urgency, and dehumanized physician-patient relationships are likely to lead to low patient satisfaction and decreased compliance rates. ■

People who live stressful lives often ride an adrenaline roller coaster produced by internal psychological threats. Their systems are frequently stimulated to prepare for action and must then readjust throughout the day.

General Adaptation Syndrome In addition to the flight or fight syndrome, a second type of response occurs for more prolonged stress. The sequence of events involved in responding to prolonged stress is known as the *General Adaptation Syndrome* (GAS) (92). Overcrowding, poverty, extreme cold or heat, and noisy work conditions are examples of stressors that can set this syndrome in motion.

The first stage of the GAS is *alarm* which leads the organism to mobilize its resources to deal with the stress. The alarm stage is somewhat analogous to the flight or fight syndrome because it too entails preparations to deal with threat, but in the GAS the response to threat involves a different hormonal system.

The alarm stage is followed by the *resistance* stage, in which the organism actively attempts to cope with the stress. Coping responses during this stage are usually successful. Nonetheless, even successful coping can have negative effects. For instance, it can suppress the capacity of the immune system to fight disease (especially upper respiratory diseases) (93). A study of this stage found that final exams lower immunity to disease, as most of you can probably attest (94).

If the stress continues over a long time period, the person will enter the *exhaustion* stage. Prolonged stress, such as job stress or unemployment, eventually exhausts the body's reserves. This exhaustion may leave people more susceptible to degenerative diseases, like cancer, and bodily dysfunctions, like ulcers (95).

Stress increases the perception of bodily symptoms and can start individuals along the road to perceiving themselves as sick (96). High levels of stress are associated with increased work absenteeism and health-care seeking (97). Stress also leads to increased alcohol and drug consumption, smoking, and eating (98), all of which place people at greater risk for some diseases.

The initial research relating stress to health found that an accumulation of stressful life changes over time (six months to a year) predisposed people to a variety of diseases (99). Stressful life changes include such events as getting divorced, losing a job, bearing the death of a loved one, experiencing foreclosure on a mortgage, and changing a residence. Subsequent research indicates that the relationship between stressful life changes and poor health is weaker than first thought, although it is still consistently found.

A more important type of stress for predicting the development of stress-related diseases consists of the frequency of daily hassles (dealing with traffic, getting angry) (100). Daily hassles may be more important than stressful life changes because daily hassles repeatedly elicit the flight or fight syndrome which may exact a heavier toll on the body's resources than more continuous coping. As you will see in the next section, the specific ways in which some people deal with stress are related to two of this country's major killers—heart disease and cancer.

Cancer

Cancer refers to a variety of disorders that are characterized by the uncontrolled growth of abnormal cells, in the form of tumors. If unchecked, cancer typically spreads through the body and eventually proves lethal. Nearly a million people in the United States are diagnosed as having cancer each year (101). The rate of cancer is on the increase, but the rate of successful treatment is also increasing. About 50 percent of people diagnosed with cancer can now be cured (102). Psychosocial factors appear to play two roles in cancer: They influence susceptibility to cancer, and they influence the growth of cancerous tumors.

Susceptibility of cancer Growing evidence shows that lifestyle choices affect the chances of getting cancer. The most dramatic example is tobacco use. It is estimated that 130,000 deaths a year are due to cancer caused by tobacco. Over 90 percent of the deaths due to lung cancer are caused by smoking (103). Another lifestyle choice affecting cancer is excessive exposure to the sun which greatly increases the risk of getting skin cancer. High levels of alcohol consumption (even the frequent use of mouthwashes containing alcohol) increase cancer rates, especially when drinking is combined with smoking. Overeating, as well as poor nutrition, places one at risk for a variety of cancers. Although the exact mechanisms responsible for the increased risk of cancer due to these factors are still in question, the fact that people can exercise control over these behaviors is not. People choose whether or not to expose themselves to these risk factors. In the last part of this chapter we will consider a model concerned with how these behaviors can be changed.

There is considerable debate about whether or not stress causes cancer. Stress reduces the number of a particular type of cell, aptly called killer cells, in the immune system. These cells are capable of killing invading bacteria. In animals, low levels of killer cells make the animals more susceptible to cancer (104). In humans, high levels of recent life changes are associated with lowered killer cell activity (105). It is possible that these lowered levels of killer cells also make humans susceptible to cancer. Consistent with this thesis are studies demonstrating that life stress, job stress, and the loss of a loved one are associated with the development of some types of cancer (leukemia, lung cancer, cervical cancer) (106).

A particularly interesting line of investigation suggests that the manner in which some people cope with stress could affect the risk of cancer. In a study of a large group of physicians whose lives were followed for over 30 years, those who suppressed their emotions were more predisposed to cancer than those who acted out their emotions (107). The suppression of anger may be particularly important as a predisposing factor (108). Unfortunately, nearly all of these studies of the relationship between stress and cancer are methodologically weak so it is not possible to draw strong conclusions from them.

Growth of cancerous tumors Although the role of stress in contracting cancer is still being debated, the evidence that stress affects the rate of tumor

■ *Come fry with me: Voluntary behaviors such as sunbathing play an important, but often unrecognized, role in causing disease. (WGS)*

(Courtesy American Cancer Society)

growth is better established. Studies on animals clearly indicate that exposure to uncontrollable, unpredictable stress increases the rate of tumor growth (109). In humans, stress and strong emotions lead to the release of hormones which increase the rate of growth of some types of cancerous tumors (110). Again, lowered levels of killer cells appear to play a role in this process (111).

Paralleling the finding for the role of coping styles in susceptibility to cancer, there is evidence of faster tumor growth in patients who suppress anger and other emotions than in patients who are emotionally expressive (112). The patients whose cancer progresses most rapidly are characterized by a feeling of helplessness and hopelessness (113). The passivity resulting from these feelings has been found to be associated with low levels of killer cells

in a study of women with breast cancer, suggesting such cells play a role in the progression of cancer, as well as in contracting it (114). It has also been found that levels of social support are associated with slower tumor growth (115), perhaps because social support helps people to deal with stress.

The data from all of these studies might be compared to circumstantial evidence in a trial. The evidence is consistent and nearly all of it indicates psychological and social factors play a role in cancer, but the case has not been proven beyond a reasonable doubt. The problem is that most of the data come from animal studies, which may or may not apply to humans, or correlational studies on humans, which cannot establish the causal role of psychological or social factors. It might be said that we lack eyewitness reports on exactly how stress and other psychological and social factors affect cancer at the cellular level. However, the enormous amount of money and effort currently being devoted to this question increases the likelihood of finding answers in the near future.

Heart Disease

Coronary heart disease (CHD) is the major cause of death in this country for people over 45 (116). In the United States, approximately 1.5 million people have heart attacks each year (117). CHD refers to illnesses resulting from the narrowing of the coronary arteries. Narrowing of the arteries reduces the flow of oxygen and nutrients to the heart. If this flow is reduced too much, a heart attack results. The behavioral factors that place people at risk for having heart disease include smoking, lack of exercise, obesity, and a diet heavy in cholesterol and saturated fats.

In addition, certain types of people are at risk for heart disease because of the way they cope with stress. These people, labeled *Type A* personalities, are characterized by competitive achievement striving, impatience, and aggressiveness (118). The early research on Type As found that they were more than twice as likely to develop CHD as people with Type B personalities, who lack these traits. However, more recent studies indicate that it is primarily the hostile, aggressive component of the Type A personality that is associated with CHD (119).

Research at the cutting edge of knowledge often yields results that are difficult to interpret, and so it is in the case of explanations for the association of Type A behavior and CHD (120). The current thinking is that Type A is linked to CHD through the "flight or fight" syndrome. Type As react more strongly to threatening and challenging situations than Type Bs (121). The higher the Type As are on hostility, the more reactive they are (122).

When Type As react to threatening situations, the ensuing flood of adrenaline causes lipids and fatty acids to be released into the bloodstream. The excessive amounts of these substances may then contribute to the formation and growth of the plaques that eventually lead to narrowing of the arterial walls (123). Type A men appear to be more reactive to stress than Type A women which may be one reason why CHD is so much more prevalent in men (124).

The hard-driving, competitive nature of Type As may lead them to seek out exactly the types of situations to which they react so strongly. Can they be persuaded to modify their behavior? We turn to this question next (Box 17-3).

Preventing and Treating Disease

In addition to their examination of the social psychological causes of disease, social psychologists interested in medicine have studied techniques of improving disease prevention and treatment. A problem plaguing medical practitioners from the beginning has been the difficulty in getting people to engage in behaviors that prevent disease or that help to cure disease. Even when people know how they should behave to maintain good health, many do not do so. For a person suffering from a disease, following the doctor's orders may be essential to getting well. For instance, people with diabetes must severely limit sugar intake, and people suffering from intestinal parasites must take particular medicines at set intervals for a specified time.

Given the importance of following medical advice, it is amazing it is not followed more faithfully.

A review of studies on this topic reveals that adherence to long-term medical regimens occurs in only 57 percent of the cases (133). Adherence to short-term regimens is a little worse, 54 percent. These figures indicate many people will not recover from their diseases, or will recover more slowly than necessary, simply because they fail to follow the doctor's orders.

The *health belief model* was developed to understand the factors that affect people's willingness to change health-related behaviors (134). According to this model, health-related behaviors are primarily influenced by two factors. The first factor consists of *beliefs about health threats*. These beliefs include general health values, perceived susceptibility to specific diseases, and the perceived severity of the diseases. The second factor consists of *beliefs about health behaviors* that can reduce the threat. These beliefs include perceptions of the effectiveness of proposed changes, one's self-efficacy or ability to make the changes, and perceptions of the costs and benefits of making the necessary changes. Thus, this is a model that stresses the individual's perceptions of the situation as determinants of health-related behavior (Figure 17-3). We will consider each facet of the health belief model.

Beliefs about health threats　Social class, ethnicity, and religion all affect *general health beliefs* and corresponding health behaviors (135). To illustrate, one group may consider personal hygiene and exercise to be essential elements of maintaining good health, but they may be considered unimportant by other groups in society (136). Also, some people place a higher value on good health than others.

People also differ in their beliefs about their *susceptibility to disease*. People who believe they are more susceptible to a given disease, such as cancer or tuberculosis, are more likely to seek screening for that disease (137). Similarly, people who fear a relapse of a disease are more likely to follow their medical regimens than those who do not fear a relapse. A major problem with both help-seeking and compliance to medical regimens is that people tend to underestimate their susceptibility to disease.

BOX 17-3

Feelings of Control and Health

Recent research suggests that feelings of control play an important role in a variety of health-related situations and that perceptions of loss of control and helplessness can have negative effects on responses to life crises. For instance, placing elderly people in nursing homes can precipitate a major health crisis in their lives (125). The effects of this crisis depend in part on the degree to which these elderly people feel they have some control over what is happening to them. Elderly people placed in nursing homes involuntarily often do not live as long as elderly people who enter nursing homes voluntarily (127).

When new residents enter a nursing home, increasing their perceptions of control has beneficial effects. When people who have entered nursing homes are given orientation lectures telling them that they will be able to control many aspects of their lives, they maintain better health than if they are given orientation lectures stressing the willingness of the staff to help them in any way they can (127). Simply providing incoming nursing home patients with information that makes their new environments more predictable and understandable enhances their sense of physical and emotional well-being (128). Consistent with these findings, if nursing home patients are given help in ways that underscore their dependence, even when the help is very well-intentioned, the patients decline in self-confidence (129). Thus, interventions that increase perceptions of control enhance well-being, while those that decrease perceptions of control can reduce well-being.

In other studies, postsurgical patients who believed that they had control over the stress they were experiencing needed fewer pain-killing drugs and sedatives than patients treated normally (130). The rate of recovery of heart attack patients is also related to their perceptions of control over their current situations and their lives. Therapy programs specifically designed to increase the patients' feelings of control during the recovery period have beneficial effects on rates of recovery (131). Another study found that the psychological well-being of people with spinal cord injuries was related to their perceptions of control over important aspects of their lives (132). Taken together these studies demonstrate the powerful influence that perceptions of control have on psychological and physical health. Once again we see how important perceptions and beliefs are as determinants of behavior. ∎

Figure 17.3 ■

Health Belief Model

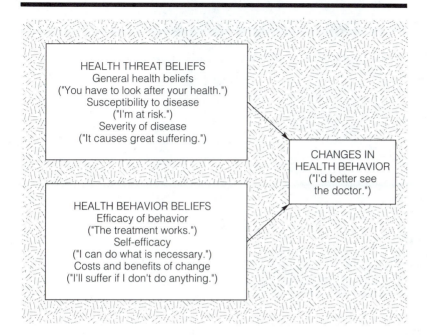

These underestimates undercut their perceptions of the need to change their behavior (138).

By now it should not surprise you to learn that the actual *severity of a disease* is not as closely related to the likelihood that people will follow medical advice as their *perceptions* of the severity of the disease. Many smokers underplay the seriousness of lung cancer and thus do not change their behavior. Although believing a disease is less severe than it actually is may be self-protective in the sense that it reduces anxiety, it may be very dysfunctional because it can lead people to avoid seeking needed medical care.

Beliefs about health behavior One critical belief concerns the *efficacy of treatment or behavior change.* If people do not believe that a behavior change will have the desired effect, they will be reluctant to

make the change. Again, the actual success rate may not be as important as the perceived success rate. People who believe a screening procedure for cancer will detect it early enough to make it treatable are more likely to be screened than those who do not believe the screening is effective. Similarly, people who believe an immunization against a disease will prevent it are the most likely to be immunized (139).

A second important belief concerns *self-efficacy*—the belief that one is capable of changing one's behavior. Even if people believe that a given behavior change works for others, if they do not think they are capable of carrying it out, they may not attempt it. People who believe they do not have the self-discipline to change their diet or increase their exercise levels may not even try.

The *perceived costs and benefits of change* also affect behavior. The costs of seeking care or following

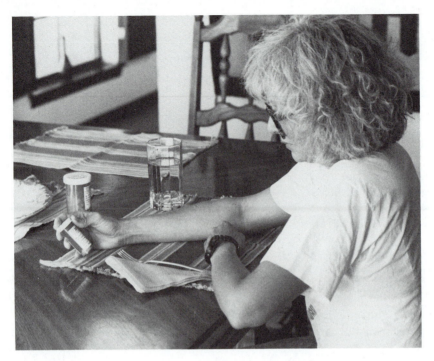

■ *Pill 'er up: Compliance with medical regimens is a major problem for medical practitioners and patients. (WGS)*

advice are not only monetary, but involve time, effort, pain, and the risks involved in changing (side effects of a treatment) (140). The barriers to seeking treatment or changing behavior consistently show up as one of the most important determinants of health-related behavior. These costs of seeking treatment are weighed against the benefits, such as avoiding future pain and suffering.

Some of the reasons why patient compliance rates are so low should now be clear. The absence of any of the factors in the health belief model can lead to noncompliance. The lack of supportive general health beliefs, or a belief that one is not at risk, that the disease is not severe, that the treatment regimen is not effective, that the individual is not capable of carrying it out, or that the costs of change are great and the perceived benefits are low, will make compliance unlikely.

Over time the health belief model has been modified to increase its utility. It is now recognized that some of the variables in the model have effects on one another. For instance, the perception that one is susceptible to dental disease increases the chances of getting a dental checkup, but getting a checkup decreases one's perceptions of his or her susceptibility to dental problems (141). Also, attitudes toward the physician and the treatment facility, demographic variables (especially sex and socioeconomic status), and cues to action (symptoms, reminders from others) have been incorporated into the model.

The health belief model has been effectively used to predict who will seek health examinations, vaccines, dental care, and health screening programs, and make changes in their dietary and smoking habits (142). In using the health belief model in clinical practice, attempts have been made to increase people's beliefs in their susceptibility to disease and

BOX 17-4

Prevention of Breast Cancer

Breast cancer is the second leading cause of death among women in the United States (147). The chances of surviving breast cancer are directly related to the size of the cancer at the time of diagnosis. This means that early detection is very important. Breast self-examination (BSE) is a proven prevention technique. Women who practice it are more likely to discover their own cancer, have tumors that are smaller at diagnosis, and have higher survival rates than those who do not. Yet, only 37 percent of women engage in monthly BSE, despite the fact that 87 percent know how to perform the exam.

Older and less well-educated women are least likely to do BSE. Many women rely on their physicians to do their examinations, but few see their physicians as often as they should to have their breasts examined. In accordance with the health belief model, women who perceive barriers to doing BSE are unlikely to do it (148). Also, consistent with the health belief model, self-efficacy in doing BSE and a belief in the effectiveness of BSE are related to the practice of BSE (149). Likewise, belief in one's susceptibility to breast cancer is associated with practicing BSE (150). Simply providing information and demonstrations has often proven unsuccessful in increasing BSE rates, but receiving monthly reminders (a cue to action) does increase BSE (151).

When a lump is detected in the breast, many women do not immediately see a physician. One study suggests that women who delay seeking treatment do so because they fear the disruption this will cause in their own lives and the lives of others; they believe they can maintain control over their lives by delaying treatment; and they believe delay will not have negative health consequences (152). Unfortunately, such delays can be costly to their health.

If you are a woman, has reading this information changed your intentions of doing a monthly BSE? If not, what are the beliefs and barriers that prevent you from doing it? ■

the seriousness of disease. Perceptions of seriousness are often increased by fear-provoking messages, a persuasion technique discussed in Chapter 10. These techniques can be very effective when combined with information about the efficacy of available treatments (143).

Other techniques, particularly behavioral ones, have been used to increase people's perceptions of self-efficacy by training them to perform the appropriate preventive or treatment behaviors. For example, muscle relaxation training and stress management programs have been successfully used to alter Type A and other CHD risk behaviors (144). These training techniques are most successful when they lead to changes in the beliefs that behavioral changes will be effective in preventing heart attacks (145). In one study reductions in hypertension were related to the patients' increased beliefs in their control over their disorder, presumably because these self-efficacy beliefs led them to make needed changes in their behavior (146) (Box 17-4).

In addition to attempts to use the health belief model to modify health-related behavior, many other programs have been developed to try to change health behavior. Informational campaigns have not proven to be very successful, although part of the problem is that they are rarely extensive enough. In one of the most fascinating studies to date, an entire community was subjected to a large scale mass media campaign based on social learning theory. This campaign used television, radio, pamphlets, and posters to motivate people to change CHD-related behaviors (153). In a second community, the mass media campaign was supplemented by intensive face-to-face contact treatments. These subjects were informed of the medical factors that placed them at risk, and they were provided with three months of instructions on how to change their lifestyles to reduce these risk factors. A control community did not receive any treatment.

The results indicated that over a 3-year period the mass media campaign was effective in reducing blood pressure and cholesterol levels. In addition to these changes, the face-to-face treatment condition was successful in achieving reductions in smoking and increases in physical exercise (see Table 17.1). This study indicates that massive information campaigns can work, but they are more effective if accompanied by face-to-face advice. Of course, educational techniques can be very expensive. However, for some diseases, like AIDS, educating the public may be one of the only techniques available to change behavior, since many of the people who most need to change (intravenous drug users) are least likely to consult with physicians—until it is too late.

In few of the areas we have presented in this text are the contributions of the two social psychologies as intermingled as they are in the case of the social psychology of health and illness. Sociological social psychologists are primarily responsible for studying the road from health to illness, but major contributions to understanding the perception of symptoms come from psychological social psychology. The effects of stress have been studied by both disciplines. Work on the psychosocial factors contributing to cancer and heart disease has been done predominantly by psychological social psychology, but important contributions have been made by sociological social psychology.

Table 17.1 ■

Results of the Stanford Three-Community Study

	Percent Change		
	Mass Media Campaign	Face-to-Face Instruction	Control Community
Cholesterol consumption	−38.6%	−42.3%	−13.4%
Blood pressure	−8.7	−6.6	−2.0
Smoking	−11.3	−50.0	−14.9
Physical activity	−11.8	8.6	−12.8
Weight	0.4	−0.4	−0.8

Note: The numbers indicate the percent change from baseline three years after the study began.
Adapted from Meyer et al., 1980.

The health belief model has its origins in the work of Lewin, the German psychologist who proposed the person/situation model discussed in Chapters 12 and 13. It has grown through the nearly equal contributions of both social psychologies. Thus, in the area of health and illness we see the two social psychologies coming together in a truly interdisciplinary way. In our estimation this is a prime example of the most productive way to study complex problems.

■ SUMMARY

In our discussion of the jury system we showed that juries often have difficulty overcoming negative pretrial publicity. Juries may become unrepresentative or lack impartiality because of problems in the way the jury pool is created or as a result of the *voir dire* process of questioning jurors. Juries in capital offense cases are often selected in such a way that the jurors are disposed to convict the defendant. In presenting evidence to the jury, studies suggest that it is best for the defense to take its first opportunity to make its opening statement. Leading questions by attorneys pose a problem because witnesses may be misled into making false statements. Witnesses also may unintentionally try to tailor their responses to suit the attorney asking the questions. Witnesses giving answers in a powerful way are most credible.

Eyewitnesses may be unreliable, but if they are confident they are likely to be believed. Eyewitnesses are most likely to be accurate when they have ample opportunity to observe the crime, are attending to the crime and are not highly stressed while doing so, give accurate initial identifications, and when there is a short time interval between the observation of the crime and identification of the criminal. Although certainty is related to accuracy, the relationship is very weak. Judicial instructions to the jury can sometimes overcome the potentially negative effects of inadmissable testimony, but they are less successful at eliminating the influence of information about prior convictions.

Most juries start their deliberations with an orientation phase, proceed through an open conflict stage to a conflict resolution state, and end with a reconciliation stage. The initial opinions of the jurors usually predict the final verdict. This verdict depends primarily on informational influence processes, but normative considerations are relevant in some instances. There are reasons to question the external validity of mock jury studies because they differ so much from actual jury trials.

Because chronic degenerative diseases now take more lives than acute diseases, the focus of medicine has been changing in recent years. Biopsychosocial models of disease suggest that behavioral and social factors play an important role in understanding the causes, prevention, and treatment of disease. On the road from health to illness people first encounter symptoms that they must perceive and interpret as significant. If they define the symptoms as requiring treatment, they may seek treatment if they are able to or can overcome the tendency to delay seeking treatment. If people decide they are ill they may adopt the sick role in which they are excused from normal role functioning and are expected to try to get well.

Social and psychological factors affect health through the health-related behaviors and through the ways people react to stress. Acute stress leads to the flight or fight syndrome, while chronic stress elicits the general adaptation syndrome. During the latter there is an initial alarm stage, followed by a resistance stage, and terminating in an exhaustion stage. Stress reduces the body's capacity to fight disease and leads to behavioral changes that can put people at risk for disease. Both life changes and daily hassles are associated with poor health.

Lifestyle choices play an important role in cancer, as does the manner in which people react to stress. People who react by suppressing strong emotions such as anger appear to be more susceptible to cancer and survive for shorter periods of time after they have contracted cancer than people who express their emotions.

Reactions to stress also appear to play a role in heart disease: Type As are more likely to have heart disease than Type Bs. The hostility component of this personality syndrome seems to be more important than the hard-driving, achievement-oriented component in causing heart disease.

The health belief model has been used to create prevention and treatment programs. It suggests that health behavior is caused by six factors: general health beliefs, susceptibility to disease, severity of disease, efficacy of behavior, self-efficacy, and the costs and benefits of changing. The model has been used to understand who will change their health behavior and to design treatment programs.

■

REFERENCES

1. Evans, W. M., 1980, *The Sociology of Law,* New York: The Free Press.
2. Greenberg, M. S. and R. B. Ruback, 1982, *Social Psychology of the Criminal Justice System,* Monterey, CA: Brooks/Cole.
3. Loftus, E. F., 1979, *Eyewitness Testimony,* Cambridge, MA: Harvard University Press.
4. Constantini, E. and J. King, 1980–1981, "The Partial Juror: Correlates and Causes of Prejudgment," *Law and Society Review* 15: 9–40; J. S. Carroll, N. L. Kerr, J. J. Alfini, F. M. Weaver, R. J. Maccoun, and V. Feldman, 1986, "Free Press and Fair Trial: The Role of Behavioral Research," *Law and Human Behavior* 10: 187–201.
5. Padewar-Singer, A. and A. Barton, 1975, "The Impact of Pretrial Publicity," in R. J. Simon (Ed.), *The Jury System in America,* Beverly Hills, CA: Sage.
6. Carroll et al., 1986, op. cit.; R. W. Davis, 1986, "Pretrial Publicity, the Timing of Trial, and Mock Jurors' Decision Processes," *Journal of Applied Social Psychology* 16: 590–607.
7. Cahn, E., 1983, "Winning Big Cases with Trial Simulations," *American Bar Association Journal* 69: 1073–1077.
8. Horowitz, I. A., 1980, "Juror Selection: A Comparison of Two Methods in Several Criminal Cases," *Journal of Applied Social Psychology* 10: 86–99.
9. Hans, V. P. and N. Vidmar, 1982, "Jury Selection," in N. L. Kerr and R. M. Bray, *The Psychology of the Courtroom,* New York: Academic Press; J. R. Hepburn, 1980, "The Objective Reality of Evidence and the Utility of Systematic Jury Selection," *Law and Human Behavior* 4: 89–102; M. Saks and R. Hastie, *Social Psychology in Court,* Princeton, NJ: Van Nostrand-Reinhold.
10. Christie, R., 1976, "Probability vs. Precedence: The Social Psychology of Jury Selection," in G. Bermant, C. Nemeth, and N. Vidmar (Eds.), *Psychology and the Law,* Lexington, MA: Lexington Books.
11. Hans and Vidmar, 1982, op. cit.
12. Loh, W. D., 1984, *Social Research in the Judicial Process,*

New York: Sage; B. J. Winnick, 1982, "Prosecutorial Peremptory Challenge Practices in Capital Cases: An Empirical Study and a Constitutional Analysis," *Michigan Law Review* 81: 2–98.
13. Cowan, C. L., W. C. Thompson, and P. C. Ellsworth, 1984, "The Effects of Death Qualification on Jurors' Predispositions to Convict and the Quality of Deliberation," *Law and Human Behavior* 8: 53–80; R. Fitzgerald and P. C. Ellsworth, 1984, "Due Process vs. Crime Control: Death Qualification and Jury Attitudes," *Law and Human Behavior* 8: 31–51.
14. Fitzgerald and Ellsworth, 1984, ibid.; *Hovey v. The Superior Court of Alameda County,* 168 California Reporter 128, 1980.
15. Quoted in D. Myers, *Social Psychology,* 2d ed., New York: McGraw-Hill, p. 386.
16. Wells, G. L., L. S. Wrightsman, and P. K. Miene, 1985, "The Timing of the Defense Opening Statement: Don't Wait until the Evidence Is In," *Journal of Applied Social Psychology* 15: 758–772.
17. Loh, 1984, op. cit.
18. Pyzczynski, T., J. Greenberg, D. Mack, and L. S. Wrightsman, 1981, "Opening Statements in a Jury Trial: The Effects of Promising More Than the Evidence Can Show," *Journal of Applied Social Psychology* 11: 301–313.
19. Loftus, E. F., D. G. Miller, and H. J. Burns, 1978, "Semantic Integration of Verbal Information into a Visual Memory," *Journal of Experimental Psychology: Human Learning and Memory* 4:19–31.
20. Loftus, E. F. and G. Zanni, 1975, "Eyewitness Testimony: The Influence of the Wording of a Question," *Bulletin of the Psychonomic Society* 5: 86–88.
21. Sheppard, B. H. and N. Vidmar, 1980, "Adversary Pretrial Procedures and Testimonial Evidence: Effects of Lawyer's Role and Machiavellianism," *Journal of Personality and Social Psychology* 39: 320–332.
22. O'Barr, W. M. and J. M. Conley, 1976, "When a Juror Watches a Lawyer," *Barrister* 3: 8–11, 33.
23. Miller, G. R. and J. K. Burgoon, 1982, "Factors Affecting Assessments of Witness Credibility," in N. L. Kerr and R. M. Bray, op. cit.; G. L. Wells, T. J. Ferguson, and R. C. L. Lindsay, 1981, "The Tractability of Eyewitness Confidence and Its Implications for Triers of Fact," *Journal of Applied Psychology* 66: 688–696.
24. Whitley, B. E., Jr. and M. S. Greenberg, 1986, "The Role of Eyewitness Confidence in Juror Perceptions of Credibility," *Journal of Applied Social Psychology* 16: 387–409.
25. Devlin, L. P., 1976, "Report to the Secretary of State for the Home Department of the Departmental Committee on Evidence of Identification in Criminal Cases," London: Her Majesty's Stationery Office.
26. Buckhout, R., 1980, "Nearly 2,000 Witnesses Can Be Wrong," *Bulletin of the Psychonomic Society* 16: 307–310.
27. Brigham, J. C., A. Maass, L. D. Snyder, and K. S. Spaulding, 1982, "Accuracy of Eyewitness Identifications in a Field Setting," *Journal of Personality and Social Psychology* 42: 673–681.
28. Lindsay, R. C. L., G. L. Wells, and C. M. Rumpel, 1981, "Can People Detect Eyewitness Identification Accuracy within and

across Situations?" *Journal of Applied Psychology* 66: 79–89; R. S. Malpass and P. G. Devine, 1981, "Eyewitness Identification: Lineup Instructions and the Absence of the Offender," *Journal of Applied Psychology* 66: 482–489.

29. Brigham, J. C. and M. P. Wolfskeil, 1983, "Opinions of Attorneys and Law Enforcement Personnel on the Accuracy of Eyewitness Identifications," *Law and Human Behavior* 7: 341–349.

30. *Manson* v. *Braithwaite,* 432 U. S. 98, 1978.

31. Ellis, H. D., 1984, "Practical Aspects of Face Memory," in G. L. Wells and E. F. Loftus (Eds.), *Eyewitness Testimony,* Cambridge, MA: Cambridge University Press.

32. Penrod, S., E. Loftus, and J. Winkler, 1982, "The Reliability of Eyewitness Testimony: A Psychological Perspective," in N. L. Kerr and R. M. Bray, op. cit.

33. Paterson, K. E. and A. D. Baddeley, 1977, "When Face Recognition Fails," *Journal of Experimental Psychology: Human Learning and Memory* 3: 406–407; P. Shapiro and S. Penrod, 1986, "A Meta-analysis of the Facial Recognition Literature," *Psychological Bulletin* 100: 139–156.

34. Penrod, Loftus, and Winkler, 1982, op. cit.

35. Tooley, V., J. C. Brigham, A. Maass, and R. K. Bothwell, 1987, "Facial Recognition: Weapon Effect and Attentional Focus," *Journal of Applied Social Psychology* 17: 845–859.

36. Lieppe, M. R., G. L. Wells, and T. M. Ostrom, 1978, "Crime Seriousness as a Deterrent of Accuracy in Eyewitness Identification," *Journal of Applied Psychology* 63: 345–351; M. S. Greenberg, C. E. Wilson, R. B. Ruback, and M. K. Mills, 1979, "Social and Emotional Determinants of Victim Crime Reporting," *Social Psychology Quarterly* 6: 156–162.

37. Yuille, J., 1980, "A Critical Examination of the Psychological and Practical Implications of Eyewitness Research," *Law and Human Behavior* 4: 335–346.

38. Davies, G. M., J. W. Shepherd, and H. D. Ellis, 1979, "Effects of Interpolated Mugshot Exposure on Accuracy of Eyewitness Identification," *Journal of Applied Psychology* 64: 232–237; G. W. Gorenstein and P. C. Ellsworth, 1980, "Effect of Choosing an Incorrect Photograph on a Later Identification by an Eyewitness," *Journal of Applied Psychology* 65: 616–622.

39. Bahrick, H. P., P. O. Bahrick, and R. P. Wittlinger, 1975, "Fifty Years of Memory for Names and Faces: A Cross-sectional Approach," *Journal of Experimental Psychology: General* 104: 54–75.

40. Bothwell, R. K., K. Deffenbacher, and J. C. Brigham, 1986, "Correlation of Eyewitness Accuracy and Confidence: The Optimality Hypothesis Revisited," University of Texas at El Paso; Penrod, Loftus, and Winkler, 1982, op. cit.; G. L. Wells and D. M. Murray, 1984, "Eyewitness Confidence," in G. L. Wells and E. F. Loftus, op. cit.

41. Deffenbacher, K. F., 1980, "Eyewitness Accuracy and Confidence: Can We Infer Anything about Their Relationship?" *Law and Human Behavior* 4: 243–260.

42. Wells and Murray, 1984, op. cit.

43. Wells, G. L., R. C. L. Lindsay, and T. J. Ferguson, 1979, "Accuracy, Confidence, and Juror Perceptions in Eyewitness Identification," *Journal of Applied Social Psychology* 64: 440–448.

44. Wells, G. L., T. J. Ferguson, and R. C. L. Lindsay, 1981, "The Tractability of Eyewitness Confidence and Its Implications for Triers of Fact," *Journal of Applied Psychology* 66: 688–696.

45. Penrod, Loftus, and Winkler, 1982, op. cit.

46. Shepherd, J. W. and H. D. Ellis, 1973, "The Effect of Attractiveness on Recognition for Faces," *American Journal of Psychology* 86: 205–211.

47. Cutler, B. L., S. D. Penrod, and T. E. Stuve, 1988, "Juror Decision Making in Eyewitness Identification Cases," *Law and Human Behavior* 12: 41–55.

48. Loftus, 1979, op. cit.; N. Hatvany and F. Strack, 1980, "The Impact of a Discredited Key Witness," *Journal of Applied Social Psychology* 10: 490–509; H. I. Weinberg and R. S. Baron, 1982, "The Discredible Eyewitness," *Personality and Social Psychology Bulletin* 8: 60–67.

49. Loftus, E. F., 1980, "Impact of Expert Psychological Testimony on the Unreliability of Eyewitness Identification," *Journal of Applied Psychology* 65: 9–15; E. F. Loftus, 1983, "Silence is Not Golden," *American Psychologist* 38: 564–572.

50. Greene, E. L., 1983, "Judges' Instructions on Eyewitness Testimony: Evaluation and Revision," unpublished doctoral dissertation, University of Washington; F. G. Kline and P. H. Jess, 1966, "Prejudicial Publicity: Its Effects on Law School Mock Juries," *Journalism Quarterly* 43: 113–116; E. A. Lind, 1982, "The Psychology of Courtroom Procedure," in N. L. Kerr and R. M. Bray, op. cit.

51. Frank, J., 1930, *Law and the Modern Mind,* New York: Tudor.

52. Carroll et al., 1986, op. cit.

53. Doob, A. N., 1976, "Evidence, Procedure, and Psychological Research," in G. Bermant, C. Nemeth, and N. Vidmar, op. cit.; V. Hans and A. Doob, 1975, "Section 12 of the Canada Evidence Act and the Deliberations of Simulated Jurors," *Criminal Law Quarterly* 18: 235–253; R. L. Wissler and M. J. Saks, 1985, "On the Efficacy of Limiting Instructions," *Law and Human Behavior* 9: 37–47.

54. Archer, R. L., H. C. Foushee, M. H. Davis, and D. Aderman, 1979, "Emotional Empathy in a Courtroom Simulation: A Person-Situation Interaction," *Journal of Applied Social Psychology* 9: 275–291; R. Hastie, S. D. Penrod, and N. Pennington, 1983, *Inside the Jury,* Cambridge, MA: Harvard University Press; N. L. Kerr, R. S. Atkin, G. Stasser, D. Meek, R. W. Holt, and J. H. Davis, 1976, "Guilt Beyond a Reasonable Doubt: Effect of Concept Definition and Assigned Decision Rule on the Judgments of Mock Jurors," *Journal of Personality and Social Psychology* 34: 282–294; A. P. Sealy and W. R. Cornish, 1973, "Juries and the Rules of Evidence," *Criminal Law Review April:* 208–223; S. Wolf and D. A. Montgomery, 1977, "Effects of Inadmissible Evidence and Level of Judicial Admonishment to Disregard on the Judgments of Mock Jurors," *Journal of Applied Social Psychology* 7: 205–219.

55. Thompson, W. C., G. T. Fong, and D. L. Rosenhan, 1981,

"Inadmissible Evidence and Juror Verdicts," *Journal of Personality and Social Psychology* 40: 456–463.

56. Tanford, S. and S. D. Penrod, 1986, "Jury Deliberations: Discussion Content and Influence Processes in Jury Decision Making," *Journal of Applied Social Psychology* 16: 322–347.

57. Miller, G. R. and N. E. Fontes, 1979, *Videotape on Trial: A View from the Jury Box,* Beverly Hills, CA: Sage.

58. Hastie, Penrod, and Pennington, 1983, op. cit.

59. Loh, 1984, op. cit.

60. Loh, 1984, ibid.

61. Kalven, H. and H. Ziesel, 1966, *The American Jury,* Boston: Little, Brown.

62. Hastie, Penrod, and Pennington, 1983, op. cit.; R. James, 1959, "Status and Competence of Jurors," *American Journal of Sociology* 64: 563–570; J. Kessler, 1973, "An Empirical Study of Six and Twelve Member Jury Decision Making Processes," *University of Michigan Journal of Law Reform* 6: 712–734.

63. Hastie, Penrod, and Pennington, 1983, op. cit.

64. Hans and Doob, 1975, op. cit.; Kalven and Zeisel, 1966, op. cit.; Kline and Jess, 1966, op. cit.

65. Hawkins, C. H., 1960, "Interaction and Coalition Realignments in Consensus-seeking Groups: A Study of Experimental Jury Deliberations," unpublished doctoral dissertation, The University of Chicago, cited in Hastie, Penrod, and Pennington, 1983, op. cit.

66. Hastie, Penrod, and Pennington, ibid.

67. Kalven and Zeisel, 1966, op. cit.; R. J. Simon, 1980, *The Jury: Its Role in American Society,* Lexington, MA: Lexington Books; Tanford and Penrod, 1986, op. cit.

68. Stasser, G., N. L. Kerr, and R. M. Bray, 1982, "The Social Psychology of Jury Deliberations: Structure, Process, and Product," in N. L. Kerr and R. M. Bray, op. cit.

69. Nemeth, C., 1977, "Interactions between Jurors as a Function of Majority vs. Minority Decision Rules," *Journal of Applied Social Psychology* 7: 38–56.

70. Stasser, G., N. L. Kerr, and J. H. Davis, 1980, "Influence Processes in Decision Making Groups: A Modeling Approach," in P. B. Paulus (Ed.), *Psychology of Group Influence,* Hillsdale, NJ: Lawrence Erlbaum.

71. Tanford and Penrod, 1986, op. cit.

72. Simon, 1980, op. cit.

73. Loh, W. D., 1981, "Perspectives on Psychology and Law," *Journal of Applied Social Psychology* 11: 314–355.

74. Fitzpatrick, R. M., 1986, "Social Concepts of Health and Illness," in D. L. Patrick and G. Scambler (Eds.), *Sociology as Applied to Medicine,* London: Bailliere Tindall; S. E. Taylor, 1986, *Health Psychology,* New York: Random House.

75. Taylor, 1986, ibid.; F. D. Wolinsky, 1980, *The Sociology of Health,* Boston: Little Brown.

76. Pennebaker, J. W., 1982, *The Psychology of Physical Symptoms,* New York: Springer-Verlag.

77. Mechanic, D., 1978, *Medical Sociology,* New York: The Free Press; L. Nuttbrock, 1986, "The Management of Illness among Physically Impaired Older People: An Interactionist Interpretation," *Social Psychology Quarterly* 49: 180–191.

78. Scambler, A., G. Scambler, and D. Craig, 1981, "Kinship and Friendship Networks and Women's Demand for Primary Care," *Journal of the Royal College of General Practitioners* 26: 746–750.

79. Dunnell, K. and A. Cartwright, 1972, *Medicine Takers, Prescribers, and Hoarders,* London: Routledge & Kegan Paul.

80. Nuttbrock, 1986, op. cit.

81. Krantz, D. S., N. E. Grumberg, and A. Baum, 1985, "Health Psychology," *Annual Review of Psychology* 36: 349–383.

82. Parsons, T., 1951, *The Social System,* New York: The Free Press; T. Parsons, 1972, "Definitions of Health and Illness in Light of American Values and Social Structure," in E. G. Jaco (Ed.), *Patients, Physicians, and Illness: A Sourcebook in Behavioral Science and Health,* 2d. ed., New York: The Free Press; T. Parsons, 1975, "The Sick Role and the Role of the Physician Reconsidered," *Milbank Memorial Fund Quarterly* 53: 257–278.

83. Svarstad, B., 1974, "The Doctor-Patient Encounter: An Observational Study of Communication and Outcome," unpublished doctoral dissertation, University of Wisconsin, cited in R. M. DiMatteo and D. D. DiNicola, 1982, *Achieving Patient Compliance,* New York: Pergamon.

84. DiMatteo and DiNicola, 1982, ibid.

85. Stiles, W. B., S. M. Putnam, M. H. Wolf, and S. A. James, 1979, "Verbal Response Mode Profiles of Patients and Physicians in Medical Screening Interviews," *Journal of Medical Education* 54: 81–89.

86. Barnlund, D. C., 1976, "The Mystification of Meaning: Doctor-Patient Encounters," *Journal of Medical Education* 51: 716–725.

87. Ley, P. and M. S. Spelman, 1965, "Communication in an Outpatient Setting," *British Journal of Social and Clinical Psychology* 4: 114–116.

88. Mechanic, 1978, op. cit.

89. DiMatteo, M. R. and D. D. DiNicola, 1981, "Sources of Assessment of Physician Performance: A Study of Comparative Reliability and Patterns of Intercorrelation," *Medical Care* 19: 829–842.

90. Cohen, S., T. Kamarck, and R. Mermelstein, 1983, "A Global Measure of Perceived Stress," *Journal of Health and Social Behavior* 24: 385–396; D. C. Glass and J. E. Singer, 1972, *Urban Stress: Experiments and Noise and Social Stressors,* Hillsdale, NJ: Lawrence Erlbaum.

91. Cohen, S., G. W. Evans, D. Stokols, and D. S. Krantz, 1986, *Behavior, Health, and Environmental Stress,* New York: Plenum.

92. Selye, H., 1956, *The Stress of Life,* New York: McGraw-Hill.

93. Jemmott, J. B. and S. E. Locke, 1984, "Psychosocial Factors, Immunologic Medication, and Human Susceptibility to Infectious Diseases, How Much Do We Know?" *Psychological Bulletin* 95: 52–77.

94. Kiecolt-Glaser, J. K., R. Glaser, E. C. Strain, J. C. Stout, K. L. Tarr, J. E. Holliday, and C. E. Speicher, 1986, "Modulation of Cellular Immunity in Medical Students," *Journal of Behavioral Medicine* 9: 5–17.

95. Baum, A., R. J. Gatchel, and M. A. Schaeffer, 1983, "Emotional, Behavioral, and Physiological Effects of Chronic Stress at Three Mile Island," *Journal of Consulting and Clinical Psychology* 51: 565–572.

96. Krantz, Grumberg, and Baum, 1985, op. cit.; Pennebaker, 1982, op. cit.

97. House, J., 1975, "Occupational Stress as a Precursor to Coronary Disease," in W. D. Gentry and R. B. Williams (Eds.), *Psychological Aspects of Myocardial Infarction and Coronary Care,* St. Louis, MO: C. V. Mosby.

98. Grumberg, N. E. and A. Baum, 1985, "Biological Commonalities of Stress and Substance Abuse," in S. Shiffman and T. A. Wills (Eds.), *Coping with Substance Abuse,* Orlando, FL: Academic Press.

99. Garrity, T. F. and M. B. Marx, 1979, "Critical Life Events and Coronary Heart Disease," in W. D. Gentry and R. B. Williams (Eds.) *Psychological Aspects of Myocardial Infarction and Coronary Care,* 2d ed., St. Louis, MO: C. V. Mosby; T. H. Holmes and R. H. Rahe, 1967, "The Social Readjustment Rating Scale," *Journal of Psychosomatic Research* 11: 213–218; J. W. Mason, W. L. Buescher, M. L. Belfer, M. S. Artenstein, and E. H. Mougey, 1979, "A Prospective Study of Corticosteroid and Catecholamine Levels in Relation to Viral Respiratory Illness," *Journal of Human Stress* 5: 18–25.

100. DeLongis, A., J. C. Coyne, G. Dakof, S. Folkman, and R. Lazarus, 1982, "Relationship of Daily Hassles, Uplifts, and Major Life Events to Health Status," *Health Psychology* 1: 119–136; M. Weinberger, S. L. Hiner, and W. M. Tierney, 1987, "In Support of Hassles as a Measure of Stress Predicting Health Outcomes," *Journal of Behavioral Medicine* 10: 19–27; J. J. Zarski, 1984, "Hassles and Health: A Replication," *Health Psychology* 3: 243–251.

101. Levy, S. M., 1985, *Behavior and Cancer,* San Francisco: Jossey-Bass.

102. Levy, 1985, ibid.

103. Levy, 1985, ibid.

104. Heberman, R., 1982, "Mediating Links between Behavior and Natural Killer Cell Activity," in S. M. Levy (Ed.), *Biological Mediators of Behavior and Disease,* New York: Elsevier-North Holland.

105. Locke, S., M. Hurst, and J. Heisel, 1978, "The Influence of Stress on the Immune Response," American Psychosomatic Society, April, cited in S. M. Levy, 1983, "Host Differences in Neoplastic Risk: Behavioral and Social Contributors to Disease," *Health Psychology* 2: 21–44.

106. Blaney, P., 1985, "Psychological Consideration in Cancer," in N. Schneiderman and J. T. Tapp, *Behavioral Medicine,* Hillsdale, NJ: Lawrence Erlbaum; Levy, 1985, op. cit.; L. S. Sklar and H. Anisman, 1981, "Stress and Cancer," *Psychological Bulletin* 89: 369–406.

107. Shaffer, J. W., P. L. Graves, R. T. Swank, and T. A. Pearson, 1987, "Clustering of Personality Traits in Youth and the Subsequent Development of Cancer among Physicians," *Journal of Behavioral Medicine* 10: 441–456.

108. Greer, S., 1979, "Psychological Attributes of Women with Breast Cancer," *Cancer Detection and Prevention* 2: 289–294.

109. Sklar, L. S. and H. Anisman, 1979, "Stress and Coping Factors Influence Tumor Growth," *Science* 205: 513–515.

110. Lippman, M. E., 1985, "Endocrine Responsive Cancers in Man," in R. Williams (Ed.), *Textbook in Endocrinology,* Philadelphia: Saunders.

111. Levy, 1985, op. cit.

112. Derogatis, L. R., M. D. Abeloff, 1977, "Psychological Aspects of Management of Primary and Metastatic Breast Cancer," in A. C. W. Montague, G. L. Stonesifer, and E. F. Lewison (Eds.), *Breast Cancer: Progress in Clinical and Biological Research,* Vol. 12, New York: Liss; L. R. Derogatis, M. D. Abeloff, and M. Melisaratos, 1979, "Psychological Coping Mechanisms and Survival Time in Metastatic Breast Cancer," *Journal of the American Medical Association* 242: 1504–1508; S. Greer, T. Morris, and K. Pettingale, 1979, "Psychological Response to Breast Cancer: Effect of Outcome," *Lancet* 2: 785–787.

113. Visintainer, M. A., J. R. Volpicelli, and M. E. P. Seligman, 1982, "Tumor Rejection in Rats after Inescapable or Escapable Shock," *Science* 216: 437–439; A. Greenberg, D. Dyck, and L. Sandler, 1984, "Opponent Processes, Neurohormones, and Natural Resistance," in B. Fox and B. Newberry (Eds.), *Psychoneuroendocrine Systems in Cancer and Immunity,* Toronto: Hogrefe; S. Greer, T. Morris, K. Pettingale, and J. Haybittle, 1985, "Mental Attitudes to Cancer: An Additional Prognostic Factor," *Lancet* 1: 750.

114. Levy, 1985, op. cit.

115. Levy, S. M., and others, 1985, "Prognostic Risk Assessment in Primary Breast Cancer by Behavioral and Immunological Factors," *Health Psychology* 4: 99–113.

116. Krantz, D. S. and R. Schulz, 1980, "A Model of Life Crisis, Control, and Health Outcomes: Cardiac Rehabilitation and Relocation of the Elderly," in A. Baum and J. E. Singer (Eds.), *Advances in Environmental Psychology,* Vol. 3, Hillsdale, NJ: Lawrence Erlbaum.

117. *Newsweek,* February 8, 1988, p. 50.

118. Krantz, Grumberg, and Baum, 1985, op. cit.; C. S. Carver, E. L. Diamond, and C. Humphreys, 1985, "Coronary Prone Behavior," in N. Schneiderman and J. T. Tapp, op. cit.

119. Chesney, M. and R. Rosenman, 1985, *Anger and Hostility in Cardiovascular and Behavioral Disorders,* New York: Hemisphere/McGraw-Hill; K. A. Matthews, 1982, "Psychological Perspectives on Type A Behavior Pattern," *Psychological Bulletin* 91: 293–323.

120. Carver, Diamond, and Humphreys, 1985, op. cit.

121. Glass, D. C., L. R. Krakoff, J. Finkelman, B. Snow, R. Contrada, K. Kehoe, E. G. Manucci, W. Isecke, C. Collins, W. F. Hilton, and E. Elting, 1980, "Effect of Task Overload upon Cardiovascular and Plasma Catecholamine Responses in Type A and B Individuals," *Basic and Applied Social Psychology* 1: 199–218; M. C. Ward, M. A. Chesney, G. E. Swan, G. W. Black, S. D. Parker, and R. H. Rosenman, 1986, "Cardiovascular Responses in Type A and Type B Men to a Series of Stressors," *Journal of Behavioral Medicine* 9: 43–49.

122. Carver, Diamond, and Humphreys, 1985, op. cit.

123. Krantz, D. S., U. Lundberg, and M. Frankenhausen, 1987, "Stress and Type A Behavior: Interactions between Environmental and Biological Factors," in A. Baum and J. E. Singer (Eds.), *Handbook of Psychology and Health,* Vol. 5, Hillsdale, NJ: Lawrence Erlbaum.

124. Krantz, Lundberg, and Frankenhausen, 1987, ibid.

125. Krantz and Schulz, 1980, op. cit.

126. Ferrari, N., 1963, "Freedom of Choice," *Social Work* 8: 105–106.

127. Langer, E. J. and J. Rodin, 1976, "The Effects of Choice and Enhanced Personal Responsibility for the Aged: A Field Experiment in an Institutional Setting," *Journal of Personality and Social Psychology* 34: 191–198; R. Schultz and B. H. Hanusa, 1977, "Facilitating Institutional Adaptation of the Aged: Effects of Predictability-enhancing Intervention," paper presented at a meeting of the American Gerontological Society, San Francisco.

128. Schulz, R., 1980, "Aging and Control," in J. Garber and M. E. P. Seligman (Eds.), *Human Helplessness,* New York: Academic Press.

129. Avorn, J. and E. J. Langer, 1982, "Induced Disability in Nursing Home Patients: A Controlled Trial," *Journal of the American Geriatric Society* 30: 397–400.

130. Langer, E. J., I. L. Janis, and J. A. Wolfer, 1975, "Reduction of Psychological Stress in Surgical Patients," *Journal of Experimental Social Psychology* 11: 155–165.

131. Cromwell, R. L., E. C. Butterfield, F. M. Brayfield, and J. J. Curry, 1977, *Acute Myocardial Infarction: Reaction and Recovery,* St. Louis, MO: C. V. Mosby; R. F. Klein, V. A. Kliner, D. P. Zipes, W. G. Troyer, and A. G. Wallace, 1968, "Transfer from a Coronary Care Unit," *Archives of Internal Medicine* 122: 104–108; E. Roskies, 1980, "Considerations in Developing a Treatment Program for the Coronary-prone (Type A) Behavior Pattern," in P. O. Davidson and S. M. Davidson (Eds.), *Behavioral Medicine: Changing Health Lifestyles,* New York: Brunner/Mazel.

132. Schulz, R. and S. Decker, 1985, "Long-term Adjustment to Physical Disability: The Role of Social Support, Perceived Control, and Self-blame," *Journal of Personality and Social Psychology* 48: 1162–1172.

133. Sackett, D. L. and J. C. Snow, 1979, "The Magnitude of Compliance and Noncompliance," in R. B. Haynes, D. W. Taylor, and D. L. Sackett (Eds.), *Compliance in Health Care,* Baltimore, MD: Johns Hopkins University Press.

134. Rosenstock, I. M., 1966, "Why People Use Health Services," *Milbank Memorial Fund Quarterly* 44: 94–124; I. M. Rosenstock, 1974, "The Health Belief Model and Preventive Health Behavior," *Health Education Monographs* 2: 354–386.

135. Kirscht, 1983, "Preventive Health Behavior: A Review of Research and Issues," *Health Psychology* 2: 277–301.

136. Jenkins, C. D., 1976, "Recent Evidence Supporting Psychological and Social Risk Factors for Coronary Disease," Taylor, 1985, op. cit.

137. DiMatteo and DiNicola, 1982, op. cit.

138. Weinstein, N.D., 1982, "Unrealistic Optimism about Susceptibility to Health Problems," *Journal of Behavioral Medicine* 5: 441–460.

139. DiMatteo, and DiNicola, 1982, op. cit.

140. Chen, M and K. C. Land, 1986, "Testing the Health Belief Model: Lisrel Analysis of Alternative Models of Causal Relationships between Health Belief and Preventive Dental Behavior," *Social Psychology Quarterly* 49: 45–60.

141. Chen and Land, 1986, ibid.

142. Taylor, 1986, op. cit.

143. Becker, M., M. Maiman, J. Kirscht, D. Haefner, and R. Drachman, 1977, "The Health Belief Model and Prediction of Dietary Compliance: A Field Experiment," *Journal of Health and Social Behavior* 18: 348–366; D. Haefner and J. Kirscht, 1970, "Motivational and Behavioral Effects of Modifying Health Beliefs," *Public Health Beliefs* 85: 478–484.

144. Gatchel, R. J., F. A. Gaffney, and J. E. Smith, 1986, "Comparative Efficacy of Behavioral Stress Management versus Propranol in Reducing Psychophysiological Reactivity in Post-myocardial Infarction Patients," *Journal of Behavioral Medicine* 9: 503–513; S. H. Lovibond, P. C. Birrell, and P. Langeluddecke, 1986, "Changing Coronary Heart Disease Risk-factor Status: The Effects of Three Behavioral Programs," *Journal of Behavioral Medicine* 9: 415–427; M. Friedman, C. E. Thoreson, J. J. Gill, L. H. Powell, D. Ulmer, L. Thompson, V. A. Price, D. D. Rabin, W. S. Breall, T. Dixon, R. Levy, and E. Bourg, 1984, "Alteration of Type A Behavior and Reduction of Cardiac Reoccurrences in Postmyocardial Infarction Patients," *American Heart Journal* 108: 237–248.

145. Kaplan, R. M., C. J. Atkins, and S. Reinsch, 1984, "Specific Efficacy Expectations Mediate Exercise Compliance in Patients with COPD," *Health Psychology* 3: 223–242.

146. Stanton, A. L., 1987, "Determinants of Adherence to Medical Regimens by Hypertensive Patients," *Journal of Behavioral Medicine* 10: 377–388.

147. American Cancer Society, 1986, *The Cancer Book,* New York: Doubleday.

148. Calnan, M. W. and S. Moss, 1984, "The Health Belief Model and Compliance with Education Given at a Class in Breast Self-examination," *Journal of Health and Social Behavior* 25: 198–210; D. Hill, G. Gardner, and J. Rassaby, 1985, "Factors Predisposing Women to Take Precautions against Breast and Cervix Cancer," *Journal of Applied Social Psychology* 15: 59–79; L. M. Strauss, L. J. Solomon, M. C. Costanza, J. K. Worden, and R. S. Foster Jr., 1987, "Breast Self-examination Practices and Attitudes of Women with and without a History of Breast Cancer," *Journal of Behavioral Medicine,* 10: 337–353.

149. Alagna, S. W. and D. M. Reddy, 1984, "Predictors of Proficient Technique and Successful Lesion Detection in Breast Self-examination," *Health Psychology* 3: 113–127.

150. Hill, Gardner, and Rassaby, 1985, op. cit.; P. T. Kelly, 1979, "Breast Self-Examinations: Who Does Them and Why?" *Journal of Behavioral Medicine* 2: 31–38.

151. Craun, A. M. and J. L. Deffenbacher, 1987, "The Effects of

Information, Behavioral Rehearsal, and Prompting on Breast Self-exams," *Journal of Behavioral Medicine* 10: 351–363.

152. Timko, C., 1987, "Seeking Medical Care for a Breast Cancer Symptom: Determinants of Intentions to Engage in Prompt or Delay Behavior," *Health Psychology* 6: 305–328; E. M. Turnbull, 1978, "Effects of Basic Preventive Health Practices and Mass Media on the Practice of Breast Self-examination," *Nursing Research* 27: 98–102.

153. Maccoby, N. and J. Alexander, 1980, "Use of Media in Lifestyle Programs," in P. O. Davidson and S. M. Davidson, (Eds.), *Behavioral Medicine: Changing Health Lifestyles*, New York: Brunner/Mazel; A. J. Meyer, J. D. Nash, A. L. McAlister, N. Maccoby, and J. W. Farquhar, 1980, "Skills Training in a Cardiovascular Health Education Campaign," *Journal of Consulting and Clinical Psychology* 48: 129–142.

NAME INDEX

A

Abramson, L. Y., 133
Adair, G., 82
Adams, G. R., 313
Adams, J. S., 51
Aderman, D., 344
Agnew, R., 218
Aguirre, B. E., 476
Akers, R. L., 218
Ajzen, Icek, 14, 281
Alexander, C. N., 132, 251
Alexander, J., 19
Allen, V. L., 193
Allport, Gordon, 434, 443, 445
Allyn, J., 282
Alwin, D. F., 51
Anderson, J. R., 251
Anderson, Leon, 67, 68
Anderson, N. H., 252
Antill, J. K., 312
Apple, M. W., 219
Archer, R. L., 133
Aronfreed, J., 108, 193
Aronson, Elliot, 444
Asch, Solomon, 176–177, 182, 246

B

Babbie, E., 81
Back, K. W., 193
Bakal, C., 343
Bakeman, Roger, 74–75
Bales, Robert, 410–411
Bandura, A., 51, 108
Barash, D. P., 343
Bargh, J. A., 253
Baron, R. A., 345
Barry, H., III, 109
Baruch, G., 164
Basow, S. A., 163

Batson, D., 344, 345
Baumeister, R. F., 132
Beci, E. L., 281
Becker, B. J., 163
Becker, Howard, 7–9, 218
Beckman, R. L., 476
Begley, T. M., 477
Bell, L., 251
Bem, Daryl, 117, 267
Benbow, C. P., 163
Benedict, Ruth, 54
Berg, David, 180
Berg, J. H., 312
Berger, J., 51
Bergmann, B. R., 165
Berk, R. A., 219
Berk, S. F., 165
Berkowitz, L., 344, 346
Berlyne, D. E., 251
Berman, J. S., 252
Bernard, J., 164
Berndt, T. J., 252
Bersheid, E., 252, 313, 314
Best, J., 20
Best, R., 163
Bickman, L., 343, 344
Biddle, B. J., 51
Bielby, D. D., 164
Billy, J. O. G., 312
Blau, Peter, 425
Blauner, Robert, 422
Bloch, M. N., 163
Blum, L. M., 164
Blumer, Herbert, 25–26, 476
Bochner, S., 283
Boggiano, A. K., 281
Bond, C. F., Jr., 253
Bourne, E., 251
Brabant, S., 163
Breault, K. D., 19, 311
Brehm, M. L., 281
Brim, O. G., Jr., 108, 109

Brock, T. C., 282
Bronfenbrenner, U., 108
Brown, J. D., 163
Brown, R. W., 108
Brownmiller, Susan, 364
Bruner, J. S., 253
Bryan, J. H., 109, 346
Buck, R., 50
Burger, J. M., 132
Burgess, R. L., 314
Bush, D. M., 109
Buss, A. H., 192
Buss, D. M., 313
Byrne, D., 312, 313

C

Callaway, M. R., 193
Callero, P., 51, 345
Campbell, D., 343
Cantor, M. G., 163
Cantor, N., 251, 253
Caplan, P. J., 163
Caplow, T., 345
Cardwell, J. D., 50
Carlston, D. E., 253
Carnevale, P. J. D., 345
Cartwright, D., 20
Carver, C. S., 192
Castro, Fidel, 465
Chaiken, A. L., 133, 219
Chaiken, S., 281, 282
Chapman, Mark, 196
Charters, W., 192
Chase-Lansdale, P. L., 165
Chelser, P., 165
Chi, M. T. H., 108
Chodorow, Nancy, 145–146
Cialdini, R. B., 132, 193, 344
Clark, R. D., III, 343
Cleary, P. D., 164

Clore, G. L., 313
Cogle, F. L., 163
Cohen, Albert, 198
Cohen, E. G., 194
Cohen, R., 343
Collins, R. L., 20
Condon, J. W., 312
Converse, P. E., 476
Conway, F., 283, 476
Cooley, Charles Horton, 111–112, 113, 387–388
Cooper, J., 281
Cooper, V. W., 163
Coopersmith, S., 133
Corder, J., 165
Costrich, N., 252
Coverman, S., 165
Covington, J., 218
Crandall, C. S., 193
Crano, W. D., 282
Crocker, J., 252
Crosby, F., 192
Cross, P., 253
Croyle, R. , 282
Cunningham, M. R., 344
Czitrom, D. J., 108

D

Daniel, Beth, 124
Darley, John, 322, 326
Darwin, Charles, 22–23, 318–319
David, D. S., 165
Davidson, B., 312
Davis, J. C., 477
Davis, K., 108, 314
Davis, M. H., 344
Deaux, K., 163
Deci, E. L., 132
Dembroski, T. M., 282
Denzin, N. K., 108
DePaulo, B. M., 251
Deutscher, I., 281
Dewey, John, 111
Dion, K. K., 282, 313
DiPrete, T. A., 164
Dobbins, G. H., 164
Dovidio, J. H., 344, 345, 356
Driscoll, R., 314
Durkheim, Emile, 3, 4, 286, 388–389, 403
Durkin, L., 163
Dutta, S., 254
Dutton, D., 314

E

Eagly, A. H., 163, 164, 282, 346
Eccles, J., 163, 164
Eisenberg, N., 164, 193
Elliot, D. S., 218
Emmons, R. A., 192
English, Horace, 440
Enzle, M. E., 132
Epstein, C. F., 164
Epstein, S., 253
Erikson, Erik, 102–104
Ermann, M. D., 218
Eslinger, K. N., 312
Etaugh, C., 165

F

Fagot, B. I., 162, 163
Farina, A., 219
Farrell, W., 165
Fasteau, M. F., 165
Fazio, R. H., 281, 282
Felson, R. B., 132, 193
Ferree, M. M., 477
Festinger, L., 81, 132, 193, 281, 312, 476
Field, M., 345
Fincham, F. D., 251
Fine, G. A., 108, 192
Fisbein, Martin, 14
Fisher, J. D., 345
Fiske, S. T., 251, 252, 253
Flavel, J. H., 108
Fox, R., 109
Fraser, Scott, 72
Frazer, Sir James, 54, 55
Freedman, D. G., 50
Freedman, Jonathan, 72, 193
French, J. R. P., Jr., 193
Freud, Sigmund, 11, 91–93, 103–104, 107, 179, 201, 375
Fridlund, A. J., 50
Froming, W. J., 132

G

Gaertner, S. L., 346
Gandhi, Mahatma, 407–408, 410
Garfinkel, Harold, 30
Gaziano, C., 476
Gecas, V., 108, 133
Gergen, K. J., 133, 345

Gerson, K., 164
Gibbons, F. X., 344
Gibbs, J. P., 192, 218, 219
Gifford, R., 253
Gilbert, D. T., 251
Gillagan, C., 109
Ginossar, Z., 252
Giordano, P. C., 108
Glass, J., 109
Glasser, Ira, 443
Glenn, E. K., 164, 165
Glenn, N. D., 314
Glick, P., 133, 346
Goethals, G. R., 282
Goffman, Erving, 28–29, 49, 120, 205, 212–213, 289
Gonzales, M. H., 312
Goode, W. J., 312
Goodlad, J. I., 219
Goranson, R. E., 345
MGortner, Marjoe, 465
Goslin, D. A., 109
Gottleib, J., 344
Gouldner, Alan, 46, 336
Gove, W. R., 164, 219, 251
Grant, P. R., 252
Grasmick, H. G., 218
Grebler, L., 108
Greeley, A. M., 81
Greenberg, M. S., 345
Griffitt, W., 312, 313
Gross, A., 82, 345
Gruder, C. L., 282, 346
Gurr, T. R., 477

H

Hagan, J., 219
Hager, J. C., 50
Hall, C. S., 108
Hamill, R., 252
Haney, C., 194
Hansell, S., 311
Hareven, T. K., 109
Harris, M. B., 344
Harrison, A. A., 312
Hartshorne, H., 109
Hartup, W. W., 163
Hatfield, E., 312, 345
Hays, R. B., 3121
Hass, C. I., 282
Heider, F., 313
Heiss, J., 51, 251
Helmreich, Robert, 74–75

Hendrick, C., 252, 312, 314
Hendrick, S. S., 133, 313
Herman, L. M., 108
Herr, P. M., 250
Hertel, P. T., 250
Herzog, A. R., 164
Higgins, E. T., 254, 282
Hill, C. T., 312, 313
Hill, R. J., 281
Himmelfarb, S., 283
Hinckley, John, 214, 215
Hirschi, Travis, 201, 219
Hite, Shere, 60–61
Hodgkinson, V. A., 343
Hoffman, L. W., 165
Holahan, C. J., 344
Holden, R. T., 51
Homans, George, 44–45, 46, 337
Hornik, J., 193
Horowitz, I, 345
House, J. S., 19, 131, 344
Hovland, C. I., 282
Howard, J. A., 164, 251
Hoyenga, K. B., 163
Hume, David, 55
Humphrey, R. H., 192, 193
Huston, A. C., 162, 163
Huston, T. L., 313, 344
Hyde, J. S., 163, 164

I

Iacocca, Lee, 410
Inkeles, A., 108
Isen, A. M., 254, 344
Izard, C. E., 50

J

James, William, 22, 111–112
Janis, I. L., 193, 283
Jemail, J. A., 253
Jenkins, 477
Jones, E. E., 132, 193, 251, 252, 281

K

Kahneman, D., 252
Kallgren, C. A., 281
Kaplan, Howard, 202
Kaplowitz, S. A., 283
Karabenick, S. A., 345

Katz, D., 280
Keech, Mrs., 470
Keeter, S., 476
Keilbowicz, R. B., 477
Kelley, Harold, 232
Kelley, K., 345
Kelman, H. C., 193
Kennedy, M. D., 477
Kerckhoff, A. C., 312, 314
Kessler, R. C., 164
Killian, Lewis, 466, 475
Klandermans, B., 477
Klapper, J. T., 282
Kluegel, J. R., 51
Kohlberg, Lawrence, 94–95
Kohn, Melvin, 10
Kollock, P., 164
Kort, C., 343, 344
Krebs, D., 345
Krohn, M. D., 218
Krosnick, J. A., 283
Kubler-Ross, Elizabeth, 106
Kuhn, Manford, 26

L

Lamb, M. E., 165
Lambert, W. E., 192
Langer, E., 109, 251
Langlois, J. H., 313
LaPiere, Richard T., 263
Larsen, O. N., 108
Latané, Bibb, 322, 326
Lauer, R. H., 50, 51
LeBon, Gustave, 464, 475
Lefcourt, H. M., 192
Leippe, M. R., 283
Lemert, E. M., 218
Lerner, M. J., 52, 219
Leslie, L. A., 164
Lesnik-Oberstein, M., 312
Leventhal, H., 283
Levinger, G., 313, 314
Lewin, Kurt, 11–12, 327–328, 502
Lewis, O., 219
Lichter, D. L., 20
Likert, R., 280
Linder, D. E., 281, 282
Lindesmith, A. R., 19
Lingle, J. H., 253
Link, B. G., 219
Linton, R., 51
Liska, A. E., 218, 282
Locksley, A., 252

Lofland, J. F., 476
Long, T. E., 283
Lopreato, J., 343
Lynn, David, 145

M

McAdam, D., 477
McArthur, L. Z., 252
McCall, George, 298
McCandless, B. R., 108
McCarthy, J. D., 477
McCauley, C., 476
Maccoby, E. E., 108, 163
McCord, J., 218
McGovern, L. P., 345
McGuire, W. J., 132, 251, 282
McLuhan, Marshall, 89
McPhail, C., 20, 476
Majors, B., 192
Malcolmson, W., 165
Manning, M. M., 133
Manson, H. H., 281
Marcos, A. C., 218
Margolin, L., 313
Markus, H., 132, 253
Marx, G. T., 476
Mason, K. O., 162
Masur, E. F., 108
Mathews, K. E., Jr., 343
Matza, D., 218
Mead, George Herbert, 25–26, 31,
    111–112, 130
Mead, Margaret, 135
Medrich, E. A., 163
Meltzer, B. N., 51
Merrens, M., 344
Merton, Robert, 197, 199
Mettee, D. R., 313
Meyer, J. P., 346
Michaels, J. W., 313
Middlemist, R., 82
Milgram, Stanley, 187–189, 192, 476
Miller, D. L., 132
Miller, G. T., 192
Miller, H. L., 313
Miller, J., 20
Miller, N., 252, 282, 283
Mills, C. W., 312
Minuchin, P. P., 163
Mirowsky, J., 51, 52, 312
Mischel, W., 164, 194
Mita, T. H., 312
Money, John, 142

Monte, C., 81
Moore, D. W., 476
Moore, K., 165
Moreland, R. L., 312
Morgan, C. J., 344
Morgan, S. P., 314
Moscovici, S., 192
Motley, Marion, 430
Mueller, C. W., 344
Munroe, R. H., 163
Myrdal, Gunnar, 420

N

Nathanson, C., 164
Neisser, U., 251
Newcomb, T. M., 192, 253

O

Oberschall, 477
Olson, M., 476
Orive, R., 193
Orne, M., 81
Osgood, C. E., 280
Oskamp, S., 81, 476

P

Page, S., 219
Paludi, M. A., 164
Pampel, F. C., 109
Pancer, S. M., 346
Pantin, H. M., 344
Papageorgis, D., 282
Park, B., 251
Parks, Rosa, 58
Parsons, J. E., 162
Patch, M. E., 193
Patterson, F., 108
Pearlin, L. I., 164
Peterson, R. D., 219
Pettigrew, T. F., 81
Petty, R. E., 283
Piaget, Jean, 94–95
Pickford, J. H., 313
Piliavin, J. A., 343, 344, 345, 346
Piotrkowski, C. S, 165
Pomazal, R. J., 345, 346
Pratkanis, A. R., 282
Premack, D., 108
Pritchett, W. D., 193

Przybyla, D. P. J., 344
Pursell, S. A., 313

Q

Quigley-Fernandez, B., 281

R

Rabban, M., 164
Rabbie, J. M., 281
Read, S. J., 251
Reeves, R. A., 193
Rhodewalt, F., 282
Richardson, Laurel, 64–65
Ridgeway, Cecilia, 69–70
Ridley, M., 3343
Riggio, R. E., 250
Ring, K., 82
Rinn, W. E., 50
Robins, L. N., 251
Robinson, Brooks, 124
Robinson, Jackie, 430, 443
Robinson, R., 51
Rodin, J., 109
Rogers, M., 344
Rogers, R. W., 283
Rogoff, B., 108
Rosch, E., 253
Rosenbaum, M. E., 312
Rosenberg, M., 19, 132, 133
Rosenblatt, P. C., 313
Rosenhan, David, 64–66, 69, 344
Rosenthal, Robert, 208
Ross, C. E., 165
Ross, L., 82, 193, 251, 253
Roy, M., 165
Rozin, P., 81
Rubin, K. H., 109
Rubin, Lillian, 62–63
Rubin, Z., 314
Ruggerio, J. A., 163
Rushton, J. P., 343
Russell, D. E. H., 165
Rutkowski, G. K., 344, 345
Ryan, W., 52, 219

S

Sabido, M., 51
Sakauri, M. M., 193
Sarbin, T. R., 51

Sayles, 477
Scanzoni, J. H., 165, 312
Schachter, S., 314
Schafer, R. B., 312
Scheff, Thomas, 190, 219
Scheier, M. F., 132
Scherer, K. R., 250
Schlenker, B. R., 132
Schmitt, R. L., 132
Schneider, D. J., 253
Schneider, F. W., 344
Schofield, J. W., 253
Schooler, C., 165
Schuman, H., 81, 281
Schur, Edwin, 148
Schwartz, L. A., 164
Schwartz, S. H., 345
Scott, S., 132
Scov, R. B., 252
Secord, P. F., 314
Seeman, M., 31
Seiber, S. D., 51
Selman, R., 108
Sheffield, C. J., 164
Shepelak, N. J., 51
Sherif, Carolyn, 17
Sherif, Muzafer, 17, 181–182
Shields, J. M., 253
Shotland, L. R., 343, 345
Shumaker, S. A., 345
Shweder, R. A., 253
Simmel, Georg, 3, 4–5
Simmons, J. L., 218
Simons, H. W., 282
Singer, E., 192
Skinner, B. F., 185
Skowronski, J. J., 253
Sloane, D. M., 218
Slusher, M. P., 252
Smelser, Neil, 467, 469
Smith, R. H., 192
Smith, S. S., 82
Smith-Lovin, L., 194
Smithson, M., 344, 346
Snarey, J. R., 109
Snow, David, 67, 68, 476
Snyder, M., 133, 251, 252, 253, 313
Soloman, L. Z., 344
Spencer, J. W., 251
Spitze, G., 314
Sprecher, S., 312
Squire, S., 476
Staub, E., 345
Steinberg, L., 314
Stephan, C. W., 51, 165, 313, 346

Stephan, W. G., 51, 81, 252, 253, 346
Stokols, D., 219
Stouffer, S. A., 192
Straus, M. A., 165
Strauss, A. L., 192
Strodtbeck, F. L., 193
Stryker, Sheldon, 28
Sutherland, Edwin, 200
Sutton, S. R., 283
Swanson, G. E., 108
Swap, W. C., 312
Swidler, A., 108
Szasz, T. S., 219

T

Takooshian, H., 344
Tallichet, S. E., 162
Tannen, D., 251
Taylor, D. G., 81
Taylor, S. E., 251, 252
Tedeschi, J. T., 132
Tesser, A., 192, 312, 313
Tetlock, P. E., 252
Thibault, J. W., 312
Thio, A., 218
Thoits, P. A., 219, 311
Thomas, J. R., 163
Thomas, W. I., 3, 5, 24
Thompson, W. C., 344
Thorndike, E. L., 20, 253, 313
Thurstone, L. L., 280
Tichenor, P. J., 476
Tietjen, A. M., 109
Tilly, C., 477
Tipton, R. M., 346

Tittle, C., 164, 218
Tobey, E. L., 133
Treiman, D. J., 164
Trivers, R., 343
Troiler, T. K., 252
Trope, Y., 252
Tunnell, G., 253
Turner, J. H., 19
Turner, Ralph, 35, 115–116, 466, 475

U

Underwood, B., 345
Useem, B., 476

V

Vasudev, J., 109

W

Wahrman, R., 193
Walsh, E. J., 477
Walster, E., 282, 312, 313, 345
Ware, M. C., 163
Warner, R. M., 250
Weber, Max, 3, 4, 410, 411
Webster, M., Jr., 194
Weiner, B., 345
Weiner, F. H., 344
Weinstein, E. A., 132
Weinstein, N. D., 253
Weiss, D. S., 253
Wells, L. E., 132

West, S. G., 346
West, M. A., 109
Weyant, J. M., 193
White, G. L., 312, 313, 314
Whitley, B. E., Jr., 163
Wicker, A. W., 281
Wiggins, J. S., 253
Williams, C. E., 251
Willis, Bill, 430
Wilson, Edward O., 320
Wilson, T. D., 281
Wishner, T., 253
Wispe, L. G., 346
Wolff, K. H., 19
Wood, M. R., 132
Wooley, S., 476
Wrong, D. H., 109
Wu, C., 282
Wylie, R., 253

Y

Yinon, Y., 345
Young, J., 476

Z

Zadny, J., 252
Zajonc, R. B., 312, 313
Zanden, James Vander, 429
Zimbardo, Philip, 189–191, 192
Zuckerman, M., 251
Zurcher, Louis, 117, 476
Zwiegenhaft, R. L., 251

SUBJECT INDEX

A

Acculturation, 422–423
Affect, 11
Affirmative action, 442–443
Agape, 305, 306
Age grading, 97
Aggression, 349–350, 362, 377–379
  anger and, 362–364
  battering, 350–353, 377
  child abuse, 353–355, 377
  consequences of, 370–371
  misattribution of arousal, 365–367
  rape, 355–362, 377–378
  sexual arousal and, 364–365
  situational factors, 367–370
  three-factor theory, 363
  TV and, 371–376
  victims, 376–377
Aging, 97, 105–106, 107
AID (Agency for International Development), 394
AIDS (Acquired Immune Deficiency Syndrome), 171–172, 460–461
Altruism, 316–318, 319, 328, 335, 336
  biological base, 319–320, 342
  cost and reward, 332–334, 342
  helper personality, 327–332
  mood, 330–331
  motivation, 331–332, 342
  personal norms, 339, 343
  reciprocal, 319–320, 337–338
  situational, 332–339
  social base, 320–322, 339–343
  social norms, 334–338, 342–343
American Socialist Party, 426
Anger, 362–364
Anomie, 197
Anorexia nervosa, 458
APA (American Psychological Association), 79
Arkansas v. *McCree,* 483

ASA (American Sociological Association), 79
Asiatic Exclusion League, 426
Assimilation, 422, 448–449
  macrosocial theory, 425–426
  perceptual, 432–434
Assortive mating, 291
Attitude, 256–259
  behaviorial inconsistencies, 259, 261–263, 268
  change, cognitive, 264–270, 280
  change, persuasive, 270–279, 280
  function, 257–258
Attraction, 285–288
  balance theory, 299–300, 310–311
  exchange theory, 288–293, 308–310, 311
  filtering theory, 307
  four-stage theory, 307
  gain-loss theory, 297–299, 310–311
  misattribution, 300–302, 310–311
  physical, 294–297, 298
  reinforcement-affect theory, 293–297, 310–311
Autokinetic effect, 181
Avoidance, 429

B

Battering, 350–353, 377
Behavior, 38, 40–43, 464–475
  collective, 454–455
  crowd, 461–464
  mass, 455–461
  panic, 458–461
  social movement, 470–475
  balance theory, 299–300, 310–311
Belief in a just world, 48
Biological evolution, 318–320, 342
Bogus pipeline, 260

Boomerang effect, 273
Brainstorming, 398
Brown v. *Board of Education,* 427, 440, 441, 442, 444
Bulimia, 182, 458
Bureaucracies, 411, 413

C

Capital punishment, 372–373
Causality, 56
Charisma, 410
Chicago school, 25–26, 31
Child abuse, 353–355, 377–378
Cognitions, 11
Cognitive control, 42–43
Cognitive developmental theory, 94, 96, 107, 144–145, 161
Cognitive dissonance theory, 264–267
Cognitive information processing, 231–233. *See also* perception processing
Cohesion, group, 402–404, 414
Collective behavior, 454–455
  panic, 458–461
  social movements, 470–475
  theories of, 464–475
  types of, 455–464
Collective locomotion, 461
Communication structures, 393–394, 414
Comparison level of opportunities, 45
Compliance, 176–179, 191
Conflict, intergroup. *See* Robbers Cave Study
Conformity, 167, 176, 182–186, 191
  deindividuation, 189–191, 192
  groups, 172–176
  obedience, 186–189
  societal, 168–172

Consensus, 170–172
Contagion, 462, 464
Cooperation, intergroup. *See* Robbers Cave Study
Correspondent, inference theory, 226–230
Craze, 457
Criminal law, 479–482, 487–488
    evidence, 483–487, 503
    jury, 482–483, 484–485, 488–489
Crowds, 456, 461–464
    convergence theory, 464–466, 475
    emergent norm theory, 466–467, 475
    Lebon, 464, 475
    relative deprivation theory, 471–475
    resource mobilization theory, 472–474, 475
    value-added theory, 467–469, 475
Cult, 454
Cultural assimilator technique, 446
Cultural continuity, 97–98

D

Date rape, 356–357
Death, 106–107, 108
Definition of the situation, 5, 24
Deindividuation, 189–191, 192
Demand characteristics, 72
Dependent variables, 70, 80
Desegregation, 441–446
Deviance, 196–197, 216–217
    control theory of delinquency, 201, 217
    differential association theory, 200–201
    goal-means gap theory, 197
    labeling theory, 203–210, 216–217
    self theory, 202, 217
    status frustration theory, 198
    strain theories, 197–200
Discrimination, 420–421. *See also* racism
    institutional, 426–429
    minority reactions, 429, 431
    polarized response, 437–439, 450
Display rules, 23
Distancing, 68
Dramaturgical school, 28–29, 30, 49, 120–121

E

Ego, 93
Egocentrism, 245
Egoistic self-concern, 328
Elaboration likelihood model, 275
Elitist, 456
Emergent norm theory, 466
Empathic concern, 328
Empathy, 328–329
Enactive learning, 37
Encoding perceptions, 238, 248–249, 250
    influences, 240–242
    models, 238–240
Enthnomethodology, 29–30
Equity theory, 46, 330
Eros, 304, 306
Ethics, 77–80, 81
Ethnic pluralism, 423
Ethnocentrism, 436
Ethnomethodology, 29
Exchange theory, 43–49, 50, 288–293, 310–311, 402
    marital breakdown, 308–310
Expectations, 228–230
Experiments, field, 72–74, 80–81
Experiments, laboratory, 69–72, 80

F

Facilitation, social, 400–402
Fad, 457
Family, 87–88, 136–137
Fashion, 457
Feminist theory, 351, 377
Fictive storytelling, 68
Field experiments. *See* experiments, field
Field studies, 74–77, 81
Fight or flight syndrome, 493
Folkways, 168
Frame, 29
Fundamental attribution error, 231

G

Gain-loss theory, 297–299, 310–311
    symbolic interactionist, 298–299
GAS (General Adaptation Syndrome), 493

Gender roles, 135–136, 158, 160–162
    consequences to men, 157–158, 159, 161
    consequences to women, 148–157, 161
    sex and power, 147–148
    socialization, 136–139, 146, 158
Generalized ohter, 112
Generic norm of ingroup-outgroup bias, 435
Gestalt, 11
Gestures, 25
Group dynamics, 402–404, 414
    minority influence, 406–407
    polarization, 404–406
Group formation. *See* Robbers Cave Study
Group leadership. *See* leadership
Group performance, 397–400, 414
Group structures
    communication, 390, 393–394, 414
    interpersonal attraction, 390, 394–397, 414
    power, 390–391, 393, 414
Groups, 386–387, 389, 398–400, 412, 414
    facilitation, 400–402
    primary, 387–388, 390–391, 414
    types, 387–389

H

Halo effect, 248
Health, 498. *See also* medicine
    beliefs and, 499–504
Helpfulness, 327–332. *See also* altruism
    situational, 332–339
Hispanics, 423–425, 448

I

Id, 92–93
Identification, 176, 179–181, 191
Identities, 222, 223
    negotiating, 225–226
    situated, 224–225
Identity, 230–233
Identity salience theory, 28
Illusory correlation, 241

Impression formation, 221–222
Independent variables, 70, 80
Information integration model, 274
Ingroups, 4
Institutions, 6
Internal colonialism, 422
Internalization, 93, 176, 181–182, 191
Interpersonal structures, 390, 394–397
Intervention, bystander, 322–332,
      342–343. See also altruism
Interviews, 57–61
Interviews, unstructured, 62–63, 80
Iowa school, 26–28, 31

J

Japanese-Americans, 426–427
Jigsaw classroom, 444

K

Knowledge gap, 457

L

Labeling theory, 203–210, 216–217,
      234–235
Labeling theory
   deviance, 203–210, 216–217
   mental illness, 210–216
Law of distributive justice, 46
Law of effect, ll, 293
Law of parsimony, 275
Laws, 168
Leaders, charismatic, 410, 415
Leadership, 411
      group, 407–415
      style, 410–411
      traits, 409–410
      transaction, 413–414
Learning. See social learning theory
Libido, 91
Life space, 11
Likert scales, 258–259
Love, 302–310
      stages, 306–307
      styles, 304–306
Ludus, 304, 306

M

MADD (Mothers Against Drunk
      Driving), 470, 472, 473

Magic, imitative, 54–55, 57, 80
Manson v. Braithwaite, 486
Mass behavior, 455–461
Mass media, 88
Media, 137–139
Medicine, 490–493
   cancer, 496–497, 501, 503
   health and control, 498
   heart disease, 497
   patient-physician relationship,
      494–495
   prevention and treatment, 497–
      504
   stress, 493–496, 503–504
Mental illness, 210–216
Mere exposure effect, 287
Mexican-Americans, 423–425, 448
Minorities, group influence, 406–
      407, 414
Misattribution, 300–302
Moral development, 94–97
Mores, 168
Motherhood, 159–160
Motivation, 118–119

N

NAACP (National Association for the
      Advancement of Colored
      People), 448, 473
National Institute of Mental Health,
      371
Nature of Prejudice, The, 434
NFL (National Football League), 430
NORC (National Opinion Research
      Center), 58–59
Norms, 168, 339, 454

O

Obedience, 186–189
Observational learning, 37, 39–41
Observational methods, 57–63, 68
Observational techniques, 63–69, 80
Occupational self-direction, 11

P

Panic, 458–461
Parsimony, 275
Peer groups, 89, 90, 137

Perception processing, 238–242
   person factors, 235–238
   prototypes, 242
   retrieval, 248–249, 250
   schemata, 243–244, 246
   situational factors, 234–235
Perceptual assimilation, 432–434
Personality and social structure, 5–
      10, 16
Personality theories, implicit, 246–248
Persuasion. See also attitude
   appeal, 272–273
   audience, 273–274
   credibility, 271–272
   elaboration likelihood model,
      275–278, 280
   polarization, group, 404–406
Pornography, 364–365
Power structures, 45, 390–391, 393,
      414
Pragma, 305, 306
Prejudice, 420, 431, 448–450
   attribution error, 435–436
   in-group–out-group bias, 434–435,
      449
   principle of least effort, 434
   reducing, 439–441, 446–450
Problematic behavior, 197
Prototype, 2452
Propaganda, 456
Psychic energy, 91
Psychoanalytic theory, 91–93, 96,
      107, 145–146, 161
Psychological social psychology, 11–
      16, 19
   aggression, focus on, 339
Psychosexual stages, 92
Psychosocial stages, 102–104, 107
Public opinion, 456–457, 459

Q

Questionnaires, 57–62, 80
Qualitative methods, 7
Quantitative methods, 7

R

Racism. See also discrimination
   institutional, 426–429, 430
   internal colonialism, 422
   modern, white, 438–439
   sports, 430

Random smapling, 58
Rape, 355–362, 377–378
    pornography and, 364–365
    psychopathology theory, 356–357
    symbolic interactionist theory, 357–362
Reciprocity, 336
Reference groups, 173–176
Reinforcement-affect theory, 293–297, 310–311
Reinforcement control, 41
Reinforcement theories, 288, 310–311
    exchange theory, 288–293
    gain-loss theory, 297–299
Relationships, romantic, 64–65. *See also* love
Replicability, 56
Research ethics, 77–80, 81
Residual social norms, 211
Resocialization, 104–106, 107
Riot Commission, U. S., 368
Risky shift, 405
Robbers Cave Study, 17–18
Role differentiation, 34, 99
Role, 32, 33, 35
Role negotiation, 34, 99
Role strain, 35
Role-taking, 112
Role theory, 23, 30, 48–50
Romeo and Juliet effect, 301

S

Sampling, nonrandom, 60–61
Schemata, 243–244
Schemata theories, 119–120
Schools, 88, 137
Scientific method, 55–57, 80
Scripts, 246
Self-awareness, 125
Self-concept, 114–117, 130
Self-development theories, 111–114
Self-disclosure, 126–127, 131
Self-efficacy, 128–130
Self-esteem, 127–128, 129, 131
Self-fulfilling prophecy, 207–208
Self-monitoring, 125–126
Self-perception theory, 117–119, 131, 267–270, 280
Self-presentation, 121–127, 131
Self-reinforcement, 41
Semantic differential scales, 259
Sensitizing concepts, 26

Sentiment relationships, 299
Sex differences, 139, 141, 143–146, 162
    intellectual abilities, 139–140, 141–143
    personality traits, 140, 143
Sex stereotypes. *See* stereotypes
Sexual preference, 136
Significant others, 113–114
Significant symbols, 25
Situated identity, 224–225
Sleeper effect, 272
Social class and justice, 47
Social comparison, 115
Social construction of reality, 7
Social evolution, 320–322, 342–343
Social exchange theory, 23. *See also* exchange theory
Social facilitation, 400–402
Social integration, 286
Social interaction, 24
Social learning theory, 23, 36–37, 49, 50, 93–94, 107, 143–144
    enactive learning, 37
    observational learning, 37, 39–41
    modeling, 38
Social loafing, 398
Social movements, 470–475
Social psychology, 2–3, 6
    criminal law and, 479–490
    ethics, 77–80, 81
    medicine and, 490–504
    synthesis, 15–18
Social status, 6
Social structure, 6
Social structure and personality, 5–10, 16
Socialization, 84–85, 86, 107
    adults, of, 100–102
    agents of, 87–90
    aging and, 105–107
    gender role, 136–139
    media, 137–139
Socialization, reciprocal, 98–99
Sociobiology, 318
    biological evolution, 318–320, 342
    social evolution, 320–322, 342–343
Sociogram, 394
Sociological social psychology, 3–5
    aggression, focus on, 339
    perspectives, 5–11
Solidarity, 473
Spatial ability, 140
Spacial proximity, 286–287

Status, 30, 205
Stereotype, 420–421, 431, 448–450
    categorizing, 431–434, 449
    reducing, 439–441, 446–450
    sex, 135, 146–148, 161, 162
Stigma, 29
Stimulus control, 41–42
Strain theories, 197–200, 217
Stress, 493–496, 503–504
Suggestibility, 464
Superego, 93
Superordinate goals, 18
Support networks, 396–397
Symbolic interactionism, 5–10, 16, 18, 298–299, 357–362
    premise, 23–25, 49
    schools of, 25–30
Symbols, 25
SYMLOG, 412

T

Tasks, 398–400
Terrorism, 462–463
Theory of reasoned action, 14–15, 262–263
Transactional theories, 413–414
TST (Twenty States Test), 26, 117
TV violence, 371–376

U

Ultimate attribution error, 435
Unit relationships, 299

V

Value-added theory, 467
Variables, 70, 80
Victim blaming, 208–210
Vocabulary of motives, 288
Voir dire, 484–485, 503

W

Women and Love, 60–61
Worlds of Pain, 62